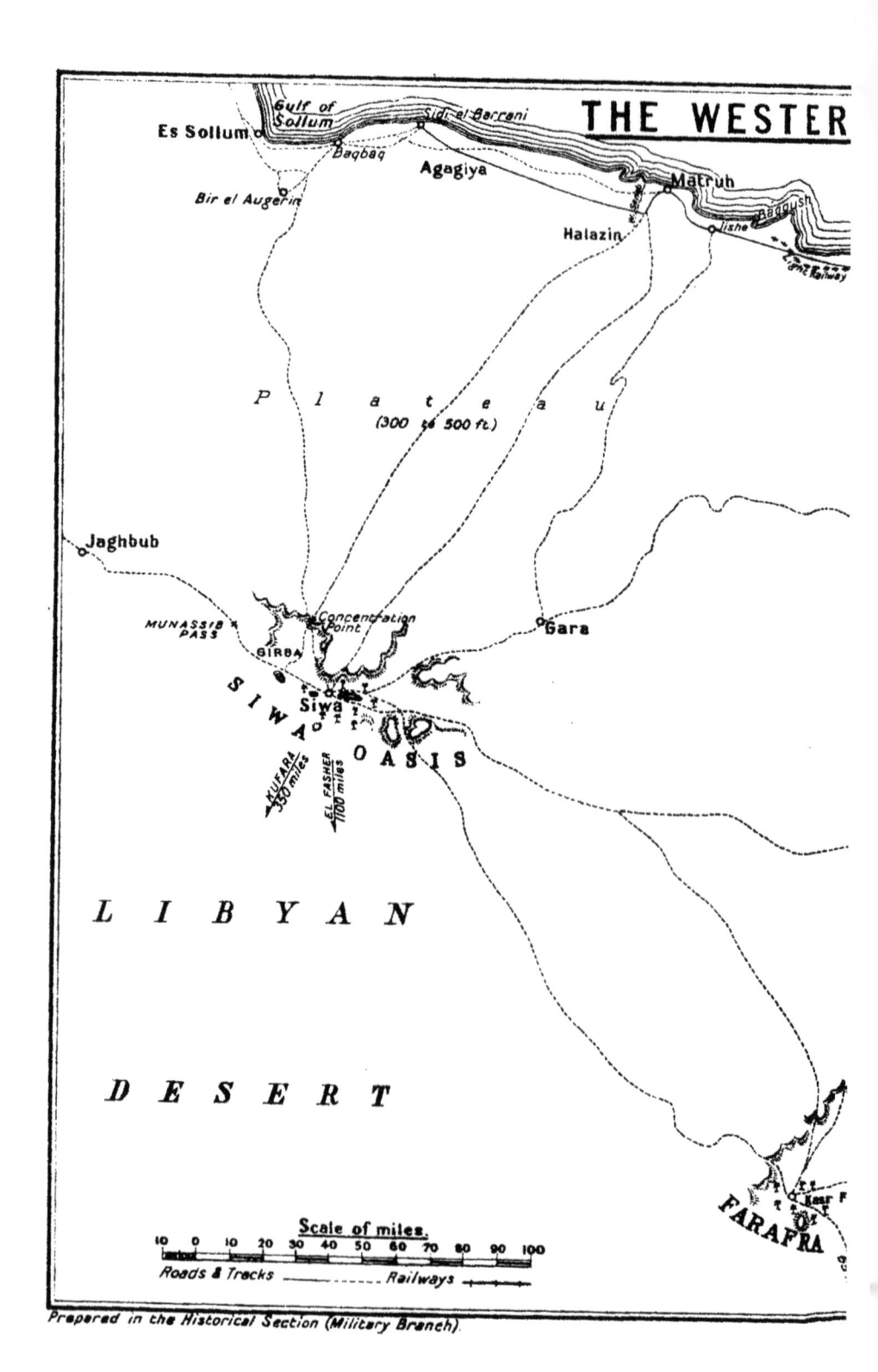

THE WESTER

Gulf of Sollum — Es Sollum — Baqbaq — Sidi el Barrani — Agagiya — Matruh — Bagoush — Bir el Augerin — Halazin — Iishe — Cairo Railway

Plateau (300 to 500 ft.)

Jaghbub

MUNASSIB PASS — GIRBA — Concentration Point — Gara — SIWA OASIS — Siwa

KUFARA 350 miles
EL FASHER 1100 miles

LIBYAN DESERT

FARAFRA — Qasr F

Scale of miles
10 0 10 20 30 40 50 60 70 80 90 100

Roads & Tracks ——— Railways ----

Prepared in the Historical Section (Military Branch).

Sketch A.

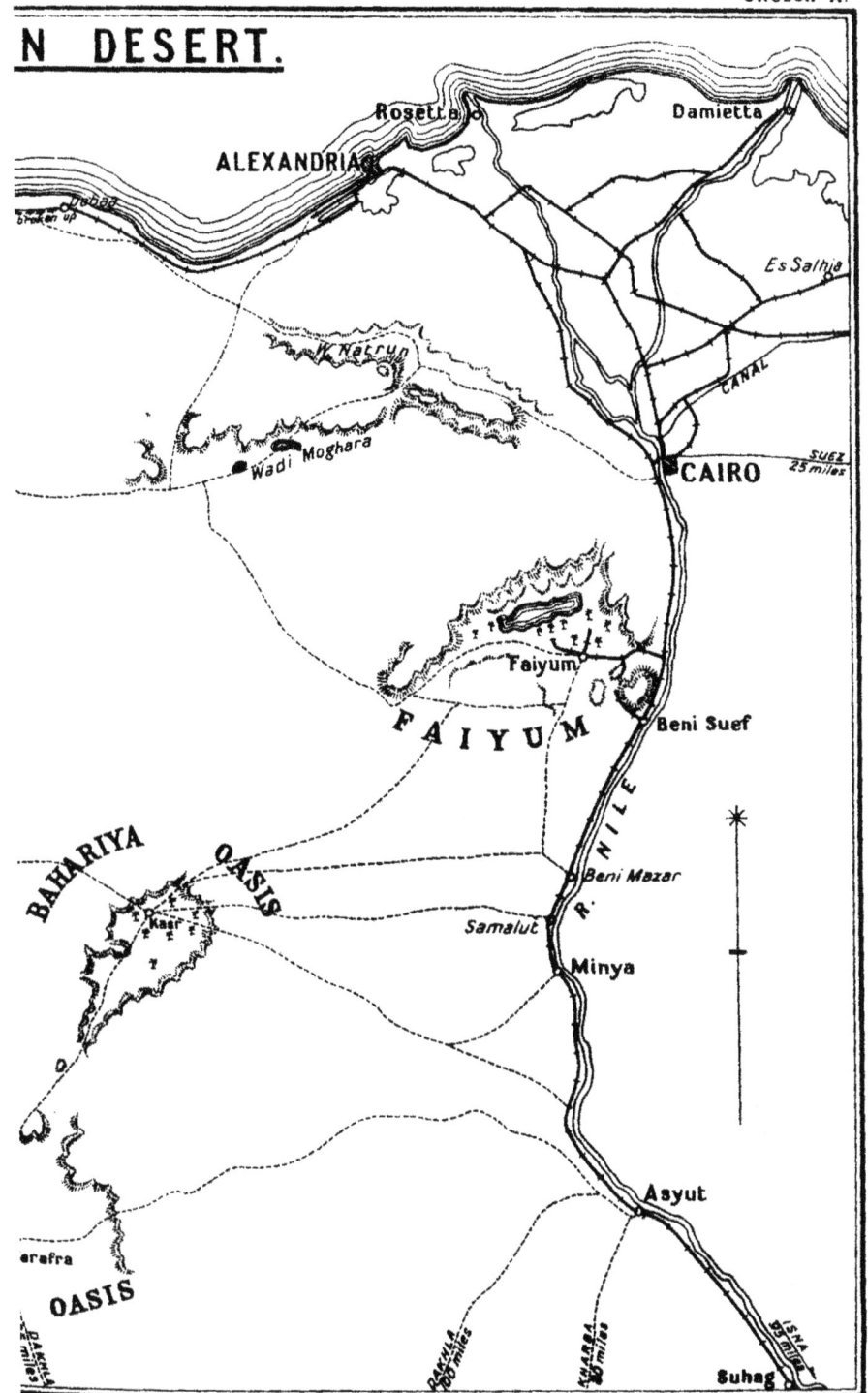

Ordnance Survey, 1927.

History of the Great War.

MILITARY OPERATIONS.

HISTORY OF THE GREAT WAR
BASED ON OFFICIAL DOCUMENTS
BY DIRECTION OF THE HISTORICAL SECTION OF THE
COMMITTEE OF IMPERIAL DEFENCE

MILITARY OPERATIONS EGYPT & PALESTINE

FROM THE OUTBREAK OF WAR
WITH GERMANY TO
JUNE 1917

COMPILED BY
Lieut.-General SIR GEORGE MACMUNN
K.C.B., K.C.S.I., D.S.O. (LATE R.A.), p.s.c., AND
Captain CYRIL FALLS
LATE 11TH R. INNIS. FUS. AND GENERAL STAFF

The Naval & Military Press Ltd

Published by
The Naval & Military Press Ltd
5 Riverside, Brambleside, Bellbrook
Industrial Estate, Uckfield, East Sussex,
TN22 1QQ England
Tel: +44 (0) 1825 749494
Fax: +44 (0) 1825 765701
www.naval-military-press.com
www.military-genealogy.com
www.militarymaproom.com

In reprinting in facsimile from the original, any imperfections are inevitably reproduced and the quality may fall short of modern type and cartographic standards.

PREFACE.

THIS history is designed to provide an authoritative account of British military operations during the war in Egypt, Palestine and Syria, and of certain minor operations more or less connected with them: the Arab Revolt against the Turks in the Hejaz, the expedition against Darfur, and the Turkish attack on Aden. The Arab Revolt brought considerable assistance to the British campaign against the Turks in Sinai and Palestine; the Darfur and Aden operations, besides being of smaller scope, affected it little, but the Darfur expedition was made necessary by the German and Turkish plan to retain by threat of attack the largest possible number of British troops in Egypt, whilst events at Aden are connected more closely with Egypt and Palestine than with any other theatre of war.

The present volume covers events from the outbreak of war with Germany—though Great Britain remained at peace with Turkey until three months later—to June 1917, when, after deadlock had followed the Second Battle of Gaza, the War Cabinet decided upon the invasion of Palestine and despatched General Sir E. H. H. Allenby to succeed General Sir Archibald Murray. It is therefore a record of nearly three years; whilst the second and final volume will cover a period of less than eighteen months, but a period of larger and more continuous active operations. The first volume is concerned with the defence of Egypt against invasion, both against the Turks from the east, and their allies, the tribesmen of the Western Desert who fought under the banner of the Senussi; with the period when Egypt formed the base of the Gallipoli Campaign; with the concentration of the Mediterranean Expeditionary Force in Egypt after Gallipoli's evacuation; with the advance to the Turkish frontier and the expulsion of the enemy from the Sinai Peninsula; and with the First and Second Battles of Gaza. It also includes the earlier stages of the Arab campaign against the Turks in the Hejaz.

Of previous history and current political events enough only is said to explain the presence of a British force in Egypt and the employment of that country as a *place d'armes*. A short account of the position of Islam as a religious and temporal power has been considered necessary to explain the Arab Revolt, and also to show why the proclamation of a Holy War by Turkey caused the British Government so great anxiety with regard to its effect upon Moslem subjects and neighbours in various parts of the world.

The military documents available were considerable in quantity, except for the years 1914 and 1915, when inadequate staffs and an improvised organization did not always permit the keeping of full records. They include, with this reservation, the war diaries of every staff and unit engaged, special reports of actions, messages received and sent, both those passing between the War Office and the command in Egypt and those between commanders and their troops. Material from the side of the enemy is scantier, but, on the whole, sufficient. It consists mainly of certain published records by German officers and of the replies of the Historical Section of the Turkish War Office to a questionaire addressed to it after the war. No Turkish official history of operations in this theatre has been published, and there is no material from which to compile detailed Turkish orders of battle for the period covered by the first volume.

As the Navy took a prominent part in the defence of the Suez Canal, and, indeed, in the whole campaign, an outline of its operations has been included. These are, of course, narrated in detail in the official naval history. Official histories of the Royal Air Force, Medical Services and Veterinary Services have appeared, or are in course of publication. Here is included only sufficient record of their work to explain the course of military operations.

The text, in typescript or printed proof, has been read by a number of commanders, staff officers and regimental officers who took part in the events described. The compilers have been greatly assisted by their criticisms and suggestions, for which they desire to tender their sincere thanks. In this connexion, there is one acknowledgement to be made of somewhat unusual character, for it cannot be often that one combatant's record of a campaign has been checked in draft by the commander of the other side. The chapters devoted to the operations against the Senussi have had the benefit of the criticism of Ja'far Pasha el Askeri, C.M.G., lately diplomatic representative of Iraq in London, and now Prime Minister of his country; who commanded

PREFACE

the troops of the Senussi in all the engagements of 1915 and 1916, and afterwards rendered striking service to the Arab cause in the Hejaz.

In accordance with the method followed in other volumes compiled by the Historical Section, Military Branch, two sets of maps have been prepared. Those of one series, described as "sketches," are bound in the volume; the others issued separately. The former are sufficient for the general reader, whilst the latter have been prepared for the use of students of warfare; but in the case of several of the smaller actions a "sketch" has been found adequate for the purpose of readers of both classes. All the maps have been compiled from data and sketches in the war diaries under the supervision of Major A. F. Becke, late R.F.A., and drawn by the principal draughtsman attached to the Branch, Mr. J. S. Fenton, late R.E. The compilers are deeply indebted to Mr. W. B. Wood, M.A., late of Worcester College, and Mr. C. T. Atkinson. M.A., of Exeter College, for their very careful revision of the text in proof. Special assistance in the compilation of the volume has also been given by Mr. E. A. Dixon.

June, 1927.　　　　　　　　　　　　　　　　　　G. F. M.
　　　　　　　　　　　　　　　　　　　　　　　　C. B. F.

NOTES.

The convention commonly observed in the British Army regarding the distinguishing numbers of Armies, Corps, Divisions, etc., is here followed; that is to say, they are written in full for Armies, in Roman figures for Corps, and in Arabic for smaller formations and units. It has been customary to give the numbers of Artillery Brigades in Roman figures, but, with the formation of the New Armies and the numbering of the Territorial field artillery brigades (previously known by Territorial titles) this sometimes results in an unwieldy set of figures, e.g. CCLXVII Brigade R.F.A. It has therefore been decided to retain Roman numerals for numbers up to one hundred and employ Arabic for all numbers above this point. We have thus: Second Army, II Corps, 2nd Division, 2nd Infantry Brigade, 2nd Cavalry Brigade, II Brigade R.F.A., but 267th Brigade R.F.A.

Turkish formations and units, to distinguish them from British, are printed in italic characters, thus: *Fourth Army, IV Corps, 4th Division.*

Abbreviations of regimental names have been frequently used in the narrative; for example, "4/K.O.S.B." for 1st/4th Battalion the King's Own Scottish Borderers. In the case of Territorial battalions, numerous in this theatre, where a number is divided in this way by a stroke from the abbreviated title, it is to be understood that the battalion described belongs to the First Line. A Second-Line battalion is printed thus: "2/4th Queen's." The 4th Australian Light Horse Brigade is generally abbreviated to "4th L.H. Brigade," the 4th Australian Light Horse Regiment to "4th A.L.H.," the New Zealand Mounted Rifles Brigade to "N.Z.M.R. Brigade," or "New Zealand Brigade."

Other abbreviations commonly used are G.H.Q. for General Headquarters Egyptian Expeditionary Force, E.E.F. for Egyptian Expeditionary Force, M.E.F. for Mediterranean Expeditionary Force.

The spelling of Arabic names varies greatly on maps printed at various periods, and that employed in reports and orders is far from uniform. Here the list drawn up by the

NOTES

"Permanent Committee on Geographical Names for British Official Use" and issued by the Royal Geographical Society has been followed, so far as it applies. The use of this list results in the appearance of names possibly unfamiliar to readers who took part in the campaigns; *e.g.* Wadi Ghazze for the commoner Wadi Ghuzze, Qantara and Qatiya for Kantara and Katia; but that has not seemed sufficient reason to abandon this, the most scientific transliteration yet carried out. On Maps 1 and 2, which are reprints of parts of official publications, the spelling does not follow this list, but where the names differ markedly from those in the text a foot-note has been inserted giving the map spelling.

A list of the meanings of a number of place-names in Palestine and Syria, and a glossary of terms found in components of place-names in Egypt, Sinai, and Palestine, are given in Appendix 15. These were compiled by Major A. F. Becke and Mr. J. S. Fenton. Acknowledgement must be made of the kindness and courtesy of the Director-General of the Survey of Egypt in checking them, and also a much longer list intended to be included in the second volume.

CONTENTS.   PAGE

INTRODUCTION 1

CHAPTER I.
THE OUTBREAK OF WAR.
Egypt in August 1914 7
The Immediate Military Problem 12
War with Turkey 15

CHAPTER II.
THE COMMENCEMENT OF HOSTILITIES AND THE THREAT TO THE SUEZ CANAL.
November and December 1914 19
The Canal Defences 22
Syria and Sinai 25
The Advance of the Turks 28
Notes: I. Disposition of Troops in the Canal Defences, 15th January 1915. 31
    II. Engineer Work on the Canal Defences. 33
    III. The Expedition against the Canal, from German and Turkish Sources 34

CHAPTER III.
THE ATTACK ON THE SUEZ CANAL, 1ST–10TH FEBRUARY 1915.
The Attack 37
The Days succeeding the Attack 46
Note: The Attack, from German and Turkish Sources 50

CHAPTER IV.
EGYPT IN THE SPRING OF 1915: THE GALLIPOLI CAMPAIGN.
The Sinai Front in February 53
The Gallipoli Campaign 54
The Sinai Front, March–June 60
The Western Frontier, the Sudan and the Red Sea .. 65
Note: Troops and Details in Egypt on 9th July 1915. 68

CHAPTER V.
EGYPT AND THE EVACUATION OF GALLIPOLI.
Egypt during the last phase of the Gallipoli Campaign .. 69
The Levant Base 73
The Evacuation of Gallipoli and the Problem of Egypt's Defence 76
Notes: I. The Beersheba Railway 85
    II. The Armenians 86

CONTENTS

CHAPTER VI.
EGYPT AFTER THE EVACUATION OF GALLIPOLI.

	PAGE
The Concentration in Egypt	87
The Suez Canal Defences	89
The Reorganization of Commands in the Mediterranean	94
The Imperial Strategic Reserve	97
Notes: I. Instructions from the Secretary of State for War to Lieut.-General Sir A. Murray	98
II. Supplementary Instructions to Sir A. Murray from Sir W. Robertson	99

CHAPTER VII.
THE WESTERN FRONTIER IN 1915.

Islam, Egypt, and the Senussi	101
The Outbreak of Hostilities	106
The Affair of the Wadi Senab	110
The Affair of the Wadi Majid	113

CHAPTER VIII.
THE CONTINUATION OF THE OPERATIONS AGAINST THE SENUSSI.

The Affair of Halazin	119
Preparations for the Reoccupation of Sollum	123
The Action of Agagiya and Reoccupation of Sidi el Barrani	125
The Reoccupation of Sollum	129

CHAPTER IX.
THE WESTERN OASES AND THE SUDAN.

The Western Oases	135
The Raid on Siwa	140
Events in the Sudan	145
Operations in Darfur: the Affair of Beringia	147
The Affair of Giuba	151
Note: The Organization of the Forces on the Western Frontier	153

CHAPTER X.
THE BEGINNING OF THE ADVANCE TOWARDS PALESTINE.

Egypt in the Spring of 1916	154
The Advance into Sinai	159
The Affair of Qatiya	162
Notes: I. The Composition of the Turkish Force at Qatiya	170
II. Sir A. Murray's Appreciation	170

CONTENTS

Chapter XI.
The Battle of Romani.

The British Occupation of Romani	175
The Turkish Advance	179
The Turkish Attack on the 4th August	184
The Pursuit on the 5th August	190
The End of the Pursuit	194
The Results of the Battle	199
Notes: I. Turkish and German Forces engaged	202
II. Distribution of E.E.F., 27th July 1916	203
III. The State of the Royal Flying Corps in Egypt at the Time of the Battle of Romani	203
IV. The Evacuation of the Wounded	204

Chapter XII.
The Arab Revolt Against Turkey.

Islam, Arabia and Turkey	205
Arabia at the Outbreak of War	209
Great Britain and the Sherif of Mecca	211
The Sykes–Picot Agreement	217
The Outbreak of the Arab Revolt	220
The Turkish Attack on Aden	221

Chapter XIII.
The Arab Campaign Against Turkey.

The Opening Phase	225
The Stotzingen Mission	228
The Problem of Rabegh	230
The Attack of Wejh	234
The Affair of Abu el Lisal and the Capture of Aqaba	239

Chapter XIV.
The Advance to El Arish.

Affairs on the Eastern Front, September–November 1916	242
Sir A. Murray's Appreciation	246
The Turkish Retirement and the Affair of Magdhaba	251
Note: Telegrams between Sir A. Murray and the C.I.G.S.	258

Chapter XV.
The Action of Rafah and Preparations for Advance into Palestine.

The Action of Rafah	262
Reconstruction and Preparation	271
Before Gaza	276

xiv CONTENTS

CHAPTER XVI.

THE FIRST BATTLE OF GAZA.

	PAGE
The Situation in late March 1917	279
The Plan of Attack	283
The Preliminary Moves and Approach March	286
The Fog at Dawn on the 26th March	289
The Envelopment of Gaza by the Mounted Troops	290
The Opening of the Main Attack	293
The Attack on Gaza by the Mounted Troops and the Advance of Relieving Columns	297
The Capture of Ali Muntar	301
Note : The Artillery of the Eastern Force	304

CHAPTER XVII.

THE FIRST BATTLE OF GAZA (CONTINUED).

The Decision to withdraw the Mounted Troops	305
The Withdrawal of the Mounted Troops and Evacuation of Ali Muntar	308
The Reoccupation of Ali Muntar and Turkish Counter-Attacks	311
The Withdrawal to the Wadi Ghazze	313
The Causes of Failure and the Reports to the War Office	315
Notes : I. The Battle, from German and Turkish Sources	320
II. Telegrams between Sir A. Murray and the C.I.G.S.	322
III. The Evacuation of the Wounded	325

CHAPTER XVIII.

THE SECOND BATTLE OF GAZA.

The Situation after the First Battle of Gaza	326
The Plan of Attack	329
The First Phase of the Attack	332
The Plan of the Second Phase	334
The Attack of the Eastern Force	337
The Operations of the Desert Column	343
The Situation at Nightfall on the 19th April	346
Note : The Battle, from German and Turkish Sources	349

CHAPTER XIX.

AFTER THE SECOND BATTLE OF GAZA.

The Consolidation of the Position	351
British Policy after the Second Battle of Gaza	354
Communications and Water Supply	358
Minor Operations	362
Egypt and the War	364
Note : Table showing Use of Water from the Pipe-Line	367

CHAPTER XX.

SIR A. MURRAY'S RECALL 368

CONTENTS

TABLE OF APPENDICES.

		PAGE
1.	Tabular Record of Operations	374
2.	Order of Battle of the E.E.F. April 1916	380
3.	Order of Battle of the E.E.F. April 1917	396
4.	The Staff and Administrative Services in the early Stages of the War	408
5.	The History of Senussism	409
6.	No 3 Section Headquarters, Telegraphic order of 4th August 1916 (Battle of Romani)	411
7.	No 3 Section Headquarters, Telegraphic order of 5th August 1916 (Battle of Romani)	412
8.	Eastern Force Operation Order No 33, 24th March 1917 (First Battle of Gaza)	413
9.	Desert Column Operation Order No. 25, 25th March 1917 (First Battle of Gaza)	415
10.	53rd Division Operation Order No. 27, 25th March 1917 (First Battle of Gaza)	418
11.	53rd Division Operation Order No. 28, 26th March 1917 (First Battle of Gaza)	420
12.	Eastern Force Operation Order No 40, 12th April 1917 (Second Battle of Gaza)	421
13.	Eastern Force Operation Order No 41, 16th April 1917 (Second Battle of Gaza)	424
14.	Eastern Force Operation Order No 43, 18th April 1917 (Second Battle of Gaza)	427
15.	(i) Meanings of Place-names; (ii) Glossary of Terms in components of Place-names	429

SKETCHES, MAPS AND PHOTOGRAPHS.

SKETCHES.

(Bound in Volume.)

Sketch A	The Western Desert	*At beginning*	
,, B	The Eastern Desert	*At end*	
,, 1.	Attack on Suez Canal, 3rd February 1915..	*Facing p.*	39
,, 2.	Affair of the Wadi Senab, 11th/13th December 1915	,,	109
,, 3.	Affair of the Wadi Majid, 25th December 1915	,,	113
,, 4.	Affair of Halazin, 23rd January 1916	,,	121
,, 5.	Action of Agagiya, 26th February 1916	,,	125
,, 6.	Operations at Girba and Siwa, 3rd/4th February 1917	,,	141
,, 7.	Operations against the Sultan of Darfur, March–December 1916..	,,	147
,, 8.	Affair of Qatiya, 23rd April 1916..	,,	161
,, 9.	Turkish Railway Communications, August 1916	,,	174
,, 10.	Battle of Romani, August 1916 ..	,,	179
,, 11.	Arabia and Syria, June 1916 ..	,,	207
,, 12.	Affair of Magdhaba, 23rd December 1916	,,	253
,, 13.	Action of Rafah, 9th January 1917..	,,	263
,, 14.	First Battle of Gaza, 26th March, 1917	,,	281
,, 15.	First Battle of Gaza, 27th March 1917	,,	305
,, 16.	Second Battle of Gaza, 19th April 1917	,,	327
Diagram I.	Water Supply, Eastern Frontier Force, November 1916	,,	271
,, II.	The Sinaitic Peninsula (5 Sections)	,,	278

MAPS.

(In Separate Case.)

Map 1. Egypt, 1/2,000,000.
 ,, 2. Southern Palestine, 1/250,000.
 ,, 3. Attack on Suez Canal, February 1915.
 ,, 4. Attack on Suez Canal, Timsah to Great Bitter Lake, February 1915.
 ,, 5. Western Desert (Matruh to Sollum)—Theatre of Operations against the Senussi.

MAPS

Map 6. Affair of the Wadi Majid, 25th December 1915.
,, 7. Suez Canal Defences, July 1916.
,, 8. The Desert Campaign (layered map).
,, 9. Battle of Romani, 3rd August 1916.
,, 10. Battle of Romani, 4th August 1916.
,, 11. Action of Rafah, 9th January 1917.
,, 12. First Battle of Gaza, 26th March 1917.
,, 13. Second Battle of Gaza, the Battlefield.
,, 14. Second Battle of Gaza, 17th April 1917.
,, 15. Second Battle of Gaza, 19th April 1917.

PHOTOGRAPHS.

Ali el Muntar from Mansura Ridge .. .. .. *Facing p.*	285
Gaza from Ali el Muntar .. .. ,,	301
Tank Redoubt from Sheikh Abbas .. .. .. ,,	335
Looking North from Lee's Hill over Gaza and Lambeth Wood .. .. ,,	341
Dunes south-west of Gaza from Samson Ridge .. ,,	343
Khirbet Sihan and Atawine from south of Sheikh Abbas.. .. .. ,,	345

LIST OF BOOKS TO WHICH MOST FREQUENT
REFERENCE IS MADE.

OFFICIAL.

CORBETT: "Naval Operations," Vols. I and II. By Sir Julian S. Corbett (Longmans.)
 The Official British Naval History of the War.

GULLETT: "The Australian Imperial Forces in Sinai and Palestine." By H. S. Gullett. (Sydney: Angus and Robertson.)
 Vol. VII of the Official History of Australia in the War. Referred to as "Australian Official History."

POWLES: "The New Zealanders in Sinai and Palestine." By Lieut.-Colonel C. Guy Powles, C.M.G., D.S.O. (New Zealand: Whitcombe and Tombs.)
 Vol. III of the Official History of New Zealand's Effort in the Great War. Referred to as "New Zealand Official History."

STEUBER: "'Jildirim': Deutsche Streiter auf heiligen Boden." By Obergeneralarzt Steuber. (Oldenburg: Gerhard Stalling.)
 A Reichsarchiv monograph, by the head of the Medical Services in Palestine in 1917 and early 1918. It is an interesting record, but lacking in military detail. The author only took over his duties in the autumn of 1917, so that but little of the ground of the present volume is covered by his book.

UNOFFICIAL.

DJEMAL: "Memories of a Turkish Statesman." By Djemal Pasha. (English Translation, Hutchinson.)
 The author commanded the Turkish *Fourth Army* throughout the period of the present volume, but his record is not of great value.

DOUIN: "L'Attaque du Canal de Suez." By Georges Douin, Lieutenant de Vaisseau. (Paris: Delagrave.)
 An excellent account by an author who was on the spot, who evidently received from British officers at the time information which has not always been preserved, and has also had access to the records of the French Ministry of Marine.

LIMAN: "Fünf Jahre Türkei." By General der Kavallerie Liman von Sanders. (Berlin: Scherl.)
 The best of the books dealing with the War in the East from the German–Turkish side. The author was, however, in Turkey—and part of the time engaged in defending Gallipoli—during the period covered by this volume, and he gives but a general sketch of operations in Sinai and Palestine. As Chief of the German Military Mission to Turkey his statements regarding policy are of importance.

"SINAI" ("Zwischen Kaukasus und Sinai"). 3 Vols. (Berlin: Mulzer & Cleemann.)
 An annual, published for three years by the German "Bund der Asienkämpfer" (Association of Combatants in Asia). Vol. I, published in 1921, is of greatest value, owing to the contribution of General Freiherr Kress von Kressenstein, who held important staff appointments and commands in Palestine. The various contributors are referred to by name: thus "Sinai": Kress, "Sinai": Dieckmann.

INTRODUCTION.

THE British Army, its organization and expansion, has been described in the volumes dealing with the war in the Western Theatre. The troops which from time to time composed the forces operating in Egypt and Palestine were drawn from the New Armies, the Territorial Force, from Australia, New Zealand and South Africa (the origin and organization of whose military forces are described, or are to be described, in their own official histories), and from the Indian Army. The garrison of Egypt at the outbreak of war between Great Britain and Germany consisted of troops of the British Regular Army, but these returned within two months to the United Kingdom. The defence of the Suez Canal in 1914 and 1915 was carried out almost entirely by Indian troops; a number of these were present in Egypt throughout the campaign in Sinai; they took some part in the offensive operations of the autumn of 1917, and a major part in those of the autumn of 1918.

When Lord Kitchener became Commander-in-Chief in India after the South African War, the three Presidential Armies of Bombay, Madras and Bengal, and corps such as the Punjab Frontier Force, always under the direct control of the Government of India, were amalgamated, renumbered as one Line, and made uniform in organization and training. The divisional system having been introduced in the United Kingdom, Lord Kitchener followed suit in India, grouping the Army into nine divisional commands, exclusive of Burma. The composition of Indian divisions differed from that of British chiefly in that the former were considerably weaker in artillery.

With the formation of one Line, the racial constitution of the regiment became of great importance. Ethnological study was undertaken with a view to the improvement of those regiments which drew their recruits from the less martial races or from those in which generations of the *Pax Britannica* had weakened the instincts of self-preservation. The results of the regrouping of races then instituted proved very satisfactory. The regiments of the Indian Army consisted partly of Mohammedans, partly of Hindus, and usually contained both Mohammedan and Hindu squadrons or companies. The behaviour of the adherents of the former religion was a matter of some anxiety after the proclamation of a Holy War by Turkey. Islamic fervour did in fact cause a few desertions, but the Indian Moslem soldiers, with rare exceptions remained true to their salt.

The menace of Russia had for many years been the chief preoccupation of Indian military policy. The Indian Army existed mainly for the defence of India, and it was only the appearance of Russia in the ranks of the Allies that freed Indian troops for service in Europe and in other theatres. Another threat, that of Afghanistan and of the 150,000 fanatical tribesmen in the North-West Frontier, remained. After providing the Indian Corps and Indian Cavalry Corps for the Western Front, a division for the Persian Gulf, and a small contingent for East Africa, it was a matter of some difficulty to find the collection of units which were formed into the 10th and 11th Indian Divisions and conducted the defence of the Suez Canal. These troops consisted either of formed brigades (in which the British battalion normally attached had been replaced by a fourth Indian battalion), or brigades created for the occasion by the grouping together of hitherto unallotted battalions. The proportion of artillery in India was far less than in the British Expeditionary Force, and only one mountain artillery brigade was available to accompany " Indian Expeditionary Force E " (as it was afterwards called) to Egypt. This force also included troops of the Native States of India, known as Imperial Service Troops, the organization and training of which had for thirty years been modelled upon those of the Indian Army. In the course of the war the Government of India raised many new units, some of which took part in the final victorious campaign in Palestine. This was a matter of great difficulty owing to the weakness of the Indian Army in reserves, either of British officers or native rank and file.

The Egyptian Army, of which mention will be made, was required mainly for the defence of, and maintenance of security within, the Sudan, and was not employed, except on a very small scale, against the Turks. The principal exceptions were the presence of a single Egyptian battery on the Canal during the attack of February 1915, and the despatch of a small contingent, under native officers, to assist the Arabs in the Hejaz in 1916.

INTRODUCTION

In August 1914 the Egyptian Army consisted of two squadrons of cavalry, three companies of mounted infantry, six batteries of field and mountain artillery, one Maxim battery, three garrison artillery companies, and seventeen infantry battalions.[1] Of this force, one field battery, one garrison company and three battalions only were stationed in Egypt, the remainder being in the Sudan.

The Turkish Army was the only civilized enemy, with the exception of small German and very small Austrian contingents, which had to be faced by the British throughout the campaigns of Egypt and Palestine. Statistics regarding the Ottoman Empire are never reliable, but it is believed that its population, not including that of Arabia, consisted of about twenty millions, of whom fourteen millions were Moslems. Taking into consideration the high losses of Turkey in recent wars, the large number of officials, the needs of factories, there were about a million men of an age rendering them liable for military service at the outbreak of war.

Service in the Turkish Army was compulsory, with numerous loopholes and exemptions. Each man was required to serve two years in the Active Army, or *Nizam*, and liable for service as a member of the Active Army Reserve for sixteen years. The peace strength of the army was 10,000 officers and 200,000 other ranks, and though nearly the whole of the Reserve was called up at the outbreak of war, it is known that a large number of men were later sent back to their occupations. The *Nizam* troops were chiefly armed with the excellent 7·65 mm.[2] Mauser, those of the Reserve and the older Territorial troops with the 9·5 mm. and many older types, including the Martini, and there were instances of men in the same company being armed with different types of rifle. The artillery also was of various types and ages.

The country was divided into four Army Inspectorates, with headquarters at Constantinople, Erzinjan, Damascus and Baghdad. The number of army corps in these Inspectorates varied, that in the Constantinople being five, whilst the Third Inspectorate, with which we are here mainly

---

[1] Eight Egyptian, 7 Sudanese, 1 Arab, 1 Equatorial; 1 company Nuba Territorials and 6 companies Sudanese Reserves. There were also the necessary corps and services: medical, works, supplies, stores and ordnance.

[2] Or, in terms more familiar to English readers, ·298 inches.

concerned, consisted of two only. The normal number of divisions to the army corps was three, and there were therefore six in Syria and Palestine. A *Nizam* division normally consisted of three regiments, each of three battalions, a regiment of field artillery of from six to nine 4-gun batteries,[1] three machine-gun companies; engineers being corps troops. In some cases mountain artillery was substituted for a part, or even for the whole, of the field artillery allotted to a division.

Some modernization of the Turkish Army had taken place as a result of the teaching and advice of Field-Marshal von der Goltz, who was attached to the Turkish General Staff for twelve years from 1883 onwards, but purely in an advisory capacity. In 1913 a large German military mission was despatched to Constantinople, and its head, Liman von Sanders Pasha, became Inspector General of the Army. In the short time at his disposal, he had undoubtedly accomplished a good deal, both with regard to training and organization, but the influence of the mission had not extended much beyond the corps in Europe. The further they were from the capital, the worse armed, equipped and trained were the troops. Training was in general weak, being for the most part confined to the barrack square. Another serious drawback was the shortage and indifferent quality of the transport. Mechanical transport there was none, and horse transport included vehicles of every possible type. It was, in fact, laid down that the first act of a Turkish formation on mobilization was to seize all the local transport available. The medical services were deplorably bad, sometimes virtually non-existent.

These deficiencies it was beyond the power of the German mission to remedy, certainly in so short a time. There was, however, another aspect of the German tuition, which is not always understood. German officers could not instil into the Turks their own methods, and there is evidence that the attempt to do so was in some respects positively harmful. The Turks often acquired from their masters rigidity without precision, and lost the habit of rough but fairly effective improvisation which had carried them through so many campaigns.

---

[1] It is doubtful whether this strength of nine batteries was often attained; probably it never was in Syria, whilst some divisions had less than six batteries.

INTRODUCTION

The fighting qualities of the best Turkish troops have always been extremely high, but the increasing complication of war left them at some disadvantage with nations which had a better standard of education. This was particularly the case with regard to the officers, who were sharply divided into two classes: those who had risen from the ranks and could scarcely read or write, and the product of the military schools. The former class was disappearing in the Active Army, but mobilization brought a great number of virtually illiterate officers back to the colours. Of the other races which made up the Turkish Army, the Arabs were inferior to the Turks, though good enough soldiers if well trained and led, but political events were to make them unreliable. The Christians were bitterly disaffected, and were largely employed in labour battalions.

Yet the Turkish Army was, now as ever, a formidable opponent. Its disadvantages in shortage of equipment and transport were partly compensated for by the frugality and hardiness of the Turkish peasant. It was impossible to prophesy when war broke out to what extent Turkey's other handicaps, material and intellectual, such as lack of munition factories or industries which could be converted to supply munitions, on the one hand, and lack of education on the other, would be lightened by German aid.

CHAPTER I.

THE OUTBREAK OF WAR.

(Map 1; Sketch B.)

EGYPT IN AUGUST, 1914.

THE situation of Egypt at the outbreak of war between Great Britain and Germany was of peculiar complexity. On the one hand, the British occupation was based, like many of our country's institutions, upon an unwritten convention. The chief British official bore the modest title of Consul-General, a title borne also by the agents of certain other States. In theory he had no authority greater than that of his colleagues, yet, while their functions were merely diplomatic, he was in practice, as representative of the Protecting Power, " the ultimate authority in the country " in all those matters . . . which the protecting power " chose for the moment to regard as calling for the exercise " of its control."[1] In theory again, Egypt was still a province of the Turkish Empire; in practice she was, save in certain minor matters, independent of Turkey. By reason of the Capitulations and other complications of her constitution, which are outside the scope of a military history, she was actually far more dependent upon some of the Great Powers than upon Turkey, her nominal suzerain.[2] On the other hand, her importance in a great war was immeasurable, mainly, though not entirely, owing to the Suez Canal. The Canal was, indeed, in the popular German phrase, the "jugular vein" of the British Empire. Half-way between England and India, on the route which was to be taken by troops from that country and later from Australia and New Zealand, on that

Map 1.

---

[1] Lord Milner: " England in Egypt," p. 30.
[2] The Constitution of Egypt, one of the most complicated in the world, cannot be dealt with apart from its history during the nineteenth century. To describe it even in outline would occupy space which cannot be afforded in these volumes. The attention of readers seeking further enlightenment on this subject is directed to Lord Cromer's " Modern Egypt," to Lord Milner's " England in Egypt," and to " Egypt and the Army," by Lieut.-Colonel P. G. Elgood, which is largely concerned with the internal affairs of Egypt during the war.

followed by the bulk of the trade between Europe on the one side and Asia and Australasia on the other, it was the most vital focal point upon the communications of the world.

By means of the Suez Canal Egypt connects the eastern seas with the Mediterranean. Through the province of Sinai she connects Asia and Africa. Even before the cutting of the Canal the Isthmus of Suez had been a trade route and of military importance also. When England fought France in Egypt over a century ago the struggle was for the road to the East. On that occasion the former had drawn reinforcements from India and South Africa by the Red Sea.[1] The route which runs along the northern coast of Sinai, though but a scarce-defined camel track, has seen the movement eastward and westward of many armies and of many famous soldiers, among them Ramases, Alexander, Selim and Napoleon. In some degree perhaps forgetful of its history, Great Britain had come to look upon the Sinai Desert solely as a barrier, which kept the Turk in Palestine at arm's length. A barrier it was to a great extent, but it had served also as a highway for thousands of years and as a military highway it was to serve again before many months were passed and throughout the course of the war.[2]

It was, however, the waterway, the Suez Canal, which had, since its opening in 1869, chiefly influenced British policy and now caused chief concern. As a line of communication it was invaluable, but scarcely less so as a potential base, for which the well-equipped ports of Alexandria, Port Said, and in lesser degree Suez, rendered it particularly suitable in view of Egypt's geographical situation. The maintenance of its integrity as an open highway had long been one of the keys to British policy and had been the determining cause of British intervention. In short, the occupation conferred on Great Britain, and through her on

---

[1] On the 8th June 1801 Sir David Baird landed at Qoseir on the Red Sea with 5,000 troops from India and the Cape, marched across the desert to Qena, on the Nile north of Luxor, and thence to Cairo, to join hands with the British force which had captured the city after the Battle of Alexandria. During the Crimean War the 10th Hussars from India landed at Suez and marched to Alexandria on its way to the Crimea.

[2] In Napoleon's Syrian campaign the advance across Sinai of the main body under Kléber was ordered on the 31st January 1799. Kléber arrived at El Arish on the 12th February, and was joined by Napoleon (who had quitted Cairo on the 10th) on the 17th. Gaza was occupied on the 24th. The force consisted of about 10,000 infantry and 1,600 artillery, with 36 field guns, and there were 16 medium guns and mortars in the park.

her Allies, very great advantages. The disadvantages of the situation were to Britain alone. The occupation necessitated from the moment of the outbreak of war with Germany a garrison stronger than the small British force which was maintained in the country in time of peace, and also naval defence of the Canal and of Alexandria. Should Turkey join the Central Powers, as seemed probable, the defence of the Canal from attack by land would be an added commitment. Moreover, this possible hostility on the part of Turkey brought a host of new problems up for solution. The Sultan of Turkey was not alone Egypt's traditional if nominal overlord, he was also the religious head of the greater part of the Mohammedan world. Egypt was a Moslem country, and it was the flaming up of religious fervour which had involved Britain in intermittent operations, under difficult conditions, for seventeen years, from the Revolt of Arabi Pasha in 1881 to the Battle of Omdurman in 1898. There was in the country little affection for Turkey, but the suzerainty of the Sultan had for the people a certain significance and his position as head of their faith considerably more.

For some years there had been a decline, if not in the prestige, at least in the popularity, of Britain in Egypt. The detached philosopher, considering how the occupation had brought the country, for bankruptcy and tyranny, prosperity and justice; how irrigation had transformed its agriculture; how increasing wealth and security had doubled its population between 1882 and 1914; might exclaim against the ingratitude of man; but the decline was in fact inevitable. Its causes are inherent in human nature, and it represents a reaction that has to be faced by every nation which undertakes the regeneration of a derelict state. It was this very prosperity which had altered the point of view of the Egyptians. A new generation had grown up which did not remember the bad old days. No people will for long recognize a foreign power as the source of its well-being. The happy situation of the country, as compared with the turmoil of fifty years back, was taken for granted; there was now little or no recognition that it was due to British administration. The aspect of the occupation uppermost in the minds of those who thought about the problem was that a nation alien in race and religion had imposed its control upon Egypt. Certain sections of the former governing classes, whose occupation was gone, helped to inflame this grievance, though their aspirations had nothing in common with those of the masses of the people. In this they took their tone from the Palace, always bitterly hostile to the occupying power.

In 1914, owing to the personal prestige of the Consul-General, Lord Kitchener, the activities of nationalism were less pronounced than they had been for some years. Various matters of difference were dormant, but they were by no means composed, nor could the effect of the excitement of war upon them easily be calculated.

To add to the eastern menace and internal anxieties there was a lesser danger in the Western Desert, from the powerful and ambitious religious leader known as the Senussi, then at war with Italy. His material interests were dependent on his friendly relations with Egypt and the British; his religious sentiments, on the other hand, brought him into sympathy with the Khalifate. Should a *Jihad*, or Holy War, be proclaimed in Constantinople, it was probable that he would instruct his followers to answer the call and that the men of the desert, in whom religious fervour burns the brighter if fed by the prospect of plunder, would attempt to invade Egypt, remarkably open and defenceless from the west.

In the Sudan all was quiet. This huge territory, stretching from Halfa on the Nile to within four degrees of the Equator, a distance of some 1,800 miles, largely desert but elsewhere of great possibilities, had been lost to Egypt through the inefficiency of her government. Jointly reconquered by Great Britain and Egypt, it had since then been jointly held. But its reconquest had allowed the former to set about the work of administration with a clean slate. Here there was no shadowy Turkish overlordship, no foreign interference, none of those cumbersome and intricate international institutions which the force of circumstances had imposed upon Egypt. Under direct administration the Sudan, left in anarchy by war, was advancing slowly but surely to a prosperity hitherto undreamt of. Among its simpler peoples in an earlier stage of civilization those growing pains of nationalism which vexed Egypt's health were not present. Public opinion, so far as it existed, had been won and held, so much so that, on the subsequent outbreak of war with Turkey, the Governor-General was

RELATIONS OF TURKEY AND EGYPT

given remarkable demonstrations of loyalty and devotion to the British cause, accompanied by outspoken denunciation of Turkey's action, by chiefs and religious leaders all over the country. It must, however, be added that the position of the British in the Sudan was a cause of dissatisfaction to Egyptian Nationalists, who sought to exploit it as a great Egyptian grievance. They argued that, as the Sudan controlled the head waters of the Nile, on which the economic life of Egypt depended, Egypt should control the Sudan.

1914.
Aug.

In August 1914, the Consul-General, Lord Kitchener, was absent in England, and Sir Milne Cheetham was acting as *Chargé d'Affaires*. The commander of the British garrison, which was known as the Force in Egypt and numbered some five thousand men,[1] was Major-General the Hon. J. Byng. General Sir Reginald Wingate was Governor-General of the Anglo-Egyptian Sudan and Sirdar of the Egyptian Army.

It will be clear from this short sketch of the political situation that the constitution of Egypt was not easily adapted to a state of war. Egypt was virtually free of Turkey, had been in fact semi-independent of her since the day of the great Albanian viceroy Mehemet Ali, but foreign diplomatic agents in the country were still officially accredited to the Porte. When hostilities broke out with Germany and Austria the first anomaly appeared: that the Powers with which Britain was at war were diplomatically represented in a country in which she maintained an army of occupation. It was at this stage important to avoid giving offence to Turkey, whose attitude was still uncertain, but it was not possible to allow the German and Austro-Hungarian representatives to remain, and they were ordered to leave the country. The incident did not, however, result in any serious protest from Turkey. There still remained the task of the prevention of espionage and the control of the numerous subjects of the Central Powers.

Great Britain's first care was to keep open and protect the Suez Canal. By an international convention the freedom of the Canal to navigation was guaranteed by the

---

[1] The troops of the Force in Egypt in August 1914 consisted of the 3rd Dragoon Guards, " T " Battery R.H.A., 7th Mountain Battery R.G.A., 2nd Field Company R.E., 2/Devonshire, 1/Worcestershire, 2/Northamptonshire, 2/Gordon Highlanders, with auxiliary services.

European Powers.[1] The Canal was administered by a French company, which actually owned the strip of land on either side of it, with here and there wider stretches for the development of its stations and workshops. When war was declared enemy shipping made straight for the Canal to avoid capture. After reaching it, certain captains made improper use of their wireless, which was accordingly dismantled. Sir J. Maxwell records that in September a German sailor swam round a British warship, waving a German flag and shouting abuse, without being molested. The incident, trifling in itself, illustrates the curious international situation at the time. Eventually it was decided that there was no right of asylum in the Canal, and the Egyptian Government called on these ships to leave its waters, escorting them with Egyptian forces beyond the three-mile limit. Outside this limit they were liable to capture by the cruisers of the Allies and to be treated as prize. The Suez Canal Company was naturally sensitive regarding its position. All difficulties as to its line of conduct were eventually solved when Turkey entered the war, and thenceforward it put its ample resources and admirable organization wholeheartedly at the disposal of the Allies.

The Immediate Military Problem.

The protection of the Suez Canal from attack by sea had long been recognized as an important part of Great Britain's naval responsibilities. The command of the Eastern Mediterranean was now assured, the British Mediterranean Fleet having effected a junction with the powerful French fleet under Admiral Boué de Lapeyrère at the entrance of the Adriatic on the 15th August.[2] Several British cruisers passed through to the Red Sea and assured the safety of the southern entrance to the Canal. Its defence against attack by land had also been considered by the War Office and the

---

[1] This Convention was signed in April 1888. The British Government then stipulated that it was not to come into force so long as the British occupation of Egypt lasted. Under the Anglo-French Agreement of 1904 Great Britain agreed to put the Suez Canal Convention of 1888 into force, with certain minor exceptions.

[2] By a convention of the 6th August the British Mediterranean Fleet was to come under the orders of the French Commander-in-Chief, who was responsible for watching the Austrian Fleet and for the protection of British trade. " Naval Operations," vol. i, pp. 83-8.

military authorities in Egypt, but so long as this country was at peace with Turkey the land problem belonged only to a possible future. The chief precautions taken in August were against damage to any portion of the Canal or the State Railways by acts of sabotage. It was, however, vitally important that there should be in Egypt sufficient troops for its defence and internal security should Turkey abandon her neutrality in favour of the cause of the Central Powers. The British garrison of Regular troops was, moreover, urgently required to complete divisions to be sent to France.

1914.
Aug.

On the 9th August orders were received from the War Office in London that two infantry divisions and a cavalry brigade would be despatched from India as soon as possible, organized for subsequent service in France. Later, Major-General Byng was informed that the Bikanir Camel Corps, placed at the Viceroy's disposal by the Maharajah of Bikanir, would also be sent to him. On relief by these forces the British fighting troops, with almost all the personnel of the administrative services, were to return to England, taking with them the greater part of the gun and small arms ammunition in the country.

Nine days later the new Secretary of State for War, Lord Kitchener, telegraphed that it had been decided by the Cabinet that the two Indian divisions should go straight to Marseilles without disembarkation in Egypt and that the British garrison should be replaced by a Territorial division. Another Indian infantry brigade would be sent to Egypt on the heels of the divisions destined for France, while, should the situation worsen, permission was given to retain temporarily a brigade of the leading division. At the same time it was announced that Lieut.-General Sir John Maxwell was to take command of the Force in Egypt and that Major-General Byng would return on relief to the United Kingdom. Sir J. Maxwell had, since Tell-el-Kebir in 1882, passed a great part of his military career in Egypt, had commanded the Force in Egypt from 1908 to 1912, and was thoroughly acquainted with the situation in all its complexities, military, political, and religious.

On the 31st August the Egyptian Camel Corps was ordered to the Canal as a measure of precaution, but orders were issued that troops were not to leave the banks save in case of a raid. The Sinai Peninsula, in normal times controlled by a handful of police, had been evacuated, and it was

1914.
Sept. considered that the appearance in it of British troops might cause agitation at Constantinople, where the atmosphere was already sufficiently heated.

On the 8th September Sir J. Maxwell arrived and took over command. On the same date the first transports of the Lahore (3rd Indian) Division were arriving at Suez and the War Office enquired how soon it could be sent on to Marseilles. Sir J. Maxwell replied that, the situation being quiet, he would retain only the 9th (Sirhind) Brigade and III Mountain Artillery Brigade, as he had been given permission to do. The remainder of the Lahore Division sailed from Alexandria on the 19th.

Map 1.
Sketch B. There were reports from beyond the Turkish border of new work on roads and water supply, and military intelligence showed that ere long 100,000 troops might be available in Syria and Palestine for action against the Canal. On the 23rd September Sir J. Maxwell reported an act of aggression; the frontier having been crossed near Rafah by a small body of armed Bedouin. The only reply to this move was the despatch of a small column of Egyptian Coastguard to destroy the wells at Nekhl, 70 miles east of Suez. But the serious view of the situation taken by Lord Kitchener was shown by a message sent on the 27th, the date of the disembarkation of the East Lancashire Division (T.F.)[1] in Egypt. He countermanded the embarkation of part of the original British garrison and informed Sir J. Maxwell that, besides the Sirhind Brigade and the East Lancashire Division (the latter of which was deficient of two artillery brigades), he was sending him two regiments of Yeomanry. Sir J. Maxwell was not unduly anxious. He knew that the next Indian convoy, with the Meerut (7th Indian) Division, had reached Aden, and he had placed the Sirhind Brigade on the Canal. The garrison being already embarked, he did not propose to retain it, and it sailed from Alexandria on the 30th September.

Oct. The strain in France, however, soon compelled Lord Kitchener to press for the despatch of even the Sirhind Brigade, which now constituted the only trained troops in Egypt. Sir J. Maxwell pointed out that news from Palestine was most disquieting. Large parties were at work repairing roads at Gaza and even El Arish, within the Egyptian border.

---

[1] Afterwards known as the 42nd (East Lancashire) Division.

THE OUTBREAK OF WAR

1914.
Oct.

German officers were visiting the frontier posts. There had been a report that a party, disguised as Arabs and carrying explosives, was moving on the Canal at Qantara. The War Office was reassuring in its reply, pointing out that a large force for the protection of Egypt was under orders from India. The Lucknow Brigade was being sent to replace the Sirhind Brigade, which would be allowed to remain until the former had arrived in Egypt. In addition to the Bikanir Camel Corps, already promised, an Imperial Service cavalry brigade, a composite Imperial Service infantry brigade,[1] and eight Indian battalions were shortly to embark, while three more brigades of native Indian infantry were to follow. These promises put a better complexion on affairs, especially as the East Lancashire Division was rapidly improving in military fitness.

WAR WITH TURKEY.

As October drew on the situation between Great Britain and Turkey grew worse and signs of excitement appeared in Egypt.[2] On the 30th all doubts were ended. It was war.[3]

---

[1] The Imperial Service troops were those maintained by Native States for the service of the Empire. The Imperial Service Infantry Brigade was to have one regular battalion, the 33rd Punjabis, and three battalions of Imperial Service troops (Alwar, Gwalior and Patiala Infantry).

[2] During this period much of the correspondence regarding policy was conducted by means of semi-official letters between Lord Kitchener and Sir J. Maxwell, in accordance with a custom prevalent in the British Army, strengthened in this case by the writers' long association and the familiarity with Egyptian affairs which they had in common. On 16th October General Maxwell wrote :—

"There is rather more nervousness in Egypt, but everything is
"quiet. It is part of the German propaganda that a revolution in
"Egypt is imminent, and that there are agents all over the country
"fomenting the natives against the British. We can find little evidence
"in support of this. There are, however, far too many able-bodied
"reservists, German and Austrian, all over Egypt. I have just finished
"a general registration and, though I have not yet the exact figures,
"there must be at least 600, and there must be another 200 from the
"crews of captured ships. This is a danger. I have wired you asking
"to have them all interned at Malta. They can do no harm there. On
"Monday I am trying before a military court an undoubted spy of
"Enver's. He is a German and an officer of the Alexandria Police, and
"he had on him when arrested a secret code, maps of the Suez Canal, and
"two boxes of detonators . . . . ."

" As we are not going to hold our Sinai frontier and will destroy as
"many wells as possible, I expect all the Bedouin will join the Turks if
"they come over. As I cannot send out patrols I do not know much
"about what is going on on the frontier lines. I expect there will be
"raids before long. The Turks seem to be doing a lot of work in road-
"making, building forts, etc., all over Palestine and Syria, which looks

The East Lancashire Division marched through the streets of Cairo next morning to impress the populace. Prominent and dangerous Turkish subjects were at once arrested and interned, but there could be no question of incarcerating the 70,000 Turkish nationals in Egypt. Martial law was proclaimed on the 2nd November and quietly received. It simplified the constitutional problem, as it was now possible for the military authorities to carry out the necessary action through the medium of the Prime Minister. In a further proclamation, announcing the actual declaration of war, Sir J. Maxwell sketched its causes, adding that Great Britain accepted its sole burden.

In other respects the difficulties anticipated from Turkey's entry into the war had arisen. The Egyptian Government viewed with alarm the prospect of taking part in hostilities against the Suzerain and Khalif. This dread did not imply devotion to the Ottoman cause so much as doubt on the part of the ministers regarding the result of the conflict and their own position in the event of victory attending Turkey and the Central Powers. In Turkey, Greece, Bulgaria, and Rumania, belief in Teutonic invincibility had become a superstition, impervious to argument. To the governments of these states, their corps of officers, their official and, indeed, the bulk of their educated classes, the alliance of Germany and Austria created the vision of a military colossus, the overthrow of which by the Entente was an impossibility. This hypnotism was not quite so general in Egypt, but the belief engendered by it was widespread and those Egyptians on whom official responsibility lay could not

---

"as if they expected attack from us, but their tendency is to move south, "and this can only mean attack upon Egypt. With the eight battalions "from India, two mountain batteries, the Bikanir Camel Corps and the "Coastguard, the Canal ought to be safe."

On 13th October, in reply to a suggestion from Sir J. Maxwell that a patrol should be sent out to Bir el Abd, 45 miles east of the Canal on the Mediterranean coast route, Lord Kitchener had telegraphed that this was inadvisable, as the situation between the peace and war parties in Constantinople was still doubtful and the latter was using the presence of Indian troops in Egypt as a lever for action. A move of this sort might therefore result in further pressure being put upon the peace party.

³ The *Goeben* and *Breslau* bombarded Odessa, Sevastopol and Theodosia on 29th October, and on the 30th the British and French Ambassadors to the Porte demanded their passports. Great Britain and France formally declared war on Turkey on the 5th November. It is now known that war was virtually inevitable from the first, Germany and Turkey having signed an offensive and defensive treaty on the 2nd August 1914. (Karl Kautsky: "Die Deutschen Dokumente zum Kriegsausbruch," Nr. 733.)

wholly escape its influence. Some of them showed anxiety to avoid that responsibility by resigning their posts. Much therefore depended upon the manner in which Great Britain handled the situation within the space of the next few weeks.

1914. Dec.

The most difficult of the problems concerned the position of the Khedive. Abbas Hilmi had throughout his reign opposed, so far as he could and dared, the British administration. He had been in Turkey ever since the outbreak of war with Germany, and was actively and openly pro-Turk. His absence had been fortunate enough, since the position of Regent was filled by the moderate and capable Prime Minister, Rushdi Pasha, but affairs could not be allowed to continue in this fashion. The British Government took a decisive step. Egypt was proclaimed a Protectorate on 18th December; on the following day the absent Khedive was declared to be deposed, and Prince Hussein Kamel Pasha, his uncle, raised to the throne in his stead, with the title of Sultan. At the same time the title of the British representative was changed from Consul-General to High Commissioner.[1]

The last strand of the tie with Turkey was thus severed. The accession of the new Sultan, respected for his character by Europeans and Egyptians alike, was on the whole well received, but these important constitutional changes were viewed by the people with greater indifference than might have been expected. Sentiments and interests were diverse enough to prevent any general expression of opinion. There was latent hostility to Great Britain and sympathy with Turkey as a Moslem Power, but there were also expectations of some benefit to Egypt from the new *régime* and recognition that the Protecting Power was, for the present at least, in a strong position. The populace acquiesced, while waiting for the solution of the riddle as to which way victory would lean in the coming struggle. Long before that riddle could be solved Egypt was to have impressive testimony to the military resources of the British Empire in the constant passage of troops through the Suez Canal.

The Sultan and his ministers cordially supported the High Commissioner and Sir J. Maxwell in utilizing the resources of Egypt as they were required. As the calls upon

---
[1] Sir Milne Cheetham, the *Chargé d'Affaires*, remained in Egypt as acting High Commissioner until 9th January 1915, when Sir Henry M'Mahon took up the appointment of High Commissioner.

them increased, the presence in the departments of the Egyptian Government of many retired officers of the British Army enabled demands to be met with a smoothness that would have been otherwise unattainable. The natural desire of these officers to rejoin their units was in some cases acceded to, the result being one of the causes of subsequent unrest, when native subordinates on occasion employed the regulations of martial law to their own advantage. For the moment, however, there was surprisingly little trouble. Such disaffection as there was did not extend to the *fellahin*, though they, as well as the larger landowners, were temporarily crippled by the crisis in the cotton trade. The outbreak of war had closed so many markets and diverted or laid up so much shipping that a proportion of that year's crop rotted in the ground. Later on war was to have a contrary effect on cotton production, making it the most profitable industry in the Delta.

After the declaration of war by Britain and France, the Sultan of Turkey caused the chief religious functionary at Constantinople, the Sheikh ul Islam, to issue, on 11th November, a *Fatwa*, or decree, proclaiming a Holy War against the Allies. On the 14th the Sultan, as Khalif, proclaimed a *Jihad* on all those making war on Turkey or her allies. It was the final call to Moslems to range themselves in defence of their faith. How wide would be the response none could tell, but its general failure or success was to Great Britain of vital importance and to France of moment hardly less.

CHAPTER II.

THE COMMENCEMENT OF HOSTILITIES AND THE THREAT TO THE SUEZ CANAL.

(Maps 1, 3, 8; Sketches B, 9.)

NOVEMBER AND DECEMBER 1914.

On the 9th November the German commerce raider *Emden* was destroyed at Cocos Islands. Remote though the scene was, the effect of her disappearance was at once felt in Egypt. As soon as her menace to shipping east of Suez was removed a number of warships urgently required in Mediterranean waters were ordered westward and passed through the Canal. In the Indian Ocean there remained only one small group on the East African coast and another assisting the Persian Gulf Expedition. The Admiral of the East Indies station had in these circumstances little to occupy him, and the Admiralty decided that he could do better service in Egypt and on the Syrian coast. Vice-Admiral R. H. Peirse therefore rehoisted his flag in the *Swiftsure* at Suez on the 1st December.[1] On an average about four ships, British and French, were available for the defence of the Canal, being changed from time to time as circumstances required.

Meanwhile, on the 16th November, the Indian troops destined for the defence of Egypt reached Suez,[2] and battalions were moved as quickly as possible to Ismailia and Port Said. Major-General A. Wilson, arrived from India, was appointed G.O.C. Canal Defences. The Sirhind Brigade was relieved and sailed on the 23rd to rejoin its division in France. At the same time Sir J. Maxwell was informed of Lord Kitchener's project of bringing the Australian and New Zealand contingents to Egypt for war training. The intention was to send them later to France, but temporarily they would be available as reserves in Egypt, where their appearance would undoubtedly impress public opinion

---

[1] "Naval Operations," ii, p. 73.
[2] See p. 15.

On the 20th November occurred the first hostilities. A patrol of 20 men of the Bikanir Camel Corps, under Captain A. J. H. Chope, was attacked at Bir en Nuss, 20 miles east of Qantara, by 200 Bedouin, who approached it under a white flag. The party extricated itself creditably, though with casualties amounting to more than half its numbers. Unfortunately this affair proved that the loyalty of the camel troopers of the Egyptian Coastguard, several of whom accompanied the Bikanirs as guides, was extremely doubtful, since they allowed themselves to be made prisoners in a manner virtually amounting to desertion.

There was for a considerable period no further contact with the enemy, and for the rest of the year the headquarters of the Force in Egypt and of the Canal Defences had time to prepare defences and organize the troops. The Australian and New Zealand contingent, a magnificent but still only partly trained force, landed early in December.[1] The Indian troops were organized into two divisions, the 10th and 11th.

Lord Kitchener discussed with Sir J. Maxwell the possibility of some action against the Turkish communications with Syria. It was at this time that a diversion in the Gulf of Iskanderun, a project that was to reappear more than once in the course of the war, was first considered and rejected, after some preliminary preparations had been made.[2] The importance of Alexandretta at this period is not made clear by a first glance at the map, because the railway line to this town from west of the Amanus Mountains is a dead end. This branch line represented the originally planned course of the Baghdad Railway, which had been altered for strategical reasons. Turkey was still a great military, but no longer a great maritime Power, and the line following the shore of the Gulf of Iskanderun was peculiarly vulnerable from the sea. The railway was therefore

---

[1] The original Australian contingent consisted of one light horse brigade and one infantry division complete with artillery; that of New Zealand of 2,500 mounted troops, 5,000 infantry and one field artillery brigade.

[2] "If any diversion is contemplated, I think the easiest, safest and "most fruitful in results would be one at Alexandretta. There . . . . . "we strike a vital blow at the railways and also hit German interests very "hard. . . . . Alexandretta would not want a very large force. All "other places—Rafah, Jaffa, Acre, Beirut—are too far from the Turkish "lines of communications." Sir J. Maxwell to Lord Kitchener, 4th December, 1914.

carried over the Amanus and then, *via* Islahie, to Aleppo. At the outbreak of war the Bagche tunnel, west of Islahie, was not pierced. Some eighty miles further west, in the Cilician Taurus, was another gap in the line. Troops and supplies from Constantinople had to be detrained at Bozanti, west of the Taurus gap, and moved down by road to Tarsus, whence they were railed to Alexandretta. There they took to the road again and moved by it to Aleppo or a station just west of it before returning to the railway. The alternative to the Alexandretta route was to continue along the main line to the Amanus gap, there detrain, follow the mountain road to Islahie, and again entrain for Aleppo. The Alexandretta route was the better and quicker.[1]

Alexandretta, therefore, though a railhead, was a vital point on the improvised Turkish line of communications. If it were held by an enemy, Turkish troops moving to Syria would have to scramble and struggle over the Amanus road. Traffic between Turkey and Syria would be virtually stopped between January and March, and relatively small quantities of munitions could be brought through at any time of the year. The objections to the scheme were, however, at least at this period, very great. An organized field army, with modern means of transport and equipment for the landing of stores, would have been required and could have ill been spared, even if it could have been found. The Navy would have been called upon to make the bay secure against submarines and protect the sea route thereto. The landing of a British force for any operation greater than a raid would probably have resulted in risings of Armenians and of tribes such as the Nasariyeh and Ismailiyeh in the Amanus, so that, once embarked upon the enterprise, Britain would have found it almost impossible to withdraw, however urgent the reasons, and leave friends to Turkish vengeance. These considerations, the first above all, convinced Lord Kitchener and the Cabinet that in existing circumstances the passive defence of the Canal itself, on the line of the Canal, was the only possible method of protecting Egypt from attack by land.

---

[1] The Amanus road was not suitable for wheeled traffic till the German engineer Klinghart had finished work on it in 1916 (" Sinai ": Kress, i, p. 19). A traveller who crossed in January 1915 states that the mud was over his ankles and that there was no transport on the road but pack-mules and camels.

It seemed, however, that the expected Turkish invasion was a long time brewing. Admiral Peirse was therefore instructed to employ light cruisers to harry Syrian ports, particularly Alexandretta, Beirut and Haifa, with a view to stopping the movement of supplies. Early in December he had available the *Doris* and the Russian *Askold*, which had been put at his disposal. The *Askold* cleverly cut a German ship out of Haifa, while in the latter part of the month the *Doris* had a series of remarkable adventures. She began on the 13th by bombarding earthworks at El Arish and landing a party. She next landed a party at Sidon, which cut telegraph wires running along the coast and inland towards Damascus. But her most notable exploit was in the Gulf of Iskanderun, when she landed parties which blew up bridges, derailed trains, cut telegraph lines. Finally at Alexandretta, under threat of bombardment of the station, she forced the Turks to blow up two locomotives, lending them gun-cotton for the purpose. The torpedo-lieutenant sent ashore by Captain Larken to supervise their destruction was solemnly given Turkish rank for that day to preserve Turkish dignity. The end of the comedy is said to have been a claim by the Baghdad Railway Company against the Turkish Government for wanton and malicious damage to the former's property by a *Turkish* officer.[1]

The raids, though justifiable by the usage of war, were afterwards discontinued in view of reprisals threatened by the Turks against Allied subjects in their hands, and it was left to the enemy to take the next step. News of the occupation of El Arish, within the Egyptian border, caused Lord Kitchener to enquire if it were not possible, with the aid of the Navy, to carry out a landing and strike at the Turks. Sir J. Maxwell replied that shallows and a choppy sea made such action difficult, adding that the force at El Arish consisted mainly of Bedouin, who would retire inland at the first appearance of British warships.

The Canal Defences.

By December the defence of the Suez Canal had been organized. The force to which it was entrusted consisted of the 10th and 11th Indian Divisions and the Imperial Service

---

[1] "Naval Operations" ii, p. 74 *et seq.*

THE CANAL DEFENCES

1914.
Dec.

Cavalry Brigade. Owing to the demand for British Regular troops in Europe the normal allotment of one British battalion to each brigade had been abandoned and the two divisions were entirely composed of Indian troops. The artillery with these troops—which, it will be recalled, had not been sent from India as divisions—consisted of three mountain batteries only. Two field artillery brigades of the East Lancashire Division and a pack-gun battery of the Egyptian Army were added to the Canal Defences, but it was upon the presence of warships in the Canal, prepared to act as floating batteries, that chief reliance for its artillery defence was placed.

The Canal was divided into three sectors for defence: Suez to the Bitter Lakes; Deversoir, north of the Great Bitter Lake, to El Ferdan; El Ferdan to Port Said. Force headquarters and the general reserve were at Ismailia. Small detachments were employed in guarding the Sweet Water Canal and garrisoning the important supply depot at Zagazig, on the main line between Cairo and Ismailia.[1]

Map 3.
Sketch B.

With the exception of its artillery, the troops of the East Lancashire Division were not employed, as Sir J. Maxwell was averse to taking them from their training. That division, however, as well as the Australian and New Zealand contingents, formed a reserve, which could be swiftly railed from Cairo to Ismailia and thence in either direction along the Canal.

The troops in the Canal Defences were equipped with first-line transport only. In January it was decided to form a small Camel Transport Corps to act as second-line transport. Five hundred camels were assembled at Abu Sueir, close to Ismailia. They were divided into eight sections, the native drivers being commanded by British officers, civilians given temporary commissions for this duty. Such was the beginning of a corps of which the numbers were to rise in the next three years to upwards of 25,000 drivers and over 30,000 camels.

1915.
Jan.

The Suez Canal was an obstacle which would have been serious to any army, but was particularly so to one which had to march to its attack dragging artillery and bridging train across a wide sandy desert. Though the distance, as

---

[1] For details of the formations and distribution by sectors and posts, see Note I at end of chapter.

the crow flies, from Port Said to Suez was upwards of one hundred miles, 22 miles were taken up by the great sheet of water known as the Great and Little Bitter Lakes and 7 by Lake Timsah. These lakes formed the natural boundaries of the defensive sectors which have been described, and considerably diminished the frontage against which an attack was practicable. The position was admirably served by a lateral railway; it had water behind it, while for the sustenance of an attacker from the desert in front were only a few brackish wells.

There had therefore never been any question but that a Turkish attack from Palestine should be met and fought upon the line of the Canal. The pre-war scheme of defence, while suggesting that a force of camelry should occupy Nekhl, to harass the enemy and keep touch with Ismailia, had definitely laid it down that " the obvious line of actual " defence of the eastern frontier of Egypt is the Suez Canal." That argument was now all the stronger because when it was framed it had not been contemplated that warships would be sent into the Canal or that the Navy would do more than render Egypt immune from a hostile landing at Suez or Port Said and, in the event of aggression from the east, patrol the Canal and the lakes with armed pinnaces.[1] After the decision that, in the event of attack from Sinai, warships should enter the Canal and assist in its defence by gun-fire, the potential strength of the position was greater than ever.

These advantages were sufficient to determine the policy of the defence in the circumstances prevailing, but it was not forgotten that there was another side to the picture. The mere interruption of navigation through the Canal, inevitable in case of an attack, would result in loss of time, serious at a period when troops and supplies were wanted hurriedly and when every extra hour that British shipping was employed on any mission meant the loss of a valuable hour which should have been given to another. Such short interruptions were, however, the least of the dangers to be contemplated. A ship sunk in the Canal was a more serious possibility.

---

[1] This is perhaps an example of extreme " blue-water " naval theory affecting military plans. It was held that warships could not be spared for the defence of the Canal because the Navy would be wholly occupied in seeking out and destroying the enemy's fleet. The Navy's object proved, however, to be the obtainment and preservation of the command of the sea, and in defending the Suez Canal the older ships of Britain and France were fulfilling their part to that end.

A temporary success to the enemy might permit him to do, 1915. in a few days, damage to the Canal which it would take many Jan. weeks to repair. Great as were the advantages of the policy of defence upon the line of the Suez Canal, that policy represented, in sum, the employment of the Empire's main line of communication as an obstacle in front of a fire trench.

The defensive work carried out along the Canal was simple by comparison with the elaborate system which was to be constructed in 1916. A series of posts was dug, the trenches revetted with sandbags and protected by barbed wire, on the east bank, principally to cover ferries and provide facilities for local counter-attack,[1] while a more extensive bridgehead was prepared at Ismailia Ferry Post. On the west bank trenches were dug at intervals between the posts. The Suez Canal Company, which put all its resources, including small craft, at the disposal of General Wilson, rendered great assistance in the construction of works and crossings. The ferries under its administration were put at the service of the defence, and a number of new ones added. Three floating bridges were assembled : the heaviest at Ismailia, and lighter ones at Kubri, half way between Suez and the Little Bitter Lake, and at Qantara.

In order to narrow, by flooding a portion of the desert, the frontage open to attack, a cutting was made in the Canal bank at Port Said on the 25th November. The plain to the east is here very low, in places below the surface of the Mediterranean, and the resultant inundation reached El Kab, north of Qantara, thus barring 20 miles of the Canal to approach. The water subsided somewhat in January, but left the area which had been covered impassable for some time longer. On the 2nd January a further cutting was made in the Asiatic bank north of Qantara, which resulted in good protection being afforded to the flank of that fortified zone. Minor inundations were created between Qantara and Ismailia.

Syria and Sinai.

The terms " Syria " and " Palestine," the former of which included the latter, were prior to the post-war settlements vague in meaning. Syria was generally taken to

---

[1] These posts were prepared, from north to south, at Port Said, Ras el Esh, Tina, El Kab, Qantara, Ballah, El Ferdan, Bench Mark, Ismailia, Tussum, Serapeum, Deversoir, Geneffe, Shalluffa, Gurkha Post, El Kubri, Baluchistan Post, Esh Shatt (see Map 3). Details of the engineer work on the Canal Defences are given in Note II at the end of chapter.

mean the strip of fertile country on the Mediterranean shore from the Cilician Gates to the Egyptian frontier at Rafah; Palestine," from Dan to Beersheba," extended from the neighbourhood of Tyre to the same frontier. Neither term corresponded to the political divisions of Turkey, the occupying Power. These divisions were the *Sanjaks*[1] of Adana and Jebel-i-Bereket (from the Adana *Vilayet*[1]) and the *Sanjak* of Aleppo (from the Aleppo *Vilayet*), these three including the country from near Tarsus to just north of Alexandretta; the *Vilayet* of Beirut, from Alexandretta to north of Jaffa; the *Vilayet* of Damascus, including the country east of Lebanon and the Jordan, from Hama in the north to Aqaba in the south; and the independent *Sanjak* of Jerusalem, from north of Jaffa to the Egyptian frontier and east to the Dead Sea. The province of the Lebanon had a special administration from Constantinople, created to put an end to the blood-feuds of its inhabitants: Druses, Maronites, Christians and Turks.

When Turkey declared war the *Fourth Army*, with headquarters at Damascus, consisted of some 60,000 troops with 100 guns, comprising the *VI Corps* in the north with headquarters at Adana and the *VIII Corps* in the south with headquarters at Damascus. The Turkish Army had been mobilized since the 2nd August. It was expected to be formidable, as Turkish troops have always been, but it had not fully recovered from the demoralization and disorganization consequent on the Balkan and Tripolitan Wars. This applied particularly to formations distant from the capital and so less under the influence of the German Military Mission than those in Turkey proper.

Sketch 9.

The railway communications with Turkey were unsuited to warfare on a large scale, but capable of carrying and supplying as many troops as could be transported over the hundred miles of desert between the Egyptian frontier and the Suez Canal. From Haidar Pasha Station at Scutari, opposite Constantinople, to Rayak on the Litany River, 25 miles north-west of Damascus, the line was the single-track standard gauge of the Anatolian-Baghdad Railway; its value greatly lessened by the gaps already mentioned.

---

[1] The Turkish administrative area known as the *vilayet* may be taken to correspond to the French "department"; its subdivision, the *sanjak*, to the "arrondissement."

At these gaps twenty tunnels were uncompleted, the break 1915. in the Taurus being 20 miles in length and that of the Jan. Amanus, at the Bagche Tunnel, 5 miles long. Though work was being pushed on, these gaps were not covered by rail for a considerable time to come,[1] but had to be bridged by motor and animal transport of all kinds. As far as Muslimie, north of Aleppo, this line had also to bear the traffic for the Turkish forces in Mesopotamia.

At Rayak the standard gauge ceased and a 1·05 metre-gauge line ran through Damascus to Dera'a, 50 miles south of that city. Here it bifurcated, running south to the Hejaz and west to Haifa. There was also a branch running from Rayak over the Lebanon to the sea at Beirut. From Affule, south-east of Haifa, a branch to Jerusalem *via* Nablus had been begun, which the Turks diverted and began to extend southwards along the Plain of Sharon after the commencement of hostilities. The Jerusalem-Jaffa line, belonging to a French company, was unconnected with this system and of a slightly different gauge (1 metre). Apart from the demerits of this railway system where the feeding of large armies was concerned, the patrolling of the coast by the Navies of Britain and France prevented the arrival of coal by sea. There were no local mines of any value and, as may be imagined, but little coal could be sent across the Taurus and Amanus. Supplies from two large colliers which were in the port of Haifa at the outbreak of war provided coal for the transportation of the troops employed in the attack on the Suez Canal to railhead, then a short distance south of Nablus. Thereafter the Turks were forced to fall back upon wood-fuel for their engines.

The problem before Sir J. Maxwell was, however, con- Map 1 & 8 cerned less with the numbers of troops of which Turkey Sketch B. could dispose in Syria or with the quality of her railway communications from Constantinople than with her power to cross the desert between the frontier and the Suez Canal. The Sinai Peninsula, mountainous in its southern half, sand desert in its northern, was crossed by no modern communications. Even the " Way of the Philistines," along the Mediterranean shore, was no more than a camel track. This

---

[1] The Amanus gap was covered early in 1917, the Taurus tunnels pierced for a light railway about the same time, but the first through train from Haidar Pasha Station to Rayak (about 900 miles) did not run till September 1918.

track ran from El Qantara (the bridge : formerly the crossing of the old Pelusiac branch of the Nile) through Romani, Qatiya and El Arish to Gaza, within the Turkish frontier. It was watered by occasional oases, with brackish wells, more frequent as it approached Egypt, and threaded its way through areas alternating in shifting sand-dunes and a firmer surface of flint and pebble. The other principal track ran *via* Nekhl, from Suez to Aqaba ; and at Nekhl alone, an Egyptian military and civil post, was there any appreciable water supply. Between these two routes was a third but difficult one, even less well watered, through Jifjaffa, to the Canal at Ismailia. How many troops could be brought across and at what season ? What route would they follow ?

In a War Office estimate made in 1906 it had been suggested that 5,000 men and 2,000 camels represented the largest possible force. The whole question, in fact, depended upon the water-supply, which was not constant. Apart from the wells, there were here and there stone cisterns, remnants of a bygone civilization, in which winter rain-water was collected by the Bedouin. After these rains also considerable pools often existed for short periods, during which there was no reason why much larger numbers than those suggested should not subsist in Sinai. It befel that, though for several years there had been little rain in Sinai, in the winter of 1914 there were some heavy storms. This unusually great supply of water made practicable the central Sinai route for considerable numbers of troops.

The Advance of the Turks.

Egypt was watchful and fairly well informed. The British aeroplanes available were incapable of long flights.[1] The French seaplanes, put at Sir J. Maxwell's disposal in November, of which there were seven in the *Aenne Rickmers* —a captured cargo steamer equipped as a seaplane carrier—

---

[1] The detachment, under Major S. D. Massy, 29th Punjabis, consisted of three Maurice Farmans sent from Avonmouth in November, two Henri Farmans taken over in Egypt, and one B.E2a which arrived from India in December. The aerodrome was at Ismailia, with a landing ground at Qantara. For long reconnaissances into Sinai it was found necessary to send out troops to prepare temporary landing grounds some miles east of the Suez Canal. The longest flight ever carried out was 176 miles, for which a specially large petrol tank had to be fitted to the machine. This, however, was after the Turkish attack on the Suez Canal.

ADVANCE OF THE TURKS

at Port Said, were better, though far from powerful enough for the work they were called upon to perform. Hard driven by an energetic commander, Lieutenant de Vaisseau de l'Escaille, they carried out reconnaissance flights which were remarkable, particularly in view of the fact that the forced descent of a seaplane on land meant almost certain death for pilot and observer.[1] From information obtained by them and from the reports of agents it became clear that the attack would not be much longer delayed, and almost certain that it would come through Central Sinai. It was known to the headquarters of the Force in Egypt that a large force, including the *10th, 23rd,* and *27th Divisions,* was assembled close to the frontier about Beersheba.

1915. Jan.

On the 11th January it was thought desirable to issue to the Egyptian Press a statement that an attack was imminent, in order that excitement might be, so far as possible, discounted and allayed. Nekhl had by this date been held by a small body of the enemy for more than a week. On the 25th a force, estimated at one regiment, was reported to be marching on Qantara.

The trenches prepared on the west bank had not been occupied till the 22nd, and then only by small detachments. When, on the 26th, Moiya Harab, 25 miles east of the Little Bitter Lake, was reported to be occupied by some 6,000 men, and at the same time, 40 miles to the north-west, the British covering troops exchanged fire in front of Qantara with an enemy who fell back in the afternoon, it was decided to take up the positions for the defence.

Map 3. Sketch B.

Two battalions of the 32nd Indian Brigade were sent to hold the trenches along the west bank from Bench Mark Post, north of Lake Timsah, to Ballah, of which sector Br.-General H. D. Watson was put in command. All along the front the trenches on the west bank were reinforced

---

[1] Thus in December Lieutenant de Vaisseau Destrem, with a British officer as observer, on two occasions flew up the Wadi Arabi from Aqaba and strove to surmount the steep range east of the valley, in order to reconnoitre Ma'an, on the Hejaz Railway. The task was beyond the power of the 80 h.p. engine, but attempts were continued by him and others until Sir J. Maxwell ordered them to stop, fearing that they would cost him one of his invaluable pilots. In the same month Lieutenant de Vaisseau Delage took off from the *Doris* off El Arish, flew over Gaza, then turned south-east to Beersheba. On his return his engine stopped while he was still ten miles from the sea. The wind just carried the seaplane over the water, but it was in a sinking condition when the *Doris* steamed up from Al Erish (a distance of 35 miles) to its rescue.

from local reserves. The New Zealand Infantry Brigade was brought up the same day from Cairo, the Otago and Wellington Battalions being sent to El Kubri in the 1st Sector, while headquarters with the Auckland and Canterbury Regiments detrained at Ismailia, where they were held in reserve. H.M.S. *Swiftsure, Clio, Minerva*, the armed merchant cruiser *Himalaya*, and H.M.S. *Ocean* entered the Canal, taking stations near Qantara, Ballah, Shallufa, Gurkha Post, and Esh Shatt respectively. The French coastguard ship *Requin* was already in Lake Timsah, where the Canal Company had dredged a berth for her east of the main channel.

Next day (the 27th) the enemy was found to have established himself astride the El Arish-Qantara road, 5 miles east of Qantara, in the 3rd or northern Sector; while in the early hours of the morning he also approached the Canal in the 1st or southern Sector, making slight attacks on the Baluchistan and Kubri posts. Major-General Wilson appreciated these feints at their proper value and, confident that the main attack would fall on some part of the 2nd Sector, reinforced Serapeum, its central post, by the 2nd Rajputs from Moascar.

Additional warships now entered the Canal, the French cruiser *D'Entrecasteaux* taking station just north of the Great Bitter Lake and the *Proserpine* at Port Said. On the 1st February the Royal Indian Marine ship *Hardinge* took station just south of Lake Timsah and north of Tussum. The ships defending the 2nd Sector were, it will be seen, stationed either at the extremities of the section of the Canal forming it or, in the *Requin's* case, in Lake Timsah, since from these points only, owing to the height of the eastern bank about Tussum, could they bring oblique fire to bear upon an enemy advancing on that front. The Canal was now closed each night and reopened each morning, so that the interruption to traffic was not serious.

On the 28th aeroplanes located a force of between three and four thousand 8 miles east of Deversoir in the central Sector, which was next day observed to have increased considerably. A reconnaissance by the enemy on the morning of the 28th against the Qantara bridgehead, on the east bank, which reached the barbed wire, resulted in six casualties among the Sepoys of the 14th Sikhs and the 1/6th Gurkhas in the post. The Turks left three dead in front of the wire and dragged away several wounded.

BRITISH DISPOSITIONS

On the 30th January the enemy closed in generally, the greatest concentration being observed east of Bir Habeita, about nine miles east of the Canal at Serapeum. He had been unable to disguise his intentions, and General Wilson awaited the main attack upon the 2nd or central Sector, with sufficient forces deployed upon the Canal and with strong reserves.

1915.
Jan.

NOTE I.
DISPOSITION OF TROOPS IN THE CANAL DEFENCES, 15TH JANUARY, 1915.

G.O.C., Canal Defences.—Major-General A. Wilson.
Chief Staff Officer, Canal Defences.—Br.-General A. H. Bingley.

SECTOR I.
(Port Tewfik to Geneffe, both inclusive.)

Headquarters—Suez.

Troops.
30th Brigade (24th and 76th Punjabis, 126th Baluchis, 2/7th Gurkha Rifles).
1 Squadron Imp. Service Cavalry.   1 Coy. Bikanir Camel Corps.
½ Coy. Sappers and Miners.   1 Bty. R.F.A. (T.).
1 Indian Field Ambulance.

Posts in Sector.
Esh Shatt	..	.. 1 Coy. Indian Infantry.
		1 M.G. Section.
Baluchistan		.. 1 Coy. Indian Infantry.
El Kubri	..	.. 1 Squadron Imp. Service Cavalry.
		1 Coy. Bikanir Camel Corps.
		½ Coy. Sappers and Miners.
		1 Bn. (less 2 coys.) Indian Infantry.
		1 Battery R.F.A. (T.).
		2 M.G. Sections (Indian Infantry).
Gurkha	..	.. 1 Coy. Indian Infantry.
Shallufa	..	.. 1 Coy. Indian Infantry.
		1 M.G. Section (Indian Infantry).
Geneffe	..	.. 14 men, Indian Infantry.
Suez	..	.. 2½ Battalions (local reserve).

SECTOR II.
(Deversoir to El Ferdan, both inclusive.)

Headquarters—Ismailia Old Camp.

Troops.
22nd Brigade, less 3rd Brahmans (62nd and 92nd Punjabis, 2/10th Gurkha Rifles).
28th F.F. Bde. (51st and 53rd Sikhs, 56th Punjabis, 1/5th Gurkha Rifles).
1 Squadron Imp. Service Cavalry.
Bikanir Camel Corps (less 3½ Coys.).
M.G. Section of Egyptian Camel Corps.
1 Brigade R.F.A. (T.).
1 Battery Indian Mountain Artillery.
2 Field Ambulances.

BRITISH DISPOSITIONS

Posts in Sector.
- Deversoir .. .. 1 Coy. Indian Infantry.
  7 men Bikanir Camel Corps.
- Serapeum E. .. 2 Coys. Indian Infantry.
  7 men Bikanir Camel Corps.
- Serapeum W. .. 22nd Brigade (less 2 battalions and one half-coy.).
  1 Bty. R.F.A. (T.).
  1 Field Ambulance.
- Tussum .. .. 1 Coy. Indian Infantry.
  7 men Bikanir Camel Corps.
- Gebel Mariam .. Observation Post.
- Ismailia Ferry .. 1 Squadron Imp. Service Cavalry.
  Bikanir C.C. (less 3½ Coys.) and M.G. Section Egyptian Camel Corps.
  1 Bn. Indian Infantry.
  1 Bty. R.F.A. (T.).
  1 Section Indian Mountain Artillery.
  1 Wireless Section (T.).
  1 Field Ambulance.
- Ismailia Old Camp 28th Bde. (less one battalion and one coy.).
  21st Bty. Indian Mountain Artillery.
  (Local Reserve.)

SECTOR III.

(El Ferdan, exclusive, to Port Said, inclusive.)

Headquarters—Qantara.

Troops.
29th Bde. (14th Sikhs, 69th and 89th Punjabis, 1/6th Gurkha Rifles).
1 Bn. 22nd Bde. ½ Coy. Sappers and Miners.
1 Squadron Imp. Service Cavalry. 2 Coys. Bikanir Camel Corps.
2 Batteries R.F.A. (T.). 26th Bty. Indian Mountain Artillery.
Armoured Train with ½ Coy. Indian Infantry.
Wireless Section (T.). Indian Field Ambulance.
Detachment R.A.M.C. (T.).

Posts in Sector.
- Ballah .. .. 2 Platoons Indian Infantry.
- Qantara E. .. 29th Bde. (less 1 coy.).
  1 Squadron Imp. Service Cavalry.
  2 Coys. Bikanir Camel Corps.
  ½ Coy. Sappers and Miners.
  1 Bty. Indian Mountain Artillery.
  Wireless Section (T.).
- Qantara W. .. Armoured Train, etc.
  2 Batteries R.F.A. (T.).
- El Kab .. .. ½ Platoon Indian Infantry.
- Tina .. .. ½ Platoon Indian Infantry.
- Ras El Esh .. 1 Platoon Indian Infantry.
- Salt Works .. 1 Company Indian Infantry.
- New Canal Works.. 1 Company Indian Infantry.
- Port Said .. .. 1 Bn. Indian Infantry (less 2 coys.).

ADVANCED ORDNANCE DEPOT, ZAGAZIG.

Troops.
1 Bn. 32nd (I.S.) Brigade.

ENGINEER WORK

DEFENCE OF RAILWAY AND SWEET WATER CANAL.

Troops.
1 Troop Imp. Service Cavalry. ¼ Coy. Bikanir Camel Corps.
¼ Coy. Indian Infantry.

GENERAL RESERVE CAMP, MOASCAR.

Troops.
31st Brigade (less 1 coy.), (2nd Q.V.O. Rajput L.I., 27th Punjabis, 93rd Burma Infantry, 128th Pioneers).
32nd (I.S.) Bde., less 1 battalion (33rd Punjabis, Alwar, Gwalior, and Patiala Infantry).
Imp. Service Cav. Bde. (less 3 squadrons and 1 troop).
1 Egyptian R.E. Section (Camels), 1 Egyptian Mountain Battery.
2 Sections Field Artillery with Cavalry Brigade.
3 Indian Field Ambulances.

NOTE II.

ENGINEER WORK ON THE CANAL DEFENCES.

The construction of the Suez Canal Defences prior to the Turkish attack was a work of great difficulty owing to the shortage of Engineer units. There were available :—

(1) Divisional Engineers, East Lancashire Division (Nos. 1 and 2 Field Companies) ;
(2) Queen Victoria's Own Sappers and Miners (No. 10 Field Company) ;
(3) Australian Divisional Engineers (No. 3 Field Company, detached from the division at Cairo) ;
(4) Military Works Department, Egyptian Army (an unarmed detachment of about 110 all ranks and a small mobile section mounted on camels) ;
(5) The 128th Pioneers.

Of these, one of the Territorial field companies was withdrawn from the Canal on 6th January 1915 ; and the other did not arrive till 6th February, after the attack. The Q.V.O. Sappers and Miners were not present till the 22nd December 1914, nor the Australian Engineers till mid-January. Thus, when the bulk of the work was in hand, only two field companies were available, and for about ten days in the middle of January only one, for two divisions defending a front of 95 miles. There were no Engineer officers available as C.R.E. or Field Engineers, save a single R.E. officer, Captain R. E. M. Russell, lent by the Egyptian Army, who was attached to the headquarters of the G.O.C. Canal Defences. The shortage of skilled supervision had its result in a lower standard of work on the trenches and posts than would have been the case with a normal engineer establishment. Fortunately, the State Railways and Telegraphs Departments were largely managed by ex-officers of the Royal Engineers, and undertook many of the duties which would, in ordinary circumstances have been carried out by Engineer units of the Force in Egypt.

The principal works carried out were, first, the laying out and construction of trenches on the west bank and of bridgeheads on the east bank. Secondly, there was the bridging, which included the construction and working of lighter bridges at El Qantara and El Kubri, a boat bridge at Ismailia Ferry Post, and eight bridges over the Sweet Water Canal. The Engineer units were also employed on the construction of aeroplane hangars; the laying on of filtered water to the camps at Moascar, Ismailia, and Suez; the distribution of filtered water by boat from the Canal Company's filters at Port Said, Ismailia, and Suez to the posts on the Canal; the storage of two days' supplies of water at 1¼ gallons per head in these posts; the cutting of the Canal bank for the inundations described in this chapter; the drawing of large-scale maps of the defences and for use with range-marks by the land and Naval artillery, for which they had the assistance of a Survey Section equipped by the Egyptian Survey Department; the installation of searchlights for the armoured train, and at Qantara, Ismailia Ferry Post and El Kubri. The mobile section accompanied reconnaissances on several occasions, prepared landing grounds for aeroplanes, drained water pools and controlled the water supply during expeditions into the desert.

NOTE III.

THE EXPEDITION AGAINST THE CANAL, FROM GERMAN AND TURKISH SOURCES.

The chief authority as to the happenings on the Turkish side is a German officer, Oberst Freiherr Kress von Kressenstein, who also appears to have been the soul of the expedition against the Canal and responsible for the details of its undoubtedly excellent organization. This officer has written an account[1] which is interesting without being of high value in the early stages from the historian's point of view, as he there seldom mentions the numbers of formations and appears to have written rather from memory than from a diary, still less from official archives.

From his story, it appears that from the very date of mobilization on the 2nd August 1914, months before Turkey entered the war, the commander of the Turkish *Fourth Army* at Damascus, Br.-General Zekki Pasha, was instructed to make plans for an attack on the Canal. The conquest of Egypt was not then contemplated. That idea came only with the appointment of the Minister of Marine, Djemal Pasha, as Commander-in-Chief in Syria and Palestine. It may even then have been due merely to the desire of the new general to arouse by propaganda enthusiasm for the liberation of Mohammedans from unbelievers, and to urge on the troops against what was certainly an admirable country to pillage.

It was soon discovered that neither Zekki Pasha nor his Chief of the Staff was qualified for the task. Enver then put it in the hands of the commander of the *VIII Corps* at Damascus—Colonel Djemal Bey (known as Djemal *Kuchuk*, the " little Djemal ")—and sent him a German staff of six, with Kress as its chief. In November—about the date of the declaration of war, Zekki was succeeded by the energetic and vigorous Djemal Pasha, who brought as his Chief of the Staff Oberst von Frankenberg und Proschlitz. The preparations now went forward much more speedily. Camels were purchased, roads made, supplies of all kinds collected, as was duly reported in Egypt. In mid-January the expedition, consisting, according to Kress, of 20,000 men, with 9 batteries of field artillery and one 15-cm. howitzer battery, moved out from Beersheba in two echelons.

Kress had made a very careful reconnaissance of the Desert of Sinai, and his appreciation is interesting. He was evidently a bold and resolute man, who was not daunted by conditions that appeared at first sight most unfavourable, but were in the end overcome with comparative ease by good organization. The main difficulty for an expedition crossing the desert was, as he recognized, the water supply. Whilst a part of the

---

[1] " Sinai," i., pp. 2–18.

hinterland of the desert was covered with dunes almost impassable to large bodies of troops, the rest had, as has been stated, a better surface, covered with what Kress describes as a "ready-made macadam." This, however, was broken by islands of deep, shifting sand, up to several square miles in extent, across which the Turks with extraordinary patience constructed brushwood tracks.

The few thousand nomad Bedouin who, as Kress puts it, eke out a scanty livelihood by robbery and cattle raising, he found unreliable as soldiers or traders, but states that they gave invaluable service as guides, and so long as the Turks and Germans were masters of the desert served them, with rare exceptions, faithfully. This, he considered, was due to their hostility to the British, rather than their friendship for the Turks. The former, he declares, had done nothing to improve the material existence of the Bedouin, their policy being to maintain the desert as a barrier between Palestine and the Canal. Except at a few of their evacuated stations, he and his expedition, he somewhat naïvely complains, came upon no wells sunk by British.

Disregarding all the precedents, as he declares with pride, of the **Map 8.** invaders of history, the force marched through the desert instead of follow- **Sketch B.** ing the coast. The old road along which marched so many great armies, through El Arish, was threatened by hostile ships. That from Ma'an, through Nekhl, to Suez, was also under the guns of British warships in the neighbourhood of Aqaba. The water supply was under the control of the German Major Fischer, who had 5,000 camels carrying water. Thanks to his organization, and to the fact that the season had been wetter than usual, there was never any water shortage. The invaders found springs at Kossaima, 45 miles south of El Arish, and, at Hubr um Mukhsheib, 20 miles east of Deversoir, a pool of rainwater that sufficed them during the halt in front of the Canal. On the march not a man or a beast was lost.

The main body marched from Beersheba, through El Auja and Ibni, between the hill-ranges of Maghara and Yelleg, through Jifjafa upon Ismailia. Smaller detachments moved by El Arish upon Qantara and through Nekhl against Suez. The object of these two latter was merely to keep the enemy in doubt as to the point at which the main attack was to be made. The only trouble of the main body was bombing by British and French aeroplanes. These, it is admitted, caused panic at first, but the troops soon got used to them.[1] The Turkish force was provided neither with aeroplanes nor weapons of defence against them.

Kress makes one very illuminating statement:—" The Army Commander, Djemal Pasha, had expected that his appearance on the Canal " would be followed by a rising of the Egyptian Nationalists.[2] In this hope " he was deceived. There remained, however, an attainable goal, to force " his way suddenly astride the Canal, hold the crossing a few days, and in " that time close the Canal permanently."

If we take the latter as Djemal's real aim, the only one which he cherished seriously, though doubtless ready to seize what opportunities fortune offered of greater results, the whole expedition, which otherwise appears as crazy in aim as admirable in organization, becomes comprehensible. If the Turkish commander had any knowledge of the numbers of

---

[1] The aerial bombs of that day were, it will be recalled, small—not more than 20 lb. in weight—and not effective weapons against troops in the open, particularly when they fell in sand.

[2] Sir J. Maxwell had information of a plot, hatched by the agents of Baron Oppenheim, the German explorer, for a rising in Cairo and the murder of Europeans to take place at the same time as the attack on the Canal. The presence of the Australians in the capital put a stop to any such attempts.

British and Colonial troops in Egypt, he cannot have thought that a rising was likely to do more than slightly embarrass Sir J. Maxwell. The conquest of Egypt was only possible through an extraordinary stroke of luck.

Djemal himself, according to his own account, had singularly overestimated general Egyptian sympathy for the Turks and the energy and courage of their would-be supporters in the country. He told his troops that the Egyptian patriots would rise behind the British when the Turks appeared. He was by no means sure of the ultimate success of the campaign, but, he states, he "had staked everything upon surprising the "English and being able to hold the stretch of the Canal south of Ismailia "with five or six thousand men at the first rush, so that I could bring up the "*10th Division* and have a force of ten thousand rifles securely dug in on the "far bank." Thereafter his intention was to take Ismailia, and hold it four or five days. Meanwhile the *8th Division* was to be hastened across the desert.

This programme sounds over-sanguine. But to grip the Canal for three days and destroy it was a more feasible enterprise. The enemy, in the event of a temporary success, might have been enabled to sink half a dozen ships in the Canal, for at least that number appears to have been moored in the Timsah. There is no record of whether adequate explosives accompanied the force.

CHAPTER III.

THE ATTACK ON THE SUEZ CANAL,

1ST—10TH FEBRUARY 1915.

(Maps 3, 4 ; Sketches B. 1.)

THE ATTACK.

FROM the 31st January onwards the British troops stationed along the Canal expected the attack at any moment and, having had ample warning of its approach, awaited it with confidence.

1915. Feb. Map 3. Sketch B.

The dispositions of the enemy, so far as they could be discovered, were on the 1st February as follows :—

At Bir Habeita, 6 miles east of Serapeum, at least 2,500 infantry and apparently two guns ; at Moiya Harab, 30 miles to the south-east and in a position such that they might be intended either to reinforce the former body or to strike at the 1st Sector in the neighbourhood of Shallufa, about 8,000 men ; further north, at Bir el Mahadat, 10 miles E.N.E. of El Ferdan, about 3,000 men. On the other hand, trenches which had been dug by the Turks 5 miles north-east of Qantara now seemed to have been evacuated, and behind, at Bir ed Dueidar, only about 300 men could be seen, though the palm grove of this oasis was certainly large enough to conceal many more. In rear, on the northern Sinai route at Bir el Abd, 40 miles east of the Canal, and at El Arish on the Palestine frontier ; on the southern route at Nekhl ; there appeared to be further considerable forces.

No move by the Turks was detected on this day but for a slight advance opposite Ismailia Ferry Post, as a result of which the bridgehead there and Bench Mark Post, 2 miles to north of it, were reinforced. A little further north small bodies of the enemy in the desert east of El Ferdan were scattered by the fire of H.M.S. *Clio* from her station near Ballah.

On the morning of the 2nd February it was discovered by patrols from Ismailia Ferry Post that there had been a further advance opposite that point during the night. Small detachments which moved out from the bridgehead made contact with the enemy and were in action till about 3.30 p.m. A high wind, which had grown stronger as the day wore on, whipped up the sand till the troops found themselves almost in darkness, and aerial reconnaissance became impossible. The enemy showed no immediate intention of coming to close quarters. He apparently entrenched himself in the evening 2½ miles south-east of the British defences.[1]

Not only at the Ferry Post but on the whole twenty-mile front from Deversoir to El Ferdan the British outposts were in touch with the enemy during the day. The *Clio* again came into action, driving the groups on which she fired out of range.

Map 4.
Sketch 1.

It was now more than ever certain that the attack would fall upon the central Sector, though still unknown whether its main weight would be directed north or south of Lake Timsah. In view of the enemy's activity in front of El Ferdan further reinforcements were brought up to that point: an armoured train with four platoons of New Zealand infantry, and two platoons to support the 5th Gurkhas in the post on the east bank. In that part of the

---

[1] A French naval officer, Enseigne de Vaisseau Potier de la Morandière, thus describes the reconnaissance from the Ferry Post :—

"On the hills, ten or fifteen kilometres from the Canal, we could see numerous traces on the sand of the columns which had moved forward during the night. But in the plain there was nothing. The desert, in its high light, looked like a smooth cloth, but was reality cut by numerous depressions in which troops could be hidden.

"The first patrols which moved out were met by rifle fire. They were reinforced; then artillery was sent out to their support.

"At my side was a battery of Indian mountain artillery, commanded by a young English officer, the only European in it. He had just been ordered to go forward. A sharp command and, in a few seconds, before we could see how it was done, the guns which had been in position were packed on the mules and the column was on the move.

"Meanwhile there had sprung up a sand storm which hid everything from view. I went out on to a dune with the English colonel in command of the post. But there it was even worse. Even to keep one's eyes open was horrible torture. And to think that people were fighting out in that!

"In the evening the detachments came in, one after another, the officers cursing the sand, the wind and the enemy, who had fallen back before them. Then quiet fell and we began to think there had been a false alarm."

Sketch 1.

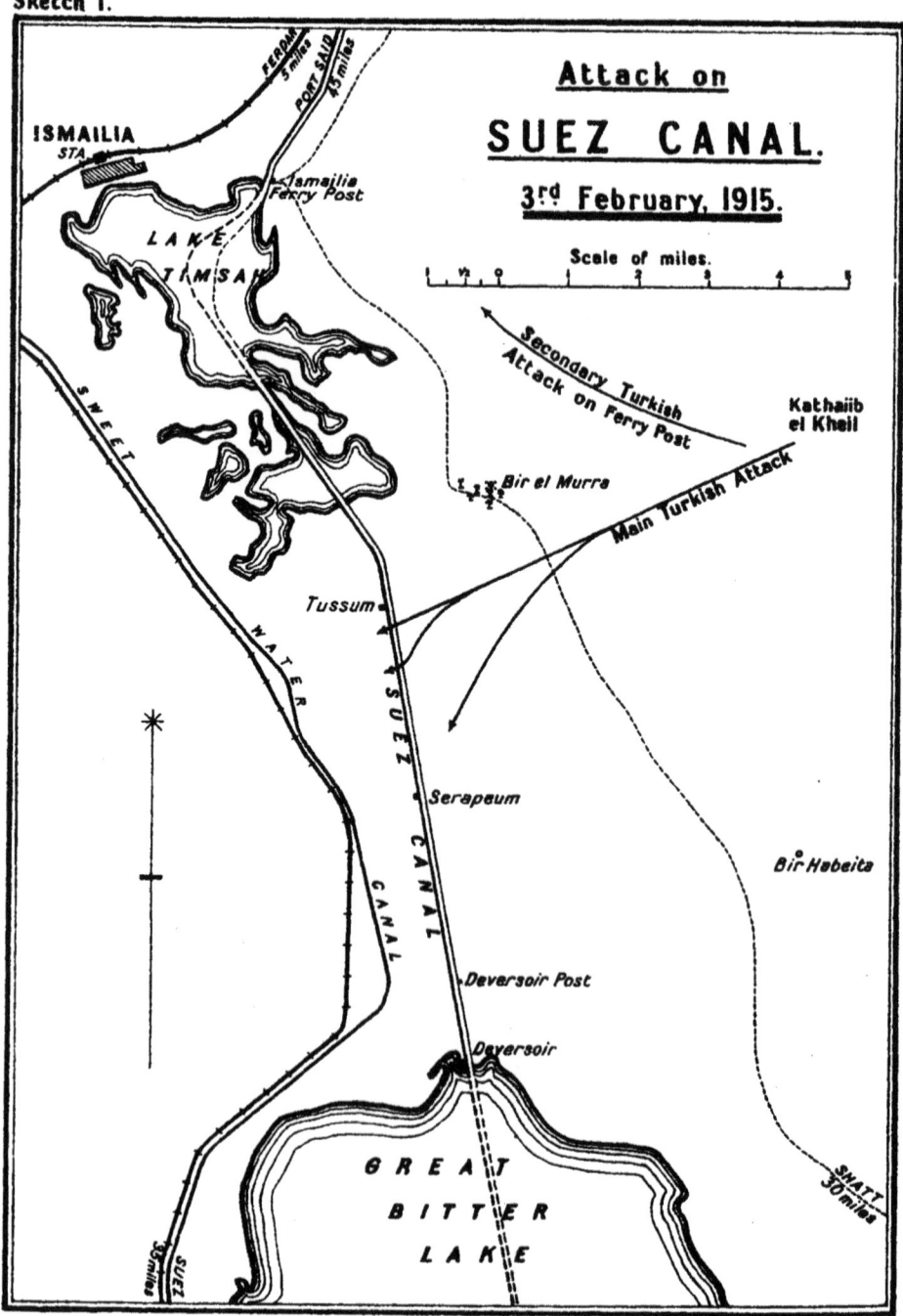

Attack on SUEZ CANAL.
3rd February, 1915.

sector between the Great Bitter Lake and Lake Timsah there were now the following troops :—
    19th Lancashire Battery R.F.A. (T) (four 15-pdrs.) ;
    5th Battery Egyptian Artillery (four mountain guns and two maxims) ;
    1st Field Company East Lancashire Royal Engineers (T) (two sections) ;
    22nd Indian Infantry Brigade, less 3rd Brahmans (62nd and 92nd Punjabis, 2/10th Gurkha Rifles) ;
    2nd Q.V.O. Rajputs ;
    Two Platoons 128th Pioneers (escort to the Egyptian battery) ;
    137th (Indian) Field Ambulance.

Of these there were six companies on the east bank ; two of the 92nd Punjabis in the Tussum Post, two of the 92nd in that of Serapeum, and two of the Gurkhas at Deversoir. On the west bank were eleven posts each held by two platoons,[1] each platoon on a frontage of some 600 yards and finding three sentry posts 200 yards apart. In reserve at Serapeum were three companies. At the first sign of the attack a company of the 62nd Punjabis was ordered up from here to the danger point, mile-post 47·4, a little south of Tussum, and this company was subsequently reinforced by six platoons of the 2nd Rajputs.

    The sand storm continued into the night. The Indian sentries, peering into the darkness, their faces screened in their puggarees and the breeches of their rifles wrapped round with rags, saw and heard nothing till 3.25 a.m. on the 3rd February, when an observation post at Tussum heard troops passing south-east of the post and towards the Canal bank. A moment later loud shouting and howling broke out south of the post.[2] Major T. R. Maclachlan, who was in command, moved a machine gun and half a platoon down to the southern flank of the post to rake the east bank. The shouting thereupon ceased and the enemy replied with ineffective machine-gun fire.

---

[1] The total number of posts between the two lakes was twelve, but No. 1 Post on the left, which was protected by the large lagoons at the southern end of Lake Timsah, consisted of a half platoon only. It manned an observation post on a dune known as Gebel Mariam, just west of the point where the Canal channel enters the lake.

[2] The noise, in defiance of strict orders, was made by irregulars, " the Champions of Islam," calling upon Allah and adjuring the attackers to die for the faith.

Still there was nothing to be seen. Then the moon, only two days past full, emerged from the clouds, and dark masses were discerned moving slowly down the gullies on the east bank towards the water. Presently these masses were discovered to be pontoons and rafts carried by squads of men. At 4.20 a.m. the Egyptian battery, which had moved to this point the previous day and dug in on the top of the high west bank in order to obtain a field of view, opened fire, with good results, for it was soon observed that the two foremost pontoons had been abandoned. With the assistance of rifle fire from the 62nd Punjabis and 128th Pioneers at Post No. 5, the battery checked most of the attempts of the enemy to carry his craft down to the water.

It is not clear whether the Turks had intended to make their first crossing at this point or whether the other detachments moving on the Canal had been slightly delayed in the darkness by the rough ground. At all events, within a few minutes gangs carrying pontoons appeared upon the east bank on a frontage of a mile and a half from a short distance north of the point of the first attempt. The rapid fire of the defenders caused most of the craft to be abandoned on the bank, while the pontoons which reached the water were quickly holed and sunk.

Three pontoons only crossed the Canal, under cover of heavy machine-gun and rifle fire now opened by the enemy from the sand-dunes close to the east bank. To the south, a boat-load of Turks landed opposite mile-post 48·3, on the front of Post No. 6. The party was instantly charged with the bayonet by a small body under Major O. St. J. Skeen, 62nd Punjabis, and all killed or wounded. The other two boat-loads landed at the original point, opposite mile-post 47·6. This party was at once attacked by Captain M. H. L. Morgan and Lieut. R. A. FitzGibbon with small detachments of the 62nd Punjabis and 128th Pioneers from Post No. 5.[1] Six Turks were killed and four wounded; about twenty escaped and hid under the west bank, where they were later rounded up and captured by a party of the

---

[1] Both officers were wounded, the latter mortally, though, after being hit, he ran a considerable distance with a message to the Egyptian battery of which he commanded the escort.

2nd Rajputs. The small parties which made these gallant attacks were the only Turks to cross the Suez Canal, save as prisoners, in the course of the war.[1]

1915.
3 Feb.

The fire from the east bank was intense and well directed, and casualties among the defenders began to mount up. But as the light improved it was seen how roughly the enemy had been handled. His iron pontoons, rafts[2] and other abandoned material littered the east bank, along which also lay many dead. His surprise crossing had been a complete failure.

Yet the Turkish command had by no means abandoned hope. At dawn an attack was launched against Tussum Post, and the enemy artillery began to shell the British positions, the warships in the Canal, and merchant shipping moored in Lake Timsah. The *Hardinge* and *Requin* in turn opened fire upon parties of Turkish infantry in the desert, as they became visible, and by the time it was daylight the action was general. It was now discovered that the Turks were holding a trench 200 yards south of Tussum Post, facing westward. Enfilade fire from the machine guns in the post practically destroyed this party. It was next found that a larger body of the enemy, some 350 strong, had made a lodgment in the British day trenches east and south of the post. At 7 a.m. a counter-attack from the southern flank of the post, led by Captain H. M. Rigg, 92nd Punjabis, recaptured a portion of these trenches and took 70 prisoners. At 11 a.m. a further counter-attack was carried out against the day trenches by Lieut. J. W. Thomson-Glover, 35th Sikhs, attached 92nd Punjabis, from the northern end of the post. This was completely successful, though not until 3.30 p.m. were the whole of the trenches regained. In all 7 Turkish officers and 280 other ranks were captured or killed and a quantity of material taken in these trenches.

Br.-General S. Geoghegan, commanding the 22nd Indian Brigade, observing at 6.30 a.m. that there was no

---

[1] Six months later a few raiders swam the Canal near Qantara and placed sticks of dynamite on the railway line. These, however, were probably native smugglers, who had taken Turkish pay when their peacetime occupation was gone. (See Chap. V.)

[2] The pontoons were of the German service pattern, of galvanized iron, each capable of holding about 20 men. There were also a number of rafts, subsequently found to consist of a light wooden framework filled with empty kerosine tins. They were 15 feet long by 12 feet wide and equipped with long-necked crutches to enable them to be rowed across.

sign of an attack south of Serapeum, decided to collect at that point sufficient troops to clear the Turks still in front of or south of Tussum Post out of the trenches and sandhills. Two companies of the 2/10th Gurkhas with their machine guns moved up from Deversoir to Serapeum, where six platoons of the 2nd Rajputs had also been collected. Crossing by the ferry, two platoons of the Rajputs with the two companies of the 92nd Punjabis from the post on their right, began at 8.40 a.m. to advance up the east bank towards Tussum. As this movement continued, the enemy broke in surprisingly large numbers from hummocks and sandhills in the neighbourhood of the point from which his southern boat-load had crossed during the night. But at the same moment a considerable Turkish force came into the open some three miles to the north-east, deployed, and, supported by two batteries,[1] began to advance in the direction of Serapeum Post.

Against this superior force the British counter-attack was unable to continue. The Rajputs, pushing on along the bank, came under heavy fire and lost the officer commanding the detachment, Captain R. T. Arundell, before they were brought to a standstill. The Punjabis were concentrated on the right to face the Turkish attack, and six platoons of the 2/10th Gurkhas moved up into support, the whole detachment on the east bank being now under the command of Lieut.-Colonel F. G. H. Sutton, 2/10th Gurkha Rifles. But the little force held its ground and its determined front brought the enemy's attack to a standstill, nowhere nearer than 1,200 yards to the British line. A second cause of the failure on the part of the Turks to press the attack was probably the fire of the French warships *Requin* and *D'Entrecasteaux*, of which more will be said later.

The abandoned pontoons lying along the Asiatic bank constituted a certain danger, as there was a possibility of their being again employed after the fall of darkness, should the enemy re-establish himself in force upon the bank. About 7.45 a.m. Br.-General Geoghegan requested Lieut.-Commander G. B. Palmes, R.N., in command of T.B. *043* at

---

[1] The force which carried out this attack was afterwards found to have been the *74th Regiment, 25th Division*; the other two regiments of that division, the *73rd* and *75th*, having already been committed to the attack against Tussum Post and the Canal immediately south of it. Behind the *74th Regiment* the *28th* of the *10th Division*, Djemal Pasha's reserve, also advanced, though how nearly it approached the Canal is not clear.

ACTION OF THE WARSHIPS

Deversoir, to destroy these. The torpedo boat moved up the Canal, firing two rounds from its 3-pdr. into each pontoon. Lieut.-Commander Palmes then landed to see if any still lay behind the east bank, and succeeded in blowing up two more with gun-cotton. Finally he almost walked into a trench full of Turks, but succeeded in regaining his dinghy.

1915.
3 Feb.

While the attacks on Tussum and Serapeum were in progress, another Turkish force, advancing from the southeast, threatened Ismailia Ferry Post, on the other side of Lake Timsah.[1] This attack was never seriously pressed, the enemy's advanced troops entrenching some eight hundred yards from the defences. On the other hand his artillery, well handled, speedily became menacing. It appeared that the two field batteries were in action in support of the infantry, while from far out in the desert a 15-cm. howitzer battery also opened fire.

At 8.15 a.m. these guns, which had been directed against the *Hardinge* but had hitherto been shooting short, began to straddle the ship. First a ricochet carried away the wireless aerial. A few minutes later a high explosive shell struck the forward funnel, another the base of the after funnel; next a shell from one of the heavy howitzers burst over the fore part of the ship, causing casualties to the guns' crews. The steering gear was damaged and the fore stokehold rendered untenable. It was only too evident to Commander Linberry that the heavy guns had his range exactly. If he remained where he was there was considerable risk that his ship, unarmoured and highly vulnerable, would be sunk in the channel. At 8.45 a.m., therefore, the *Hardinge* slipped and proceeded to anchor in Lake Timsah, outside the fairway. The heavy howitzers fired only three or four rounds more at her, then switched to another target.

The artillery defence of Tussum now fell largely upon the *Requin*,[2] the only warship in the area, except the armed tug *Mansourah* and T.B. *043*, both armed with light guns. She was searching for the enemy's field artillery and shelling small groups of infantry in front of Ismailia Ferry Post with her 10-cm. guns when she came under the fire of the 15-cm. howitzers which had previously engaged the *Hardinge*.

---

[1] This force consisted of the *68th Regiment, 23rd Division*.

[2] The *Requin*, whose specially dredged berth had been long chosen, had made preparation for the defence of the Sector by placing numerous range-marks in the desert. Her role was, in fact, that of a floating battery.

She could not find the enemy battery, the shooting of which became more and more accurate. Presently it straddled the ship and the situation became uncomfortable. The crews of the 10-cm. guns, which had no protection, were moved beneath the shelter of the steel deck, and a bigger head of steam raised in case the ship should have to shift her moorings. One 27·4-cm. turret gun alone remained in action, at first without effect. But at 9 o'clock a puff of smoke was observed in the desert, corresponding with the fall of a big shell near the ship. It was estimated that the Turkish howitzers were firing from a point 9,200 metres distant. Fire was accordingly opened with the turret gun at ranges varying from 9,000 to 9,500 metres. After the third round the heavy howitzer fire ceased suddenly and was not resumed, a serious danger to the Canal being thus removed.

The *Requin* did further good work opposite Tussum and Serapeum, aided by the cruiser *D'Entrecasteaux*. The latter had received orders to move up and replace the disabled *Hardinge*. Subsequently these orders were cancelled, as the flagship *Swiftsure* was on her way down from Qantara to carry out that task. The *D'Entrecasteaux* therefore moved about three-quarters of a mile north of Deversoir and then received the wireless message:—
" Repulse the attack on Serapeum." She could see *Requin's* shells bursting east of that point and she herself at once opened fire with her 14-cm. guns. The crossfire from the heavy guns of the two French ships was now therefore directed upon the area of the Turkish deployment. It was probably in great measure owing to the moral effect of the melinite that the Turkish troops could not here be induced to advance.

The enemy had now been definitely repulsed between Serapeum and Tussum. His artillery continued to shell the west bank intermittently till 2 p.m., when fire ceased. The silence that followed indicated that the action had been broken off, and bodies of Turks were soon seen moving eastward, to be hastened on their way by the 24-cm. gun of the *D'Entrecasteaux*, firing at extreme range. The force under Lieut.-Colonel Sutton which had carried out the counter-attack now withdrew to its former position north of Serapeum. About half an hour later a small body of the enemy occupied the ridge which it had evacuated, but was shelled off it by the British artillery.

THE SECONDARY ATTACKS 45

Opposite Ismailia the enemy's artillery persisted longer, numerous shells falling in the bridgehead and camp, though without causing any casualties. But at 3.30 p.m. the *Requin* apparently silenced a battery firing on the shipping in the Timsah, and here, as further south, the action now died down.

1915
3 Feb.

Reinforcements of the 31st Indian Brigade, which began to arrive at Serapeum at 4.30 p.m., were not required, but they were retained in positions of close support at various points in view of the possibility that the offensive would be renewed. Major-General A. Wallace, commanding the 11th Indian Division, took over command of the front between the Great Bitter Lake and Lake Timsah. The *Swiftsure* had now taken up the former berth of the *Hardinge*, the *Ocean* had also moved to this part of the front, and the *Hardinge* had been sent to replace the *Swiftsure* at Qantara.

Further reinforcements for the front at Ismailia, consisting of Headquarters 2nd Australian Brigade, with the 7th and 8th Battalions Australian Infantry, arrived in the town during the evening. All was ready for the fresh attack which, it seemed probable, would have to be met in the morning. The night passed quietly, save for some musketry fire from the east bank south of Tussum Post.

Elsewhere the attacks on the Canal had been of minor importance, nowhere pressed with energy sufficient to give Major-General Wilson a moment's inquietude or uncertainty as to the enemy's real plan. In the Suez sector the enemy did not come to close quarters. Fire was exchanged between a small detachment and the post on the east bank at El Kubri, after which the Turks withdrew.

Map 3.
Sketch B.

Against El Ferdan, the northernmost post of the 2nd Sector, the infantry attack was equally feeble. There had been some firing on this part of the front before dawn, and daylight discovered two lines of trenches dug about two and a half miles from the Canal. On these the *Clio* opened fire. Soon after 9 a.m. two Turkish field guns began firing on the railway station, making good practice and securing several direct hits. The *Clio* located and engaged these guns within less than half an hour, whereupon the Turks turned their attention to her, continuing to do remarkably pretty shooting. She was hit twice and had some small damage done to one of her guns, but she sustained no casualties among her crew. By 10.30 a.m. she had silenced the Turkish guns. During the afternoon she had further practice against bodies of the enemy seen falling back towards the northeast.

At Qantara, in the 3rd Sector, there was a rather stronger attack, between 5 and 6 a.m., upon two piquets furnished by the 89th Punjabis. The machine guns and rifles of the piquets caused heavy loss to the enemy when he came up against the British barbed-wire defences, and he was driven off without difficulty. Thirty-six prisoners were subsequently brought in here and 20 dead found outside the wire. These figures did not represent the whole of the enemy's losses, as he carried off further dead and wounded in his retirement.

These feint attacks had all been conducted with so little resolution as to fail completely in their object. There were known to be further detachments of the enemy in the Suez Sector in the neighbourhood of posts other than at El Kubri, but they did not appear within machine-gun range of Baluchistan, Gurkha or Shallufa.

The Days Succeeding the Attack.

**1915.
4 Feb.**
To the astonishment of the garrison of the central Sector, expecting a renewal of the attack, it was discovered when day broke that the bulk of the Turkish force had disappeared. There were, however, at least some snipers south of Tussum Post, about mile-post 48·3, whence shots had been fired during the night. Br.-General Geoghegan ordered Captain L. F. A. Cochran to advance north along the east bank with two companies 92nd Punjabis from Serapeum Post and clear the area between it and Tussum.

**Map 4.
Sketch 1.**
Captain Cochran moved along the bank with one company, extending the other widely on his right to cut off the enemy's retreat to the east or north-east. At 8.40 a.m. he reached a hummock, on ascending which his company was fired on by a party of the enemy 120 yards away. His men lay down and returned the fire. Five minutes later some fifty Turks jumped up from their trench, holding their rifles butt uppermost, while one who looked like an officer waved something white. Captain Cochran advanced

ACTION NEAR TUSSUM POST

towards them, signalling to them with his hand to come over. A few unarmed Turks responded, then firing broke out again and several Sepoys fell.[1]

1915.
4 Feb.

Major T. N. Howard, brigade-major of the 22nd Indian Brigade, who had been watching from the west bank, saw that the number of the Turks was considerable and that they were strongly entrenched. He galloped back to Serapeum, whence Br.-General Geoghegan despatched a company from each of the 27th[2] and 62nd Punjabis and 128th Pioneers,[2] under the command of Major Maclachlan, to Captain Cochran's assistance. A fire fight of about an hour followed, but, just as the British detachment was about to charge, the enemy surrendered. Six officers and 292 men, of whom 52 were seriously wounded, were captured, with three machine guns. The dead found in the position numbered 59, among them being the German staff officer who had supervised the crossing, Hauptmann von dem Hagen.

Opposite Ismailia and Qantara it was found that the enemy's trenches were deserted. At noon Br.-General W. A. Watson, commanding the Imperial Service Cavalry Brigade, with his own brigade, two infantry battalions and an Indian mountain battery, moved out from Ismailia Ferry Post. Seven miles north-east of Tussum a body of the enemy, estimated at three or four regiments, was seen. There was no sign of a general retreat, though further north a body of infantry was observed moving eastwards. The reconnaissance returned to the bridgehead after taking 25 prisoners and 70 camels, part of the Turkish water column.

On the morning of the 5th February aerial reconnaissance discovered that the enemy opposite the 2nd Sector was concentrated east of Bir Habeita in his old camp, upon which bombs were dropped. This force was subsequently seen to deploy and advance some distance as if about to renew the attack, but it passed out of sight into a valley and did not again emerge. To the north the enemy's right column was seen withdrawing through Qatiya, on the

5 Feb.

---

[1] There is no evidence of deliberate treachery in this affair. The Turks were divided in their intentions, and in any case the display of a white flag is more properly a request for a parley than a signal of surrender.

[2] These two regiments belonged to the 31st Indian Brigade, in general reserve at Moascar, and the companies were part of the reinforcements brought up the previous afternoon. (See p. 45.)

Mediterranean route. To the south a small detachment of New Zealand Infantry, the 2/7th Gurkhas, a squadron of Imperial Service Cavalry, and a battery of East Lancashire Artillery, encountered 7 miles north-east of Esh Shatt a body of about 100 Turks, which fell back at its approach. On the 6th February mounted patrols from Qantara found Ed Dueidar evacuated by the Turks but were fired on by Bedouin. A camp of about a regiment was located at Rigum, east of the Great Bitter Lake, and another south-east of it at Moiya Harab. By the 10th February the only enemy reported in the neighbourhood of the Suez Canal was a body of 400 at Rigum.

No counter-offensive, it will be seen, was launched on the morning of the 4th February, when it was discovered that the enemy had fallen back from the neighbourhood of the Canal. The opportunity for the destruction of the Turkish central force unfortunately could not be taken. In the first place, though there were 70,000 troops in Egypt, only the Indian infantry brigades, and not all of them, were highly trained, while it was necessary to retain considerable strength in Cairo and elsewhere. The only point in the central Sector at which there were facilities for moving troops quickly to the east bank was at the floating bridge at Ismailia, the ferries being very slow and limited in carrying power for the purpose. The mounted troops at General Wilson's disposal on the morning of the 4th February were the Imperial Service Cavalry Brigade and the eight companies of the Bikanir Camel Corps. Certain squadrons and companies of these formations were distributed among the three sectors of the defence,[1] the remainder being held in the neighbourhood of the bridge, over which the cavalry brigade made its reconnaissance on the afternoon of the 4th, as previously recorded. Late on the 3rd February Sir J. Maxwell ordered the Yeomanry stationed in Cairo[2] to move by train next morning to Ismailia, where it arrived on the evening of the 4th, but even then the cavalry consisted of 16 squadrons only, most of them, particularly the Indian troops, far from advanced in training. There were no

---

[1] See pp. 31–3.
[2] This unbrigaded force consisted of the Hertfordshire Yeomanry, the Westminster Dragoons, and one squadron Duke of Lancaster's Own (See p. 14).

LORD KITCHENER'S INSTRUCTIONS 49

water convoys in existence, the only water-carrying transport being the pack animals for water carriage in the first-line transport of the Indian units. The force was therefore unsuitable in both composition and equipment for a counter-stroke beyond the immediate vicinity of the Canal.

1915. Feb.

What was still more important—for, had an offensive policy been contemplated, there would have been time to have organized camel or donkey water transport before the enemy's advance—was that Sir J. Maxwell had been warned by Lord Kitchener not to risk a reverse, which would have had far-reaching effects. It had therefore been decided that, unless an exceptional opportunity offered itself, only local counter-attacks, followed by pursuit up to a distance of 10 miles, were to be attempted. Another factor was uncertainty as to the enemy's strength and intentions. Thus, on the 6th February, orders issued for a reconnaissance by a force of all arms from the Ferry Post were cancelled on receipt of information from agents that the enemy expected considerable reinforcements. The Turks were in fact on that date in full retreat, but it was not until the middle of the month that Sir J. Maxwell was assured that the troops which he had reason to suppose might be in reserve had not left Beersheba. The inability of the intelligence services to discover that these reserves had not crossed the frontier was largely due to the break-down of the hard-worked French seaplanes, those which attempted at this critical moment to reconnoitre Beersheba failing owing to mechanical trouble.[1]

Traffic on the Canal was suspended for a few nights and during the daylight hours of the 3rd February; otherwise communications with the East were not disturbed by the attack. Nor were the British casualties heavy, the total being 163, including ten naval, most of them suffered by

---

[1] For over a fortnight they had been flying practically from dawn to dusk. On the 19th January El Arish was reconnoitred, on the 22nd Lieutenant de Vaisseau Delage dropped bombs on a camp at Bir el Abd, was forced to descend into the sea owing to engine trouble, and was brought back by a torpedo boat to Port Said. On the 23rd Lieutenant de Vaisseau de Sazieu reported columns between El Auja and Kossaima and 10,000 men at Beersheba, returning with numerous bullet-holes in his wings (Paul Chack: "On se bat sur Mer," p. 216).

the *Hardinge*.[1] The losses of the enemy are difficult to fix with precision, but they were estimated by British Headquarters at over 2,000.[2]

These losses were not great, taking into consideration the strength of the force and the hazardous nature of its enterprise. The defeat suffered by the enemy was, however, a blow to Turkish prestige, though its damaging effect was lessened by the fact that the expedition had been able to disengage itself and return unmolested to its base. In Egypt the effect of the action was excellent, Sir J. Maxwell and the High Commissioner finding their difficulties much lightened. Turkey had fallen in the estimation of her admirers, while those whose sympathies were with the British, above all the Egyptian Government, were relieved of fears regarding their situation and confirmed in the attitude they had adopted.

NOTE.

THE ATTACK, FROM GERMAN AND TURKISH SOURCES.

The Turkish right, or northern, column consisted of a squadron of cavalry and some mounted irregulars and Bedouin, with detachments of infantry from the *80th* and *81st Regiments, 27th Division*.

The central and main column marched in two echelons. The first consisted of the *VIII Corps Headquarters* (Major-General Djemal Pasha, Kuchuk, with Kress as Chief of the Staff), the *25th Division* and the *68th Regiment, 23rd Division*, three or four squadrons *29th Cavalry Regiment*, a camel squadron, the *4th* and *8th Engineer Battalions* (both with pontoons), irregulars such as the "Champions of Islam," and mounted Bedouin.

---

[1]

Killed.

	British.	Indian.	Egyptian.
Officers	2	1	1
Other Ranks	2	24	2

Wounded.

	British.	Indian.	Egyptian.
Officers	7	1	—
Other Ranks	11	109	2

One civilian was wounded, the Canal Company's pilot, Mr. George Carew. After having had a leg shot off and an arm broken, he brought the *Hardinge* into the Timsah. He was awarded the Legion of Honour by the French Government.

[2] Between 30th January and 9th February 716 prisoners were captured; between 28th January and 4th February 238 dead were buried, while a number of Turks were drowned in the Canal. The figures given by Kress ("Sinai" i, p. 16) are 192 killed, 371 wounded and 727 missing. These figures probably only refer to the central column, while it never appears to have been the custom of the Turkish command to record casualties suffered by their Bedouin allies and other irregulars. Prisoners reported that there were 200 killed opposite Qantara, probably Bedouin for the most part.

GERMAN AND TURKISH ACCOUNTS

The second echelon consisted of the *10th Division*, with cavalry and auxiliary troops. With this marched Army Headquarters, Djemal Pasha, *Biyuk* ("the Great") with Colonel von Frankenberg as Chief of the Staff. The total artillery with this column was one two-gun battery of 15-cm. howitzers and nine field batteries.[1]

The left, or southern, column consisted of the *69th Regiment, 23rd Division*, mounted gendarmerie and irregulars, and a pack battery.

Most regiments appear to have left behind their third battalion, from which it is possible that the fittest men were transferred to the other two and the weak left in Palestine. With regard to numbers, Kress speaks of the expeditionary force as composed of "about 20,000 men," without stating whether this includes the northern and southern columns. Djemal Pasha puts the total force, including these columns, at 25,000 men, and this figure may probably be accepted as correct.

Kress states that the attack at Tussum failed for three reasons. In the first place the sandstorm delayed the attempt to cross until it was almost dawn. Of that we need make small account, for the boat-attack was in any case defeated before it was light. His second reason is more plausible: that neither the troops nor the subordinate command had sufficient discipline or training for an operation such as crossing a canal over 100 yards broad in face of opposition and in darkness. The third reason given for the failure is that the Turkish command committed the error of employing an Arab rather than a Turkish division in the first assault.[2] The deep-seated, age-old hatred between Turk and Arab had been underestimated and it had been thought that a Holy War would unite the two races. The Arab soldiers proved unreliable and went over, sometimes in formed bodies, to the enemy.

Now, it is perhaps questionable whether Djemal should not have employed his best division, the *10th*, of Turkish troops, for the crossing, but the remainder of the argument does not hold water. The total number of prisoners taken on the 3rd February on the Tussum–Serapeum front was 279, of whom a number were wounded and about 26 were taken on the west bank after a most gallant crossing. The vision of the faithless Arabs surrendering in formed bodies cannot therefore be taken seriously. Liman von Sanders states that the British fire caused a panic, which probably represents the situation more accurately.

A general retirement was ordered by Djemal (by his own account against the advice of Kress) on the evening of the 3rd. Though his reserve was untouched, his pontoons were almost all destroyed,[3] and he had observed that the British position had been reinforced. Kress gives his opinion that the decision was correct and that a renewal of the attack might have led to the destruction of the force. He records that the return march was carried out in good order, undisturbed by the enemy. Dr. Paul Range, the chief authority regarding the Turkish water supply in the various campaigns, has a few words only to say on this matter, but he admits that the force had difficulties on its way back owing to lack of water.[4] The bones of its transport animals subsequently found in Sinai are even surer testimony.

---

[1] There was, however, a battery or at least a gun, of 12-cm. calibre in action north of Tussum, as was proved by fired cartridge cases picked up.

[2] The *VIII Corps* belonged, as has been stated, to the Damascus Inspectorate, the recruiting area of the *23rd Division* being Homs and that of the *25th Division* Damascus.

[3] A total of 25 pontoons was found by the British.

[4] "Sinai," ii. p. 93.

Kress concludes that, though the expedition against the Suez Canal failed to achieve the results anticipated, yet it was by no means fruitless. The fact that the Turks had been able to bring strong forces with heavy artillery across the desert caused anxiety in England and Egypt and compelled the British to hold the country strongly.

The explanation of the presence of Turkish troops at Rigum on the 10th February and of their constant appearance during the weeks that followed is that Djemal Pasha left Kress in the desert with three battalions, two mountain batteries, and a squadron of cavalry, to attempt to keep the British on the stretch by local attacks and to endanger the shipping in the Canal.

CHAPTER IV.

EGYPT IN THE SPRING OF 1915; THE GALLIPOLI CAMPAIGN.

(Maps 1, 3; Sketches A, B.)

THE SINAI FRONT IN FEBRUARY.

THE immediate menace to the Suez Canal having been removed, the next step was to disperse a small force of irregulars which was threatening the village of Tor, on the shore of the Gulf of Suez and near the toe of the Sinai Peninsula.[1] For this purpose Lieut.-Colonel C. L. Haldane, 2/7th Gurkhas, embarked with half his battalion in H.M.S. *Minerva* at Suez on the 12th February. The detachment landed the same night with all precautions against attracting attention, moved out at once with the garrison, consisting of 150 men of the 2nd Egyptian Battalion, and before dawn had surrounded the enemy's camp. The action which followed was short and sharp. The enemy lost 60 killed and 102 prisoners, including a Turkish major, and 20 camels were also captured. Not more than a few stragglers can have escaped, while the British losses were one killed and one wounded. The quality and strength of the opposing forces were doubtless so disparate that one result only was possible, but it was the speed with which the Gurkhas carried out the operation that minimised their loss. By 5.30 p.m. the force was back on board.

Map 1.
Sketch B.

A period of quiet now ensued in Egypt, the Yeomanry and the detachments of Australian and New Zealand infantry which had reinforced the Canal defences returning to Cairo to resume their training. Information was received from various sources that the Turkish troops which had crossed the desert were demoralized by their defeat and the hardships of their return march. Already, it appeared, that ill will towards the efficient but overbearing German staff officers, which was to grow as the war continued, had manifested itself among them. From further up the

---

[1] The chief importance of Tor was that its occupation by the enemy would have given him opportunities for placing mines in the Gulf of Suez.

coast the light cruiser *Philomel* brought reports that the troops in the neighbourhood of Adana and Alexandretta were badly armed and elderly. The Christian levies had been disarmed since the surrender to the *Doris* at Alexandretta, in which they had been involved, but five hundred had deserted and taken to the hills with their rifles. Other troops had openly declared that they would surrender if a landing were made by adequate British forces.

Yet the threat to the Suez Canal, though more distant, remained. On the 21st February a French seaplane reported that there appeared to be 30,000 troops still in the neighbourhood of Beersheba. Another reconnaissance on the 23rd discovered 250 tents at Nekhl and 16 tents, with some 200 regular troops moving about them, at Bir Hassana, half-way between Nekhl and El Arish. " It would appear from "this," Sir J. Maxwell cabled to Lord Kitchener, "that we "may look for another attack later on."

There was now a resumption of naval activity against the Turkish coasts. On the 24th February the French cruiser *Desaix* landed a party at Aqaba and chased the Turkish post there up into the hills. The French again took over the watch on the Syrian and Anatolian coasts, having formed a squadron under Admiral Dartige du Fournet for the purpose.[1] Admiral Peirse with his squadron was also at this period placed under the command of the French Admiral.[2]

The Gallipoli Campaign.

A great and sudden change was in store for Egypt. There was about to be initiated a new campaign which was to affect it vitally, to demand all the energies of its military command, to make of it the greatest of British bases outside the British Isles and France, to put upon Turkey a pressure such as to cause the cessation of operations on a large scale in Sinai, but, in spite of this relaxation, to denude the country to a dangerous point, at certain periods, of fighting troops.

The first official intimation to Egypt of the Cabinet's design was contained in a telegram from Lord Kitchener of the 20th February, stating that a naval squadron was

---

[1] The battleships *Saint-Louis* and *Jauréguiberry*, the cruiser *D'Entrecasteaux*, and the coastguard ship *Henri IV*.
[2] " Naval Operations," ii, p. 143.

TROOPS FOR THE DARDANELLES 55

bombarding the forts of the Dardanelles and that a force was being concentrated on the island of Lemnos to assist the Navy in occupying them, 2,000 Marines being already there, while the rest of the Royal Naval Division would follow in March. Admiral Carden, commanding the British naval squadron, might, however, require much greater military strength at Lemnos in early March, and Sir J. Maxwell was instructed to prepare a force of approximately 30,000 men of the Australian and New Zealand contingents in Egypt (which had received 10,000 reinforcements just prior to the attack on the Suez Canal) under the command of Major-General W. R. Birdwood for this service. From this time forward it may be said that the greater part of the activities of Sir. J. Maxwell and his staff were absorbed by the problem of the Dardanelles.

1915. Feb.

On the 24th February Lord Kitchener cabled his instructions for General Birdwood, who was ordered to put himself directly in touch with Admiral Carden. The brigade of Australian infantry, the despatch of which Sir J. Maxwell had suggested to the Admiral but regarding which he had not yet received a reply, was ordered to be sent at once to Lemnos. The 3rd Brigade, under the command of Colonel E. G. Sinclair-MacLagan, sailed on the 2nd March, with seven days' landing rations and two months' reserve supplies.

March.

On the 17th March Sir J. Maxwell suggested to Lord Kitchener that Lemnos, to which this force had been sent and to which he understood the 29th Division from England was being directed, was a far from ideal base.[1] He, for his part, had moved troops out of Alexandria so as to leave it clear for the Mediterranean Expeditionary Force, by which title the army in process of formation for the Gallipoli Campaign was now officially known. Port Said was also clear and available when required. General Sir Ian Hamilton, who had now arrived to take command of the M.E.F., came to the same conclusion after visiting Mudros harbour, and asked that the 29th Division should be sent to Egypt. But greater changes than this were impending. On the 18th March took place the unsuccessful naval attack upon the Narrows, which resulted in the loss of the French ship,

---

[1] The telegram was based upon information from Rear-Admiral Rosslyn Wemyss, the Commandant of the base.

Bouvet, with practically all hands, of the *Irresistible* and *Ocean*; while the cruiser *Inflexible* was put out of action for months, a second French ship, the *Gaulois*, had to be beached on Drapano Island, and a third, the *Suffren*, had to be docked. The action, of which he had arrived in time to see the disastrous ending, convinced Sir Ian Hamilton of the impossibility of forcing the Straits by means of the Navy alone. A landing on a considerable scale was, in his opinion, now necessitated and was agreed to by Lord Kitchener and the Cabinet.

At a conference at Mudros on the 17th March Sir Ian Hamilton had decided that, for lack of accommodation and the technical appliances necessary to a large base, the island of Lemnos was unsuitable, not only for the 29th Division, but for the Royal Naval Division, the greater part of which was still in its transports, and the French division under General d'Amade, which was on its way. Now that a military landing in face of the enemy had been determined upon, it became necessary to redistribute on board their transports and reorganize the troops, embarked under "long voyage" conditions. It was accordingly decided that these divisions should be moved for the purpose from the Aegean to the Egyptian bases, which Sir. J. Maxwell had provided for them. The Royal Naval Division sailed for Egypt on the 23rd March and arrived at Port Said on the 27th. On the 28th General d'Amade with the first contingent of the French Division reached Alexandria; the following day the first echelon of the 29th Division arrived at that port. On the 4th April Sir Ian Hamilton was able to inform Lord Kitchener that re-embarkation of this force and embarkation of the Anzac Corps had begun. On the 25th were carried out the historic landings.

The base of the Mediterranean Expeditionary Force was, therefore, now definitely established in Egypt, under the command of Br.-General C. R. M'Grigor. This base was a component of Sir Ian Hamilton's command, but established in a country which was under the military authority of Sir. J. Maxwell. A further complication was that the Australian base and depots were directly under General Birdwood, as representative of the Commonwealth Government. The Force in Egypt found itself cumbered with the charge of large numbers of animals and the field equipment not required in Gallipoli. Again, the M.E.F. had a call upon the garrison of Egypt, and the extent of its demands was to be limited only by the safety of that country.

1915. April.

Large quantities of local produce and stores of all kinds were required by the M.E.F. from Egypt. The Force in Egypt had its own purchases to make and knew the markets, while the operation of two purchasing agencies would have been a source of confusion and extravagence. This difficulty was solved by the " Resources Board," whereon were representatives of the civil and military authorities, which was successful in mobilizing the resourses of the country and buying at reasonable prices. As an illustration of the dependence of the Gallipoli expedition upon Egypt, it may be added that a great proportion of the drinking water for the Peninsula was sent from Alexandria in clean oil-tankers, to be conveyed to the shore in water barges. In addition, tens of thousands of tins were made in Egypt, filled, sealed, roped and despatched to Gallipoli, so that water might be carried straight to the troops in the trenches.

The embarkation of troops, the reception of, and provision of hospitals for, sick and wounded, also fell upon the Egyptian command. In fact, on Sir J. Maxwell there gradually devolved many of the responsibilities of a War Office conducting a campaign, without its co-ordinating authority. Good will and liaison between the staffs alleviated the inconveniences of the situation but did not suffice to remove them.

The despatch of further troops to Gallipoli from the garrison of Egypt followed quickly on the landings. On the 27th April the 29th Indian Brigade, under the command of Br.-General H. V. Cox, left Port Said for Helles. On the 28th Lord Kitchener cabled to Sir Ian Hamilton to call for the East Lancashire Division and instructed Sir J. Maxwell to embark it. The 2nd Mounted (Yeomanry) Division, under the command of Major-General W. E. Peyton, was on its way from England as a reinforcement to the Egyptian garrison. Its last convoy reached Egypt on the 29th April, and the cavalry transports were ordered to be used, without conversion, for the transportation of the East Lancashire Division.[1] The embarkation of that division and of 3,000 reinforcements to the Anzac Corps began on the 1st May.

On the 3rd May Sir J. Maxwell suggested to Lord Kitchener that the Australian Light Horse and New Zealand Mounted Rifles should be sent to Gallipoli as infantry. He had ascertained that officers and men were more than willing to be so employed. Lord Kitchener was apparently surprised that he was prepared to take the risk, especially as, on the departure of the East Lancashire Division, he had suggested that another should be sent to him in its place. In reply to his question, Sir J. Maxwell stated that in his opinion the greatest of all risks was that of failing to obtain a decision at Gallipoli, but again expressed the hope that further infantry would be sent to Egypt.[2] There was little hope of this for the moment, but he had at least the assurance that for the time being the 2nd Mounted Division was to be left in Egypt. Further troops were being hastened out to Gallipoli, a second French Division embarking at Marseilles early in May, while towards the end of the month the 52nd Division left England. On the other hand, Sir J. Maxwell learnt in May from the Governor-General of Australia that three more infantry brigades and a brigade of light horse were to be sent to Egypt to complete their training.

A fortnight after the arrival of the 29th Indian Brigade at Gallipoli, Sir Ian Hamilton decided that it would be unwise to employ the two Mohammedan Battalions, the 69th and 89th Punjabis, so near Constantinople, and stated his intention of returning them to Egypt. Sir J. Maxwell was alarmed lest this should be considered by their co-religionists a slight upon Mohammedan troops. Lord Kitchener came

---

[1] As a battalion of the Manchester Regiment from this division was in the Sudan, a relief had to be found for it before it could rejoin its formation. Lord Kitchener proposed that the Maori Battalion of the New Zealand contingent, which was somewhat backward in training, should be sent to Khartum, but on Sir R. Wingate's advice the need for a European battalion was recognised. Eventually the 2/3rd London Regiment was sent from Malta to the Sudan, while the Maori Battalion rejoined the New Zealanders on the Peninsula as soon as it was ready.

[2] "At present I see no reason for anxiety, but any failure on the "part of Hamilton would bring about a critical situation all over the Moslem "world, and I think we should take all legitimate risks to avoid this. If, "however, I send the bulk of the New Zealand and Australian mounted "men as infantry, I think you should send infantry to Egypt when you "can manage it."—Sir J. Maxwell to Lord Kitchener.

to the rescue. The two battalions were ordered by him to be despatched at once to France, Sir John French being instructed to send two battalions to Egypt to replace them. Eventually the 9th Bhopal Infantry and 125th Napier's Rifles, both weak and somewhat exhausted, were sent from France for this purpose, while Sir J. Maxwell despatched two more battalions of his best Indian troops, the 1/5th and 2/10th Gurkhas, to complete the 29th Brigade.

1915.

Despite the departure of troops to Gallipoli and that of the 30th Indian Brigade, which had been ordered to Basra in March for the reinforcement of the Persian Gulf Expedition, the number of men in Egypt was as great as ever, while that of animals was increasing very rapidly. On the other hand, the actual garrison was growing weaker and less efficient, with the withdrawal of the best formations. A return made to the War Office on 9th July shows that the troops numbered 70,000 officers and men (including 28,000 in the M.E.F. Base), but that there were 36,000 horses and 16,000 mules in the country,[1] a high proportion of these belonging to formations which had gone to Gallipoli. There were also 11,000 officers and men patients in hospital, 9,000 of these battle casualties and sick from the M.E.F.

A further call made upon the Force in Egypt at the end of July was disquieting. Sir Ian Hamilton asked for the Yeomanry in the country, consisting of the 2nd Mounted Division and the original two regiments and one squadron, now brigaded under the command of Br.-General J. T. Biscoe, for use as infantry. Sir J. Maxwell pointed out to Lord Kitchener that this would leave Egypt in a dangerous situation. A third Indian brigade, the 28th, was now gone to Aden (in circumstances to be recorded later), and he had sent a brigade of the 2nd Mounted Division to replace it on the Canal. All the duties in Cairo and most of those in Alexandria were carried out by this division. Recently he had sent out to Gallipoli practically all the trained Australians and New Zealanders, and had grouped the three new Australian infantry brigades (the 5th, 6th and 7th) for training. He did not consider that the safety of Egypt could be assured if the country were left without any formations of British troops.

July.

---

[1] See Note at end of chapter.

Nevertheless he at once made arrangements to despatch to Gallipoli Major-General Peyton, 300 officers and 5,000 men of the 2nd Mounted Division and Biscoe's Yeomanry Brigade. Lord Kitchener intervened. He had, he pointed out to Sir Ian Hamilton, placed the garrison of Egypt, including the Yeomanry, at his disposal, but only in case of necessity and for a short time. He had not contemplated that it should be called upon before troops specially sent from home for the M.E.F. were employed; whereas the 53rd Division was now actually at Alexandria and the 54th in process of arrival.[1] Sir Ian Hamilton replied that he would employ these troops before calling on the Yeomanry. But Sir J. Maxwell had no long respite; the division sailed on the 16th August.

Meanwhile the last great offensive of the Gallipoli campaign had been launched. On the night of the 6th August took place the landing in Suvla Bay.

THE SINAI FRONT, MARCH—JUNE.

Map 1.
Sketch B.

We turn again to Sinai and to the minor operations carried out by the Turks with the evident intention of detaining British troops in Egypt. One of the first effects of the Gallipoli campaign had been the disappearance of the British naval forces from the Suez Canal. The *Swiftsure*, Admiral Peirse's old flagship, *Ocean* (sunk, as has been recorded, on the 18th March) and *Minerva* had been sent to the Dardanelles. At the beginning of March the Admiral was ordered to leave Egypt in the *Euryalus* and meet *Swiftsure* and *Triumph* in the Gulf of Smyrna. He took with him the Russian *Askold* and Sir J. Maxwell's invaluable servant, the seaplane-carrier *Aenne Rickmers*, now anglicized as *Anne*. No sooner was the Admiral gone than a cable from Whitehall ordered him to send six French seaplanes to the Dardanelles, "keeping three in Egypt." As a fact there had never been more than seven French seaplanes; two had been lost, three were gone in the *Anne* to the Gulf of Smyrna, where Admiral Peirse was bombarding the forts, and two were at the moment in another prize, the *Rabenfels* (now the *Raven*), off Gaza, waiting for a chance to fly over

---

[1] The 10th, 11th, 13th and 52nd Divisions had previously been despatched from England and had joined Sir Ian Hamilton.

MINES IN RED SEA 61

Lydda. The Force in Egypt was, in fact, deprived of its eyes, and the Turks might have doubled their troops at Beersheba without information of the fact reaching Egypt for a fortnight. Nor could their work in extending their railway in that quarter be observed. Admiral Peirse was ordered on the 15th March to return to Egypt, but without the battleships *Swiftsure* and *Triumph*, which proceeded to Mudros to take part in the attack on the Narrows. The *Anne* was during the operations disabled by the Turkish torpedo boat *Demir Hissar*, but was eventually patched up and returned to Port Said.[1]

1915. March.

The period of quiet on the Sinai front now came to an end. On the 9th March (the day after the receipt of the order to despatch the 30th Indian Brigade to Basra) eight mines were fished out of the Red Sea. On the 15th the defence against mine-laying in the Canal was weakened by the withdrawal of the torpedo boats, and it was necessary to make shift with armed launches and the Company's hoppers for the patrolling of the Bitter Lakes.

In the early hours of the 22nd March a patrol of nine men of the 56th Rifles, 28th Brigade, was returning to Gurkha Post, north of El Kubri, when two Turks were seen 2 miles south of the post. On advancing to seize these men, the patrol was fired on by a number of others. It subsequently appeared that there had been four or five hundred in the vicinity. Havildar Subar Singh, in command of the patrol, succeeded in bringing back all but two of his men, who were killed, though the Turks, with fixed bayonets, constantly attempted to surround his little party.

Map 3.

At the sound of firing, detachments were sent out from Gurkha Post, and the Turkish force, which included camelry and men mounted on mules, fell back. The situation was sufficiently disquieting. It was known that there were some 4,000 Turkish troops with guns at Nekhl, and the force seen might well be the advanced guard of a much stronger one, about to attack the Canal. The provision of adequate floating defence was difficult ; the only battleship, the old French *Henri IV*, having just been despatched to the Dardanelles to replace the lost *Bouvet*, and all the torpedo boats being gone. *Requin*, the cruiser *Bacchante* from Suez, and the light cruiser *Philomel* took station in the Canal.[2]

---

[1] " Naval Operations," ii, pp. 209–10.
[2] " Naval Operations," ii, p. 292.

THE SINAI FRONT

The Royal Indian Marine ship *Dufferin* was already near Shallufa. That night there was an attack by the enemy on Shallufa Post. Fire was at once opened by the garrison and *Dufferin* turned her searchlight upon the scene. The enemy thereupon withdrew slowly. As there had been reports that he was entrenching 10 miles east of the Canal, orders had already been issued that he was to be dislodged. A column, consisting of two squadrons Hyderabad Lancers, 1/5th Lancashire Battery, a detachment of the Bikanir Camel Corps, the 51st and 53rd Sikhs, and a half battalion 1/5th Gurkhas, under the command of Lieut.-Colonel G. H. Boisragon, moved out at daylight from El Kubri. To ensure a decisive success against the wary Turk it would have been preferable to have attacked him at dawn instead of after a march in daylight. This had been recognized, and it had been intended to complete the crossing at least three hours earlier. It was, however, a wild night, with strong wind and current, so that the use of the pontoon bridge, kept moored along the west bank at Kubri, was unsafe. The troops had therefore to be ferried across, a slow process with a force of this size.

1915.
23 March. After a march of 9 miles the infantry, supported by the battery of artillery, deployed and went straight through the position, the Turks fleeing in disorder after suffering 50 casualties. Unfortunately, owing to the softness of the sand, the cavalry, which had been despatched north-eastward to cut the line of retreat, arrived too late to intercept the enemy. The losses of the British were 3 killed and 16 wounded, all Indian ranks. A considerable quantity of ammunition was captured, all that could be carried being brought in and the remainder buried in the sand.

Despite this prompt attack, there was still cause for anxiety as to the intention of the enemy, whose scouts and patrols remained in the neighbourhood of the Canal in the Suez Sector. There had been a heavy fall of rain in Sinai, which by providing water facilitated enemy movement, though it was insufficient to maintain the inundated area as a barrier.[1] As precautionary measures the Royal Naval Division, during its short stay in the country, detached eight companies to Qantara for a few days, and the French

---

[1] The inundation now extended no further south than Ras el Esh, eight miles south of Port Said, or a third of the original distance.

TURKISH "PIN-PRICKS"

armoured cruiser *Montcalm* arrived at Ismailia. But the Turkish forces had now drawn off and the alarm was over. The *Bacchante* and *Euryalus* were sent to Tenedos; the *Goliath*, on arrival at Suez from the East African coast, was also ordered to carry on to the Aegean.[1] The detachment of the Royal Naval Division returned to Port Said. There had been no appreciable interruption in the despatch of troops to Gallipoli as a result of the Turkish demonstration.

1915. March.

During the next fortnight the most important events were the attempted assassination of the Sultan of Egypt[2] —the would-be murderer being arrested and afterwards executed—and the discovery of a mine in the Canal. The mine must have been three days in the water when it was found. A hostile patrol appeared near Qantara on the morning of the 8th April. Later in the day tracks were found leading up to and away from the east bank opposite mile-post 20. These having been patiently followed eastward through the sand no less than 15 miles, a large packing case was found. The Canal was then dragged and the mine brought up on the night of the 10th. Several ships had passed over the spot in the time intervening.

April.

On the 28th April Turkish detachments again approached the Canal. A patrol of 100 men of the Bikanir Camel Corps, searching for ammunition reported to have been buried by the enemy 12 miles east of Ismailia Ferry Post, came upon a body of from two to three hundred Turks and Bedouin, with which it fought an indecisive action. Other parties were reported at several points, a large one at Qatiya. There were now three new and good French seaplanes at Port Said, so that adequate aerial reconnaissance was possible. At dusk the enemy's camp was located at Hawawish, 13 miles east of the Canal at a point mid-way between Ismailia and El Ferdan. Br.-General W. A. Watson, with a column consisting of eight squadrons of the Imperial Service Cavalry Brigade, a half battalion 27th Punjabis and a section of Egyptian artillery, left Ismailia that night with the intention of surprising him. The Turkish force, however, moved while it was still dark and made an attack on Bench Mark Post, which was easily beaten off. It then retired, but was located by an aeroplane at dawn at Bir el

---

[1] "Naval Operations," ii, p. 293.
[2] Two months later, on the 9th June, there was another attempt on the Sultan's life, a bomb being thrown at him, which failed to explode.

Mahadat, not far from its former position. General Watson, on receiving this information, marched in that direction. Unfortunately only a small rear guard could be brought to action, the main body slipping away. The rear guard was put to flight, some 30 Turks being killed and 12, including an officer, taken prisoner, while the British had 11 casualties. It was ascertained that the main body had mountain guns and a machine gun.

There were now in the Canal only the three old French ships *Saint-Louis*, *Montcalm* and *Requin*, and the old British light cruiser *Proserpine*, the *Philomel* being away on special duty. It was proposed to apply to Admiral de Robeck, who had succeeded Admiral Carden in command of the Eastern Mediterranean Squadron at the Dardanelles, for the *Euryalus* and *Bacchante* or equivalent ships. The French, however, were prepared to help, and Admiral Dartige du Fournet sent the cruisers *Jeanne d'Arc* and *D'Entrecasteaux* and the light cruiser *D'Estrées* into the Canal on the 30th April. But the danger was over; no Turkish forces were now in touch with the British troops on the Canal.

The Canal Defences had a full month's respite from this harrying before fresh activity developed on the 30th May. On that date a party of 20 men approaching the bank between Ballah and Ferdan was detected and fired upon. At daybreak a mine was found buried in the sand, three-quarters of a mile from the east bank. On the night of the 2nd June the Qantara outposts were shelled at long range. A small mixed force was sent out, and the enemy fled, a Turkish officer and an Arab being captured. These minor offensives brought the enemy one important success on the 30th June, when the Holt liner *Teiresias* struck a mine in the Little Bitter Lake, despite the fact that the lake had been regularly patrolled by three armed launches, manned by naval ratings. The ship swung round across the channel and blocked it completely, but the Canal Company was able to reopen it for traffic that night.

This represented the last activity of any importance on the part of the enemy in Sinai until the autumn. The majority of his Regular troops and almost all his officers of experience had been transferred to the Dardanelles. The pressure upon Turkey at that point had, though the effort to make it enfeebled Egypt, removed the threat of a further offensive against the Suez Canal.

THE WESTERN FRONTIER, THE SUDAN, AND THE RED SEA.

The anxieties and responsibilities of the British commander in Egypt were not confined to the defence of the Canal and the difficult role he had to play in the Gallipoli campaign. On every hand German and Turkish agents were at work to make trouble, seeking out weak points, blowing the smouldering coals of religious hatred. From Sinai, from the Western Desert, from Arabia, from Darfur, their influence converged upon Egypt, which had already become Britain's base for operations in the Near East, a rich source of supplies, an ideal camp and training ground for her military reserves. Their efforts were methodical and obviously co-ordinated.

1915.

Signs of unrest appeared in early spring on the Western Frontier. Sayed Ahmed, the Senussi, head of a powerful Mohammedan sect, was encamped outside Sollum, close to the Mediterranean shore. Since the Tripolitan War, which had resulted in the formal occupation of Cyrenaica by Italy, his ascendency had kept the tribesmen in arms against her and limited her range of authority to that of her ships' guns. Even on the coast she had no post east of Tabrouk, over 50 miles from Sollum and the frontier. The Senussi expressed bitter hatred for the Italians, against whom he had won certain successes, but still professed friendship for the British. Yet, as Sir J. Maxwell reported to Lord Kitchener on the 7th May, he had at his side Nuri Bey, Enver's half-brother, certainly no good influence. On the 19th May it was reported that a party of three German and a number of Turkish officers,[1] with a large supply of rifles, ammunition, machine guns and pack artillery, had reached him, landing west of Sollum. Further difficulties were caused by his demand that an Italian prisoner, who had escaped him and fled to Egypt, should be given up. This was obviously out of the question, but tact was required to explain the fact politely to a chieftain who knew naught of Hague Conventions. The entry of Italy into the war at the end of May slightly improved the situation, as it gave prospect that the intrigues in Rome by Germans, Turks and renegade Egyptians might be checked.

Map 1. Sketch

May.

---

[1] The number was put as high as fifty, but the Arab agent is given to exaggeration and there were probably not more than a fourth of that number of officers.

The Senussi in his communications with the British High Commissioner and Sir J. Maxwell still preserved a tone more or less friendly. How far from friendship he had already moved was revealed by an event which took place on the 7th June, though Sir J. Maxwell did not hear of it until two months later. A Turkish sailing ship captured by the French Navy off Crete had on board a mission to the Senussi of two Turkish officers and five non-commissioned officers, together with costly presents, £5,000 in Turkish gold, decorations, ammunition and grenades. There was also an autograph letter from the Sultan of Turkey, in which he acknowledged one from the Senussi. He conferred upon the latter the title of Vizir and authorized him to proclaim a *Jihad* against Great Britain, France and Russia. Of Italy he made no mention, save to congratulate the Senussi on his successes against her.[1] He declared that the Turks would drive the British and French at Gallipoli into the sea.

This news reached Sir J. Maxwell on the very day of the landing in Suvla Bay. It was the first evidence he had had that Sayed Ahmed was communicating directly with Constantinople, and it came at a time when anxiety regarding the issue of the Gallipoli campaign was growing among Britain's best friends in Egypt. He had, however, earlier proof that the Germans were interested in the sect. On the 20th July the *Dufferin* brought to Alexandria a German lieutenant, Baron von Gumpenberg, captured on the high seas. This officer, who had assumed the name of Roeder and carried forged American passports, had been in Tripoli, undoubtedly on a mission to the Senussi.

The threat in the Western Desert continued to grow, till it culminated in the autumn in war, involving the prolonged operations which will be later described. In the Sudan also there were sporadic disturbances. These were due in part to the uneasiness which Great Britain's war with the Khalifate aroused among the Moslem population, but still more to the propaganda of Turkish emissaries, who put about rumours that the British had been defeated on the Suez Canal, enlarged upon the reverses suffered by Russia and later upon the lack of success of the Gallipoli campaign.

---

[1] The letter was doubtless written before Italy entered the war against Austria.

TURKISH THREAT TO ADEN

The operations necessitated by these outbreaks were of minor character and were conducted by General Sir R. Wingate with the Egyptian and Sudanese troops at his disposal. The Governor-General had been promised by Sir J. Maxwell British reinforcements, should they be required, but he was able not only to dispense with these but to assist Egypt and the M.E.F. with personnel and material, particularly by the despatch of British Regular officers. There was, however, more serious trouble brewing on the western frontier of the province of Kordofan, in the Sultanate of Darfur. The Sultan, though treated with the greatest forbearance, assumed an attitude more and more intransigent. So long as he refrained from active hostilities no move was made by the British. His turn did not come until his obvious designs upon the Sudan made an expedition against him inevitable.

In June Sir J. Maxwell was informed that a Turkish force had made an attack on Perim Island, in the Bab el Mandab, and that the Government of India were desirous that he should despatch an expedition against the Turks on the mainland at Sheikh Said, one hundred miles west of Aden. He decided to send Major-General Sir G. Younghusband's 28th Indian Brigade, with "B" Battery H.A.C. and the Berkshire Battery R.H.A. (T.).[1] It was possible to defer the expedition for a short time, but, on the development of a direct threat to Aden, the force sailed on the 13th July for that port. This was the third Indian brigade to leave Egypt, besides all British officers who could be spared. From the 1st June the divisional organizations of the 10th and 11th Indian Divisions were broken up, the Indian troops being now directly administered by the G.O.C. Canal Defences.

The operations in the Sudan, the campaign against the Sultan of Darfur, the attack by the Turks on Aden and their repulse by General Younghusband's expeditionary force, will be recorded later in some detail. They are mentioned here because the unrest and aggression in their distant areas all had a certain effect upon Egypt, adding in greater or less degree to the preoccupations of its command with the defence of the Suez Canal, the support of the Gallipoli campaign, the watch upon the Western Desert and the maintenance of order within the country.

---

[1] These batteries belonged to the artillery of the 2nd Mounted Division.

NOTE.

TROOPS AND DETAILS IN EGYPT ON 9TH JULY 1915.

	Off.	O.R.	Horses.	Mules.
Yeomanry Brigade	62	992	1,076	—
2nd Mounted Division	424	7,818	6,841	506
* Indian Expeditionary Force " E "—			2,179	3,124
British	308	109	—	—
Indians	491	15,032	—	—
† Part of 5th Australian Brigade.	36	1,116	149	—
6th Australian Brigade	130	3,930	178	—
A. & N.Z. Army Corps Training Depot.	276	9,635	10,977	134
Army Corps Details	23	108	—	—
29th Divisional Supply Column.	3	309	—	—
Regulars, Details	57	398	81	91
Depot	10	364	5,928	13
Mediterranean Expeditionary Force Base.—			8,645	12,827
British	337	25,397	—	—
Indians	24	2,376	—	—
	2,181	67,584	36,054	16,695

* The 29th and 30th Indian Brigades had gone. The 28th Brigade was under orders for Aden, but is here included.

† The 5th, 6th and 7th Brigades were in process of arriving. Some troops of the 7th Brigade had landed on the 2nd July and are probably included in the A.N.Z.A.C. Training Depot.

CHAPTER V.

EGYPT AND THE EVACUATION OF GALLIPOLI.

(Maps 1, 8; Sketches B, 9.)

EGYPT DURING THE LAST PHASE OF THE GALLIPOLI CAMPAIGN.

THE Suvla Bay landing had not achieved the results which had been hoped for from it, but the time had not yet come for the abandonment of the Gallipoli enterprise to be contemplated. For the moment the chief problem was to supply the M.E.F. as speedily as possible with the reinforcements and drafts which it urgently required. Lord Kitchener cabled to General Maxwell on the 11th August that the latter's returns showed large numbers of officers and men at the base. Could he not find more for Gallipoli? The figures represented, in fact, apart from drafts actually awaiting transport to Mudros, men unfit or temporarily unfit, men untrained, and those looking after from three to six horses apiece, belonging to the light horse on Gallipoli and to the divisions there which had left behind the greater part of their transport in Egypt.

Lord Kitchener added that he was sending to Egypt the Scottish Horse, dismounted, three Territorial battalions from Malta[1] and two from Gibraltar. Sir J. Maxwell was, as has been recorded, on the point of despatching to Gallipoli the 2nd Mounted Division as an infantry brigade. He had also some unexpected reinforcements for the M.E.F. The 4th Light Horse Brigade had arrived from Australia with one regiment only mounted; this regiment he proposed to allot as divisional cavalry to the newly formed 2nd Australian Division,[2] and the other two as drafts to the three light horse brigades already on the Peninsula. Lord Kitchener approved of the suggestion. The 2nd Australian Division

1915.
Aug.

---
[1] These three battalions belonged to the 2nd Line of the London Regiment of which one battalion had, as already stated, been sent to the Sudan.
[2] This division was formed in Egypt of the 5th, 6th and 7th Brigades, already in the country.

itself was now also despatched to Mudros, the 5th Brigade sailing from Alexandria on the 16th August and the other two following. Sir J. Maxwell also arranged with Sir Ian Hamilton that all troops from the United Kingdom, Gibraltar, Marseilles and Malta, with the exception of a garrison battalion required for the Sudan and four Territorial battalions (two very deficient in training) for his own needs, should sail direct to Mudros, without touching at Alexandria.

Next Lord Kitchener enquired if the 28th Indian Brigade, about to return from its two months' expedition to Aden, was suitable for employment against Mohammedans. A fortnight later the War Office offered the 51st and 53rd Sikhs from this brigade to Sir Ian Hamilton. The latter was anxious enough to have them, though he would have preferred units with no Mohammedans in their ranks.[1] General Maxwell, however, protested against their withdrawal. He was now again beginning to be troubled by pin-pricks on the Canal front, where, he pointed out, his Indian troops had barely two nights' sleep a week. His contention was upheld, and neither the 28th Brigade nor any of its battalions were sent to Gallipoli.

In the latter part of September there was a sudden and remarkable development of the situation in the Near East. The Bulgarian Army had mobilized, with the obvious intention of invading Serbia from the east at the moment when she was engaged in facing an Austro-German offensive from the north; the Serbian Government called upon Greece for the aid which they had right to expect in such circumstances, under the terms of the treaty between the two countries. The Greek Government in turn requested the Allies to send troops to Salonika in order to enable Greece to give this support. Great Britain and France promised to send 150,000 men between them; of these it had been decided that some would have to come from Gallipoli, which, however, was not to be abandoned. On the 25th September, the day on which he received this information

---

[1] The 28th Brigade had already been employed against Mohammedan troops in the defence of the Suez Canal and at Aden. The implication in Lord Kitchener's question was whether it was suitable for employment so near Constantinople as the Peninsula. With regard to the two Sikh battalions, these had Mohammedan companies. There had been a few desertions among Moslem troops in the early days on the Suez Canal, and it was not yet realized how small had been the effect of the proclamation of *Jihad*.

THE SALONIKA CAMPAIGN 71

from the War Office, Sir Ian Hamilton was informed by 1915.
General Bailloud, the French commander under his orders,
that the latter's Government had ordered him to send one of
his two divisions to Salonika. Then came an order from
Lord Kitchener to concentrate the 10th Division at Mudros.

The Salonika campaign began with changes of plan. Oct.
On the 3rd October, while the Force in Egypt was hurriedly
organizing a Yeomanry regiment from details of the 2nd
Mounted Division for the new expedition, the French
transports which had sailed from Mudros returned to the
harbour. The despatch of the British 10th Division was
cancelled. The Greek Prime Minister, M. Venizelos, an
ardent supporter of the Allies and of the Serbian treaty,
had fallen and the pro-German party, backed by the Court,
had come to power. As a result, the Greek authorities had
suddenly withdrawn their invitation to land at Salonika.
But on the 7th the movement of the 10th Division and of the
Yeomanry from Egypt was ordered to continue. The
Allies had decided to support Serbia, with or without the
assistance of Greece, and were now launched upon yet
another campaign.

During the summer, as has been stated, the Egyptian Sketch B.
command was happily little troubled by hostile activity
against the Suez Canal; nor were the Turks in a position,
with the coming of cooler weather, to renew operations, even
on the scale of those which had followed their defeat at
Ismailia in February.[1] There are but two incidents worthy
of note on this front from the beginning of August until the
end of 1915.

On the 13th August seven men (probably hashish
smugglers, accustomed to swimming the Canal by night in
times of peace) swam across to a point north of Qantara
and placed dynamite cartridges on the railway line, which
here follows the western bank. The dynamite was exploded
by a passing train, but no damage resulted. The only
military operation occurred on the 23rd November. It had Nov.
been discovered the previous day that a hostile column
about 200 strong was at Bir el Mahadat. Two columns

---

[1] The actual number of divisions in Syria and Palestine, eight in
November 1914, appears to have been merely reduced to five a year later,
but it is obvious from the statements of Kress and other sources of information
that the numbers of the *Fourth Army* had sunk in proportion far
greater.

therefore moved out at night, from El Ferdan and Qantara, to drive the enemy from the vicinity of the Canal. The first column reached Mahadat to find that the enemy had fled. The Qantara column, consisting of two squadrons Mysore Lancers, the Bikanir Camel Corps, and a half battalion 2/2nd Gurkhas,[1] reached the Hod el Aras, 12 miles E.S.E. of its starting point, at 4.25 a.m. After a two hours' halt the mounted troops resumed their march eastward. At 8.5 a.m., emerging from the shelter of a valley, the column came under fire from a small force, and another body of the enemy was seen about four miles off, hastily retreating on Qatiya. It soon appeared that there was no chance of catching this latter party and the cavalry, which had moved off at once in pursuit, was recalled by galloper and ordered to cut the retreat of the rear guard.

This party was quickly overtaken and scattered, the remnant being pursued for 12 miles. Twenty Bedouin and 13 camels were shot or captured. Prisoners stated that some 60 regular Turkish camelry had formed part of the force, but had fled at top speed when the Indians were sighted, leaving to the Arabs the unenviable task of acting as rear guard. In this action a well-known Bedouin leader, responsible for several mine-laying raids on the Canal, Sheikh Ridalla Selim Dadur, was killed. His death had great effect in Sinai and thenceforth for some time to come all was quiet on that front.

Egypt had now reached a curious situation with regard to the war. She was the base for two campaigns, with a third momentarily dormant on her eastern frontier, and a fourth imminent upon the western. Yet the people themselves were still relatively little affected by warfare, save in so far as they were enriched by it. Observers from Great Britain were, indeed, often indignant that there appeared to be so little interruption of normal existence, or even of the sports and amusements of the European colonies in Egypt. Such critics misunderstood the situation. It was part of the deliberate policy of Sir H. M'Mahon and Sir J. Maxwell that war-time restrictions and regulations should be felt by the civilian population as little as was compatible with

---

[1] This battalion was attached to the Garhwal Brigade, Meerut Division, which had just arrived in Egypt on its way to Basra from France.

safety and the efficient conduct of operations. At home, apart from the efforts required of them, it was necessary that the people of Great Britain should realize that, in the current phrase, " there was a war on." For the Egyptians it was neither necessary nor desirable that they should have the fact brought home to them more forcibly than the conditions of warfare already impressed it. If there was a war on, it was not theirs, certainly not in the sense in which it was Britain's.

This policy had, in fact, resulted in considerably more enthusiasm—and not passive enthusiasm only—for the Allies than would have appeared had Egypt been dragooned into a fuller identification of herself with their cause. Throughout this period the Government responded readily to all calls made upon them by the High Commissioner and the military authorities; their loyal co-operation checked the activities of spies and propagandists; the requisitioning of supplies and material was effected without hardship to the people, who remained fairly contented and cheerful. Well-to-do Egyptians came forward of their own accord in response to appeals for the work of the Red Cross Society and similar organizations, appeals originally addressed to European residents and Christians only. Religious feeling in the Delta remained calm, though to be stirred slightly by the action of the Senussi. Internal affairs moved more smoothly than could have been expected by the most sanguine.

The Levant Base.

If all in this respect was well, the military machine was over-worked. The strain upon it had steadily increased as the troops engaged in the Gallipoli campaign were augmented, though the development of Lemnos as an advanced base had permitted the despatch of a proportion of the shipping from the United Kingdom direct to Mudros and thus lessened the congestion at Alexandria and Port Said. In spite of the opening of several general hospitals at Lemnos, the flow of wounded and sick from the Dardanelles necessitated constant expansion of hospital accommodation. The Egyptian Government offered its civil hospitals and various public buildings, while many hotels were requisitioned. Between the 1st April 1915 and January 1916 the number of beds rose from 3,500 to 36,000, and 104,000 cases passed through. While awaiting the arrival of proper establishments from the United Kingdom, Australia and New Zealand, improvised nursing personnel was mobilized to supplement the scanty medical assistance available. The *hôtels de luxe* of the Nile, down to Assouan, were organized as convalescent hospitals in order to avoid the evacuation of the lighter cases to Great Britain and ensure that they should be sent as early as possible after recovery to the reinforcement depots.[1]

A small headquarters, still organized upon the system which prevailed in time of peace, was also burdened with embarkation duties upon a great scale, with the movement of large bodies of troops by rail, with the provision of supplies and stores, and with many other duties for which it had not been devised.[2]

When the Salonika campaign was instituted it became clear that some administrative reorganization in Egypt was necessary. It was decided in the first place, as the War Office informed General Maxwell in a telegram of the 26th October, greatly to enlarge the base at Alexandria, in order to provide for increased requirements of the Force in Egypt itself and for those of all forces in the Levant. That alone did not meet the situation. The operations of these forces were under different commanders, and it was impossible for the officers charged with the issue of supplies and stores to decide upon the priority of demands which might well conflict. There was also the possibility of a new campaign in the Levant—in the Gulf of Iskanderun, for example —being suddenly decided upon and given first call upon available supplies.

One authority alone could conveniently be made responsible for the maintenance in the field of these different forces and for the provision of resources for any further enterprise: the Quartermaster-General at the War Office.

---

[1] The Atlantic liners *Britannia* and *Mauretania* were now running as hospital ships between England and the Levant. Their size prevented them from entering the Egyptian harbours, but they could go into Mudros. The sick and wounded from Egypt destined for England were therefore despatched to Mudros in smaller ships and there transferred to the great vessels.

[2] In Appendix 4 is a note on the staff and system of administration in Egypt in the early stages of the war, on railways, embarkation, remount, and veterinary, and medical services.

It was essential, therefore, that he should control supplies, and that the Adjutant-General should have a similar measure of control in Egypt where man-power and hospitals were concerned. Such was the principle on which was established the Levant Base. Major-General G. F. Ellison was appointed to the command of the base in October, until Lieut.-General E. A. Altham could be spared from the M.E.F.

The Levant Base was a great military depot, under the direct control of the War Office, with all resources, including drafts of men, at its command. Its function was to estimate the requirements of Egypt, Gallipoli, Macedonia and any other theatre of war in the Mediterranean, and to arrange with the War Office to meet them. All applications were made direct to the G.O.C. Levant Base, who, if any demand were likely to exhaust his stock or if demands appeared to conflict, referred to the War Office for instructions.

It had previously been found that, without some co-ordinating authority, it was difficult to obtain the best results from the hospitals. Before the establishment of the Base, in June 1915, the Adjutant-General sent to the Mediterranean Surgeon-General W. Babtie, as Principal Inspector of Medical Services, to ensure that the fullest use of hospital accommodation was made for the sick and wounded from Gallipoli. This officer had his headquarters in Egypt and joined that of the Levant Base on its formation.

In one respect the reorganization was not completed: with regard to the local purchase of supplies. In strict logic, the new scheme demanded that the Levant Base should buy the large quantities of supplies drawn from Egypt, and that the Force in Egypt should be placed in the same relation to the Base as the other forces in the Levant. Common sense and business convenience made it desirable that the Egyptian military authorities, who worked in close co-operation with the Egyptian Government and had an intimate knowledge of the country, should continue to do the buying. In this case, therefore, an exception was made, General Maxwell and his staff purchasing on behalf of the Base.

The Levant Base was a virtual necessity to the conduct of several campaigns under different commanders. Its usefulness was diminished when the Gallipoli Peninsula had been evacuated and over when an efficient base had been established at Salonika.

The Evacuation of Gallipoli and the Problem of Egypt's Defence.

On the 11th October Lord Kitchener put to Sir Ian Hamilton the fateful question : what was his estimate of the losses that would be incurred if it were decided to evacuate the Gallipoli Peninsula ? The Commander-in-Chief of the M.E.F. replied that the operation would be of extreme difficulty and probably extremely costly. Four days later he was ordered home to give a fuller explanation of his views. He was to be succeeded in the command by Lieut.-General Sir Charles Monro.

Evacuation was not yet decided upon, but the very mention of the word sufficed to call up the problem of Egypt. Turkey, once freed from the grip in which she was held by the Allies on Gallipoli, would almost certainly renew her attack upon the Suez Canal. The trend of Lord Kitchener's thought is clearly revealed by his immediate and urgent demand from Sir J. Maxwell for a report on the Turkish communications in Asia Minor and Syria. The former had been considerably improved since the attack on the Suez Canal. True, neither of the gaps round the Gulf of Iskanderun were yet closed, twenty tunnels in the Taurus, aggregating 3,000 yards, still remaining to be completed; but on the other hand the road from Bozanti to Tarsus had been remade. And so rapid had been the progress of the Bagche tunnel that it appeared likely to be pierced before the year 1915 was out.

Sketch 9.
But the most important development was in Palestine. Mention has already been made of the branch line from Affule to Jerusalem, which had, at the outbreak of war, reached Sileh, north-west of Nablus, and had been diverted by the enemy from its original difficult route over the Judæan Hills into the Plain of Sharon. With Meissner Pasha, the constructor of the original Hejaz Railway, in control of the work, the line was pushed quickly southward over the flat plain, far enough from the coast to be secure from naval bombardment. From Lydda to the Wadi Sarar, the " Junction Station " of Sir E. Allenby's day, the French Jaffa-Jerusalem line was followed, it being merely necessary

to alter the gauge from 1 metre to 1·05.¹ Entering now rather more difficult country, it was brought across the highlands known as the Shephelah to Beersheba, which it reached at almost the same moment that Lord Kitchener called for a report upon it. From Beersheba a metalled road had been completed to El Auja, on the Egyptian frontier. Though the railway was single and of narrow gauge, though it worked on wood fuel, it vastly increased the importance of Beersheba as a base for operations against Egypt. Rail and road constituted not an immediate danger, while the British held the enemy at Gallipoli, but a serious future menace to the Suez Canal and to Egypt.

1915. Oct.

In the message calling for this information Lord Kitchener also enquired what were Sir J. Maxwell's plans for meeting a renewed Turkish offensive. To this question an answer was not easy, in the absence of definite data. General Maxwell replied that his scheme of defence must depend upon the garrison available ; at present he never knew from one day to another what new calls would be made on him by Gallipoli. His Indian troops were efficient, but all, and especially the Imperial Service units, required more British officers. It was urgently necessary to augment the Royal Flying Corps. Speaking generally, his plan in the event of another attack would be similar to that of February, save that he would arrange for a counter-offensive, which lack of water transport and the tenor of his instructions had on that occasion prevented.

On the heels of Sir C. Monro, Lord Kitchener himself now came out to the Aegean to survey the highly complicated situation on the spot, to view with his own eyes the position in Gallipoli, and to study the future defence of Egypt. On the occasion of his visit the project of a landing in the Gulf of Iskanderun made the second—and certainly the most dramatic—of its periodical appearances upon the military scene.

The evacuation of Gallipoli would set free considerable Turkish forces. Now that Bulgaria had entered the war and the Serbians had been driven from the Constantinople

---

¹ The word used in the German report (" Sinai:" Dieckmann, ii, p. 63) is " umgenagelt," which implies that one rail had to be taken up and respiked. The difference in gauge was about 2 inches. For an account from German sources of the progress of this railway, see Note I at end of chapter.

railway, thus affording Germany increased facilities for the reinforcement and equipment of the Turkish Armies, these might be expected to be more formidable than ever. The railway activity in Palestine was in itself sufficient proof that Turkey had not abandoned the idea of an attack upon Egypt. Early in October Enver Pasha was reported to have declared in the Turkish Parliament that the first expedition had been no more than a highly successful reconnaissance, to prepare the way for a much greater effort. Operations on a large scale would be instituted later. "The "conviction resulting from this enterprise," he had concluded, "is that the campaign against Egypt will take place."

Sir J. Maxwell considered that the evacuation of Gallipoli would have disastrous effects, morally as well as materially, unless Britain struck hard at Turkey elsewhere. His thoughts turned again to the Gulf of Iskanderun and to the possibility of cutting the Turkish communications, not only with Syria, but with Mesopotamia, where Major-General C. V. F. Townshend, in his advance, had defeated the Turks at Kut el Amara on the 28th September. A landing in the Gulf, he suggested to Lord Kitchener prior to the latter's departure from England, should be made before the evacuation of the Gallipoli Peninsula.

From France, on his way out, Lord Kitchener cabled some of his objections, laying stress upon the submarine peril and the large numbers of troops which the enterprise would require. General Maxwell had taken these objections into account, but thought that the advantages outweighed them. His estimate of the troops required was 100,000 men, and he pointed out that occupation of a strategical position in the Gulf would enable Egypt to be held and the position in Mesopotamia to be maintained with far fewer troops than would otherwise be needed. The importance of the question had been recognized at home; in October the General Staff and Admiralty War Staff had prepared jointly an appreciation, reaching the conclusion that the Syrian problem and that of the defence of Egypt had two solutions only :—

    (i) Military operations on a large scale against the Gulf of Iskanderun ;
    (ii) Defence of the line of the Suez Canal.

On the 7th November Lord Kitchener sailed from Marseilles for Mudros, and the next day Sir J. Maxwell,

THE ALEXANDRETTA PROJECT

1915.
Nov.

Sir H. M'Mahon and Sir C. Monro left Egypt to meet him there. They were joined at Mudros by Admiral de Robeck and General Birdwood (in command at Gallipoli since Sir Ian Hamilton's departure), who came over from Imbros. Lord Kitchener arrived on the morning of the 10th November and at once began an examination of the Alexandretta scheme. That evening he cabled to the Prime Minister :—

"This morning everyone met me and we discussed "possible plans for the future.

"Maxwell will have prepared you for the great "difficulty that would be experienced in defending Egypt "if Peninsula is evacuated, unless some other action is "at once taken elsewhere to counter disastrous effect on "the Mohammedans and the Arab world. M'Mahon "holds strongly to the same opinion, having consulted "with Maxwell and Monro in Egypt, and all three are of "opinion that a landing in the neighbourhood of Alexandretta "should be undertaken before the Peninsula is evacuated. "Ayas Bay is the place chosen in order to cut and hold "the railway between Amanus and Taurus at Missis,[1] "preventing the Turks moving east, and thus protecting "Egypt and Baghdad.

"In order to carry out this project we consider "it is essential that two more first class divisions should be "sent from France as soon as possible after the six ordered,[2] "and of course in addition to the Indian divisions going "to Mesopotamia.

"We can arrange to send to Salonika from Gallipoli "a number of men equivalent to the 27th and 28th "Divisions, thus keeping these divisions intact in Egypt. "The 26th would go with the 22nd to Salonika, thus com-"pleting our force there to five divisions. For the landing "at Ayas Bay we should require in the first place two "divisions and some 3,000 mounted troops (which latter "could be obtained from Egypt and here), to be closely "followed by the other two divisions already ordered from "France and subsequently by troops from the Peninsula, "when Gallipoli is evacuated. The positions that would

---

[1] Missis is 40 miles east of Tarsus and 13 miles from the sea at Ayas Bay (see Sketch 9).
[2] The six divisions then under orders for the Levant were the 22nd, 26th, 27th, and 28th for Salonika ; and the 31st and 46th for Egypt.

"be held in Asia Minor would be roughly from the marshes "south of Ayas Bay, along the ridge of hills south-east of "Jeihan river to Missis.

"We are working out a plan of considerable reduction "of the lines now held on the Peninsula, so as to reduce the "garrison and enable us to send to Salonika the Naval "Division, the 53rd and 54th Divisions, together with certain "details from Alexandria to replace the 27th and 28th "Divisions. The Admiral is working out the naval part "of the scheme, which he considers feasible. You might "let the staff work out any possible objections to the proposal, "which all here consider would be the most effective "method of dealing with the present situation. The greatest "secrecy should be observed if these proposals are agreed "to. The 28th should be stopped and the 27th diverted "to Alexandria at once, and the troops we have designated "will be sent to replace them at Salonika."

Lord Kitchener had asked for criticism from the General Staff; it responded heartily. Its objections may be summarized as follows :—

(i) The locality was favourable for the concentration of large Turkish forces;
(ii) The expedition would have to force its way 25 miles inland. It would then have to hold a perimeter of 50 miles and for this at least 160,000 infantry would be required;
(iii) Drafts to replace battle casualties and those from exposure were estimated at 20 per cent. monthly for the first three months and 15 per cent. monthly thereafter;
(iv) This expenditure of force would not weaken Germany in the main theatre, whereas an equal expenditure in France would weaken the Germans to at least an equivalent degree;
(v) Granting that there was to be a withdrawal from Gallipoli and Macedonia, we should nevertheless be for a time engaged in all three ventures at once, which would cause a dangerous dispersion of military and naval force;
(vi) Eventual withdrawal would be difficult, perhaps impossible;

THE ALEXANDRETTA PROJECT

1915.
Nov.

(vii) The scheme offended against a fundamental principle of strategy : to retain the power of concentrating strength for a great offensive in a decisive theatre of war.

These criticisms Mr. Asquith forwarded to Lord Kitchener. He might have added that the Admiralty also was inclined to be unfavourable to the scheme. Ayas Bay, the War Staff admitted, was well protected from the weather and could easily be protected from submarine attack. If, however, a landing were carried out there before Gallipoli was evacuated, it was doubtful whether enough small craft and lighters could be found in the Mediterranean for the second venture, while to tow these out from the United Kingdom in winter was no easy matter. Above all, a new transport route of 400 miles (that is, from Port Said) would be added to the Navy's responsibilities.

Sir C. Monro was requested by Lord Kitchener to reply. Newly arrived from the Western Front, his point of view was more detached than that of Sir J. Maxwell, burdened with the care of Egypt. He agreed with the General Staff that the scheme, regarded purely as a military operation, was open to objections. But, as he was informed that, politically, the defence of Egypt in Egypt was undesirable, protection must be offered from outside, as a counterpoise to the evacuation of Gallipoli ; and this scheme involved fewer difficulties than any other landing. It was estimated by the Intelligence Section in Egypt that a surprise landing would not be opposed by more than 5,000 troops and that it would take the enemy seven days to assemble 15,000. By the time that Gallipoli was evacuated the British defensive positions would therefore be secure. The perimeter to be held need not, he thought, exceed 40 miles. The major part of this front was protected by a great river, which could only be crossed by large bodies of troops at well-defined points. He adhered to the estimate of 100,000 men, or eight divisions. He did not contemplate evacuation before the end of the war, as it would result in a further massacre of Armenians.[1] The wastage figures of the General Staff he accepted ; they were no higher than might be expected in any part of the Near East.

---

[1] For the massacre referred to by Sir C. Monro and for an account of Armenian refugees in Egypt, see Note II at end of chapter.

The discussion continued for some days. Finally a new consideration was thrown into the scale ; the French objected to the proposed expedition. Their criticisms from the naval and military points of view were sound: that preparations would be so slow and complicated as to render secrecy almost impossible, whereas secrecy was the most important factor of success ; also that the risks of a landing under fire would be very great. But it was clear that their chief objections were political. On the 13th November Colonel the Vicomte de la Panouse, their Military Attaché in London, presented to the Chief of the Imperial General Staff a note, of which the following is a translation :—

"Should the British Government be considering a
"disembarkation of troops in the Gulf of Alexandretta in
"order to cut the railway to Palestine, they will have to
"take into consideration not only the economic interests
"but also the moral and political position of France in
"these countries.

"French public opinion could not be indifferent to
"any operations attempted in a country which it considers
"as destined to form part of the future Syrian state ; and
"it would require of the French Government not only that
"no military operations should be undertaken in this partic-
"ular country without previous agreement between the
"Allies, but also that, should such action be taken, the
"greater part of the task should be entrusted to French
"troops and the French generals commanding them.

"In order to avoid any subsequent misunderstanding,
"the French Military Attaché believes it to be his duty to
"direct the attention of the British Imperial General Staff
"to this state of affairs, so that it shall be thoroughly realized
"from this moment that any plan of operations must be
"considered jointly and in accordance with the views stated
"in this note."

That ended the matter, for France herself was not in a position to conduct such an enterprise. The Prime Minister and some of his colleagues crossed to France on the night of the 16th for a conference with the French Government and the naval and military authorities. On the 19th he informed Lord Kitchener that, as a result of this conference and after consideration of the maritime position in the Mediterranean, His Majesty's Government had decided against the proposed expedition to Ayas Bay.

1915.
Nov.

It was necessary, therefore, to approach the problem from another angle. Lord Kitchener's appreciation coincided with that of the combined staffs at home : that there was no alternative to the Ayas Bay scheme but defence of the Suez Canal. In this Generals Maxwell, Monro and Birdwood, as well as the High Commissioner, were in agreement with him. Plans for the evacuation of Gallipoli were now being worked out, though there was question of Helles being retained even if the Anzac and Suvla positions were abandoned. That was not Egypt's sole danger. The menace of the Senussi had been growing steadily all through autumn and winter and came to a head while Sir J. Maxwell was absent at Lemnos. The steps leading from comparative friendship to open war between the Senussi and the British in Egypt will be traced a little later in this narrative. Here it suffices to point out that, in addition to the defence of the Suez Canal and the maintenance of order in Egypt, becoming disquieted by the already apparent failure of the Dardanelles enterprise, a force was required to defend the country from the west and to defeat the Senussi.

Sir J. Maxwell reported that, to ensure the safety of the Canal against a first-class offensive, under conditions based upon the latest experience gained in France, 12 infantry divisions, a cavalry division, and 20 batteries of heavy and siege artillery would be required ; two additional divisions would be necessary for the defence of Egypt itself, the protection of communications and the maintenance of order ; and for the defence of the Western Frontier three infantry brigades, with cavalry and artillery. The War Office considered this estimate excessive, but General Maxwell, in consultation with Lord Kitchener, had founded it upon a system of defence 12,000 yards east of the Canal. It was also suggested that a light railway should be laid to Qatiya, on the coast road to Palestine, and a strong position there created, to deny to the enemy the only approach to the Canal relatively well supplied with water. In preparing such a system of defence native labour could be employed to a large extent, but it was obvious that men, materials and munitions would be required on a huge scale, comparable only to that of the Western Front.[1]

General Maxwell considered that if the Turks attempted another attack it would be on a scale very much larger than the last. He estimated that the enemy would be in a position to begin operations early in February and saw no reason why the Turks should not, if their railway worked well, remain in the desert after March, despite the heat, and open out trenches in front of the British defences. He was not inclined to count upon the good will of Egypt if once a powerful Turkish force appeared within striking distance of the Canal.

When the General Staff at the War Office came to work out the figures on its own account, it certainly cut down somewhat Sir J. Maxwell's estimate of the force required, but reached one strikingly high when the weakness of the garrison then in Egypt is taken into consideration. For the defence of the Suez Canal it suggested that five mounted and eight infantry divisions would be necessary, together with 19 batteries of siege and heavy artillery, armoured cars and additional aircraft; for the Western Frontier two mounted and two infantry brigades, with proportionate field artillery; for Egypt itself one mounted brigade and 15 garrison battalions.

Lord Kitchener sailed from Mudros on the 24th November, but had time before leaving to give his attention to the defence of Egypt after having been informed of the Government's decision against a landing in Ayas Bay. He sent

---

[1] Lord Kitchener, in a telegram to the War Office, stated the requirements as follows :—

"Royal Engineers, with material; wire for defences; telephonic "and cable communications for a front of 87 miles. Water arrangements "for troops holding these lines will have to be made locally, by pumping-"stations along the Sweet Water Canal and syphon connection across the "Canal, with piping to the front. Transport by tugs, barges and armed "craft to be arranged on the Canal. Heavy gun positions on west bank "to be selected and connected by railway. With regard to the Royal "Engineers, there will be required not less than fifteen companies, in "addition to those available from the M.E.F. Aeroplane establishment "proportionate to the force should also be sent. Two divisions of Indian "cavalry should be sent to Egypt at once from France and these should be "followed by English infantry. Artillery to complete all troops of M.E.F. "to be collected in Egypt. Heavy guns at three-quarters of the scale of "the present allotment per mile in Flanders and ammunition at full scale, "in order to form a reserve, should be provided. Severely wounded and "sick not likely to recover in six weeks to be evacuated to England."

THE BEERSHEBA RAILWAY

back to Egypt with Sir J. Maxwell, Major-General H. S. Horne, who had accompanied him to the Near East, so that the latter's experience of the Western Front might be available for the reconnaissance of a new line of defence. Sir J. Maxwell returned to face an unhappy situation. Fresh calls had come from Mesopotamia, where affairs had gone ill, the advance on Baghdad had failed, and the Battle of Ctesiphon been followed by the retreat of General Townshend to Kut and its investment by the enemy in the first week of December. The 28th Indian Brigade and a number of individual Indian battalions were despatched to Basra. There were 60,000 troops still in Egypt, but the vast bulk of these were details of various formations and recruits from Australia and New Zealand, which had been organized into temporary battalions for training. There were no staffs and no formations, save those of the remaining Indian brigades. The Force in Egypt was almost reduced to the functions of a training and reinforcement camp.

1915.
Nov.

NOTE I.

THE BEERSHEBA RAILWAY.

The railway to Beersheba was the fruit of Djemal Pasha's eagerness to attack Egypt. It was he who, on his arrival in Syria, summoned from Baghdad the celebrated German engineer Meissner Pasha, and his energy which organized the work. There was no shortage of rails, for reserves amounting to 200 miles lay in the dumps of the Hejaz Railway. There were, however, only 30 miles of sleepers. So, first the twelve-mile section of the French line from Jaffa to Lydda, and then the sixty-five mile French line from Damascus to Mezerib (which could the more easily be spared since it practically doubled the section of the Hejaz Railway from Damascus to Dera'a) were torn up to provide iron sleepers. Wooden sleepers were cut from eucalyptus and pine trees of the Lebanon. The line was well laid, the bridges and culverts being solidly built of stone by local contractors. The section of over one hundred miles to Beersheba was open by the 17th October 1915.[1] There it would have ended, at least till it had been possible greatly to augment its carrying power, had the advice of Kress been taken, but Djemal insisted upon at once continuing it towards El Auja on the frontier and later to Kossaima. Had he been permitted, he would have robbed the British of the achievement of laying the first railway across Sinai.

Sketch 9.

The difficulties regarding fuel were serious. The two colliers at Haifa, of which mention has been made, supplied coal enough for the concentration against the Suez Canal, permitting the despatch of 126 military trains of 13 wagons apiece to Sileh within a fortnight. When that store was expended difficulties began. The German officials exercised all their wonted ingenuity. Their attempts at blockade-running having failed, they opened abandoned mines in the Lebanon, but the coal, scanty

---

[1] "Sinai": Dieckmann, ii, pp. 63–4.

86   THE ARMENIANS

in quantity, was full of brimstone, and spoiled their engines. Then they fell back upon wood fuel, which diminished their engine power by 30 per cent and caused fires in their trains from sparks. The supply of lubricant was equally precarious. Within a few months their stores of grease were used up. They experimented with a wood tar produced in the Taurus, but heated bearings resulted from its use. They then manufactured fair substitutes from the olive oil of the country and the sesame cultivated in the plains about Haifa.[1]

NOTE II.

THE ARMENIANS.

The Armenian massacres of 1915 put into shade even the exploits of like nature of Abdul Hamid in the Nineties and of his successors, the Young Turks, in 1909. They followed the Turkish defeats by the Russians in Georgia, being begun against those Armenian settlements which had aided the Russians and then extended to the Mediterranean shore at Alexandretta. The general system was the announcement of wholesale deportations, the defenceless columns being then set upon by bands of ruffians organized for the purpose, but sometimes by the gendarmerie conducting them and even by regular troops, and butchered by thousands. The men not killed were impressed into labour battalions; women and girls were violated and stabbed to death with bayonets, but for a certain number carried off into Turkish harems. Many succeeded in escaping to the Russians, and in a few cases the deportations were actually carried out as ordered—small colonies of Armenians being found among the Arabs of Trans-Jordan in the advance of 1918—but it is probable that half a million perished.

A settlement of Armenian refugees was one of the embarrasments of Sir J. Maxwell. In August 1915 the French squadron, under Admiral du Fournet, was cruising off the Syrian coast south of Alexandretta, when an Armenian priest swam out and was taken aboard. He told the French that the neighbouring Armenian villages had been attacked by the Turks. The men had defended themselves while their ammunition lasted and then, after heavy losses, retreated toward the sea with their women and children. The French Admiral contrived to take off the remnant, from a dangerous beach and under fire from the enemy, and brought them to Port Said, where they were put into camp. Many more refugees eventually found their way to this haven.

The Armenians have virtues, but not such as are adaptable to the conditions under which these found themselves, and it must be recorded that most of the refugees were lazy, dirty, insubordinate, and disinclined to undertake any enterprise in the cause of their hosts. Service in raids against the Syrian coast had no appeal for them, nor would they volunteer for an auxiliary transport corps required at Salonika. Finally a French military mission, under Colonel Romieu, was more successful in its appeal. It not only induced every able-bodied man to enlist for combatant service, but brought in Armeniens from many parts of the world, even from the United States, till the *Légion Arménienne* amounted to 4,000 rifles. Three battalions served in 1918 under General Allenby and not without distinction.

---

[1] " Sinai ": Dieckmann, ii, pp. 53–8.

CHAPTER VI.

EGYPT AFTER THE EVACUATION OF GALLIPOLI.

(Map 7; Sketch B.)

THE CONCENTRATION IN EGYPT.

THE unkindly fates which had from the first attended the Gallipoli Campaign would take no denial. In some fear as to the result, but to avoid worse evil, it had been decided to evacuate Anzac Cove and Suvla Bay, while retaining Cape Helles for the time being. It had also been agreed, as we have seen, that no other landing on Turkish territory was to be attempted as a counterpoise to that abandonment. The Suez Canal must be defended in Egypt; therefore to Egypt the troops from the Dardanelles must be sent.

1915. Dec.

It was certain that, however successful the evacuation, the troops from Gallipoli would not be a formidable weapon, even for passive defence, for some time to come. The formations were very weak, and thousands of men were in the trenches who would in any other campaign have been in the hospitals. Those in better case were yet low in health from continuous strain and indifferent food. Rest, reorganization, training and complete re-equipment were necessary before any campaign that involved marching could be undertaken. For the purpose no better situation than Egypt could have been found. Its climate from November to March is as healthy and invigorating as any in the world. Hard work on digging trenches, in the stimulating air of Sinai, with ample food, was an excellent recipe for the restoration of troops debilitated by exposure and nervous strain.

The first arrival in Egypt was the 2nd Mounted Division, which landed at the beginning of December. It, however, came not from Gallipoli, but from Mudros, where it had been resting. Meanwhile, as has been stated, Sir J. Maxwell had been ordered to send the 28th Indian Brigade and other Indian battalions—a total of eleven—to Basra.[1] They were

---

[1] 3rd Brahmans, 125th Rifles, 9th Bhopal Infantry, 128th Pioneers, 6th Jats, 92nd Punjabis, 2nd Rajputs, 41st Dogras, 56th Rifles, 51st and 53rd Sikhs. These battalions joined the Indian Corps, now on its way to Mesopotamia from France.

to be replaced by seven battalions from France, but these reliefs had not arrived when, on the 1st December, their embarkation began. There was, however, to be little delay in the reinforcement of Egypt, for Lord Kitchener was deeply impressed by the danger in store for the country when the hands of the Turks were freed. Sir J. Maxwell was informed that the 14th and 46th Divisions from France and the 31st from the United Kingdom were to be sent to him, the last named beginning embarkation on the 6th December. He was to receive 250 machine guns, a welcome reinforcement, since he was particularly weak in this respect; and 2,000 rifles a week for the Australian troops, now arriving without arms. In the 8th Australian Brigade, for example, which landed in the first week of December, only ten per cent of the men had rifles. The ration strength of the Force in Egypt had by the 7th December risen, in round figures, to 100,000 men and 50,000 animals, but these still represented mainly drafts, transport and administrative services. On the Canal at this date there were twelve battalions only.

On the morning of the 20th December the evacuation of Anzac and Suvla was complete; its success affording some mitigation of all the disappointments the campaign had caused. Everyone breathed more freely when it became known that, by a combination of good organization and good fortune, all had been smoothly carried through and the disaster which had ever appeared possible had been escaped. Troops now poured into Egypt, all those evacuated and not required for the defence of Helles being despatched as soon as transport could be provided, save for the Royal Naval Division, which was to remain to garrison the Aegean islands under the Admiralty. The 53rd and 54th Divisions, very weak and without artillery, arrived on the 14th December. The 1st and 2nd Australian Divisions, the New Zealand and Australian Division, and the 29th Indian Brigade were *en route* by the end of the month. The 31st Division, from England, arrived at Port Said on the 22nd December. The move of the 14th Division from France was, however, cancelled, and the 46th was recalled in January before all its troops had disembarked. The remainder of the M.E.F. was sent to Egypt as soon as possible after the evacuation of Cape Helles, which was completed on the night of the 8th January.

THE SUEZ CANAL DEFENCES.

The policy of defending the Suez Canal upon its own banks had now been definitely abandoned. It had been decided, as has been recorded, that the line of resistance must be far enough to the east to deny the Canal to the fire of hostile artillery, and that a system of active defence, should be adopted. On the 10th December General Horne completed the reconnaissance to make which he had been sent to Egypt, and the proposed alignment of the outer defences was telegraphed to the War Office. They were to run roughly 11,000 yards east of the Canal and the lakes, through Ayun Musa, Gebel Murr, Kathib el Habashi, Kathaiib el Kheil, and thence, skirting the eastern edge of the inundations in the Plain of Tina, to the sea.

Some advanced posts were spoken of as possibilities, but there was no mention of the Qatiya district, the centre of important oases. This area had occupied a prominent place in the Imperial General Staff's estimate, mentioned in the last chapter, of the force required for the defence of Egypt. It was upon the best-watered route to Egypt from Palestine, that which had been followed by Napoleon and many other great leaders of armies. It was calculated by the General Staff that, were the Turks permitted to occupy this district, they might be able to bring against the Delta a force of 200,000 men by the end of January, which might be increased to 300,000 a month later. How unduly pessimistic from the British point of view was this estimate the subsequent course of operations was to prove.[1] Kress had avoided this apparently obvious route for his main force in January 1915, because he had not command of the sea. By January 1916, however, the activities of German and Austrian submarines in the Mediterranean had somewhat altered the situation, making it difficult and dangerous for the Allied Navies to approach the coast and take station to interrupt an advance.

If the Qatiya district were denied to the enemy, the scale of the attack would, it appeared to the General Staff, be greatly diminished, since the Turks would then have to

---

[1] The appreciation is dated 11th December 1915. A War Office appreciation dated 9th February 1916 put the highest possible number of Turks that could be brought against the Canal by the end of the following month at 130,000. For an estimate of Turkish resources in 1916 see Chapter X.

advance over almost waterless country. It was considered that not more than 50,000 troops could operate against the Qatiya district if the latter were in British hands, and estimated that two divisions and two cavalry brigades would suffice to hold such a force in check.

Sir A. Murray, the newly appointed Chief of the Imperial General Staff,[1] at once took up this question with Sir J. Maxwell, calling upon him to give his reasons if he were not in favour of the occupation of Qatiya. General Maxwell disagreed with the premises on which the General Staff's argument was based: he did not consider that Qatiya by any means marked the end of the water-bearing district on the northern route. To deny to the enemy a fairly well-watered line of approach he thought it would be necessary to advance as far as Bir el Abd, a distance of 45 miles. In any case, the maintenance of sufficient strength at Qatiya would consume all the railway material as yet available and thus weaken the defence of the central route, by which the enemy's railway was advancing.[2] He was of opinion that nothing should be allowed to interfere with the construction of the main line of defence. Time pressed; for the wet season, most favourable for the advance of the enemy across Sinai, was at hand. Lord Kitchener asked for the view of General Horne, now on his way home, and was informed that he also was opposed to the occupation of Qatiya in the circumstances. There, for the time being, the question remained, and the advance to Qatiya was postponed until the construction of the defences had made considerable progress.

Parallel to the outer line of defences was to be a second, at an average distance of 4,500 yards behind it. This position, though it surrendered some points from which observation of the Canal was possible, was yet sufficiently far advanced to prevent any serious bombardment of the waterway. The third and last line of defence was to consist of a series of mutually supporting works covering bridgeheads and vital points on the east bank. The second and third lines of defence could be covered by the fire of warships in the Canal and the lakes.

---

[1] General Murray was C.I.G.S. from September to December 1915.

[2] The Turkish railway was now being extended towards El Auja, which it reached in May.

SUEZ CANAL DEFENCES

The task was enormous, and it was clear that it could not be carried out by military labour. The General Staff had, in fact, decided that no field companies could be spared to superintend the work, though the services of 27 officers of the Royal Engineers were promised, of whom 13 arrived early in January. Fortunately Egypt possessed ample labour and high technical skill to organize and direct it. Sir Murdoch MacDonald, Under Secretary for Public Works, was appointed to take charge, with the title of Deputy Director of Works, Canal District, and allotted an executive staff of civil engineers, who were given temporary military rank. His task was the control of all work other than that on the actual defences, under the direction of Colonel H. B. H. Wright, R.E., Chief Engineer in Egypt. The purely military work of planning and supervising the construction of the defensive positions was entrusted to Colonel P. G. Grant, R.E., who had collaborated with General Horne on their reconnaissance. Railway construction was entrusted to Sir George Macauley, Egyptian State Railways, a retired officer of the Royal Engineers, who was appointed for the purpose Director of Railway Services. To co-ordinate the work and to accelerate progress by direct control on the spot, Sir J. Maxwell appointed Major-General Sir H. V. Cox his representative in all matters relating to the defences.

1915. Dec.

In describing the work undertaken it is convenient to follow the classification made by Sir J. Maxwell in his report to the Secretary of State for War, dated the 31st January 1916. He divided the scheme into the following branches :—

(i) Engineer Services, exclusive of defence works ;
(ii) Engineer Services on defences ;
(iii) Services in connection with railways.

The first branch was sub-divided into :—

(a) Water supply ;
(b) Communications, other than railways.

(a) The sole source of water to the Canal district was the Sweet Water Canal, running west of and roughly parallel to the Suez Canal. To supply troops on the east bank from this the obstacle of the Canal had to be passed, while filtration had to be devised to render the water fit for British troops to drink. The general system adopted was the establishment of a series of reservoirs on the east bank, connected by syphons with filtration plants on the west bank. At certain points this method was impracticable; at Kabrit, for example, on the shore of the Great Bitter Lake, the reservoir had to be filled from boats; at Esh Shatt opposite Suez, the water was led down by pipe-line from the reservoir at El Kubri, the next further north. The reservoirs were made of reinforced concrete, with a capacity of 50,000 gallons each. From these the water was pumped through pipe-lines to the advanced positions, where distribution was carried out by means of auxiliary tanks.

(b) The original scheme of road communications was very extensive. It comprised lateral communication along the east bank, branch roads forward from each of the bases on the Canal to the advanced positions, and lateral communication along the second line of defence. Owing to lack of labour and material, it was found necessary to modify this scheme and to carry out only the second part of the programme. There were some difficulties with contractors, as a result of which up to the end of 1915 only 2,500 men were employed on road-making, but in January 1916 this number was nearly quadrupled. Road-metal was brought in tugs and barges to the Canal bases at which the roads started, while, as each road progressed, Decauville railways were used to carry it forward.

The floating bridges were increased and improved, and personnel specially trained to operate them so that they could be swiftly formed up and dismantled. Three heavy bridges, of large lighters and capable of carrying heavy artillery, were projected at Kubri, Shallufa and Qantara, with five medium bridges to take cavalry, field artillery and infantry in fours, at Serapeum, Ismailia, Ferdan, Ballah and Kilometre 40, 3 miles north of Qantara. Ferries already established supplemented these. Landing stages were to be the special task of the Canal Company.

(ii) The work on the defences was begun by the establishment of a series of posts, at varying intervals, at points of particular importance. As further labour and material became available the number of these posts was increased, with a view to linking them up at a later date into a continuous or semi-continuous line. The shortage of skilled labour and material was serious in the initial stages, while, since native workmen were largely employed, covering parties had to be found, as much for their moral reassurance as for their protection from actual danger, and water had to be taken out to them by camel convoys. The digging of the works was easy, keeping them open very difficult. A hurdle-factory and saw-mills were established at Port Said to provide material for the revetment of trenches.

1915. Dec.

(iii) Between Egypt proper and the Canal the sole means of communication was the Cairo–Ismailia Railway, of which the last 50 miles, from Zagazig, was single. At Ismailia this railway branched north and south, following the west bank of the Canal to Port Said and Suez. It was decided to double the section of single line from Zagazig to Ismailia and, in order to provide a second avenue of communication, to continue to the Canal at Qantara the branch line which ran from Zagazig to Salhia.

The first of these enterprises was the first undertaken in order to relieve the growing congestion on the line. Orders to this effect were issued on the 25th November. Work began on the 1st December. Thirty-six days later, on the 6th January, the work was completed and the double line open for traffic. This was a remarkable achievement, having involved the shifting of nearly 400,000 cubic yards of earth and the transport of over 150,000 tons of material; the more notable in that during the whole period, nine and a half military trains, on an average, were run daily in each direction, in addition to the full normal traffic. Fifteen thousand men were employed upon this task. It was not possible to begin work on the Salhia–Qantara line until the other task was completed.

While the troops from the Dardanelles, England, and France were arriving Sir J. Maxwell set about the organization of camel convoys to enable them to operate in the desert. Difficulty was experienced in finding sufficient camels of suitable type. The camel trade with Arabia had ceased owing to the war, which meant that Egypt had lost an annual supply of 30,000 animals of the best class, desert-bred, hardy, accustomed to working without water for long periods. There were vast numbers of camels in the Delta, but those bred there were considered inferior for military purposes, and had to be watered daily, though they could be taught, by a considerable period of training, to do without water for several days. It was hoped to provide from Egypt 30,000 camels and that the remaining 20,000 of the estimated requirements could be procured from India and Somaliland. Of some 150,000 animals brought up during

December and January for inspection by officials of the Ministry of the Interior only 13,000 were considered fit for purchase.[1] A number of these were later required to make mobile the force which had been assembled on the Western Frontier for operations against the Senussi.

The Reorganization of Commands in the Mediterranean.

The Cabinet had waited only for the evacuation of Anzac and Suvla to include the Mediterranean in a reorganization of command, which had begun in the Western Theatre. Next day, the 21st December, Sir C. Monro was informed of its scope. He himself, having accomplished the work for which he had been sent to the Near East, was to return to France to take over the command of the First Army, vacant owing to the promotion of Sir Douglas Haig to the chief command. General Birdwood was to remain in command of the force on Gallipoli, and Sir Brian Mahon was to command the Salonika Army, which had now grown to five divisions.

The headquarters of the M.E.F. had already, soon after the opening of the Salonika campaign, moved to Lemnos from Imbros, a new headquarters being formed on the latter island under General Birdwood. Headquarters M.E.F. was now to move to Egypt, from which it was to control and supervise the operations at Salonika.

Its most important function was, however, to be in Egypt itself. The War Office considered that Sir J. Maxwell was so fully occupied with the internal military affairs of Egypt and the defence of the Western Frontier that he had not time for the control and reorganization of the large forces which were now assembling in the Canal zone. For this purpose it was thought necessary to have a separate

---

[1] Mange was evidently the chief cause of rejection. From sixty to seventy per cent of Egyptian camels suffer in some degree from this disease. When camels were bought in large numbers at a later period it was found necessary to purchase those not too severely affected and cure them before issue to the troops. Thus from the 1st January to the 31st March 1916, 16,067 camels, mostly affected at the time of purchase, were admitted to camel hospitals for the treatment of mange. Several other camel diseases were also prevalent. Some account of the organization of the Camel Transport Corps is given in Appendix 4.

command, and since the M.E.F. headquarters staff was in existence, it was convenient to employ it. Lieut.-General Sir Archibald Murray, who had been succeeded by Sir William Robertson as Chief of the Imperial General Staff, was appointed to succeed General Monro. 1915. Dec.

Sir A. Murray brought with him special instructions from the Secretary of State regarding the new system of command in the Mediterranean. He was to have his headquarters in Egypt, to command the troops assembling and refitting in that country and to be responsible for the defence of the Suez Canal; while the force at Salonika was to be under his " general supervision."[1] He was to make his own arrangements with Sir J. Maxwell as to what troops were to be under the latter's command for the protection of the Western Frontier and the maintenance of order in Egypt, and as to the line of demarcation between the M.E.F. and the Force in Egypt; the general principle being that he should, so far as possible, keep all formed divisions directly under his own orders, while unattached brigades and units should be under Sir J. Maxwell.[2]

Such were the first arrangements made to meet the new conditions. As early as the 9th January they were modified owing to a change of plan at Salonika. Sir A. Murray was now informed that the British force there was to come under the orders of the French commander, General Sarrail, for operations, and that his responsibility would be limited to the supervision of administration. Even that function he was to exercise only until the following September, when the Salonika Army became completely independent. 1916. Jan.

On the 9th January General Murray arrived, and took over command from General Monro the following day. He found the Canal a scene of great activity. Fleets of *dahabiehs* had been brought from the Nile to the Canal and were carrying stone and railway material to the termini of the roads and railways on the east bank and pipes for the pipe-lines which were to run out into the desert at right angles to the line of the Canal. Light railways in the Delta had been picked up and transferred to the Canal Zone. Hundreds of *dahabiehs* sailed each day from Port Said with

---

[1] It was not explained whether this phrase implied command, administration or training. It actually comprised all these.

[2] For the text of Lord Kitchener's memorandum see Note I at end of chapter.

hurdles, unloaded these at various points, then went on to Suez to fetch road-metal. The pipes came in the first place from India, about 130 miles of piping being obtained from this source. Thereafter it had to be purchased in the United States, and its arrival was awaited with anxiety. A single submarine might at this stage throw all plans out of gear and delay progress for many weeks.

It was fortunate that the foundations of the new scheme of defence had been laid by Sir J. Maxwell. It demanded a great effort from all departments of the Government, intimate knowledge of men, of resources, of procedure, and the tact which only experience can fully develop. A new commander and staff would have found it a matter of extreme difficulty to set in motion this complicated machinery; they certainly could not have achieved so much in the time with all the good will in the world.

The three succeeding chapters are devoted to the campaign against the Senussi, which was conducted by Sir J. Maxwell, as G.O.C. Force in Egypt. Having described the origin of the dual command in Egypt, it is here convenient to anticipate and to relate how the system came to an end. The arrangement whereby Sir J. Maxwell was in command in Egypt, except for the Canal area, had secured his presence in the country at a difficult moment, which was what Lord Kitchener particularly desired. It was, however, anomalous that the headquarters of the major force should have no voice in the country's affairs, which were interwoven with the administration of the M.E.F. The War Office also found difficulty in dealing with the separate staffs. Sir A. Murray, when his opinion on the matter was called for, stated that there was not room for two independent commanders in Egypt. He would, he said, gladly stand down himself in the interests of unity. Sir J. Maxwell also pointed out that the system led to difficulties, especially since the actual base and communications of the M.E.F. were in his area, and was wasteful into the bargain. Each commander asked that, in coming to a decision, no attention should be paid to any personal claim which he might have. On the 10th March a telegram was received from the Secretary of State informing Sir A. Murray that the Government had decided to unite the two forces in Egypt under his command and that Sir J. Maxwell would return home.

At the same time the Mediterranean Expeditionary Force, now including the Force in Egypt, was renamed Egyptian Expeditionary Force, thus taking its title from the country to which its responsibility for operations was now confined. The Levant Base ceased to exist shortly afterwards, General Altham became Inspector General of Communications, and the various Directors of the E.E.F. took over their duties in a normal organization.

1916.
March.

The Imperial Strategic Reserve.

Sir A. Murray brought with him to Egypt, in addition to the memorandum from Lord Kitchener, supplementary instructions from the new Chief of the Imperial General Staff, General Sir William Robertson, who, in view of the greater responsibilities now attached to his office, was taking measures to obtain fuller control over the forces in the various theatres. In these instructions[1] there was enunciated the principle of the Imperial Strategic Reserve. As such the force under Sir A. Murray's command was definitely to be regarded.

For the moment, the memorandum went on to point out, it was impossible to forecast the future action of the enemy in the East and Near East. The main effort of Turkey might be made in Mesopotamia, against Egypt, or possibly even in the Balkans. The War Committee had decided that, where Great Britain was concerned, France was the main theatre of war. It was therefore important that, once the situation in the Near East became clearer, no more troops than necessary should be retained there. Both for the defence of Egypt and for the creation of an effective strategical reserve for the Empire, the first requirement was the reorganization of the tired and depleted divisions from Gallipoli. For his part the C.I.G.S. promised that everything needed to bring these divisions up to war establishment should be despatched from the United Kingdom.

There has been much comment from military opinion throughout the world on the size of the concentration in Egypt, while less attention has been paid to the speed

---

[1] For the text of Sir W. Robertson's instruction see Note II at end of chapter.

98 IMPERIAL STRATEGIC RESERVE

with which this concentration was broken up. A list of the infantry divisions in the Imperial Strategic Reserve, with their subsequent destinations, shows how soon its bulk was transferred.

11th Division (to France, 28th June).
13th Division (to Mesopotamia, 15th February).
29th Division (to France, 15th March).
31st Division (to France, 28th February).
42nd Division (remained in Egypt).
46th Division (to France, 4th February).
52nd Division (remained in Egypt).
53rd Division (remained in Egypt).
54th Division (remained in Egypt).
1st Australian Division (to France, 22nd March).
2nd Australian Division (to France, 16th March).
4th Australian Division (to France, 3rd June).[1]
5th Australian Division (to France, 18th June).[1]
New Zealand Division (to France, 6th April).[1]

It will be seen that of the fourteen divisions from Gallipoli, from France and the United Kingdom, or (in the case of the last three in the above list) formed in Egypt, six were gone before the first quarter of 1916 was out and four more by the end of the first half of that year. Divisions were sent away in the order in which they stood in military value, which meant that all the best troops were taken. Four Territorial divisions only remained, and of these the 42nd also was to be withdrawn early in 1917.

NOTE I.

Instructions from the Secretary of State for War to Lieut.-General Sir A. Murray, K.C.B., appointed General Officer Commanding-in-Chief, Mediterranean Force.

Dec. 29th 1915.

Sketch B. 1. You are appointed General Officer Commanding-in-Chief the forces protecting Egypt against attack from the East, and you will furthermore supervise the operations at Salonika. Your headquarters will be in Egypt, the locality to be fixed by yourself after arrival in that country, subject to the approval of the War Office.

2. Lieut.-General Sir J. Maxwell, commanding in Egypt, will maintain his present command except as stated in these instructions, and will be responsible for the security of the Nile Delta and Nile Valley except

---

[1] Not all these divisions were in Egypt at one time, the 4th and 5th Australian Divisions not being formed till March, when several others had left the country. The New Zealand Division also was formed in Egypt from the New Zealand and Australian Division and troops which arrived from New Zealand.

in respect to attack from the East. He will furthermore have charge of all reserve troops and depot formations in Egypt other than those which may unavoidably be stationed within the area allotted to your command as defined in the next paragraph.

3. The line of demarcation between your area of command and Sir J. Maxwell's will be fixed approximately five miles west of the Suez Canal and the Great Bitter Lakes, but should include Tell el Kebir and Zagazig. You may find it necessary to modify this to some extent by agreement with him.

4. After arrival in Egypt you will inform Sir J. Maxwell as to the forces in that country and on their way to that country, which are to be included in your command. These in principle are to consist of all organised divisions and to comprise all independent brigades, over and above those which may be considered necessary for the defence of Egypt and the Nile Valley against attack from the west, and for supporting such purely garrison troops as may be detailed to maintain order within the Nile Delta and in the Nile Valley.

5. You should maintain as active a defence as possible, subject to so framing your arrangements as to ensure that no formed bodies of the enemy shall come within artillery range of the Suez Canal. Every care must also be taken that small hostile parties should not reach the Canal by night or day and interfere with its navigation. You should use every endeavour, by aircraft or otherwise, to interfere with the Advanced Base and Lines of Communication of the enemy. In arranging for the security of the Canal, and in carrying out any operations based on the sea east of the Canal line, you will act in close co-operation with the Senior Naval Officer on the spot.

6. Troops in transit through the Canal will only be under your orders should it be necessary to disembark them temporarily in the immediate vicinity of the Canal for any special purpose, on an emergency or in consequence of an accident.

7. The Levant Base and the Lines of Communication extending from that Base to the Eastern Frontier will be under your command.

8. The force at Salonika is under your general supervision, and you are authorized to proceed there should you be satisfied that your presence is needed and that you can be spared for the time being from personal command of the forces protecting Egypt against attack from the East. As regards the Balkans, the policy of His Majesty's Government is to defend the town and harbour of Salonika in co-operation with the French forces in the neighbourhood.

NOTE II.

Supplementary Instructions to Sir A. Murray from Sir W. Robertson.

To Lieut.-General Sir A. Murray, K.C.B., K.C.M.G., C.V.O., D.S.O.
December 29th 1915.

I desire to supplement the instructions you have received on appointment as Commander-in-Chief of the Mediterranean Force to the following effect :—

1. You will realize that the Force under your command in Egypt is of the nature of a general strategical reserve for the Empire.

It is at present quite uncertain what the future action of the enemy in the East and Near East may be. The Turks may elect to make their main effort in Mesopotamia, while demonstrating against Egypt, or they may make their main effort against the latter country. Again, they may decide to employ their forces in Europe, set free by the vacation of Gallipoli, to assist the Central Powers and Bulgaria in operations in the Balkans or against Rumania.

The War Committee has decided that, for us, France is the main theatre of war. It is therefore important that as soon as the situation in the East is clearer, no more troops should be maintained there than are absolutely necessary, but circumstances may make it necessary to reinforce our troops either in Mesopotamia or in India or in both. You should therefore be prepared to detach troops from Egypt when and if the situation makes this advisable.

2. Both for the defence of Egypt and the creation of an effective strategical reserve, the first requirement is to reorganize the troops in Egypt, and to get the depleted and tired divisions from Gallipoli in a condition to take the field.

Efforts are now being made to despatch to Egypt as rapidly as possible everything that is required to bring these divisions up to war establishment.

3. I should be glad if you will keep me regularly informed as to the general military situation in your theatre, and as to the organization and condition of your troops. Will you please let me have a report as to the latter, as soon as possible after your arrival. I also desire to have all important information about the enemy which you may obtain. A daily communiqué should be addressed to me, each evening.

CHAPTER VII.

THE WESTERN FRONTIER IN 1915.

(Maps 1, 5, 6; Sketches A, 2, 3.)

ISLAM, EGYPT, AND THE SENUSSI.

WE leave now for the time the main channels of the war to study the minor campaign on the western borders of Egypt. The *Jihad*, which had caused anxiety so great to those Powers with numerous Moslem subjects, had been in general a failure. In the Western Desert, where its natural appeal was backed by the unceasing propaganda of Turkish and German agents, it was to have one of its few successes among people not of Turkish race.

Map 1.
Sketch A.

The operations which resulted from these intrigues were of minor character, and it may perhaps seem that they are here given prominence out of proportion to their size. To that criticism there are several answers. It is, in the first place, impossible to preserve proportion in these matters, for a frontier skirmish would shrink to vanishing point if the actions of single battalions and squadrons in its course were given no more space than they receive in a description of the Battle of the Somme. In the second place, the size of the forces engaged does not always indicate the importance of the campaign, especially in desert areas. Lastly, these operations are of considerable interest and among the most remarkable of the many small wars, often conducted under great difficulties, which the Great War bore along with it: eddies created afar by its tremendous current. They differ also from most of the small wars in which Britain engaged in earlier days, in that these were usually carried out with seasoned and well trained troops. In the operations on the Western Frontier the command in Egypt was forced to employ for the most part troops inadequately trained in open fighting, and as a consequence the force lacked, during the earlier stages of the campaign, the qualities needed in the desert. The officers had not acquired the craft, the almost universal attribute of the British Regular regimental officer, required to bring their men through climatic and geographical difficulties. These factors added both to the anxieties of the command and to the credit of the troops when the affair was brought to a successful issue.

During 1914 and the first part of 1915 the presence in Egypt of large forces prevented any outbreak in the country or on its borders. But as these troops moved to other theatres of war and as the operations conducted by Britain against Turkey were seen to fall short of decisive success, there was some religious excitement within and without. The great prestige of Sayed Ahmed invited Turkish intrigue, for his support meant much to the Ottoman Government. At a moment when the Grand Sherif of Mecca was known to be lukewarm, if not disaffected, the assistance of the Grand Sheikh of the Senussi was invaluable to them, not merely locally, but in the whole world of Islam. On the other hand, Sir J. Maxwell and Sir H. M'Mahon realized that he himself had no real hatred for Great Britain, and they were intent upon avoiding, or at worst postponing, a rupture of peaceful relations.

The western frontier of Egypt was at the outbreak of war not exactly defined, negotiations with Turkey on the subject having been interrupted by the Tripolitan War and then made of no avail by the cession of Tripoli to Italy, but it ran south from the coast just west of Sollum. Between the Nile and its Delta, to which the vast bulk of Egypt's population is confined, and this imaginary line ruled across the sands is an area of upwards of two hundred thousand square miles, which is officially part of Egypt. This country is semi-desert along the coast, inland purely desert, but contains a number of oases, some of them of great size and supporting considerable populations, administered by the Egyptian Government. Among them roam Bedouin[1] tribes, repairing to them for water when desert pools fail, and trading for dates and other necessities with the settled inhabitants.

There was a possibility that the Senussi might stir up the Bedouin to invade the Nile Valley by way of these oases, driving the hardy desert tribesman in a fervour compound of puritanical zeal and lust for robbery upon lax and wealthy Egypt. It was less probable but not impossible that he

---

[1] " Bedouin " is the term generally applied to the nomad, as opposed to the settled Arab. It is, in fact, a plural form, the singular being " Bedu "; the latter is, however, little used by Europeans, who employ " Bedouin " as a singular or plural noun and also as an adjective.

might raise a wave of religious sentiment such as would carry along even the peaceful Egyptian *fellahin* as soldiers of the Crescent. From both dangers it was essential to protect the country. The measures taken to meet them were so successful as to create the subsequent impression that the anxieties of the Egyptian authorities had been exaggerated. But those who know the history of past explosions of feeling among Moslem peoples, those who study that of the outbreak in Egypt immediately after the war, will realize that the situation might at any moment have become serious. The British attitude to the Senussi was conciliatory in the extreme; forbearance was carried to a point beyond which it would have implied dangerous weakness; all without avail. Gradually but inevitably we drifted into open warfare with this important figure in the Mohammedan world.

Sayed Ahmed, the Senussi,[1] was descended from the founder of a Mohammedan sect, which dated from the beginning of the last century. The sect had arisen to reform and purify the faith, and though, like other reformers, its adherents incurred the charge of unorthodoxy, they were very strict followers of their religion. In theory the Senussi had no claim to temporal power, but Sayed Ahmed's predecessor, the ambitious and masterful Mohammed el Mahdi, had set him in this respect a dangerous example, which he had followed, though perhaps unwillingly. War with Italy in 1911 virtually forced him to assume the temporal rulership of the tribes which opposed the Italian attempt to occupy Cyrenaica, and by the time hostilities with Britain broke out in 1915 he had visions of making himself Sovran of a vast Libyan State.[2] He was a man of considerable ability and character, but lacked equipment of equal importance in that difficult hour: understanding of the modern world and its forces. His personal position was not over secure, since his nomination had come to him accidentally and had been made as a temporary expedient. At the death of the Senussi, Mohammed el Mahdi, his son Mohammed Idris was too young to succeed him in his functions. For this reason his nephew Sayed Ahmed, the

---

[1] Sometimes spoken of as the "Grand Senussi."
[2] In Appendix 5 is a short account of the rise and tenets of the sect, and of the part played by it in the Tripolitan War.

eldest of the family, had been appointed to the office. Now, however, Mohammed Idris was old enough, and many of the sect considered him their rightful leader. He was, moreover, strongly opposed to the policy towards Great Britain which Sayed Ahmed was being led by Turkish influence to pursue.

Sayed Ahmed was, like his predecessors, to some extent a nomad. At the end of 1914 he was encamped at M'sead, near Sollum, the outpost of Egypt on the west, among the tribesmen of the Aulad Ali, a people who had not previously seen him. Thousands of them came to pay him their respects, and he collected supplies from them, sometimes in a high-handed manner. At Sollum Lieut.-Colonel C. L. Snow, of the Egyptian Coastguard, was in charge of the Western Frontier. Upon this officer, intimately acquainted with the local Bedouin, fell the hard task of negotiating with the Senussi, preventing, so far as possible, intrigues in Egypt through the channel of his followers in the country, and at the same time preserving the Moslem leader's indubitable respect for British authority and good faith.

The worst influence with the Senussi was, as has been recorded, that of Nuri Bey, who arrived in February 1915. The Turk was unfavourably received and at first ordered to live at Bir Waer, two miles from the camp, almost as a prisoner. He was, however, well supplied with money, and soon acquired influence over the Senussi. His object was to embroil Sayed Ahmed, whether or not the latter desired it, with Great Britain. For example, a raid on Sollum was secretly planned for the night of the 15th June. Fortunately the Senussi heard a bugle-call and demanded its meaning. Finding out what was afoot, he sent the men back to their quarters and had the leaders flogged the next day. Nuri himself denied complicity in this affair.

In the end Nuri was given command of the troops, with Ja'far Pasha, a Baghdad Arab trained at the Military School at Constantinople, as second-in-command. The two set about augmenting the small force at the camp by training levies of the Aulad Ali. And as the Senussi's armed power grew, so his attitude became more haughty and intractable.

In August occurred a serious incident. After a very rough night on the 15th, Lieutenant Norman Holbrooke, the submarine commander who had sunk the Turkish cruiser *Messudieh* in the Dardanelles, approached calm water north-west of Sollum. On the shore he saw some Arabs and a European, who waved a white flag. Lieutenant Holbrooke got into his boat and rowed alone towards the shore, but, observing that the men were armed and being unpleasantly impressed by a closer view of the European, began to row back to the submarine. The party ashore then opened fire, which the submarine returned with a machine gun, one British sailor being killed and a number of Arabs hit.

For a few days it seemed that war must follow. But, in reply to Sir J. Maxwell's urgent demand for an explanation, the Senussi expressed regret for what had happened, declaring that Italian warships frequently fired on the coast and that his people had taken the submarine to be Italian. The excuse was obviously disingenuous, but it was equally obvious that the Senussi personally had had nothing to do with the affair, which was probably another deliberate attempt to force his hand.

Hardly giving the warmth caused by that incident time to cool, the followers of the Senussi began conducting about the fort at Sollum what they were pleased to call night manœuvres, which consisted in training artillery and machine guns upon it at short range. Then there came accidentally into General Maxwell's hands a packet of letters addressed by the Senussi to Moslem potentates and journalists all over Arabia and India, inciting them to a *Jihad* and informing them that he was the representative of the Khalif in Northern Africa. Despite all this, the High Commissioner and Sir J. Maxwell were directed to persevere in a friendly policy. Britain had no desire, especially at a moment when she was engaged in the negotiations with the Sherif of Mecca, which will be chronicled later, to earn the enmity of any section of the Arab world. Moreover, Colonel Snow was still convinced that the Senussi himself was not really hostile.[1]

As late as the 30th September Colonel Snow had a cordial interview with the Senussi, afterwards lunching with

---

[1] This opinion is confirmed by Ja'far Pasha el Askeri, in London in 1925, who comments on this passage :—" The Grand Senussi was not "really anxious to fight against England, knowing that he had to deal "with the Italians in Tripoli and the French in the south. German money, "however, and German agents, with Enver's influence strongly exerted "from Constantinople, dragged him into the war."

There is evidence from the British side that Ja'far himself made every effort to avoid war.

Ja'far. This young Baghdadi, who spoke eight languages and had served in the German Army, was an excellent trainer of men. He opened his heart to his guest, as one who had undergone the same experience, on the difficulty of applying a veneer of discipline to desert tribesmen and the speed with which it wore off when put to the test. He described to him how, after the engagement of Certe,[1] in March of that year, when the Italians had been defeated and their native levies had fled in disorder, he had lost the opportunity of destroying their force, because he could not induce the Arabs to pursue it when they saw that there was booty to be got in the captured camp. Colonel Snow was left with the impression that the troops of the Senussi would be formidable opponents. A few days later came a report that they had won another victory over the Italians near Tripoli, capturing guns, numerous prisoners and a large sum of money.

The Outbreak of Hostilities.

Map 5.
Sketch A.
The month of November saw a decisive step taken by the Senussi. In the first week the armed steamer *Tara* and the transport *Moorina* were torpedoed by German submarines, the crews being landed at Port Sulieman in Cyrenaica and handed over to troops of the Senussi. Strong protests were made to Sayed Ahmed, who pretended at first that he knew nothing of the affair. A last effort for peace was made and negotiations opened to induce the Senussi to dismiss his Turkish advisers in return for a sum of money, but without success.

The activity of German submarines along the coast had encouraged the Senussi in his attitude. On the 6th November one of them attacked two Egyptian coastguard gun-boats in Sollum Bay, sinking the *Abbas* at her moorings and damaging the *Nuhr-el-Bahr*. On the night of the 17th a small party fired into the Egyptian camp at Sollum; another party killed two friendly Bedouin and cut the coastwise telegraph line. Next night the *Zawiet*[2] at Sidi el Barrani, 48 miles east of Sollum, was occupied by a force of 300 *Muhafizia*,[3] the Senussi's regular troops, and on the

---

[1] Certe or Sirte, in Libya on the Gulf of Sidra.
[2] Zawiet or zawiyat, literally a cell, monastery or hermitage. See Appendix 5.
[3] Muhafiz, literally a commander, defender or guard.

DECISION TO EVACUATE SOLLUM

night of the 19th the barracks were fired on, one coastguard being killed. On the 20th there was an attack on an Egyptian post 30 miles south-east of Sollum. There was now no alternative to the recognition of a state of war. The external danger was as yet comparatively small, but serious unrest had appeared about Alexandria as a result of these events. It was important that the Senussi should be defeated but equally important to move carefully and risk no initial reverse.

1915. Nov.

The conditions were difficult. Sollum was too far—280 miles in the direct line—from Alexandria to be a suitable base for an expedition ; its roadstead was open to submarines, and Admiral Peirse was without sufficient fast armed patrols to protect shipping in it. Mersa Matruh, 120 miles further east, was a superior base for operations and comparatively well supplied with water. It was therefore resolved to withdraw the Western Frontier posts to Matruh and there concentrate a force sufficient to deal with the situation, if necessary reinforcing the place gradually by small bodies of troops in trawlers, and using the Khedivial Railway, with railhead at Dabaa,[1] 75 miles east of Matruh, as a second line of communication.

On the 20th November orders were issued for the formation of the Western Frontier Force, under Major-General A. Wallace, and its assembly at Matruh. It was to consist of a Composite Yeomanry brigade, under the command of Br.-General J. D. T. Tyndale-Biscoe,[2] a Composite infantry brigade under Br.-General the Earl of Lucan,[3] a detachment of the Egyptian Army Military Works Department (no Royal Engineers being available), and the Divisional Train of the 1st Australian Division.

A force consisting of the 2nd Battalion New Zealand Rifle Brigade,[4] one company 15th Sikhs, detachments of the Bikanir Camel Corps, and an armoured train manned by Egyptian artillery, was despatched by rail on the 21st to Dabaa, to make good the railway and patrol to the Moghara

---

[1] Spelt Dhabba on Map 1.
[2] Three composite Yeomanry regiments (from details of the 2nd Mounted Division), one composite regiment of Australian Light Horse (from details of the Australian Light Horse Brigades), the Notts Battery R.H.A. and Ammunition Column.
[3] 6th Royal Scots, 2/7th and 2/8th Middlesex, 15th Sikhs.
[4] The 1st and 2nd New Zealand Rifle Brigade had arrived in Egypt from New Zealand a few days earlier.

Oasis. Later the 1/1st North Midland Mounted Brigade with attached artillery was sent to preserve order in the Faiyum and a small force to the Wadi Natrun, 45 miles south of Alexandria.

On the night of the 23rd November three trawlers left Alexandria with 300 men of the 15th Sikhs. Their orders were to take these troops to Mersa Matruh and then to carry on to Sollum to embark its garrison. The Egyptian force at Sollum, which numbered a little more than one hundred, had, however, already embarked in the coastguard cruiser *Rasheed*, and it arrived at Mersa Matruh at the same time as the trawlers. The garrison of Sidi el Barrani, having beaten off an attack on the evening of the 22nd, left by road before dawn and reached Matruh on the 24th. Baqbaq, 100 miles west of Matruh, was also evacuated. The unreliability of the Egyptian Coastguard was shown in the course of this march when 14 native officers or cadets and 120 other ranks deserted to the Senussi, taking with them arms, equipment and 176 camels. A small force of Egyptian infantry and artillery, whose loyalty was doubtful, was at once withdrawn from Matruh. No sooner was Sollum evacuated than small steamers and sailing-ships began to enter the harbour with munitions for the enemy.

By the 3rd December the garrison at Matruh amounted to 1,400. By the 10th the whole force above-mentioned had arrived and in addition " A " Battery Honourable Artillery Company, one section (two 4-in. guns) of the Royal Marine Artillery heavy battery at Alexandria, and two aeroplanes of the 17th Squadron R.F.C. The force was the best that could be found in Egypt but by no means well adapted to its task. The staffs had been hastily collected, the second-line Territorials had not completed their training, while the Composite Brigade of Yeomanry was made up from some twenty regiments. For the protection of the Line of Communication were allotted the 161st Brigade of the 54th Division, recently returned from Gallipoli, two armoured trains and two more aeroplanes of the 17th Squadron, with headquarters at Hammam, 36 miles from Alexandria on the Khedivial Railway.

Meanwhile there were gatherings of the Senussi's followers south and west of Matruh. The detachments varied in strength from one to five hundred; the total was possibly 2,500. The Senussi himself maintained his usual

Sketch 2.

THE AFFAIR OF THE WADI SENAB.

(a) 11th Dec., 1915.

(b) 13th Dec., 1915.

enigmatic attitude. He repudiated the actions of Nuri Bey and his own brother Hilal, who had organized hostilities. He was reported to have recalled his *Muhafizia*, but, if so, they had not obeyed. The Bedouin between Dabaa and Sollum were apparently in sympathy with him, which meant simply that they anticipated his success. That the British had been driven out of Sollum by submarines was taken all along the coast for evidence that their power at sea was gone.

1915.
Dec.

The country in which the Western Frontier Force was to operate was difficult. Along the coast, fringing the true desert, is a strip of land which to-day just affords grazing for camels and African sheep and is here and there rudely cultivated by the Bedouin. Water can generally be found by digging; in fact, two thousand years ago there were pleasure resorts and villas along this coast, and Cleopatra is said to have visited Matruh, or Paraetonium, as it then was. But the existing wells and cisterns are uncertain and often great distances apart. The soil, dusty in summer, becomes gluey in the wet season, and rain is fairly plentiful between December and March. In this season the heat of the day is not unduly great, and the nights are often very cold. It was within this narrow strip that all the earlier operations took place.

South of this coast belt is a plateau of bare limestone hills, some fifty miles wide south of Dabaa and thrice as much at the longitude of Sollum. Then comes the desert proper, wherein soft, rolling sand-dunes stretch away southward for many hundreds of miles. One hundred and sixty miles south of Sollum is the large oasis of Siwa, one of the chief centres of the Senussi's influence, on the desert's edge. Eastward of Siwa lies a series of oases, of which some are within striking distance, for Bedouin camelry, of the Nile Valley.

From Alexandria the single standard-gauge railway, built by the ex-Khedive Abbas Hilmi, followed the coast. It was directed upon Sollum and had at the outbreak of war reached Dabaa. From the railhead ran a track, cleared of stones and roughly levelled where necessary, which bore the somewhat magniloquent title of the Khedivial Motor Road and had indeed a fair surface in dry weather. But the wet season was at hand, and it was evident that the force would find movement a matter of great difficulty.

The Affair of the Wadi Senab.

Major-General Wallace decided to strike a blow, even if he had the power only to strike a light one, as soon as possible. It was important to diminish the prestige of the Senussi and also to bring him to action before he received reinforcements from the west. There were reports that he had demanded large numbers from his commander facing the Italians at Certe.

Sketch 2.

On the 11th December General Wallace sent out a column to disperse a body of the enemy reported to be at Duwwar Hussein, 16 miles west of Matruh. It was under the command of Lieut.-Colonel J. L. R. Gordon, 15th Sikhs, and consisted of a section of the Notts Battery, a detachment of the Royal Naval Armoured Car Division,[1] the 2nd Composite Yeomanry Regiment, and his own regiment, less two companies. The column marched at 7 a.m., the infantry following the track beside the Matruh–Sollum telegraph line, the cavalry, cars and guns moving south-west down the Khedivial Motor Road. The cavalry had advanced some nine miles when its right flank guard was suddenly fired on at short range. This was moving so fast at the time that the scouts had been unable to keep far enough ahead. An attempt was made to turn the enemy's right with the aid of the armoured cars, but the fire was so hot that Major J. T. Wigan, commanding the column, recalled this attack. The guns now came into action, and after the arrival of a squadron of Australian Light Horse from Matruh in the afternoon the enemy was driven out of the Wadi Senab with considerable loss. His force, about three hundred strong, had fought stoutly and had lost about 80 killed and 7 prisoners. The British losses were 1 officer and 15 other ranks killed, 2 officers and 15 other ranks wounded. The officer killed was Lieut.-Colonel Snow, who was acting as Intelligence officer to the Western Frontier Force. His death at this juncture was a great loss.[2]

Lieut.-Colonel Gordon had heard the firing and learnt from a message dropped by an aeroplane that the cavalry was heavily engaged. Since the forces were separated by

---

[1] Four armoured cars, 3 Fords, and a Wireless car.
[2] Colonel Snow lost his life trying to save that of a wounded Bedouin in a cave, whom he approached in an endeavour to persuade him to surrender. He believed that he was so well known in the desert that no Arab would fire upon him.

6 miles, while his own was small and had a considerable amount of baggage for a long trek, he decided not to move to the assistance of the cavalry, rightly judging that it would be reinforced by General Wallace from Matruh. He therefore continued his march, mending some gaps cut in the telegraph line with his regimental telephone wire as he advanced. In the afternoon he selected a camp at Umm er Rakham, where there were wells sufficient for the whole force. Here he was rejoined by the cavalry at night.

Owing to the fatigue of the Yeomanry horses nothing could be done on the following day, the 12th, beyond rounding up some cattle and camels, with 25 prisoners, from the neighbourhood. Colonel Gordon was instructed by General Wallace, by telephone from Matruh, to continue the reconnaissance as far westward as possible next day, returning to Umm er Rakham at night. But as the enemy was reported by aeroplane to be in some strength at Duwwar Hussein, 7 miles to the south-west, he suggested that he should follow the telegraph westward as far as the Wadi Hasheifiat and then move up the wadi to Duwwar Hussein, near its source, rather than leave his flank open to the enemy. General Wallace concurred and also promised to send four armoured cars by the Khedivial Motor Road towards Duwwar Hussein to co-operate. On the night of the 12th Colonel Gordon was joined by the 6th Royal Scots, less two companies, with a convoy of stores from Matruh.

The track west of Umm el Rakham was reported unfit for heavy wheels, so reserve ammunition and extra water were transferred to the pack mules of the 15th Sikhs. The machine-gun limbers, however, accompanied the column, which marched at 8.30 a.m., leaving one of the two Sikh companies to guard the camp. The mounted troops were in the van, extended over a wide front; one company 15th Sikhs formed the advanced guard, two platoons of the Royal Scots the left flank guard.

At 9.15 a.m., when the main body had covered scarcely two miles and was a few hundred yards east of the Wadi Hasheifiat, heavy firing broke out on the left flank. Colonel Gordon galloped up on to the ridge on his left and saw his flank guard retiring hastily northward, pursued by a body of men so like British troops that for a moment he believed two parties of the Royal Scots were firing on one another in error. Examination through field-glasses, however, showed that the attackers were troops of the Senussi. They were advancing in open formation, firing from behind cover as they moved, and certainly doing credit to Ja'far's training. A small body only was at first visible, but it soon became clear that a considerable force was advancing on Colonel Gordon's flank and that he must fight it on the edge of the plateau. He decided to hold the attack with his main body, while the advanced guard and cavalry enveloped the enemy's left. He ordered a company of the Royal Scots to occupy a position on the ridge and to support the retiring flank guard. His message took some time to reach the cavalry, as it was then over a mile ahead of the advanced guard, which had wheeled to its left and become heavily engaged. Fresh bodies of the enemy appeared on the front of the cavalry when it came into line on the right, and Colonel Gordon estimated that the total force attacking him numbered from a thousand to fifteen hundred. Just before 10 a.m. the enemy opened fire with one or two guns firing 4-inch shell. His shooting was extremely bad, but three machine guns which he brought into action were well handled.

There was some risk that the advanced guard would be cut off from the main body. Colonel Gordon, for this reason and because the Royal Scots had not advanced to the ridge, ordered it to withdraw in the direction of headquarters. The officer commanding reported, however, that he could not comply with the order unless he abandoned his wounded and that he was therefore obliged to hold his ground.

The Royal Scots being still unable to advance, Colonel Gordon sent a helio message to the camp at Umm Rakham, ordering up all reinforcements that could be spared. In reply he was informed that the machine-gun section of the Royal Scots and 75 men of the Australian A.S.C., who were armed with rifles, were being sent. The former did not arrive until the action was over, but the Australians came up in time to be of excellent service. Then, at 2.15 p.m., it was reported by helio from Umm Rakham that, in response to a telephone message earlier in the day to Matruh, two squadrons Australian Light Horse had come up and were escorting the two guns of the Notts Battery. Owing to the difficulty of the ground the guns came into action close to the camp, at

Sketch 3

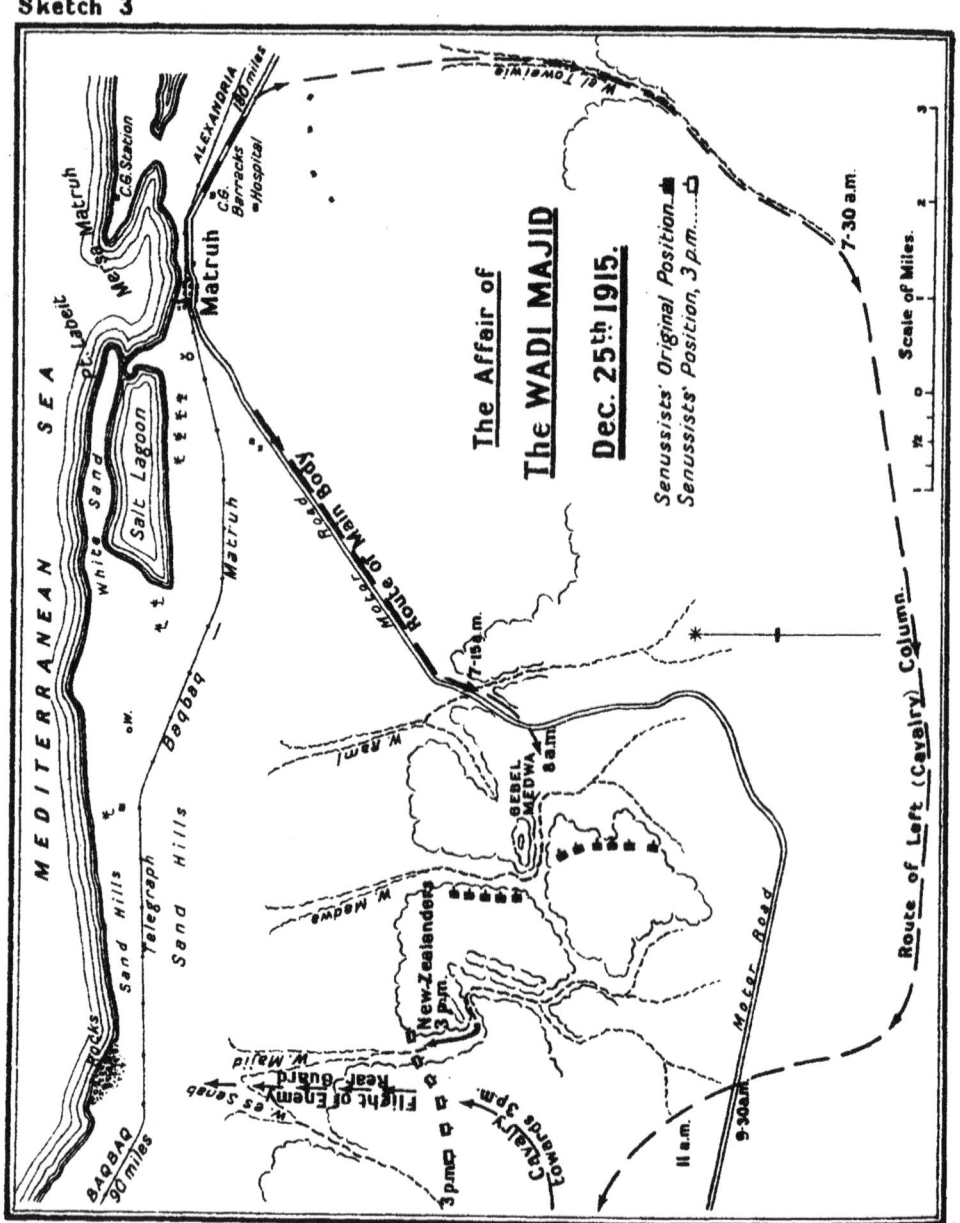

The Affair of The WADI MAJID
Dec. 25th 1915.

THE ENEMY'S WITHDRAWAL

3.15 p.m., at long range, but a lucky shell fell in the midst of one of the largest bodies of the enemy, which scattered and disappeared.

1915.
13 Dec.

This was the turning-point of the action. All along the line the enemy began to retreat and the Royal Scots advanced to the ridge. There was, however, no hope at this hour of the afternoon of any decisive result, so Colonel Gordon, the ridge secure in his hands, withdrew his troops to camp. His losses were 9 killed and 56 wounded. Those of the enemy were estimated at 250.[1] The column returned to Matruh next day, the troops in a state of great fatigue.

The enemy had been driven off, but had been able to retire unmolested, and must be given credit for the surprise and the vigour of his attack. Had the standard of training and the experience of the whole column been equal to those of the 15th Sikhs, the Senussi might have been heavily defeated.

THE AFFAIR OF THE WADI MAJID.

From the 15th December to Christmas Eve the weather was unfavourable and no operations were undertaken. The period was devoted to further reorganization of the Western Frontier Force, which was strengthened by the arrival of the 1st Battalion New Zealand Rifle Brigade. Meanwhile the enemy had concentrated astride the Khedivial Road at Gebel Medwa, 6 miles south-west of Matruh. It was estimated from aerial reconnaissance and other sources of information that his strength was upwards of 5,000,[2] with a considerable proportion of *Muhafizia*, four guns and several machine guns. General Wallace decided to make an attempt to surprise him by a night advance from Matruh.

Map 6.
Sketch 3.

---

[1] Ja'far Pasha states that his losses were only 17 killed and 30 wounded. These figures do not include those of his Bedouin allies, but probably the total was less than half the British estimate.

[2] Ja'far Pasha states that there were under his orders three battalions of *Muhafizia* of 300 men each, four mountain guns and two machine guns. Another battalion, with one gun and two machine guns, had been sent by him on the 21st towards Dabaa to interrupt communication with Alexandria. The Senussi and Nuri had a further force of three battalions, four mountain guns and eight machine guns at Halazin, 15 miles south-west of Gebel Medwa. He adds: "Besides the regulars there were of "course numerous nomads from the neighbourhood. These would take "part with us in an action if they saw we were going to be successful, "but, if the contrary, would retire to their camps and lie low."

1915.
25 Dec.
At 5 a.m. on the 25th December the force moved out in two columns, organized as follows :—

Right Column—
  Commander : Lieut.-Colonel J. L. R. Gordon.
  Royal Bucks Hussars.
  1 Section Notts Battery R.H.A.
  15th Sikhs.
  1st New Zealand Rifle Brigade.
  2/8th Middlesex.
  Notts & Derby Field Ambulance.
  Water Section Australian Train.

Left Column—
  Commander : Br.-General J. D. T. Tyndale-Biscoe.
  Brigade Staff and Signal Troop, Composite Yeomanry Brigade.
  2 Troops Duke of Lancaster's Own Yeomanry.
  1 Troop Derbyshire Yeomanry.
  2 Troops City of London Yeomanry.
  1 Squadron Herts Yeomanry.
  Composite Regiment Australian Light Horse.
  Notts Battery R.H.A. (less 1 Section).
  Yeomanry Machine Gun Section.
  Yeomanry Field Ambulance.

The right column was to advance down the Khedivial Road upon Gebel Medwa while the left column made a detour, moving south of Matruh down the Wadi Toweiwia and thence westward round the right flank of the enemy, to cut off his retreat. H.M.S. *Clematis* was to support any action within range.

The cavalry itself was clear of the Wadi Toweiwia by 7.30 a.m. Bringing the guns and ammunition limbers through was, however, a matter of considerable difficulty which the squadron of Herts Yeomanry took two hours to accomplish.[1] The remainder of the left column continued its sweep, with the intention of striking the Khedivial Road 12 miles from Matruh.

This road runs almost straight south-west from Matruh for 5 miles, then turns left-handed to avoid some rough and difficult country, a tangle of hills cut by deep wadis and crowned by the dominating height of Gebel Medwa.

---

[1] Afterwards, the main body of cavalry being far ahead, this squadron moved in to assist the right column.

BRITISH ADVANCE

Down the road the right column marched in complete silence. The morning was dark, but the stars gave light enough for a good pace to be maintained. The prospect of a surprise seemed rosy, but soon after 6 a.m., just as day was breaking, the enemy's outposts gave the alarm by lighting a huge bonfire. Two troops of the Bucks Hussars, advancing in the direction of the flare, became engaged, and the column was halted until it was light enough to see. The enemy was then visible in large numbers moving along the hills in a southerly and south-easterly direction. There had been at least a partial surprise. It was probably due to this fact that the height of Gebel Medwa itself was not occupied by the enemy and also that one only of his four guns ever came into action.

1915.
25 Dec.

Colonel Gordon ordered the officer commanding the 15th Sikhs to send one of the two companies of the regiment forming the advanced guard to occupy Gebel Medwa and secure his right flank, then to continue his advance down the road. At 7.30 a.m. the advanced guard moved forward and the Sikh company seized the height of Gebel Medwa without opposition. At 8 a.m. the enemy began to shell the road with one gun. The shooting was much more accurate than in the previous action, but some of the shells were blinds, and small loss was caused. Colonel Gordon, who had galloped up to the ridge held by the advanced guard, saw the position which the enemy was taking up along the ridge west of Gebel Medwa and located the gun with his telescope. He ordered the section of the Notts Battery to engage the gun, which was soon afterwards silenced from a range of 2,000 yards. Shells fired by the *Clematis* from a range of 10,000 yards were now also falling upon the enemy's position.

Colonel Gordon ordered the 15th Sikhs to attack that portion of the ridge, south-west of Gebel Medwa, which appeared to be the key to the position, and requested General Wallace to relieve the company on Gebel Medwa. A company of the Middlesex was sent up for the purpose, but the Sikh company was not in action with its own battalion till 10 a.m.

On coming under fire the Sikhs had opened out into artillery formation, astride, but well clear of, the road. At 8.45 a.m. the battalion advanced on a frontage of 200 yards, with the 1st New Zealand Rifles following. Meanwhile the Middlesex and Bucks Hussars were ordered by General Wallace to make a containing attack on the enemy's left.

The advance went briskly. As it progressed Colonel Gordon sent up one company of the New Zealand Rifles to attack the south bank of a gorge on the left of the Sikhs and another to reinforce their right. At 9.30 a.m. the Sikhs, who had advanced very steadily across an open plateau, were ordered to halt and maintain a heavy fire on the enemy's line, now 800 yards distant. There being as yet no signs of the cavalry and the enemy beginning a retirement, it was clear that there was no object in waiting longer. The advance was resumed, the New Zealand company on the left being transferred to the right flank to join the other company of its regiment.

Shortly after 10 a.m. the whole ridge was in British hands. The enemy broke and fled, some small parties taking refuge in caves and gullies, in which many were shot or bayoneted and a few captured. Colonel Gordon led up the guns and the two reserve companies of the New Zealanders to the west edge of the plateau overlooking the Wadi Majid, from which point considerable loss was inflicted on the retiring enemy.

Had the cavalry been up in time the enemy's force might have been destroyed, but the left column had been considerably delayed by hostile mounted troops. It had first come into action at 8 a.m. against camelry and cavalry 4 miles due south of Gebel Medwa, evidently so placed to deal with just such a turning movement as General Wallace had projected. This force was dispersed by machine-gun fire, but the column did not resume its advance till 9 a.m. Later it manœuvred in the plain south-west of the hills endeavouring to turn and drive back upon the infantry small bodies of the enemy in retirement.

Colonel Gordon, having no signal section attached to his column, endeavoured to communicate with the cavalry through the regimental signallers of the 15th Sikhs. He first saw the mounted troops two miles to the south and moving southward at 11 a.m. Not until 12.45 could he get an answer to his calls and even then it was some time before his urgent requests that the cavalry should advance straight upon the Wadi Majid and engage the enemy retreating from the infantry had any result.[1]

It was not until about 3 p.m. that the left column reached the required position between the Wadis Senab and Majid, and it was then too late. The Sikhs had meanwhile crossed the Wadi Majid and the New Zealanders had cleared the northern end of the wadi, driving the enemy's rear guard, which numbered about 150, towards the shore, and burning his camp in the wadi's bed. Over one hundred dead were here counted, a number of prisoners were taken with 80 camels and other live stock, besides artillery and small arm ammunition.

The line was now facing north, the enemy's rear guard between it and the sea. The bulk of the enemy's force, with his herds, had, however, escaped westward. After 4 p.m. darkness began to fall, saving the rear guard, which, though broken and demoralized, was still resisting. The remnant issued from the Wadis Senab and Majid and fled to the rocky sea-shore, whither the cavalry was unable to follow. At 5 p.m. Colonel Gordon broke off the infantry pursuit, ordering the New Zealand Rifles to withdraw to Gebel Medwa, where the right column was to bivouac. The mounted troops returned that evening to Matruh. The infantry passed a Christmas night of bitter cold, and welcomed the order to move in the early morning. The column reached Matruh at 6.45 a.m. on the 26th December.

The operation had been successful in that the enemy had been heavily defeated and his prestige lowered. Unfortunately it had not been found possible to clinch the success. Had the cavalry been able to intercept the enemy's main body the campaign might have been virtually ended then and there.

The British losses were light : 13 killed and 51 wounded. Those of the enemy were certainly heavier. It was estimated that there were over three hundred dead on the

---

[1] At 12.45 p.m. Colonel Gordon sent the following message :—" Move due north and reinforce infantry. Enemy retiring north-west." At 1.10 p.m. he sent :—" Move on Wadi Majid. Your assistance urgently required." At 2.45 p.m. he sent :—" Work north-east and round up the enemy in front of the infantry." Major G. Pennefather-Evans, commanding the 15th Sikhs, having read Colonel Gordon's first message, also signalled :—" Message from O.C. Column begins : 'Move due north and reinforce infantry. Enemy retiring north-west.' Ends. I do not need reinforcing. Push on north. From O.C. 15/Sikhs."

ground, while 20 prisoners were taken.[1] A number of the dead were deserters from the Egyptian Coastguard, in their old uniforms. Among the booty were the office and personal effects of Ja'far Pasha. A subadar and eleven sepoys, captured by the enemy in the transport *Moorina*, escaped from their guards during the action and rejoined.

General Wallace had now breathing time to deal with the situation in his rear, between Matruh and Dabaa, where large numbers of Bedouin had congregated.[2] After giving his troops a rest, he despatched a column,[3] under the command of Br.-General Lord Lucan, to Bir Gerawla, 12 miles south-east of Matruh. Leaving Matruh on the afternoon of the 28th December, the column returned on the evening of the 30th. No resistance was met, the Bedouin fleeing from their encampments on its approach. Eighty tents and a quantity of grain were destroyed, 100 camels and 500 sheep brought in. The operation had a salutary effect upon the Egyptian Bedouin of the coast area.

---

[1] This figure is from the War Diary " A. & Q.", Western Frontier Force. Sir J. Maxwell's despatch states that 82 prisoners were taken. It is possible that the latter figure includes non-combatants taken with the camels, as the Despatch states that 34 were captured in the Wadi Majid alone.

[2] There was also a battalion of *Muhafizia*, of the presence of which the British were unaware. See footnote 2, p. 113.

[3] Six squadrons of cavalry, two sections of artillery, the 15th Sikhs and 2/7th Middlesex (less two companies). The 1st New Zealand Rifle Brigade operated further south.

CHAPTER VIII.

THE CONTINUATION OF THE OPERATIONS AGAINST THE SENUSSI.

(Maps 1, 5; Sketches A, 4, 5.)

THE AFFAIR OF HALAZIN.

THE operations of Lord Lucan's column mentioned in the last chapter had not apparently broken up all the enemy concentrations in rear of the Western Frontier Force, for on the 1st January 80 tents were seen from the air at Gebel Howeimil, 35 miles south-east of Matruh and 15 miles south of the coast at Baqqush.[1] It was, however, impossible owing to torrential rains to make any move against this camp for the next ten days. On the 9th the weather cleared but a further delay was necessary to give the country time to dry. A mixed column[2] under the command of Br.-General Tyndale-Biscoe moved out of camp on the 12th and reached Baqqush on the afternoon of the 13th, after many delays due to guns sticking in the mud. Next day it advanced to Gebel Howeimil. The largest camp was found deserted,[3] but at smaller camps camels and live-stock were taken and all tents burned. The column returned that night to Baqqush, the cavalry having marched nearly 50 miles since morning. Under cover of the operation the telegraph line between Matruh and Dabaa was mended by the R.N. Armoured Car Division. On the 15th the section of "A" Battery H.A.C., and two squadrons Australian Light Horse, which were to return to Egypt, left the column at Baqqush to march to Dabaa. The remainder of the column reached

1916.
Jan.
Maps 1, 5.
Sketch A.

---

[1] Baqqush is spelt Bakshuba on Map 1.
[2] One section "A" Battery H.A.C., six squadrons cavalry, machine-gun and signal sections, 2/7th Middlesex (less two companies), 15th Sikhs (less two companies), 1st S. Midland Field Ambulance, 137th Field Ambulance, Water Section, detachment 1st Australian Divisional Train.
[3] Ja'far Pasha states that this was the camp of the force sent towards Dabaa. (See footnote 2, p. 113.) It was recalled after the defeat at the Wadi Majid on Christmas Day.

Matruh on the 16th, the horses much fatigued by long marches on heavy ground with scanty rations. Thirteen prisoners, 140 camels and 50 cattle were brought in.

Sir J. Maxwell now proposed to the War Office that he should reoccupy Sollum, as soon as naval assistance could be given him and the Western Frontier Force made really mobile. The recapture of the place was in his opinion not yet a military necessity but advisable on political grounds. On the 27th he was informed by Sir W. Robertson that the Admiralty had instructed the Commander-in-Chief East Indies Station to report when he was ready to co-operate. Destroyers would be necessary to keep off German submarines should a landing be attempted. But the Navy had its hands full at the moment, and the Admiral was informed that the reoccupation of Sollum was not a matter of urgency.

Two letters, "couched in terms of injured innocence," as Sir J. Maxwell reported, were received from Sayed Ahmed, one of them addressed to Lord Kitchener. The Senussi blamed the British for the outbreak of hostilities, but as he refused to surrender the survivors of the *Tara* and *Moorina*, on the ground that they were hostages handed over to him by the Ottoman Government, it was clear that he was not disposed to be friendly. No reply therefore was sent to his letters.

The return of troops from Gallipoli now made it possible to amend the improvised organization of the force. The 1/2nd South Midland Mounted Brigade was ordered to join General Wallace and was to consist of the Bucks, Berks, and Dorset Yeomanry, with the Notts Battery R.H.A. The Composite Yeomanry Brigade was to consist of the Herts and 2nd County of London Regiments, with a squadron each of Duke of Lancaster's and Surrey Yeomanry. The former brigade did not, however, reach Matruh till after the Affair of Halazin, and the Bucks Yeomanry and a squadron of Dorset Yeomanry already there remained detached from it and under the orders of the Composite Brigade.

On the 19th January an aeroplane located the main enemy camp at Halazin, 22 miles south-west of Matruh. It consisted of over three hundred tents, among which the pilot, Captain L. V. Royle of the Coastguard, recognised that of the Senussi himself. It was decided to attack as

Sketch 4.

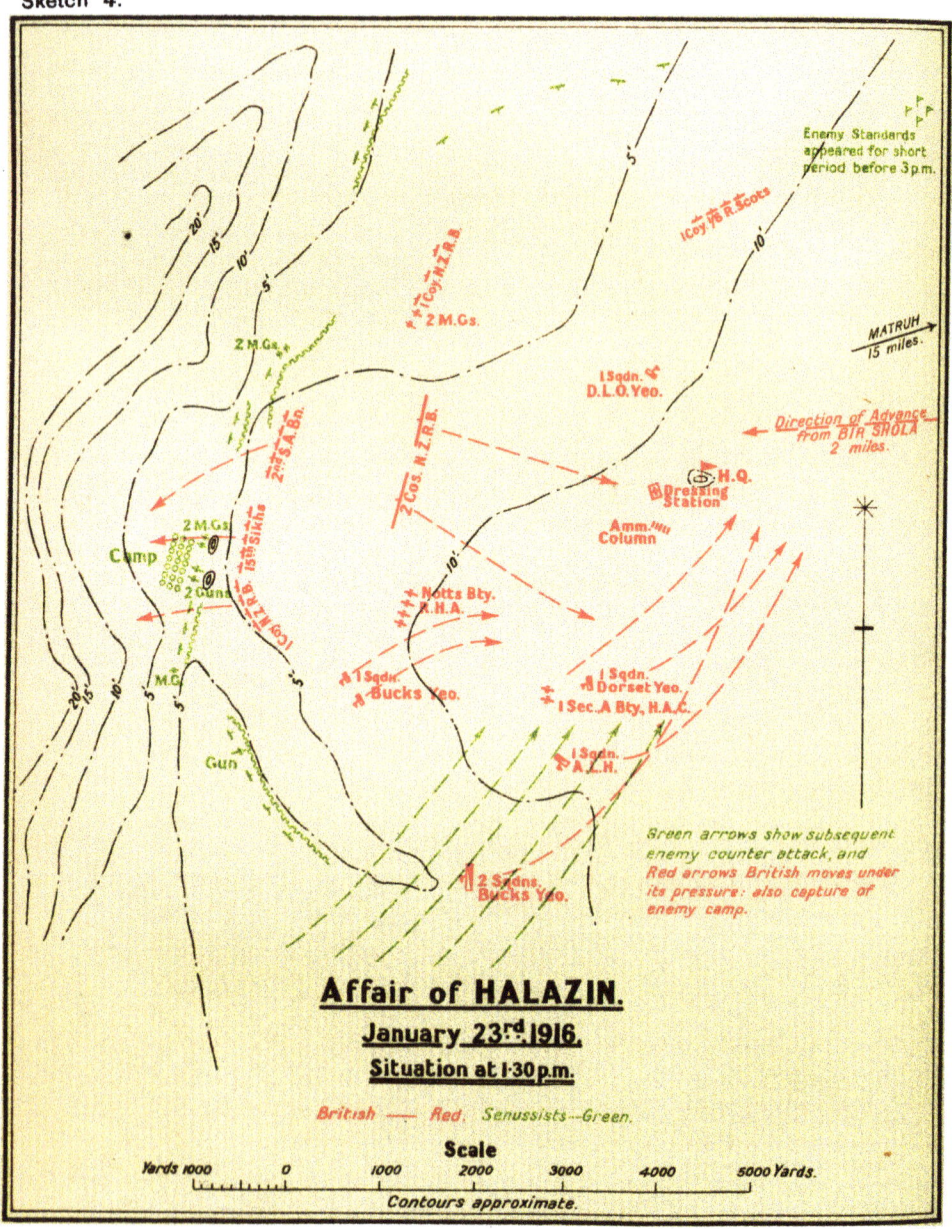

Affair of HALAZIN.
January 23rd 1916.
Situation at 1.30 p.m.

British — Red. Senussists — Green.

BRITISH ATTACK 121

soon as the 2nd South African Infantry should arrive. This unit reached Mersa Matruh, in trawlers from Alexandria, on the 21st.[1]

1916.
22-23 Jan.
Sketch 4.

Major-General Wallace left Matruh at 4 p.m. on the 22nd January and formed a perimeter camp at Bir Shola, 12 miles to the south-west, where a miserably wet night was passed. At 6 a.m. on the 23rd he advanced on Halazin in two columns;[2] the right, or infantry, column on a compass bearing to the reported position of the enemy's camp; the left, or cavalry, echeloned to the left front of the infantry. The train had to be parked outside Bir Shola owing to the difficulty of ascending the rising ground, sodden with rain. Motor ambulances stuck repeatedly and had to be extricated by teams from the train. The detachment of the R.N. Armoured Car Division which accompanied the force was sent back to Matruh, as it was feared that the cars would be unable to return after the track had been further cut up by traffic. The right column moved forward with small mixed detachments as advanced and right flank guards, the former in touch with that of the left column. At 8.25 a.m., after 7 miles had been covered, the left column reported parties of the enemy 2 miles ahead of its screen, which was in action an hour later. It was then decided by Major-General Wallace that the infantry should attack, while the cavalry manœuvred against the enemy's right.

At 10 a.m. the 15th Sikhs advanced in open order, supported by the 2nd South African Infantry and 1st New Zealand Rifles, and covered by the fire of the Notts Battery. The enemy appeared to be extended over a front of a mile and a half, but mirage prevented accurate observation. He was evidently falling back gradually upon a prepared position in rear, and he showed considerable skill in the

---

[1] The whole brigade had been put at Sir J. Maxwell's disposal, but only this battalion was in time for Halazin. It had reached Alexandria from England on the 10th January.

[2] Right Column (Lieut.-Colonel J. L. R. Gordon) :—one squadron Duke of Lancaster's Own Yeomanry, Notts Battery, 15th Sikhs, 2nd S. African Infantry, 1st N.Z. Rifle Brigade.

Left Column (Br.-General J. D. T. Tyndale-Biscoe) :—Bucks Hussars, one squadron each Herts and Dorset Yeomanry and Australian Light Horse, two troops Surrey Yeomanry, machine-gun section, " A " Battery H.A.C. (less one section).

Reserve ($\frac{1}{2}$ mile in rear of Right Column) :—2 troops Herts Yeomanry, 6th Royal Scots (less two companies).

Baggage Escort :—2/8th Middlesex (less two companies).

withdrawal, also handling well at least three mountain guns and five machine guns. A body of the enemy now appeared on the British right, and at 11.45 Colonel Gordon reinforced the right of the Sikhs with two companies of South Africans. Shortly afterwards the enemy appeared on the British left also, while the right flank guard reported that it was being driven in by a strong party with machine guns. This movement was countered by sending up a company of New Zealanders with machine guns, which checked the enemy's advance but was in turn outflanked by another body. A company of the Royal Scots put an end to the pressure on this flank.

On the left the enemy's enveloping movement was stronger and more persistent. The advance of the left column was held up at 1.30 p.m., and although it was reinforced from the reserve, it was gradually driven in. The remaining two companies of the New Zealanders were now sent to this flank (one company having been moved up on the left of the 15th Sikhs) and the enemy's advance brought to an end.

By this time the force was in a curious position. The flanks had been driven back while the Sikhs advanced in the centre and the whole force was in horse-shoe formation.[1] The determination to press the main attack, however, brought its reward. By 2.45 p.m. the Sikhs, South Africans and New Zealand company reached the enemy's entrenchments, from which the defenders streamed back into the desert, abandoning their large camp. The flanking attacks now melted away, but the horses of the mounted troops, which had had no water, were too exhausted for serious pursuit. Had the ground permitted the use of the armoured cars the enemy would not have escaped so easily.

This was a costlier action than those which had preceded it, the British casualties numbering 312,[2] while, according to the statements of the few prisoners taken, those of the enemy were about 200 killed and 500 wounded. The Senussi had been dealt another severe blow, but once again the result was indecisive, and his force remained in being.

---

[1] The two troops Surrey Yeomanry are not shown on Sketch 4. They were acting with the D.L.O. Yeomanry.
[2] One British officer and 20 other ranks killed; 10 British, 3 Indian officers and 278 other ranks wounded.

PREPARATIONS FOR ADVANCE

Owing to the fatigue of troops and animals and the fact that his field ambulance and ammunition column were stuck in the mud, General Wallace decided to bivouac 2 miles east of the captured position. The troops spent the night in great discomfort, without coats, blankets, and in most cases food, without water for man or beast save that found in pools left by the rain. Only two ambulance carts could be got away to Matruh; the rest of the wounded had to remain with the column and share the conditions of its bivouac.

Next morning the column started back to Bir Shola. After a wet night the mud was worse than ever. All vehicles had to be dragged by parties of troops and such of the wounded as could not sit horses carried on stretchers, till the train was met 3 miles west of Bir Shola. The night of the 24th also was wet and cold, but the conditions were vastly different. Fresh water, coats, blankets and food were now available, and 16 bell tents, with stretchers and medical comforts, had been sent out from Matruh to meet the column, so that the more seriously wounded were well cared for. Next morning the weather cleared and the column marched back to Matruh in good spirits.

Preparations for the Reoccupation of Sollum.

Sir J. Maxwell and Br.-General N. Malcolm, his Chief of the General Staff, visited Matruh on the 1st February to study the question of the reoccupation of Sollum. Two thousand camels had now been allotted to the Western Frontier Force, which thus for the first time became completely mobile, able to advance a considerable distance from Matruh and remain in the desert for a long period. The force itself was changing in composition. It had been joined by the headquarters and the remaining troops of the 2nd Mounted Brigade.[1] The R.N. Armoured Car Division, the heavy cars of which had been found unsuitable for desert warfare in the wet season, had left it on the 27th January, being replaced by the Cavalry Corps Motor Machine-Gun Battery, with 17 light armoured cars and 21 motor bicycles. Next day the 15th Sikhs, under

---
[1] The Composite Yeomanry Brigade was broken up shortly afterwards, its troops coming under the command of the 2nd Mounted Brigade.

orders for India, began leaving Matruh by detachments. In the early days of the force this battalion had been its only trained unit and had borne the brunt of every action hitherto fought. The 1st South African Infantry arrived to relieve it, shortly afterwards followed by the 3rd Battalion. Br.-General H. T. Lukin, commanding the South African Brigade, arrived with his staff at Matruh on the 4th February. A detachment of Egyptian engineers was also added to the force.

According to General Maxwell's information, the enemy's main body was in the neighbourhood of Barrani, while there was a smaller force at Bir Waer, outside Sollum. There was a choice of two courses: to advance on Barrani along the coast and simultaneously land a force at Sollum; or to carry out the whole operation by land, using Barrani after its capture as a base to supply the force so far as possible from the sea. The difficulty inherent in the former course was that Sollum Bay was commanded by encircling heights and that, as there were mines at the harbour's mouth to be removed before a landing could be effected, surprise was out of the question. These conditions favoured resistance to a landing and made it probable that heavy casualties would be incurred if one were attempted. Sir J. Maxwell therefore decided on the second of the alternatives, though this had its own special difficulty, the route from Barrani to Sollum having few wells along its course. The first step in the operation was obviously to defeat the enemy covering Barrani, to occupy that place and establish there a depot for the further advance of 50 miles to Sollum.

Major-General Wallace, long incommoded by an old wound, did not feel himself capable of withstanding the physical strain which this prolonged desert operation would certainly involve. He therefore tendered his resignation to Sir J. Maxwell, who appointed Major-General W. E. Peyton to be his successor in the command of the Western Frontier Force.

General Peyton arrived at Matruh on the 10th February. His first step was the establishment of an intermediate depot between Matruh and Barrani, which are 80 miles apart as the crow flies and 90 miles by march route. He chose for his purpose Unjeila, exactly half-way,

Sketch 5.

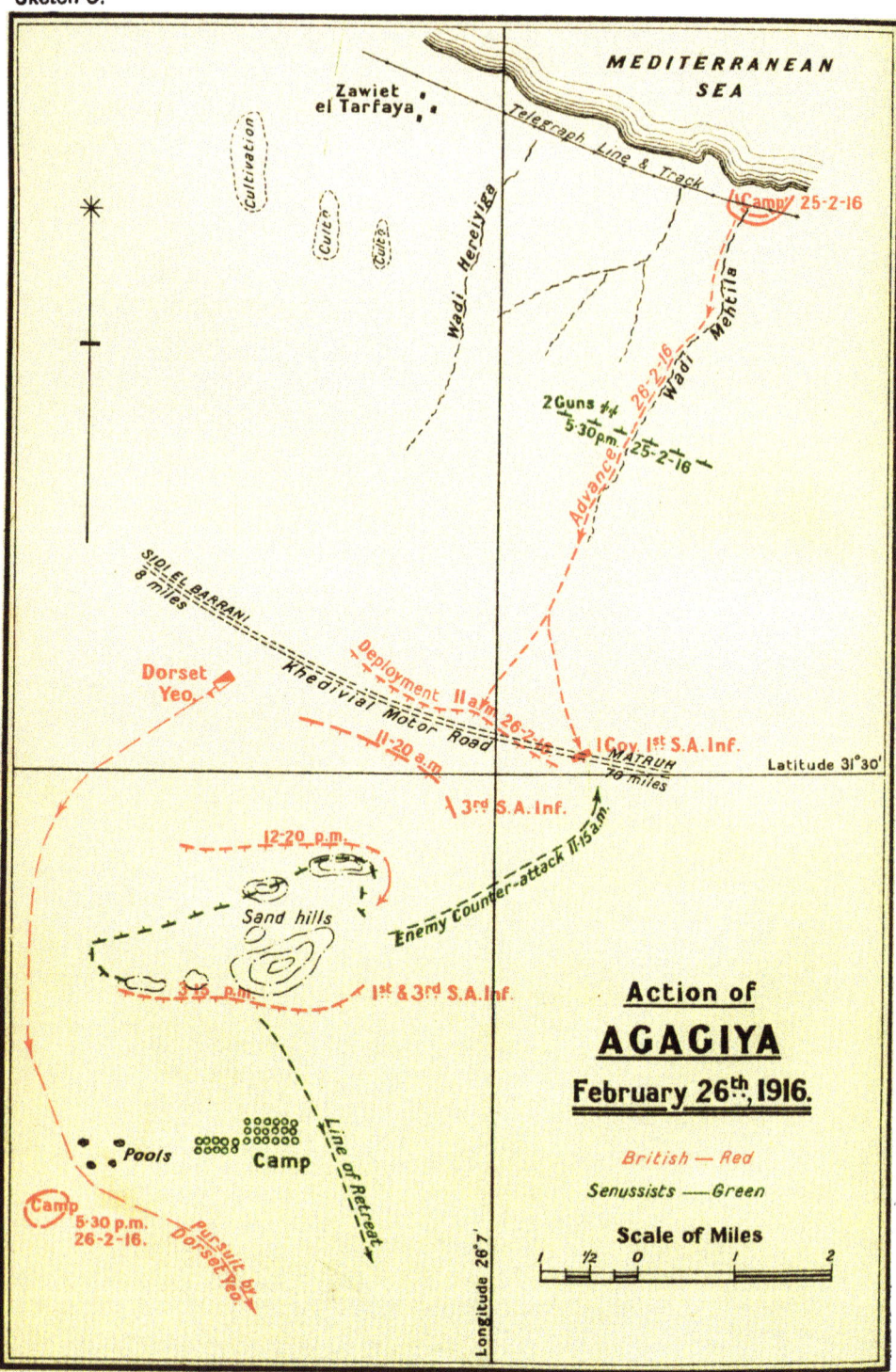

Action of AGAGIYA
February 26th, 1916.

British — Red
Senussists — Green

GENERAL LUKIN AT UNJEILA

where there were adequate wells. On the 13th a column[1] was despatched thither under the command of Lieut.-Colonel H. T. Fulton, 1st New Zealand Rifles, with a convoy of 800 camels carrying 28 days' mobile rations, for 1,400 men, 200 horses and for the camels themselves. The column reached Unjeila without molestation after a three days' march. It was followed by a convoy of wheeled transport with further stores, escorted by the 2nd South African Infantry. The 3rd Battalion having arrived at Matruh by sea from Alexandria, General Peyton was now ready to despatch, under the command of Br.-General Lukin, the main force destined to capture Barrani.

Sir J. Maxwell felt some anxiety lest the Senussi should take alarm on receiving news of these preparations and draw off his forces inland. Great Britain had borne in mind the adage to beware of entrance to a quarrel, but, being in, desired that the opponent should be taught to beware of her. Rumours were therefore spread in suitable quarters that the Western Frontier Force was about to withdraw from Matruh. The story was current in Cairo almost at once and doubtless reached the Senussi before long.

The Action of Agagiya and the Reoccupation of Sidi el Barrani.

On the 20th February Br.-General Lukin marched out to join the force at Unjeila with the 1st and 3rd South African Infantry, 6th Royal Scots, Dorset and one squadron Bucks Yeomanry, Notts Battery (less one section), and a field ambulance. On the 22nd he reached Unjeila and took command of the troops there. His orders from General Peyton were to advance on Barrani as soon as possible. Even at this stage he had a long line of communication, open to attack by the Bedouin throughout. On the very day of his arrival the 2nd South African Infantry had to be sent back to Matruh to escort transport returning empty for further supplies.

Aerial reconnaissance during the march had shown that the enemy was encamped at Agagiya, 15 miles

---

[1] 1st N.Z. Rifle Brigade, one section Notts Battery, one troop Dorset Yeomanry, one signal section, detachment Egyptian Engineers, detachment field ambulance.

south-east of Barrani. Bedouin reported that both Nuri and Ja'far were in camp. Sayed Ahmed himself had left for the Siwa Oasis, whence he was engaged in directing against Egypt another operation of which mention will be made in the next chapter.

Sketch 5. Leaving the New Zealanders and Royal Scots to hold his supply depot at Unjeila, General Lukin marched on the 23rd to Shammas (12 miles) and next day to the Wadi Mehtila (16 miles), at both of which places there was sufficient water. An entrenched camp was formed on the shore at the mouth of the Wadi Mehtila. The force was now 8 miles north-east of the enemy's camp among the sand-hills at Agagiya. General Lukin decided to rest his troops on the 25th, then move out under cover of darkness and attack the enemy at dawn. Ja'far Pasha, however, did not wait to be attacked. At 5.30 p.m. two guns and a machine gun opened fire on the British camp. They were silenced by the British artillery and driven off, but it seemed probable that another attack would follow, and disturbance had been created sufficient to cause General Lukin to abandon his project of a night march.

1916.
26 Feb. The enemy showed no further activity that night and, when the Yeomanry moved out at 5 a.m. next morning to reconnoitre, it was found that he had made no general advance and had, in fact, no outlying detachments, being concentrated in his former position among the sand-hills. It was estimated that his strength was 1,500,[1] with three guns and five machine guns. His dispositions were excellent, especially for defence against an enemy not very strong in artillery. He held a series of large yellow sand-dunes upon a slight plateau, a mile in length and two miles in depth. This area had been entrenched and at certain points wired. As at Halazin, there was no cover for a force advancing from the northward to the attack.

At 9.30 a.m. General Lukin, having received the Yeomanry's report, moved out from camp to attack the position, and ordered Lieut.-Colonel H. M. W. Souter, commanding the Dorset Yeomanry, to be prepared to cut off the enemy's retreat. The Yeomanry, less one squadron on the British left, thereupon moved round the western flank of the position and occupied some sand-hills, from

---

[1] Ja'far Pasha states that the force numbered 1,600.

which a good view was to be had. A dismounted advance was then carried out with the object of pinning the enemy to his ground. Two armoured cars operating with the Yeomanry on this flank were of great assistance in keeping down the enemy's machine-gun fire, though they found difficulty in moving on the soft sand.

1916.
26 Feb.

Meanwhile the infantry column advanced, the 3rd South African Battalion leading. At 11 a.m., when the head of the column was $5\frac{1}{2}$ miles S.S.W of the British camp, the order was given to deploy for the attack, to be carried out by the 3rd Battalion supported by the 1st. At 11.20 a.m. the advanced screen came under fire. The battalion now advanced in line, the men at two paces' interval, with machine guns on the flanks, and the Notts Battery opened fire to support the attack. From the enemy's side also broke out heavy machine-gun and rifle fire, and the three guns came into action. The advance of the South Africans against an enemy they could not see, over ground without cover and swept by his fire, was admirably steady. At long range loss was slight, but as the sand-hills were approached casualties began to mount up.

Ja'far Pasha now adopted his favourite tactics and attempted a swift outflanking movement against the British left. On this occasion they were less successful than at Halazin. A company of the 1st South African Battalion was moved up in echelon to cover the threatened flank, and drove off the counter-attack. General Lukin at once threw in his reserves and ordered the assault.

Advancing with a rush, the infantry quickly captured the front line on the edge of the sand-hills. But there was depth in the position, and small bodies of the enemy made a running fight through the dunes. Progress in such conditions was slow, and it was not until 3.15 p.m., just three hours later, that the 1st and 3rd South African Battalions reached the southern edge of the hills, where they halted and concentrated. By this time the enemy had disappeared.

Lieut.-Colonel Souter had been told by General Lukin that the assault had been launched. He decided to let the enemy get well clear of the sand-hills, with their wire and entrenchments, and moved forward parallel to, and about a thousand yards west of, the line of retreat. At 2 p.m. the whole retiring force was seen, extended over a mile, camels and baggage in front escorted by Bedouin,

Muhafizia with machine guns forming flank and rear guards. Colonel Souter now had with him his own three squadrons of Dorset Yeomanry, but the Bucks squadron had moved off in pursuit of a small camel convoy which had broken away from the enemy's column, and it could not be recalled in time to take part in the notable charge that followed. Colonel Souter dismounted his men to breathe the horses, while the officers examined the ground, which ascended slightly in the direction of the enemy but offered no obstacle to cavalry action.

The reconnaissance over, the attack was made in two lines, the horses galloping steadily. Several machine guns opened fire, well handled at first, but as the Yeomanry approached the shooting became wilder and finally ceased. Fifty yards from the rear guard[1] Colonel Souter gave the order to charge, and, cheering loudly, the Dorsets dashed at the enemy. Steady hitherto, the rear guard broke its ranks to escape the sword, while the Bedouin with howls of dismay scattered and fled into the desert. Colonel Souter's horse was shot under him, and its dying strides threw him almost at the feet of Ja'far Pasha. There was a moment's uncertainty, for the Dorsets had suffered heavily, but the arrival of the machine-gun section decided the issue. Ja'far, who was wounded, and two other Turkish officers who did not join in the flight, were captured. Nuri was for some time believed to have been killed, but escaped from the field.

The enemy was pursued far into the desert, considerable numbers being killed with the sword. Thirty-nine prisoners were captured and 60 camels loaded with dates and 40,000 rounds of ammunition. A large number of tents were burnt after the action. The enemy's losses were estimated to be five hundred, while those of the British were 184.[2]

It is not too much to say that the charge of the Dorset Yeomanry was the outstanding event of the campaign. But for it the enemy would once again have slipped away,

---

[1] The rear guard is stated by Ja'far Pasha to have been 150 strong, with three machine guns.

[2]

	Killed.	Wounded.
Officers	6	7
Other Ranks	41	130

The Dorset Yeomanry had 5 officers and 27 other ranks killed, 2 officers and 24 other ranks wounded.

and the action would have resembled the Affairs of the Wadi Majid and Halazin—indecisive successes. After Agagiya the forces of the Senussi never again stood to await a British attack. The capture of Ja'far Pasha was in itself a most fortunate result of the charge. Deprived of the qualities of character and leadership which he had shown, the Senussi and his forces were henceforth far less formidable. The campaign on the Western Frontier was to drag on for many months, but the enemy had lost his sting and there was to be no more serious fighting. The task before General Peyton was still difficult enough, but it was the desert and its conditions rather than human opposition with which he now had to battle.

After resting his troops and burying the dead, General Lukin marched into Barrani without opposition on the 28th February.

1916. Feb.

The Reoccupation of Sollum.

On the 2nd March an aeroplane was sent to General Lukin to reconnoitre the country between Barrani and Sollum. The Western Frontier Force now had possession of a harbour 90 miles nearer to Sollum than was Mersa Matruh. Barrani was, however, an indifferent landing-place, its utility being dependent on good weather, while to feed a force there by land, as had to be done until the Navy was ready, was a matter of difficulty.[1] To husband supplies, General Peyton had ordered General Lukin to send back from the battlefield of Agagiya all his mounted troops but one squadron and two guns. As soon as he was established at Barrani he sent back every other horse he could spare and all artillery personnel but the gun detachments. From Matruh to Unjeila was for a camel convoy a two days' march, from Unjeila to Barrani two more. Escorts of from fifty to one hundred men had to accompany each of these convoys.[2] The victualling of Barrani from the sea was for the Navy an anxious affair owing to the presence of German submarines along the coast. It was skilfully

March. Map 5. Sketch A.

---

[1] The advance had been begun some days earlier than Sir J. Maxwell had originally intended and the Naval authorities had been led to expect.

[2] Convoys moved at one or two days' interval in both directions. The first came straight through from Matruh. Thereafter there were organized two chains—from Matruh to Unjeila and Unjeila to Barrani.

carried out by Commander B. M. Eyres Monsell and completed by the 4th March, just as the weather was breaking.

There was now no shortage of supplies at Barrani, and General Peyton was able to bring up the bulk of his force, establishing his headquarters there on the 7th. The Composite Yeomanry Brigade had been broken up, the 1st New Zealand Rifles and the 1st Australian Divisional Train had left the Western Frontier Force for Egypt, but it had been strengthened by the formation of a headquarters signal section, and by the arrival of the Hong Kong & Singapore Mountain Battery, a detachment of the Kent Field Company Royal Engineers, and a company of Australian Camel Corps. These troops, together with the 2nd Mounted Brigade, the 4th South African Infantry, and other units which had been on the Line of Communication, moved to Barrani. But before the concentration was complete the advance on Sollum began. The force did not come into action till after this move was finished, but the march illustrates so well the difficulties of desert warfare that it deserves to be recorded in some detail.

The direct route to Sollum was the Khedivial Motor Road, following the coast. But the escarpment, which at Barrani is 25 miles from the sea, runs thence north-west to the Gulf of Sollum to end in cliffs above the shore. To climb it there, with the forces of the Senussi installed atop of the plateau, as they were now reported to be, would have probably entailed heavy losses. General Peyton decided to follow a route further inland and ascend the plateau by the Median Pass, 20 miles south-east of Sollum, thus establishing himself on the high ground and denying to the enemy the advantages which he would have gained from a dominating position at Sollum. The only doubt regarding the inland route was whether the water supply would suffice. General Peyton learnt that there was a good supply in the wells of Augerin, near the foot of the pass, and large cisterns at Median and Siwiat, on the plateau. He therefore determined to use this route, moving his force in two echelons so as not to draw the wells dry. Br.-General Lukin with the South African Brigade and the rest of the slow-moving troops was to advance on the 9th March, *via* Baqbaq, to Augerin, timing his march so that he should arrive at daybreak on the 12th and then seizing the Median and Eragib Passes. The mounted

DIFFICULTIES OF THE MARCH

column, consisting of the 2nd Mounted Brigade, artillery, and camel corps, under the command of Br.-General Lord Hampden, was to leave Barrani on the 11th and rejoin General Lukin on the 13th. The force would then be concentrated at Augerin, with outposts on the plateau and the passes in its possession.

1916. March.

The first part of the programme was carried out. General Lukin reached Baqbaq at 1 p.m. on the 11th March, on which day Lord Hampden moved to Alem Abu Sheiba, half way between Barrani and Baqbaq. On the 12th General Lukin marched to Augerin, armoured cars pushing ahead and seizing the Median and Eragib Passes. It was then discovered that the reports regarding water had been over optimistic; the wells would not suffice for the mounted troops, and the route along the plateau had a supply inadequate for the movement even of General Lukin's whole force. General Peyton, however, refused to abandon the strategic advantage to be gained by establishing himself on the top of the escarpment, but he had to alter his plans, and it is significant of his difficulties of communication that several of his messages of the next few days are marked " by flag."

General Lukin was ordered to move up on to the plateau with two battalions—he took the 1st and 4th S.A. Infantry—the Hong Kong Mountain Battery and a small detachment of the Field Ambulance. The 2nd and 3rd Battalions and details were sent back under the command of Lieut.-Colonel W. E. C. Tanner to Baqbaq, where General Peyton formed a third column of slow-moving troops under his personal command, which was to follow the coast-line. Lord Hampden's mounted column was also directed to move along the coast instead of by the inland route, as previously ordered.

On the 13th March General Lukin moved up on to the plateau, using both the Median and Eragib Passes, and halted at Bir el Siwiat. On the same day General Peyton advanced to Bir Tegdida, 19 miles from Sollum. Lord Hampden was to have joined General Peyton, but, receiving an incorrect report that there was lack of water at Tegdida, he remained all day at Baqbaq, which he had reached on the 12th. On the 14th the three columns concentrated near the Halfaiya Pass, 3 miles S.S.E. of Sollum, the cavalry having to make a long march to come up with the other troops. General Lukin brought his water supply on camels, there being no water on the plateau north-west of Siwiat. General Peyton then sent up another battalion, the 2nd S.A. Infantry, through the Halfaiya Pass, continuing his own course along the coast.

There was no general engagement at the end of this long and difficult approach. Sollum was hastily evacuated by the enemy and occupied in the afternoon by the cavalry and the 2nd and 3rd S.A. Infantry. The rest of the force followed next morning, when the first of the supply ships entered the bay. It had been a remarkable march, for the number of troops involved was far greater than usually employed in desert operations of this nature, in which water was scarce, fodder very scanty, and railhead distant 240 miles from the final goal.[1]

While the cavalry was moving into Sollum the armoured cars, under the command of Major the Duke of Westminster, were ordered to move on Bir Waer, which it was reported by aeroplane was being evacuated, and if the enemy was gone, to pursue him "with reasonable boldness." Bir Waer was found deserted, and the cars took up the pursuit to the westward. Doubtless the enemy commander believed, from previous experience, that if his highly mobile force put itself a day's march from the British it was safe. But the Derna road, and indeed the surface of the whole desert, were surprisingly hard, so that a speed of 40 miles an hour was actually reached at times. Hundreds of armed Bedouin fleeing westward were passed, but no attention was paid to them. Then, 25 miles west of Sollum, the main force of the enemy was seen a mile south of the track, and was at once attacked.

Now the moral results of Agagiya were plainly shown. The enemy at once fled into the desert, with the exception of a few Turks, who stood pluckily to their guns and machine guns, but were shot down by the advancing cars. Three guns (all the enemy had on this front), nine machine guns and a quarter of a million rounds of small arm ammunition were taken. Thirty prisoners were captured, including two officers. The pursuit was kept up for 10 miles, many more of the enemy being shot down. The British suffered no casualties.

---

[1] Alexandria to Dabaa by rail 100 miles; Dabaa to Matruh 90 miles by march route, 75 in a straight line; Matruh to Sollum 150 miles by march route, 125 in a straight line.

EXPLOIT OF THE ARMOURED CARS

There remained the question of the prisoners from the *Tara* and a few survivors of the transport *Moorina*, handed over to the Senussi in November 1915. A letter from Captain R. S. Gwatkin-Williams, commander of the *Tara*, addressed to the British troops in Sollum, which he did not know had been evacuated, was found by great good fortune in an Arab house, and indicated the place of their confinement. Captain Royle, after having questioned the Arab prisoners, fixed it with greater certainty at El Hakkim, a post consisting merely of two old Roman wells, a sheikh's tomb and a block-house, nearly 120 miles west of Sollum.

1916.
17 March.

Then was carried out the exploit which won such wide attention, even at the height of the Battle of Verdun. The Duke of Westminster, with about equal numbers of light armoured cars and ambulances, 45 in all, set out from Sollum at 1 a.m. on the 17th. A high average speed was kept up, considering that the route was of soft sand or strewn with boulders and that it was absolutely unknown, but the cars did not reach their destination till nearly 3 p.m. The prisoners were found. The ambulances drew up beside their tents. "In a moment," writes Captain Gwatkin-Williams, "we were tearing bully-beef, bread and "tinned chicken, and drinking condensed milk out of tins. "We tore our food like famished wolves, with tears in our "eyes and wonder in our hearts."

The prisoners, 91 officers and other ratings,[1] after they had eaten their fill, were packed into the cars and ambulances. The convoy then returned, but could not make Sollum that night and halted at Bir Waer, where the Australian Camel Corps was on outpost duty. Next day the prisoners were brought to Sollum and put aboard a hospital ship for Alexandria.

They had suffered occasional brutalities, but had been in general kindlily treated, according to the lights of their captors. The fact was that the Senussi's own forces were by this time near starvation in many districts, while an Arab can live on half the food required by a European. And so these unfortunates were in process of starving to death. Few, probably, would have survived another four

---

[1] They included one British officer of Indian cavalry and one civilian, a Portuguese cook.

months. Four had died at El Hakkim, mainly from starvation. Disease, dysentery and lice, cold by night, heat by day, had made horrible their existence.

With the reoccupation of Sollum the campaign on the coast may be said to have been ended. The Aulad Ali, who had joined the Senussi in hopes of being led to raid the Delta, came in and surrendered in large numbers to General Peyton. They also were feeling the pinch of hunger. The effect in Egypt was excellent, and the unrest in the Alexandria district was greatly diminished. British prestige had recovered whatever had been lost by the original evacuation of Sollum, and that step had been amply justified.

Early in April the South African Brigade returned to Alexandria by sea, the transport marching to railhead on the Khedivial Railway. Two battalions of the Composite Brigade, one company Camel Corps, and two guns of the Hong Kong Battery, with light armoured cars and aeroplanes, remained at Sollum. By July the Western Frontier Force had been reduced to the 6th and 22nd Mounted Brigades,[1] the 2nd, 3rd, and 4th Dismounted (Yeomanry) Brigades, with aeroplanes and auxiliary troops.

---

[1] 6th and 22nd were the new numbers given to the 1/2nd South Midland and 1/1st North Midland Brigades respectively.

CHAPTER IX.

THE WESTERN OASES AND THE SUDAN.

(Map 1; Sketches A, 6, 7.)

THE WESTERN OASES.

THE coast route was not the only one by which the **Map 1.** Senussi could advance against Egypt. Over three hundred **Sketch A.** miles west of the Nile at the latitude of Beni Suef is the great Oasis of Siwa, once the Oasis of Jupiter-Ammon, where a European god was identified with an Egyptian and Alexander the Great deified as his son. From Siwa are two routes to the Nile Valley, through chains of oases.[1] The northern leads east, with several small oases and wells upon its course, to the great Oasis of Bahariya, of which the eastern edge is less than one hundred miles from the Nile at Minya. The southern runs south-east, through Farafra and Dakhla, to another large oasis, that of Kharga, which is one hundred miles from the Nile at Suhag and rather more from Isna. Siwa had long been one of the chief centres of the Senussi's influence.

Those behind the Senussi contemplated a double attack upon Egypt: along the coast and from Siwa through the oases. These operations were, moreover, to coincide with an attack upon the Sudan by the Sultan of Darfur. The Senussi's influence extended through the heart of the desert down into Darfur, and there is evidence that, despite the vast distance which separated the two potentates, there was co-ordination in their measures of hostility. The strategic conception behind their actions was remarkable, but it was not that of Sayed Ahmed or Ali Dinar. Subsequent information suggests that the former's inner motive was the creation of a Libyan state, not necessarily including any Egyptian territory. He seems to have supposed that by making himself troublesome on the Western Frontier he might incline Britain to favour this project on terms satisfactory

---

[1] There is a third track, through Gara and Moghara to Alexandria, but it has no importance in the present record.

to herself. Britain's unwavering support of Italy was to checkmate this ambition. But the objects of those who inspired him and Ali Dinar were in general to create unrest in north-eastern Africa, and in particular to secure the retention of the greatest possible number of British troops in Egypt. It is also probable that the invasion had been originally planned to synchronize with an attack on Egypt from Palestine, which the campaign in Gallipoli forced the Turks to postpone.

1916. Feb. Just as Major-General Peyton was about to begin his advance from Matruh upon Sollum, Sir J. Maxwell learnt that a battalion of the Senussi's troops, 500 strong, had occupied the Bahariya Oasis on the 11th February. The camp was bombed by British aeroplanes, whereupon the troops scattered among the inhabitants of the oasis, who numbered 6,000, and thus avoided further attack from the air. About the same time the Farafra Oasis was also occupied, but was soon afterwards vacated, the enemy moving forward to Dakhla, which was seen from the air to be occupied on the 27th.

To guard the Nile Valley in anticipation of such a move, Sir J. Maxwell had, as already stated, despatched the 159th Brigade to the Wadi Natrun, north-west of Cairo, and the 1/1st N. Midland Mounted Brigade to the fertile and thickly inhabited area known as the Faiyum, of which the centre is 60 miles south-west of Cairo, with smaller detachments along the Nile Valley. He now strengthened these detachments and constituted a command known as the Southern Force, under Major-General J. Adye, with headquarters at Beni Suef, to cover the approaches to the Nile Valley from the west. As General Peyton's successes rendered attack along the coast impossible, General Adye was enabled to shift his strength to the south, till by the end of March his most southerly post was at Isna.

As soon as Dakhla was occupied by the enemy, Sir J. Maxwell withdrew the Egyptian officials from Kharga, which was connected by a light railway with the main railway following the Nile. He decided not to send a force to protect that oasis, still less to attempt to turn the enemy out of the others. The Arabs were, in fact, in a strong position. They might not be formidable in fighting qualities, were probably far less so than the battalions under Ja'far on the coast, but they were desert bred, and with a small amount of camel transport could cover very great distances. As a consequence, they were within striking distance of the Nile Valley at several points on a wide front, but were for the time being out of reach of the British forces, which were not mobile or inured to the conditions of desert warfare. There was additional danger in that Upper Egypt, threatened from Kharga, contained a large and highly excitable population, with a considerable proportion of Copts, against whom the flame of religious fanaticism was easily fanned. Sir J. Maxwell restricted Major-General Adye to defensive measures and at the same time kept the oases under constant observation from the air. When, on the 19th March, he handed over his command to Sir A. Murray, the Senussi was still threatening the Nile Valley, but, on the other hand, the situation on the coast had been completely cleared up and the Senussi's forces in the oases had evidently become discouraged and showed a less aggressive spirit.

Soon afterwards, of their own accord, they evacuated Kharga. On the 15th April Kharga was reoccupied by the British, the troops being moved out by the light railway and a force of 1,600 of all arms concentrated in the oasis.[1] On the 27th a post was established in the small oasis of Moghara, 95 miles west of Cairo, which had hitherto only been occasionally visited by patrols. Sir A. Murray decided to extend the Kharga light railway to the western edge of the oasis, to construct another from Beni Mazar on the Nile to Bahariya, and to establish a line of blockhouses along the Darb el Rubi,[2] from Samalut on the Nile to Bahariya, the route which the railway was to follow.

Now began the organization of the remarkable force which was to bring the Western Desert under control to an extent that a little earlier would have appeared impossible.

Much, in the first place, was accomplished by the Imperial Camel Corps, the formation of which had been authorized in November 1915. A detachment was, it will

---

[1] The "Kharga Detachment," commanded by Lieut.-Colonel A. J. McNeill, Lovat Scouts, consisted of three weak battalions of dismounted Yeomanry (1/1st Fife and Forfar, 1/1st and 1/2nd Lovat Scouts), a half flight R.F.C., the Hong Kong Mountain Battery, and small detachments of Egyptian Cavalry, Imperial Camel Corps, Royal Engineers and auxiliary services. The Camel Corps marched, timing its arrival to synchronize with that of the first train.

[2] Darb, a way. The name does not appear on Map 1, but the track is shown, from Samalut, through Hajar es Salam and Galeb el Moashat to Bahariya.

be remembered, under General Peyton's command at the time of the reoccupation of Sollum. It was built up company by company (remaining for a considerable period purely on a company organization, while certain companies acted independently throughout the war) from the 1st and 2nd Australian Divisions, the Australian Light Horse, the New Zealand troops, and the British Yeomanry and Territorial Infantry, but was predominantly Australian. The Australians, particularly the light horsemen from the country districts, took to the work at once. The county yeomen, with their high standard of physique, soon made excellent camelry; the town-bred men took longer to accustom themselves to desert conditions; but the whole corps, which by the end of 1916 had grown to a brigade, had become at home in the desert before the major portion was moved to the eastern front.

The Imperial Camel Corps was the backbone of the defence of Egypt from the west. But the use of camelry in war is ancient, and it was the internal combustion engine which now completely altered the situation. The capacity of the light car patrols of Ford cars, and to a rather less extent the light armoured motor batteries,[1] for long distance raids and patrols not only brought the Bedouin under control but resulted in the acquisition of most valuable information regarding the desert and its conditions. Where tens of miles had been patrolled by camelry, hundreds of miles were now patrolled by the light cars. The distances between the bases on the Nile were very great, so that lateral co-operation was almost impossible and each patrol had to rely upon its own base for support. Nevertheless, within a very short period the patrolling was so thorough that not only were the enemy detachments deprived of all communication with the Nile Valley, but each occupied oasis was practically isolated from the rest. The work was exceedingly arduous; heat, flies, fever and the monotony of the sand were its accompaniments; while, if danger from the enemy was less than on many other fronts, death from thirst, following a breakdown in the desert, was a possibility which always had to be faced.

---

[1] By April 1917 there were six light car patrols and three light armoured motor batteries in what had originally been the Western Frontier and Southern Forces, then combined as the Delta and Western Force.

By the end of May four blockhouses had been established along the Darb el Rubi, and all through the summer the railway towards Bahariya was pushed on, the work proving difficult and slow. At this time the main enemy concentration was in Dakhla, the richest of the oases, and it was estimated that the force there numbered 1,800. By October, Sir A. Murray was ready to reoccupy Bahariya, and instructed Major-General W. A. Watson, who took over command of the Western Force on the 4th, to advance against it. News of the impending move reached Sayed Ahmed, who had recently moved up to Bahariya from Dakhla, and he himself with the bulk of his force quitted the oasis for Siwa between the 8th and 10th. Sickness and shortage of food in the oasis probably contributed to his decision to retreat. An attempt to cut off the rear guard west of Bahariya by a concentration of light cars was unsuccessful owing to the great distance to be covered and the nature of the country.

It was now known that the force in Dakhla was much diminished and probable that it also would be shortly withdrawn. General Watson decided on a bold stroke: to attack at once with a small column of cars, supported by a company of Camel Corps from Kharga, which, however, could not hope to arrive on the scene of action till 48 hours after the cars. The cars[1] reached Dakhla on the 17th, but it was found, perhaps fortunately, that the greater part of the enemy force had already left. A party of 120 was captured at Budkhulu, in the centre of the oasis. On the 19th the Camel Corps, after a remarkable forced march from Kharga, reached Bir Sheikh Mohammed, almost on the western edge of Dakhla, and took 40 more prisoners. During the next few days drives took place in all directions, resulting in the capture of 50 more of the enemy and many political prisoners, and by the end of the month the great oasis, which contained 20,000 inhabitants, was clear of the enemy and of enemy influence. Permanent garrisons were established both here and in Bahariya and the civil government restored, to the content of the inhabitants. In November a patrol was sent out from Bahariya to the distant Farafra oasis, where further prisoners were captured.

---

[1] One Rolls Royce armoured car and one tender; six Ford cars and twelve motor bicycles. The personnel consisted of 2 officers and 58 other ranks, with two Vickers and two Lewis guns.

The Raid on Siwa.

We have now reached a point far ahead of that to which the record has been brought on the Sinai front, but it is convenient to conclude the account of operations in the Western Desert and deal with those in the Sudan and Darfur before returning to events in Egypt's main theatre of war.

In the coast area the successful campaign of Major-General Peyton had left no organized enemy force in Egyptian territory, but Nuri was still established within the Italian frontier with the remains of that which had then been so heavily defeated. In preventing any resurgence of the Senussi's power the light armoured cars and Fords were here also of great value. On the 7th April 1916, four light armoured cars with the machine-gun section of the 2/7th Middlesex carried out a raid from Sollum on an ammunition depot at Moraisa, 18 miles north-west, in which twenty-one boxes of 8·9-cm. Mantelli gun ammunition and 120,000 rounds of small arm ammunition were destroyed. In the course of the month another 167,000 rounds were discovered in various depots. The Italians were now able to co-operate, having established a post of two battalions at Bardia.[1] On the 25th and 26th July an important raid was carried out from Sollum by a detachment of light armoured cars under the command of Captain C. G. Mangles, 20th Hussars, assisted by Italian cars from Bardia, supported by half a company *u*.perial Camel Corps and the Italian armed yacht *Misurat* The objective was a party of *Muhafizia* established in Italian territory in the Wadi Sanal, 40 miles west of Ras el Mehl, who had been robbing friendly Bedouin under pretence of collecting taxes for the Senussi. The raid was successful in breaking up the concentration but still more important in the proof which it gave to the tribes that Great Britain and Italy were henceforth in a position to work together for the pacification of the area. Patrolling was active throughout the year, the most notable exploit being the capture of a camel convoy 20 miles north-west of Jaghbub, the Senussi's chief centre of influence, which is 135 miles from Sollum. Further raids with Italian co-operation were carried out during the winter.

It is necessary to hark back for a moment to political affairs. It has been mentioned that Sayed Idris, cousin to

---

[1] Mersa Burdi Suleiman on Map 5.

Sketch 6.

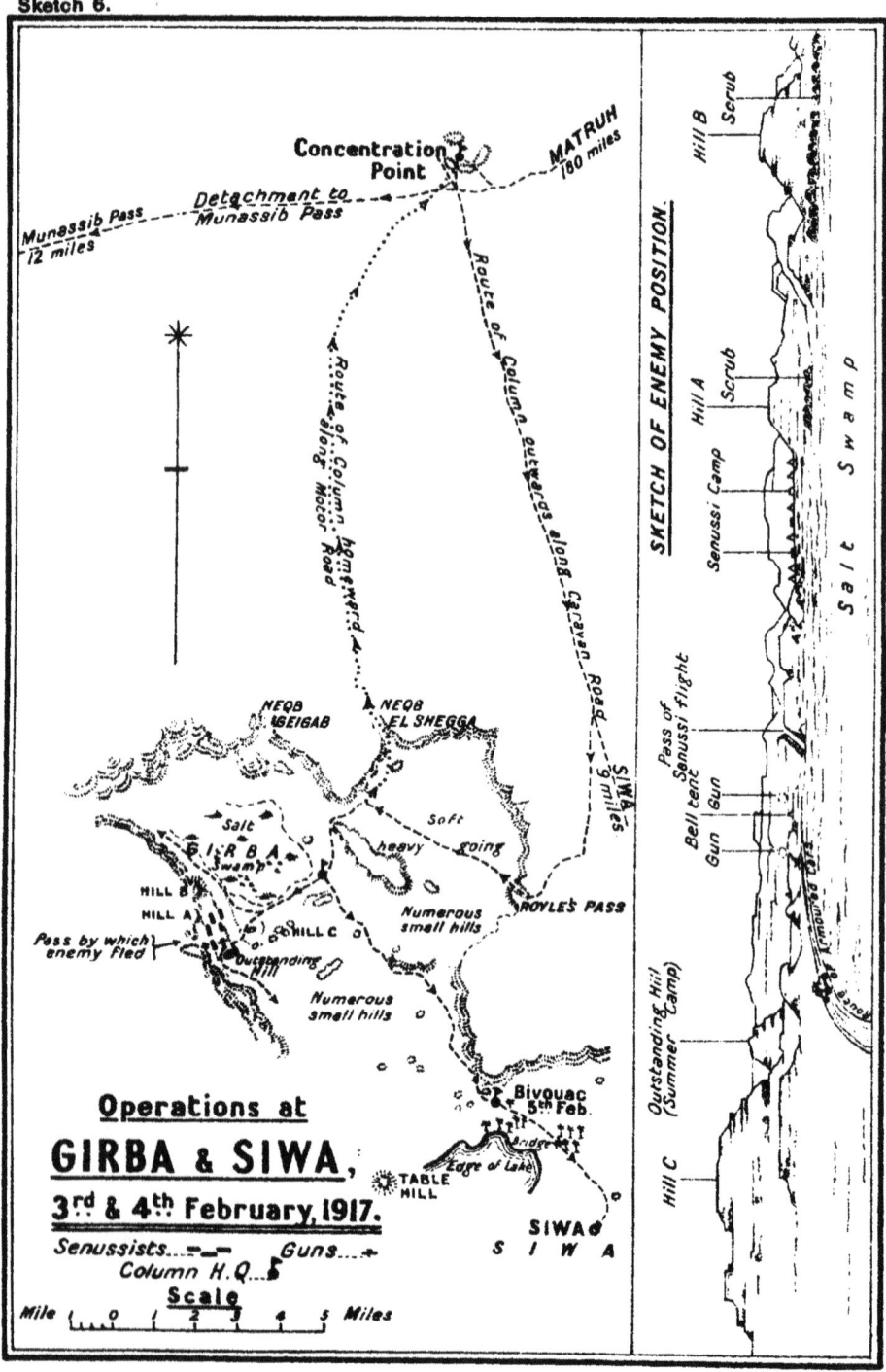

NEGOTIATIONS WITH SAYED IDRIS

the Grand Sheikh, had by blood a better claim to the headship of the Confraternity than Sayed Ahmed, but had been passed over on account of his youth on the death of his father, Mohammed el Mahdi, in 1902. The strength of the position of Idris was recognized by his cousin, who in 1915 appointed him Emir of Cyrenaica and Tripoli and named him his successor. It has also been recorded that Sayed Idris disapproved of the Grand Sheikh's policy of aggression against Egypt. He was quite prepared to go on fighting Italy, but foresaw disaster to the Confraternity and his family in a conflict with Great Britain. When he found it impossible to dissuade his cousin from the adventure he wrote to Sir J. Maxwell dissociating himself from it, and then retired with his followers into Western Cyrenaica to await what appeared to him the inevitable result of Sayed Ahmed's folly.

Sayed Idris's position of authority made him second only in importance to Sayed Ahmed. After the latter had suffered complete defeat at the hands of the British and Sollum had been reoccupied, Idris came forward as the one Senussi leader with whom the British and Italian Governments could negotiate a peaceful settlement. In July 1916 a joint British and Italian mission met him, at his own request, at Zuetina, south of Benghazi, in Cyrenaica. The representative of the Anglo-Egyptian Government was Colonel the Hon. M. G. Talbot, who was accompanied by two Egyptian notables distantly related to Idris. In the same month Great Britain and Italy came to an agreement that neither would conclude peace without the other, and that both would recognize Idris as the religious head of the Confraternity, but would grant him no territorial concessions, independence, or autonomy.[1] One of the chief British conditions of peace to Sayed Idris was the surrender of all British prisoners in the hands of the Senussi. These prisoners were released, and Sayed Idris made no difficulty about accepting all the British terms. Negotiations temporarily broke down in September on the question of the conditions of release for Italian prisoners, but affairs had already made considerable progress, and it was arranged to hold another Anglo-Italian conference with Idris as soon as possible.

---

[1] In March 1917 a Tripartite Agreement was concluded between Great Britain, France and Italy, which pledged these Powers to make no agreement with the Senussi except after understanding with each other, and provided for military and naval co-operation if necessary.

The British Government, then, having tacitly recognized Sayed Idris as religious head of the Confraternity, and intending to give him formal recognition in the agreement which it was hoped to conclude, decided that Jaghbub, the Holy Place of the Confraternity, though it was within Egyptian territory, should be excluded from further military operations against Sayed Ahmed and his followers. These operations were now to be directed against Siwa and Girba, Egyptian oases still held by Sayed Ahmed and the remnant of his forces.

By January 1917, all Sayed Ahmed's plans had collapsed, and he felt himself no longer safe even in Siwa. Sir A. Murray learnt that it was his intention to retire, with his chief commander, Mohammed Saleh, and his permanent force of 1,200 retainers, to Jaghbub. On the 21st January the Commander-in-Chief gave orders for operations to be carried out by a mixed force of armoured cars and camel corps, to capture Sayed Ahmed if possible and to inflict loss upon his followers. Preparations for the advance of a force of this nature across the 200 miles of waterless desert between Matruh and Siwa were expected to take a month, but almost immediately there came news that the departure of Sayed Ahmed was imminent. Sir A. Murray then took the bold step of ordering Brigadier-General H. W. Hodgson to carry out an attack at once, with cars alone.

Map 1.
Sketch 6.
The Oases of Girba and Siwa are close together—are, in fact, practically one—Girba lying north-west of Siwa. It was known that the enemy's main force was established in the former. General Hodgson's plan was to attack the camp at Girba and send a detachment of two armoured motor batteries to block the Munassib Pass, near Gaigab and 24 miles north-west of Girba. The track from Girba to Jaghbub, which the enemy would follow if he retreated to the latter oasis, descends through this pass from the plateau. It was the old manœuvre of the Boer War, which now, owing to the motor car, could be carried out at far greater range than then.

After considerable difficulties had been overcome the force, consisting of three light armoured batteries and three light car patrols, was concentrated 185 miles south-west of Matruh and 13 miles north of the Shegga Pass, leading to

Girba and Siwa, on the 2nd February.[1] At 9 a.m. on the 3rd the main force entered the oasis by a pass subsequently known as " Royle's Pass," from the name of the officer who acted as guide, some five miles south-east of the Neqb el Shegga, and moved on to the attack on Girba. The arrival of the advanced guard, consisting of three patrols of two armoured cars each, took the enemy completely by surprise. Fire was exchanged, but unfortunately the cars were unable owing to the nature of the ground to advance closer than 800 yards to the enemy. Later in the day light cars succeeded in approaching to within 400 yards of his position and kept it under machine-gun fire.

1917.
3-4 Feb

From deserters it was learnt that the enemy at Girba was 850 strong and that the Senussi was at Siwa with Mohammed Saleh and about four hundred more troops. It was subsequently discovered that Mohammed Saleh left to take command at Girba on the opening of the action, while Sayed Ahmed and his party at once began a retreat westward.

The night was fairly quiet, but at 5 a.m. the enemy again opened fire with guns and machine guns, bonfires were seen in his camp, and it was evident that he was burning stores. As day broke he was seen retiring through a pass directly behind his position, and shortly afterwards the whole force had disappeared. During the day his camp was destroyed and reconnaissances carried out towards Siwa, which was entered the following morning without opposition. A parade was held in front of the court-house, at which the local sheikhs were assembled. The inhabitants received the British troops with friendliness and were evidently content to be rid of Sayed Ahmed.

The party sent to hold the Munassib Pass had left the point of concentration at the same time as the main body. Its chance of destroying the retreating enemy was ruined by the steepness of the escarpment, which forced the armoured cars to remain 18 miles from Munassib. The light cars and one armoured car only managed to descend the escarpment and take up their position in accordance with instructions. On the 4th this detachment seized a small enemy convoy moving in from the west with mails. Next day it intercepted and routed the leading parties retreating from Girba,

---

[1] The concentration point is shown on Map 1 and Sketch A.

but the enemy then established a post out of reach of the cars and warned the succeeding columns to turn off into the sand-dunes instead of moving through the pass. The cars were then obliged to return to the point of concentration. The total loss inflicted on the enemy was estimated to be 40 killed and 200 wounded, while a quantity of rifles and ammunition was destroyed and 40 camels killed. The British losses were three officers slightly wounded. The whole force returned to Matruh on the 8th February.

As Sayed Ahmed and Mohammed Saleh had both escaped with most of their following, the expedition cannot be said to have been completely successful, but it had proved to the Senussi and all the dwellers in the Western Desert how long was now the British arm, had finally removed all danger in that quarter, and generally enhanced British prestige. That of the Senussi, defeated yet again, driven off the one road and painfully making his way across the heavy sand-dunes of the desert to Jaghbub, was proportionately diminished.

* * * * *

As it turned out, the defeat of Sayed Ahmed at Siwa had a decisive effect upon the Anglo-Italian negotiations with Sayed Idris. These had been resumed at Tabruk, in Eastern Cyrenaica, late in January, Colonel Talbot being again the British representative. They made slow progress, owing to difficulties between the Italians and Idris, until the latter comprehended the full effect upon his prospects and position of the action at Siwa. In that affair, occurring as it did while the conference was sitting, there was convincing proof that Great Britain regarded him as head of the Confraternity and his cousin as a rebellious rival. It made him anxious to seize his opportunity without further delay, and also brought over to him doubters and waverers from the following of Sayed Ahmed, if only because it was now apparent that the policy of refusing to attack Great Britain had been the wiser one. On the 12th April 1917 Sayed Idris accepted the British conditions, which may here be briefly summarized. Idris agreed to hand over to the nearest British or Italian post all persons of British, Egyptian or Allied nationality, and of any nationality if travelling in a British ship, who might be compelled to land on his coast by reason of injury to their ship. He also agreed to hand over to the British Government, or, as an alternative, to

AGREEMENT WITH SAYED IDRIS

1917.
April.

send out of Africa, all Turkish officers, and officers of enemy countries who might fall into his hands. With the exception of 50 police, who might be maintained at Jaghbub, he agreed to allow no armed force to remain there, at Siwa, or elsewhere on Egyptian territory On their part, the British Government agreed to afford facilities for trade through Sollum—a matter of great importance to Idris—so long as the conditions of his agreement were carried out. Another clause declared that, though Jaghbub remained within the Egyptian frontier as before, its internal administration would be entrusted to Sayed Idris, so long as he carried out his engagement regarding armed forces on Egyptian territory.

Meanwhile the Italian delegates and Sayed Idris had overcome their difficulties. On the 14th April, the date on which he, as representative of the Senussi Confraternity, signed with the British Government the agreement just outlined, he concluded another agreement, in the nature of a *modus vivendi*, the terms of which do not here concern us, with the Italian Government.

Nor are we greatly concerned with the subsequent affairs on the Western Frontier, which henceforth disappears from the sphere of military operations. But it is due to Sayed Idris to explain that he was able to establish himself firmly as head of the Confraternity, and that as such he kept his engagements with Britain. Though he voluntarily left Cyrenaica in 1923 to live in Egypt, the cause lay in differences with the Italian Government which it was beyond his power to overcome.

Sayed Ahmed remained in the country for over a year, but was almost impotent, and eventually, in August 1918, embarked on an Austrian submarine, and after reaching Constantinople became for a time a figure of importance in the Pan-Islamic propaganda of the Turkish Government.

EVENTS IN THE SUDAN.

The Sudan in 1914 and 1915 was, as has been stated, remarkably quiet. The few and very minor military operations during this period, like the more important Darfur campaign in 1916, were conducted by General Sir Reginald Wingate, the Governor-General, with Sudanese troops. In December 1914 small patrols were despatched to restore order and protect friendly tribesmen in the Duk Fadiat district of the Mongalla Province and to punish the Nuer tribesmen of the Lau district, Bahr el Ghazal Province, who had attacked a mission station. A rather larger affair was the Lokoia patrol of January 1915, to punish the tribes of Jebel Lyria and Jebel Luch, in the Mongalla Province, who were openly defying the Government. This patrol, consisting of a half company of 9th Sudanese, a company and a half of the Equatorial Battalion, and a detachment of the Medical Corps, under Major C. C. MacNamara, Royal Irish Rifles, achieved its purpose with slight loss. Other small patrols were despatched, in February 1915, to punish raiders in the Zeraf valley of the Upper Nile Province, in March to punish the Sheikh of Abujok, and in August to restore order in the Torit district of the Mongalla Province.

The most important of these expeditions was that sent against Mek Fiki Ali of Jebel Miri, in the Nuba Mountains Province. This chief, long loyal, had been corrupted by intrigue and propaganda. At the end of March 1915, he attempted to capture the Government post at Kadugli, then, his plot having been discovered, withdrew to his stronghold and fortified it. All endeavours to persuade him to interview the Governor failed, and it became necessary to vindicate authority as swiftly as possible.

The Miri group of hills, of which the central stronghold, Jebel Tuluk, is 2,600 feet high, is about thirty miles in circumference and consists of a tangled mass of rocky and unsurveyed heights, very steep and separated by deep ravines. It is 52 miles from Talodi, the headquarters of the Nuba Mountains Province. A force of all arms, of a total strength of 46 officers and 1,007 rank and file,[1] was concentrated at Kadugli on the 13th April under Captain H. J. Huddleston, the Dorset Regiment.[2] After a careful reconnaissance of the difficult position, Captain Huddleston attacked Jebel Tuluk at dawn on the 20th April, with three columns, each consisting of a company of the Camel Corps. The Nubas, well armed with small-bore rifles, kept up a heavy fire during the advance, but eventually the summit of the hill was practically surrounded. The fire of snipers,

---

[1] One squadron cavalry, one section artillery, one Maxim section, three companies Camel Corps, two and a half companies 11th Sudanese, one company 7th Battalion Egyptian Army and administrative services.

[2] Afterwards Brigadier-General commanding the 232nd Brigade, 75th Division, in Palestine.

Sketch 7.

Operations against the Sultan of DARFUR.
March - December, 1916.

however, prevented its occupation. On the morning of the 22nd numbers of the enemy surrendered, but Fiki Ali escaped through a gap in the long piquet-line.

The next task was to hunt down the Mek, exhausting work in the hottest season of the year. Owing to his knowledge of the country he escaped for several weeks, but eventually gave himself up to Captain D. Balfour, whom Sir R. Wingate had sent to demand his surrender. The troops returned to their quarters on the 12th June, the expedition having had an excellent effect in the province. Over two hundred rifles and a large quantity of ammunition were brought in or destroyed.

None of these affairs caused much anxiety or difficulty, and they were hardly more numerous or serious than those which occurred in the Sudan in time of peace. Generally speaking, the Great War made little impression on the people, while their leaders were conspicuously loyal. On the 8th November 1914 Sir R. Wingate had held a meeting of sheikhs at Khartoum, explaining to them the causes of war between Britain and Turkey. His address had been enthusiastically received and followed by spontaneous messages expressing their loyalty from chiefs all over the huge area of the Sudan. Even when rumours spread that the Turks had won a victory on the Suez Canal in February 1915, there was no serious trouble, though there was comment a little later upon the defeats of the Russians and the lack of success of the Dardanelles expedition.

Operations in Darfur: The Affair of Beringia.

Evidence of co-ordination in the German and Turkish plans to detain British troops in Egypt appeared when the same week in February which saw the advance of the Senussi from Siwa saw also the concentration on the Sudan frontier of the forces of Ali Dinar, Sultan of Darfur. The Governor-General had been, in his turn, gradually reinforcing the detachments of Camel Corps on the frontier with infantry and artillery, and it was apparent that hostilities would not be long delayed. Sketch 7.

The Sultanate of Darfur, which lay to the west of the Kordofan Province of the Sudan, was one of the old Central-African Kingdoms, of which to-day Abyssinia only survives. Conquered and annexed to the Egyptian Sudan in 1874, it had been freed by the revolt of the Mahdi. The night before the Battle of Omdurman, Ali Dinar, then one of the Khalifa's lieutenants, deserted the Dervish army with some thousands of his followers, fled to Darfur and established his authority in its capital, El Fasher, a town of 50,000 inhabitants. Eventually, with the sanction of Lord Kitchener, he made himself Sultan. Up to the outbreak of war with Turkey he had paid a nominal tribute to the Sudan. Then his attitude had changed, he had refused to pay the tribute and proclaimed a *Jihad* against the British Government. He was probably not ill disposed, but propaganda through the Turkish mission to the Senussi had had its effect upon him and he had surrounded himself with religious fanatics, who poisoned his mind and distracted him by false reports and crazy exhortations. Intercourse with him became gradually more and more strained. An interview with a British official might have had satisfactory results, but unfortunately he would not admit one to his capital. He was treated with forbearance and given repeated opportunities to retreat from a position which in saner moments he probably regretted having assumed. So long as he refrained from active hostilities he was let alone. His turn did not come until Sir R. Wingate discovered, at the end of 1915, that he was planning an invasion of the Sudan in conjunction with the attacks of the Senussi upon Egypt. This discovery led to a campaign remarkable for the distances covered in waterless country and for the revival of the old Dervish tactics of attempting to rush a square.

At the beginning of 1916 the Governor-General concentrated a force of two thousand at Nahud,[1] 90 miles east of the frontier of Darfur. In March he himself visited Nahud and ordered the commander of the force, Lieut.-Colonel P. V. Kelly, 3rd Hussars, to cross the frontier and occupy the wells of Um Shanga and Jebel el Hilla. The advance began on the 16th, and Um Shanga was occupied by the mounted troops without trouble. Owing to lack of water, the move on Jebel el Hilla was more difficult, and Colonel Kelly took a bold course in advancing with only 30 mounted

---

[1] Two companies mounted infantry, two batteries artillery (six 12¼-pdr. mountain guns and two Maxims), one Maxim battery, five companies Camel Corps, six companies Sudanese Infantry, two companies Arab Infantry, three companies Egyptian Infantry, with medical and supply detachments.

ADVANCE INTO DARFUR

infantry, 240 Camel Corps, and eight Maxim guns to seize it. He accomplished his purpose after a brush with a force of 800 enemy horsemen.

1916. March-May.

The advance helped to restore British prestige, weakened by the defiance of the Sultan, in the Western Sudan. But Ali Dinar's main force of from four to six thousand riflemen and numerous spear-armed auxiliaries remained at El Fasher, and there was no prospect of security until it had been dispersed. An advance on the capital was an undertaking of difficulty and risk, since from Nahud to El Fasher was a distance of 250 miles, at this season almost waterless and always without roads. General Wingate decided to supplement the camel transport on which the troops depended by a service of light lorries from railhead at Rahad to Nahud, as soon as a rough road could be constructed. This he hoped subsequently to extend to El Fasher, a distance of 360 miles in a direct line (and another hundred miles by the course which the road eventually followed) from Rahad.

During April, Berusk, Um Kedada and Abiad, further within the frontier, were occupied after some resistance from the enemy, and preparations were made for the advance on El Fasher. Sir A. Murray lent a flight of four aeroplanes, for which tent-hangars were put up at Abiad. He also despatched 15-pdr. guns and ammunition, pack wireless and light mechanical transport. He had taken over responsibility for the defence of the Assouan-Halfa reach of the Nile, which he arranged with the Naval Commander-in-Chief, East Indies and Egypt, Vice-Admiral Sir R. E. Wemyss, should be patrolled by armed steamers manned by naval ratings. He had sent to the Sudan, seriously denuded of troops by the Darfur expedition, Egyptian Engineers from Sollum and, at an earlier period, relieved the 2nd Egyptian Battalion at Tor and Abu Zenima by Indian troops, in order to strengthen the force at the disposal of the Governor-General. Finally, he sent to Khartoum three British officers and 45 other ranks to man a Maxim battery.

To have awaited the wet season would have ensured a better water supply for the advance on El Fasher, but the rain would have made the country more difficult. For this reason and because delay might be interpreted as weakness, Sir R. Wingate instructed Colonel Kelly to be ready to move during the full moon in May. Colonel Kelly concentrated his striking force at Abiad, where he was unsuccessfully attacked by an enemy force 500 strong on the 5th. Owing to the shortage of water it was decided to leave Abiad in two columns[1] on the 15th and 16th, the forces reuniting 40 miles west of Abiad and 28 miles short of Melit, where there was a good supply of water and only a small enemy garrison.

On the morning of the 15th May a party of mounted infantry scouts cleverly captured an enemy observation post on a ridge 2 miles from the British camp. In consequence, as was subsequently ascertained, news of the advance did not reach El Fasher until the force was within striking distance of Melit. This village was bombed from the air and thereupon evacuated by the garrison. It was occupied by Colonel Kelly's whole force on the morning of the 18th.

1916.
22 May.
Owing to the fatigue of the troops the further advance was postponed till the 22nd May. The force struck camp at 5.30 a.m. and advanced in square formation, as large parties of enemy horsemen and camelry were visible from the first. The country was rough and covered with small sand-hills, across which it was difficult to see more than a few hundred yards in any direction. At 10.30 a.m. the enemy was found to be occupying a strong position ahead, but was quickly shelled out of his advanced trenches.

The square now advanced to a better position, close to the village of Beringia, and carried out hasty entrenchment, the enemy's main line being the other side of the village. Colonel Kelly was preparing to attack when the enemy suddenly left his position and advanced against the south face of the square. The assault was delivered with that fanatical bravery in which few races can match the tribes of the Sudan, despite the fire of two mountain batteries and four sections of Maxims manned by British detachments. Some of the attackers fell within ten yards of the firing line. But the troops held their ground steadily, and forty minutes after the launching of the attack there were signs of wavering in the enemy's ranks. Colonel Kelly at once ordered the "advance" to be sounded. In face of the counter-attack, delivered with dash, the enemy broke and fled.

---

[1] Sixty mounted scouts, eight guns and fourteen maxims, four companies Camel Corps with two maxims, eight companies infantry (13th and 14th Sudanese and Arab Battalion).

The losses of the tribesmen were estimated at over a thousand, more than three hundred dead or seriously wounded being counted within five hundred yards of the square. It appeared from the rude parade states afterwards found at El Fasher that the strength of the enemy was 3,600, besides auxiliaries. The casualties of Colonel Kelly's force numbered 26.

1916. May-Oct.

There was a further attack by the enemy before El Fasher was reached, but it was not serious. At 10 a.m. next morning Colonel Kelly entered the town with his mounted troops. Ali Dinar fled south with his remaining adherents, numbering about two thousand, who were bombed as they emerged from the town by Lieutenant J. C. Slessor, Royal Flying Corps. Four guns, many rifles, much ammunition and a plant for the manufacture of gunpowder were captured.

Danger to the Sudan from the Sultan of Darfur was now at an end, but there was no hope of tranquility whilst he himself was at large.

THE AFFAIR OF GIUBA (JEBEL JUBA).

Ali Dinar was reported to have fled towards the Marra Mountains, some fifty miles south-west of El Fasher. Colonel Kelly was unable to order an instant pursuit owing to the exhaustion of his transport animals and the shortage of supplies. Soon afterwards envoys from the Sultan came in to discuss terms. Negotiations continued till the 1st August, when, it being evident that the enemy's sole object was to gain time, they were broken off by Colonel Kelly.

Sketch 7.

Meanwhile Ali Dinar had not prospered in his affairs. Some of his followers revolted and fighting followed. Eventually he was left with not more than a thousand men, a force which might, however, swell rapidly if not interfered with, and was large enough to carry out raids for supplies and keep the district in turmoil. It was decided therefore to establish posts at Kebkebia, 80 miles west of El Fasher, and Dibbis, 110 miles south-west, as soon as the country had dried somewhat after the August rains. Kebkebia was occupied without opposition early in September. In October, Major H. J. Huddleston was despatched by Colonel Kelly with a force of 200 rifles (13th Sudanese and Camel Corps), two guns and four Maxims, to Dibbis, which he reached on the 13th.

He encountered a body of 150 riflemen and 1,000 spearmen under Ali Dinar's son and dispersed it after a short skirmish. Ali Dinar again opened negotiations, but again it was discovered that he was not acting in good faith. Colonel Kelly therefore reinforced Major Huddleston with 100 rifles, 13th Sudanese.

Hearing that the Sultan's force at Kulme, 50 miles west of Dibbis, was suffering from disease and hunger and that no serious resistance was to be expected from it, Major Huddleston decided to march to attack it, without waiting for further reinforcements. Kulme was occupied on the 3rd November, after slight opposition. Here most of the Sultan's remaining arms and ammunition were captured, while several hundred followers, including men and women of his family, came in to surrender.

Ali Dinar now fled to Jebel Juba, or Giuba, south-west of Kulme. Leaving behind half his force, which there was no prospect of being able to feed, Major Huddleston set out on the 5th November with 150 rifles, one gun and four maxims, mounting the troops on horses taken from the enemy or lent by friendly Arabs.[1] At dawn on the 6th he came upon the camp, on which he was able to open fire at 500 yards, whereupon the Sultan's followers scattered and fled in all directions. A mile from the camp the body of Ali Dinar was found. He had been shot through the head.

The Province of Darfur, now pacified except in its remote north-west corner, was once again part of the Sudan, to the population of which it added a million inhabitants. For a time, as was the case after wars in Europe in the Middle Ages, bands of armed and masterless men roamed the country pillaging the defenceless, but they were gradually hunted down and broken up, and the administration was soon firmly established. Co-operation by the French in Wadai checked intrusion from the north of the Senussi's followers.

The danger of the rising is not to be measured by the relative ease with which it was suppressed, or by the small number of troops engaged, any more than is the larger-scale campaign against the Senussi. It is not difficult to stamp out a spark travelling along a fuze to a powder-barrel, but the

---

[1] It may be noted that the Arab inhabitants of Darfur had always been hostile to Ali Dinar. The powerful Rizeigat tribes of the south-west had more than once rebelled and defeated him.

task is one demanding speed and resolution. How disastrous might have been the explosions planned by Germans and Turks in Kordofan, in Upper Egypt, in the Faiyum and the region of Alexandria, they alone knew who bore the responsibility for the safety, not only of those areas, but of all Egypt and the Sudan.

NOTE.

THE ORGANIZATION OF THE FORCES ON THE WESTERN FRONTIER.

The organization of the forces on the Western Frontier varied from time to time, and changes of commanders were frequent. The following summary will make clear the organization and its alterations.

(i) In November 1915, when hostilities with the Senussi developed, the Western Frontier Force was formed, under the command of Major-General A. Wallace.

(ii) In January 1916, when the oases west of the Nile were threatened, the Southern Force was formed. Major-General W. E. Peyton was actually appointed to the command, but within a fortnight relieved Major-General Wallace in command of the Western Frontier Force, and Major-General J. Adye took over command of the Southern Force.

(iii) On the 31st March 1916 the Southern Force was amalgamated with the Western Force, which was divided into a N.W. and S.W. Section. Major-General J. Adye became Adjutant-General to the E.E.F. Major-General Peyton took over the whole Western Frontier Force, but was given a new appointment while on leave in England and did not return to Egypt.

(iv) On the 11th May, Lieut-General Sir B. Mahon took over the command, but was invalided from sunstroke within a few days. Major-General A. G. Dallas, who had been temporarily in command during General Peyton's absence, continued in that position.

(v) On 20th June, Major-General Sir C. M. Dobell assumed command. The N.W. and S.W. Sections disappeared and a new Coastal Section was formed.

(vi) On the 4th October, Major-General W. A. Watson took over command from Major-General Dobell, who went to command the Eastern Frontier Force in Sinai.

(vii) On the 5th March 1917, the quietude of the area permitted the amalgamation of the Delta Command with that of the Western Frontier Force, under Brig.-General H. G. Casson. The amalgamated command had two sections: Coastal and Southern.

CHAPTER X.

THE BEGINNING OF THE ADVANCE TOWARDS PALESTINE.

(Maps 7, 8; Sketches B, 8, 9.)

EGYPT IN THE SPRING OF 1916.

Map 7.
Sketch B.
IN Chapter VI the general narrative was carried up to the arrival of the troops from Gallipoli in Egypt: there to be re-equipped, restored in health, and finally either despatched to the Western Front or employed to protect Egypt and the Suez Canal against the Turkish offensive then expected. In the same chapter the amalgamation of the two Egyptian commands in March was anticipated, the return of Sir J. Maxwell to England and Sir A. Murray's assumption of command of the combined Mediterranean Expeditionary Force and Force in Egypt, under the name of the Egyptian Expeditionary Force, being recorded. Though that point has been disposed of, it must be remembered in reading the pages which follow that until the 19th March Sir A. Murray's command included only Sharqia, the easternmost province of Egypt, and Sinai, and that his attention was concentrated on the defence of the Canal. For these reasons he established his headquarters at Ismailia.

The administrative work of the first six weeks was very heavy. Every day during that period ships arrived at Alexandria and Port Said with troops, guns, transport and stores of the Dardanelles Army; every formation in need of reorganization and re-equipment. Before the last units reached the country or the components of this great mass has been disentangled, the move of troops from Egypt for service elsewhere began, further to complicate the administration. In both material and personnel the formations from Gallipoli were incomplete, and training was one of the most urgent problems to be faced.

A training centre for Australian and New Zealand reinforcements was at once formed at Tell el Kebir, and a machine-gun school at Ismailia. Sir J. Maxwell had already organized at Zeitun the Imperial School of Instruction

REORGANIZATION OF M.E.F.

on a considerable scale. When this passed under the control of Sir A. Murray in March, he expanded it and merged in it the machine-gun school, concentrating all training, except that of the Australian reinforcements, at Zeitun, under the command of Lieut.-Colonel the Hon. E. M. Colston, Grenadier Guards. Classes were formed for (i) officers, (ii) non-commissioned officers, (iii) machine gunners, (iv) Lewis gunners, (v) signallers, (vi) artillery, (vii) Stokes gunners, (viii) grenadiers. Between the 7th January and 31st May, 1,166 officers and 5,512 other ranks passed through the various courses of instruction.

1916. Jan.-March.

The organization of the signal services was also of importance. The signallers from Gallipoli had to be almost entirely re-equipped in material and reorganized to suit Egyptian conditions, while fresh personnel had to be trained to replace their heavy casualties.[1] Until this period the civil administration had worked the telegraph system for the army, employing mainly native operators. New units had to be formed, equipped and trained to take over this work on the Sinai front, on the coast of the Western Desert as far as Sollum, and for the force defending the Nile Valley from the west.

Yet another piece of work, on the importance of which Sir A. Murray lays stress in his Despatches, was the survey on a large scale of the Canal Zone and certain areas east of the advanced line. This was initiated by Mr. E. M. Dowson, Director-General of the Survey of Egypt, who put his resources at Sir A. Murray's disposal, and carried out by the Topographical Section of the Intelligence Branch, working in co-operation with the Royal Flying Corps. By the end of May the survey had approached Qatiya.

Sir A. Murray found the work on the Canal Defences, the plan and organization of which have been outlined, fast progressing. No part of the advanced line was as yet occupied by troops, mainly because there had been delays in establishing the water supply caused by lack of piping. But on the 13th January Sir A. Murray ordered his Corps Commanders to the Canal, to take over the work and prepare schemes of defence.

---

[1] Up to the 31st May 94 officers and 1,305 other ranks were trained in signal duties at Zeitun and Alexandria.

The Canal was divided into three sections,[1] each held by a corps, as follows :—

    No. 1 Section (Southern)—Suez to Kabrit.—IX Corps (Lieut.-General the Hon. Sir J. G. H. Byng) ; 29th, 46th, and 10th Indian, Divisions. Headquarters, Suez.

    No. 2 Section (Central)—Kabrit to Ferdan.—Anzac Corps (Lieut.-General Sir W. R. Birdwood) ; 1st and 2nd Australian, and New Zealand and Australian, Divisions. Headquarters, Ismailia.

    No. 3 Section (Northern)—Ferdan to Port Said.—XV Corps (Lieut.-General H. S. Horne) ; 11th, 13th and 31st Divisions. Headquarters, Port Said ; Advanced Headquarters, Qantara.

The VIII Corps (Lieut.-General F. J. Davies), consisting of the 42nd and 52nd Divisions, was at first concentrated at Tell el Kebir and later, as other divisions moved to France, broken up. General Davies then succeeded General Byng, who had returned to the Western Front, in command of the IX Corps.

In addition to these eleven divisions, there were the 53rd and 54th, in Sir J. Maxwell's command, the former guarding the Nile Valley, the latter at Cairo. By the end of February, after the departure of the 13th, 31st and 46th Divisions and the break-up of the 10th Indian, the distribution was as follows :—

    No. 1 Section.—IX Corps ; 29th and 42nd Divisions.

    No. 2 Section.—Anzac Corps ; 1st and 2nd Australian, and New Zealand and Australian, Divisions.

    No. 3 Section.—XV Corps ; 11th and 52nd Divisions.

Then the Anzac Corps and its troops went to France, and on the 27th March the II Anzac Corps, commanded by Lieut.-General Sir A. J. Godley, and consisting of the 4th and 5th Australian Divisions and the Australian and New Zealand Mounted Division, came into being and took over No. 2 Section.[2] By this time, though the defences were not yet complete, the advanced line was occupied.

---

[1] The military term employed in this connection is generally "sector." As, however, "section" is used in Sir A. Murray's Despatches and the official titles of the headquarters were subsequently "Headquarters No. . . . Section," the latter has been retained.

[2] The 3rd Australian Division went to England direct from Australia.

PROSPECTS OF TURKISH ATTACK 157

Sir A. Murray, however, was not content to adopt a system of passive defence. He was already buying camels in order to organize large mobile columns in each section. He was engaged in preparations for pushing out a railway to the Qatiya district, to permit of its occupation, in accordance with the appreciation made by him when C.I.G.S.[1] But he now contemplated an advance much greater than to Qatiya. In a letter addressed to Sir W. Robertson on the 15th February, 1916,[2] he stated that in his opinion the best method of defending Egypt from the east was to advance across Sinai to El Arish, and that fewer troops would be required for this undertaking than for the passive defence of the Suez Canal. With regard to the danger of a Turkish invasion he stated that during the early spring it would be possible for the Turks to bring down to Beersheba and push across the desert a force of 250,000 men, but added that there was no sign of their attempting such an enterprise and that the time available was short. Replying on the 27th, Sir W. Robertson agreed that Qatiya should be occupied if possible; an advance to El Arish was a far bigger question, on which no decision could for the moment be made. For his part, he thought it extremely unlikely that more than 100,000 Turks could be brought against Egypt.

We see then that as late as mid-February the command in Egypt still contemplated the possibility—though not the probability—of a force of 250,000 Turks advancing to the attack on Egypt, and that the C.I.G.S. considered two-fifths of this force to be the maximum which the enemy could concentrate for the purpose. In view of the scanty information available from the Turkish side regarding this period, it is difficult to ascertain exactly what the enemy's intentions were. That an offensive was contemplated in February we know from both Kress and Liman.[3] The question to which

1916.
Feb.
Map 8.

---

[1] See pp. 89–90.
[2] This letter is given in full in Note II at end of chapter.
[3] "Sinai": Kress, i, p. 21; Liman, p. 181. Both speak of it as "eine grössere Expedition," meaning a major expedition. The Historical Section of the Turkish General Staff speaks somewhat vaguely of an expedition consisting of seven divisions and 100,000 strong (57 battalions, 23 batteries) having been contemplated. But this was first projected in April 1915 and then found impossible owing to the drain of Gallipoli. Later it was hoped to carry out the expedition in October 1916, but "patience was not "exercised" and "for some urgent reasons" the small-scale advance which led to the Battle of Romani took place in the hottest season of the year.

we must attempt to find an answer is: How far were the British estimates justified, and why was the Turkish expedition postponed until July and then limited to a single reinforced division?

Sketch 9.   There is no evidence that the Turks ever contemplated, still less made preparation for, an expedition approaching the strength of 250,000 men. In February 1916 their troops between the Cilician Gates and the Suez Canal numbered from forty to sixty thousand men, but of these the bulk were in Northern Syria, where the enemy was concerned for the safety of his communications at Alexandretta. Three Turkish Armies, the *First*, *Second* and *Fifth*, were in Thrace, where, as Liman von Sanders caustically remarks, there was no enemy.[1] As an example of the slow rate at which Turkish troops in large numbers were transported to a distant theatre of war, it may be mentioned that when the *Second Army* was transferred to the area south-west of Lake Van in Armenia, the move began in April and lasted until August.[2] Communications with Palestine were better, and the ten divisions of this army might have been concentrated in Southern Palestine in a shorter period, but not before the end of the wet season. With the forces already in Syria there might then have been 150,000 men between Jerusalem and the Sinai frontier. But if they had come they could hardly have been fed, as we now know, even in Southern Palestine, far less in Sinai; for in the summer of 1917 the 40,000 combatants holding the Gaza-Beersheba line were seriously under-nourished and their transport animals half-starved. Turkish troops can subsist on less than any European troops, the Russians not excepted, but the resources of Palestine in food were comparatively small, all munitions of war had to come from Constantinople (when not from Berlin), and the railway system, which has been described in detail, was quite inadequate to maintain a quarter of a million men even at Beersheba.[3]

---

[1] Liman, p. 159.
[2] Liman, p. 161.
[3] As to the equipment of the Turkish reserves at this period, the following telegram sent by Liman to the Turkish Ministry of War from Balikisri in Asia Minor on the 14th March is instructive: "Saw to-day " depot regiment over 8,000 strong, with only 1,050 rifles of various models. " Not a single bandolier, and a great proportion of those who had rifles " without side-arms." (Liman, p. 157.)

Turkish plans were, perhaps, as Sir A. Murray subsequently stated in his Despatches, upset by the campaign of the Grand Duke Nicholas, which resulted in the capture of the fortress of Erzerum on the 15th February and in April of Trebizond, the best Turkish Black Sea harbour in the zone of operations. This campaign did not result in the withdrawal of troops from Syria to any great extent, but it may have kept reinforcements from being sent there, and certainly kept the Baghdad Railway fully employed in transporting the *Second Army* to Ras el Ain, whence it was to march towards Erzerum. As a result, the German and Austrian reinforcements sent to Palestine, small in numbers though valuable in quality, were delayed till the summer, when Sinai was at its driest and hottest, and no move against the Canal was made until July. This, however, does not affect the contention that the M.E.F.'s estimate of Turkish resources was altogether excessive. Sir W. Robertson's figure of 100,000 represented their means and intentions much more nearly, and this appears, in the light of present knowledge, to be the extreme limit of any concentration ever contemplated by Turkey, or in her power to effect. That the exaggeration of the former estimate was quickly recognized by the Imperial General Staff is shown by the speed with which British divisions were transferred from Egypt to the Western Front, even before the end of the wet season in Sinai.[1] It will be noted that Sir A. Murray lays down in his appreciation that after the beginning of the hot weather, that is from about the 15th April, one corps of three divisions on the Canal, one division holding Qatiya, and three mounted brigades for all purposes, would suffice for the defence of Egypt from the east.

The Advance into Sinai.

Until the middle of February the troops were fully engaged in reorganization, training, and work upon the Canal Defences, in the making of roads and laying of light railways and pipe-lines, without which these defences could not be occupied. Reconnaissances by the Royal Flying Corps and the seaplanes of the Royal Naval Air Service (a squadron of which now succeeded the French seaplane detachment at

---

[1] See p. 98.

160 ADVANCE INTO SINAI

Port Said)[1] established the fact that there were no considerable Turkish forces in Sinai and no signs of a concentration in Southern Palestine for an attack on Egypt. During the latter half of the month the XV Corps pushed its mounted patrols out 20 miles, to Bir en Nuss and Hod Umm Ugba, finding this area clear of the enemy and practically deserted by the Bedouin. From Tor, at the southern end of Sinai, which was garrisoned by the 2nd Battalion Egyptian Army and had come under General Murray's control by arrangement with General Maxwell, a reconnaissance was carried out, and a small force of the enemy—chiefly Bedouin with a few Turkish officers—ejected from a camp established several miles inland. In No. 2 (the Central) Section a force about a squadron strong of the 8th and 9th Australian Light Horse and a detachment of Bikanir Camel Corps carried out between the 11th and 15th April a raid to Jifjafa, a distance of 52 miles, captured an Austrian engineer officer and 33 men, and destroyed a well-boring plant which had been at work for five months. At the same time the IX Corps in the Southern Section reconnoitred 30 miles to Bir el Giddi and the tracks leading east therefrom.

Meanwhile the standard-gauge line from Qantara towards Qatiya had been begun. On the 10th March the first shipload of rails and sleepers arrived at Qantara, and in four weeks 16 miles, including sidings, were laid. The line followed the caravan track for 5 miles and was then to make a sweep north to avoid the large and shifting sand-dunes of Romani, curving back to the caravan route near

---

[1] The "East Indies and Egypt Seaplane Squadron" was formed in late January 1916, and consisted of British seaplanes which had been employed in the Gallipoli campaign and of the French seaplane detachment. There is no record of the precise date at which the French detachment was withdrawn from Egypt, but its last reported flight took place on the 16th April. Squadron Commander C. L'Estrange Malone was the first commander of the East Indies Squadron, Commander C. R. Sampson, R.N., taking over command in May 1916. The seaplane carriers at the disposal of the squadron were the *Ben-my-Chree*, *Anne*, *Raven*, and *Empress*, but the last named was sent to Mudros in May. The depot included a training base for observers, who were supplied by the Army, and an intelligence report centre. The squadron carried out remarkable work in reconnaissance, photography, and bombing along the Syrian coast throughout 1916 and 1917, and was also employed in the Red Sea and at Aden. An interesting account of its activities is to be found in "In the Side Shows" by Captain Wedgwood Benn (Hodder and Stoughton).

Sketch 8.

OCCUPATION OF QATIYA BASIN

the Oghratina Oasis, 5 miles east of Qatiya. A subsidiary 2 ft. 6 in. line was also begun from Port Said along the shore.

1916. April. Sketch 8.

The railway having passed through the advanced line of the Canal Defences, it became necessary to establish permanent posts ahead of it in the Qatiya Oasis to protect it from attack by the enemy and to ensure the Egyptian labourers against interference from armed Bedouin. On the 6th April, Br.-General E. A. Wiggin, 5th Mounted Brigade (the mounted troops in the XV Corps Section), was appointed to the command of the Qatiya district, and made responsible to Lieut.-General Horne. Three days afterwards the latter was recalled to a command in France and succeeded by Major-General the Hon. H. Lawrence, hitherto commanding the 52nd Division. The XV Corps Headquarters was broken up and General Lawrence was given a reduced corps staff, known as Headquarters No. 3 Section.

On the 9th April a squadron of the Worcester Yeomanry found the Turks in some strength at Bir el Abd, 15 miles east of Qatiya. By the third week of the month the whole of the 5th Mounted Brigade was disposed to cover the railway: headquarters and Gloucester Hussars at Romani, Worcester Yeomanry at Qatiya, Warwick Yeomanry (less one squadron on the Canal) at Bir el Hamisah, 3 miles south of Qatiya. The 2/2nd Lowland Field Company, R.E., 52nd Division, was attached to the brigade for the development of wells. The brigade had no artillery, the ground being soft sand over which wheels could scarcely move and the water supply for horses still far from plentiful. On the 21st and 22nd two squadrons (less one troop) Worcester Yeomanry with a detachment (4 officers and 60 other ranks) of the Field Company were pushed out to the Oasis of Oghratina, and replaced in Qatiya by a squadron of Gloucester Hussars until the arrival of the 5th Australian Light Horse. This regiment had been ordered to reinforce General Wiggin, in view of signs of renewed activity on the part of the enemy, an outpost of the Warwick Yeomanry from Bir el Hamisah having been attacked by Turkish or Bedouin cavalry before dawn on the 19th and having had its horses stampeded. The Light Horse was due to arrive at Qatiya on the 24th.

Thirteen miles S.S.W. of Qatiya, on the track from Qantara, the small oasis of Dueidar was held by 120 rifles 5th Royal Scots Fusiliers, a few Yeomanry and men of the Bikanir Camel Corps, 156 rifles in all. Five miles behind this post, at Hill 70 in the advanced line of the Canal Defences, was the 4th Royal Scots Fusiliers, of the 52nd (Lowland) Division, which was holding this portion of the front. Railhead was on the 21st near El Arais and 4 miles west of Romani, so that the time had come when Qatiya could be held in greater strength and more easily supplied. At the very moment when this reinforcement was about to take place, the enemy struck a blow which for combined speed, skill, daring, and success is hardly to be matched in the records of the campaign.

THE AFFAIR OF QATIYA.

1916.
22-23 April.
Sketch 8.

Br.-General Wiggin had received a report that the enemy party which had raided his outpost on the 19th was at Bir el Mageibra, 8 miles south-east of Hamisah, and that it was about two hundred strong. With the approval of General Lawrence, he arranged to carry out a raid from Hamisah against the camp. This raid he decided to command in person. He arrived at Hamisah on the 22nd, bringing with him headquarters, one squadron and one troop of Worcester Yeomanry from Qatiya. The dispositions of his force that evening were therefore as follows :—

> Oghratina :—Two squadrons (less one troop) Worcester Yeomanry, detachment 2/2nd Lowland Field Company R.E.
> Qatiya :—One squadron and machine-gun subsection, Gloucester Hussars, 40 dismounted details Worcester Yeomanry, details R.A.M.C., A.V.C., and camel transport.
> Hamisah :—Warwick Yeomanry (less one squadron), one squadron and one troop Worcester Yeomanry.
> Romani (in reserve) :—Gloucester Hussars (less one squadron and machine-gun subsection).

As luck would have it, the raid coincided with the Turkish advance. General Wiggin arrived at Mageibra at dawn on the 23rd and found a considerable but almost empty camp. He dispersed a handful of Turkish troops, captured six prisoners, and destroyed the camp. He was back at Hamisah by 9 a.m., having marched 16 miles, his horses tired and in need of water but not exhausted. On his arrival, as will be recorded later, he heard of the Turkish attack, to which we must now turn.

Oghratina, on the morning of the 23rd April, had been occupied only about thirty-six hours by one squadron and the detachment of Royal Engineers and twelve hours by the second squadron, so that not much entrenching had yet been carried out. The camp was, however, alert, and stood to arms at 4 a.m. in a dense sea-fog, which is not uncommon in the early morning at this season. Suddenly the sound of pumps at the wells 500 yards south-west of the camp and at the foot of the slope on which it stood was heard by the sentries of "D" Squadron, on the left of the line. It was thought that a patrol of "A" Squadron must be watering, but Captain E. S. Ward ran down the hill to investigate. He almost ran into the midst of a party of about sixty Turks in a hod south of the wells. He rushed back, collected what men he could find in the mist, opened fire on the Turks at pointblank range, inflicted heavy casualties on them, and forced them to retreat headlong. Captain Ward followed, but was at once met by very heavy rifle fire, showing him all too plainly that it was no small party which he had surprised. He therefore fell back to the line held by his squadron.

Soon afterwards "A" Squadron on the right was heavily attacked and by 5.15 a.m. the whole camp was assaulted from north, east and south-east in overwhelming strength. Almost from the first the troops were engaged from a range of fifty yards or less. Major F. S. Williams-Thomas, in command of the detachment, had orders to retire if attacked in force, but found himself unable to do so without leaving in the lurch the dismounted men. He felt it his duty to stand by the engineers, but for whom, he considered, he might have been able to disengage his two squadrons and fight a rear-guard action back to Qatiya. The remnants of "D" Squadron were driven back upon the second line of defence, held by the engineers, but that position was speedily forced also, and then the Turks had the whole camp at their mercy. By 7.45 a.m., he states, 11 Yeomanry officers and 135 other ranks were casualties. Half the rifles of those still unwounded were clogged with sand. Further resistance would have meant that the whole force would have been slaughtered to no useful end, and the remnant of the detachment surrendered.

At Qatiya "A" Squadron Gloucester Hussars, under Captain M. G. Lloyd Baker, stood to arms and saddled up at 3.30 a.m. A patrol came in to report having seen and heard nothing in the mist. Soon afterwards a small patrol of the enemy approached and fired into the camp, then retired swiftly. Heavy firing was heard from Oghratina and a message received at 6 a.m. that an attack had been repulsed. Half an hour later came a message that it had been renewed, and a mounted orderly from Romani reported that Dueidar, far away to the right rear, had also been attacked. At 7.45 another enemy patrol was driven off. All firing at Oghratina had ceased and there was for an hour complete quiet, while the fog gradually dispersed.

At 8.45 a.m. a patrol, sent out toward Oghratina, saw two lines of troops in open order, about three hundred in each line, advancing on Qatiya, and a mile and a half distant. Behind them were further troops in a formed body, and cavalry could be seen advancing south-west, doubtless to surround the post. At 9.45 a.m. a battery of mountain guns opened fire from near Er Rabah, north-east of Qatiya. The first twenty shells fell beyond the camp, but then a correction was made and shells began to burst in the horse-lines, killing or maiming most of the horses within a few minutes. An enemy aeroplane came over very low, spotting for the artillery. As the guns opened the enemy advanced, crawling forward in small parties, covered by rifle fire.

Meanwhile, on his arrival at Hamisah, General Wiggin had learnt that Oghratina was surrounded, and soon afterwards was informed of the advance on Qatiya. He ordered Lieut.-Colonel Coventry, commanding the Worcester Yeomanry, to water the Worcester squadron first and advance with it on Qatiya. Watering at a few small desert wells was slow work, and, before it was completed, shells were seen bursting at Qatiya. Colonel Coventry then moved off at once, at 9.50 a.m. As he approached Qatiya he saw that the camp was heavily engaged. He dismounted his squadron three-quarters of a mile west of the camp and led it up on foot to prolong the line of the Gloucester squadron to the left. This considerably relieved pressure on that flank, where the enemy fell back some distance. A heavy fire battle then continued for several hours. The enemy's artillery had ceased fire after destroying the horses, but the volume of his rifle and machine-gun fire was great, and under its cover his infantry gradually pressed in on front and flanks.

The first of General Wiggin's remaining squadrons (of Warwick Yeomanry) having watered at Hamisah, moved off at 10.30 a.m., he himself following with the second a quarter of an hour later. His intention was to attack the enemy in rear in the neighbourhood of the Hod um Ugba, north-east of Qatiya. Half-way between Hamisah and the camp he became engaged with the enemy's flanking troops. He fought his way slowly forward for about a mile. But now, at 1.45 p.m., the opposition became very strong, and his own men and horses were tired out. He saw soon afterwards a commotion among the camels in Qatiya camp and that some of the tents were burning. He decided that he could do no more to help and that his best course was to fall back on Hamisah, whence he had heard a burst of machine-gun fire, and pick up a detachment of 20 men guarding the camp, a quantity of stores and a number of camels. On his return he discovered that the firing had been no more than an exchange of shots between a body of Turks retiring from Dueidar and British aeroplanes pursuing them. It must be added that the firing and the safety of his detachment at Hamisah had had no serious weight in deciding General Wiggin to retire.

Lieut.-Colonel R. M. Yorke, in command at Romani, moved out with five troops and a machine-gun subsection, Gloucester Hussars, at 10.15 a.m. His intention was not to advance to the support of Qatiya, of the attack on which he had not heard, but to intercept a column of 500 Turks, which he was informed was retiring south-east from Dueidar in a disorganized condition. But shortly after leaving Romani he heard firing from Qatiya, and, on reaching some high ground, was able to see the Turkish artillery north of Er Rabah shelling the camp. He changed direction and advanced towards it, whereupon it ceased fire and a quarter of an hour later withdrew some distance.

At 10.45 a.m. Colonel Yorke's advanced guard came under fire north-west of Er Rabah. He pressed on, driving the enemy back to the high ground south of the Hod um Ugba. Here the enemy was reinforced and his rifle fire became so heavy that Colonel Yorke found himself unable to make any further progress. He began a gradual withdrawal, with long halts to let his wounded get clear to Romani, and was followed up by the Turks at 1 p.m., their battery reopening fire from a new position, but with little result.

It will be noted that his advance had been almost simultaneous with that of General Wiggin on the other flank of the enemy. Unfortunately, he was not aware of the presence of the other force to south of Qatiya, nor was it till after General Wiggin's troops had begun their retirement, about 3 p.m., that Colonel Yorke, who was then a mile east of Abu Hamra, caught sight of them.[1] At 3.30 he saw that Qatiya was in the hands of the enemy and decided to retire at once to Romani. There he remained till midnight, when, on being informed that no infantry could be sent up to support him, he fell back on railhead.

From the time—about 1 p.m.—when the two relieving forces had failed in their object, the garrison of Qatiya was doomed. The enemy pressed in closer and closer. Soon after 1.30 p.m. Colonel Coventry asked Captain W. H. Wiggin, commanding the squadron of Worcester Yeomanry, if he thought he could get back to the horses and bring up the horse-holders, as every man was needed. Captain Wiggin crawled down the hill, but before he reached the horses, by what proved to be extraordinary good fortune for himself and other survivors, fainted from the effect of a wound received earlier and lay about an hour unconscious. Meanwhile the shelling was renewed and the enemy closed to within fifty yards. At 3 p.m. the Turks charged with the bayonet, and the remnant of the little garrison was forced to surrender. Captain Wiggin, now recovered, was leading forward the numbers-three when he saw the camp rushed by the enemy. But, seeing some men running back from the line, he had the presence of mind to gallop horses up to meet them, and rescued a number of them. In all, including the horse-holders, about eighty escaped. Captain Wiggin himself was the only officer at Oghratina or Qatiya not either killed or captured.

There remains to be recorded an episode incidental to the Turkish expedition against Oghratina and Qatiya: the attack on Dueidar. This post was in a small oasis, measuring 450 yards from east to west and 150 from north to south, and was defended by half a dozen small works clear of the date trees. Its garrison, as previously stated, consisted of 156 rifles.

---

[1] General Wiggin had seen Colonel Yorke's force on the horizon an hour earlier and had tried to communicate with it by helio.

DEFENCE OF DUEIDAR

1916. 23 April.

At 4 a.m. it was found that communication with Qatiya was interrupted. A linesman was sent out and the commander of the garrison, Captain F. Roberts, 5th Royal Scots Fusiliers, visited his posts. He then sent out a Yeomanry patrol to the south-east and ordered the troops to stand to arms. The patrol returned without having seen anything in the dense mist. At 5.17 a.m. a large body of men suddenly appeared in front of the principal redoubt, to the south-east of the oasis. As the sentry who had seen them fired, the Turks dashed forward. The garrison of the redoubt was creditably alert, when it is considered that it had no reason to suppose there was an enemy nearer than Mageibra, 20 miles away. The fire of a Lewis gun under 2nd Lieutenant G. McDiarmid and of every one of the fifty rifles in the redoubt swept the Turkish ranks. The enemy recoiled, leaving about twenty dead and wounded on the ground.

Fire was now opened by a mountain gun out of the mist, but the shooting was hopelessly erratic, doubtless because no observer could see the British position. The rifle fire increased, and at 7 a.m. the enemy attempted to outflank the position to the south. This move was checked by the fire of a little work on that flank, containing only one N.C.O. and six men. Shortly afterwards the Turks shouting " Allah ! " again charged the south-eastern redoubt. Again they were routed by the steady fire of the defence, some being brought down within twenty yards of the wire. Thenceforward they confined themselves to ineffective artillery, machine-gun and rifle fire.

At 6.25 a.m. Major H. Thompson, 4th Royal Scots Fusiliers, at Hill 70 on the railway, 5 miles in rear, received orders to reinforce Dueidar with two companies. He moved off forty minutes later with " C " and " D " Companies and 11 men of the Glasgow Yeomanry as scouts. On approaching the palm grove he sent up a small detachment to reinforce the south-eastern redoubt, where the action appeared hottest, and went forward himself to ascertain the situation and take over command. He found that the enemy had a firing line south of the Dueidar-Qatiya track, 200 yards distant from the principal redoubt. North of the track there were apparently no Turks ; at least no attack had been made in that quarter.

Major Thompson then sent a party out to an isolated work, north-east of the grove and not hitherto held, to engage the enemy with enfilade fire. Shortly afterwards the mist cleared somewhat, and a British aeroplane dropped a message to the effect that the enemy's main body was in retreat and that the firing line in front of the position now amounted to no more than about one hundred and fifty rifles. At noon a squadron of the 5th Australian Light Horse arrived and moved off south-east in pursuit of the enemy's main body, leaving the rearguard to the garrison of Dueidar, which issued from the oasis and attacked it all along the line. The Turks broke and fled. They were pursued for a mile and a half and 17 unwounded prisoners taken, while several wounded men were brought in later. The remainder of the 5th Australian Light Horse arrived at 1.30 p.m., having marched from Qantara, and took up the pursuit, capturing a few more prisoners. The total captures were one officer and 31 other ranks, and 75 dead were left on the field. The British casualties numbered 55, and 52 camels were killed in the lines beside the oasis.

At 9 p.m. Br.-General Wiggin arrived at Dueidar with his two squadrons,[1] and the outer line of defence now became from railhead to Dueidar. Both positions were reinforced, the 2nd Australian Light Horse Brigade moving up to railhead the following morning. But the attack was over and the enemy in retreat. On the 24th aeroplanes of the 5th Wing followed various columns, bombing them and firing on them with machine guns.

An interesting point regarding this series of actions was later brought to notice. An observer of the 14th Squadron R.F.C., discovered from tracks in the sand the lines of advance of the enemy. The main force, which attacked Oghratina and Qatiya, advanced along the caravan route from Bir el Abd. On the other hand, the track of the column which attacked Dueidar—consisting mainly if not wholly of camelry—ran from Mageibra through Bir Gharif ed Dukhan. There is therefore no doubt that this was the force reported at Mageibra to General Wiggin. While he was on the march to attack it, as he hoped by surprise, it was on the march to attempt the surprise of Dueidar.

---

[1] On the following day he was ordered to take the remnants of his brigade back to Qatiya.

It must be added that it was not the intention of Major-General Lawrence to make a serious resistance in the oases to a Turkish attack, and that in such circumstances General Wiggin's orders were to retire on Dueidar or railhead. The difficulty regarding these orders was the presence of dismounted troops with the outposts. The engineers at Oghratina could scarcely have marched 14 miles from Oghratina to railhead without being caught by the enemy's camelry, which could have brought them (and the Yeomanry if it attempted to succour them) to action until the Turkish infantry came up. Had there been no sappers at Oghratina it is possible that the Yeomanry might have slipped away in the fog. It is also probable that the presence of dismounted details at Qatiya made Captain Lloyd Baker hesitate to retire during the short period that such a course was open to him, before his horses were destroyed.[1]

1916. April.

The affair at Qatiya was a lamentable occurrence, resulting as it did in the total loss of three and a half squadrons of Yeomanry. Otherwise it had no effect, except to delay the progress of the railway for a few days. On the 24th Major-General Chauvel, commanding the A. & N. Z. Mounted Division, was put in command of the advanced positions, including the 52nd Division's post at Dueidar. Romani was reoccupied that day, but General Chauvel, taught by the unhappy experience of the 5th Mounted Brigade, established a considerable camp there and controlled the area by vigorous patrolling rather than by maintaining dangerously isolated detachments at the other oases.

---

[1] It should, however, be noted that Captain Lloyd Baker was in telephonic communication with Br.-General Wiggin after 9 a.m., that he informed the latter of the advance of 600 men in open order with a formed body behind them, and that he was not ordered to retire. He was told that both General Wiggin and Colonel Yorke were moving to his assistance.

The details of the capture of these two posts were not known till after the Armistice, when information became available from officers who had been prisoners of war. This information, which has been embodied in the foregoing narrative, tends to relieve the Yeomanry of the charge of having been completely surprised. It may be said that patrols from Oghratina were not apparently far enough out, and that a mounted outpost of this type should have had standing patrols far ahead in the direction of the enemy. But at Qatiya there was not any suggestion of surprise, and it is difficult to see in what respect Captain Lloyd Baker (who was killed) could have acted differently. In both cases the defence was gallant in the extreme.

The delay to the railway's progress was small. By the 29th April four trains a day were running regularly to railhead, and a special company had been formed to work the line.[1] The subsidiary narrow-gauge line from Port Said had reached Mahamdiyah on the coast. By the 19th May the main line was open for traffic up to Romani,[2] and it was decided to link up Romani and Mahamdiyah by a branch of standard gauge. This was completed by the 9th June. It was now possible to garrison Romani with infantry on a considerable scale, to construct a strong position, and to maintain there a certain amount of artillery for its defence.

NOTE I.

THE COMPOSITION OF THE TURKISH FORCE AT QATIYA.

The composition and strength of the Turkish force is given in detail by the Historical Section of the Turkish General Staff. It was commanded by Colonel Kress von Kressenstein and consisted of the *1st* and *2nd Battalions* and one company *3rd Battalion, 32nd Regiment* (afterwards to distinguish itself at Romani), an irregular camel regiment of four companies, two independent camel companies, a 75-mm. battery of the *8th F.A. Regiment* and two guns of the *9th*, two field ambulances and an ammunition column. Its strength was 95 officers and 3,560 other ranks (2,668 rifles), 6 guns, 4 machine guns, 225 horses, 1,009 dromedaries (presumably riding camels), 756 camels (presumably baggage camels), 96 donkeys. In his Despatches Sir A. Murray estimated the enemy force at 3,500, which is almost exactly its ration strength.

The account of the raid given by Kress is laconic. He writes:
"In March 1916 we heard for the first time that the English were "making a railway from Qantara in the direction of Qatiya. A fighting "reconnaissance, which I carried out in April with two battalions, an Arab "camel regiment and one and a half batteries, against Qatiya and Dueidar, "led to the capture of an English cavalry regiment and half a company of "engineers, and confirmed the accuracy of the reports."

NOTE II.

SIR A. MURRAY'S APPRECIATION.

G.S. Z.33.

15th February 1916.

THE CHIEF OF THE IMPERIAL GENERAL STAFF.
    War Office,
        London, S.W.

I.

Map 8. 1. It is clear that the security of Egypt against an attack from the
ketches A, east is not best assured by the construction of a great defensive position
9. in proximity to the Suez Canal—among other reasons because such a

---

[1] No. 276 Railway Company.

[2] During the week ended 26th May the following tonnage was carried: 1,125 tons supplies, 420 tons engineering material, 960 tons water (215,000 gallons), 150 tons railway material, 150 tons miscellaneous stores, and 60 tons troops (about 700 men).

position is wasteful in men and material. In order to effect the object aimed at, it would be far preferable to push out across the Sinai Peninsula towards the Egyptian frontier, making dispositions for an active defence. Less troops will actually be required for an active defence than for a passive or semi-passive defence of the Canal Zone.

2. In the Sinai Peninsula itself there are four chief points of importance, namely, El Arish, El Hassana, Nekhl, and El Kossaima. The three latter are important road centres—the course of the roads in Sinai being determined by water supply—which any hostile invading force, except one marching by the northern coast road and El Arish, must pass on its way to Egypt. Of the three, El Kossaima is of greater importance than either of the others, for enemy forces, moving down from Syria and Palestine, must pass El Kossaima or between El Kossaima and the northern Sinai Coast, whether the subsequent line of march is *via* Nekhl or El Kossaima.[1]

3. Strategically, therefore, the true base of the defensive zone of Egypt against invasion from the east is not the 80 or 90 miles of the Canal Zone, but the 45 miles between El Arish and El Kossaima.

II.

1. The first factor which it is necessary to weigh is the extent and magnitude of the danger implied in the word "invasion." At present, and during the early spring, it would be possible for the enemy, given adequate arrangements on the Syrian railways, to bring down to Beersheba and to push across the Sinai desert a very considerable force, say, 250,000 men. The water difficulties which would confront him during this season would be reduced to a minimum, and with sufficient previous preparation his other difficulties could be surmounted. We have, however, so far, no definite information of an enemy movement on a really large scale in this direction. Our intelligence does indeed tend to show that the Turks themselves are anxious to undertake the invasion of Egypt, but it also tends to show that their German military advisers in Turkey are averse at the moment to this undertaking. The time at their disposal is already becoming short, even if it be assumed that they have two months for the completion of their preparations and for the inception and achievement of their undertaking. The forces at our disposal for the defence of Egypt are now considerable, and so long as they remain in this country the enemy can have little hope of a successful issue to his enterprise.

2. When once the hot weather begins, the enemy's difficulties will necessarily be largely increased. Heat of itself is no bar to operations; but both men and animals require considerably more water during the hot weather, and the supply of water along the roads which cross the Sinai Peninsula is naturally far more difficult during that period. In the hot weather the enemy will be confined to the existing wells or to carrying the water required by his troops.

3. At El Arish it is estimated that a force of 40,000 to 50,000 troops could be concentrated without experiencing any great difficulty in obtaining water even during the hot season.

It may be noted here that if El Arish were in our occupation we should be in a comparatively advantageous position with regard to water, since the water-bearing area lies comparatively close to the sea and within range of naval gunfire. An enemy attack on El Arish would, on the other hand, be hampered by water difficulties, since it appears that he would mainly have to depend on water supply from the south of Magdhaba (20 miles S.S.E. of El Arish) and from Rafah (28 miles E.N.E. of El Arish).

---

[1] *Sic*. It would appear that "*via* Nekhl or El Hassana" is meant.

It is estimated that it is possible for the enemy to bring up 60,000 men to attack, but he would fight with a comparatively waterless country immediately in rear of him.

If El Arish is not in our possession and the Qatiya district is, the hostile forces advancing from El Arish to, say, Bir El Abd, would be obliged to cross a region of 30 or 40 miles with a very indifferent water supply and to fight with this behind them. The difficulties of the road are also considerable, and it is estimated that the Turks could not bring a larger force than 25,000 men to attack at Bir El Abd after early spring.

If we occupy neither El Arish nor Qatiya it is possible that the enemy might gradually collect troops in the latter district, and with good arrangements and care it is considered that 80,000 men is not an excessive estimate of the number for whom it would be possible to find sufficient water, even in the hot weather.

4. On the central road *via* El Hassana the water supply is very limited. The enemy has been laying a pipe-line from Kossaima towards El Hassana, but the difficulties are apparently very great and it seems doubtful if the prolongation of the pipe-line westwards—certainly beyond El Hassana—is possible ; and even so, El Hassana is about 90 miles from the Canal. A hostile advance on this line in spring or summer would, therefore, appear impracticable for a force of any size.

On the southern roads from Nekhl, where perhaps 20,000 men could be concentrated, there is an almost waterless stretch of 40 miles between Nekhl and Ain Sadr,[1] and a second waterless stretch, also of 40 miles, between Ain Sadr and the Suez Canal, necessitating the carrying of water for an invading force over, say, three stages. The roads are also in bad order at present, and pass through defiles which would render water-transport difficulties very great. It is estimated that these roads could hardly be used in the hot weather by any forces exceeding 10,000 men.

5. To summarize, therefore, the enemy is working upon a very narrow margin of time if he contemplates any really serious efforts during the next six or eight weeks. The fact that the present season has been unusually wet may, indeed, increase this margin, since his difficulties as regards water may perhaps not become serious so early in the year as usual. During the hot season, however, providing that the Qatiya district be occupied by us, the limit of the possibility in this way of an invasion from the east would seem to be an advance of, say, 40,000 troops, with their transport, if the enemy should use all available roads.

III.

1. In the first part of this paper, stress has been laid upon the strategic importance of El Arish. In the second part, the factors limiting the enemy's power to strike have been briefly considered.

In any case the enemy's first step must be to collect his forces, either towards Beersheba, or further south, say about Ma'an, on the Hejaz railway. The latter is not considered a very likely contingency, since the Pilgrim road from Ma'an, to Nekhl is very difficult for wheeled traffic, while the roads from Nekhl to the Canal, as has already been stated, are in bad order, cross a difficult country with little water, and during the hot season will hardly admit of the passage of any large force.

If, however, the enemy concentration should take place in the Beersheba region, his main forces must advance to the invasion of Egypt by way of El Kossaima and El Arish, or between those places.

---

[1] Ain Sadr, or Ain Sudr, halfway between Nekhl and Suez, is just south of the southern limit of Map 8.

2. From the point of view of the permanent security of Egypt, therefore, it is highly desirable that El Arish should be occupied by us with mobile forces of sufficient size :—

   (a) To be able to meet and oppose such enemy forces as might attempt to march against Egypt by the northern coast road.

   (b) To be able to attack in flank any enemy forces attempting to move against Egypt by way of the central or southern roads which cross the Sinai Peninsula, diverging from El Kossaima.

   (c) To be able to undertake rapid offensive operations against enemy concentrations, or the heads of enemy columns, in southern Palestine (Beersheba region).

If El Arish could be held, the permanent occupation of other points in the Sinai Peninsula outside the Canal Zone would appear to be unnecessary, unless the concentration about Ma'an should necessitate reconsideration of the desirability of occupying Nekhl.

3. The importance of El Arish emerges more and more clearly the further the problem is considered. To undertake its occupation immediately in sufficient strength is, however, out of the question. It would be necessary to employ a considerable number of troops, and sufficient camel transport is not yet available to maintain a force of the required size at a distance of seven marches from the Canal. The question of the possibility of supplying the force from the sea from a depot within, or near the eastern end of, the Bardawil Lagoon, has been fully gone into with the Navy; and it has been found that the formation of the coast would render this impracticable.

4. In these circumstances it appears certain that it will be necessary to build a railway for the maintenance of any considerable force pushed out across the northern part of the Sinai Peninsula. Our reliance on the railway, yet to be constructed, necessarily limits the possibilities to a gradual forward movement.

5. The first step seems to be clear, namely an advance to a suitable position east of Qatiya and the construction of a railway to that place. Even apart from the question of El Arish, the occupation of the Qatiya district is most necessary. By pushing out to the neighbourhood of Bir El Abd, east of Qatiya, we should deny this comparatively well-watered region to the enemy. So long as we do not occupy Qatiya it is open to the enemy gradually to concentrate a considerable force within two marches of the Canal; and his force would be limited only by the amount of water obtainable, which is estimated to be sufficient for as many as 80,000 troops, even in summer.

6. Preparations for this preliminary movement are now, therefore, being actively pressed on. The question of the construction of the necessary railway has already been taken up, and it is anticipated that sufficient camels will be available to equip a force of one Division and one Mounted Brigade with camel transport very shortly. A force of the size named is considered sufficient to clear and occupy the Qatiya district and to hold the eastern end of it, with a reserve at Qantara. Once occupied, a Turkish attack on the line of the northern coast road could only be made in very difficult circumstances. As has already been pointed out, the enemy would have to deliver his attack with a 40-mile desert zone, and with bad roads on the line of which the water supply is very indifferent, behind him.

7. Finally, the question arises as to what number of troops it is necessary for us to maintain in Egypt for the defence from the east. At present, and until the hot weather begins, i.e., about 15th April, no very material reduction in the strength of our forces actually in the country is deemed advisable. From the beginning of the hot season, however, it would appear that one Army Corps of three Divisions on the Canal would be sufficient, provided that we held the Qatiya district with one additional Division, and that three Mounted Brigades were available

for all purposes. As the extent of front to be watched and patrolled is extensive, it is necessary that units should be at full war strength, otherwise four Divisions will not be sufficient. It must be remembered that day and night the whole 80-mile length of the Canal has to be carefully watched to prevent the enemy placing mines in the Canal or Bitter Lakes, which feat has already been accomplished, and that every ship and boat passing up and down has to have its guard for the same purpose.

If the reoccupation of El Arish should eventually be practicable, it is considered that, besides an Army Corps and two Mounted Brigades in the Canal Zone, two mobile Divisions and two Mounted Brigades would be needed to undertake an effective offensive-defence from El Arish and to occupy that place. This would involve the retention in Egypt of a fifth Division; but against the disadvantage of increasing the size of the force left in Egypt must be set the fact that a sufficient mobile force operating from El Arish should go far to render the defence of Egypt from the east permanently secure, irrespective of seasons.

A. J. MURRAY,
General, Commander-in-Chief,
Mediterranean Expeditionary Force.

15/2/16.

Sketch 9.

TURKISH RAILWAY COMMUNICATIONS.
August, 1916.

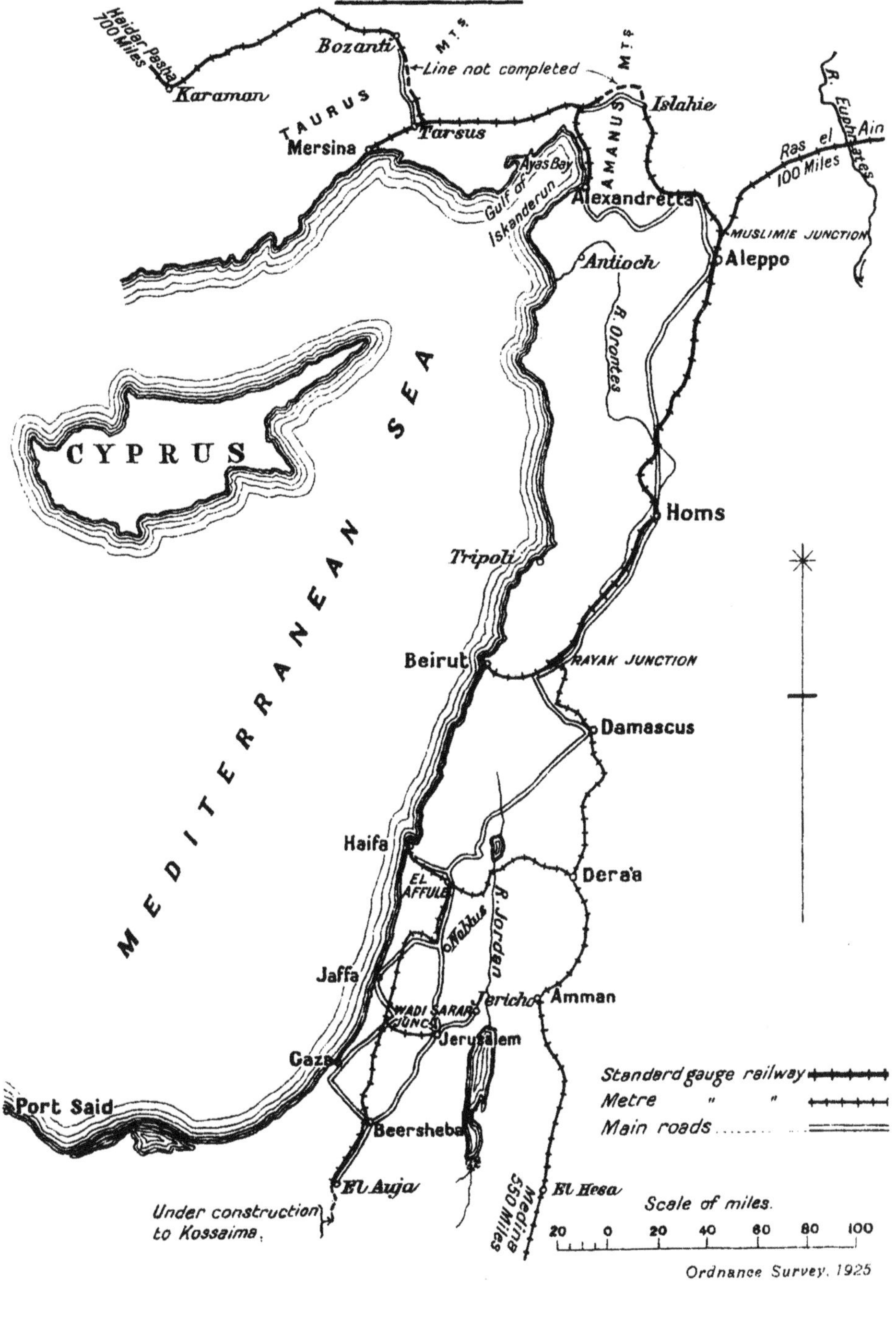

CHAPTER XI.

THE BATTLE OF ROMANI.

(Maps 8, 9, 10 ; Sketches B, 10.)

THE BRITISH OCCUPATION OF ROMANI.

BETWEEN the 11th May and the 4th June the 52nd (Lowland) Division moved to Romani, where a strong position was gradually developed, its left flank on the sea, its right rounded off to cover the new railhead at Romani Station. It was supplied by both the main line from Qantara and the narrow-gauge line from Port Said to Mahamdiyah. A 6-inch pipe-line was laid beside the main railway, but owing to the heavy demands on piping by the Canal Defences, lagged considerably behind railhead. By the 4th June, 17 miles of this pipe had been laid from Qantara, "pipehead" being then west of Pelusium Station. The troops at Romani had therefore still to be supplied with water either by means of trucks from Qantara or by convoys of camels from pipehead. Local water was impregnated with salts to such an extent that it could not be used in the boilers of the engines, and on the 30th June Sir A. Murray informed the War Office that every drop of water drunk at Romani came from the Nile, that the 6-inch pipe was now inadequate, and that he required a 12-inch pipe. This the War Office promised, and three months later the first consignment arrived.

1916.
May-June.
Map 8.
Sketch B.

The mounted troops originally established at Romani, Qatiya, and Oghratina had subsisted on the local well water, but the coming of the extreme summer heat, during which a temperature of 123° Fahrenheit was registered inside a tent, altered the situation. British troops could not now march and fight on the saline water ; the horses often refused it, and, if they drank it, quickly lost condition.[1]

---

[1] A condensing plant was installed at Mahamdiyah to supplement the supply, but it proved expensive in coal and the intake sucked in so much sand that the pipes were choked. When it was finally put into working order the further advance across the desert had begun and its need was almost over.

It must be added that both troops and horses gradually accustomed themselves to the local water, and were able to subsist upon it for short

The defensive position at Romani ran southward from Mahamdiyah along a line of high sand-hills, which marked the eastern edge of an area of very soft and shifting sand. East of this natural line of defence the ground sloped down to much lower dunes and harder sand. Movement here was easier, nor were the dried gypsum pans by which the area was broken, in general serious obstacles. Within sight of the Romani heights were the large groves forming the Qatiya Oasis.

Map 9.

The principal tactical point in the position was a dune known as Katib Gannit, at its southern end, standing 100 feet above its neighbouring hillocks. Between the shore at the western end of the Bardawil Lagoon and Katib Gannit, on the eastern slopes of the Romani heights, were constructed in first line twelve works, on an average 750 yards apart, with another series curving westward, then northward, in the form of a hook, to protect the right or southern flank. The total number of works was eighteen[1]; when fully garrisoned they held from 40 to 170 rifles apiece, with an average of 100 rifles. In addition to Lewis guns an average of two Vickers guns was also allotted to each. The works were prominent, since concealment could not be obtained without sacrificing field of fire. They were well wired, though at the opening of the Battle of Romani the spaces between them were not covered by wire, except on the right of the position.

After the middle of May the heat in Sinai is very great, becoming fiercest between mid-June and the end of July. By night it is reasonably cool, and often cold, but day after day, when once the sun is well up, the desert throws back its heat like metal. Plate-laying on the railway could not in these conditions be carried out after 10 a.m. Worse than

---

periods. Better water than that in existing wells, which were fouled by decaying vegetable matter, was frequently obtained by sinking new ones in their vicinity. The digging of a well in the sand was, however, a long and arduous task. Great saving of time and trouble was effected by the use of the "spear-point" pump, first employed by the Australian Field Squadron. A section of 2¼-inch piping was brought to a point and perforated above that point, the perforation being covered with wire gauze. This was driven into the sand, and additional lengths screwed to it till the required depth was attained, when a service lift-and-force pump was attached. Water was thus obtained without difficulty in any water-bearing area and far more quickly than from most of the wells in the oases.

[1] Maps 9 and 10 show only 16 works; apparently the two remaining were in rear of these.

AIR RAIDS

the sun is the hot southerly wind, or *Khamsin*,[1] which turns all the atmosphere to a haze of floating particles of sand. In camp at Romani the troops suffered severely, but the Scotsmen more than the Australians, many of whom, coming from the ranges of the interior, were accustomed to great summer heat and scanty water supply. No major operations took place within this period, for the Turks retained in Sinai only small scattered garrisons, out of reach of the British force. In the air, however, there was considerable activity. Turkish aeroplanes appeared over the Suez Canal twice during the month of May, dropping bombs on Port Said, but causing no material damage and only 23 casualties to troops and civilians. On the 18th a successful bombardment of the town and aerodrome of El Arish was carried out from the sea and air in reprisal for the first of the Turkish raids. On the 22nd the R.F.C. bombed all the enemy camps on a front of 45 miles parallel to the Canal.

1916.
May-June.

The activity of the Turkish aeroplanes was, however, increasing, and Colonel W. G. H. Salmond, commanding the 5th Wing, planned a big raid on the 18th June upon their aerodrome at El Arish. To gain the advantage of surprise, the eleven British machines kept out to sea until past El Arish, then turned inland and approached their objective from the south-east. Two Turkish machines were destroyed on the ground, two of the ten hangars set on fire, and four others hit by bombs. Successful attacks with bombs and machine guns were also made on several parties of Turkish troops. The British aeroplanes were subjected to heavy fire and three brought down. Of these, one fell into the sea, the pilot being rescued by a motor-boat; a second fell north of the aerodrome and was burned by its pilot, Captain R. J. Tipton, R.F.A., before the Turks could reach him. The third aeroplane was observed on the ground by one of the escorting machines, piloted by Captain S. Grant-Dalton, Green Howards, who landed beside it, took off its pilot, Captain H. A. Van Ryneveld,[2] and carried him 90 miles back to Qantara.

Map 8.
Sketch B.

---

[1] *Khamsin*, fifty. The Bedouin believe this wind blows once every fifty days. It lasts sometimes for only a few hours, sometimes for several days.
[2] Now Colonel Sir H. A. Van Ryneveld, Director of the South African Air Services, who flew from London to Cape Town *via* Cairo in 1920.

On the ground constant patrolling and reconnaissances took place. In one such expedition, to Bir Bayud, 19 miles south-east of Romani, made on the 16th May, a day of particularly intense heat, the 6th A.L.H. narrowly escaped disaster from lack of water, many men lying for hours unconscious in the groves of Qatiya. On the 31st a successful raid on the enemy's post at Bir Salmana, 22 miles E.N.E. of Romani, was carried out by the New Zealand Brigade, supported by the 1st A.L.H. Two Turks were captured and 15 killed, while British aeroplanes caused further loss to the retreating enemy, especially in camels.

During the month of June an operation was carried out from No. 2 Section of the Canal Defences to deny to the enemy the large supplies of water in the Wadi um Mukhsheib and at Moiya Harab, 25 miles east of the Little Bitter Lake, which had been used by the Turks in their attack on the Canal the previous year. A composite force of the 9th and 10th A.L.H. (3rd L. H. Brigade), with detachments of engineers and of the Bikanir Camel Corps, under the command of Lieut.-Colonel T. J. Todd, moved out on the 9th June to the Wadi um Mukhsheib, and a detachment of Middlesex Yeomanry advanced to Moiya Harab. The ancient stone cisterns, sunk beside the wadi's bed to catch its overflow, were pumped dry. Patches of clay which were holding water in large pools were ditched by explosives, to drain off the water into the sand. Three days' work in intense heat disposed of five million gallons of water, the cisterns being then sealed to prevent them from refilling after the next season's rains. As a result, the use by the enemy of the Central Sinai route, by which he had advanced in 1915, was made practically impossible and the area of a serious Turkish offensive narrowed down to the coast route, where preparations had been made to meet it.

At the beginning of June the revolt of the Arabs in the Hejaz against the Turks broke out. This, together with the events which led up to it, will be described in the chapters that follow. One result may be mentioned here: Sir A. Murray was now directed by the C.I.G.S. to consider seriously that advance to El Arish which had previously been merely a vague possibility. Sir W. Robertson did not, however, contemplate that such an advance would be possible before October.

Sketch 10.

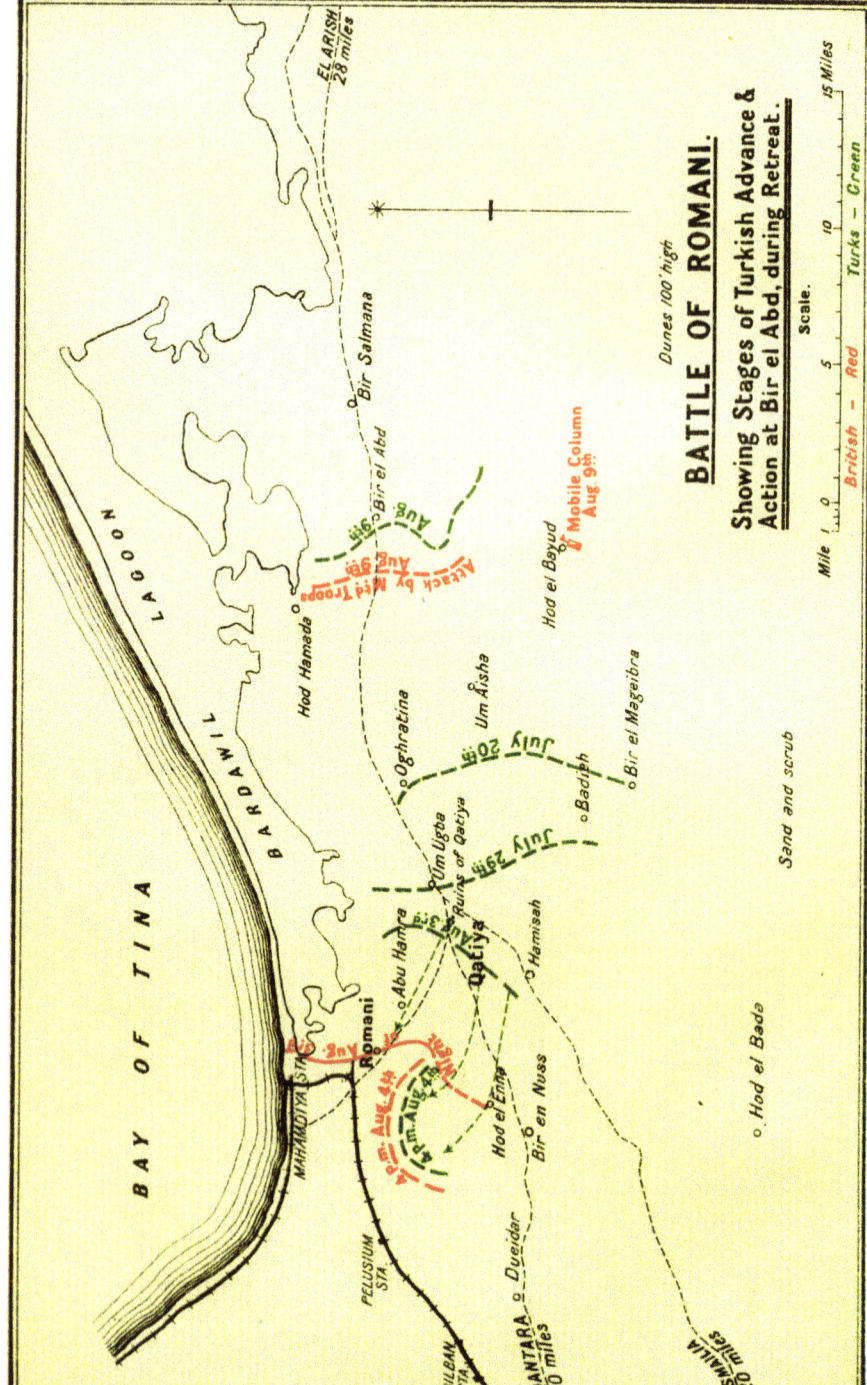

The Turkish Advance.

July opened quietly. Active patrolling was continued, one reconnaissance reaching Bir Salmana on the 9th and finding it unoccupied. The most advanced Turkish camp was at Bir el Mazar, 42 miles east of Romani, where upwards of 2,000 troops were believed to be concentrated, but the garrison showed no sign of aggression. It appeared that, the season being so far gone, the long anticipated Turkish offensive would now be postponed until the winter.

1916.
July.
Map 9.
Sketch 10.

Suddenly the situation changed. On the 17th July enemy aircraft showed great activity over the Romani area. The German aeroplanes were faster and better climbers than any which Sir A. Murray had at his disposal, and though they did not prevent the British machines from reconnoitring the country ahead, they established a definite superiority in the air which was long to endure.[1] On the 19th July a British aeroplane, with Br.-General E. W. C. Chaytor, commanding the New Zealand Mounted Rifles Brigade, acting as observer, discovered that a force estimated at 2,500 had occupied Bir Bayud and that there was a somewhat smaller concentration at Gameil.[2] On the northern route there was a force of equal strength at Bir el Abd, where tents were visible among the groves. Some 6,000 camels were also seen at the camps or moving between Bir el Abd and Bir Salmana. By the morning of the 20th there had been another move forward. Three thousand men were now entrenched at Mageibra, and Bir el Abd had evidently been made an advanced depot for supplies and stores. There was also a small force so far forward as Oghratina, which had grown to 2,000 by the following morning. It was obvious that the Turkish offensive was after all about to be launched.

On receipt of General Chaytor's report, G.H.Q. took steps to reinforce the Romani position, still known as No. 3 Section Canal Defences and commanded by Major-General the Hon. H. A. Lawrence. Two battalions of the 42nd Division were moved up from No. 2 Section to Qantara and the 158th Brigade of the 53rd Division sent out to Romani on the 20th. The troops already at General Lawrence's disposal were the

---
[1] For a statement of the situation, see Note III at end of Chapter. The new German *300th Flight Detachment* is mentioned in Note I.
[2] Gameil, a small oasis, not marked on Map 8 or Sketch 10, is west of Bir Bayud.

52nd Division and the A. & N.Z. Mounted Division, less the 3rd L.H. Brigade. On the night of the 22nd the dispositions in No. 3 Section were as follows :—

On the main position :—155th Brigade on the right (Redoubts 23, 22, 21 and 1 to 5) ; 158th Brigade (less one battalion) in the centre (Redoubts 6 to 10a) ; 157th Brigade on the left, holding the remainder of the line to the sea ; 156th Brigade and one battalion 158th in reserve at Romani Station.

At Romani :—1st and 2nd L.H. Brigades.
At Dueidar :—5th A.L.H.
At Hill 70 :—N.Z.M.R. Brigade (less 5th A.L.H.),[1] and Composite Regiment 5th Mounted Brigade.[2] (Section Mounted Troops.)
At Hill 40 :—1st Dismounted Yeomanry Brigade.

The total rifle strength was about 14,000.

A relatively small proportion of the available artillery had been brought up owing to the shortage of water for the teams. The guns in position, including those sent up within the next few days, consisted of one battery 60-pdrs., two batteries 4·5-inch howitzers, and four 18-pdr. batteries. The Ayr and Leicester Batteries R.H.A., with the A. & N.Z. Mounted Division, brought the total up to 36 guns.[3]

The water supply, which limited the amount of artillery that could be maintained at Romani, had a similar effect

---

[1] The Wellington Regiment was attached at this time and throughout the Battle of Romani to the 2nd L.H. Brigade, and the 5th A.L.H. to the N.Z. M.R. Brigade.

[2] The 5th Mounted Brigade had been in process of reorganization on the Canal after its losses at Qatiya and was gradually being brought up to Hill 70. A composite regiment of two squadrons Gloucester Yeomanry and one squadron Worcester Yeomanry, was moved up on the 20th. The third squadron of the Gloucester Yeomanry was at Pelusium when the Turks attacked the Australian outposts on the 4th August.

[3] Two 18-pdr. batteries 263rd Brigade, in position south of the railway, to fire south and south-east ; one 60-pdr. battery, 2 howitzer batteries 262nd Brigade and one 18-pdr. battery 260th Brigade in the centre, within the loop formed by the railway ; one 18-pdr. battery 260th Brigade on the shore near Mahamdiyah.

The employment of " ped-rails "—short wooden planks fastened to each wheel of the guns and wagons—had greatly increased the mobility of field artillery in the desert. Their object was to distribute the weight resting at any moment on the sand over a considerable surface, and thus minimize the sinking of the wheel. They were used throughout the campaign in Sinai and only removed when the comparatively firm soil of Southern Palestine was reached.

with regard to troops. Sir A. Murray decided not to increase the force of four infantry brigades, but moved up the 160th and 161st Machine-Gun Companies, of the 53rd and 54th Divisions respectively, thus greatly increasing his fire power at a comparatively small cost in water. Meanwhile with the possibility of offensive action before his eyes, he ordered the concentration of a small mobile column of mounted troops and Imperial Camel Corps in No. 2 Section,[1] under the command of Lieut.-Colonel C. L. Smith, Imperial Camel Corps, and assembled the camel transport necessary to enable the 42nd Division to advance into the desert.

1916. July.

The two brigades of the A. & N.Z. Mounted Division at Romani redoubled their activity in patrolling. On the 20th July the 2nd L.H. Brigade, with two guns of the Ayrshire Battery, demonstrated against Oghratina and captured several prisoners, from whom the enemy's order of battle was learnt. It appeared that the Turkish force was commanded by Kress in person and consisted of the *3rd Division*, of which one regiment had proved its marching and fighting qualities at Qatiya, and a regiment of camelry; with a number of special machine-gun companies, heavy and mountain artillery, officered and partly manned by Germans and Austrians.[2] From this date until the opening of the battle one of the two Light Horse brigades at Romani marched out each morning towards Qatiya at 2 a.m., and bivouacked till dawn in front of the position. It then advanced on a wide front until it had drawn the enemy's fire. If the Turkish outposts were weak, they were driven in; if the enemy appeared disposed to counter-attack, the brigade retired slowly. It returned to camp at nightfall, and the second brigade carried out an identical manœuvre next day.

Until the 28th the enemy remained quiet, but that morning he was found to have occupied the Hod um Ugba, 5 miles east of the British line. Lieut.-Colonel W. Meldrum, commanding the Wellington Regiment, proposed to eject him from this position, which did not appear to be strongly held. Approval was given to his suggestion, and a brisk

---

[1] 11th A.L.H. (less one squadron), City of London Yeomanry (less one squadron), 4th, 6th, and 9th Companies Imperial Camel Corps.
[2] Fuller details of the enemy's force, from Turkish sources, are given in Note I at end of Chapter.

attack by two squadrons, supported by two guns and several machine guns, drove the Turks from the hod, with the loss of 8 prisoners of the *31st Regiment*.

The enemy's hesitation, his cautious advance and careful entrenchment of successive positions, was puzzling to G.H.Q., which asked for nothing better than an attack upon the Romani defences. We now know that the long pause was due simply to the fact that the Turks were awaiting their heavy artillery, delayed by the necessity for constructing tracks through the areas of heaviest sand and even then compelled to move by very short stages. But to the British command it seemed possible that Kress was not, after all, contemplating an attack, and that he would content himself with sitting down and blocking the British advance. In this case it was probable that he would soon receive reinforcements, and it was therefore necessary to be prepared to attack him before they arrived. The Commander-in-Chief considered it scarcely possible that the Turks could attack in force elsewhere than on the northern route, and was prepared to reduce the troops in Nos. 1 and 2 Sections to a minimum. He calculated that all his preparations for the equipment of his force with camel transport would be complete by the 3rd August, but he decided to give the enemy another ten days, and instructed General Lawrence to be prepared to attack about the 13th, the date of the full moon, unless himself attacked earlier.

Sir A. Murray also discussed with Vice-Admiral Sir R. E. Wemyss, commanding the East Indies Station, the possibility of a landing at El Arish and the destruction of the Turkish base there. It was proposed to land an infantry brigade 3,000 strong, with detachments of engineers, and to construct entrenchments which it might be necessary, on that treacherous coast, to hold for several days while awaiting weather conditions favourable for re-embarkation. The C.I.G.S. cordially approved of the proposal and in fact agreed with reluctance to its abandonment when the victory of Romani and the retreat of the enemy towards El Arish had altered the situation.

The advance to the Hod um Ugba on the 28th, disturbed though it was by the Wellington Regiment, proved to be the beginning of the Turkish offensive. Next morning the enemy's line again ran through the hod, stretching for a short distance north of the caravan route and about six miles

SIR A. MURRAY'S PLAN

south of it, to a point west of Badieh.¹ By the morning of the 3rd August it was evident that he was at last about to launch his attack, for he had moved forward to Qatiya. His line now ran north-east and south-west, from the Bardawil Lagoon to east of Qatiya, with his left flank thrown well forward.

1916.
3 Aug.

To Sir A. Murray it appeared that the enemy commander was bound down to one plan of operations. It was incredible that he should throw his main weight against the prepared defences. What was anticipated was a containing attack against these defences and an attack with all available strength against the British right south of Katib Gannit. A manœuvre of this nature would obviously expose the Turkish left flank to an attack by mounted troops, an arm in which the British were strong and the enemy weak. To meet an attack designed to turn his right and pass round it against the camps at Romani and the railway, Sir A. Murray's plan was as follows. In the first place, the enemy was to be delayed and made to pay as dearly as possible for every foot of ground won south of Katib Gannit; then, when he was thoroughly committed and, it was hoped, in some degree disorganized, he was to be attacked in flank by the Section Mounted Troops from Hill 70 and Dueidar, and by the 3rd L.H. Brigade from the Canal Defences, while the Mobile Column already described operated more widely against his flank and rear.

The former of these two elements in the scheme of defence was ensured by a concealed prolongation of the right flank south of Katib Gannit. Major-General Chauvel, after a careful reconnaissance, had selected a position from Katib Gannit to the Hod el Enna, some four miles long, with a second position covering the series of parallel gullies, running south-east and north-west, which gave access to the area of soft sand in rear of the Romani defences. No entrenchments were made, as they would have betrayed the position to the active enemy aircraft, but telephone lines were laid down and the officers of the 1st and 2nd L. H. Brigades made themselves thoroughly acquainted with the ground. It was on these two brigades, under the command of General Chauvel, that was to fall the task of

---

¹ See Sketch 10.

holding up the enemy till he could be taken in flank by the rest of the mounted troops, echeloned in rear. These were on the 3rd August disposed as follows :—

    At Dueidar :—5th A.L.H.[1]
    At Hill 70 :—N.Z.M.R. Brigade (less 5th A.L.H.) and 5th Mounted Brigade.[2]
    At Ballybunion, the railhead of the metre-gauge railway from Ballah :[3]—3rd L.H. Brigade.
    At the railhead of the metre-gauge railway from Ferdan :—Mobile Column.

The 42nd Division had been concentrated at Qantara between the 20th July and the end of the month, and by the 3rd August moved out along the railway and disposed as follows :—

    At Gilban Station :—127th Brigade.
    At Hill 70 :—126th Brigade.
    At Hill 40 :—125th Brigade.

As it seemed probable that the enemy would attack next morning, the 1st L.H. Brigade was ordered to occupy at dusk the skeleton position south-west of Katib Gannit, with two regiments in line and one in reserve. The 1st and 2nd L.H. Brigades had had heavy and trying work in the desert heat and were both below strength, so that when horse-holders and other details were deducted neither had more than eight hundred rifles available for dismounted action.

The preparations were now complete. British monitors had been lying off Mahamdiyah for some days, shelling the assembling Turkish force. An armoured train was in a siding at Qantara, ready to assist in the defence of the right flank. All available aircraft had been collected at Ismailia, Qantara, Port Said and Romani.

The Turkish Attack on the 4th August.

Map 10.

    The Turks were fully prepared to play the role allotted to them by the British command. The account given by Kress of his plan of attack shows that it was exactly what

---

[1] This regiment which, as has been stated, temporarily formed part of the N.Z.M.R. Brigade, was sent forward at night to reconnoitre the Turkish left, the Auckland Regiment taking its place at Dueidar.
[2] Still Section Mounted Troops, that is, under General Lawrence's direct command.
[3] See Map 7 (inset enlargement).

had been anticipated. He intended to bombard the line of redoubts with his heavy artillery but to employ only weak infantry detachments against them. His main attack was to be launched against the British right and rear.[1]

1916.
3-4 Aug.

The night of the 3rd August was mild and still. There was a slight haze, but the shimmer of the sand made it possible to distinguish objects moving at a hundred yards' distance. A shot or two fired out in the desert to the south-east had put the long piquet line of the 1st and 2nd A.L.H. thoroughly on the alert, but it was almost midnight when a post reported a large body of men to its front. It afterwards became known that the enemy had followed the 2nd L.H. Brigade in its usual evening retirement from before Qatiya, hoping to pass round the flank of the British position on its heels. The regularity of the Australians' method of patrolling exposed them to a risk of this sort.

As soon as he was assured of the Turkish advance, Lieut.-Colonel J. B. Meredith, commanding the 1st L.H. Brigade, called up his third regiment. Finding the gullies held, the enemy came to a standstill, and there was silence for an hour. Then a sudden heavy fire burst out along the whole front, and, making their way forward in considerably superior strength, the Turks were by 2 a.m. in many places within fifty yards of the Australian line.

The squadrons on the left near Katib Gannit were hard pressed, but it was against Mount Meredith, a high dune in the centre, that the full weight of the attack developed. At 2.30 the Turks charged the hillock with loud shouts. Their masses, visible against the silver sheen of the sand, offered excellent targets to magazine fire and their first assault was beaten back with heavy loss, the fallen rolling down the steep slope. But steady pressure on its flanks speedily rendered the hill untenable, and at 3 a.m. it was abandoned. The squadron to the right of it was now taken in flank and suffered considerable loss, but was ordered to hold its ground until the position in rear was occupied. At 3.30 all the Australians immediately south of the hill, having been forced back upon their led horses, succeeded in mounting, disengaging themselves, and falling back to the second position. The Turks followed up swiftly and a machine gun on Mount Meredith swept the Australian lines.

---

[1] See Note I at end of Chapter.

Day broke, revealing to the enemy how slenderly the position was held and to the Australians that their right was outflanked by strong forces. The second position was therefore abandoned, and the brigade withdrew slowly to Wellington Ridge, troop covering troop, and by steady and accurate fire staving off a general attack with the bayonet, which might have meant the annihilation of the defence. The enemy now opened artillery fire upon the infantry defences and the camps in rear. The shrapnel caused some loss, but the high explosive shell was smothered in the soft sand.

At 4.30 a.m. Colonel J. R. Royston's 2nd L.H. Brigade came up from Etmaler. After its return from reconnaissance, it had almost immediately been ordered to turn out in readiness to support the 1st Brigade. General Chauvel, however, relying on the latter's steadiness,[1] had refused to allow the 2nd Brigade to be committed to the fight until daylight had disclosed the general situation. He now ordered two of its regiments to move up on Colonel Meredith's right. Despite the reinforcement, the enemy's pressure continued and his advance up the valley between Wellington Ridge and Mount Royston, a dune about the same height as Katib Gannit and Mount Meredith, and $2\frac{1}{4}$ miles west of Wellington Ridge, continually forced back the right. Between 5 and 6 a.m. the light horsemen were compelled to retire slowly from the ridge, though the 6th and 7th A.L.H. still held the western edge. Finally, at 6.15, Colonel Meredith was ordered to withdraw his brigade behind the line occupied by the 7th A.L.H. to a position north of Etmaler camp. At 7 a.m. the 6th and 7th A.L.H. retired squadron by squadron from the remainder of Wellington Ridge. The enemy did not appear on the crest until an hour later, but then poured a heavy fire into the camp, only a few hundred yards away. The fire of the Ayr and Leicester Batteries, however, quickly drove him off it, and the immediate danger was averted.

The situation was now somewhat threatening, for the enemy's outflanking movement was steadily progressing, pushing along the slopes of Mount Royston and turning the right of the 2nd L.H. Brigade. Its third regiment, the Wellington M.R., had meanwhile been thrown in. Major

---

[1] It was General Chauvel's old brigade, which he had commanded at Gallipoli.

C. E. Turner, commanding " D " squadron of the Gloucester Hussars at Pelusium Station,[1] saw in the distance infantry moving about Mount Royston. He had had no report as to the situation, but at once marched his squadron towards the advancing enemy. His prompt action checked the outflanking movement, which made no further progress during the next two hours. Ugly as the aspect of the battle appeared, the enemy had already virtually failed in his bold attempt. His programme had been upset by the resistance of the two light horse brigades, his troops were fatigued and having drunk the water in their water-bottles, had now to face the growing heat without any.

1916.
4 Aug.

Meanwhile, frontal attacks had been made on the main defences, but without ever causing anxiety to Major-General W. E. B. Smith, commanding the 52nd Division. At 8 a.m. extended lines of infantry advanced against Work 4. It was evidently the enemy's intention, though his attack was mainly for the purpose of holding the British infantry to their ground, to overwhelm Works 4 and 5 with heavy artillery fire and thus make a breach for an infantry attack. The shelling was heavy and accurate,[2] but the Turkish attack broke down completely 150 yards from Work 4 under the fire of the divisional cyclist company and of the supporting artillery. Subsequent attempts to advance were less resolute.

Headquarters No. 3 Section, at Qantara, had already begun to put in train the movement against the Turkish left. At 5.35 a.m. General Lawrence ordered the 5th Mounted Brigade at Hill 70 to move towards Mount Royston. The Composite Regiment at once moved off and the remainder of the brigade prepared to follow. Then, as the situation became clearer, at 7.25, General Lawrence ordered the N.Z.M.R. Brigade to advance on Mount Royston *via* Dueidar, picking up its outlying regiment (the Auckland) at that point, and to " operate vigorously so as to cut off the " enemy, who appears to have got round the right of the A. " & N.Z. Mounted Division." The 3rd L.H. Brigade at Ballybunion was ordered to move forward to Hill 70 and send one regiment to Dueidar. G.H.Q. at the same time ordered the Mobile Column to march on Mageibra.

---

[1] See footnote 2, p. 180.
[2] At the day's end it was found that 108 shells had fallen inside Work 4 and 61 within the perimeter of its wire defences ; 89 shells in Work 5 and 43 within its perimeter.

While the mounted troops were advancing the fight became almost stationary on the front of the A. & N.Z. Mounted Division. At 10 a.m. it faced south from a point 700 yards north-west of Work 22, north of Wellington Ridge, to the sand-hills north of Mount Royston. As the line had fallen back, the 2nd and 3rd Regiments had come in between the 6th and 7th, and the order from right to left was now 6th A.L.H., 3rd A.L.H., 2nd A.L.H., 7th A.L.H., Wellington M.R. A mile N.N.W. of Mount Royston "D" Squadron, Gloucester Hussars, held its ground. The Composite Regiment, 5th Mounted Brigade, arriving in advance of the rest of the brigade, came up very opportunely on the flank of this squadron, to a position 1,500 yards west of Mount Royston, taking in enfilade a strong body of Turks attacking "D" Squadron and forcing them back to the higher slopes of the hill.

At 10 a.m. General Chauvel, who knew that the N.Z.M.R. Brigade was on its way, but had as yet seen no signs of its advance, sent a staff officer to Br.-General E. S. Girdwood, commanding the 156th Brigade, in reserve, proposing that the latter should move up his fresh infantry to relieve the 1st and 2nd L.H. Brigades, whereupon the Australians, after watering their horses, would swing round the enemy's left flank and co-operate with the New Zealanders and 5th Mounted Brigade in enveloping it. General Girdwood replied, however, that it was the intention of Major-General Smith to make an attack eastward when the moment seemed favourable and that he himself was in reserve for that operation.

The orders received by the N.Z.M.R. Brigade were to move on Dueidar and operate against the enemy's flank. When these orders were issued Mount Royston was not in the enemy's hands, and the situation was different when the brigade approached Dueidar. The enemy's line had now swung round until it faced north, and a dune known as Canterbury Hill, east of Pelusium Station, was the last defensible position between it and the railway. A mile short of Dueidar Br.-General Chaytor received orders to move north to Canterbury Hill. He reached it about 11.30 a.m. and found the Composite Yeomanry Regiment in action against the Turks on Mount Royston. He was still without the 5th A.L.H., which had not received orders of recall and remained out on the Turkish left. Seeing 2,000 of the enemy entrenching on Mount Royston, General Chaytor swung right to attack that position. About the same time the 127th Brigade of the 42nd Division, sent up by rail, began detraining at Pelusium Station.

1916.
4 Aug.

General Chauvel's brigades first found touch with the advancing New Zealanders by heliograph, and then Colonel Royston galloped across and explained the situation. General Chaytor decided to move up between the right of the Australians and the Yeomanry (which was shortly afterwards joined by the remainder of the 5th Mounted Brigade under Br.-General Wiggin) and attack Mount Royston.

Supported by the Somerset Battery, the two New Zealand regiments began an advance upon the hill about 2 p.m. But, moving dismounted over heavy sand, exposed to the fire of an almost invisible enemy, their progress was very slow. At 4 p.m. General Chaytor arranged with General Wiggin to push home the attack an hour later. Lieut.-Colonel R. M. Yorke led one squadron Gloucester Hussars and two troops Worcester Yeomanry at a gallop against the southern spur of Mount Royston and took it, the enemy on the crest not awaiting the onset. Down below large numbers of the enemy were concentrated about a battery of pack guns in action. The teams were shot down by the Gloucester squadron on the crest, and numbers of Turks came running up the ridge, holding their hands up. By 6 p.m. the whole position was taken by the New Zealanders and Yeomanry, who were supported in the final stages of the attack by the leading battalions of the 127th Brigade. Five hundred prisoners and two machine guns in addition to the pack battery were taken, and the outer flank of the enemy's force was completely routed.

Just before the recapture of Mount Royston the enemy on the inner flank had made a last effort to advance across Wellington Ridge, but was driven back by artillery fire. Fresh frontal attacks were also launched upon the main defences, which can have had no other object than of preventing a British advance while the Turkish heavy guns were withdrawn. They broke down completely, the enemy apparently suffering considerable loss.

At 5.5 p.m. Major-General Smith had ordered the 156th Brigade to attack Wellington Ridge on the left of the A. & N.Z. Mounted Division and in conformity with the counter-attack upon Mount Royston. A bombardment of the ridge was begun by the artillery at 6.45 and just before 7 p.m. the 7th and 8th Scottish Rifles moved south from behind Work 23. But it was now becoming dark, and on the rough ground direction was hard to keep. The 8/Scottish Rifles advanced to within a hundred yards of the crest of Wellington Ridge, but was there held up by heavy rifle fire. Br.-General Girdwood ordered the two battalions to advance no further until daylight, but to keep the enemy closely engaged all night, as it appeared to him that by such tactics he might hope to make a larger haul of prisoners in the morning than if the enemy were dislodged and scattered in the darkness.

The day's fighting was therefore over. The Turks, after a bold and skilful attack, had completely failed in their object. So far, they had not lost heavily in prisoners, but the British had at their disposal for the morrow's operations five mounted brigades : one (the 3rd L.H. Brigade) not yet engaged, two (the 5th Mounted and N.Z.M.R. Brigades) still fairly fresh, while the 1st and 2nd L.H. Brigades, after twenty hours in action—but almost all that time dismounted —were still capable of new efforts. There was yet a possibility of destroying the opposing force.

The 1st and 2nd L.H. Brigades spent the night on the battlefield. The N.Z.M.R. and 5th Mounted Brigades withdrew on the water supply and their supply camels at Pelusium Station, where the brigades of the 42nd Division were also assembling. The 3rd L.H. Brigade halted at Hill 70, and the Mobile Force at the Hod el Bada, 14 miles south of Romani Station.

THE PURSUIT ON THE 5TH AUGUST.

Maps 8, 10. Sketches B, 10.

As soon as he was acquainted with the situation, General Lawrence issued orders for a general advance to take place at 4 a.m. next morning. The A. & N.Z. Mounted Division was to press forward with its right on the Hod el Enna and its left in close touch with the 156th Brigade of the 52nd Division, advancing on Mount Meredith. The 3rd L.H. Brigade was to advance towards Bir en Nuss and attack the Hod el Enna from the south, keeping touch with the A. & N.Z. Mounted Division or the 5th Mounted Brigade, which, under the orders of Major-General Sir W. Douglas, commanding the 42nd Division, was to assist in linking up the right of the A. & N.Z. Mounted Division with the 3rd L.H.

RECAPTURE OF WELLINGTON RIDGE

1916.
5 Aug.

Brigade. The 42nd Division[1] was to advance on the line Canterbury Hill to Mount Royston to the Hod el Enna and drive back any opposition to the advance of the mounted troops, while part of the 52nd Division was to act in a similar manner towards Mount Meredith. The G.O.C. 52nd Division was also instructed to prepare for an advance eastwards towards Abu Hamra, which, however, was not to be undertaken without further orders from Section Headquarters.[2]

As day broke on the 5th August the 8/Scottish Rifles, which had passed the night just short of the crest of Wellington Ridge, advanced in company with the 7th A.L.H. and Wellington M.R. on their right. The attack was covered by the 7/Scottish Rifles on the left, who had during the night brought a total of 16 machine guns and Lewis guns into a position from which they were able to sweep the crest and reverse slopes of the ridge. Well as the Turks had fought hitherto, they knew now that they had been abandoned, and the lines of bayonets in the dim light were too much for their exhausted nerves. A white flag was hoisted and a forest of arms held high. Eight hundred and sixty-four men surrendered to the 8/Scottish Rifles and a great number more to the Light Horse and Wellingtons, who breasted the rise a few minutes later. In all, 1,500 prisoners were taken in the neighbourhood of Wellington Ridge. Other bodies of Turks, pinned to the ground by fire from the works further north, were likewise unable to join in the general retirement, and at 6 a.m. a further 119 surrendered to the infantry in Work 3. Most of the prisoners were in a pitiable state of fatigue and had long been without water.

While this rear guard was being rounded up it had become apparent that the Turks were in full retreat. At 6.30 a.m. General Lawrence ordered General Chauvel to take command of all the mounted troops[3] and move in pursuit. But, as already stated, the brigades were somewhat scattered, and the troops of the 1st and 2nd L.H. Brigades had to be collected and mounted. The N.Z.M.R.

---

[1] Only two brigades were ready for the move, and the 126th Brigade remained in reserve at Pelusium Station.
[2] These orders are given in Appendix 6.
[3] That is to say, of the Section Mounted Troops (N.Z.M.R. and 5th Mounted Brigades) and the 3rd L.H. Brigade, but not the Mobile Column, which was under the orders of the G.O.C. No. 2 Section.

Brigade reached Bir en Nuss at 8.30 a.m., where it found the 3rd L.H. Brigade still watering. The latter brigade was ordered by General Chauvel to move on Hamisah, beyond which it had been ascertained that the enemy's left flank extended, though his main body had fallen back on Qatiya. Thence, the brigade was to wheel left towards Qatiya, to co-operate in a general attack by the mounted troops. Its advanced guard moved off to fulfil this mission at 9 a.m.

The general mounted advance began at 10.30. By noon the troops under General Chauvel's command were on a line from west of Bir Nagid to south of Katib Gannit; the 3rd L.H. Brigade on the right, advancing on Hamisah, then the N.Z.M.R. Brigade and the 1st and 2nd L.H. Brigades, with the 5th Mounted Brigade on the left.

There were greater delays before the infantry divisions were on the move. In the case of the 42nd Division this was not of great importance—save that it involved a very trying advance in the heat of the day—because the division's role was only to advance to the Hod el Enna in support of the mounted troops, and it is doubtful whether it could in any event have gone further; actually the Turkish rear guard was routed and largely captured without its assistance being required. But, as a matter of fact, the first message sent to the 127th Brigade, which was to lead the advance, miscarried, and the second, despatched at 2.45 a.m., did not reach it till 5.40 a.m.[1] Nor did the brigade's first-line camels arrive till after this, and the troops had then to fill their water-bottles. The brigade marched at 7.30 a.m. and reached the Hod el Enna between 9.30 and 10 a.m., considerably fatigued. The 125th Brigade at Pelusium, delayed by the troops' ignorance of the handling of camels, moved off at 5.15 a.m. and arrived in rear of the 127th Brigade at 11.15, having suffered still more severely in its longer march.

In the case of the 52nd Division, the delay was more serious. Immediately after ordering General Chauvel to take command of the mounted troops and pursue the enemy, General Lawrence, at 6.37 a.m., sent a message to the 52nd Division instructing it to carry out the advance eastwards on Abu Hamra which had been anticipated in his orders

---

[1] Divisional headquarters had just arrived at Pelusium Station, and there appears to have been extraordinary pressure on the single signal station there. But brigade headquarters was only 4 miles away at Mount Royston.

ADVANCE ON QATIYA

1916. 5 Aug.

of the previous night. On receiving this message General Smith ordered the R.F.C. squadron at Mahamdiyah, which was at his disposal, to reconnoitre while his brigades were completing their preparations. At 10.15 a.m. General Lawrence urgently repeated his order, but it was some time longer before the 155th and 157th Brigades were able to march. Here again the distribution of water from the camel *fanatis*[1] was the chief cause of delay. There was delay also in distributing food to the men, and it was highly necessary that the troops should have a meal after the night's work, with the prospect of a march and possibly a battle in the sun before them. It was not till noon that the 157th Brigade, followed by the 155th, moved out from the defences, and Abu Hamra was not reached till nightfall.

Meanwhile the 3rd L.H. Brigade had gained a striking success against the enemy on the high ground west of Hamisah. The 9th A.L.H. under Lieut.-Colonel W. H. Scott, boldly galloped to within a few hundred yards of the Turkish line and then attacked on foot under cover of the fire of the Inverness Battery and machine guns. The enemy hastily abandoned his position, but 425 prisoners and seven machine guns were captured. Unfortunately the brigade then came under fire of the heavy guns behind Qatiya, and withdrew late in the afternoon to Bir Nagid, 2½ miles west of Hamisah, before receiving an order from General Chauvel to protect his right.

Between 12 noon and 1 p.m. the four brigadiers of the N.Z.M.R., 1st and 2nd L.H. and 5th Mounted, Brigades reconnoitred the enemy's position from a sandy ridge 2 miles west of Qatiya. Many stragglers had been passed in the course of the advance, and it seemed possible that the enemy holding the position was in a demoralized condition and that brusque tactics might result in large captures of men and guns. It was accordingly decided that the three Australian brigades should advance mounted on Qatiya, while the 5th Mounted Brigade, also mounted, attacked the enemy's right flank.

The three brigades advanced on Qatiya at 3.30 p.m., the Yeomanry on the far left. Reaching the edge of the

---

[1] *Fantasse*, plural *fanatis*, an Arabic word adopted by the Army. The *fantasse* was a small metal tank of which each camel carried two. It had a capacity of 12 gallons. The water supply was carried by the 1st-Line camels, and each division had also a camel convoy with one day's water.

white gypsum bed which lay before them, they formed line and, fixing bayonets to give at least moral effect to mounted action, advanced at a gallop, cheering loudly. But as the oasis was neared the ground became so swampy that the horses were at once checked. The regiments then dismounted and continued the advance on foot. The 5th Mounted Brigade (which was, unlike the others, armed with the sword) likewise found a mounted advance impossible owing to the intensity of the enemy's fire and was obliged to send back its horses.

Of the expected demoralization in the Turkish ranks there was no sign. Their fire was hot and well directed, while their artillery out-gunned the supporting Ayr and Somerset Batteries. By sunset the advance had ceased, seeing which, from his position 3 miles in rear, General Chauvel ordered a retirement to Romani.

When the 1st and 2nd L.H. Brigades reached camp some of the horses had not been watered for sixty hours. The men of the 2nd and 3rd A.L.H. had been during practically the whole of that period in action or in the saddle. Both sides were almost at their last gasp. While the British mounted troops were moving back to Romani, men sleeping as they rode, the Turks were struggling back to Oghratina under cover of darkness.

The infantry brigades were disposed for the night as follows:—The 155th and 157th Brigades at Abu Hamra, the 127th Brigade at Hod el Enna, the 125th Brigade on its left, in touch with the 156th Brigade, which had its left on Work 21. The Mobile Column, which had found Mageibra evacuated, spent the night there.

The End of the Pursuit.

The foresight of Kress in preparing successive lines of defence with each step forward was rewarded after his defeat at Romani. He had lost between three and four thousand prisoners, but he had saved all his artillery except one battery and had kept his tired troops in hand. He had fought one successful rear-guard action at Qatiya and was now prepared to meet an assault at Oghratina.

General Lawrence's orders for the 6th August directed the mounted troops (less the 1st and 2nd L.H. Brigades, whose horses were unfit to move) to press forward vigorously

SUFFERINGS OF THE INFANTRY

1916.
6 Aug.

against the enemy, who was believed to have left a rearguard of one regiment on the Qatiya line, and to attempt to cut off the retreat of men and material. The 42nd Division was to advance eastwards at 4 a.m. and occupy the line from Bir el Mamluk to Bir Qatiya, supporting the mounted troops as required. The 52nd Division was to advance from Abu Hamra at the same hour and prolong the line of the 42nd to the north-east. It was stated that Section headquarters would move to Romani at noon.[1]

At dawn the N.Z.M.R. Brigade, followed by the 5th Mounted Brigade, advanced on Oghratina, but found the enemy as well placed as on the previous day. The 3rd L.H. Brigade on the right advanced in the direction of Badieh, but the Turkish left was well secured and little progress could be made.

Meanwhile, the 42nd and 52nd Divisions had carried out their orders, but there was never the remotest chance that they would be able to support the mounted troops against the Oghratina position. The heat was again terrific, and the heavily burdened infantry—especially that of the 42nd Division, not yet hardened to desert conditions or trained in the conservation of water—suffered tortures on its march. The 127th Brigade did not reach Qatiya till evening was drawing on, and from it alone 800 men had fallen out by the way. The 125th, 155th and 157th Brigades also had many casualties from the sun. The medical services worked their hardest, but their efforts did not suffice. Next day it was necessary to employ the Bikanir Camel Corps, a detachment of Yeomanry and even aeroplanes to search the desert for the unfortunates who had fallen out on the march and now lay upon the sand, often in a state of delirium. The four brigades struggled on to the line upon which they had been directed, but that was the end of the pursuit so far as the infantry was concerned. It was now, indeed, obvious that its employment was useless in the present conditions, and, if persisted in, would cause many deaths. In the course of the day the Mobile Column had been in touch with the enemy between Bayud and Mageibra, but could make no impression on his flank.

On the 7th August the same three mounted brigades again probed the enemy's position at Oghratina, but once

---
[1] Appendix 7.

again found it too strong. Next morning it was discovered that the position had been evacuated, and patrols found the enemy back upon the old position at Bir el Abd, where he had first appeared three weeks earlier. On this day the Mobile Column did succeed in getting round the enemy's flank but was too weak to embarass him seriously, and fell back at night to Bir Bayud.

To General Chauvel it appeared that there was still a possibility that a bold attack on the enemy's position would be successful, if all the mounted troops were put at his disposal. His plan, to which General Lawrence gave his approval, was as follows :—The 1st and 2nd L.H. Brigades, now restored by their rest, were to march out to Qatiya under the command of Colonel Royston, water there, march through the night to the Hod Hamada, 4 miles north-west of Bir el Abd, timing their movement so as to arrive at 3 a.m. on the 9th August. There they were to bivouac for an hour and a half, and then advance to a point 2 miles north-east of Bir el Abd, to co-operate with the N.Z.M.R. Brigade in an attack on the enemy's position at 6.30 a.m. The 3rd L.H. Brigade was to attempt to work round the enemy's left flank and cut off his retreat ; the 5th Mounted Brigade was to be in reserve.

The scheme was in the nature of a gamble. If the enemy were demoralized, it had a chance of success ; if not, very little, since it involved an attack supported by four horse artillery batteries on a prepared position held in superior strength and covered by double the number of guns, including heavy howitzers, and strong in machine guns.[1] Yet it appeared a legitimate gamble, because the attacking troops were more mobile than the defence and could be drawn off if the task was found to be beyond their capacity.

1916.
9 Aug.
The four attacking brigades began their advance before daylight, the 3rd L.H. Brigade leading on the right with the object of finding and turning the Turkish left. The New Zealanders in the centre advanced at 4 a.m., with a gap of a mile between them and the 3rd Brigade. The remaining two Australian brigades moved off at 5 a.m., with the

---

[1] The five brigades of General Chauvel's force, exclusive of horse-holders, did not number more than 3,000 rifles. The enemy had probably double that number at Bir el Abd.

ATTACK ON BIR EL ABD

intention of enveloping the Turkish right while the New Zealanders gripped the centre. As these brigades came up into line, their left on the Bardawil Lagoon, there was a further gap of half a mile between their right and the New Zealanders. The four brigades covered a front of 5 miles, which, counting the 5th Mounted Brigade in reserve, gave them less than a rifle to three yards of frontage.

1916.
9 Aug.

By 5 a.m. the New Zealanders, advancing astride the caravan route, had driven in the enemy outposts and reached some rising ground which overlooked Bir el Abd and the Turkish centre. But the enemy quickly realized how thin was the line opposed to him and at 9 a.m. issued from his trenches to counter-attack. The fire of the Somerset Battery and of the brigade machine guns checked his advance, but a hot fight for fire supremacy followed and the New Zealanders found it extremely difficult to maintain their position. The Australian brigades on right and left were likewise held up.

At 7.30 the Turks again attacked, making for the gap between the New Zealanders and the 2nd L.H. Brigade, but the breach was partially closed by a squadron of the the 5th A.L.H. from reserve, and the Turkish advance came to a standstill. A little later General Chauvel, seeing that the 3rd L.H. Brigade on the right was unable to fulfil its mission of turning the Turkish flank, ordered it to close in towards the New Zealanders.

Turkish transport could be seen moving eastward from Bir el Abd; columns of smoke were pouring up from burning stores. It was therefore clear that the enemy was uneasy regarding his power of resistance. The New Zealanders redoubled their efforts, but only succeeded in advancing sufficiently to expose their line to flanking attacks, as the Australian brigades were unable to conform to the movement. By 10.30 all progress was over. Moreover, Br.-General Chaytor, in view of renewed pressure on the gap on his left, was compelled to ask for assistance, whereupon the Warwick Yeomanry was sent to him, one squadron dashing up at a gallop to a position on his left.

The enemy, realizing now that he could hold his position, returned to the offensive at midday, launching another heavy attack upon the Canterbury and Auckland Regiments and the squadron of the Warwicks. Again he was beaten back, but by 2 p.m. the attack had extended to the British left flank. The Ayrshire Battery, supporting Colonel Royston's force, came under very heavy shell fire and lost so many horses that for a short time it was immoblized and ran some risk of capture, the riflemen in front of it having been compelled to give ground. Eventually the guns were withdrawn, but only just in time, as Colonel Royston's troops were now retiring. A further withdrawal of the 3rd L.H. Brigade on the right made the situation of the New Zealanders critical.

At 5.30 p.m. General Chauvel gave orders for a general retirement. It has been remarked that he had decided upon the attack only because the mobility of his troops gave them an opportunity to disengage themselves if necessary. But it was now proved that for dismounted cavalry in action at comparatively short range against superior numbers to break off the fight is no easy matter. It was only their tenacity and the welcome fall of darkness that saved the New Zealanders. The Machine-Gun Squadron, under Captain R. Harper, had at the end of the action all its guns in line, some of them firing at a range of one hundred yards. Under cover of these machine guns and of squadrons of the 5th Mounted Brigade the brigade was finally able to withdraw. The British losses in the action were just over three hundred, including 8 officers and 65 other ranks killed.

General Lawrence was anxious that the force should bivouac as near as possible to Bir el Abd, in case another attack should be practicable next day. But General Chauvel, in view of the strength of the Turkish position and the exhaustion of his troops, felt compelled to withdraw to Oghratina, where the force bivouacked, leaving the 3rd L.H. Brigade out to watch Bir el Abd.

The Mobile Column had not been placed under General Chauvel's orders and co-ordination had had to be arranged through Section headquarters. Owing to failure of communications it did not directly co-operate in the action at Bir el Abd. It had, however, a sharp brush with an enemy at Hod el Bayud in the morning, the Turks leaving 21 dead on the field.

There was no further serious fighting. Bir el Abd was found evacuated on the 12th August and the enemy back upon a new position at Salmana, 5 miles to the east, where he was engaged by the horse artillery batteries. He then drew off to his starting point, El Arish, leaving an outpost at Bir el Mazar.

The Results of the Battle.

Romani was a considerable British victory. The enemy completely failed in his object and lost nearly four thousand prisoners, a mountain battery, 9 machine guns, 2,300 rifles and a million rounds of ammunition, 100 horses and mules, 500 camels, and two complete field hospitals. At Bir el Abd he destroyed a great quantity of his own stores. Judging by the number of Turkish dead found, Sir A. Murray put his total casualties at 9,000, and though according to the evidence of the enemy they were much lower, the number of prisoners alone represents nearly a quarter of the force.[1] In contrast to these heavy losses, the British casualties numbered only 1,130, with a low proportion of killed and a very small proportion of missing.[2]

Nevertheless it was disappointing that the enemy should have been able to retire with his force in being and his artillery practically intact, after a complete defeat which had appeared to offer opportunities for his destruction. The causes of his escape will, it is hoped, have been made clear by the foregoing account, but it may be well to recapitulate them shortly.

In the first place, the retreat, especially the withdrawal of the heavy guns, was undoubtedly conducted with great skill by Kress and his staff.[3] The devotion of the troops, their extraordinary powers of endurance and of marching in the sand and heat, their swift restoration when they had fallen back on water and supplies, however meagre, constituted another important factor.

---

[1] Liman states that the losses were one third of the force. This would be about 5,500 if only the attacking force at Romani is counted, or perhaps 6,000 if a fresh regiment believed to have been engaged at Bir el Abd is included.

[2]

	Killed.	Wounded.	Missing.
Officers	22	81	1
Other Ranks	180	801	45

Of these losses the majority were in the A. & N.Z. Mounted Division. It is improbable that more than about twenty of those reported missing fell into the hands of the enemy.

[3] Kress's chief staff officer was apparently a Turk, Major Kadri Bey.

In the second place, Sir A. Murray's carefully prepared plan of enveloping the Turkish left had, as has been shown, to be modified and weakened owing to the Turkish advance through the skeleton position held by the 1st and 2nd L.H. Brigades having been more rapid than had been anticipated. In the words of his Despatch, "the result of the somewhat "rapid advance of the Turks from the south was that General "Lawrence was obliged to divert the cavalry originally "destined to operate against the enemy's rear to strengthen "the line of resistance to the north." Br.-General Chaytor, it will be recalled, first received orders to move through Dueidar on Mount Royston, to take the enemy in flank and rear, but the progress of the Turks north-east of Mount Royston made it necessary for him to swing north-east to Canterbury Hill, and his attack was eventually almost a frontal movement. Yet it is possible that had Sir A. Murray's intentions been strictly carried out, without regard to the threat to the railway, the operations of the mounted troops would have resulted in a far greater haul of prisoners, and the main force of the enemy would have been virtually destroyed. Sir A. Murray himself had never been greatly concerned for his communications, considering that the Turks would be worn out by their exertions and exhausted by the heat if they ever reached them, and recognizing that a blow against the left flank or even left rear of the enemy would be infinitely more devastating than a frontal attack.

With regard to the question of co-ordination between infantry and cavalry, General Lawrence had decided, after careful consideration, not to move his battle headquarters to Romani, and did not do so till noon on the 6th August. At Qantara he was in communication with all parts of his front and behind the troops waiting at their water supply for the counter-attack.[1] Had he felt that circumstances permitted him to move earlier to Romani, it is possible that the delays on the 5th August might have been reduced. At least he would have seen why his reiterated orders to

---

[1] The lines of cable communication were:—(i) Qantara—Pelusium Station—52nd Divisional Headquarters at Romani; (ii) Qantara—Port Said—Mahamdiyah—Romani. The first was extremely congested and also interrupted by shell fire during the battle; the second proved slow. Communication between the 52nd Division and its brigades was excellent, that in the 42nd Division, which had recently been moved out, not nearly so good.

advance were not more quickly obeyed. Even then it is by no means certain that the infantry could have been moved forward in time to grip the retreating enemy, owing to the difficulties of water supply and—in the case of the 42nd Division—the inexperience in handling camels. Once on the move, the British infantry proved incapable, in the intense heat and soft sand, of approaching the speed of the Turks. Indeed, Sir A. Murray, in a telegram to the C.I.G.S. on the 8th August, stated that the latter could march almost as fast as his mounted troops.[1]

Yet another factor, though probably of less importance, was a certain lack of co-ordination in the movements of the mounted troops. The failure of the 3rd L.H. Brigade to support General Chauvel on the morning of the 5th August was serious, as this brigade constituted his freshest troops. The fact that Colonel Smith's Mobile Column was never under General Chauvel's command has been criticised, but the point is largely theoretical. Its failure to co-operate usefully, though it was boldly handled, was, like that of the 3rd L.H. Brigade on the 5th, due to difficulties of communication, owing to the fact that it was operating so wide on the flank.

Regrettable as the escape of the Turkish main body was, the enemy had suffered heavy defeat, the full consequences of which only appeared some time later. The Battle of Romani marks the end of the campaign against the Canal. Further attacks might be projected in Constantinople, but they were always found to be impracticable. The offensive had passed from the enemy. In the next few months Sir A. Murray, advancing steadily and methodically, was to drive him back across the Egyptian frontier and advance on his heels into Palestine.

---

[1] "I cannot pursue with all the vigour I should like, because my "infantry and the horses of the Mounted Division are exhausted. There "were 800 men missing in one brigade of the 42nd Division on arrival at "Qatiya, after a short march on 6th August. I am informed by the General "Officer Commanding 52nd Division that many of his men are physically "quite incapable of making a sustained effort. My cavalry are hardly "faster in the desert than the Turkish infantry, who are fine active men in "good condition. In other respects the situation is quite satisfactory, but "I should have liked to have hunted the Turks east of Bir el Abd. Con- "sidering that we are operating in the Sinai Desert in the month of August, "I think you may feel assured that we are doing, and shall continue to do, "all that is physically possible. Myself and all ranks have much "appreciated your message."

NOTE I.

TURKISH AND GERMAN FORCES ENGAGED.

Germany was now able to assist her Turkish ally with more than the few staff officers who had represented her first contribution in Palestine. For the attack on Egypt she had organized a contingent of all arms and auxiliary services. This force received the code name of "Pasha," and later, when preparations were made to despatch a second and stronger contingent, was known as "Pasha 1." Its constitution was as follows:—

A machine-gun battalion of 8 companies;[1]
5 anti-aircraft groups;
60th Battalion Heavy Artillery:—[2]
   1 battery 100-mm. guns [2].
   1 battery 150-mm. hows. [4].
   2 batteries 210-mm. hows. [2 each].
2 trench-mortar companies;
300th Flight Detachment;
Wireless detachment;
3 railway companies;
2 field hospitals;
A number of mechanical transport companies for work in the Taurus.

Austria provided two mountain howitzer batteries of six guns each.

All the above units, with the exception of two 210-mm. howitzers, the trench mortars, (and, of course, the railway and mechanical transport companies) took part in the expedition to Romani. The remainder of the force consisted of the *3rd Division* (of twelve battalions), a Turkish regiment of camelry, the *3rd Regiment of Mountain Artillery* (three 4-gun batteries), and auxiliary services. The ration strength was about 16,000. In addition to the above there is some evidence that the *81st Regiment* of the *27th Division* advanced as far as Bir el Abd and took part in the defence of the position there. Nearly 5,000 camels and 1,750 horses accompanied the columns.

The object of the expedition was not to cross the Canal, but to capture the Romani position and then establish strong entrenchments opposite Qantara and bring the Canal under the fire of the heavy artillery. Liman (p. 183) describes the objective as "not whole and not half; it makes one think of a man trying to wash his hands without wetting his fingers." But it appears that further troops were to have been brought across Sinai had the first attack succeeded.

The advance was made in three successive columns on account of the scanty water supply, the troops marching by night. The transport of the heavy guns was an extraordinary feat. According to prisoners' reports, boards were laid down over the smaller islands of soft sand and picked up again when the wheels had passed over them. Over large areas of this nature tracks for the wheels of the gun-carriages were dug and packed tight with brushwood. Considerable quantities of ammunition, both artillery and small arm, must have been carried, for it was used without stint at Romani. It is believed, however, that the supply ran short after the 4th August.

---

[1] Five companies according to Steuber, the official German historian, 8 according to others, Kress speaks of "personnel and matériel for 8 companies," and it seems certain that 8 of 4 guns each were formed, with the addition of Turkish personnel as drivers, etc.

[2] The personnel of the batteries was apparently German as to officers, N.C.O.s and leading numbers, the remainder Turkish.

NOTE II.

DISTRIBUTION OF E.E.F., 27TH JULY, 1916.

(Smaller Units, R.A., and R.E. not included.)

Eastern Frontier :—
No. 1 Section.—8th Mounted Brigade.
                54th Division (less 163rd Brigade).
                20th Indian Brigade.
                29th Indian Brigade.
No. 2 Section.—3rd L.H. Brigade (brought into No. 3 for Battle of Romani).
                160th Brigade (53rd Division).
                163rd Brigade (54th Division).
                British West Indies Brigade.
No. 2a Section.[1]—42nd Division (brought into No. 3 for Battle of Romani).
No. 3 Section.—A. & N.Z. Mounted Division (less 3rd Aust. L.H. Brigade).
                5th Mounted Brigade.
                52nd Division.
                158th Brigade (53rd Division).
                1st Dismounted Brigade.

Western Frontier :—
6th Mounted Brigade.
22nd Mounted Brigade.
Part of 53rd Division.
2nd Dismounted Brigade.
4th Dismounted Brigade.

NOTE III.

THE STATE OF THE ROYAL FLYING CORPS IN EGYPT AT THE TIME OF THE BATTLE OF ROMANI.

The 5th Wing R.F.C., had two squadrons only in Egypt at the time of the Turkish advance: No. 14 Squadron, with detachments at Ismailia, Qantara, Port Said and Sollum ; and No. 1 A.F.C. Squadron, with two flights at Suez, one at Kharga, and one forming at Heliopolis.

From the 19th July onwards all available machines were concentrated at Ismailia, Port Said and Qantara, even the half-flight at Sollum flying to Ismailia. An advanced landing ground was established at Romani. Continuous reconnaissance was carried out from this date onwards. The enemy's machines were single-seater Fokkers and two-seater Aviatiks, and were much faster than the B.E.2.C's, which formed three-fourths of the British aeroplanes, and five miles an hour faster even than the De Havilands, of which there were only three in Egypt. The fact that the Fokkers had interrupter gear, enabling the machine gun to fire through the propeller, gave them a further important advantage. Despite this fact, the British air service was able, from the beginning of the operations to the end, to give a considerable amount of information as to the enemy's movements. During the period of the operations it had, however, five machines damaged in fighting and one destroyed.

---

[1] This Section was formed on 16th June 1916, under the direct command of G.H.Q. Its area was between the northern boundary of No. 2 Section, and a line drawn east through Kilometre 50, south of Qantara. It was abolished on the evening of July 27th.

NOTE IV.

THE EVACUATION OF THE WOUNDED.

The evacuation of the wounded in a terrain such as Sinai was of very great difficulty. Neither motor ambulances nor horsed ambulances could be employed. At the period of the Battle of Romani no ambulance trains had yet been taken across the Canal, so that the evacuation of wounded from Romani, and from Mahamdiyah on the light coast railway, had to be carried out on open trucks. However, the distance which wounded had to be carried by rail was comparatively short, since No. 31 General Hospital was in the Canal Works on the east bank at Port Said, and No. 26 Casualty Clearing Station also east of the Canal, at Qantara East, the starting point of the desert railway.

The majority of the wounded and the only cases that caused difficulty were from the A. & N.Z. Mounted Division. The division had four mounted field ambulances: the New Zealand, and 1st, 2nd, and 3rd Australian Light Horse Field Ambulances. Prior to the battle mobile sections of each of these were organized with eight sand-carts (a two-wheeled cart with an awning) and a number of camel *cacolets*.[1] Sand-sledges, which the Australian troops, it is claimed by their official historian, were the first to use, were also employed. The tent divisions were immobile and remained in positions further back as main dressing stations. The camel transport was found unsuitable in front of these main dressing stations, and sand-carts and sledges were chiefly employed between them and the advanced stations near the firing line. The wounded suffered very severely during their transport to Qantara in the intense heat.

---

[1] Camel *cacolets* were of two kinds: a small collapsible chair for sitting cases, and a sort of bed for lying cases. Both were carried slung to a camel, one each side.

CHAPTER XII.

THE ARAB REVOLT AGAINST TURKEY.

(Sketch 11.)

ISLAM, ARABIA, AND TURKEY.

THERE has in the preceding chapters been allusion to the effect of the war upon Islam, and to the danger lest the proclamation of *Jihad* by the Sultan of Turkey should unite Moslems against the Allies and stir the many millions of his faith in the empires of Great Britain and France. In Chapter XI reference was made to the outbreak of the Arab revolt against Turkey. This revolt and its political genesis must now be described; its later stages will be followed in the volume recording the operations in Palestine of the winter of 1917 and 1918, to which they are related. In Moslem countries religion and the civil power have always been closely connected,[1] and the Sultan of Turkey had for centuries been the recognized head of orthodox Islam. It is therefore desirable, before dealing with Arab politics and the Arab revolt, to touch, as briefly as possible, upon the rise of Islam and the events which established the Sultan of Turkey as head of a religion of Arab foundation.

Mohammed, the Prophet of God, was an Arab of the tribe of the Quraish, born at Mecca in A.D. 570, who preached a new faith to the pagan tribes of Arabia: a pure monotheism, which offered a better guide to life and finer ideals than they had known hitherto, but was yet simpler, more easily understood and less unworldly than Christianity. His religious teachings were recorded from memory in the Koran after his death, which is believed to have occurred in A.D. 632 or in Year 11 of the Hegira,[2] according to the Moslem calendar.

---

[1] Moslems, in fact, theoretically make no distinction between civil and religious authority. The Khalif, or " successor " to the Prophet, was also *Imam*, " leader," and *Amir el Muminin*, " Commander of the Faithful " ; supreme in civil, legal and military administration, and leader in public worship.

[2] The accepted English form, which may be more exactly transliterated as *hijra*, meaning departure from one's country. The Mohammedan era dates from the Prophet's flight from Mecca to Medina.

After his death the leadership of the new religion passed to his " successor " (the literal translation of the word " Khalif "). The first three Khalifs were not of the Prophet's family, and one, Othman, not even of his clan, but thereafter these qualifications were considered necessary. The Khalifate was at first elective, but eventually became in practice largely hereditary. The faith spread very rapidly, advancing at the expense not only of paganism, but to some extent also of Christianity.

After the short rule at Medina of the early Khalifs, for the most part old men when they succeeded to the office, the first Ommayyad[1] Khalif rose to power in A.D. 660, with his capital at Damascus. Thirteen Ommayyad Khalifs reigned at Damascus and then the Abbasid[2] dynasty arose, with its capital first at Damascus, then at Baghdad. By this time one of the great empires of the world's history had been created by the swords of a long succession of fighting Khalifs. The dynasty, coming under control of the Seljuk Turks in the middle of the eleventh century, fell before the Mongols in 1258, but Abbasid Khalifs maintained a shadowy power in Egypt till the Ottoman Sultan Selim captured the last in 1517. It has generally been accepted that the title of Khalif was held by the Sultan in virtue of succession to this captive Khalif, who died in 1538, but modern research has shown that the title had long been assumed by him and had descended from Sultan to Sultan. It was the temporal power of the Turks, first dominating, then succeeding, the crumbling Arab empire, which secured them their spiritual power and placed a prince, not of Arab birth, at the head of the orthodox Mohammedan faith. The Turkish Khalif was accepted for practical reasons: temporal power has always been recognized by Mohammedans as desirable in the Khalif, and no other Mohammedan ruler rivalled the Sultan in this.

It is not necessary here to do more than mention the chief great schism of Islam and the division of believers into the two main sects of Sunni, the orthodox, and Shiah, who believe that the Khalifate is in abeyance. But it may be noted that there has always been considerable enmity

---

[1] That is, in the succession and line of Omar, the Prophet's son-in-law.
[2] Descended from Abbas, the Prophet's uncle.

Sketch II.

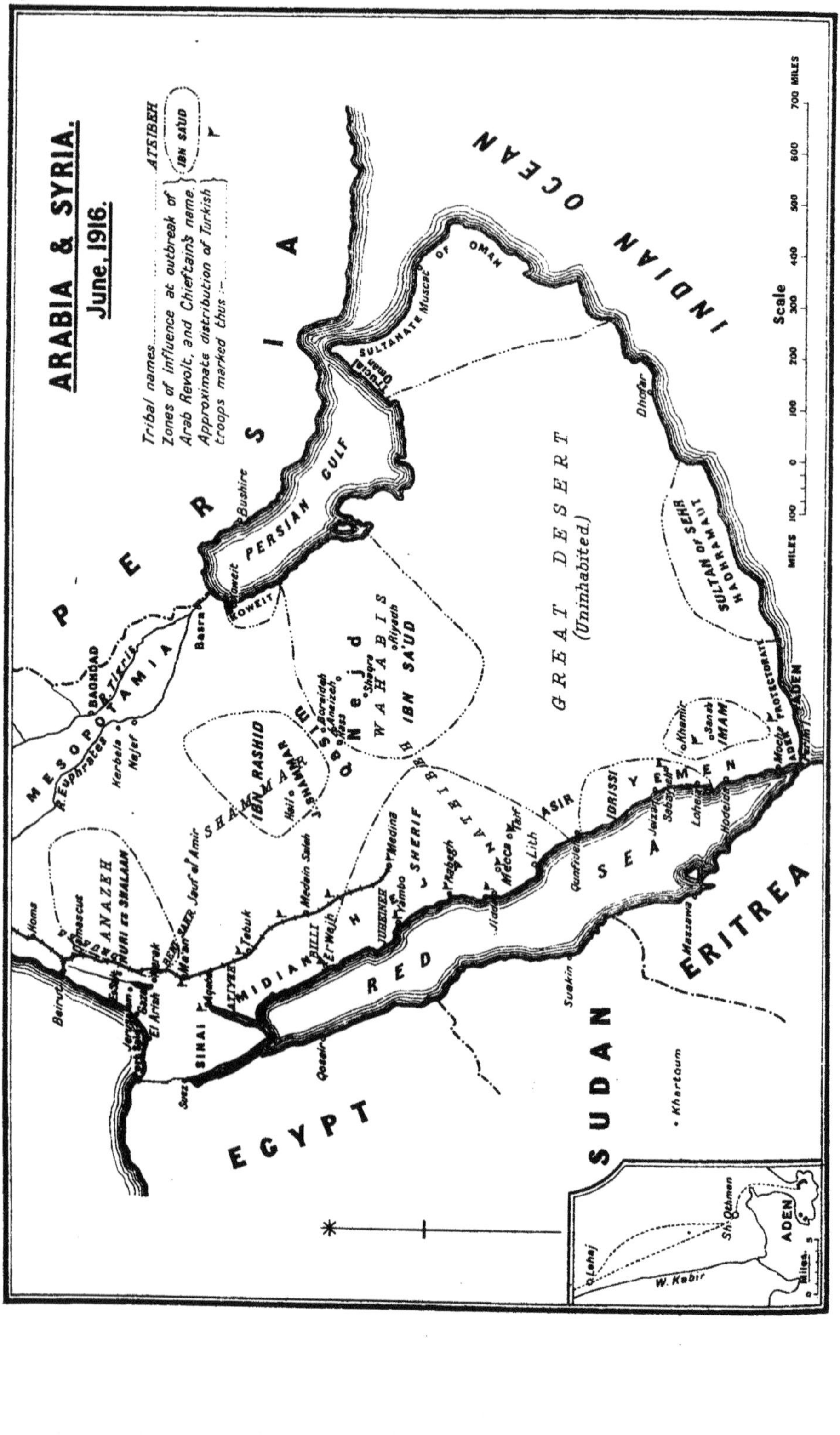

Ordnance Survey, 1928.

THE WAHABIS

between Sunni and Shiah and that it would require very powerful influences to bring them together. There are other divisions of Islam of less importance, in addition to Senussism, which has already been considered, but the only one which concerns this history is Wahabism. The Wahabis form an extremely puritanical and militant sect within the boundaries of orthodoxy. Arising in Central Arabia in 1760, this sect has periodically waged war on the sins and laxities of Islam and has at times acquired great power. Its activities before the war will be described a little later, and the part it played in the course of the year 1918 mentioned in the second volume.

To understand the Arab revolt it is also necessary to have in the mind's eye the geographical area involved and to glance through the history of Arabia during the preceding four hundred years. The popular conception of Arabia as a vast desert is more correct than are most such generalizations. This huge country, two and a half times as large as France and Germany combined, is believed to have less than six million inhabitants, of whom perhaps half are settled on the land or in towns, and half are nomadic. Its fertility is limited to a narrow ribbon along portions of the coast, to the hill-country of Asir and the Yemen in the south-west —the *Arabia Felix* of the Romans— and to the area of Qasim and a few other districts in the centre.[1]

Sketch 11.

A country of this nature, in which the most civilized and populous areas are separated from one another by vast tracts of desert, is unlikely to remain long in the hands of a single ruler. Moreover, the Arabs, physically a fine race and highly intelligent, had always shown themselves, except in the one great period when the ardour of their young religion welded them into a nation, politically frivolous, incapable of organization and more prone to disintegrate than to coalesce. Since the climacteric of the Abbasid empire of Baghdad, Arabia has not recognized a common allegiance. Various independent or semi-independent principalities rose and waned after the decline of those Khalifs, but for four hundred years before the Great

---

[1] A portion which has been termed the "fertile crescent," from Palestine east of the Lebanon, below the mountains of Anatolia and Persia to the head of the Persian Gulf, though largely inhabited by Arabs, is outside Arabia proper in the modern usage of the word.

War, though with fluctuating fortune, Turkey ruled or exercised considerable influence upon most of the habitable districts of Arabia.

In 1642 successful rebellions forced the Turks temporarily to evacuate the Yemen. One hundred years later the Wahabis overran the greater part of Western Arabia, and their power even reached the shore of the Persian Gulf. In 1811 Mehemet Ali, Pasha of Egypt, was deputed by the Ottoman Sultan to punish the Wahabis, who were accused of violating the Prophet's tomb and interrupting the pilgrimages. An Egyptian army landed in the Hejaz and after six years of warfare destroyed the Wahabi capital, Daraiya. For twenty-five years there was an Egyptian occupation of Nejd, but by 1840 it had been brought to an end by pressure from Turkey, backed by Great Britain. It had by no means killed the power of Wahabism or of its chief support, the Sa'ud Emirate, which transferred its capital to Riyadh and speedily flourished once again.

Not until 1872 was Turkey in a position to reoccupy the Yemen and instal a governor at Sanaa. Even in the twentieth century her rule in Arabia was stormy. In 1904 the Yemen rebelled and captured her garrisons. For several years the Turks employed large forces in an endeavour to crush this revolt, but in 1911 a settlement was reached, generally to their advantage. The Turks had also to deal in 1907 with the Idrissi of Sabayyeh, who was helped by the Italians from the opposite shores of the Red Sea during the Tripolitan War, and had failed to bring this chieftain to terms by 1914.

This outline of Western Arabian history is not complete without mention of the British occupation of Aden. In 1802 a treaty was negotiated with the Sultan of Aden, whereby the port was opened to British goods if carried in British ships. Later on Great Britain became desirous of obtaining a port of call and, with the advent of steam, a coaling station. In 1835 the Sultan agreed to sell the town, but when Commander Haynes with a small British force prepared to take possession, the Egyptian garrison resisted the landing and a skirmish took place. In 1839 Aden was captured by the British and has since remained in their hands, its importance having greatly increased in recent years.

ARABIA AT THE OUTBREAK OF WAR.

From the fragments of the Arab Empire there had, then, Sketch 11. grown up an Arabia more or less under Ottoman control, with the exception of the Aden Protectorate; the Hadhramut to the east of it; the Sultanate of Oman or Muscat; Trucial Oman, or the " Pirate Coast," within the Persian Gulf; Koweit, and a few minor chiefdoms on the shores of the Gulf or established on its islands; all of which were in some degree under British influence. After the subsidence of the Yemen revolt in 1911 the country remained comparatively peaceful under Turkish control. The princes with whom this history is concerned are five, three whose spheres of influence lay along the Red Sea, and two in the interior. First must be set the Grand Sherif of Mecca, Hussein Ibn Ali, ruler of the Hejaz, the country of the pilgrimage, and guardian of Mecca and Medina, the chief Holy Cities of Islam. Next in importance was the Imam Yahia of Sanaa, whose power lay in the Yemen highlands. Third stood the Idrissi, Emir of Sabayyeh, who had established himself in control of Asir. In the interior were, in the north, Ibn Rashid, Emir of Hail, whose house had always been friendly, and since 1896 closely allied, to Turkey; south of him Ibn Sa'ud, Emir of Riyadh, ruler of Nejd, and of incalculable power owing to his control of Wahabism.[1] These five rulers had constantly been at variance with one another and with the Turks, and many combinations had resulted from their ambitions. The political terms employed in describing them and their powers must not be taken to carry the weight which would be theirs if applied to European states. The boundaries of these chieftains were vague and fluctuating; independent or semi-independent princelings often existed within the territories of which they are set down as overlords, and there were areas to which two or three of them laid claim at once. It may be added that Ibn Sa'ud, and indeed Ibn Rashid, cannot be described as Turkish vassals in the same sense as the Sherif or the Imam. Of them all only Ibn Rashid, however, was strongly pro-Turk; Ibn Sa'ud, the Imam, and the Idrissi were all fairly, and the Sherif very, friendly to Great Britain.

---

[1] Certain important pastoral chiefs, with the principal of whom, Nuri esh Shalaan (see Sketch 11), this history is concerned, are not included in the above list.

The characters of the three western chiefs differed greatly, but each in his fashion was a remarkable man. Sherif Hussein, while vacillating in policy and desirous of keeping a foot in either camp as long as possible, enjoyed the great prestige due to his family and his office. The Sherifate of Mecca had endured a thousand years, and, though Hussein's branch of the clan had ruled less than a hundred, yet he was of the Quraish or tribe of the Prophet, having thus the qualification anciently laid down for the holder of the Khalifate. At the outbreak of war, he was a man of sixty, learned in Arab literature, popular with the townsmen of Mecca and Medina and the Bedouin of their neighbourhood, ambitious but cautious.

The Imamate of Sanaa was also of great antiquity. The Imam had given evidence of considerable ability, but he lived shrouded in mystery from Europeans, for, so far as is known, no Christian had ever seen him. He was in receipt of a subsidy from Constantinople and had an accredited agent at Aden when war broke out. While a treaty with the Idrissi was signed by the Viceroy of India in April, 1915, the Imam, though not bitterly hostile, never came to terms, and continued throughout the war to feed and clothe the Turkish troops in the Yemen, perhaps under compulsion. In any case, having been dispossessed of his seaboard by the Idrissi, and being troubled by a confederacy of rebel chiefs, his importance, where Great Britain was concerned, was greatly diminished.

The situation of the Idrissi differed markedly from those of the other two. Of African descent, his family had been established in Asir only since 1830, and he had in his favour none of the advantages of ancestry or kinship with the aristocracy of Arabia. He was, in fact, a self-made prince, his power being based on force of character, added to a reputation as a worker of miracles. He was, however, of all the Arab chieftains, the most uncompromising enemy of the Turk.[1]

The position of Turkey in Western Arabia had been greatly strengthened by the construction of the Hejaz

---

[1] During the war the Idrissi carried out his engagements, and though no important success resulted from the alliance with him, he contained at least one weak Turkish division and prevented it from joining in the attack on Aden. The operations of the Turks against Aden are described later in this chapter.

Railway. When we come to consider its importance, we are concerned not with Turkey alone, but also with the power which stood behind her—the German Empire. The railway was part of the vast German scheme for controlling the East and the land-routes to it. The problem of the Baghdad Railway, which was to bring Central Europe to the Persian Gulf, was fairly familiar, even to those uninstructed in international politics, before the war, but its companion venture, the Hejaz Railway, had attracted less attention, probably because its aim was so cleverly masked. A two-fold sham accompanied it. To the faithful it was a means of facilitating the pilgrimage; the Sultan Abdul Hamid, whose dearest project it was, saw in it the consolidation of his authority; Germany looked forward to controlling through him Western Arabia, to threatening British communications in the Red Sea, to decreasing the political and military, and even (though to a much smaller extent) the economic, importance of the Suez Canal.

The railway reached Medina in 1908, shortly before the fall of Abdul Hamid, having been built by German engineers, very economically from the point of view of both the Sultan and of Germany, from the subscriptions of pious Moslems throughout the world. It was to have been extended to Mecca[1] and to have had a branch to the Gulf of Aqaba, but these projects were abandoned owing partly to the anarchy which followed the revolution, partly to the Tripolitan and Balkan Wars and their drain on Turkey's resources, and partly, as regards the extension to Mecca, to the opposition of the Sherif. Hussein had made himself predominant in Mecca and its port of Jidda, reduced the Turkish Vali of the Hejaz to the position of a cipher in that area, and was shrewd enough to realize that further extension of the railway would facilitate the supply and reinforcement of Turkish garrisons and thus subject him to stronger control.

Great Britain and the Sherif of Mecca.

British policy in Arabia on the outbreak of war with Turkey had two main objects: to keep open and undisturbed communications through the Suez Canal and the Red Sea;

---

[1] The Germans even contemplated an eventual extension to the Yemen.

to nullify by all possible means the Turkish attempt to raise the Mohammedan world against the Allies by the proclamation of *Jihad*.

As to the former, Turkey was not in a position to make any serious attacks upon British shipping from the Arabian coast, but it was possible for the Hejaz Railway to bring mines and even supplies for German submarines to within easy reach of the shore of the Red Sea.[1] With regard to the latter, the attitude of the chiefs of Western Arabia and above all of Sherif Hussein was a matter of deep concern. From the moment of the proclamation of *Jihad*, Turkish agents swarmed in Northern Africa, the Sudan, Arabia, round the Persian Gulf and as far afield as Afghanistan, urging Moslems to respond to their master's call. The Hejaz, both from its geographical position and because it contained the shrines of Islam, might serve either as conduit or barrier to this propaganda, according to the temper and actions of Sherif Hussein. A *Jihad* endorsed by Mecca would have to Islam an appeal far more powerful than one dependent on Turkish religious authority alone. Important as were the other chiefs who have been named, he was far more so than they, not only because of his hereditary wardenship of the Holy Places and the pilgrim coast, his descent and the dignity of his family, but because his territory was upon the Red Sea littoral within reach of the Hejaz Railway. The whole of Western Arabia was held, though not strongly, by enemy garrisons, there being two independent divisions, the *21st* and *22nd*, in the Sanjak of Asir and Vilayat of the Hejaz respectively, and the *Yemen Army Corps*, of the *39th* and *40th Divisions*, in the Yemen. The Hejaz Railway brought these troops into communication with Turkey; without it they were cut off from home. It was therefore desirable to enter into relations with the Sherif before the proclamation of *Jihad* could have time to produce serious results in Arabia.

For some years before the war there had been dissatisfaction among the more thoughtful of the Arabs, especially those who had been brought into contact with the world outside their own countries, with their position in the

---

[1] Several mines were laid in the Gulf of Suez in December 1914, and in February 1915 large mines were transported from Ma'an on the Hejaz Railway to Aqaba and there launched. Eight were recovered by the Navy.

Ottoman Empire. The defeat of Turkey in the Balkan and Tripolitan Wars had filled their spirits with hopes of freedom. A wave of unrest had passed over Arabia and all the Arab world. The glories of the Abbasid Empire, gilded by imaginative retrospection, returned to their thoughts, and they saw the vision of a great Arab confederacy and Khalifate, held by a true successor to the Prophet and stretching north to the mountains of Taurus and Amanus. To the Sherif and his sons these dreams were familiar, and they desired that, if the confederacy came into being, it should be under his suzerainty, whether or not that suzerainty included the title of Khalif.

Lord Kitchener was well acquainted with Arab aspirations. In February 1914 the Emir Abdulla,[1] the Sherif's second son, had visited him at Cairo and privately informed him of the Sherif's ambition to secure autonomy for the Hejaz. This was a matter in which Great Britain had especial interest, by reason of the large pilgrimages from India, for which the Government had to a certain extent to cater and assume responsibility.

At the end of September 1914, nearly six weeks before the outbreak of war with Turkey, Lord Kitchener, bearing in mind that conversation, sent a message to Abdulla to enquire whether, in the event of Turkey being drawn by Germany into war with Great Britain, the Sherif and those Arabs under his influence would be for or against the latter. The Sherif's reply was friendly but cautious, and indicated that he would not of his own choice support the Turks. In October 1914, Sir J. Maxwell wrote to Lord Kitchener to urge that closer touch should be established with the Arabs of the Hejaz and the Yemen, and reported that the Turks were intriguing with the Bedouin of Sinai and the Western Desert. The *Chargé d'Affaires* at the Residency was equally alive to the importance of the question, which was being closely studied by the Foreign Office. But war with Turkey was not yet inevitable, and it was important to take no step which would precipitate it.

The day that Turkey declared war against Great Britain a more important communication was sent, in accordance with the wishes of Lord Kitchener, to the Emir

---

[1] The Emir was then representative of Mecca in the Turkish Parliament, where he had shown hostility to the Young Turks.

Abdulla. The Sherif was given the assurance that, if he and the Arabs actively assisted Great Britain in the war, she would recognize and support the independence of the Sherifate and of the Arabs generally. The Sherif's messenger reached Cairo in December with the reply that he would not adopt a policy hostile to Great Britain, but that his position in Islam made an immediate breach with Turkey impossible. His attitude was prudent and reasonable, and he was, in fact, actually sounding other Arab rulers as to their future course of action. He had already rendered service incalculably great to the Allies, for, between the despatch of the second message and its reply the Turks had, as previously stated, played their card of *Jihad*.[1] The Sherif had refused to proclaim *Jihad* from the Holy Cities; the summons therefore remained purely Turkish and failed almost completely to appeal to the Arab world.[2] Great Britain, for her part, took such further steps as were possible to counteract its effects. Proclamations were issued in India, Egypt and the Sudan that, so long as the Turks did not interfere with the pilgrimage and unless the move became necessary for the protection of Arab interests, the Holy Cities and Jidda should be immune from Allied attack. Copies of these proclamations were spread broadcast in the Hejaz by aeroplane.

In January 1915, Sir H. M'Mahon arrived in Egypt to take up the new office of High Commissioner, with instructions from the Foreign Office to foster the Sherif's friendship. Sir R. Wingate, the Governor-General of the Sudan, whose summer station near Port Sudan was opposite Jidda, was also in touch with the Sherif and, with the assistance of the Sudan notable Sayad Sir Ali Morgani, was able to send to the High Commissioner and Lord Kitchener frequent reports as to the situation in the Hejaz. There was in that quarter small change for some time to come. The Sherif's policy was a waiting one; the Turks, fully occupied with the defence of Gallipoli and Mesopotamia, troubled him little with their authority and showed no sign of reinforcing their garrisons. By the middle of the year, however, the Sherif had evidently overcome his hesitations.

---

[1] See p. 18.
[2] Very few Arabs in Asia followed the Turkish lead. In Africa the Senussi and the Sultan of Darfur obeyed the call, as has already been recorded.

He reopened negotiations by writing to the High Commissioner to request that Great Britain would guarantee the independence of all Arab lands as the reward of a revolt against Turkey. His letter was opportune, for any fresh embarrassment to Turkey would have its effect upon the campaigns in Gallipoli and on the Tigris. His demands, however, were sweeping. He proposed that Britain should acknowledge Arab independence within an area bounded on the north by Latitude 37, from Mersina to Persia; on the west by the Red Sea and the Mediterranean; on the south and east by the Indian Ocean, the Persian Gulf and the frontier of Persia. The Protectorate of Aden was excluded from these demands. In a private letter to the High Commissioner he begged for the resumption of the annual donation to the Holy Cities, which had been withheld, and for which he hoped that Great Britain would make herself responsible.[1]

The High Commissioner replied guardedly, expressing gratification at the Sherif's declaration that British and Arab aims were identical. He confirmed the friendly sentiments of His Majesty's Government, to which Lord Kitchener's previous message had given voice, but stated that discussion of boundaries in detail was premature, especially as large numbers of Arabs were fighting on the Turkish side. Great Britain, he said, would arrange for the transmission of the pious donations if the Sherif would guarantee their safety. The question of the Khalifate was not touched upon, for that was obviously the affair, neither of Great Britain nor of the Arabs, but of the whole Moslem world.

In October 1915 Sir H. M'Mahon reported to the Foreign Office that the Sherif, though in friendly fashion, complained that the British response was lukewarm. Both the High Commissioner and Sir J. Maxwell considered it essential to offer the Arabs a guarantee wide enough to ensure their entry into the war on the Allied side. Their knowledge of conditions in Arabia was by now thorough. When the Arab question first promised to become important the High Commissioner had attached to his office a number

---

[1] The question of these donations from Turkey and elsewhere was a matter of great concern to the Sherif, since the Hejaz never has been, and probably never will be, self-supporting, owing to the poverty of its soil.

of experts : travellers, archæologists and officials of the Egyptian service, intimately acquainted with the country and its politics. In February 1916 the British Government formally constituted on this foundation the " Arab Bureau." This office was charged, under the control of the High Commissioner,[1] with the study and development of British policy in Arab affairs and the collection of information. Until 1915 the Government of India, specially concerned with Aden and its hinterland, and also with the pilgrimage to Mecca, had handled Arab questions on the Red Sea coast. On the 31st March 1915 the British Government had placed the conduct of Arab affairs as far south as Lith, 80 miles south of Mecca, in the hands of the High Commissioner —an obvious improvement.

The information obtained by their intelligence services had convinced Sir H. M'Mahon and Sir J. Maxwell that there was widespread hostility to the Turks in Arabia and Syria—and among Christians as well as Moslems in the latter country—and particularly in the ranks of Arab troops in the Turkish service. This belief received striking confirmation soon after the receipt of the Sherif's letter mentioned above.

There came into the hands of the British authorities in Egypt complete information of a secret society of Arab officers in the Turkish Army, which was united with a civilian society of similar aim. This aim was an Arab Khalifate including Arabia, Syria and Mesopotamia. The members of the society had offered allegiance to the Sherif[2] and repudiated the spiritual rule of the Sultan. They seemed to realize that an Arab Empire was outside practical politics at the moment, and were aware of French aspirations in Syria, so that their immediate ambitions stopped short at a confederation of states. It also appeared that the Turks knew of the existence of these societies, but were adopting for the moment a lenient attitude, which was contrary to their custom and proof of the importance they ascribed to the movement.

---

[1] The Arab Bureau was supervised by Lieut.-Colonel (later Br.-General) C. G. Clayton, who held a triple office : Sudan Agent, head of Political Intelligence, and head of Sir J. Maxwell's Military Intelligence. He was also in liaison with the staff of the Naval C.-in-C. Its Director was Commander D. G. Hogarth, R.N.V.R.

[2] It was probably this support which had led to the Sherif's proposal to Great Britain.

AGREEMENT WITH THE SHERIF

This information was despatched to London by Sir H. M'Mahon and Sir J. Maxwell. The latter telegraphed the outline of the story to Lord Kitchener, pointing out that the question was urgent, that there were indications of the Turks being prepared to go a long way to meet the societies' demands—if only by piecrust promises—and that it was essential to send to the Arabs through the Sherif a definite statement of sympathy and support, even if it fell short of adherence to their programme. If they were driven to despair of Allied help, the Arabs might turn to Turkey, or rather to Germany, whose emissaries were often infinitely more sympathetic and far-sighted than the Turks. In that case the *Jihad*, hitherto a failure, might become only too effective. The active assistance of the Arabs, on the other hand, would be of great value in Arabia, Mesopotamia and Syria.

With this information and counsel before it, the British Government, in the latter part of October 1915, instructed the High Commissioner to send a reassuring reply to the Sherif's last letter. Hussein was informed that, subject to certain exceptions, such as the districts of Mersina, of Alexandretta, and of that portion of Syria lying west of the districts of Damascus, Homs, Hama and Aleppo, which were not purely Arab, Great Britain pledged herself to recognize and support the independence of the Arabs within the territories enclosed by the boundaries which he had proposed. A second reservation limited the assurance to those parts of the Arab territories in which Great Britain was free to act without detriment to the interests of France. A final reservation was that the Turkish Vilayets of Basra and Baghdad would probably be subjected to British control.

Sherif Hussein was generally, but not completely, satisfied with these stipulations. Like many other discussions conducted during the strain of war, these ended in agreement to take action for the common good, but with many details left over for future adjustment. In the spring of 1916 the Sherif finally decided to take action to assist in expelling the Turks from Arab territories.

THE SYKES-PICOT AGREEMENT.

Separate negotiations, not in the hands of Sir H. M'Mahon, had meanwhile been in progress between Britain and France regarding their respective spheres of influence.

218 THE SYKES–PICOT AGREEMENT

Long before the outbreak of the Arab revolt against Turkey, it had become apparent that the Arab movement would involve the interests of France in Syria. It had been, in fact, the clash of these interests with those of the Sherif which had prevented a prompt decision on the question of boundaries raised by him. France had been recognized in the sixteenth century as the protector of the Latin Church in the Ottoman Empire by Sultan Suleiman, who granted capitulations to that effect to François I. The anti-Christian spirit of the French Revolution and of Napoleon's Oriental policy had weakened her position, and, just when under Napoleon III her political influence was reviving, the Franco-Prussian War had come to blight it. In recent years France had been to some extent eclipsed by Germany in the East, but she still had a hold upon the affections of Syrian Christians, if Moslems turned rather to Great Britain. It was known that she had not abandoned her aspirations and that, if victory rested with the Allies, she would expect to have her way in Syria.

The British Government accordingly deputed Sir Mark Sykes to enter into agreement with M. Georges Picot, representing the French Government, regarding the boundaries of the prospective Arab States and of British and French spheres of influence. Agreement was reached, but the zones marked upon the Sykes–Picot map have since lost their full significance for various reasons, including the collapse of Tsarist Russia and the resuscitation of Turkish power in Asia Minor. Here it suffices to record that there were to be two areas, "A" and "B"; in the former of which France, in the latter Great Britain, were to uphold an independent Arab state or confederation of states. "A" was a rough triangle from Aleppo to Lake Tiberias to Rowanduz near the Persian frontier, including Aleppo, Homs and Damascus. "B" lay south thereof, its western boundary following the Jordan to the Dead Sea, turning west to the coast at Gaza, thence along the old Sinai frontier to Aqaba, while it extended east to Mesopotamia. There were to be two other spheres, a Blue and a Red; in the former of which France, in the latter of which Great Britain, were authorized to establish such administration as seemed suitable, after consultation with the future Arab state or confederation of states. The Blue covered approximately Syria north of Acre and west of Damascus and Aleppo, and

THE BALFOUR DECLARATION

extended into Turkey-in-Asia. The Red consisted of the valley of the Tigris and Euphrates from north of Baghdad to the Persian Gulf.   1916.

Russia also had to be taken into account, and in May 1916 Notes were exchanged between Great Britain, France and Russia, in which the spheres of influence of those countries were defined. Italian interests had already been recognized in April 1915. The Sherif was not informed of the full details of this understanding between the Great Powers until 1918, but he indulged in no illusions that there were not many difficult problems for settlement after the war.

These problems, it will be seen, were already sufficiently complicated, but the following year, in November 1917, the British Government were compelled to increase their complexity by the pronouncement regarding Palestine known as the "Balfour Declaration." The development of the war, which was ever engaging more nations and affecting more interests, the imperative pressure of Allied needs, and the international power of the Jewish race, had made desirable the recognition of Jewish aspirations for a "National Home" in Palestine. The Balfour Declaration, a public statement by Mr. A. J. Balfour, Secretary of State for Foreign Affairs, to Lord Rothschild, on the 9th November 1917, was as follows:—   1917. Nov.

"His Majesty's Government view with favour the "establishment in Palestine of a national home for the "Jewish people, and will use their best endeavours to "facilitate the achievement of this object, it being clearly "understood that nothing shall be done which may pre- "judice the civil and religious rights of existing non-Jewish "communities in Palestine, or the rights and political "status enjoyed by Jews in any other country."

The Zionist movement caused some perturbation among Syrians, particularly Mohammedans. It must be noted, as proof of the importance of the question, that immediately after the Balfour Declaration Germany entered into negotiations with Turkey in an endeavour to provide an alternative scheme which would appeal to Zionists. A German–Jewish society, the V.J.O.D.,[1] was formed, and in January 1918

---

[1] *Vereinigung Judischer Organisationen Deutschlands zur Wahrung der Rechte des Osten.*

Talaat, the Grand Vizier, gave vague promises of legislation by means of which " all justifiable wishes of the Jews in " Palestine would be able to find their fulfilment."

The Outbreak of the Arab Revolt.

Meanwhile the Turkish authorities, having discovered some compromising correspondence, had suddenly changed their attitude to the Arab movement. Early in 1916 Djemal Pasha decided that the moment was come for repression and set about his task in characteristic fashion. Executions more or less judicial were widespread, but, as so often the case with Turkish justice, the worst side of the affair was the savage vengeance of soldiery and gendarmerie upon the unfortunate Arabs and their families. The brutal methods of Djemal prevented a revolt in Syria, but his general Arab policy was, in the opinion of an observer so shrewd as Liman von Sanders,[1] a fiasco, and largely contributed to making the Arab soldiers of the Turkish Army, who were good fighting men if properly handled and led, disaffected and quite unreliable. The Sherif of Mecca was too strong thus to be struck down, and Djemal, though suspicious of him and his sons, was forced to remain on terms of outward courtesy with them. The third son, Sherif Feisal, was in Constantinople early in 1916, and it was the preparations for the despatch of fresh Turkish forces to the Southern Hejaz which he witnessed on his way home that precipitated the revolt.

Great Britain had by the spring begun the provision of the arms and munitions which she had promised to Sherif Hussein. These were despatched by Sir R. Wingate, who was closely watching the situation from the Sudan, and whose emissaries frequently crossed the narrow strip of water between the African and Asiatic shores. It was now certain that the rising would take place; indeed, Sir H. M'Mahon was urging the Sherif to delay his operations until it was possible to equip him more fully for his task. Doubtless the revolt would have had a more favourable beginning had time been allowed for the completion of preparations, yet in view of the movement southward of

---

[1] Liman, p.198.

those Turkish forces, whereof mention has been made, and of the fate which it brought upon them, it came at an opportune moment.[1]

1916.
June.

In early June Commander Hogarth and other officials of the Arab Bureau sailed to the neighbourhood of Jidda to interview a representative of the Sherif. They had expected to meet Abdulla, but it was the youngest son Zeid, little more than a boy, who awaited them on the 8th June. The reason was a good one ; the rising had begun three days earlier, on the 5th. Commander Hogarth was able to report on his return to Egypt that the revolt was genuine and inevitable, though its chances of success had been jeopardized by ignorance and haphazard methods. The Sherif asked for money, food-stuffs, at least another 10,000 rifles with ammunition, and particularly mountain artillery with Mohammedan personnel. To employ Egyptian troops to assist the Arabs in driving the Turks out of Arabia was a somewhat risky policy, which had not hitherto been contemplated. But it was evident that instant aid was required by the Sherif, and Sir R. Wingate did not hesitate to supply it. He despatched without delay two mountain batteries under their own Moslem officers, with a battery of six machine guns, all under the command of a senior Egyptian officer, Sayad Bey Ali. Three ships, with these reinforcements, 3,000 rifles, ammunition and large supplies of barley, flour, rice and coffee, sailed from Port Sudan on the 27th June and reached Jidda next day.

Thus began the Arab revolt against Turkey, a remarkable contribution to the cause of the Allies. Despite reverses, disappointments and periods of lethargy, it was to have far-reaching effects, constituting throughout the rest of the British campaign in Sinai and Palestine a steady drain upon Turkish resources and a powerful threat to the Turkish flank.

The Turkish Attack on Aden.

The blockade of Aden by the Turks, being more closely related to the history of this campaign than of any other, and also connected with the particular phase of the campaign

Sketch 11.
(inset).

---

[1] For an account of these forces and of the German Stotzingen Mission accompanying them see Chapter XIII.

now under discussion, is recorded in outline in this chapter. In an earlier one the hurried despatch to Aden by Sir J. Maxwell of the 28th Indian Brigade has been mentioned.

On the outbreak of war with Turkey there were signs of a Turkish concentration in the Sheikh Sa'ad Peninsula, 100 miles west of Aden, presumably foreboding an attack on the Protectorate. On the 10th November 1914 three battalions, moving from India to Suez, were landed near Sheikh Sa'ad, and drove the Turks inland. In June 1915 the Turks, having reoccupied the Sheikh Sa'ad Peninsula, made an unsuccessful attempt to land on Perim Island. During the latter half of the month the situation became threatening. A Turkish division advanced on Lahaj, 20 miles north of Aden, with the apparent intention of attacking the latter town.

*1915.
3-4 July.* Major-General D. L. B. Shaw, the British commander at Aden, decided to forestall the enemy at Lahaj and protect the friendly Sultan. On the 3rd July a somewhat ill-equipped force, known as the Aden Moveable Column, consisting of about a thousand rifles, chiefly Brecknockshire Battalion, with small Indian detachments, ten Maxims, six 15-pdr. and four 10-pdr. guns, set out for Lahaj, to which the Aden Troop[1] had already been despatched. It was to halt for that night at Sheikh Othman, a few miles out of Aden, but, as time was pressing, local cars were requisitioned and a small number of infantry sent forward to reinforce the Aden Troop. Nine or ten cars reached Lahaj ; the rest stuck in the sand and were abandoned. At 3 a.m. on the 4th the Moveable Column marched out from Sheikh Othman to cover the 14 miles to Lahaj.

By seven o'clock the heat had become terrific, and less than half the column had reached Lahaj. The Turks, advancing simultaneously, were delayed by the advanced guard and it was dark before they succeeded in entering the town. There was some very confused fighting, which continued through the night.[2] The Arab drivers with the camels, carrying everything except the mountain battery and not provided with an escort, fled at the first shot, in many cases

---

[1] The Aden Troop is a force of Indian Cavalry, actually more nearly approximating to a squadron than a troop, stationed at Aden for escort duties and other services within the protectorate.

[2] The Sultan of Lahaj, whose house was an old and faithful friend to Great Britain, was shot in the darkness.

RECAPTURE OF SHEIKH OTHMAN

taking their beasts and loads with them. The G.O.C., with the main body 5 miles outside Lahaj, learnt that he had lost all his stores, his water and two of his guns, while his troops were suffering severely from the heat. He decided to retreat because, were his force destroyed, the enemy would have Aden itself, with the harbour, the cables and the coal at his mercy. The Turks made no attempt to pursue, and the tired men reached Sheikh Othman without molestation, but, as the troops were shaken, it was decided to fall back upon Aden on the 7th July. At Sheikh Othman the head of the main Aden water-supply system had to be abandoned.

Such was the state of affairs when Sir G. Younghusband landed in advance of his troops and took command. The worst feature was the lack of water in the town at the very hottest time of the year. A supply of condensed water from ships in the harbour to a small extent remedied this loss.

The force from Egypt, the 28th (Frontier Force) Brigade, Berks Battery R.H.A., " B " Battery H.A.C., etc., was landed and ready to advance on Sheikh Othman by nightfall on the 20th July, ten days after receipt of orders to leave Egypt. The Aden garrison was then holding a line of outposts across the isthmus about two miles from the town. The troops bivouacked that night behind the outpost line.

At 3 a.m. on the 21st July the advance began. The Turks in Sheikh Othman were apparently taken by surprise, but as the leading troops reached the outskirts of the village fire was opened upon them from trenches to west of it, and a small counter-attack attempted against the left of the 51st Sikhs, on the left of the line. This was easily beaten off, and at 6 a.m. the Sikhs entered the village and drove out the enemy. The Aden Troop was not strong enough to interfere seriously with his retirement, and the infantry was forced to give up the pursuit after five or six miles. The casualties of the Turks were estimated at fifty, and they left behind a quantity of equipment. The British losses were 8 killed and 26 wounded.

The damage to the water supply was quickly repaired, and within twenty-four hours water was flowing into Aden. There are in Arabian warfare certain pleasant conventions, and within a few days, unhindered by the Turks, the usual camel caravans with eggs, fruit and other foodstuffs began to come into the town.

Sheikh Othman was fortified by General Younghusband, as it appeared to him to be the key to the defence of Aden. There remained to be solved the difficult problem of whether Lahaj should be recaptured. It was decided that it would be unwise to make the advance unless the place were to be permanently occupied, which would involve the locking up of a brigade for the rest of the war. General Younghusband therefore considered it his duty to hold Sheikh Othman and allow the Government to decide whether an advance to Lahaj should be carried out. Shortly afterwards the 28th Brigade was ordered back to Egypt.

Apart from numerous minor operations, the situation at Aden remained unchanged until the end of the war. The place was henceforth garrisoned by one British and four or five Indian battalions. The enemy had two divisions in the Yemen, but probably not more than 5,000 rifles all told, scattered over a very large area. In the immediate neighbourhood of Aden there were 2,000 Turkish infantry and perhaps 500 Arabs.

The authorities on the spot and in Egypt were always anxious that the Turks should be ejected from Lahaj, but the Government considered that Great Britain had enough responsibilities, without stirring up a quiet situation in that quarter. On the other hand, there is no doubt that the retention by the Turks of Lahaj and the fact that no attempt was ever made to drive them out were harmful to British prestige in Southern Arabia. Railway material was brought from India and a metre-gauge line constructed to the position at Sheikh Othman, and in October 1918 the G.O.C., Aden, was asked by the War Office what resources he required to recapture Lahaj. But the Armistice with Turkey found the Turkish force still sitting there. Ali Said Pasha, the Turkish commander, had then been at Lahaj for over three years, and for at least two completely cut off from Constantinople. During that period he had received no reinforcements or supplies and had been maintained by the Imam. After the Armistice came into force, its terms had to be conveyed to Ali Said Pasha by the British, as the Turkish Government were unable to communicate with him, and it was some time before he could be persuaded to surrender.[1]

An account of affairs at Aden throughout the war, including some of the minor operations mentioned above, is given in "The Empire at War," edited by Sir Charles Lucas, v., pp. 135-48.

CHAPTER XIII.

THE ARAB CAMPAIGN AGAINST TURKEY.

(Sketch 11.)

THE OPENING PHASE.

On the 5th June 1916, Sherif Hussein's eldest son Ali and his third son Feisal raised the standard of revolt near Medina, the terminus of the Hejaz Railway. On the following day Feisal made an unsuccessful attack upon the town's defences, while Ali marched north with the intention of cutting the railway in the neighbourhood of Medain Saleh, 180 miles north-west of Medina. The threat to Medina was never serious and the interruption of railway communication with Damascus but momentary.

1916.
5 June.
Sketch 11.

Meanwhile the Sherif was organizing attacks upon the other Turkish strongholds in the Hejaz. His prospects did not appear to be rosy. The Turkish forces in the country were believed to number upwards of 15,000, but reports from a region to a great part of which no Christian could penetrate were not reliable. The main formation was the *22nd Division*, while battalions from the *21st*, which had its headquarters in Asir, were at Lith and Qunfideh,[1] on the coast south of Mecca.

The Sherif's forces cannot be estimated, since contingents joined and went home when they chose to do so. There may have been 50,000 men in the field by the end of June, but a small proportion only had modern—or in many cases any—rifles.[2] Moreover, the Arabs were at this stage entirely without artillery or machine guns.

Hussein himself conducted the operations at Mecca. Here the Turkish commander, though he had been rendered uneasy by the attitude of armed Bedouin and must surely have heard of the revolt at Medina, was surprised. The summer garrison consisted of 1,000 men, distributed in

---

[1] Both these places surrendered to the Sherif at a later date.
[2] When the revolt broke out there were reported to be 30,000 men encamped against Medina, with only 6,000 rifles among them.

barracks in the town and in forts outside it.[1] On the 9th June, when the first open hostilities took place, he telephoned to the Sherif:—" The Bedouin have revolted against the " Government. Find a way out." The Sherif, who did not lack humour, replied:—" Of course, we shall," and at once ordered a general attack. After three days of street fighting the barracks were set on fire on the 12th, and the garrison, overcome by smoke, was captured.

On the following day the remainder of the Turkish force, with the exception of the garrisons of two of the small forts outside the town, was taken prisoner. Two guns of the Egyptian batteries, which were landed at Jidda after the capture of the town, were at once despatched to Mecca, and their fire speedily brought about the surrender of the forts.

On the 9th June also 4,000 Arabs of the Harb tribe, under their own Sheikh, attacked Jidda, the chief port of the Hejaz, but were beaten off. The Turkish garrison was provided with artillery and machine guns, so that the Arabs had little prospect of capturing the place unaided. But naval support was forthcoming. On the 11th June the Indian Marine ship *Hardinge* and the light cruiser *Fox* bombarded the Turkish positions north of the town; while seaplanes from the *Ben-my-Chree* dropped bombs on various targets. On the 16th the garrison of 45 officers and 1,400 rank and file, with 16 guns and machine guns, surrendered to the Arabs, lack of water as well as the naval action having contributed to this result. Rabegh, 100 miles north of Jidda, where there was only a handful of Turks, was also captured. On the 27th July another Red Sea port, Yambo, 200 miles north-west of Jidda, surrendered to the Sherif's followers.

Taif, 70 miles south-east of Mecca, was a much more difficult objective. It was strongly fortified and surrounded by entrenched positions, while its garrison consisted of 3,000 men with ten 75-mm. Krupp guns. The Emir Abdulla sat down before it with 5,000 tribesmen, but attempted no more than an investment, for an assault by the ill-armed and undisciplined Arabs was out of the question. The arrival of the Egyptian batteries, together with a battery of captured

---

[1] Taif was the summer station of the Turkish Governor-General and the greater part of the garrison of Mecca, owing to the heat and unhealthiness of the capital. The move to summer quarters, which left Mecca very weak, had taken place before the outbreak of the revolt.

Turkish howitzers from Egypt, also manned by Egyptian personnel, altered the situation. On the 16th July, five weeks after the beginning of the siege, this artillery opened fire and speedily silenced two Turkish guns in advanced positions north of the town. Next day the artillery was moved to within closer range of the defences and bombarded them steadily for ten days, the Turkish guns being completely dominated and the works considerably damaged. The Arabs threatened assaults on several occasions, but none took place. It is probable, indeed, that Abdulla had no intention of making a serious assault, which would have involved heavy loss and disheartened his tribesmen, since he knew that the Turkish garrison must fall eventually. The siege continued, with intermittent bombardments, till the 22nd September, when, after its request for an armistice had been refused, the garrison of Taif surrendered unconditionally. The Sherif had now captured over 5,000 prisoners, of whom a number of Arab or Syrian blood volunteered for service against the Turks.

1916. July.

Meanwhile, at Medina affairs had gone less well. On the 3rd July the Turks made a sortie from the town and defeated the Emir Feisal. They also sacked the suburb which he had occupied and carried off the surviving women and children to Damascus. After this action there was no real siege of Medina for some time to come. Ali withdrew from the railway and joined his brother south of Medina, the combined forces holding the tracks to Mecca through the hills, but attempting no more.

On the 3rd August the Turks attacked again and drove back Ali, in a running fight lasting 28 hours, to Ghadir Rabegh, 20 miles south of Medina. It was evident that as yet the Arabs could neither attack with success nor defend themselves against the attacks of their trained and well equipped enemy. The revolt had, indeed, led to a series of brilliant successes, but they had been mainly those of surprise. It seemed probable that the Turks would be able to restore the position so soon as they were prepared to make a serious effort.

Fortunately, while awaiting reinforcements at Medina, the Turks gave the Arabs time for a certain measure of organization to be introduced. General Sir R. Wingate was appointed to the command of operations in the Hejaz, which meant that he was responsible for such British reinforcements as might be sent and for advising the Sherif in his operations. The appointment was not made public, lest the fact that British officers were directing operations in the Holy territory of the Hejaz should create anti-Christian propaganda in Moslem countries and reflect adversely on the Sherif.[1] One of Sir R. Wingate's officers, Lieut.-Colonel E. C. Wilson, Governor of the Red Sea Province of the Sudan, was sent by him to Jidda to act as his representative and was for some time, prior to the arrival of a British Military Mission, charged unaided with advising the Sherif and assisting to direct the energies of his troops. Large numbers of rifles were shipped to the Hejaz, and the Arab forces were formed into three groups : one under Ali, about 8,000 strong, facing Medina on the south ; a second under Abdulla, 4,000 strong, on the east and north-east of the town ; and a third under Feisal, 8,000 strong, based on Yambo to operate against the railway.

The Stotzingen Mission.

Mention has been made of the arrival at Medina of Turkish reinforcements, which caused the premature outbreak of the Arab revolt. It was not until some weeks after fighting had begun that the British authorities learnt that these reinforcements had been accompanied by a German mission of very great importance.

When the *Dufferin* was off Yambo in June it was reported that there were several Germans, including a woman, in the town, but there had been many such stories and this was not taken seriously. Later on the truth of the information was confirmed. The party consisted of Major Freiherr Othmar von Stotzingen, an officer with distinguished service ; one Karl Neufeld, a German adventurer with a curious record well known in the Sudan, and a fluent speaker

---

[1] General Wingate continued to hold this appointment until March 1919, in conjunction with that of High Commissioner in Egypt, in which he succeeded Sir H. M'Mahon on the 1st January 1917. When General Allenby's advance began it was arranged that all Arab operations north of Ma'an on the Hejaz railway (about the latitude of Aqaba) should be under the direction of the Commander-in-Chief, E.E.F. South of Ma'an, and including those of Asir, affairs remained in General Wingate's hands. The secrecy of his position was observed so closely that his despatches concerning the operations in the Hejaz were not published till December 1919.

THE STOTINGZEN MISSION

of Arabic;[1] the latter's Kurdish wife; two German mechanics and an Indian servant, probably a Pathan deserter. There may also have been with these people a wireless officer, Lieutenant Diel, and others. Papers picked up at Qatiya after the retreat of the Turks made clear the aims of the mission. Stotzingen was charged with setting up a wireless station on the coast to communicate with the Germans in East Africa and also with the direction of propaganda in Somaliland, Abyssinia, the Sudan, and Darfur.[2]

Stotzingen had left Berlin on the 15th March, with letters of recommendation to Enver,[3] and arrived on the 12th April at Damascus. He was now only separated from the Turkish force because, as a Christian, he might not pass through Medina and Mecca. He had hoped to charter a dhow at Wejh, the next port on the coast north of Yambo, but, finding the blockade too strict, had continued his journey by land.

The new Turkish force, commanded by Khairi Bey, consisted of a mobile column 3,500 strong, including one Q.F. battery and two machine-gun companies. It had been formed in Constantinople of drafts from depots. A proportion of the troops were Syrians, which was no disadvantage, as the Turk finds the climate of southern Arabia very trying.

---

[1] Neufeld had acted as interpreter with British troops in 1884. He was one of the Khalifa's prisoners released by the British after the Battle of Omdurman. He had subsequently been allowed to live in the Sudan, but was expelled from the country on the outbreak of war as an undesirable alien. He was a man of education and a certain ability.

[2] The most important passage is as follows:—" The German Major " von Stotzingen is ordered by the German Military authorities to establish " an information post in the neighbourhood of Hodeida, for the purpose of " opening up communication with the German troops in German East " Africa. All Turkish military and civil authorities are enjoined to afford " Major von Stotzingen and his staff every assistance. The wireless " apparatus brought by Major von Stotzingen will be utilized for the " purpose of forwarding orders and information to Turkish G.H.Q."

A pocket book belonging to Lieutenant F. Grobba, another member of the Mission, picked up on the same battlefield, contained random notes, such as :—" People well disposed to us in the Sudan." " The nephew of " the Mad Mullah, Awad, of the tribe of the Dolbohanti Somalis." " Is " there a telegraph line as far as Hodeida ? " " The English have a line " from Loheia through Kamaran." (Kamaran is an island just south of Loheia.)

[3] The following naïve but doubtless effective recommendation from Countess Schlieffen is perhaps worth recording :—" He does not obtrude " his personality and has not those characteristics which often make the " Germans disliked in foreign parts."

This force had come direct by rail to Medina, bringing with it Stotzingen's heavy baggage, including the wireless material. It was to have marched to Mecca, then on to Qunfideh (where the Germans were to have rejoined it), then, apparently, to Sana'a, the Imam's capital. The expedition represented an ambitious attempt to restore Turkish prestige in Arabia, for no Turkish troops had ever previously traversed the country, the Yemen garrisons having always moved by sea. The force was small, but Arabia is a land suited to the movement of small forces only, and one in which they may have opportunity, if they be well found, disciplined, and mobile, to achieve great results. It is hard to overestimate the importance of the expedition, which might even have taken Aden by surprise. With these reinforcements the Idrissi might have been crushed and the Imam left triumphant in the south. Of not less importance would have been its influence across the Red Sea, had Stotzingen obtained touch with German agents. It might have been able to give material assistance to the "Mad" Mullah of Somaliland, who had designs upon Italian Eritrea, where the white garrison did not exceed two thousand. To have transported a Turkish battalion would have been difficult, but not impossible, since from Hodeida to the nearest point on the Eritrean coast is less than one hundred miles, so that fast dhows, with a favouring wind, could accomplish the greater part of the crossing between dusk and dawn. From Mocha the distance is about 40 miles.

All these plans and possibilities were brought to naught by the Arab Revolt. Stotzingen quitted Yambo before its occupation by the Arabs, and returned to Damascus. Some members of the Mission appear to have been killed by the Bedouin; the rest escaped northward and joined the Palestine army. The troops under Khairi Bey were, as has been stated, held up at Medina, and eventually used as drafts to bring up to strength the battalions of its garrison.

The Problem of Rabegh.

Sketch 11.

The Arab Revolt and the prospects opened up by it had an effect upon the campaign in Sinai. It was discussed by the War Committee on the 6th July 1916, when

RECOMMENDATIONS OF WAR COMMITTEE 231

Sir Mark Sykes, who had considerable knowledge of Arabian affairs, was heard.[1] The Committee made the following recommendations:—

1916.
6 July.

(i) The C.I.G.S. should direct the C.-in-C. Egypt to prepare to occupy El Arish and Aqaba, since a force established at these places would directly threaten the Turkish communications between Syria and the Hejaz,[2] and encourage Syrian Arabs; at the same time most effectively defending Egypt.

(ii) The C.I.G.S. should direct the C.-in-C. Egypt to push on at once with the Qatiya Railway, making preparations for its extension to El Arish.

(iii) The C.I.G.S. and the Admiralty should instruct the C.-in-C. Egypt and the Naval C.-in-C. East Indies to concert plans for the occupation of Aqaba.

(iv) The Admiralty should direct the Naval C.-in-C. East Indies to prevent the Turks using the Red Sea from Hodeida to Lith, if this is not already being done.

(v) The India Office should direct the Resident, Aden, to try for the co-operation of the Imam in preventing the withdrawal of the three Turkish Divisions now in Asir and the Yemen. It is understood that the co-operation of the Idrissi is secured.

(vi) The India Office should draw up a scheme for minor operations to drive back the Turkish outposts near Aden.

(vii) The Admiralty and General Staff should develop naval and military measures designed to make the enemy expect a landing at Alexandretta or Smyrna.

(viii) The War Office should take steps to meet the probable demands of the Sherif and Idrissi for arms and ammunition.

---

[1] His proposals were embodied in the following formula:—" Towards " all Arabs, whatever their condition, whether independent allies, as Ibn " Sa'ud and the Sherif, inhabitants of protectorates, spheres of influence, " vassal states, we should show ourselves as pro-Arabs, and that wherever " we are on Arab soil we are going to back the Arab language and Arab race, " and that we shall protect or support Arabs against external oppression " by force as much as we are able, and from alien exploitation."

[2] It must be remarked that the threat to Turkish communications with the Hejaz by a force at El Arish was extremely remote. A force at Aqaba would have threatened the Hejaz railway, but only if it were highly mobile. Between Aqaba and Ma'an are 60 miles of most difficult country. And a raid could do no more than temporarily cut the railway, the Turks being equipped with material and break-down trains to restore it.

These recommendations were in general carried into effect. With regard to Aqaba, however, the Sherif did not desire that a British force should land there, and no landing took place. Aqaba was eventually captured, as will shortly be recorded, by the Arabs themselves, from the interior.

For the next few months the chief problem was one which had not presented itself at the meeting of the War Committee : the defence of Rabegh, 150 miles S.S.W. of Medina. The Turks had now concentrated a strong force at Medina, and it was credibly reported that they were about to advance to the recapture of Mecca. They had formally deposed the Sherif, appointed a new one, Ali Haidar, and brought him from Constantinople to Medina, ready to make a triumphal entry into Mecca, with the Turkish holy carpet. They had reinforced the Hejaz garrisons with about eight battalions[1] and, with the Yemen force already mentioned, which was used to bring other battalions up to strength, had now about 13,000 troops there, of whom over half lay between 20 and 40 miles south of Medina, 2,000 in the town, and 1,500 along the railway to north of it. It was known that they were actively collecting transport, supplies, and forage both from the north and from their ally, the Emir of Hail.

From Medina to Mecca there are two main routes : one inland, the other through Rabegh. The former is the more difficult and the worse supplied with water, and it was thought that no considerable force could advance on Mecca without using the route through Rabegh and watering at its wells. A quantity of stores for the use of the Arabs had already been landed there by the British, who were also preparing to despatch there a flight of the Royal Flying Corps. The defence of Rabegh was of vital importance both on account of the stores and because it provided a watering place on the main route to Mecca.

Both Sir R. Wingate and the High Commissioner, Sir H. M'Mahon, advocated the despatch of a brigade of British troops to Rabegh. Sir A. Murray was opposed to this project. The arguments in its favour are too obvious to require recapitulation ; that which influenced the

---

[1] At least one battalion of the *131st Regiment, 41st Division*, was sent down; while the *42nd* and *55th Regiments, 14th Division*, were permanently detached from their division to garrison the Hejaz.

Commander-in-Chief, apart from the very important one that he could ill spare a force of this size, is less apparent, but none the less strong. He considered that though the Sherif frequently spoke as if desirous of such support, the appearance of Christian troops so near the Holy Places would alienate the sympathies of the Arabs. Then there was no certainty that the troops, if sent, would serve a useful purpose, for the Turks might, after all, be able to use the inland route. The Battle of Romani had given proof of their capabilities in desert warfare. The discussion of this difficult problem began at a conference at Ismailia between Sir A. Murray and Sir H. M'Mahon on the 13th September and continued for a considerable period, many telegrams passing between the Foreign Office, the High Commissioner, Sir R. Wingate, Sir A. Murray, and the C.I.G.S. on the subject.

In December 1916 the Turks renewed their attacks, and the Arabs were defeated south-west of Medina. The Emir Feisal had shown military ability in these encounters, but his men were demoralized by the Turkish artillery.[1] The enemy then established himself in the hills, half-way between Medina and Rabegh, while the armies of Feisal,

---

[1] Witnesses so far apart as General Liman von Sanders and Lieut.-Colonel T. E. Lawrence have testified that the Arab, with training and cool, resolute leadership, makes a good soldier, even in the conditions of modern war. But at this period the Bedouin, though unawed by rifle fire, to which they were accustomed, were terrified by artillery. The Sherif reached the heart of the problem when he stated to the High Commissioner that the only hope for his cause lay in providing a counter to the " science " and inventions of war of the enemy, which my troops do not possess."

That the Arab conceptions of warfare differ from the European is apparent from the following report of the actions mentioned above by Colonel (then Captain) T. E. Lawrence:—" When he [the Emir Feisal] " was in Wadi Yambo in early December the unexpected happened. The " Arabs under Sidi Zeid became slack and left a by-road near Khalis un-" guarded. A Turkish mounted infantry patrol pushed up along it into " Wadi Safra near Kheif. The front line of Arabs, hearing news of this "enemy six miles in their rear, broke with a rush to rescue their families and " property in the threatened villages . . . . and the astonished Turks " occupied Hamra and Bir Said unopposed . . . . He [Feisal] moved into " Nakl Mubarak with his forces and the still-trembling remnant of Zeid's " army, and after a few excited days fought a long-range action against a " strong Turkish reconnaissance. In this he found his troops lacking in " many respects : his centre and right wing held and repulsed the enemy ; " the left wing (Juheinah) retired suddenly behind his centre, without " hostile pressure. He suspected treachery, and ordered a general retreat " on Yambo, the next water supply. The defaulting left wing refused to " retire, put up an independent stubborn resistance for another twenty-" four hours, and then rejoined Feisal at Yambo. It explained that the " retirement during the action was to find an opportunity for brewing a " cup of coffee undisturbed."

based on Yambo, and of Ali, based on Rabegh, were separated, and the situation was far from satisfactory. The British R.F.C. flight had arrived at Rabegh in November, and was guarded mainly by a detachment of 600 Egyptian artillery and infantry. The stores had accumulated till they invited the Turks more strongly than ever to advance. Yet still Sir A. Murray and Sir W. Robertson held out against the despatch of British troops. The former, however, had thought it necessary to make preparation by concentrating two infantry brigades, two artillery brigades, two companies Imperial Camel Corps, two field companies R.E., with auxiliary troops, at Suez, in case he should be ordered to send an expedition to Rabegh.

Finally, there prevailed in the counsels of the War Cabinet,[1] what appears to have been a fortunate decision, from the religious and political, as well as the military, point of view. It was Lieut.-Colonel Wilson, Sir R. Wingate's representative with the Sherif, himself previously an advocate of the despatch of British troops to Rabegh, who clinched the matter by suggesting that no troops should be sent unless the Sherif would actually demand them in writing and hold himself responsible for the consequences of their appearance in the Hejaz. This Sherif Hussein was not prepared to do. In January 1917 another division was required from Egypt for France, and the Commander-in-Chief was informed that British troops need no longer be held in readiness for Rabegh. The wisdom of the decision can now scarcely be doubted, strong as were the arguments of those who advocated the despatch of troops; for the presence of a brigade on this unhealthy, ill-watered shore, might have involved the E.E.F. in a serious commitment.

The Attack on Wejh.

Meanwhile, despite the reverses in front of Medina, the prestige of the Sherif had risen in the Hejaz. Under his auspices the pilgrimage had taken place in September and had been highly successful. Ships had brought from Egypt over a thousand pilgrims and from India twice that number, while several hundreds journeyed from North-West Africa.

---

[1] The War Cabinet, with a reduced number of members, succeeded the War Committee in early December 1916, when Mr. Lloyd George succeeded Mr. Asquith as Prime Minister.

IMPROVED POSITION OF SHERIF

1916.
Sept.

In all, over six thousand pilgrims had come from outside Arabia, which was considered a remarkable number in view of the conditions of war and the shortage of shipping. The total number of pilgrims was 26,000, including many from the territory of the hostile Emir of Hail. Enthusiasm and gratitude for British aid was so great at Jidda that the local Sheikh, after being shown over the flagship *Euryalus*, officially invited the Admiral to ride at the head of the procession of the Egyptian holy carpet through the town: an honour which was " prudently if reluctantly " declined. Sir R. Wemyss throughout this period showed deep comprehension of the Arabs' point of view and of the difficulties which beset their course. He was always ready to suggest and put into action schemes for co-operation with them, as at Jidda in the summer and later at Wejh, and had become very popular with them.

In other respects the position of the Arabs had been strengthened. A Turkish officer of Arab birth, Aziz Bey el Masri, had volunteered to assist his compatriots, and had been appointed Minister for War and virtually Commander-in-Chief by the Sherif. This officer, who had a distinguished record and had been regarded a few years earlier as one of the best of the young soldiers in the Turkish army, had been living in Egypt since the Tripolitan War, in fear of assassination by Enver's party should he return to Turkey.[1] Aziz Bey subsequently became dissatisfied with his position and resigned. He was succeeded by Ja'far Pasha el Askeri, formerly leader of the Senussi's forces and a prisoner in the Citadel at Cairo since the action of Agagiya. This officer volunteered to serve the Sherif on hearing of the atrocities of Djemal in Syria, and was put in command of his trained troops, consisting mainly of Arabs who had served in the Turkish Army and had been captured in the Hejaz or Mesopotamia.

1917.
Jan.

In January 1917 a small British Military Mission, of which the senior officer was Lieut.-Colonel S. F. Newcombe, R.E., was sent to assist Lieut.-Colonel Wilson. The services rendered by the officers composing it were invaluable and resulted in many romantic exploits. Of these the most remarkable were achieved by a young archæologist, Captain T. E. Lawrence, formerly employed on intelligence duties

---

[1] Mention is made of this officer's career in Tripoli in Appendix 5.

at Cairo, who was to exercise upon the Arabs an extraordinary influence and to whom much of the final success of their campaign was to be due. A French Military Mission under Colonel E. Bremond, with two French and four Moslem officers of French Moroccan regiments, had arrived at Jidda in September 1916, with the object of watching over the interests of French subjects taking part in the pilgrimage, and of arranging for French assistance to the Sherif. A small detachment of French Moslem troops, with mountain artillery and machine guns, was also landed in the Hejaz. Arms and ammunition had been, by the end of 1916, supplied by the British in large quantities.

The danger of a Turkish advance on Mecca still existed, however, till it was dissipated by a bold move on the part of the Emir Feisal and Captain Lawrence. So early as October 1916, Feisal had proposed an advance along the coast and the formation of a new base at Wejh, 180 miles north-west of Yambo, which would threaten the rear of the enemy at Medina and his sole means of communication, the Hejaz Railway. The Arab reverses in December had altered the situation. The forces under Emirs Ali and Zeid had been severely handled by the Turks, and Feisal feared that if he himself, who was holding the tribes together by personal prestige alone, left the area, both Rabegh and Yambo would fall. A suggestion by Captain Lawrence, backed by the arguments of Lieut.-Colonel Wilson, solved the problem. The Emir Abdulla, then north-east of Medina attempting to check the supply of food to the garrison from Hail, who had not suffered defeat and enjoyed a credit equal to that of Feisal, was requested to move astride the railway at the Wadi Ais, 70 miles north of Medina. No Turkish advance on Rabegh was likely to take place unless he were first dislodged, and for that troops would probably have to be withdrawn from the Medina area. To this suggestion the brothers agreed, though with some misgiving. Emir Feisal's advance on Wejh involved a flank march of 200 miles parallel to the Turkish communications, and the abandonment of his base at Yambo and his only defensive position. It was made possible by the British command of the sea and the co-operation of the Red Sea Patrol.

The march along the coast began on the 18th January 1917. The Arab force numbered 10,000, and had with it one of the Egyptian mountain batteries, the guns having been handed over to Feisal after a detachment of his men had been trained in their use.[1] A much smaller force would have been sufficient for the enterprise, but Feisal was anxious to prove to the tribes on his route the popularity and power of his father's cause. On the 23rd January five hundred Arabs were landed at Wejh from British ships and had captured the place before Feisal's arrival. The Arab camelry in the garrison promptly deserted, leaving only 200 Turkish infantry to defend the town. This force was put to flight, a large proportion being captured by the landing party and by Feisal's advanced guard, which came up among the fugitives at dawn on the 25th. Only about one third of the Turkish force escaped.

1917.
Jan.

The advance on Wejh, though it can in reality have constituted but a very slight threat to Medina, acted like a charm. Thenceforth there was never question of a Turkish attack on Mecca. The troops at Medina, known as the *Hejaz Expeditionary Force*, though never undergoing a siege in the true sense of the term, became in effect an invested garrison, and before long began to eat their transport animals. In addition, the Turks became concerned, and in this case with more reason, for the safety of the Hejaz railway. A detachment, known as the *2nd Composite Force*, was formed at Tebuk, an important station 300 miles north of Medina. It had a ration strength of 5,000, and was commanded by Mohammed Djemal Pasha.[2] Another detachment known subsequently as the *1st Composite Force*, and still later as the *Ma'an Command*, had its headquarters at Ma'an, and was for some time commanded by Mohammed Djemal Pasha (Kuchuk). Its strength early in 1917 was four battalions, but towards the end of the year it had grown to over 7,000. The defence of the railway was parcelled out among these three forces, small garrisons being posted at each station in blockhouses.

---

[1] The great advantage possessed by the Arabs in warfare of this type was their independence of transport. The total baggage of Feisal during his march on Wejh was carried by 380 camels. He relied, of course, on stores being landed at Wejh by the Navy after the capture of the place. The mountain battery, when manned by the Egyptian gunners, had a complement of 360 camels. In the hands of the Arabs it had 80, yet they carried as much ammunition as their predecessors.

[2] Generally known as Djemal III; not to be confused with either the Commander of the *Fourth Army*, Ahmed Djemal (Biyuk—"the Great,") Djemal I; or Mohammed (Kuchuk), Djemal II, mentioned below.

238   THE ARAB CAMPAIGN

Hitherto the raiding of the line by the Arabs had been of a very primitive nature. A few rails were removed, to be relaid by the Turks, accustomed even in times of peace to such incidents, within a few hours. With the advent of British officers, who instructed the Arabs in the use of explosives and led in person expeditions against the railway, all this was altered. Damage was now done with frequency and on a scale such as to interrupt seriously the Turkish communications, and finally, but at a period with which this volume is not concerned, cut off Medina altogether.

1917.
Feb.
A single early raid may be shortly described, as typical of many which were subsequently carried out. On the 12th February, Bimbashi (Major) H. Garland, Egyptian Army, left Wejh with a party of 50 Bedouin, reaching the line south of Toweira, 120 miles north-west of Medina, after eight days' camel riding. He had been told by the Arabs that trains now ran only by day, so thought he might work at leisure under cover of darkness. He sent a party to lay explosives under a bridge south of the station, while he himself mined a section of rails further down the line. Then he heard a train from the north enter the station, stop, and quickly start again. He had a few minutes only to complete the laying of a reduced charge, and ran back when the train was within 200 yards of him. The explosion came when he was 50 yards from the line, and he saw the engine leave the rails and crash down the embankment. The Turkish guard poured out of the blockhouse at the station, but the Arab who had been at work at the bridge pluckily fired his charge also, destroyed the bridge and thus cut off the train.

Exploits of this sort, carried out in the north by Feisal's forces, in the south nearer Medina by those of Ali and Abdulla, with the aid of British and French officers and of Egyptian, Indian and French Moroccan troops, became almost of weekly occurrence. Fighting on a large scale was rare. The Turks kept to the blockhouses, and moved out to patrol or mend the line only in considerable strength, accompanied by pack artillery and machine guns. The Arabs, never attacking when the Turks were in force, played their game of tip-and-run, under the inspiration of their British advisers, with trifling loss to themselves and a steadily rising list of casualties to the enemy.

CAPTAIN LAWRENCE'S JOURNEY 239

The Affair of Abu el Lissal and the Capture of Aqaba.

In March and April 1917 the First and Second Battles of Gaza were fought and the E.E.F. definitely established within the Palestine frontier. It therefore became desirable to extend the operations of the Arabs further north and to open a new base at Aqaba. The mission was entrusted to Captain Lawrence, who carried it out in characteristic fashion. *Sketch 11.*

On the 9th May he left Wejh with Sherif Nasir, Feisal's principal lieutenant. Auda Abu Tayi, a chief of the Eastern Howeitat, and the best fighting leader who appeared among the Arabs in the course of the campaign, also accompanied him, the whole party not numbering more than about fifty camelry. His first object was to obtain the adherence of Nuri esh Shalaan, chief of the most important section of the Anazeh, and the fourth of the desert princes, after the Sherif, Ibn Sa'ud, and Ibn Rashid. It was not expected or desired that Nuri, with his chief market at Damascus, would instantly break with the Turks, but his favour was necessary for the use of his roads and for the employment of Auda's tribesmen against Aqaba. *1917. May.*

Crossing the railway between Tebuk and Medain Saleh —and cutting it with explosives as he passed—Captain Lawrence rode to Nebk, 130 miles north-west of Jauf el Amir and about the same distance north-east of Ma'an on the railway. Auda rode to Jauf to negotiate with Nuri, and while he was thus employed and his tribesmen were gathering, Captain Lawrence himself made an extraordinary journey north, riding as far as Baalbek, 30 miles north of Damascus and 500 miles as the crow flies from his starting-point. He had many interviews with chiefs, who promised to rise when the time was ripe for operations in Trans-Jordan. He was back at Nebk on the 19th June, and carried out another raid on the railway north of Amman. *June.*

Then on the 28th, the Arabs crossed the railway south of Ma'an and captured a post of Turkish gendarmerie on the Ma'an-Aqaba road. The force under Auda and Nasir, now five hundred strong and consisting of some of the hardest-fighting tribesmen of the desert, then took up a position in the hills overlooking the road at Abu el Lissal, and on the 1st July a Turkish battalion marched out from

(27793) R

Ma'an and encamped below. Fire was exchanged by the two parties throughout the 2nd, the Turks expending all the scanty supply of ammunition they had brought for their one mountain gun in fruitless shelling of the hills.

1917. 2 July. At sunset Auda collected fifty horsemen in a hollow valley 200 yards from the Turkish position and suddenly charged. The Turks broke, whereupon the rest of the Arab force dashed down the hill on their camels. The fight was over in five minutes. Captain Lawrence counted 300 dead Turks on the field; by his exertions and those of Sherif Nasir 160 were saved from death and taken prisoner. The loss of the Arabs was two killed and a few wounded. The effect of the Affair of Abu el Lissal, as it has officially been named, was far-reaching. The Arabs, with only local surprise in their favour, had annihilated an equal or superior force of trained Turkish infantry. Their achievement bred in them new confidence.

On the following day the party marched to Guweira, half-way between Ma'an and Aqaba, and received the surrender of the garrison of 120 men. Thence, it moved seaward to Kethira, where it overran a Turkish post of 70 infantry and 50 mounted men, capturing most of them.

Then at Khadra it came in contact with the Aqaba garrison, 300 strong, which had moved inland to be out of view from the sea and on the road to Ma'an and safety. But the local tribesmen, having had news of the Arab successes, were up and surrounding the entrenched camp of the Turks. On the arrival of Nasir with the Sherif's banner they demanded that an assault should be carried out. Captain Lawrence desired, however, that it should be spread abroad that the Arabs took prisoners, and, after some negotiations, he persuaded the whole Turkish force to surrender. On the 6th July the Arabs marched into Aqaba with over 600 prisoners, including 20 officers and a German N.C.O., who had been superintending the boring of wells. Within a few days they had killed about the same number of Turks, with small loss to themselves. They had also obtained the base which was to serve them throughout their successful campaign of 1918.

One event of some political importance must be mentioned before concluding the account of this period of the Arab activities. In October 1916, Sherif Hussein, without consulting his British advisers, announced his assumption of the title of " King of the Arab Nation." The step was of doubtful wisdom, since none of the greater chiefs of Arabia were likely to accord him that rank ; while Ibn Sa'ud, though most friendly to Great Britian, was displaying hostility to his pretensions. British officers, in his own interest and that of the common cause, were instructed to address him as " His Lordship," or, if a title could not be avoided, as " King of the Hejaz," an honour which could not wound the susceptibilities of other Arab rulers.

CHAPTER XIV.

THE ADVANCE TO EL ARISH.

(Map 8; Sketches B, 12.)

AFFAIRS ON THE EASTERN FRONT, SEPTEMBER–NOVEMBER 1916.

Map 8. Sketch B. AFTER the defeat of the Turkish attack upon Romani, the first necessity was the rest and restoration of the troops, who had suffered severely from the intense heat in which the battle had been fought and the pursuit conducted. The Australian and New Zealand mounted troops, to whose tenacity and physical endurance the victory had been largely due, now set about making the Sinai Peninsula their own. Reconnaissances were pushed further than ever afield, largely with the object of bringing under control the Bedouin, among whom numbers of rifles had been distributed by the enemy. This object was but partially attained. Watchful, long-sighted, suspicious as beasts of prey, swift in movement, these dwellers in the desert were not easily approached, and their smoke signals were means of communication as effective as the most perfect telegraph system.

It will be recalled that the War Committee had decided that the goal of the E.E.F. was now El Arish,[1] but that this goal was not expected to be attained till winter. The laying of railway and pipe-line was resumed immediately after the enemy had retired to El Arish. On the 24th September the first ship from America, which had had special naval escort through the Mediterranean, arrived at Qantara, with 5,000 tons of 12-inch piping.[2] The fact that the railway was already working enabled this pipe-line to be laid with

---

[1] See pp. 178 and 231.
[2] A proportion of 10-inch piping was included in the cargo, and, as it was necessary to start work at once without awaiting the second consignment (which arrived a month later), both diameters were employed in the line from Qantara to Romani.

great speed,[1] but considerable difficulties were encountered in training screwing gangs, in altering the threads, which were not all of the same standard, and in teaching the Egyptian labourers to handle these huge sections, which weighed half a ton apiece. Serious trouble was also caused by the absence of expansion joints, the sun affecting the metal so much that heavy leakage occurred when water was first run into the pipe. But by the 17th November the 12-inch pipe was filling reservoirs at Romani which had previously been prepared.

As the railway had assisted the pipe-line, so now the pipe-line assisted the railway. As soon as water was laid on to Romani the railway was freed of the burden of hauling it out in great quantities for the supply of the troops. Progress on the railway was accelerated, but as it once again drew ahead of the pipe-line the old difficulty reappeared.

The railway did not entirely obviate the necessity of a road. A metalled roadway had been laid from Qantara as far as Gilban Station, but it was obviously impossible to continue this across Sinai. Experiments were made with brushwood, which afforded a useful temporary track, but a far more satisfactory method was discovered to be the employment of wire netting, three or four strips in breadth, laid on the sand and pegged down. From Gilban onwards this was laid close to the railway line, and later ahead of it. The hooves of horses cut the wire, so mounted troops were forbidden to use the track, but it was of great value to infantry, while Ford cars could also be driven along it. Even under the weight of traffic it seldom sank more than an inch or two in the sand.

On the 17th August Sir A. Murray reported that, active operations in Sinai having been for the time being brought to an end by the enemy's retreat, he proposed to move his headquarters from Ismailia to Cairo. He also recommended that a properly organized corps headquarters should be

---

[1] Where the pipe-line was to be laid close to the rails, pipes were rolled one by one out of the train while it was in slow motion, the Egyptians thoroughly enjoying this new game and becoming very expert at it. There were, however, points where the pipe-line necessarily deviated from the rail. In such a case the pipes were off-loaded in heaps and dragged to their destination by Holt tractors, of which six were despatched from England for the purpose.

created for the command of the troops in Sinai, to relieve him of detail. Since the return to France of Lieut.-General Horne, No. 3 Section of the Canal Defences had been commanded by an improvised section headquarters, which had conducted the operations of Qatiya and Romani.

The move of G.H.Q. to Cairo had the disadvantage that it withdrew the Commander-in-Chief from touch with his troops in the desert. But it must be recalled that this touch had been established only seven months and that it was no more than five since Sir A. Murray had taken over the functions of the Force in Egypt, the commander of which had always lived in Cairo. Sir A. Murray was now discovering that the internal affairs of Egypt made constant demands upon him. The representatives of foreign nations, who had adopted a tone quiet enough while Egypt seemed in danger of invasion, began to take their stand upon their formal rights under the Capitulations, and their demands often clashed with the requirements of martial law, however leniently administered. The problems raised by the Arab revolt against Turkey also required his attention and his close association with the High Commissioner in the capital.

Whether, on balance, the transfer was or was not justified, it is not within the province of this history to suggest. But it is important that its causes should be fully understood. For the moment the Eastern Front was one only of the Commander-in-Chief's responsibilities. The War Office recognized his difficulty and agreed to his proposal. It also approved of the appointment of Major-General Sir Charles Dobell to command the troops on the Canal and in Sinai, with the rank of lieutenant-general and the title of G.O.C. Eastern Frontier Force.[1] Major-General Dobell had conducted with success the operations in the Cameroons and had since the previous June been in command of the Western Frontier Force. G.H.Q. opened at Cairo on the 18th October, Sir C. Dobell's Eastern Force headquarters taking its place at Ismailia. The headquarters of the Inspector-General of Communications, which had been established at Cairo, was merged in G.H.Q., and Lieut.-General Sir E. Altham returned to England.

1916.
18 Oct.

---

[1] Generally known as "Eastern Force," by which title it will be referred to henceforth.

During the months of September, October, and November, there were no operations of importance. The enemy continued to show an aggressive spirit in the air, and carried out an important raid on the 1st September against Port Said. This resulted in some casualties to both troops and civilian inhabitants,[1] but no damage to the port. In reply the R.F.C. bombed the aerodrome at El Arish. Two large raids by mounted troops were carried out during the period, in accordance with the policy of keeping the desert under control. Both entailed long marches and consequently the most elaborate arrangements for the carriage of water. In both cases, however, the commanders received instructions not to become involved in heavy fighting if the enemy were encountered in strength.

The first raid was directed against El Mazar, on the main coastwise track to El Arish. Here, it will be remembered, the enemy had left a post on his retirement after the Battle of Romani. The force was commanded by Major-General Chauvel and consisted of the 2nd and 3rd L.H. Brigades, three companies Imperial Camel Corps, two horse artillery batteries and two guns of the Hong Kong & Singapore Battery.[2] It assembled at Bir Salmana, 20 miles west of Mazar, on the 16th September, but the palm groves gave insufficient concealment, and it was attacked by German aeroplanes. The hope of surprising the garrison of Mazar, believed to be from five to seven hundred strong, had therefore to be abandoned. Nevertheless the column started that evening, marched through the night, and attacked the Turkish outposts at dawn on the 17th. But the place was found to be well fortified and its garrison thoroughly alert; the horse artillery, misled by its guide, was late; so General Chauvel, to the disappointment of his troops, decided to break off the action. Shortly afterwards the Turks withdrew their post from Mazar.

The other raid was a more difficult undertaking directed against a Turkish post at Bir el Maghara, 50 miles south-east of Romani, on the northern spurs of the Sinai hills. North of the hills, to the coast about Mazar, stretches the bleakest and most completely desert portion of the sand-dune

---

[1] Military: 1 killed, 11 wounded. Naval: 8 wounded. European civilians: 9 killed, 17 wounded. No bombs fell in the Arab quarter.
[2] The 1st L.H. Brigade followed and remained during the action 10 miles in rear.

country, while the ascent to Maghara is by way of a steep, narrow and rocky gulley. The force, commanded by Major-General A. G. Dallas, consisted of the 11th and 12th A.L.H., 1st City of London Yeomanry, 300 men Imperial Camel Corps, and one section Hong Kong Battery. It marched out from Bir Bayud (where, since Romani, numerous wells had been dug) on the evening of the 13th October. After two night marches the enemy was found on the morning of the 15th occupying a strong position on the steep hills of Gebel el Maghara. He was driven from his advanced position, 18 prisoners being captured. A two hours' engagement followed, but General Dallas, perceiving that there was no likelihood of taking the second position without considerable loss, then drew off in accordance with his instructions, reaching Bayud on the 17th.

During the first half of November Br.-General P. C. Palin led a small column from No. 1 Section Canal Defences to Gebel Bishr, 30 miles south-east of Suez, and drove off a body of the enemy which had established itself in the hills.

On the 7th December, Lieut.-General Sir Philip Chetwode, Bt., took command of a new force, the "Desert Column," which comprised, roughly speaking, the troops of the old No. 3 Section Canal Defences, but varied in composition from time to time. The railway had now reached Mazar, to which General Chetwode soon afterwards advanced his headquarters from Bir el Abd.

Sir A. Murray's Appreciation.

Map 8. Sketch B. The force and the railway had now covered more than half the distance between Qantara and the Palestine frontier. The mounted troops had on more than one occasion penetrated to the outskirts of El Arish, only 27 miles from the frontier at Rafah. British railhead at Mazar was 60 miles north-west of Turkish railhead at Kossaima, and a short further advance would bring the British line parallel to the Turkish. A vast organization had been built up to render Sinai habitable by British troops. Hundreds of miles of rail, roadway and piping had been laid; filters supplying one and a half million gallons a day and reservoirs to hold far greater quantities had been constructed. Qantara, a desert village on the bank of the Canal, had grown into a great port. And in the words of Sir A. Murray's Despatch, "the desert,

SUBJUGATION OF THE DESERT

1916.
21 Oct.

"till then almost destitute of human habitation, showed the "successive marks of our advance in the shape of strong "positions firmly entrenched and protected by hundreds of "miles of barbed wire, of standing camps where troops could "shelter in comfortable huts, of tanks and reservoirs, of railway "stations and sidings, of aerodromes and of signal stations and "wireless installations, by all of which the desert was subdued "and made habitable, and adequate lines of communication "established between the advancing troops and their ever-"receding base."

With all this organization, with a ration strength of 150,000 British and 6,000 Indian troops, and of 13,000 Egyptian Labour Corps, Sir A. Murray was yet not in a strong position for an advance into Palestine. Since the Battle of Romani drafts had come slowly for his infantry divisions; one of his mounted brigades, the 8th, had been despatched to Salonika on the 16th November; while five of his Yeomanry regiments which had not been given horses since their return from Gallipoli had been formed into two infantry battalions and also sent to Salonika. His appreciation of his position and of the future is contained in a letter addressed to the C.I.G.S., on the 21st October. This, together with a number of telegrams which succeeded it, is of the highest importance, as showing the development of British policy with regard to the campaign.

Sir A. Murray began by stating that he had been instructed that the policy of the E.E.F. must in the near future be defensive, though, subject to this decision, the occupation of El Arish was desirable. With this view he felt himself to be in accord. An active defence of Egypt would, he considered, most effectively be based on El Arish. But, he pointed out, he had estimated his requirements for the occupation of this place to be five divisions and four mounted brigades. At present he had four divisions only, and these were 6,000 under strength, but he had six mounted brigades.[1]

---

[1] That is, 1st, 2nd and 3rd L.H., N.Z.M.R., 5th and 6th Mounted Brigades. The last was transferred a few days later from the Western to the Eastern Force, but was retained in the Suez Section. Sir A. Murray did not include the Imperial Service Cavalry Brigade, presumably not considering it suitable for the work in hand, or the 22nd Mounted Brigade which he proposed to keep on the Western Frontier.

If the sole problem had been the defence of Egypt, the position at Bir el Abd which had now been established would have constituted the limit of advance necessary, since all the water-bearing area was now in British possession.

Sir A. Murray considered that something more was demanded of him. He should at least prevent the withdrawal of enemy troops from Syria and Palestine to other theatres. He was therefore of opinion that, though he had four divisions only instead of the five for which he had asked, his advance on El Arish should continue.

This decision might have to be reconsidered. Should the Turks largely reinforce their troops in Sinai, or should his own force be further reduced, he would probably be compelled to withdraw to a previously prepared position at Bir el Abd or Salmana.

As to the first of these contingencies, the arrival of considerable enemy reinforcements seemed at present unlikely, since the Turks were everywhere hard pressed. Opposed to him in Palestine and Sinai were the *3rd* and *27th (Arab) Divisions*, which he estimated at 6,000 and 10,000 effective rifles. In addition to this force on his immediate front, there were in Syria the *41st, 43rd* and *44th Divisions*, but he assumed that the *43rd* would remain in Lebanon, while at least one division must be held in the Alexandretta district.[1] It thus appeared that only one other division was available for the reinforcement of Southern Palestine. Withdrawals from other theatres were improbable, except from the Caucasus, whence it was just possible that a corps of 30,000 men might be sent. In that case the British might have to meet 55,000 men. That he considered to be the maximum for some time to come, nor did he believe that such a concentration could be effected without his knowledge.

Meanwhile the leading British division was within 40 miles of El Arish. The enemy had three alternatives open to him in face of the British advance. He might strengthen

---

[1] General Murray omits the *23rd Division*, which was at Tarsus and Mersina during the summer and included in the *Fourth Army* early in 1917. The other three divisions are given correctly, though at least one battalion of the *41st* was in the Hejaz. These divisions must have been extremely weak, for the Turks state that the rifle strength of the coast defence forces, including Gendarmerie battalions, was 12,000 in the following March. The reference to the Lebanon is due to the fact that it was reported to be disturbed.

El Arish and attempt to bar further progress; he might himself begin an advance from his railway along the route through Central Sinai towards Ismailia; or he might evacuate Sinai altogether. Which course he would take it was impossible to foresee, but in any event Sir A. Murray anticipated being able to drive him out of El Arish.

1916.
21 Oct.

In case the enemy should be reinforced, defensive positions were being prepared as the advance continued. The strong Romani defences were being maintained, and work was about to begin on a line at Bir el Abd. A more advanced line had been reconnoitred 5 miles east of Salmana. The construction of these two latter positions would be the task of the Egyptian Labour Corps.

On the Western Frontier affairs were satisfactory. The blockade and the activity of the armoured cars had obliged the Senussi, from sheer want, to retire to Siwa. Thither Sir A. Murray did not intend to follow him,[1] but he could now reduce his strength on this front to reinforce Sinai. The situation might still change for the worse, because the Italian blockade was not yet effective, and in that case the Western Frontier might again have to be reinforced. Meanwhile, it was proposed to reorganize its defence on the basis of patrolling a front of one thousand miles. The area of occupation was to be restricted to the coast belt (Sollum, Matruh and Dabaa), the Oases of Moghara, Bahariya and Kharga, with reduced detachments at Wadi Natrun and the Faiyum.

By this means the forces on the Western Frontier could be reduced immediately by one dismounted Yeomanry brigade, one mounted brigade, two batteries R.H.A., one battery R.F.A.; while, as more camelry became available, it was hoped to withdraw a second mounted brigade. These troops were to be transferred to Sinai or the Canal Defences.

In short, it was Sir A. Murray's intention to continue the advance on El Arish, holding Sections 1 and 2 of the Canal Defences and the Western Desert as lightly as possible. His object was to secure El Arish as a base for offensive action against the Turks in Southern Syria. This project he was prepared to carry out with the troops at his disposal,

---

[1] On this point, as has been recorded in Chapter IX, the Commander-in-Chief changed his policy, and carried out a raid on Siwa in the following February.

but he would have to reconsider it either if the Turks were heavily reinforced or if his own strength were materially reduced for any length of time.

There followed upon this letter a prolonged discussion, conducted by telegram, between Sir A. Murray and Sir W. Robertson as to the extent of the operations to be undertaken, the requirements of the E.E.F., and the possibility of reinforcing it.[1] On the 12th November, Sir A. Murray telegraphed that after occupying El Arish it was his intention, while having due regard to his primary duty of defending Egypt, to harass the enemy in Syria with his mobile forces, thus, he hoped, attracting to his front Turkish troops which would otherwise be employed in other theatres.

In studying the further correspondence on this subject, certain conflicting tendencies of British policy must be kept in mind if the tone of the telegrams is to be understood. The Imperial General Staff was opposed in principle to operations which might deflect British resources from the main theatre in France and Belgium. But the new Prime Minister, Mr. Lloyd George, attached great importance to the effect which the expulsion of the Turks from Jerusalem would have upon the opinion of the world. The C.I.G.S. endeavoured to give effect to the Prime Minister's policy regarding Palestine, while maintaining the general British policy that France was the main theatre of war. Thus, on the 9th December, two days after Mr. Lloyd George had kissed hands, Sir W. Robertson telegraphed to Sir A. Murray pointing out the value of a big success on his Eastern Front and enquiring what additional troops would be required for action beyond El Arish. Sir A. Murray replied next day that he needed two additional divisions if he were to cross the Palestine frontier, and suggested that these might be lent him from Mesopotamia. On the 12th the C.I.G.S. telegraphed that the Prime Minister had seen Sir A. Murray's last message and desired that the maximum effort should be made during the winter. No troops could be withdrawn from Mesopotamia till the spring, so that any reinforcements sent before then would have to come either from France or Salonika. He enquired how soon the two additional divisions would be needed, whether the water supply would permit of six divisions being employed in offensive operations,

---

[1] These telegrams will be found in the Note at end of Chapter.

and what was the Commander-in-Chief's estimate of the force which he would have to face at the various stages of his advance.

1916. Dec.

Sir A. Murray promised to make the greatest effort in his power. He still considered a fifth division necessary, but would try to reach Rafah without it. For a subsequent advance to Beersheba he would need the full six divisions, but not until about the 15th February. He would be forced to keep one division on the Canal to secure the waterway and one between Qantara and railhead. He estimated that the enemy might oppose him with 40,000 men in a month's time and with another 12,000 if the Hejaz were abandoned. And then, on the 15th December, came a message that, despite all the previous discussion, the primary mission of the E.E.F. was still the defence of Egypt.

It will be seen, therefore, that future policy remained somewhat indefinite, though no doubt was left in the mind of the Commander-in-Chief as to the immediate action required of him. He was still limited to the defence of Egypt, and while he was enjoined to do his utmost to obtain a success against the enemy, the reinforcements which had been discussed had faded into the background. Yet within the limits thus imposed, the Force, after its year of "walking through this great wilderness,"[1] was about to be enabled to quit it for a land where there was at least verdure to ease the eyes, though the vines and fig trees and pomegranates and oil olive of the Biblical promise were still far off.

THE TURKISH RETIREMENT AND THE AFFAIR OF MAGDHABA.

The Turkish garrison at El Arish was believed to be 1,600 strong and known from the reports of the R.F.C. to be well entrenched. Twenty-five miles south-east of the town, on the banks of the great Wadi el Arish, "the River of Egypt," were further camps at El Magdhaba and Abu Aweigila, protecting the Turkish railhead at El Kossaima. The Turkish defences at El Arish covered all the water in that area; between them and the British railhead there was none. An advance upon El Arish therefore necessitated the establishment of a very large supply at railhead and the concentration of large numbers of camels to carry it forward.

Map 8. Sketches B, 12.

---

[1] Deuteronomy, ii, 7.

Preparations were not complete till the 20th December. By that date material to lay the railway to Rafah was in sight, and the War Office had despatched eight tanks and some heavy guns and howitzers to Egypt.

On the very day that all was ready for the advance, the R.F.C. reported that the enemy had evacuated his position. Though it was not certain that some resistance would not be encountered, there was now no need to rely upon the slow advance of the infantry The A. & N.Z. Mounted Division and the Imperial Camel Brigade (which had completed its concentration and received its title only the day before)[1] were ordered to move on El Arish that night. After a march of 20 miles the town was surrounded on the morning of the 21st and found to be indeed empty of Turks.[2] The local Arabs professed unbounded joy at their departure and the arrival of the British. The 52nd Division reached El Arish on the 22nd. Mine-sweeping was at once commenced in the roadstead and the construction of a pier begun. By the 23rd the first ship from Port Said was landing supplies in boats.

The night march of the mounted troops to El Arish, otherwise uneventful, marked the escape from the desert. As they rode in the darkness the men, to their delight, felt their horses pass from the sand which they had known so long to firm soil. And with morning light, though sand-dunes mile on mile lay to south and east of them, their eyes were gladdened by green patches of cultivation, with wheat and barley just sprouting, and many palms.

General Chetwode, commanding the Desert Column, arrived at El Arish by boat on the 22nd December and at once gave orders for the pursuit of the enemy. To render this possible he had arranged for a special camel convoy with rations and fodder to arrive at El Arish at 4.30 p.m. that day. There was still uncertainty as to the movements of the Turkish force which had evacuated El Arish; whether it had moved along the coast to Rafah or south-east along the

---

[1] To this brigade was attached the Hong Kong & Singapore Battery of mountain artillery, which had Indian personnel. The brigade at this date consisted of three battalions.

[2] "Sinai": Kress, i, p. 24. "As our troops were not strong enough "to defend the town of El Arish, which was unhappily situated and exposed "to the fire of British warships, we were obliged in December to evacuate "this place also."

Sketch 12.

Wadi el Arish in the direction of the railway at Kossaima. Nor was it known whether Rafah and the posts along the wadi were held in strength. The first orders issued to General Chauvel were to move down the wadi on Magdhaba and Abu Aweigila with the bulk of his force, while sending a detachment of the Camel Brigade to operate against Rafah. During the afternoon, however, an aeroplane report was received which showed that there was a considerable garrison at Magdhaba. General Chetwode thereupon cancelled the Rafah enterprise and ordered General Chauvel to advance on Magdhaba with all available troops of his division[1] and the Camel Brigade.

1916.
22 Dec

There was at this date no running water in the wadi, nor had the bold reconnaissances of the Australian Field Squadron, working up to it at night while El Arish was yet held by the Turks, found any by such boring as they had been able to carry out. Water had therefore to be carried for the needs of the force. This caused an unexpected delay, for the long camel train carrying it was crossed in the darkness by the incoming columns of the 52nd Division, which thus checked the advance. General Chauvel's force was, therefore, unable to move out until midnight.

The ground was firm, the night clear and cold, so that the march, once begun, was swift. At 3.50 a.m. on the 23rd December the bivouac fires of Magdhaba came in sight, and an hour later the force halted in an open plain, 4 miles from the settlement. Day broke while General Chauvel with his brigadiers and staff was making a reconnaissance of the enemy's position ; the fires then disappeared and the whole valley was shrouded in smoke, which made observation very difficult. It appeared, however, that the Turkish position lay astride the Wadi el Arish, that it was roughly square, about two miles from east to west, and rather less from north to south, and consisted of about half a dozen redoubts and certain connecting entrenchments. At 7.50 a.m. a report was received from an airman that he had been fired on from one of the redoubts north of the wadi and from several points in its bed. Another welcome report from the air was that there was no sign of reinforcements for some distance beyond Ruafa, 8 miles south-east of Magdhaba,

23 Dec.

---

[1] That is, less the 2nd L.H. Brigade, which had been withdrawn for a rest, and the Ayr and Leicester Batteries.

and only a handful of troops there. General Chauvel's time was therefore limited only by his scanty water supply and not by any threat from the enemy.

Orders for the attack were at once issued. The 3rd L.H. and N.Z.M.R. Brigades under Br.-General Chaytor were to move north of Magdhaba and attack from the north-east; the Camel Brigade (Br.-General C. L. Smith) to advance straight on Magdhaba north of the El Arish road; the 1st L.H. Brigade was to be held in reserve. The signal for the advance was to be the opening of fire of the artillery, consisting of the Inverness and Somerset Batteries R.H.A. and the Hong Kong Battery. As the troops began their advance a further report from the air showed little movement within the area of the defences, though the rifle pits in the redoubts were being reinforced. Nothing could be seen of the Turkish artillery.

By 9.25 Br.-General Chaytor was established 3 miles north of Magdhaba. He ordered Br.-General Royston, commanding the 3rd L.H. Brigade, to send a regiment right round the position, through Aulad Ali, and cut off the enemy's retreat to the south and south-east. General Royston led the 10th A.L.H. and two sections of the Machine-Gun Squadron forward at a gallop, and was just in time to catch a number of prisoners in the wadi, portions of the garrison having already begun a retirement. At 9.55, without waiting for the Camel Brigade's attack to be pushed home— this arm being necessarily slower in movement than the Light Horse, since it could not advance mounted so close to the position—General Chaytor directed the Canterbury Regiment on Hill 345, on the south side of the wadi, and the Wellington on its right against Magdhaba itself. The Inverness and Somerset Batteries now for the first time located the enemy guns by the dust of their discharge.

At 10 a.m. an airman dropped a message on General Chaytor's headquarters reporting that the enemy was making off and might yet escape the enveloping movement.[1] The report was at once sent to General Chauvel, who ordered

---

[1] This retreat was inexplicable at the time, as, on the one hand, a large number of prisoners were captured by the 10th A.L.H. in its sweep and, on the other, it was speedily found that all the redoubts were held and prepared to make a stout resistance. It is made clear by a statement of the Historical Section, Turkish General Staff, that a number of Arab soldiers left their position in a body.

SLOW PROGRESS OF ATTACK

Br.-General Cox, commanding the 1st L.H. Brigade, to move straight on Magdhaba. General Cox led out his brigade at the trot. He speedily came under shrapnel fire from the enemy's mountain guns, whereupon he changed direction slightly and increased his pace to a gallop. The enemy opened heavy fire with machine guns and rifles. The range was over a mile, but it was clear now that there had been no general evacuation of the position and that a further mounted advance in face of the musketry fire would involve heavy casualties. General Cox therefore swung his two regiments right-handed at the gallop and took cover in a tributary of the main wadi. Thence, at 10.30, he began a dismounted attack with the 3rd A.L.H. up the wadi's broad bed.

1916.
23 Dec.

At 11.50 a.m. General Chauvel reported the situation to the Desert Column. The N.Z.M.R. Brigade (less Auckland Regiment in reserve) was attacking from the north. The 3rd L.H. Brigade (less 10th A.L.H.) was still held in reserve by General Chaytor. The 10th A.L.H. was moving round the eastern flank of the position at Aulad Ali. The Camel Brigade (less one battalion in reserve) was advancing directly on the village. The 1st L.H. Brigade on its right was working up the wadi in the same direction. The artillery was in action, but had difficulty in obtaining targets owing to the nature of the ground and to mirage. Immediately afterwards General Chaytor threw into the fight the remainder of the 3rd L.H. Brigade, ordering it to fill the gap between the Wellington and Canterbury Regiments and to attack the most easterly of the Turkish works. The 8th and 9th A.L.H. advanced at a gallop and dismounted under heavy fire to advance against the redoubt on foot.

Fire from the redoubts was now very hot, and little progress was being made. The Camel Brigade in particular, which had to advance over ground dead flat and devoid of cover, was seriously checked, and it was upon the fire power and weight of numbers of this force that General Chauvel had chiefly relied for the success of the attack. At 1.5 p.m. the G.O.C. had bad news from Bir Lahfan, 14 miles down the wadi from Magdhaba. There he had left a field troop of engineers to dig for water, and he now learned that none was obtainable. Unless Magdhaba was taken there was no water nearer than El Arish, and most of the horses had had none since the beginning of the march. He therefore reluctantly decided that it was necessary to break off the action, as there appeared no immediate prospect of capturing Magdhaba. At 1.50 p.m. he telegraphed an account of the situation to the Desert Column and stated that he proposed to order a withdrawal.

Meanwhile, however, the 3rd A.L.H., steadily working up the wadi, had obtained touch with the Camel Brigade within 100 yards of Redoubt No. 1, north of the wadi, which had been the principal bar to progress on this flank. A wide, level patch of the wadi's bed, devoid of cover, had to be crossed before the redoubt, which lay on the edge of the right bank, could be assaulted. But a spirited charge was carried out by two companies of the Camel Brigade in conjunction with the light horsemen. With loud cheers the former on the plain above, the latter from the wadi, dashed at the redoubt. They were met by heavy fire, and a high proportion of the losses incurred in the whole action were suffered here. But the enemy did not await the bayonet. The garrison sprang to its feet and surrendered, three officers and 92 other ranks being taken prisoner.

This was in fact the climax of the fight. When he learned what had happened, at 2.30 p.m., General Chauvel telephoned to General Chetwode that he had now no doubt regarding his ultimate victory. The G.O.C. Desert Column promised that if possible a convoy with water should be sent to meet the column on its return journey.

Soon after 2 p.m. General Chauvel had learnt from General Chaytor that the enemy showed signs of withdrawing from the buildings of the village and that success was now imminent on his front also. The 3rd L.H. Brigade was then in touch with the two New Zealand regiments and within 600 yards of the enemy's trenches. Meanwhile (though this was unknown to General Chauvel) the 10th A.L.H. had carried out its encircling movement with great success. After capturing 300 prisoners at Aulad Ali, it had crossed the Wadi el Arish, rounded Hill 345, swung north and attacked Redoubt No. 4. The ground here was hilly and afforded good cover, so that the light horsemen were able to approach in a series of mounted rushes till close to the Turkish trenches. One party actually galloped through Redoubt No. 3, though without capturing it.

At 4 p.m. Redoubt No. 2 was captured by the 1st L.H. Brigade, with Khadir Bey, commanding the *80th Regiment*,

CAPTURE OF MAGDHABA

1916.
23 Dec.

who was in command of the garrison. The New Zealanders and 3rd L.H. Brigade also swept over the northern trenches and advanced on the houses and huts of the village. By 4.30 p.m. all organized resistance was over and the remainder of the garrison was everywhere surrendering in small batches.

General Chauvel at once rode into Magdhaba and ordered the Auckland Regiment to clear the battlefield, arranging that a small convoy should be sent up with its supplies. The remainder of the force, which had been able to water some of its horses in Magdhaba, he ordered to assemble at once at his headquarters and begin the return march. On the way back water and food were drawn from the convoy sent up by the Desert Column. Men and horses, after marching and fighting for thirty hours without pause, and having been in many cases three nights without sleep, were completely exhausted on their return to camp. The wounded suffered very severely on the jolting camel *cacolets*, and, to add to their discomfort, the night was very cold. The capture of a Turkish field hospital, however, enabled them to receive better attention before evacuation than would otherwise, in the conditions of the operation, have been possible.

Altogether 1,282 prisoners, including Khadir Bey and his two battalion commanders, were captured. Ninety-seven Turks were buried by the troops left to clear the battlefield. The garrison consisted of the *2nd* and *3rd Battalions, 80th Regiment* (*27th Division*), one mountain battery, and 50 camelry. Not more than the merest handful can have escaped. In addition to the four mountain guns, 1,200 rifles, a great quantity of ammunition, 40 horses and 51 camels were captured. The British losses were 146.[1]

The action will be remembered as a notable instance of the effective employment of mounted troops against isolated fortifications in open country. It proved also the value of the new Camel Brigade. Less mobile than the Light Horse, now that the shifting sands of the desert, for use in which it had been organized, had been left behind, and slower in coming into action, the dismounted strength of its three

---

[1]

	KILLED.	WOUNDED.
Officers	5	7
Other ranks ..	17	117

Fifty-one horses were killed or wounded.

battalions almost equalled that of two light horse brigades.[1] When acting, therefore, with the other mounted troops it greatly increased their offensive power. General Chauvel attributed his small casualty list to the bad shooting of the Turkish infantry, even though firing was maintained up to very close quarters. His threefold superiority in artillery was also undoubtedly a factor. The Inverness Battery fired 498 rounds during the action, a remarkable expenditure of ammunition in this country, 50 miles from railhead.

On the 22nd December a small column from No. 1 Section Canal Defences had found the country half-way between Suez and Nekhl clear of the enemy. As a result of the occupation of El Arish and the destruction of their rear guard at Magdhaba, the Turks withdrew the remainder of their posts from Sinai. Bir el Maghara, Nekhl, Bir el Hassana, were all evacuated by New Year's Day. For the first time since the outbreak of war the Sinai Peninsula was now virtually clear of the Turks.

NOTE.

TELEGRAMS BETWEEN SIR A. MURRAY AND THE C.I.G.S.

From—General Officer Commanding-in-Chief, Egypt.
To—Chief of the Imperial General Staff.
No. A.M. 1251.   12th November 1916.

Map 8. Sketch B.   I intend as soon as possible to occupy El Arish and there to protect Egypt and clear the province of Sinai. I also propose, while having due regard to my primary duty of defending Egypt, to harass the Turks in Syria with my mobile forces to the full extent of my strength. I thus hope to attract to myself Turkish forces which would otherwise be engaged against the Sherif, or the Russians, or in Mesopotamia. I hope by acting on the defensive-offensive to gain full value from my Egyptian army field force which a purely defensive role would not achieve. The sending of any detachment to Rabegh weakens my offensive and has the natural drawbacks inherent in dispersion of force. . . . . . . The Egyptian field force must always be necessary and to reduce it below a certain figure, which I consider has now been reached, relegates it to a purely defensive role which might lead to its being ignored, whilst if we keep it at its present strength the offensive action it is capable of must draw enemy forces against it, and a strategic reserve is hence available for the purpose of meeting the unforeseen.

---

[1] The Camel Brigade, when going into action, usually left the same proportion of its strength with the camels—one fourth—as the cavalry left with the horses when acting dismounted.

From—Chief of the Imperial General Staff.
To—Sir Archibald Murray.
No. 26174, cipher.   9th December 1916.

To-day Prime Minister mentioned to me desirability of making your operations as successful as possible. I am in entire agreement. Wire précis of action proposed beyond El Arish, stating what additional troops you would require for advance, if any. I cannot help thinking that in view of importance of achieving big success on Eastern front, and the effect this will have, you might risk having fewer troops on Western. A success is badly needed, and your operations promise well.

From—General Officer Commanding-in-Chief, Egypt.
To—Chief of the Imperial General Staff.
No. A.M. 1380   10th December 1916.

Your No. 26174, 9th. I have always thought important results might be secured by an advance by us from Arish into Syria. At the present moment I am endeavouring to make as large a success as I can at Arish, which place and Masiada are strongly entrenched. Our railhead is within 20 miles of Arish now, and I propose when it has advanced about 8 miles further, i.e., in about 10 days' time, to move 42nd and 52nd Divisions on Masiada and Arish, and my Mounted Division and Camelry well south and then east, so as to cut off the enemy should they attempt withdrawal. My own fear is that the enemy may, before I am near enough to strike, evacuate Arish. After occupation of Arish I propose to push on 42nd and 52nd Divisions to Rafah, constructing railway from Arish to Rafah as rapidly as possible. I am in urgent need of railway track demanded from War Office for this railway extension. Immediately Arish is occupied I intend to send mounted force towards Kossaima, with a view to dealing with enemy detachments at that place, and at Magdhaba and Abu Aweigila, as well as with any other which may retire from Maghara and Bir El Hassana eastward. My action subsequent to reaching Rafah must naturally be dictated by situation at moment, and by main consideration that the enemy must be defeated in the field. My idea, however, if circumstances permit, is to advance from Rafah on Beershaba, where enemy's main concentration appears to be. Occupation of this place would, moreover, have advantage of placing me on a railway.

At Beersheba I should be only 70 miles from Hejaz line, against which my aircraft could co-operate daily. Further, I cannot but think our appearance at Beersheba would result in a rising of Arab population in southern Syria, who are known to be very disaffected towards Turks. As regards additional troops, I fully realize shipping difficulties, as well as submarine danger and undesirability of taking troops from main theatre, but if my operations progress as I hope, I shall have a long line of communication, and I also require more infantry if I am to operate with any sort of rapidity. Would it not be possible to lend me temporarily two divisions from Mesopotamia and any spare mounted troops there may be, either there or in India, if it is not out of place for me to make a suggestion I should like to have suggested sending a cavalry division from France, but realize that this may be out of the question in view of shipping difficulties. One point I wish to make clear is that after Arish my operations cannot be rapid, as in the absence of local supplies I am dependent on my railway, though by making a sea base at Arish, and subsequently at Rafah, I hope to supplement this. You may rely on me, however, to push on as rapidly as I possibly can. I shall not stop acting offensively until I see that I am in danger of risking the defence of Egypt. My rearward entrenched positions will be carefully maintained. Given rails and pipes, which up to now have been supplied me generously, I can make my weight, small or large, felt by the Turks.

From—Chief of the Imperial General Staff.
To—General Officer Commanding-in-Chief, Egypt.
No. 26289, cipher.   12th December 1916.

Your A.M. 1380, 10th December, has been seen by Prime Minister, who wishes you to make the maximum possible effort during the winter. Until the spring we cannot send any troops from Mesopotamia, and if you need reinforcements before then they must be drawn either from France or Salonika.

At what stage would you require the two divisions for which you ask? Do you want these additional troops to enable you to reach Rafah, or to advance from Rafah to Beersheba?

With two additional divisions you would have six and your mounted troops. Can you water so large a force as this, as I assume that you intend, when you have cleared the Sinai Peninsula, to employ all the troops you have offensively on the Eastern front?

What do you estimate as the maximum force enemy can bring against you at various stages of your operations, and when do you estimate hot weather will stop your operations?

From—General Officer Commanding-in-Chief, Egypt.
To—Chief of the Imperial General Staff.
No. A.M. 1389.   13th December 1916.

Your No. 26289 cipher. The greatest effort will be made. Have noted what you say regarding reinforcements. You make no specific mention of mounted troops, which would very greatly help me if they can be spared. In my first appreciation I said that an additional division, making five in all, would be necessary to hold and operate from Arish. I still consider this necessary in order to ensure security, though I shall do my best to push forward from El Arish to Rafah without it, commencing about 15th January. For my further advance from Rafah to Beersheba, I feel justified in asking for a second division, but this would not be required until about 15th February. I must always keep one division on Canal to ensure 80 miles of waterway not being interfered with by raiders, mines, &c., and one division, Qantara to railhead, as protection from raiders from the south. El Arish will be held as a strongly entrenched position, thus leaving me, if reinforced by two extra divisions, between three and four infantry divisions plus mounted division for advance into Syria. Water troubles are apparently at an end after passing the line of Gaza-Khelasa-Asluj. In 1916 hot weather never stopped my force, and I hope that in 1917, with increased experience and better water facilities, we shall do no worse. Enemy can now bring 25,000 against me; in a month's time, 40,000; if he abandons Hejaz, another 12,000. Any further additions must come from Europe, Mesopotamia or Caucasus.

From—Chief of the Imperial General Staff.
To—General Officer Commanding-in-Chief, Egypt.
No. 26624, cipher.   15th December 1916.

Your No. A.M. 1389 of 13th December. In order that any possibility of misunderstanding may be removed, I wish to make it clear that notwithstanding the instructions recently sent to you to the effect that you should make your maximum effort during the winter, your primary mission remains unchanged, that is to say, it is the defence of Egypt. You will be informed if and when the War Cabinet changes this policy.

By the occupation of El Arish you cover the only line of approach to Egypt which can be used by any considerable force, and therefore employ the troops required for the defence of Egypt in the most economical and effective way. Also, at the same time, your advance should encourage the Arabs of Southern Syria to throw in their lot with the Sherif, and it may enable you to get into touch with them by aeroplane. Also, by threatening the Hejaz railway it should reduce the probability of a Turkish advance on Mecca, and if you are able to provide for the security of Egypt and at the same time by advancing beyond El Arish gain successes over the Turks and increase your chance of assisting the Sherif, you should do so.

It is impossible to send you any cavalry, and the possibility of sending further infantry divisions mainly depends on whether we can persuade the French to agree to release troops from Salonika. In the meantime you should be as aggressive as possible with the troops at your disposal subject to your main mission of defending Egypt. In this connection, I do not quite understand why, when you have occupied El Arish and cleared the enemy from Northern Sinai, it should be necessary to keep a whole division on the Canal and another on your line of communication in addition to the considerable number of troops you have in excess of the establishment of divisions. The danger of raids on the Canal should be small while you are pressing the enemy in superior force, and your aeroplanes should be able to give you ample notice of any such raids.

CHAPTER XV.

THE ACTION OF RAFAH AND PREPARATIONS FOR ADVANCE INTO PALESTINE.

(Maps 8, 11 ; Sketches B, 13 ; Diagram 1.)

THE ACTION OF RAFAH.

Map 8.
Sketch B.
THE Turks had been dealt a heavy blow at Magdhaba, but it was impossible to follow up the advantage immediately. The Force was still condemned to wait on rail and pipe. It was reported by the R.F.C. that the enemy was entrenching a position at El Magruntein, south of Rafah, which was occupied by about two battalions with mountain artillery. The Turks had again left an isolated detachment within striking reach of the British mounted troops, for no other encampment could be located within ten miles, the next position being apparently on the left bank of the Wadi Ghazze about Weli Sheikh Nuran and Shellal. General Chetwode, commanding the Desert Column, considered that a cutting-out raid, like that at Magdhaba, offered reasonable prospects of success against Rafah. As the advance of railway and pipe-line could not be made rapid enough to permit of the occupation of this place for some time to come, General Dobell and Sir A. Murray concurred—the Commander-in-Chief with the proviso that at this stage no undue risks should be run.

On the 28th December the 1st L.H. Brigade carried out a reconnaissance to Bir el Burj, 12 miles along the El Arish—Rafah road, which was found to be in fair condition and suitable for cars and guns. General Chauvel then ordered a more important reconnaissance, to Sheikh Zowaiid, 20 miles from El Arish and only 10 from the Turkish position. This was carried out by the 1st L.H. Brigade, which marched out on the morning of the 30th December, bivouacked that night at Sheikh Zowaiid, and returned to camp the following afternoon. About a hundred friendly inhabitants were found in the village, where water

Sketch 13

Action of RAFAH.
Jan. 9th, 1917.

was plentiful. Some cultivation, it has been stated, had been seen about El Arish, but the brigade brought back tidings of still better country, with rolling stretches of pasture and young crops, brightly starred with poppies and other wild-flowers. A small advanced guard, pushing forward to rising ground beyond Sheikh Zowaiid, had seen great activity at El Magruntein.

For a few days it was necessary to send back to railhead the N.Z.M.R. and 3rd L.H. Brigades to save transport. They returned to El Arish on the 5th January. The difficulty regarding supplies at El Arish was not yet over, though nearing its end. On the 4th January the first construction train reached the town, but it was to be some time before railhead, with the large station and sidings necessary, could be established there. The landing of supplies from the sea, on an exposed beach and in squally winter weather, was both slow and dangerous. The arrangements made by Vice-Admiral Sir R. Wemyss had, however, resulted in the first consignment of stores being put ashore in boats and lighters on the 23rd December and in the landing of 1,500 tons in the ensuing fortnight.

While the infantry was entrenching El Arish plans were being made for the raid against the enemy's position at Rafah. The troops which had captured Magdhaba, that is the A. & N.Z. Mounted Division (less 2nd L.H. Brigade) and Camel Brigade, were to be employed in this operation, and in addition the 5th Mounted Brigade and No. 7 Light Car Patrol.[1] General Chetwode decided to command the raid in person. On the 7th January his orders were issued, with instructions for the concentration of the force at Sheikh Zowaiid.

At 4 p.m. on the 8th January the force moved out from El Arish, the 5th Mounted Brigade leading. After the Yeomanry had enveloped Sheikh Zowaiid, the column advanced and bivouacked about 10 p.m., the main body closing up to the cross roads west of the village.

At 1 a.m. on the 9th January the advance was resumed, all wheeled vehicles except the guns remaining at Sheikh Zowaiid. The A. & N.Z. Mounted Division, followed by the Camel Brigade, moved along the track to Karm Ibn Musleh, the 1st L.H. Brigade as advanced guard. The 5th

1917.
Jan.

9 Jan.

---

[1] 4 gun-cars and 3 store-cars.

Mounted Brigade, leaving two troops of the Worcester Yeomanry for the protection of Sheikh Zowaiid,[1] moved off by the same route at 2.3 a.m., except for a squadron of the Worcester Yeomanry, which followed the historic El Arish—Rafah road. Half a mile outside Sheikh Zowaiid a Bedouin camel patrol was overrun by the advanced guard and fortunately captured to a man. The R.F.C. had during the previous afternoon prevented observation of the column's advance by Turkish aircraft, so that the enemy was still in ignorance of the impending attack.

Map 11.
Sketch 13.
At 3.30 a.m. the column reached Point 250, the road-junction 4½ miles south of Rafah, halted for an hour, then continued the advance eastward. The left flank guard of the 3rd L.H. Brigade captured two Turks, though not before they had put up a flare. The signal was not repeated elsewhere and probably was not seen.

At 5.15 a.m., the N.Z.M.R. Brigade, led by Major C. L. Barlow, an intelligence officer who knew the country well, and a native guide, was detached from the column to round up the native encampments about Karm Ibn Musleh and Shokh es Sufi. The population consisted of old men, women and children, with no arms but a few swords and revolvers. They gave a warning, however, before the New Zealanders could reach them—the long-drawn Arab "lu-lu-lu!" which travels a great distance—and as dawn appeared smoke signals went up from one Bedouin camp after another. At 6.15 a.m. the Auckland Regiment crossed the frontier, a dramatic and significant moment in the course of the campaign. The action that followed was to be fought in two continents, Asia and Africa.

Br.-General Chaytor reported to General Chauvel that there was a good position of assembly for the division in the neighbourhood of Karm Ibn Musleh. General Chauvel then moved up to this spot, dropping the Camel Brigade on the way. By 6.45 a.m. the 1st and 3rd L.H. Brigades and the artillery were just south of Karm Ibn Musleh, thus cutting off the retreat of the enemy to the south-east; the N.Z.M.R. Brigade was rather over a mile to the north, and the Camel Brigade three-quarters of a mile to the west.

---

[1] Two troops of the 1st L.H. Brigade were also left as baggage-guard, and probably similar detachments from the other brigades, though this is not recorded.

The 5th Mounted Brigade and General Chetwode's headquarters remained at Point 210, 4½ miles west of Karm Ibn Musleh. A patrol of the Wellington Regiment was sent out to cut the telegraph line running east from Rafah in the direction of Shellal.

General Chauvel and his C.R.A. now reconnoitred the Turkish position. From Karm Ibn Musleh, where the ground was slightly higher, it was clearly visible and proved to be extremely strong. The approaches were devoid of cover and the immediate neighbourhood of the entrenchments almost a glacis. In the centre was a formidable keep, known as "the Reduit," on a smooth grassy knoll.[1] South of this, in a rough semi-circle, was a series of three systems of works, known as " A," " B," and " C," the " B " works forming a first line of defence against advance from the south. The works were well dug and excellently sited, with a perfect field of fire up to 2,000 yards in almost every direction. But they were not wired, and this fact gave the attackers a chance of success. Desert Column headquarters sent a message to General Chauvel that a deliberate artillery preparation was necessary in view of the position's strength. General Chetwode announced that when targets had been selected he would cross the fire of the divisional artillery (consisting of the Leicester, Inverness and Somerset Batteries R.H.A.) with that of " B " Battery H.A.C., attached to the 5th Mounted Brigade, to obtain a greater concentration of fire.

At 8.30 General Chauvel, having received from the air reports that the roads east and south-east of Rafah were clear but for a few patrols, issued his orders. The N.Z.M.R. and 1st L.H. Brigades were to attack the " C," or eastern, group of works, and the Camel Brigade the " B " group. Artillery preparation was to begin at 9.30 a.m., and continue for half an hour, at the end of which time the attack was to commence. The 3rd L.H. Brigade was to remain in divisional reserve. General Chetwode was holding the 5th Mounted Brigade in column reserve.

By 9.45 a.m. the attacking troops had approached mounted to within 2,000 yards of the entrenchments. As they advanced, a camel train with an infantry escort was

---

[1] Officers who took part in the action state that after the capture of the position it was found that the enemy had extended the Reduit to include Point 265, after the compilation of the map on which Map 11 is based.

observed leaving Rafah on the Khan Yunis road. The Canterbury Regiment headed straight for Rafah itself and quickly captured the village, with 45 prisoners—Germans, Turks and armed Bedouin—and a number of camels, horses and mules. The regiment, with the Auckland on its left and the Wellington in support (the latter after despatching two troops to the northward to observe Khan Yunis), then advanced dismounted due south against the ridge at Point 265. Brigade headquarters advanced to the boundary pillar a mile south of Rafah, whence there was an excellent view of the greater part of the Turkish position. The 1st L.H. Brigade advanced dismounted from the east against the " C " group of works, but was able to make little progress against shrapnel and heavy machine-gun fire.

On the south, the attack of the Camel Brigade had been launched, the 1st Battalion being directed on B4, the 3rd Battalion being in support and the 2nd in reserve. At 10.30 a.m. the 5th Mounted Brigade, ordered by General Chetwode to demonstrate against the works further west, moved off from Point 210, Warwick Yeomanry on right and Gloucester on left. The remaining squadron of the Worcester (two troops having been left, as recorded, at Sheikh Zowaiid, one detached to watch the left flank, while one squadron was acting as escort to " B " Battery H.A.C.) followed in reserve. On arrival upon the plateau, 2,500 yards from the enemy's position, the Warwick Yeomanry was ordered to engage Works B1 and B2, and the Gloucester sent to the left along the edge of the sand-dunes (which here ran 2 miles inland) to attack the right of A1, the most westerly of the works. The troops dismounted and went into action at a range of 2,000 yards, at once coming under the fire of machine guns and two guns firing shrapnel.

All exits to the north being now stopped by the New Zealanders, orders were issued for the reserves to be thrown in and the attack pressed home. The 3rd L.H. Brigade (less 8th A.L.H., left with divisional headquarters) was to attack C3 and C4 on the left of the 1st L.H. Brigade and in touch with it. Br.-General Cox, commanding the 1st L.H. Brigade, was to reinforce his line and push home an attack against C4 and C5, keeping touch with the N.Z.M.R. Brigade on his right. The Camel Brigade was to close with its original objective, the " B " trenches.

ENVELOPMENT OF POSITION

At 11 a.m. the position of the troops, from right to left, was as follows:—Canterbury and Auckland Rifles, two squadrons 1st A.L.H., one squadron 2nd A.L.H., 3rd A.L.H., 10th A.L.H., 1st Battalion Imperial Camel Corps, Warwick and Gloucester Yeomanry. The Inverness Battery was covering the N.Z.M.R. Brigade, the Leicester and Somerset Batteries the two Australian brigades, the Hong Kong Battery the Camel Brigade; while the H.A.C. battery shelled the " C " works from a point three-quarters of a mile northeast from Point 210.

By 12.15 p.m. the N.Z.M.R. Brigade (the Wellington now having moved up between the other two regiments) was within 600 yards of the enemy's position, and shortly afterwards its right found touch with the left of the 5th Mounted Brigade, the cordon of troops round the enemy's fortifications being thus complete. The 2nd Battalion of the Camel Brigade was thrown in to thicken the line of the 1st and prolong its right. The batteries pushed forward boldly over the open ground, " B " Battery H.A.C. advancing 1,500 yards from its former position to within about the same distance from the enemy and switching its fire from the " C " works to support the attack of the 5th Mounted Brigade. The 7th Light Car Patrol had been put at Br.-General Wiggin's disposal and he had ordered it to support the left of his line, which was in trouble from Turkish machine-gun fire. The cars were boldly and smartly handled. They bumped across country till they reached the Rafah road, rushed along it under fire past the flank of the Turkish position to a sunken portion which gave them just sufficient cover, and there came into action at a range of 1,600 yards, bringing oblique fire to bear on A1 and A2.

Step by step, during the next two hours, the troops from all sides pressed in upon the position. But the very slight undulations of the ground gave hardly any cover, and every yard seemed to be beaten by machine-gun fire. The advance became slower and slower. At 2.30 p.m. General Chauvel called for a fresh effort against the Reduit (by the N.Z.M.R. Brigade) and the " C " works at 3.30 p.m.; the artillery keeping up an intense fire on them till that hour.[1] In the interval he received somewhat serious news from the New

1917.
9 Jan.

---

[1] The Inverness Battery had by now only 19 rounds left, and was withdrawn to divisional headquarters.

Zealanders. A patrol had caught in the open near Rafah a Turkish officer and some Germans, who had stated on interrogation that the *160th Regiment*[1] had left Shellal to relieve the garrison of Rafah as soon as the action had begun. Confirmation of the report quickly followed, for the New Zealand patrols saw troops in artillery formation, about two battalions, advancing over the ridges west of Shellal. At 4.15 p.m. the flank guard in the direction of Khan Yunis also reported that a force of about 500 was advancing on Rafah. Messages received by General Chauvel from his own formations all indicated that little or no progress was being made. The situation of the column was now exceedingly difficult.

At 4.30 p.m. General Chauvel had a conversation on the telephone with General Chetwode, who decided that, owing to the advance of the Turkish reinforcements and the poor prospect of capturing the position quickly enough, it might be necessary to break off the action and that preparatory arrangements should be made to do so. Orders to this effect were actually written by the staff of the A. & N.Z. Mounted Division, but before they were issued the turning point of the action had come and the General himself caught sight of the New Zealanders topping the green hill at Point 265.

At the moment when he was speaking to the G.O.C. Desert Column, the N.Z.M.R. Brigade was being launched to the final assault on the Reduit. The troops swept up the slope with the bayonet, and after a few minutes' fighting the central position was in their hands.[2]

An attack against C5 was at once organized, but before the advancing New Zealanders reached it the Turks in the work stood up and raised their hands. The 1st L.H. Brigade, which had previously been forced by the enemy's fire to give some ground, followed up the success of the New Zealanders on its right by again advancing and capturing

---

[1] This regiment either temporarily formed part of the *3rd Division* or was attached to it.

[2] Br.-General Chaytor in his report thus describes the attack and final assault :—" This attack was carried out in a perfect manner. The " brigade had to advance for over a mile across an open, grassy slope, devoid " of any cover. The covering fire from machine guns and rifles was excellent, " made the Redoubt appear a smoking furnace, and kept the Turks' fire " down. The men covered the last 600 to 800 yards in two grand rushes, " everyone having made up his mind to get home, and the result was that " the position was taken with very little loss to ourselves."

the remainder of the enemy's position on its front, while the 3rd L.H. Brigade was equally successful. To the south the Camel Brigade, which had thrown its 3rd Battalion into the attack, launched an assault on the " B " group of works. The troops had in most cases worked their way to within assaulting distance by crawling, and were unaware of the exact position of the enemy's front line. Fortunately, when they were within 200 yards of this the Turks fixed bayonets and let them be seen above the parapet, thus marking their position for the attackers. The last 40 yards were covered in a swift rush, the men cheering loudly. As they approached the trench, white flags appeared. A short fight followed with those who would not surrender, and B2, the central work of the system, was captured by 4.50 p.m. It was one of the most strongly held, and the Camel Brigade captured 5 officers and 214 other ranks. Shortly afterwards B1 was captured by the Warwick Yeomanry, the total number of prisoners captured in the " B " works being 320. Br.-General Wiggin had meanwhile switched the bulk of his force from the " B " works to the " A," and the latter were evacuated by the enemy. Some of the Turks from these works were captured by the Australians, but a number probably escaped in the dusk.

The action was over and it was urgently necessary to withdraw as swiftly as possible. Detachments from the Wellington Regiment were already engaged at long range with parties of the enemy advancing from Shellal and Khan Yunis. Arrangements were made to collect the wounded without delay and teams hastily despatched to bring in a captured mountain battery. For the former purpose the 3rd L.H. Field Ambulance, covered by a regiment of the 3rd L.H. Brigade, was left behind. The remainder of the column marched back to Sheikh Zowaiid, where it bivouacked for the rest of the night.

It was learnt from aeroplane reports that the enemy had made no attempt to reoccupy Rafah, so on the morning of the 10th January a squadron of the 3rd L.H. Brigade and the 7th Light Car Patrol returned to the battlefield with all available limbered wagons and loaded these up with captured material.[1] The 8th A.L.H., which remained all night at

---

[1] The local Bedouin, who had remained impassive spectators of the action, were found busily engaged in looting.

Rafah, had a brush with Turkish cavalry and camelry east of Shokh es Sufi at 7 a.m., drove them off, and captured 14 prisoners.

The captures in this brilliant action were 35 officers (including the Turkish commander and one German) and 1,438 other ranks (including 10 Germans) unwounded, and 162 wounded; a total of 1,635. It was estimated that 200 of the enemy were killed. The bulk of the prisoners belonged to the *31st Regiment (3rd Division)*, two battalions of which were annihilated. Four mountain guns, 4 machine guns, 578 rifles, a considerable quantity of ammunition and other material, 83 camels, 54 mules and horses were also taken. The British losses were 487.[1] The total was more than thrice that incurred at Magdhaba, but this had been a more difficult operation, conducted against a stronger position and troops of better quality, and the casualties cannot be considered high. The enemy had defended his trenches with stubbornness and bravery. Even when they were under the heaviest fire, men could be seen exposing themselves to take deliberate aim. But the marksmanship of the Turks, as at Magdhaba, was poor. General Chetwode stated in his report to Sir C. Dobell that, excellent as was the work of all the troops engaged, the part played by the New Zealand Brigade was outstanding. That the action terminated favourably was largely due to its dashing assault upon the Reduit, for from that moment Turkish resistance began to crack.

The enemy had not learned aright the lesson of the disaster which had befallen his detachment at Magdhaba. It can only be supposed that he considered his position at Rafah to be better and more easily reinforced in case of need.[2] That this view was not altogether ill-founded is shown by the fact that, owing to the arrival of enemy reinforcements and the lack of water—available only within the

---

[1]

	KILLED.	WOUNDED.	MISSING.
Officers	3	31	–
Other ranks	68	384	1

[2] "Sinai": Kress, i, 24. Kress states that his advice was to evacuate Sinai completely, but that Djemal for political reasons would not consent to this course. He points out that the actions of Magdhaba and Rafah proved the great advantage possessed in country of this sort by a combatant very strong in mounted troops over an enemy almost without this arm. Great as was the British superiority in this respect, it was not so great as Kress declares when he describes the three brigades at Magdhaba as "two English cavalry divisions."

Diagram 1.

WATER SUPPLY TO THE E.F.F., NOV., 1916.
(Not to scale.)

C A V A L R Y
(Horses watering at local wells)

I N F A N T R Y

Camel Convoys with drinking water

RAILHEAD

2000 Egyptian labourers.

SALMANA STA. { Storage tanks for water rail-borne from ROMANI. Animals from local wells. }

Infantry, &c.
500 Egyptian labourers.

BIR EL ABD { 500,000 Gall. Reservoir under construction.
Infantry, &c.
Animals from local wells. }

Storage tanks for water rail-borne from ROMANI.

Infantry, &c.
500 Egyptian labourers.

BATTERY OF STAND-PIPES.

12" Pipe under construction

Stand-pipes for filling trucks.
500,000 Gall. Reservoir.
PIPEHEAD

ROMANI STA.

QANTARA 20 miles
12" Pipe

Ordnance Survey, 1927.

enemy's position or many miles to the rear—the British at one moment proposed to retire before the fight was won. The margin between success and failure had been slight. The decision to leave wheels behind at Sheikh Zowaiid afterwards appeared to have been unnecessary and certainly increased the column's difficulties. By 1.30 p.m. no less than four of the New Zealand machine guns were out of action for lack of ammunition. Major A. H. Wilkie, quartermaster of the Wellington Regiment, brought up a supply from Sheikh Zowaiid and, hearing that his regiment was calling for ammunition, seized a cable wagon, tipped out the contents, filled it with boxes of S.A.A., and brought it up at a gallop, just in time for the machine guns to come into action to cover the final assault.[1]

Reconstruction and Preparation.

The occupation of Sinai may be said to have begun in early April 1916. It had been extended by bounds, followed by steady consolidation and preparation for the next move, except for one important check administered by the enemy at Qatiya[2]. The fringe of cultivation was now reached, but

Map 8. Sketch B.

---

[1] "New Zealand Official History," pp. 77–8. The machine guns of the 7th Light Car Patrol would also have run out of ammunition had not the Yeomen of the 5th Mounted Brigade refilled belts from their bandoliers. That the Inverness Battery had to be withdrawn for lack of ammunition has been mentioned.

[2] The following table gives the dates of the various moves and important events in the course of the advance, with the mileage from the starting point at Qantara :—

April	Occupation of the Qatiya basin by mounted troops—25 miles.
23rd April	Turkish surprise attack on the mounted troops.
April–August	Occupation of the Romani Oasis. Railway and wire road laid to Romani—23 miles.
4th–14th August ..	Turkish attack on British position at Romani; Turks pursued to Bir el Abd by mounted troops.
17th November	Railhead 8 miles east of Salmana—54 miles. Pipehead Romani—23 miles.
1st December	Railhead east of Mazar—64 miles.
21st December	Occupation of El Arish—90 miles.
23rd December	Pursuit of Turks and destruction of rear guard at Magdhaba.
9th January (1917) ..	Capture of Turkish force at Rafah on the Palestine frontier—117 miles.

Diagram 1. the method of progress was to continue. The speed of the advance had been and was to remain dependent on that of the railway and, in rather less degree, of the pipe-line. From the 17th November onwards the supply of water was as shown in the diagram attached; that is to say, practically all water drunk by troops and labourers was drawn by tank trucks through a battery of stand-pipes from the reservoir at Romani, and carried forward to storage tanks at railhead and other points. When pipehead reached Bir el Abd a similar reservoir had already been constructed there, from which the trucks were now filled. Thereafter the pipe-line advanced at an increased pace and on the 5th February 1917 reached El Arish. It had almost caught up the railway, and had brought near the hour when offensive action in Southern Palestine would be possible, so far as water and supplies were concerned.

But the necessity of waiting while railway and water supply were constructed was not the sole trammel to progress. On the 11th January a telegram was received from the C.I.G.S. which confirmed, and indeed reinforced, that of the 15th December quoted in the last chapter.[1] The general situation, Sir W. Robertson stated, did not at present permit the despatch of the reinforcements which the Commander-in-Chief considered necessary, and the War Cabinet had therefore decided to defer the prosecution of operations on a large scale in Palestine until the autumn. The general policy during the summer was therefore to prepare for such a campaign, but meanwhile—here was the rub—to be ready to release for service in France one or two divisions. It was hoped to send some troops during the summer from East Africa and India. At the same time Sir A. Murray was promised that none of his mounted troops should be taken from him and informed that there was no intention of curtailing such activities as he considered justified by his resources. The blow fell sooner than was expected, for on the 17th January the War Office ordered a division to be prepared for despatch to France. Sir A. Murray selected the 42nd, and rearranged his forces. The 54th Division was moved up from the Canal to Romani, while the 53rd took the place of the 42nd further forward. The 42nd

---

[1] See pp. 260–1.

Division began embarkation in Egypt early in February. Once again Sir A. Murray felt it his duty to repeat to the War Office his estimate that he needed five infantry divisions in addition to his mounted troops.

1917. Jan. Map 8. Sketch B.

Sir C. Dobell, commanding the Eastern Force, had now submitted his appreciation and proposals for action. He stated, in brief, that the enemy in front of him did not number more than 12,000, but that reinforcement by another division was possible. Two lines of advance were open to the Eastern Force: by Rafah, or Auja on the Turkish railway. But as the enemy had practically withdrawn from Sinai and his railhead was in the air, there was no advantage to be gained by advancing in that direction, since an advance on Rafah would force him to fall back from Auja. Further, he must then, if he wished to defend Palestine, fight with his inadequate forces or withdraw troops from elsewhere. General Dobell therefore proposed to keep to the coast, and was now in a position to advance his mounted troops to Rafah, which had not been reoccupied by the Turks after the raid of the 9th January: keeping two divisions at El Arish, to which he would move his own headquarters. To these suggestions Sir A. Murray agreed, uttering a word of warning against pushing a small force too far forward.

For operations in normal terrain the transport extemporized for service in Sinai stood in need of some reorganization. On the 13th January the War Office concurred in Sir A. Murray's proposals to re-equip the 52nd, 53rd and 54th Divisions with wheeled trains instead of the camel trains employed in the desert; but only on condition that the personnel should be so far as possible other than European, as none would be available from home. The War Office also gave approval to his proposal that those Yeomanry brigades which were not remounted after their return from Gallipoli should be numbered the 229th, 230th and 231st Infantry Brigades and formed into a new division, the 74th (Yeomanry) Division. It was recognized that some time would elapse before artillery, engineers and auxiliary services to complete this division to establishment would be forthcoming, but the infantry material was magnificent.

The War Office likewise agreed to the proposed re-formation of the 4th Australian Light Horse Brigade from three regiments unbrigaded since the return from Gallipoli,[1] and to the organization of his mounted troops into two divisions of four brigades each:—A. & N.Z. Mounted Division (Major-General H. G. Chauvel), consisting of the 1st and 2nd L.H., N.Z.M.R., and 22nd Mounted Brigades; and Imperial Mounted Division (Major-General H.W. Hodgson), consisting of the 3rd and 4th L.H., 5th and 6th Mounted Brigades.

Considerable developments had taken place in the medical arrangements since the Battle of Romani, particularly with regard to the evacuation of wounded from the battlefield and their transport by rail. In December for the first time a hospital train was brought east of the Canal. The medical situation in Sinai, at the time of the advance to El Arish, was as follows:—

> At Railhead.—Immobile sections of divisional field ambulances, accommodating 700 casualties.
> At Bir el Abd.—No. 24 C.C.S., open for 400 cases; Nos. 53 and 54 C.C.S's. parked, with equipment for 200 each.
> At Bir el Mazar.—No. 26 C.C.S., open for 400 cases.
> At Mahamdiyah.—No. 2 (Australian) Stationary Hospital with 800 beds.
> At Qantara East.—No. 24 Stationary Hospital, with 800 beds.

Two hospital trains and equipment for an emergency train were available on the Sinai railway. Evacuation by sea was impossible, as there was no point on the coast where hospital ships could take off wounded.

The A. & N.Z. Mounted Division Field Ambulances were reorganized before the Action of Rafah. The transport allotted to each field ambulance now consisted of 10 pairs of litters, 15 pairs of *cacolets*, 12 sand-carts, 12 cycle stretchers and 6 sledges, capable of carrying 92 patients at one time. The new organization, put to the test of battle at Rafah, worked well. The time was coming, however, when motor ambulances could be employed.

The transfer of mounted troops to the Eastern Force made necessary a rearrangement of the Egyptian garrisons. For internal defence and the maintenance of order the War Office had for some time been sending out British garrison

---

[1] 4th, 11th and 12th A.L.H. The brigade was commanded by Br.-General J. B. Meredith, who had commanded the 1st L.H. Brigade at Romani.

G.H.Q. TROOPS

battalions, composed of men—in part old Regular soldiers— past marching age, and younger men incapacitated by wounds or other disabilities from more active service. These proved of value, especially for the guarding of stores at Alexandria and Port Said. Outside Eastern Force and the Royal Flying Corps, there were only three relatively small commands directly under G.H.Q.: Western Force, Alexandria District and Delta District, composed as follows :—

1917.
Jan.

Western Force—
> Bikanir Camel Corps ;
> 230th and 231st Brigades ;[1]
> Detachments R.A., dismounted (seven 15-pdr. guns, two 9-pdr. Krupp guns, two Naval 4-in. guns) ;
> 5 Armoured Motor Batteries ;
> 6 Light Car Patrols (Fords) ;
> Motor Machine-gun Battery ;
> 1 Garrison Battalion.

Alexandria District—
> 103rd Local Company R.G.A. ;
> 5th Battalion British West Indies Regiment ;
> 2 Garrison Battalions.

Delta District—
> 2nd Battalion North Lancs Regiment (from East Africa) ;
> 1/4th Duke of Cornwall's L.I. (from Aden) ;
> 5 Garrison Battalions.

The troops on the Canal itself (still forming part of Eastern Force) had been reduced as far as possible, and now consisted of the following :—

Northern Section—
> 20th (Indian) Brigade ;
> 1st and 2nd Battalions British West Indies Regiment ;
> 3 Garrison Battalions.

Southern Section—
> Imperial Service Cavalry Brigade ;
> 2 Companies Imperial Camel Corps ;
> 267th Brigade R.F.A. (53rd Division) ;
> 272nd Brigade R.F.A. (54th Division) ;
> 229th Brigade (to form part of the 74th Division).

---

[1] These brigades remained on the Western Frontier till March, when they were transferred to the Eastern Front to form the 74th Division. Delta District and Western Force were then amalgamated, a few further garrison battalions being added. The Western Desert was thereafter almost entirely controlled by the mobile forces of camelry, armoured cars and light patrols of Ford cars.

In the air the situation was unsatisfactory, though bombing attacks were carried out against the Turkish base at Beersheba with apparent success, and as late as the 7th and 8th March Sir A. Murray reported not only that his aircraft gave him complete information regarding Turkish movements, but that its activity allowed little or no movement on the Beersheba railway. On the 20th March, however, he informed the War Office that almost daily new enemy aeroplanes, which quite outclassed his best, appeared over his lines. He asked if even four fighting machines of the best type could be sent to enable him to prevent full information of his movements being gained by the enemy.[1] The Royal Flying Corps in Egypt at this date consisted of Headquarters Middle East Brigade, 5th Wing (Nos. 14 Sqdn. R.F.C. and 67 Sqdn. A.F.C.), and 20th Reserve Wing (Nos. 21, 22, 23, 57, 58 Reserve Squadrons and No. 3 School of Military Aeronautics).

BEFORE GAZA.

Map 8. Sketch B.

Pipehead had, as previously stated, reached El Arish on the 5th February. The railway was being laid ahead of that place, and a strongly entrenched position established there. By the 22nd February a further advance was possible, and on that date the A. & N.Z. Mounted Division was concentrated at Sheikh Zowaiid, the troops bivouacking on the beach. Next day it was reported that the enemy had evacuated Khan Yunis, 5 miles beyond Rafah, and the 2nd L.H. and N.Z.M.R. Brigades, under the command of Br.-General Chaytor, advanced to occupy it. Khan Yunis was, however, found to be held in some strength. After a brush with the Turkish outposts, the column withdrew in accordance with its instructions. The enemy subsequently evacuated Khan Yunis, which was occupied by the Desert Column on the 28th February. Desert Column headquarters was now at Sheikh Zowaiid, Eastern Force headquarters and the infantry at El Arish.

---

[1] "Sinai": Kress, i, pp. 32-3. "The standard of efficiency of the *300th Flight Detachment* was wonderful. Though the enemy had superiority both in numbers and quality of machines, the detachment won and kept an undoubted mastery of the air from its arrival in the desert in the spring of 1916 until the autumn of 1917."

The statement is exaggerated. The German machines were superior to the British, but the enemy frequently avoided combat because he could not replace pilots or machines and was short even of spare parts.

The enemy had possibly expected that the British 1917. would now leave the coast. Finding that they did not, the Feb. Turks were emboldened to reoccupy Nekhl and Bir el Hassana with small detachments. On the 18th February three columns were despatched against these posts. That against Bir el Hassana marched from El Arish and consisted of the 2nd Battalion Imperial Camel Corps and one section of the Hong Kong Battery. The small garrison of Hassana was surprised, 3 officers and 19 other ranks, with a quantity of stores, being captured. The two columns marching on Nekhl came from the Canal, the northern from Serapeum consisting of the 11th A.L.H., the southern from Suez of the headquarters 6th Mounted Brigade, detachments of Yeomanry of that brigade and the 58th Rifles. The enemy garrison at Nekhl, composed of about one hundred cavalry, was warned by Bedouin of the British advance and fell back towards Aqaba, leaving a field gun and 11 prisoners in British hands.

During February the reports of agents showed that the enemy had received reinforcements in the shape of the *16th Division* and two regiments of the *3rd Cavalry Division*.[1] Desertions, however, were also fairly numerous, and between the Action of Rafah and the end of February 70 deserters entered the British lines.[2]

From the date on which their detachment at Rafah had been destroyed the Turks had devoted themselves to the perfection of their position at Shellal, which was now very strong. Sir A. Murray had made all arrangements to attack this position when, on the 5th March, the R.F.C. 5 March. reported that the enemy was withdrawing. Vigorous bombing attacks were carried out by the R.F.C. against Beersheba, Tell esh Sheria (12 miles north-west, where the

---

[1] This was a new formation, the old division of that number having been dissipated and practically destroyed by hunger in the Caucasus. The Turkish cavalry was armed with the lance. Except on one occasion, just prior to the Third Battle of Gaza, it never attempted mounted action in the course of the campaign. The very great British superiority in mounted troops rendered this practically impossible. The *3rd Cavalry Division* has, however, from this point to the end of the campaign, probably the best record among the Turkish formations.

[2] Kress (" Sinai," i, p. 25) complains of heavy losses from this cause. It seems that only a very small proportion of the deserters came over to the British, by far the greater number, and especially the Arabs and Syrians, disappearing in the towns and villages of Palestine and Trans-Jordan.

railway crossed the Wadi esh Sheria) and on the junction of the Beersheba railway with the Jerusalem-Jaffa line. These attacks were intended to interfere with the withdrawal, but it was soon found that the enemy had fallen back no further than Gaza and Tell esh Sheria, 14 miles north and north-east respectively of Shellal.[1]

However, the distance which he had put between himself and the British advanced troops was sufficient to necessitate a further pause, while the railway was being laid to Rafah. Meanwhile, the British mounted troops were reorganized into two divisions and preparations pressed on for an attack upon the Turkish position at Gaza.

---

[1] " Sinai ": Kress, i, p. 25. Kress would have liked to fight on his strong position at Shellal, but found himself too weak to hold it and at the same time assure the defence of Gaza. The reinforcements promised by Enver came too late (most of them, in fact, not till after the First Battle of Gaza), and " with a heavy heart " he ordered the evacuation of Shellal. He had to dispose his force to hold up the British if they advanced along the coast, or if—though this appeared to him improbable—they attempted to advance by way of Beersheba upon Jerusalem. The last round of ammunition was successfully withdrawn.

THE SINAITIC PENINSULA

Diagram II

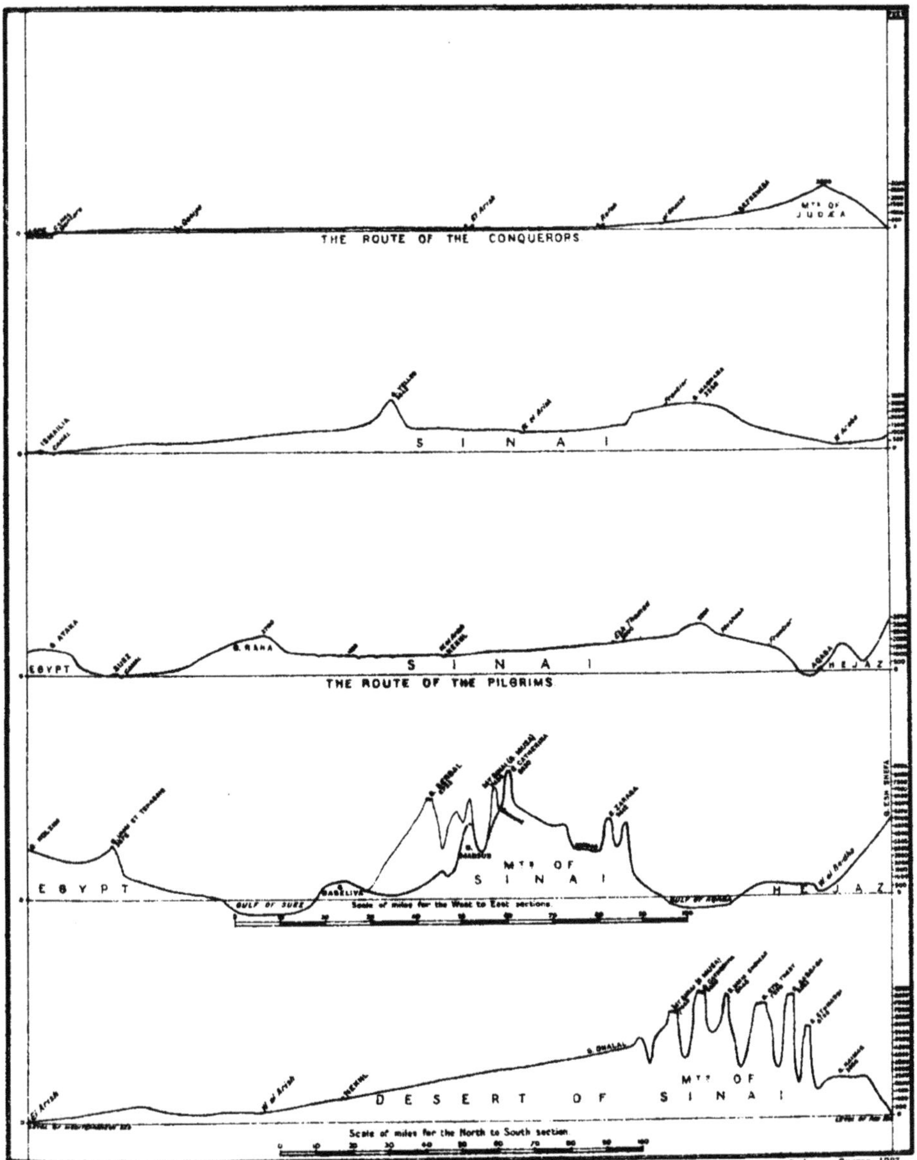

Compiled from the 1,000,000 map

Ordnance Survey, 1927

CHAPTER XVI.

THE FIRST BATTLE OF GAZA.

(Map 12; Sketches B, 14.)

THE SITUATION IN LATE MARCH, 1917.

SIR A. MURRAY'S general instructions still remained Sketch B. the negative ones contained in the War Office telegram of the 11th January : that the projected advance into Palestine and capture of Jerusalem had been postponed until the autumn.[1] The departure of the 42nd Division had left him with three infantry divisions only, the 52nd, 53rd and 54th. Pressure on the enemy was, however, about to be renewed on all fronts; in this the War Cabinet desired that he should take his share, and it was aware that he had in contemplation an attack on Gaza.[2]

By the 1st March railhead had reached Sheikh Zowaiid, 30 miles from Gaza. By the 21st Rafah Station was open[3] and the line had been extended to the neighbourhood of Khan Yunis. The pipe-line was following it closely, though, owing to a temporary shortage of 12-inch piping, smaller gauges were being employed between El Arish and Rafah. The local water supply was now improved, Khan Yunis in particular containing one remarkable well which afterwards, when a pumping engine had been installed, produced an almost unlimited quantity. But though it was now possible

---

[1] See p. 272.

[2] On the 26th February, in continuation of conferences in the previous October and November, an Anglo-French Congress assembled at Calais and decided upon the details of a great series of offensive operations to take place that spring. On the 11th March Baghdad was occupied by the British and an Allied offensive in Macedonia was begun. On the 9th April, the British in France began the series of operations known as the Battles of Arras, 1917, and on the 16th the French " Nivelle offensive " on the Aisne opened. The Russian Revolution, which accentuated the need of Allied activity on other fronts, broke out in March.

[3] It appears, however, that it was not ready for unloading supplies till after the First Battle of Gaza.

to concentrate the whole of the Eastern Force at Rafah or even further forward, there was not sufficient transport to permit of the conduct of operations at any considerable distance from railhead. There were no supply columns except those improvised from the Camel Transport Corps as required. The infantry divisions had their new horsed trains, the mounted troops still their camel trains; but there were as yet no roads fit for motor transport, even had this been then available in Egypt in sufficient quantity.

The Turkish forces were disposed in the vicinity of their railway, with a detachment at Gaza. Their locations were believed to be Abu Hureira, 10 miles south-east of Gaza, Huj and Tell en Nejile, respectively $8\frac{1}{2}$ and 17 miles due east of Gaza. The force holding Gaza was, then, more or less isolated, and the situation resembled that at the moment when the successful attack on Rafah had been made, except that in this case considerably stronger columns might be expected to move to the aid of the detached outpost if it were attacked. The total enemy forces at Gaza or in a position to intervene in its defence were estimated to be two and a half weak divisions.[1]

As a result of the advance along the coast, the British line of communications now overlapped the Turkish. The question whether the Force should follow the coast line or turn inland towards Auja on the Turkish railway had previously been discussed and the former alternative had been chosen. Now that Rafah and Khan Yunis, from which tracks left the coast route and ran towards Beersheba, had been reached, the problem required reconsideration. Sir A. Murray, however, again came to the conclusion that to turn inland was inadvisable, " since by so doing he would " be drawing his line of communications parallel to the " enemy's front, and there was no technical advantage to be " gained by linking up the military railway with the [Turkish] " Central Palestine railway, either at Beersheba or Tell esh " Sheria. The true line of advance," he decided, " was still " along the coast, since the enemy was no less effectually

---

[1] The Historical Section of the Turkish General Staff gives the strength of the forces which took part in the First Battle of Gaza, including one regiment of the *53rd Division* which advanced from the north to intervene in the battle, as 16,000 rifles.

Sketch 14.

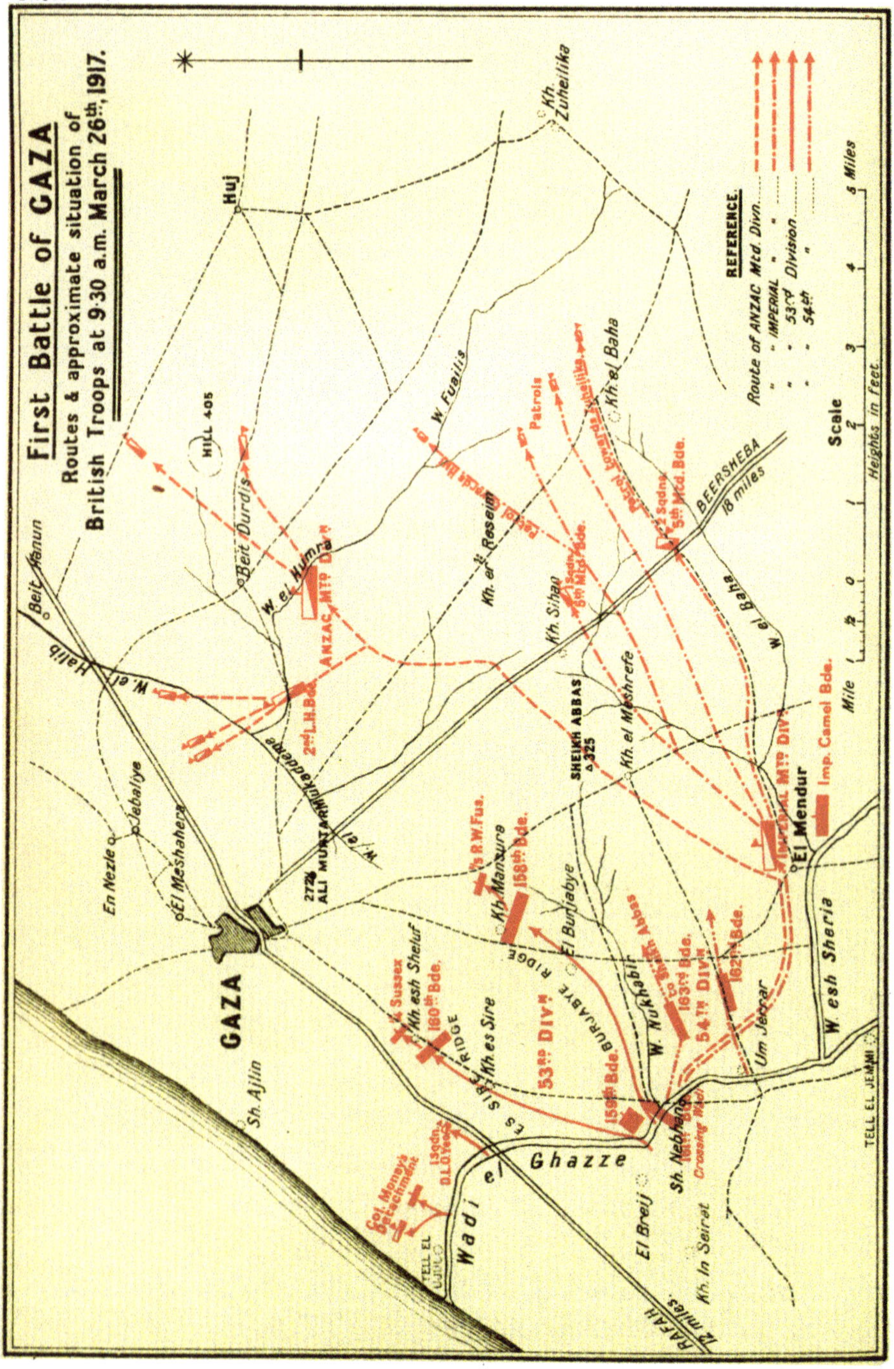

Ordnance Survey, 1925.

GAZA OF THE PHILISTINES

"threatened thereby, while his own line of communications "was more easily protected and railway construction was "more rapid, owing to the absence of gradients."

1917.
March.
Map 12.
Sketch 14.

Both the Commander-in-Chief and Sir C. Dobell were concerned lest the enemy should evacuate Gaza and withdraw out of reach before a blow could be struck at him. It was therefore necessary to act swiftly, and the only effective action within the immediate power of the British appeared to be a repetition on a larger scale of the operations which had proved so successful at Magdhaba and Rafah; that is to say, a cutting-out expedition against Gaza, after which it might be necessary temporarily to withdraw the whole force or a part of it to railhead. Sir A. Murray set three objects before Sir C. Dobell, to whom the operation was entrusted: to gain the line of the Wadi Ghazze in order to cover the advance of the railway, to prevent the enemy from withdrawing unmolested, to capture Gaza and its garrison by a *coup de main*.

Gaza, one of the five cities of the Philistine Alliance, and one of the most ancient in the world, possibly 4,000 years old,[1] has always been the gate of Palestine. It has been taken over and over again, especially by Egyptian invaders from the west, but also by armies from the north. Among its famous captors are Tiglath-Pileser III of Assyria (731 B.C.), Alexander (332 B.C.),[2] Khalif Omar (635 A.D.), Saladin (1187 A.D.), Napoleon (1799 A.D.). The Gaza of Omar, Saladin, Napoleon and the present day is not, however, on the same site as that of the Egyptians, Assyrians and Greeks, the city having been completely destroyed in 96 B.C. and rebuilt under Aulus Gabinius forty years later, slightly further south. At the time of the outbreak of war it had a population of 40,000, and carried on a considerable export of barley to Great Britain, though it had no harbour, ships anchoring a mile out to take aboard their cargoes.

The country between Rafah and Gaza, east of the coast belt of sand-dunes from half a mile to three miles broad, is a gently rolling plateau of light but firm soil, rising slowly inland and traversed by watercourses, which are dry

---

[1] The earliest mention of Gaza is in the Tell el Amarna tablets, in a letter from the governor who then held it for Egypt. The date of these letters is about 1,400 B.C.

[2] Alexander's siege lasted two months, and he was wounded in its course by a bolt from a catapult.

except in the rainy season but then often become torrents. In the spring, when covered by young crops or fresh grass following the winter rains, it has a pleasant, verdant appearance, but the summer sun scorches it brown.

Five miles north-east of Khan Yunis and 8 miles south-west of Gaza are the ruins, shrine and native village of Deir el Balah, with palm and olive groves, the only wooded area between the gardens of the two towns. Half-way between Gaza and Deir el Balah the great Wadi Ghazze runs to the sea, cut wide and deep by storm-water borne to it by innumerable tributary wadis from all the country round, but especially from the toe of the Judæan Hills, the Shephelah, and the plateau of Edom. Its bed is sandy, with steep mud cliffs on either bank, cut by numerous vertical clefts, which run for varying but often considerable distances into the higher ground beyond the banks. These nullahs were found to afford admirable cover, their sides being as steep and firm as those of well revetted trenches, while exits were easily cut in them. But they made movement in the vicinity of the wadi dangerous in the dark, and at all times demanded vigilant ground scouting from mounted troops.

After crossing the wadi the coast road passes along the western slope of a low ridge on the edge of the sand-dunes. East of this ridge is a narrow valley, from which rises a longer and higher ridge. This latter (hereafter referred to as the Es Sire Ridge) is part of a high feature east of Gaza and running from north-east to south-west, which is continued almost to the right bank of the Wadi Ghazze. Parallel to the Es Sire Ridge and separated from it by a broad valley is another tongue from the high ground east of Gaza, known as the Burjabye Ridge. On the crown of this ridge, 3 miles south of Gaza, is what may be described as an abrupt step, a slight but cliff-like ascent at Khirbet[1] Mansura. On the highest point of the Es Sire Ridge, half a mile south-east of that quarter of Gaza known as the East Town, and overlooking it by 300 feet, stands the shrine of Ali el Muntar on the hill to which Samson bore the gates of the city. West and south-west of Ali el Muntar, between it and Gaza, and extending to a mile west of the Rafah road, lay olive groves, gardens and fields, surrounded and intersected by a maze

---

[1] Khirbet, ruins. This prefix, common in a land of dead civilizations, is hereafter shortened to " Kh."

of cactus hedges. The ridges and the valleys between them were without cover and practically treeless till this area of grove and garden, extending in places over 2,000 yards from the town itself, was reached. To the east of Gaza the ground rolled away in open down, cut here and there by watercourses, yet ideal for the employment of mounted troops. But all approaches to the city were covered by the cactus hedges, which were particularly formidable on the southern side. They were of great height and thickness, destructible only by high explosive or prolonged work with cutting tools, and obstacles as efficient as any that defenders could hope to construct.

The artificial defences at this date, though they would not have been serious in face of a deliberately organized attack supported by registered artillery, and though there was little wire in them, were considerable obstacles to an assault to be carried out in the special conditions alone possible in this case. The trenches south of Gaza commanded bare slopes; the absence of any cover until close to the city, and then the high hedges, gave the position its strength and made of it a little pleasing prospect to infantry attacking from the south and south-east.

The Plan of Attack.

Sir C. Dobell proposed that the Desert Column, under the command of General Chetwode, should carry out the attack, while the remainder of the Eastern Force moved up so as to be ready to give support if required.

Eastern Force was rearranged for the operations, the Desert Column now comprising the A. & N.Z. Mounted Division (less the 1st L.H. Brigade), the Imperial Mounted Division (less the 4th L.H. Brigade), and the 53rd Division. The remaining troops, directly under the command of the G.O.C. Eastern Force, were the Imperial Camel Brigade, the 52nd and 54th Divisions, and the 229th Brigade, the only formation of the 74th Division as yet available.

The plan of operations drawn up by G.O.C. Eastern Force received the approval of G.H.Q. on the 19th March. Its essence was that, after making good the line of the Wadi Ghazze, the Desert Column should carry out the *coup de main* against Gaza, while the 54th Division moved out and stood by to protect it against a Turkish counter-stroke from the east, of which General Dobell was apprehensive. The operation orders of the Eastern Force,[1] issued on 24th March, directed the G.O.C. Desert Column to "dispose "his mounted troops so as to block the enemy's lines of "retreat from Gaza, and to watch for any movement of his "[the enemy's] main body" from the neighbourhood of Huj or Tell esh Sheria ; and then to "attack the enemy's force "occupying Gaza." The attack was to be carried out on the 26th March. The operation would involve an approach march, carefully planned to secure surprise and fit in with the difficult arrangements for the supply of water. To give the mounted troops a radius of action of 20 miles from railhead, it had been necessary to transfer to them the newly-formed horsed trains of the infantry divisions. The 53rd and 54th Divisions were given the camel trains which had been employed in the desert. It was arranged that the Navy should undertake the landing of stores and supplies at Deir el Balah as soon as they were required, pending the nearer approach of railhead to the Wadi Ghazze.

Desert Column's orders[2] were issued on the 25th March, on which date the Wadi Ghazze was reconnoitred by the divisional and brigade commanders of the Desert Column. Crossings were prepared and exits from the wadi selected, the work being covered by the A. & N.Z. Mounted Division, which put out a line of patrols, kept as thin and invisible as possible. These patrols moved some distance beyond the wadi, and under their cover Major-General A. G. Dallas, commanding the 53rd Division, made a reconnaissance of the ground between the Rafah-Gaza road and the sea, and also of the lower portion of the Es Sire Ridge.[3]

---

[1] Appendix 8.
[2] Appendix 9.
[3] The enemy's position had previously been reconnoitred and photographed by the R.F.C. The existing maps, based on the Palestine Exploration Fund map made by Lieutenants C. R. Conder, R.E., and H. H. Kitchener, R.E. (afterwards Field Marshal Lord Kitchener), were uncontoured but showed the features of the country by means of brush-hachuring. They gave an excellent general idea of the ground, but were deficient in detail for tactical purposes. Map 12, of the First Battle of Gaza, is based on these maps, form-lines being substituted for the brush-hachuring. By the time the Second Battle was fought a partially contoured map had been prepared, on which Map 13 is based. Comparing the maps for the First and Second Battles, it will be seen that the former was substantially accurate, though lacking in detail.

Ali el Muntar from Mansura Ridge.

The 53rd Division was to cross the wadi at 5 a.m., seize the high ground on the Es Sire and Mansura Ridges, and attack Ali Muntar as soon as reconnaissance and artillery registration had been completed. The Eastern Force was at this date very short of artillery. The third artillery brigade of each division was without howitzers, and in the case of the 53rd and 54th Divisions even the 18-pdr. batteries of these brigades were still in the Canal Defences. The whole force had only three heavy batteries (twelve 60-pdrs.), while to economize transport only one section (two guns) of each of these batteries was brought up for the First Battle of Gaza. The ammunition supply was by no means large. Great as had been the expansion in the production of guns and ammunition, the demands of the Western Theatre had grown correspondingly, and the secondary theatres of war were still pinched in this respect.

1917.
March.

To support General Chetwode, the 54th Division (less one brigade in Eastern Force reserve) had been ordered by Sir C. Dobell to cross the wadi immediately after the mounted troops and take up a position at Sheikh Abbas, the next ridge east of the Burjabye Ridge, to cover the rear of the 53rd Division and keep open the corridor along which it was to attack.

General Chetwode estimated the garrison of Gaza at 2,000, unaware that recent reinforcements had nearly doubled it.[1]

The orders of Major-General A. G. Dallas, commanding the 53rd Division,[2] directed the 158th and 160th Brigades to begin crossing the wadi at 3.30 a.m. and to advance up the Burjabye and Es Sire ridges respectively, the 158th to a covered position behind Kh. Mansura, the 160th to the neighbourhood of Kh. esh Sheluf. The 159th Brigade was to follow the 158th across the wadi and remain on the right bank until it received further orders. A detachment (hereafter described as Money's Detachment)[3] was to cross the wadi nearer its mouth and take up a position in

---
[1] See Note I at end of Chapter XVII. The actual date of the reinforcement is unknown; it may have been only on the night previous to the issue of General Chetwode's orders.
[2] Appendix 10.
[3] This detachment, commanded by Lieut.-Colonel N. Money, consisted of that officer's battalion, the 2/4th West Kent (160th Brigade), the Gloucester Hussars (5th Mounted Brigade, Imperial Mounted Division), and two 60-pdrs. 15th Heavy Battery.

the sand-dunes between the Rafah–Gaza road and the sea. Its mission was to divert the enemy's attention on this flank and to cover one section of the 15th Heavy Battery. A section of the 91st Heavy Battery was to enter the wadi on the Rafah–Gaza road, covered by the divisional cavalry. The third section of 60-pdrs. (10th Heavy Battery) was to form part of the 160th Brigade Group. Instructions issued with the orders explained that the position was not strongly held and that it was intended to press the attack with vigour. They also stated that the supply of artillery ammunition was limited and that it would be chiefly devoted to the bombardment of "the Labyrinth," a group of trenches due south of Gaza on the edge of the area enclosed by cactus hedges.

The Preliminary Moves and Approach March.

On the 20th March the head of the Eastern Force was at Rafah, 18 miles from Gaza, with outposts at Khan Yunis. Here were the two mounted divisions and the headquarters of the Desert Column. Advanced headquarters of the Eastern Force also moved to Rafah on this date. The remainder of the force was echeloned further west, both for convenience of supply and to avoid a concentration which would indicate to the enemy preparations for an immediate advance. The Camel Brigade, the 52nd Division, and one brigade of the 54th Division were at Sheikh Zowaiid, 29 miles south-west of Gaza, and the remainder of the 54th at El Burj, 8 miles further west. The 53rd Division was encamped upon prepared defences 4 miles south-west of Rafah. G.H.Q. was still at Cairo.

On the 21st March the first step was taken in a series of preliminary moves, arranged in accordance with the exigencies of water supply and made chiefly at night. One brigade of the Imperial Mounted Division advanced to Khan Yunis, where the groves gave considerable concealment; the 53rd Division concentrated at Rafah, and the 54th Division closed up upon its leading brigade at Sheikh Zowaiid. The next two days were occupied by preparations and the move of auxiliary units. On the 24th the advance was resumed, the 53rd Division moving from

APPROACH MARCH 287

Rafah to Khan Yunis and the 54th from Sheikh Zowaiid **1917.**
to Rafah. By midnight on the 25th the force was con- **25 March.**
centrated close to the Wadi Ghazze as follows :—

> The two mounted divisions and the 53rd Division at Deir el Balah ;
> The 54th Division at In Seirat, 2 miles east of Deir el Balah ;
> The 52nd Division at Khan Yunis ;
> The Camel Brigade at Abasan el Kebir, 5 miles south-east of Khan Yunis.

The 53rd Division thus had a march of seven miles to Deir el Balah, which began at dusk on the 25th to avoid the observation of enemy aircraft. After a halt of between three and four hours, the division then had to face another march of four miles before it reached the crossings of the Ghazze. As some three miles more of broken ground east of the wadi had to be crossed before Mansura and Esh Sheluf were reached, it will be seen that a heavy call upon the division's endurance was to be made before it was committed to the attack.

At 2.30 a.m. on the 26th the A. & N.Z. Mounted **26 March**
Division left its bivouac at Deir el Balah and moved across the rear of the 54th Division at In Seirat to the previously prepared crossing at Um Jerrar, 4½ miles east of Deir el Balah, reaching the wadi without hitch or delay, followed by the Imperial Mounted Division. The Camel Brigade left Abasan el Kebir in the early morning[1] and moved to its crossing at Tell el Jemmi, south of Um Jerrar, also arriving without mishap, though the night was of inky blackness.

The 53rd Division moved out from Deir el Balah at 1 a.m. in four columns : three brigade groups[2] and Money's Detachment, all save the last-named with orders to be at a place of assembly closs to the Wadi Ghazze in the neighbourhood of El Breij by 2.45 a.m. The 160th Brigade (Br.-General W. J. C. Butler) was to cross at 3.30 a.m., the 158th Brigade (Br.-General S. F. Mott) at 3.45 a.m., while the 159th Brigade (Br.-General J. H. du B. Travers) was to follow the 158th. The artillery was to form up at

---

[1] There is no record of the hour at which it left its bivouac.
[2] Each had only one section of a field company R.E., and one bearer sub-division of a field ambulance R.A.M.C., in addition to the establishment of the brigade.

In Seirat and cross after the 158th and 160th Brigades had advanced sufficiently to ensure its safety: the 266th Brigade R.F.A. following the 158th Brigade Group, the 265th Brigade R.F.A. and one section 10th Heavy Battery following the 160th Brigade Group.[1]

The movements all took place in accordance with orders, except that of the 158th Brigade. In its case the officer detailed as guide lost his way and the brigade was eventually led to the wadi by Br.-General Mott, arriving 50 minutes late at 4.35 a.m.

Money's Detachment moved down to the wadi near the shore, ready to cross at dawn, and the section of the 91st Heavy Battery, covered by the divisional cavalry squadron (Duke of Lancaster's Own Yeomanry) moved to a good position, previously reconnoitred, on the Rafah–Gaza road.

The development of a supply of water from the Wadi Ghazze (which, though now nearly dry, had numerous springs in its bed) by the divisional engineers was begun directly the infantry had crossed. A supply sufficient for all the troops engaged was obtained, long rows of canvas troughs being put up for the watering of horses.

Sir C. Dobell moved his battle headquarters from Rafah to just north of In Seirat, where he arrived at 6.45 a.m. and took up a position overlooking the wadi, then veiled in mist. General Chetwode also established his headquarters here, with the intention, as stated in his orders, of moving later to Sheikh Abbas. Owing to the fog, to the delay which it caused in the attack of the 53rd Division, and to the early attainment of their objectives by the mounted troops, General Chetwode did not, however, move his headquarters across the Wadi Ghazze but conducted the operation from In Seirat. He was thus able to discuss personally with Sir C. Dobell the problems which arose in the course of the day. In this there was advantage, but it was perhaps counter-balanced by the fact that the subordinate of two commanders almost inevitably feels himself cramped in his

---

[1] It must, however, be understood that though an artillery brigade marched with each of the leading infantry brigade groups, it was not at the tactical disposition of the brigadier, but at that of the divisional commander, through his C.R.A. General Dallas was influenced in making this arrangement by the fact that he had only two field artillery brigades to support three infantry brigades. He did not desire to split up his already inadequate artillery formations in order to allot batteries to the 159th Brigade.

THE FOG

1917.
26 March.

conduct of an action if his superior is "on top" of him;[1] as, for instance, when General Sir Charles Warren was conducting the Spion Kop operation in 1899, with General Sir Redvers Buller looking on. General Dallas's battle headquarters was first established at 3.45 a.m. near El Breij, on the left bank of the Wadi Ghazze.

Sir A. Murray established an advanced headquarters in a railway train at El Arish, in order to be in touch with Sir C. Dobell. He arrived at 6 p.m. on the 25th and was in telegraphic and telephonic communication with the Eastern Force exchange at Rafah.

We have thus the following chain of command: Advanced G.H.Q. at El Arish; Eastern Force headquarters, the equivalent of the Army, near In Seirat; Desert Column headquarters, the equivalent of the Corps, at the same point. But G.H.Q. was without reserves, so that its influence upon the battle was confined mainly to that of advice. The smallness of the staffs of Eastern Force and Desert Column must also be noted. The total force under Sir C. Dobell's command consisted of two mounted divisions, a brigade of Camel Corps, three infantry divisions; that is to say, it was larger and far more complicated than a normal army corps. Yet his staff was smaller than that of an army corps on the Western Front at this period. At his advanced headquarters he had three general staff officers only, of whom two were out for a great part of the first night of the battle, endeavouring to ascertain the situation. General Chetwode's staff was the equivalent of that of an infantry division, the chief general staff officer being a G.S.O. 1st Grade. When a staff is too small for its functions the price paid in battle is excessive strain, lack of sleep, and consequent liability to error.

THE FOG AT DAWN ON THE 26TH MARCH.

Map 12.
Sketch 14.

The occupation of the line of the Wadi Ghazze, unopposed by the enemy, was to be interrupted by the weather. About 4 a.m., after a still, cold and very dark night, fog rolled up from the sea, gradually thickening till by 5 a.m., just before dawn, objects could not be distinguished at 20

---

[1] The two headquarters were actually, and remained all day, side by side, in the open and without cover of any sort.

yards' distance. A large proportion of the infantry had fortunately by this time completed the crossing of the wadi. A fog of this density was unusual in March, and no provision for its occurrence—except the allowance of a margin of time—had been made in framing plans for the attack. Its appearance was the first of several accidents which marred the day and caused the loss of valuable hours in an operation against time, for the completion of which every moment of daylight was required.

To have cancelled an enveloping attack of this nature would now have been difficult, as the mounted troops were well on their way, and would, unless they could be brought back, be visible to the enemy in large masses as soon as the fog cleared. Moreover, the headquarters of Eastern Force and Desert Column were at the moment both on the move to In Seirat. To General Chetwode, whose headquarters opened at In Seirat at 6.37, a few minutes before that of the Eastern Force, it appeared that the only possible course was to allow the movement to continue and to hope for an improvement as soon as the sun made itself felt. In any case the mounted troops, heading through the fog for open country, could not easily have been stopped, nor was it to them entirely a disadvantage. If fog renders movement slow and maintenance of direction difficult, it also screens from view.

It was impossible for General Dallas to go forward, as he had hoped, to reconnoitre the ground over which he was to attack. He therefore waited at El Breij, hoping that the fog would lift, while his two leading brigades, after a slight delay, slowly and carefully felt their way forward to their positions on the ridges. The expected improvement in visibility occurred about 7.30 a.m.[1]

The Envelopment of Gaza by the Mounted Troops.

The fog was at its thickest, as has been recorded, just as the leading brigade of the A. & N.Z. Mounted Division

---

[1] There is some divergence in the various accounts as to the hour at which this took place. The war diary of the Desert Column states that the fog began to lift at 7 a.m. and was practically gone by 8; that of the E.F.F. records that it lifted at 7.30 a.m.; while Sir A. Murray in his Despatch states that it cleared at 8, and in a telegram after the battle that it lasted till 11 a.m. It would appear that it began to lighten at 7, was practically clear on higher ground at 8, but that visibility was poor everywhere for some time longer, and in the ravines and depressions the mist lay thick for several hours.

approached the Wadi Ghazze at 4.50 a.m. Owing to good guiding and the excellent sense of direction possessed by the Australian mounted troops, the movement was not seriously checked, though each section could scarcely distinguish that next in front. The 2nd L.H. Brigade (Br.-General G. de L. Ryrie) successfully crossed, covered the mile of broken ground on the right bank, and then, reaching a better surface, advanced at a smart pace, on a compass bearing. By 8 a.m., an hour after the commencement of its advance, its screen was approaching Sheikh Abbas, and the fog was lifting. Here the first encounter with the enemy took place. A Turkish patrol opened fire on the 7th A.L.H., which promptly closed upon it at a gallop and rode it down. Shortly afterwards two enemy aircraft swooped down and fired their machine guns at the leading troops, but caused no casualties and were eventually driven off by rifle fire. The regiment, widely extended, continued to advance rapidly, galloping through the small bodies of the enemy which it encountered. The men were in the highest spirits at their advance into the Turkish position, and thoroughly enjoyed riding down and capturing the surprised and fleeing Turks in this ideal grass country. They crossed the Gaza-Beersheba road, cutting the telegraph lines which ran beside it as they passed, one patrol capturing ten wagons and another a party of 30 German pioneers with pack-horses.

Soon after 9 a.m., the 2nd L.H. Brigade reached its destination of Beit Durdis, closely followed by the remainder of the A. & N.Z. Mounted Division. After a short halt to reorganize, the 2nd L.H. Brigade was despatched north-west. By 10.30 it had taken up a position on a hill overlooking Gaza from the north-east,[1] had occupied the village of Jebaliye, 2 miles north-east of Gaza and west of the road to the north, and had detached the 7th A.L.H. to envelop the northern side of the town. Half an hour later the 7th A.L.H. had extended to the sea. Two squadrons of the 6th A.L.H. were pushed out towards Deir Sneid, 7 miles north-east of Gaza, to watch for the approach of Turkish reinforcements from the north. How complete was the surprise was shown when a patrol of the 2nd L.H. Brigade captured the commander of the Turkish *53rd Division* between Deir Sneid and Gaza. The Turkish general, with a

---

[1] Afterwards known as Australia Hill. See Map 14.

small mounted escort, was driving with his staff in carriages down to Gaza to take command, in complete ignorance of the proximity of British troops, when to his astonishment and disgust his escort bolted and he found himself surrounded by a party of light horsemen, grinning at his discomfiture. The incident was, however, not altogether a good omen, for it presaged the advance of reinforcements to Gaza.

The N.Z.M.R. Brigade concentrated near Beit Durdis and despatched a squadron towards Huj and a second towards Najd, 3 miles N.N.E. of Huj.[1] The 22nd Mounted Brigade formed up south of the New Zealanders. General Chauvel's divisional headquarters was established at Beit Durdis, and communication by cable, helio and wireless opened. The wireless was, however, jammed by the more powerful Turkish installation at Gaza.

The Imperial Mounted Division, following the A. & N.Z. Division, had been somewhat delayed by the fog in crossing the broken ground east of the Wadi Ghazze, but reached its destination at Kh. er Reseim at 10 a.m. On its march it had pushed out four patrols in an easterly direction towards Abu Hureira, Tell esh Sheria, Kh. Zuheilika, and Huj. The first three were held up by small bodies of Turkish cavalry and infantry, and two squadrons of the 5th Mounted Brigade were pushed forward in support towards Kh. el Baha, south-east of Kh. er Reseim and a mile north of the Gaza–Beersheba road. Another squadron was despatched towards Huj to make touch with the patrols of the A. & N.Z. Division. In this it failed, coming under fire from a small body of the enemy. At 9.45 a.m. a squadron of the Worcester Yeomanry charged a party of Turks north-west of Kh. el Baha and captured 60 prisoners. These minor incidents represented all that was seen of the enemy for some hours. The 5th Mounted Brigade remained on the Gaza–Beersheba road, south of Kh. el Baha, in support of its outpost squadrons.

The Camel Brigade (Br.-General C. L. Smith) had crossed at Tell el Jemmi, south of the crossings of the mounted divisions at Um Jerrar, and had reached El Mendur, on the bank of the Wadi esh Sheria, before the Imperial Mounted

---

[1] These detachments were directly under the orders of the divisional commander.

ADVANCE OF INFANTRY

Division passed by on its way to Kh. er Reseim. Its outpost line was put out between the right of the 5th Mounted Brigade and the Wadi Ghazze.

1917.
26 March.

The 54th Division (Major-General S. W. Hare), less 161st Brigade and 271st Brigade R.F.A. in Eastern Force reserve, crossed according to orders behind the mounted troops, took up a position of observation on the Sheikh Abbas Ridge, and began the digging of a line of entrenchments facing east. The 161st Brigade, which had halted at Sheikh Nebhan, on the bank of the Wadi Ghazze, received orders at 8.45 to cross and advance to El Burjabye, west of Sheikh Abbas and south of Mansura, where it would be in a position to support either the 53rd or 54th Divisions.

By 10.30 a.m., therefore, the mounted troops had accomplished their first mission of enveloping Gaza and interposing their main force between the town and the Turkish encampments to the east, thus creating a corridor for the main attack. At Sheikh Abbas the 54th Division covered the right rear of that attack. It now remained for the 53rd Division to carry out its more difficult tasks : the capture of the Ali Muntar position, which dominated Gaza, and then of the town itself.

The Opening of the Main Attack.

Despite the fog, the two leading brigades of the 53rd Division reached their positions of assembly on the ridges soon after 8.30 a.m. The 160th Brigade began crossing the Wadi Ghazze at 3.45 a.m., before the fog had come up and only a quarter of an hour after schedule time. The 158th Brigade was, as already related, led down to the wadi by its commander at 4.35, fifty minutes late. It was the intention of General Dallas, when he found how thick the fog had become, to halt the two brigades north of the Wadi Ghazze till the artillery had crossed. At 6.50 he sent orders to them to push forward slowly towards their respective objectives, Mansura and Esh Sheluf. But both brigadiers, impressed with the importance of time, had already moved when these orders were received : Br.-General Butler, who was first across, long before they were sent. By 5.10 a.m., the 4/Sussex, the leading battalion of the 160th Brigade, had secured the most prominent knoll on the Es Sire Ridge. Br.-General Mott also decided to advance on Mansura as soon as his brigade was over. Bugles were heard sounding in the Turkish lines as he moved forward. By 8.30 he was in touch with the 160th Brigade, now at Esh Sheluf, and soon afterwards his leading battalion, the 5/Welch Fusiliers, reached a covered position west of Mansura, 3 miles from the wadi and 2 miles short of Ali Muntar.

The 159th Brigade had completed its crossing by 6.40 a.m., and taken up a position on the right bank according to orders. At 8.25 Br.-General Travers telephoned to divisional headquarters to ask whether he was to move forward. He was told to stay where he was, as General Dallas had not yet decided how he desired to employ him. An hour later the brigade received orders to advance to Mansura in support of the 158th Brigade.

At 9 a.m. General Dallas, who had gone to the headquarters of the 158th Brigade, rode forward to reconnoitre, summoning his brigadiers and C.R.A., Br.-General R. E. A. Le Mottée, to a conference at Mansura to discuss the detailed arrangements of the attack. It was 10.15 before they actually assembled. Br.-General Travers, who had ridden up from the wadi, pointed out that the 159th Brigade, not having received orders to advance until 9.30, nor having been properly on the move before 10, would not be ready to take part in the attack till noon.

Though a long preparatory order had been issued by General Dallas at 9.15 the previous night, the actual operation orders for the attack had not been drawn up in advance, since details depended upon the results of reconnaissance. But it had been hoped that the attack would be launched by 10 a.m. General Chetwode was, therefore, growing anxious at the delay and was also concerned because he had been for two hours out of touch with General Dallas during the move of the latter's headquarters from El Breij to Mansura.[1] At 10.18 he telephoned to him, impressing on him the need of speedy action. General Dallas replied at 10.50 that the loss of time had been due to difficulty in

---

[1] General Dallas had left an officer at the telephone at El Breij, but the latter appears to have gone forward. It should be noted, however, that it is the duty of each formation or unit to provide communication with formations or units under its command. The responsibility for communication is forward, not backward, though this does not, of course, absolve any commander from sending back information by all means in his power.

UNEXPECTED DELAYS

bringing up his artillery and that he hoped to be ready to attack at noon. **1917. 26 March.** In point of fact, the artillery was already in position south of the Mansura bluff and in the valley between the Burjabye and Es Sire Ridges, though cable had not yet been laid out to connect the brigades with divisional headquarters, and no orders had yet been sent to them. The 266th Brigade records that it had actually opened fire on Ali Muntar at 10.10, while the 265th had two batteries ready to open fire at 10.20 and had ordered the third battery to move up into line with the other two. Their progress that morning may be shortly related. The C.R.A. had ordered them to cross the wadi and take up positions to give support if necessary to the infantry in its preliminary advance to Mansura and Esh Sheluf, and both were across by 6.30 a.m. As the infantry met with no opposition in its advance to the line Mansura–Esh Sheluf, no artillery support was required at this stage. Br.-General Le Mottée had then ridden out on a reconnaissance, in the course of which he had given verbal instructions to the two brigade commanders to push forward and take up new positions to support the further advance of the infantry on Ali Muntar and the Gaza defences. The real causes of the delay were, first, the time employed at Mansura in reconnaissance, which had been delayed by the fog, and the explanation of the plan of attack to the brigadiers, who had in turn to explain it to their battalion commanders ; and secondly, the fact that the 159th Brigade had not yet arrived.

General Dallas had at 10.4 a.m. telegraphed to Desert Column asking for the position of the 161st Brigade (Br.-General W. Marriott-Dodington) and 271st Brigade R.F.A. in Eastern Force reserve, which he had been promised by General Dobell if he required them. Desert Column replied, presumably without consulting Eastern Force, that the brigade group was at Sheikh Nebhan, where he should get in touch with it, and that it was at his disposition. As we have seen, it had already crossed the Wadi Ghazze, with orders to move to El Burjabye. But Br.-General Dodington, thinking that point too exposed, had moved down into the valley between the Burjabye and Es Sire Ridges. General Dallas sent it a telegraphic message at 11.45, ordering it to move up to Mansura, but, so far as can be ascertained, the message did not reach the brigade. A staff officer was subsequently sent to find it and bring it forward, but it was not till 1.10 p.m. that General Dallas's instructions were received.[1]

At 11 a.m. General Dallas issued his formal orders —recording the outline of what had been settled at the conference—for the attack.[2] This was to begin as soon as subordinate commanders had issued their orders. Br.-General Butler had to ride back to his brigade across the valley to the Es Sire Ridge. Meanwhile the 158th and 160th Brigades, now about 2½ miles from their objective, were to push forward patrols towards Ali Muntar.

Half-an-hour later Desert Column again telegraphed, expressing the anxiety of both Generals Dobell and Chetwode with regard to the delay and ordering General Dallas to launch his attack forthwith. At 11.45 the latter ordered the attack to begin, and the 158th and 160th Brigades began their advance a few minutes later. The 159th Brigade, which was assigned a part in the attack, had not then arrived at Mansura. The 158th Brigade was to attack Ali Muntar from Mansura, the 160th Brigade the same objective along the Es Sire Ridge. The 159th Brigade was to cover the right of the 158th and attack a hummock north of Ali Muntar and on the other side of the Gaza–Beersheba road, known as Clay Hill. The sole divisional reserve was to be one battalion of the 159th Brigade, until the arrival of the 161st Brigade, for which General Dallas had asked. The two field artillery brigades were to support the infantry under the orders of the C.R.A.

The artillery bombardment began at noon, the 265th and 266th Brigades being in the positions already mentioned. Two guns of the 10th Heavy Battery came into action at the south-west end of the Es Sire Ridge, two guns of the 91st from the Wadi Ghazze where the Rafah–Gaza road crossed it, and two guns of the 15th Heavy Battery (with Money's Detachment) from the dunes north of Tell el Ujul

---

[1] The brigade was south of the final E in Es Sire, only about a mile and a half from Mansura. Major H. L. Wright, its brigade-major, states that the message received at 1.10 was by motor-cyclist. It therefore appears that it came, not from General Dallas, but from Eastern Force, which records ordering the brigade to Mansura at 12.45. Major Wright also states that he placed a patrol at the point which he took to be El Burjabye, to receive any message which might be sent, but that none was received from this source.

[2] Appendix 11.

on the coast. As the enemy's position was invisible, no definite artillery programme had been drawn up, and it was necessary to trust to the reports of forward observing officers for the support of the advance, though the heavy batteries were successfully ranged by aeroplanes.

On receiving their orders to begin the attack, the troops of the 158th and 160th Brigades, who had now been assembled for from three to four hours, began their advance with alacrity, almost at once coming under shrapnel fire. The head of the 159th Brigade reached Mansura at noon and had to wheel first right, then left, in order to take its position on the right of the line and swing in towards its objective. The battalions were immediately deployed, and, eager to catch up, covered long stretches at the double.

The Attack on Gaza by the Mounted Troops and the Advance of Relieving Columns.

By noon General Chetwode had begun to fear that if the main infantry attack met with strong opposition it would be impossible for it to capture Gaza before nightfall. On the other hand, he had as yet received no reports from the air of the movement of relieving columns, while none of the mounted troops keeping the ring had been seriously engaged. He therefore considered that if necessary he might safely employ a portion of them to attack the town from east and north, as foreshadowed in his orders. He sent a message to Generals Chauvel and Hodgson to reconnoitre towards Gaza and to be prepared to despatch a brigade each to assist the infantry.[1]

Soon afterwards General Chetwode received information from the A. & N.Z. Mounted Division which tended to confirm his anxiety. An early prisoner's report had put the infantry garrison of Gaza at two battalions only; now a sergeant of *Fourth Army* Signals had stated that

---

[1] Anzac Mounted Division.
Imperial Mounted Division.
W.O.8.   26th.
Both cavalry divisions will reconnoitre immediately with view to closing in on enemy at Gaza to assist infantry if ordered. One brigade only from each division will be employed, leaving two brigades to continue observation. No news by aeroplane of any enemy movement from any direction. Acknowledge.
                                    Desert Column, 12.5. p.m.

there were six. He therefore proposed to Sir C. Dobell that he should employ the A. & N.Z. Mounted Division in the attack and received the latter's consent. At 1 p.m. he placed General Chauvel in command of both divisions, ordered him to free his own division for the attack by moving the Imperial Mounted Division further north, and stated that he himself would replace the latter by the Camel Brigade.[1]

This order, though sent by telegram, took precisely an hour to reach General Chauvel, who at once ordered the Imperial Mounted Division to move up to Beit Durdis and take over all the outposts of the Anzacs to east and north-east, these parties being directed to rejoin their own brigades as quickly as possible. These arrangements took time, and it was nearly 3 p.m. before General Chauvel had shifted his headquarters to a knoll between Beit Durdis and Gaza, whence he would have a view of the operations. He had already summoned his brigadiers to meet him at that point, and at 3.15 p.m. he issued his orders. The 2nd L.H. Brigade was to attack from the sea to the Gaza–Jebaliye road, the N.Z.M.R. Brigade from the road to the ridge north-east of Gaza, the 22nd Mounted Brigade thence to the track leading to Beit Durdis. The attack was to start at 4 p.m.

General Chauvel had acted, it is clear, with all possible expedition, but to General Chetwode, unaware how long his orders had taken to reach him, the eagerly desired news of his attack seemed to lag. At 3.50 p.m. he again telegraphed, impressing upon General Chauvel that the success of the operation depended largely upon the vigour of his attack and that it was imperative that the position should be in British hands before dusk. He also suggested that General Chauvel should withdraw a portion of the

---

[1] Anzac Mounted Division.   53rd Division.
   Imperial Mounted Division.
W.O.10.   26th.
   Column Commander considers it most desirable that mounted troops should press in on Gaza to assistance of infantry, which is on very extended front. General Chauvel is placed in command of both mounted divisions. The I.C. Bde. will be ordered to area Kh. er Reseim. General Chauvel should order Imperial Division move to the north about Kh. Kufiye [1 mile south of Beit Durdis] or Beit Durdis, to release the Anzac Division for attack on Gaza and sandhills from N.E. Aeroplanes report no enemy activity in Akra or Hureira areas. Report action taken. Addressed Anzac Mounted Division, repeated Imperial Mounted Division, 53rd Division.   Desert Column, 1 p.m.

Imperial Mounted Division to assist his own division in the attack and added that he had ordered three batteries of armoured cars to support him. On receipt of his message General Chauvel asked General Hodgson for another brigade, and the latter detailed the 3rd L.H. Brigade (Br.-General J. R. Royston) for the purpose.

Hitherto the troops of the A. & N.Z. Mounted Division had seen little of the enemy in the vicinity of Gaza, though about noon a column of infantry passing through the suburbs had been caught by the machine guns of the 5th A.L.H., in position to the north-east. The Turkish garrison was, in fact, chiefly concerned with the main infantry attack from the south, and the advance of the mounted troops was not at first strongly opposed. The latter, aware of the need for haste, pressed in with dash. The 2nd L.H. Brigade, moving against the northern side of the town, was not seriously engaged until it reached the cactus hedges. Here it met with considerable resistance, and there was hard fighting in this enclosed area, Turks and Australians frequently firing at one another from a range of a few yards through the hedges. When dusk fell the brigade had reached the northern and western outskirts of Gaza. The N.Z.M.R. Brigade[1] advanced from the neighbourhood of Jebaliye against the east and north-east of the town. The Wellington Regiment captured two 77-mm. Krupp guns, pushed on with them to the outskirts of the town, and blew down at pointblank range several houses from which their advance was being disputed, taking prisoner twenty terrified and beplastered Turks. One squadron of the Canterbury Regiment swung south against Ali Muntar and entered the trenches just after the infantry of the 53rd Division. The 22nd Mounted Brigade (Br.-General F.A.B. Fryer) advanced at a gallop along the track from Beit Durdis to Gaza and had likewise reached its outskirts by dusk.

Meanwhile the long-expected advance of Turkish reinforcements had made itself felt. General Hodgson had issued orders at 2.20 p.m. for the move northward of the Imperial Mounted Division to take over the outposts of the A. & N.Z. Mounted Division. He intended that the 6th Mounted Brigade (Br.-General T. M. S. Pitt) should

---

[1] Only three troops of the Auckland Regiment were available, the remainder of that regiment being still in observation towards Huj and Najd.

take up a position east of Beit Durdis and that the 5th (Br.-General E. A. Wiggin), which was astride the Gaza–Beersheba road supporting its outposts in the Wadi el Baha, should fill the gap between it and the Camel Brigade, which had orders to move to Kh. er Reseim. Br.-General Wiggin, however, received with these orders instructions not to move until he was relieved, and there was a long delay in the arrival of the Camel Brigade, which did not receive Desert Column's message till some time later. The relief was not eventually completed until after 6.30 p.m., when the 5th Brigade moved about two miles further north and occupied a Turkish trench previously reconnoitred.

While the Berkshire Yeomanry of the 6th Mounted Brigade was relieving the A. & N.Z. Mounted Division's outposts east of Beit Durdis, a sudden Turkish attack from the direction of Jemmame drove in the posts on Hill 405, a mile and a half north of Beit Durdis. General Hodgson ordered the 6th Mounted Brigade, with the Berkshire Battery R.H.A., to advance and retake the hill. The brigade, had, however, just then found a small supply of water and was engaged in watering its horses. The resultant delay, slight though it was, enabled the Turks to occupy the crest of the hill at 5.15 p.m. General Hodgson had already asked General Chauvel for the return of the 3rd L.H. Brigade, which had moved westward in support of the A. & N.Z. Mounted Division. This brigade, less the 10th A.L.H., came back promptly, and Br.-General Royston, at once grasping the danger of the situation, occupied the hill north-west of Hill 405 and assisted the 6th Mounted Brigade to prevent any further advance of the enemy. The fire of the Notts and Berkshire Batteries took the Turks in enfilade and inflicted considerable loss. The latter battery was, however, caught by the concentrated fire of about three Turkish batteries and forced to withdraw. It was now, however, 6.30 p.m. and nearly dusk, and the enemy made no attempt to follow up his advantage. When General Hodgson discovered that he had for the moment lost touch with the 5th Mounted Brigade owing to the move of his divisional headquarters, he asked General Chauvel for the 10th A.L.H. to fill the gap between the left of the 6th Mounted Brigade and the Camel Brigade at Kh. er Reseim. This regiment succeeded in reaching its position in the growing darkness. The enemy advancing from the west were

GAZA from Ali el Muntar.

Sheikh Hasan WEST TOWN MEDITERRANEAN SEA EAST TOWN Sheikh Redwan Sand dunes

estimated at 3,000 infantry and two squadrons of cavalry. Three enemy columns were also reported to be moving south from the direction of Deir Sneid. A squadron of the 22nd Mounted Brigade and the 7th Light Car Patrol were despatched to the assistance of the two squadrons 6th A.L.H. holding the main road to the north. The 11th and 12th Light Armoured Motor Batteries reported to Br.-General Royston and assisted the 3rd L.H. Brigade to hold the Turkish attack from Huj. The advance of the enemy, both from the north and from the east, was successfully checked and it does not appear that he made any further serious efforts till morning light.[1]

1917. 26 March.

The Capture of Ali Muntar.

The 53rd Division had not been in action since the Gallipoli campaign. It had now reached a high standard of training, and the troops, after their winter in Sinai, were thoroughly fit and acclimatized. Its advance up the ridges was a model in precision and steadiness, and the horsemen of the Dominions, who watched it as from an amphitheatre, witnessed a good example of British infantry tradition.[2]

The left battalion of the 158th Brigade, the 5/Welch Fusiliers, reached the " cactus garden " south of Ali Muntar, and there halted to allow the other battalions, which had more ground to cover, to come up on its right. The 1/Hereford, from brigade reserve, was brought up to attack Green Hill on the left front, since it enfiladed the advance of both the 158th and 160th Brigades. The 159th Brigade had now come up on the right of the 158th and was directing its advance on Clay Hill. Heavy machine-gun fire met the troops as they approached the position, and the advance slowed down.

---

[1] See Note I. at end of Chapter XVII.
[2] The deployment of the division is shown below, the 160th Brigade being separated from the other two, until approaching Gaza, by the valley between the Es Sire and Burjabye Ridges.

(Left)	(Centre)	(Right)
160th Brigade.	*158th Brigade.*	*159th Brigade.*
2/10 Middx.	1/4 Sussex. 1/5, 1/6, 1/7 R.W.F.	1/5 Welch, 1/4 Cheshire.
2/4 Queen's.	1/1 Hereford.	1/4 Welch.
(2/4 W. Kent in Money's Detachment.)		(1/7 Cheshire divisional reserve.)

By 3.30 p.m. the 161st Brigade had reached Mansura. Assured of a new divisional reserve, General Dallas at once sent the 7/Cheshire to rejoin the 159th Brigade. The Cheshire was moved up in support of the 5/Welch on the left, which appeared to Br.-General Travers to be meeting the stiffest resistance and to have come to a standstill.

The support of the artillery had not been very effective in the early stage, partly owing to its unavoidably hurried entry into the attack.[1] The arrival of the 271st Brigade R.F.A. with the 161st Brigade Group produced a marked effect in diminishing the fire of the machine guns on Clay Hill.

At 3.50 p.m. the determination of the infantry earned its reward. Some forty men of the 5/Welch Fusiliers (158th Brigade) and the same number of the 5/Welch (159th Brigade) suddenly dashed forward through the machine-gun fire and made lodgments at two points in the trenches east of Ali Muntar mosque, capturing 20 Germans and Austrians, and 20 Turks. The grip upon the position was held fast with utmost difficulty in face of local counter-attacks, but was made secure so soon as the support of the 271st Brigade R.F.A. had checked the galling fire of a nest of machine guns on Clay Hill.

On the left the 160th Brigade had advanced more rapidly. By 1.30 p.m. the Labyrinth, a maze of entrenched gardens due south of Gaza, had been captured, and the 2/10th Middlesex was established on a grassy hill overlooking the town and half a mile from it. The 4/Sussex, advancing up the centre of the Es Sire ridge under intense fire, was less successful. After losing their commanding officer and suffering heavy casualties, the troops fell back in some disorder from the crest. At 4 p.m., reinforced from the reserve and its task made lighter by the success on its left, the battalion again advanced.[2]

---

[1] General Dallas in his report refers to the difficulty in the way of two artillery brigades giving adequate support to three infantry brigades. See also footnote, p. 288.

[2] It would appear, however, that the infantry had been considerably shaken by the artillery fire which met it, for the 265th Brigade R.F.A. reports that stragglers from the three battalions of the 160th Brigade continued to fall back through the guns till dusk.

As the 158th and 159th Brigades slowly fought their way forward, General Dallas realized that more driving force was necessary if the whole position was to be carried. Machine guns on Green Hill had delayed the 158th Brigade's advance all the afternoon, and that brigade's reserve battalion, the Herefordshire, which had been put in to attack the hill, had swung away to the right, as so often happens in attacks of this nature. General Dallas ordered the 161st Brigade, leaving one battalion in divisional reserve, to carry Green Hill and fill the gap between the 158th and 160th Brigades. The brigade began its attack at 4 p.m., 1/4th Essex on right, 1/5th on left, 1/6th in brigade reserve, and, despite heavy fire, captured its objective at 5.30 p.m. The 159th Brigade had meanwhile also been successful. The 4/Welch and 4/Cheshire stormed Clay Hill at 4.45 p.m., and the brigade's whole objective was in its hands shortly afterwards.

By 6.30 p.m. the whole position was won, the Turks everywhere running back into Gaza. The 159th Brigade had its right on Clay Hill and its left south of the Gaza-Beersheba road, the 158th Brigade held Ali Muntar, the 161st Brigade Green Hill, and the 160th Brigade was north of the Labyrinth.

So far, then, as the troops were concerned, all seemed over. By nightfall Gaza was surrounded completely, except for its south-western side. Everywhere save among the sand-dunes, where a comparatively small body held its position in front of Money's Detachment, the Turks had fallen back to the town. The British troops, weary but exultant, looked forward with confidence to the surrender of the whole garrison at dawn. Meanwhile they were consolidating the positions won and pushing forward patrols, which felt their way among the houses till in the course of the night men of the A. & N.Z. Mounted Division from the north and east met infantry of the 53rd Division in the eastern streets. Yet, while to them a brilliant victory seemed about to reward their labours and sacrifices, Generals Dobell and Chetwode at In Seirat found cause for anxiety. Though the town was enveloped, the advance of the enemy from north and east boded ill for the morrow.

NOTE.

THE ARTILLERY OF THE EASTERN FORCE.

	60-pdr.	4·5-in. how.	18-pdr.	2·75-in. gun.
A. & N.Z. Mounted Division—				
4 Batteries R.H.A. (T.) (each four 18-pdrs.).	—	—	16	—
Imperial Mounted Division do...	—	—	16	—
Imperial Camel Brigade—				
1 Camel Pack Battery (six 2·75-in.).	—	—	—	6
52nd Division—				
2 Brigades R.F.A. (each twelve 18-pdrs. and four 4·5-in. hows.)	—	8	24	—
1 Brigade R.F.A. (twelve 18-pdrs)	—	—	12	—
53rd Division do.	—	8	36	—
54th Division do.	—	8	36	—
Army Troops—				
3 Batteries (each four 60-pdrs.)	12	—	—	—
	12	24	140	6
At First Gaza the 52nd Div. Arty. was not engaged, the third brigades of the 53rd and 54th Divns. were in the Suez Canal Defences, and only four guns of each 18-pdr. battery of the 53rd and 54th Divisions and one section of each heavy battery were brought up. Therefore deduct	6	8	76	—
Total at First Gaza[1] ..	6	16	64	6

[1] The actual attack of the 53rd Division was supported only by six 60-pdrs., twelve 4·5-in. hows., and twenty-four 18-pdrs.

Sketch 15.

CHAPTER XVII.

THE FIRST BATTLE OF GAZA (CONTINUED).

(Map 12 ; Sketch 15.)

THE DECISION TO WITHDRAW THE MOUNTED TROOPS.

As the day wore on, Generals Dobell and Chetwode frequently conferred at In Seirat. It appeared to them that the delays, first that caused by the fog, secondly that owing to the progress of the 53rd Division having been slower than had been anticipated, must result in involving them in a fight with Turkish reinforcements long before the position was captured. It was, in fact, a matter of surprise to them that there was no news of serious pressure from the east until comparatively late in the afternoon, but the stubborn defence of Ali Muntar and Green Hill deprived the British of what advantage they might otherwise have gained from the tardiness of the Turkish relieving columns. Feeling certain that these columns would appear sooner or later, General Dobell, after consultation with General Chetwode, decided that unless Gaza was captured by nightfall the fight must be broken off and the mounted troops withdrawn. The state of the horses was constantly in their minds. These had been watered before midnight on the 25th, had for the most part been without water all day and would probably get little, unless Gaza was taken, until withdrawn to the Wadi Ghazze. As we have seen, some pools had been found. The information on this subject received by Desert Column was the following. At 10.25 a.m. General Hodgson had telegraphed that there was a small quantity of water near Kh. er Reseim and that he had watered the horses of one of his brigades. In the same telegram he had given the less promising news that, according to the statement of a deserter, all the wells but three in Gaza had been blown up. At 12.44 p.m. General Chauvel had telegraphed that there were a few small pools in the Wadi el Halib (by which was probably meant its tributary, the Wadi el Humra).

1917.
26 March.
Map 12.
Sketch 15.

By 4 p.m., as has been recorded, just as General Chauvel began his attack on Gaza, the long expected advance of the Turks made itself felt. From the air[1] there were no reports of the enemy being in strength until after the withdrawal of the mounted troops had been ordered, so that this order was based on reports from Generals Chauvel and Hodgson,[2] together with the fact that the 53rd Division had not yet captured its objectives.

On the strength of these reports, General Dobell, who had been from the first apprehensive of a strong counter-attack

---

[1] General Dobell had at his disposal 5 aeroplanes for general reconnaissance, 6 for artillery co-operation, and 6 for patrol duties. There was also always one machine at the disposal of Desert Column.

[2] All the messages on this subject received by the Desert Column, prior to its order to the mounted troops to withdraw, are here given, so that the precise information on which Generals Dobell and Chetwode acted shall be apparent.

Anzac Mounted Division report verbally patrol near Deir Sneid reports 3 infantry columns advancing on Gaza from Deir Sneid, estimated strength about 300.
4 p.m.

I.C.C. Brigade,
A.P.10. 26th.
Aeroplane reports at 3.45. Saw about 200 cavalry about 5 miles S. of Gaza on Hureira road halted. One battalion of infantry halted 2 miles W. of Beersheba. Ends.
4 p.m. Desert Column.

Desert Column.
G.R. 142. 26th.
Have just had report from Deir Sneid that three enemy columns are moving towards us from that direction. Body of 300 infantry are reported to have moved into sandhills W. of Deir Sneid. Have sent one squadron 22nd Brigade to oppose them and am ordering up one Brigade from Imperial Mounted Division. Can aeroplane reconnaissance be sent to verify this?
4 p.m. Anzac Mounted Division.

Desert Column. 26th.
3,000 infantry, 2 squadrons cavalry, advancing from Huj in southwesterly direction.
4.50 p.m. Moundiv. [Imp. Mtd. Divn.].

There is also the following entry in the War Diary of the rear headquarters Eastern Force (at Rafah) :—
R.F.C. reported at 6 p.m. that a column of enemy troops were marching in fours towards Gaza, and were 1½ miles S.W. of Huj. The column's length was 1½ miles, including transport. Screen of infantry in front of column and flank guards on both flanks.

This report was, of course, telephoned to General Dobell, but cannot have influenced General Chetwode when, ten minutes later, he issued orders to General Chauvel to retire across the Wadi Ghazze. Its tenor was not, in any case, very different from General Hodgson's report of 4.50 p.m.

There is no record of any other message, but General Chauvel conversed on the telephone from time to time with General Chetwode.

DECISION TO WITHDRAW CAVALRY 307

against the right rear of the force, warned the 54th 1917.
Division to be prepared to move 2 miles westward to the 26 March.
Burjabye Ridge, with its left on a point one mile north of
Mansura, where it would be in touch with the 53rd Division.
Soon afterwards, at 5.38 p.m., he ordered this movement to
take place. The headquarters of the Desert Column was
informed of the despatch of these messages, but they were
not communicated to the 53rd Division either by Desert
Column or by the 54th Division.

At this date sunset is almost exactly at 6 p.m. (Cairo
time) and darkness falls swiftly at this latitude. By that
hour no news of the fall of Ali Muntar had been received by
Desert Column, and indeed, though a lodgment in the Turkish
trenches had been effected long before, it was not, as we have
seen, till 6.30 that the whole position was captured. General
Chetwode came to the conclusion that the sands had run
out, that he could no longer leave the mounted troops with
half their numbers involved in fighting amidst the gardens
of Gaza, while the Turks attacked the other half from north
and east. At 6.10 p.m., with the approval of General
Dobell, he reluctantly issued a telegraphic order to General
Chauvel that the mounted troops should break off the
action and retire across the Wadi Ghazze.[1] He subsequently placed the Camel Brigade under the orders of
General Chauvel to assist in covering his retirement, and
instructed him by telegram that when the withdrawal was
complete the brigade should take up a line from the wadi to
the right flank of the 54th Division in the new position on
the Burjabye Ridge to which it had been directed.

Just as the order for General Chauvel's withdrawal was
being despatched, a report came in from General Dallas
that a redoubt north-east of Ali Muntar had been captured
and that the enemy was retiring stubbornly. This information did not seem to General Chetwode to warrant any
change in his orders. The extrication of the mounted troops
and the watering of their horses appeared to him to be of
the first importance. It was not until some time later that
he heard of the retreat of the enemy from the whole ridge.

---

[1] "Australian Official History," p. 282, states that General Chauvel
made a "strong protest" on receipt of these orders. No written protest
is on record, and General Chetwode states that none was made to him
verbally, by telephone, or messenger.

The Withdrawal of the Mounted Troops and Evacuation of Ali Muntar.

The withdrawal of the mounted troops was a slow and difficult affair, not because of hostile pressure, for of that there was none until dawn, but because formations were widely scattered in the darkness and frequently intermixed, while some regiments were far from their horses—the 7th A.L.H., for example, nearly four miles—and all wounded had not yet been brought in. The artillery was first sent back under escort. The Imperial Mounted Division remained in position to cover the retirement of the troops which had been attacking Gaza.

1917. 27 March. By 2 a.m. on the 27th the A. & N.Z. Mounted Division had passed Beit Durdis, and General Hodgson ordered the concentration of the 5th and 6th Mounted and the 3rd L.H. Brigades. It was not until 5.30 a.m. that the Turks attacked the 3rd L.H. Brigade in strength, just as it was crossing the Gaza-Beersheba road near Kh. Sihan. At the moment of the attack the 7th Light Car Patrol, which had had a very exciting evening and had lain up for some hours close to Ali Muntar to give its exhausted detachments a rest, advanced down the road, and very effectively covered the retirement of the 3rd L.H. Brigade.[1] Soon after daylight

---

[1] The "Australian Official History" quotes the following account from the personal diary of Lieutenant W. H. P. McKenzie, a New Zealand officer, in command of the 7th Light Car Patrol :—

"At dawn we saw we were in a sticky position [near Ali Muntar] if discovered. We slipped out on to the Gaza–Beersheba road, every now and then meeting small parties of British 'lost ones,' whom we directed towards the wadi, and then hit up the pace towards Sihan, where we hoped to meet the armoured cars. They were not there. Instead, we found the 3rd Light Horse Brigade retiring before a huge enemy force, who were bearing in heavily on them. General Royston galloped over and asked me if I could cover his retirement. This is just the kind of job we are most suited for. We ran the cars into likely positions along the ridge, and, while the brigade went by, we waited until the enemy came within range. When they were some 1,200 or 1,500 yards off, we opened fire with five machine guns. It was immense. General Royston was greatly pleased, and he asked us if we required a squadron to cover our retreat or to stand by in support. We said 'No,' so he wished us good luck, and galloped after his brigade. We were now on our own. It was the time of our lives. We placed the cars (never attempting to dismount the guns) in such positions that enemy parties, trying to avoid the fire of one, would come under the fire of another; but we could not stem a force of thousands. They kept advancing, and we retired from one ridge to another comfortably, while the 3rd Brigade got clear away across the wadi, and was secure. We had targets of mounted men and infantry, and killed at least 150 of them, and they must have had very heavy casualties altogether. We suffered no losses."

A MISUNDERSTANDING

all the troops of the Imperial Mounted Division were safely across the wadi. The Camel Brigade had moved meanwhile to its position continuing the 54th Division's right to the bank.

1917.
26 March.

We must now go back to consider the effect of this retirement upon the position of the 53rd Division. Shortly before 7 p.m. General Chetwode telephoned to General Dallas that the mounted troops were withdrawing, that his right would thus be left in the air, and that he must withdraw it sufficiently "to make touch with the 54th "Division." General Dallas protested against abandoning the ground he had won and asked that troops should be sent to close the gap between the two divisions and cover the rear of his brigades, his own reserve now amounting to only one battalion of the 161st Brigade.

Unhappily "touch with the 54th Division" meant something quite different to the two commanders. General Chetwode supposed that his own staff had informed General Dallas of the impending move of that division. General Dallas, not having received this information, was under the impression that touch was to be made at Sheikh Abbas, 4 miles from his right on Clay Hill; General Chetwode meant that touch should be made with the 54th Division's new left flank, a mile north of Mansura and not much over a mile from the 161st Brigade on Green Hill; and the misunderstanding did not become apparent in the course of their conversation. General Dallas was told that his request for more troops could not be complied with; on his further request for time in which to consider the matter, General Chetwode, after consultation with General Dobell, gave a peremptory verbal order that the right of the 53rd Division should be thrown back to meet the left of the 54th. No further order, written or verbal, was issued to the 53rd Division till nearly midnight, and it was believed to be carrying out its instructions to withdraw its right to Mansura and there make touch with the 54th Division.

At 6.35 p.m. General Dobell had informed Desert Column and the 54th Division that he contemplated withdrawing the whole force across the Wadi Ghazze if Gaza did not shortly fall. By 11 p.m., however, he had become aware of the full extent of the 53rd Division's success. He also received about this time various intercepted wireless messages between Kress at Tell esh Sheria and Major Tiller, the German officer commanding the Gaza garrison, which showed that the situation of the latter was desperate. Why these messages did not reach General Dobell earlier cannot now be determined, as the originals are not to be found. The only obvious explanation is that his advanced headquarters was far from Eastern Force exchange at Rafah, that there was heavy pressure on the line forward, and that proper discretion as to the priority of messages was not exercised. The British Intelligence (E) at Cairo had the key to the Turkish cipher, picked up all the messages, and telephoned them to Rafah always within a quarter of an hour of their being deciphered and translated, and in one case within ten minutes of the message being sent out.[1] The times of the messages are not known, but there were at least four which reached Rafah prior to 6.30 p.m., all of which would have been of immense value to General Dobell had they been earlier in his hands.

At 11 p.m., therefore, being now better informed as to the situation, General Dobell instructed Desert Column that General Dallas should "dig in on his present line," throwing "back his left flank and connecting his right with "the 54th Division." This message appeared merely confirmatory of the verbal orders which General Chetwode had already given General Dallas, and was therefore not repeated to the latter. General Dobell also stated that Eastern Force would take command of the 53rd Division—that is, withdraw it from General Chetwode—next morning as soon as communication could be arranged, and that the 52nd Division, less one brigade, would be held in reserve

---

[1] The following are extracts from the private diary of Lieut.-Colonel (then Major) H. P. T. Lefroy, I. (E) :—

"Things began to hum about mid-day, as we attacked Gaza "9 a.m. . . . Tiller anxiously reports no sign of arrival of any re-"inforcements. Von Kress assures him Divs. 3 and 16 coming to his "assistance. By evening Tiller reports British have entered town by "N. and E., and situation very bad. Von Kress asks him concerning "morale of troop commanders and troops. Tiller replies that former "refuse to face combat at dawn. . . .

"Situation at midnight (26/27) very interesting. Messages from "Gaza (VKA) pessimistic. Tiller asks von Kress to attack at 2 a.m., "when our [the British] artillery cannot see, as his troops cannot face "any further artillery fire. Kress regrets unable, but counsels him to "hold on at all costs, as he will attack with Divs. 3 and 16 from "Jemmame and Sheria at 'first morning grey.' Tiller says English "in the town and occupying 'the battery and half the position,' and "unless reinforcements sent there is very little hope. W/T personnel "VKA and VQT (G.H.Q., Sheria) exchange farewell messages, and "arrange burn all papers, and to blow up VKA. Latter done 5.40 a.m., "but our troops drew off to S.E. of town, and Gaza was not taken."

at In Seirat. The 155th Brigade had been there all day and the 157th was now on the march from Khan Yunis.

1917.
26 March.

What was actually happening on the ridges south and east of Gaza differed radically from the conception in the minds of Generals Dobell and Chetwode. With his right north of the Gaza-Beersheba road, General Dallas saw no possibility of remaining on any part of the captured position and at the same time making touch with the 54th Division at Sheikh Abbas, when the retirement of the mounted troops had uncovered him. At 10.30 p.m. he issued orders for his whole force to withdraw to a line from the caves at Tell el Ujul, near the Wadi Ghazze, on the left, through a point a mile north of Esh Sheluf, thence to Mansura and Sheikh Abbas. This move involved a retirement of little over a mile on the Es Sire Ridge, but one of three miles between Clay Hill and Mansura. The 158th Brigade was to come into divisional reserve. General Dallas had previously telegraphed to Desert Column the line he was taking up and that he would " join up with " 54th Division on western slopes of Sheikh Abbas," but the exhausted and numerically inadequate staff of General Chetwode did not even then realize the misconception of the G.O.C. 53rd Division. It was nearly midnight when General Dallas's staff discovered that the 54th Division was drawing in to north of Mansura. Had he known this movement was in progress, he would certainly not have abandoned all the captured position, probably none of it with the exception of Clay Hill. The 159th Brigade, which was to have taken over from Mansura to Sheikh Abbas, was now moved into divisional reserve. The withdrawal of the troops took a considerable time, as patrols had been pushed right into the outskirts of Gaza. Some of these did not return till dawn, but the retirement was generally complete by 4 a.m. on the 27th.

The Reoccupation of Ali Muntar and Turkish Counter-Attacks.

It was not till 5 a.m. on the 27th that General Chetwode realized that the whole position had been abandoned.[1]

---

[1] General Dallas states that he had explained on the telephone the full extent of his withdrawal to General Chetwode ; the latter states that he did not understand his subordinate to mean that he was abandoning anything like so much ground. In any case the responsibility rests upon Desert Column Headquarters, since General Dallas had telegraphed to it the line he was taking up.

Map 12.
Sketch 15.

He then issued orders that patrols of the 53rd Division and of Money's Detachment should advance and discover whether the Turks had reoccupied it.[1]

General Dallas then ordered the 160th and 161st Brigades to push forward strong patrols to the positions of the previous evening and to support them if they were able to reoccupy the line. It was a severe test, moral and physical, for troops who had been without rest (except for what they got on the ridges while awaiting the launching of the attack) for over thirty-six hours, who had gallantly captured the position and then been withdrawn from it. But Ali Muntar and Green Hill were both found to be unoccupied. One company of the 7/Essex, 161st Brigade, reoccupied Ali Muntar and two companies of the same battalion Green Hill. On the front of the 160th Brigade, after the 2/10th Middlesex had pushed forward patrols beyond Sheluf, the 2/4th Queen's was ordered by Br.-General Butler to advance and gain touch with the 161st Brigade. But while this battalion was moving up in artillery formation, it saw the patrols of the 161st Brigade to the north-east falling back. The 1/Hereford of the 158th Brigade had been ordered to reoccupy that brigade's old position, but some delay occurred, as this battalion was then refilling water-bottles and replenishing ammunition from the regimental transport, which had just come up the valley between the Es Sire and Burjabye Ridges. The Herefordshire was, however, also advancing when the companies of the 161st Brigade were seen falling back.

Br.-General Dodington, commanding the 161st Brigade, had expected Turkish counter-attacks after dawn, and his anticipations were soon fulfilled. The first was not heavy, though it caused the momentary loss of Ali Muntar and a portion of Green Hill. But before the 6/Essex, sent forward by Br.-General Dodington, came into action, the 7/Essex had re-established tself upon the positions, which were consolidated as well as circumstances permitted. Meanwhile, a further Turkish force—that which had attacked the 3rd L.H. Brigade in its retirement—had appeared on

---

[1] O.C. Cav. Regt., Imp. Mtd. Div., att'd. 53rd Divn.; 53rd Divn. A.P. 22. 27th.
Push patrols forward at once and ascertain situation west and north of Gaza. Open your helio and get touch with Eastforce H.Q., Hill 310.
5.36 a.m.   Des. Col.

Sheikh Abbas and was shelling the rear of General Dallas's position, including his reserves, medical units and transport camels. Yet, though bodies of the enemy passed down into the ravines running west of the crest, no serious attack was made upon the 54th Division in its new position on the Burjabye Ridge.

1917.
27 March.

At 8 a.m. Eastern Force had sent General Dallas a message to the effect that he was to come directly under its orders. At 9.15 his appreciation of the position was received by General Dobell. He stated that, if the present positions of the 53rd and 54th Divisions were to be maintained, it was necessary that the enemy should be driven off Sheikh Abbas and especially that the artillery harassing his rear should be driven out of action by a counter-attack. He suggested that this counter-attack should be made by mounted troops, as a deliberate advance by the 52nd Division might be too slow.

General Dobell had already warned the 52nd Division at In Seirat to be prepared to make a counter-attack eastward, its left on the right of the 54th Division, but before he had decided whether or not it was advisable to carry out this operation a further heavy blow fell upon the 53rd Division. A strong Turkish attack, launched at 9.30 a.m., quickly recaptured Ali Muntar, its garrison suffering serious losses and falling back to Green Hill. The latter was almost surrounded and the situation of the two Essex battalions appeared for a time to be critical, but eventually they extricated themselves. General Dallas then reorganized the line to eliminate the acute salient south of Ali Muntar, drawing it back to a point half-way between that hill and Sheluf.

The Withdrawal to the Wadi Ghazze.

On receipt of this information Desert Column placed the 54th Division under General Dallas's command and warned him to be prepared to withdraw both divisions across the Ghazze if necessary that afternoon. Soon after 11 a.m., General Dallas had a conversation with Br.-General G. P. Dawnay, B.G.G.S. Eastern Force, who asked him whether he considered that the position now held by the two divisions could be maintained for three or four days. He replied that he considered the position a bad one and unsuitable for defence unless Sheikh Abbas also was occupied. He had no fear as to his troops being able to hold their own, but communication by day across the Wadi Ghazze was almost impossible, since all the tracks were under the fire of batteries which the enemy had brought up to Sheikh Abbas. It should be added that the men of the Egyptian Camel Transport Corps had in the course of the morning shown remarkable steadiness and devotion to duty, bringing up food, water, and ammunition along this shell-swept corridor.

General Dobell had now to come to a definitive decision with regard to the action. It appeared to him that General Dallas's view was correct and that the line held by the 53rd and 54th Divisions had little to recommend it while he was preparing for further operations, which he considered would require all the resources at his disposal. As for putting the 52nd Division into the fight to retake Sheikh Abbas, he was strongly averse to that measure. The reorganization of all the troops would have taken considerable time, and to have brought up the necessary supplies and ammunition would have been, in his judgment, virtually impossible. The provision of water would have been the greatest difficulty of all. As he had done on the 26th, he gave Sir A. Murray on the telephone an outline of his situation and stated that in his judgment it was now necessary to break off the fight. The Commander-in-Chief regretfully agreed with this decision.

At 4.30 p.m. General Dobell issued orders by telephone, subsequently confirmed in writing, for the withdrawal of the 53rd and 54th Divisions under the command of General Dallas to the left bank of the Wadi Ghazze. General Dallas accordingly ordered the retirement to begin at 7 p.m., covered by the 158th and 163rd Brigades. The afternoon passed without incident of importance, except for considerable shelling on the fronts of the 53rd Division and the Camel Brigade, until 7 p.m., when an attack upon the 161st Brigade was beaten off without difficulty. In the evening the 22nd Mounted Brigade moved across to the coast and relieved Money's Detachment in the sand-dunes. It was withdrawn at midnight, as part of the general retirement. With these movements there was no interference by the enemy, and the whole of the 53rd and 54th Divisions were across the Wadi Ghazze before 4 a.m. on the 28th March.

The troops who took up a position on the left bank of the wadi were extremely exhausted. The 26th had been reasonably cool, the normal weather of the season, though the mid-day sun was trying. On the 27th a *Khamsin* had begun to blow, somewhat before its usual season, and the great heat which accompanied it had aggravated the sufferings of men already wearied and short of water.

1917.
28 March.

The British losses were just under four thousand, with a high percentage of lightly wounded,[1] but also, unfortunately, over five hundred missing, of whom 5 officers and 241 other ranks, wounded and unwounded, fell into the hands of the enemy. These casualties were suffered almost entirely by the 53rd Division and the 161st Brigade, of which the latter had particularly heavy losses.

The Turkish loss in prisoners was 837, including 4 Austrian officers and 37 other ranks and the divisional commander and staff of the *53rd Division*. The guns captured by the N.Z.M.R. Brigade were brought in. The total Turkish casualties were estimated by Sir A. Murray to be considerably in excess of his own, but it is now known that they were about five-eighths of that figure.[2]

The Causes of Failure and the Reports to the War Office.

Few actions of the late war have been the subject of greater differences of opinion than the First Battle of Gaza. The problem is complicated, since it is not merely whether or not the withdrawal of the mounted troops was necessary, but whether the attack of the 53rd Division could not have been launched earlier. The latter question, again, depends to a great extent upon how far the fog delayed operations. Then there is the third question, whether, notwithstanding the delay, notwithstanding the withdrawal of the mounted troops, there was any possibility on the afternoon of the 27th of acceding to General Dallas's request to retake Sheikh Abbas, and subsequently of renewing the attack on Gaza.

---

[1]

	Killed.	Wounded.	Missing.
Officers	78	176	13
Other ranks	445	2,756	499

(The only source from which these figures could be accurately obtained was a return made by the A.A.G. 3rd Echelon on the 15th April. In these circumstances the figures under "Killed" include all who died of wounds between the 27th March and that date. In a telegram of the 1st April, Sir A. Murray gave an approximate figure for the casualties which was 469 lower than the above).

[2] For Turkish casualties see Note I at end of chapter.

It will be attempted here, not to find an answer to these questions, but merely to point out all considerations which appear to have importance. With regard to the mounted troops, the situation must be judged as it appeared to General Chetwode and as he represented it to General Dobell on the afternoon of the 26th: not as it appears in the light of later knowledge. Nor in any case has the fact that the Turkish relieving columns were halted during the night much bearing on the subject. They might have been more active, but they could hardly have exercised strong pressure during the hours of darkness. Their pressure would have been strong enough as soon as dawn appeared. On the other hand, it is clear that Gaza was, in fact, virtually captured by nightfall, and it certainly seems probable that General Dobell's actions would have been different had he received earlier the despairing messages of Major Tiller—messages which he ought to have received in no case later than an hour after their despatch.

Turning to the 53rd Division, it has been shown that the fog delayed the infantry in its progress to Mansura and Esh Sheluf less seriously than has commonly been supposed. The two leading brigades had reached these positions by 8.30 a.m.; it is a reasonable calculation that they would have been there an hour earlier if unhindered by the fog, but probably not more. The 159th Brigade was across the wadi by 6.40 a.m., and could presumably have been at Mansura by 9.30. A much more important effect of the fog seems to have been its delay of the necessary reconnaissance. Even as it was, it would appear that, had the brigadiers accompanied General Dallas to Mansura, while their brigades were being led to their positions, the conference could have been held an hour earlier than 10.15 a.m., the time at which it actually began. The two field artillery brigades had five batteries out of six in position at 10.20 a.m. Granting that it might not have been possible to communicate to them the plan and arrange for their co-operation without some further delay, it is not unreasonable to suppose that the attack might have been launched an hour sooner if the conference had assembled that much earlier. Whether it would have been taking undue risk for the infantry to have advanced, covered by strong patrols, towards its objectives, without waiting for the artillery's support, is another and more difficult question. It must be remembered that the successful progress of the mounted troops does not furnish a complete analogy; they were advancing into open country, the infantry against an enemy force in position. The delay in the arrival of the 161st Brigade Group, owing to misunderstanding, was also an important factor, though less as regards its infantry than its attached artillery brigade, the support of which at an earlier hour might have led to the speedier capture of the position.

The second serious misunderstanding occurred after the order for the withdrawal of the mounted troops had been given, when General Dallas was not informed that the 54th Division was closing in to north of Mansura. This misunderstanding has been dealt with in detail, but though it accounts for the abandonment of the position gained, it does not alter the fact that the holding of the advanced line on Ali Muntar, with the Turkish artillery on Sheikh Abbas, would have been an exceedingly difficult matter, unless Gaza could be immediately taken. If the 54th Division, which had two brigades only available, withdrew to the Burjabye Ridge, it had inevitably to abandon Sheikh Abbas. The abandonment of Sheikh Abbas allowed the Turks to occupy it, to bring up their guns and (it was eventually proved) to render the new position practically untenable. Sheikh Abbas could hardly have been retained unless the mounted troops had been kept out. It could not have been retaken on the 27th unless they had been again employed, together with the two brigades of the 52nd Division then available. On the second of these cases Sir A. Murray writes in his Despatches :—

"If it had now been practicable for the General
"Officer Commading Eastern Force to advance with his
"three infantry divisions and two cavalry divisions, I have
"no doubt that Gaza could have been taken and the Turks
"forced to retire; but the reorganization of the force for a
"deliberate attack would have taken a considerable time,
"the horses of the cavalry were very fatigued, and the
"distance of our railhead from the front line put the
"immediate maintenance of such a force with supplies,
"water and ammunition entirely out of the question. The
"only alternative, therefore, was to retire the infantry."

* * * * *

On the 28th March Sir A. Murray reported to the War Office that he had advanced to the Wadi Ghazze, that he had been heavily engaged east of Gaza on the 26th and 27th, that he estimated the Turkish casualties at between 6,000 and 7,000 men in addition to 900 prisoners, and that his troops had behaved splendidly. The C.I.G.S. replied on the 30th[1] that as a result of his recent success and of British progress in Mesopotamia the situation had altered since he received his last instructions. His immediate objective should now be the defeat of the Turks south of Jerusalem and the occupation of that city. Sir A. Murray answered next day (the 31st) that he was most anxious to advance on Jerusalem, but added a warning that his difficulties must be realized and that no rapid advance could be expected. He again called attention to his former estimate of the strength required for the operations, and stated that, though he could beat the Turks in the open, it had been proved that they were exceedingly good defensive fighters. They would probably take up a series of defensive positions between the Beersheba-Gaza and Jaffa-Jerusalem lines, out of which he could not hope to turn them without considerable losses, requiring immediate replacement. In any case his progress would be measured by that of his railway, and the best he could hope for was 20 miles a month, if no great engineering difficulties were met with. He concluded by stating that he might have to ask for material to double the line from Qantara to Gaza.

Sir W. Robertson replied briefly on the 1st April, but on the 2nd, after the War Cabinet had considered Sir A. Murray's message of the 31st March, despatched a long telegram embodying its views. He had been asked to point out the great importance of the operations in Palestine. Everyone was now feeling seriously the strain of war, and the moral effect of success was extremely valuable. The War Cabinet therefore desired that Sir A. Murray's operations should be pushed on energetically. He added that there was internal unrest in Turkey, and that she was undoubtedly more exhausted than any other of Great Britain's enemies. With the reinforcements detailed for Egypt, he did not see why Sir A. Murray should not be

---

[1] Both telegrams are given in full in Note II at end of chapter.

completely successful.[1] On the 4th April Sir A. Murray telegraphed that he hoped the War Cabinet would be assured that he fully appreciated the importance of operations in Palestine. He did not believe that a single day of the past fifteen months had been wasted, or that greater energy could be displayed. Preparations were in progress for a renewed attack on Gaza, but he was anxious not to hurry over this operation, as he felt that a methodically prepared attack had chances of winning a considerable success. After taking Gaza he intended to continue the invasion of Palestine, though he had at the moment only enough rails to reach Deir el Balah. He then enumerated his reasons for proposing to continue his advance along the coast instead of the Turkish Beersheba railway, and stated his requirements in mechanical transport, Army Service Corps drivers, artillery for his new divisions, signal units and material, Royal Engineers (Army Troops), and modern aeroplanes.

1917.
April.

Meanwhile the Government had asked for a fuller report on the operations, all that had yet been received being the short telegram on the 28th March.[2] In a very long telegram of the 1st April Sir A. Murray recounted his objects (which have been given in Chapter XVI) and the conditions, and gave a sketch of the operations, estimating the Turkish casualties at 8,000. He concluded :—

" The operation was most successful, and owing to the
" fog and waterless nature of the country round Gaza just
" fell short of a complete disaster to the enemy. Our
" troops are exceedingly proud of themselves, particularly
" 53rd Division, who have not been in action since Suvla,
" and I am delighted with their enterprise, endurance, skill
" and leading. None of our troops were at any time
" harassed or hard pressed. It is proved conclusively that
" in the open the enemy have no chance of success against
" our troops, but they are very tenacious in prepared
" positions. In the open our mounted troops simply do
" what they like with them."[3]

---

[1] The reference is to troops required to bring up to strength the 74th Division and also to proposals to form another division from Territorial battalions then in India. As will appear, a mixed division of Territorial and Indian battalions (the 75th) was eventually formed instead. This telegram is given in full in Note II.

[2] Note II., first telegram.

[3] This telegram with the exception of the passage above, is given in Note II.

It will be seen from Sir W. Robertson's messages that the policy of the Government had completely changed. No longer were serious operations to be postponed until the autumn; Sir A. Murray was now urged to advance and capture Jerusalem as soon as possible. To some extent this revision of estimates and plans was accounted for by the British success in Mesopotamia, but it was governed to a greater extent by the interpretation placed by the C.I.G.S. and the War Cabinet upon Sir A. Murray's reports. There is no doubt that these reports, the first of which resulted in congratulatory messages from H.M. The King, the Imperial War Cabinet, Lord Derby, General Nivelle, with personal telegrams from Sir W. Robertson and Sir John Cowans, created in their minds the impression that the result of the battle had been more favourable, and that the enemy had been harder hit, than was actually the case. This appears to have been one of those occasions in which a commander in the field, hoping immediately to improve his situation after what has appeared to him to be only a temporary set-back, has unconsciously understated the extent of that set-back in his reports to those in ultimate authority. He may by such action avoid creating needless despondency, but he may also give rise to exaggerated hopes, deprive himself of support which a fuller representation of the case would have ensured, and finally be forced to demand it after a further check to his plans.

At the same time, even had Sir A. Murray's messages been framed in less sanguine tones, neither the C.I.G.S. nor the War Cabinet would have been likely to admit that his offensive power had vanished as a result of one indecisive action—an action which, judged by the standards of the Western Front, was small and far from costly. The War Office was fully aware of the Turkish strength in the theatre and the limits of possible reinforcement, and with some minor differences its estimate corresponded with that of G.H.Q. in Egypt. Though the renewed British offensive, preparations for which were known to be in train, might have been less confidently urged, it does not seem probable that it would in any case have been cancelled.

NOTE 1.

THE BATTLE FROM GERMAN AND TURKISH SOURCES.

The chief authority for the events of the First Battle of Gaza on the enemy side is the account by Kress in " Sinai " (i. pp. 26-9).

During the early part of March Gaza had been held by a weak detachment of two battalions and two batteries. The *16th Division* was at Tell esh Sheria, on the railway, 15 miles as the crow flies south-east of Gaza. The *3rd Division* was in reserve at Jemmame, 11½ miles almost due east of Gaza. Beersheba was occupied by a cavalry brigade and a weak regiment of the Arab *27th Division*.

In the second half of March Kress gathered from the excellent reports of his *300th Flight Detachment* that the British intended to make their attack in the direction of Gaza. He acted at once. Gaza was strengthened by a regiment of the *16th Division* and other infantry, also by Austro-Hungarian howitzers and a German battery. Its total garrison, according to Liman von Sanders, who goes into more detail than Kress with regard to the infantry, consisted of the *79th* and *125th Regiments*, and *2nd Battalion 81st Regiment* (a total of seven battalions), the two Austrian howitzer batteries (12 heavy mountain howitzers) and the German 10-cm. battery (2 long guns), from *Pasha I*; together with the original two Turkish field artillery batteries.[1] The *53rd Division*, which Djemal had held up near Jaffa in fear of a British landing, was ordered to march down the coast towards Gaza. Kress himself shifted his command post from Beersheba to Tell esh Sheria to be nearer the scene of action.

At about 8 a.m. (Cairo time) the German commander received at Tell esh Sheria a report from one of his flying officers to the effect that strong British forces, amounting to about two infantry divisions, were advancing from the south on Gaza, and that a great force of cavalry, " some three cavalry divisions," with numerous armoured cars, had burst through between Gaza and Tell esh Sheria. Telephone communication broke down, but for a time there was communication by wireless with the town. The commandant, Major Tiller, reported later that he was being attacked in great strength from south, east, and north-east. Kress ordered him to hold Gaza, whatever might happen, to the last man.

A regiment of the *53rd Division*, he records, moving down from Jaffa, was due at El Majdal (which is 13 miles north-east of Gaza along the coast) that day.[2] He ordered it to continue its march on Gaza after a short rest, but he could not count upon its reaching that point before the morning of the 27th. To the troops nearer at hand he at once sent orders to move. The *3rd Division*, in the Jemmame area, was to advance on the line Gaza—Ali Muntar. The *16th Division* was directed against the British rear, with the point where the Khan Yunis—Gaza road crossed the Wadi Ghazze for its objective. Both divisions were to attack the enemy directly they came in touch with him. Meanwhile the *Beersheba Group* was to advance by way of Shellal in the direction of Khan Yunis.[3]

The German commander hoped that the troops of the *3rd* and *16th Divisions* would be in action close to Gaza before the fall of darkness. Apparently, however, the alarm was late in reaching them, and there were delays which Liman von Sanders calls "typically Turkish" before they were on the move. Then the British mounted troops and armoured cars succeeded in checking them. By nightfall, Kress states, the Turks had covered scarcely half the distance to Gaza. Liman adds that they had not made their presence seriously felt. Kress, having regard to the state of their training and to some mixing up of units in action against the

---

[1] These details are confirmed by the Historical Section, Turkish General Staff, which states that there were also in Gaza a squadron of cavalry and a company of camelry.

[2] The second regiment was apparently at Ramle.

[3] It will be noticed that the issue of these orders justified General Dobell's anxiety for his right and his mounted troops.

British cavalry, felt that he could not order them to continue their advance that night. He sent orders, however, that it was to be resumed at dawn with the original objectives.

After the British retirement Kress was inclined to pass to the offensive, but was forbidden to do so by Djemal. He admits that the commander of the *Fourth Army* was correct in his decision.

The enemy's casualties are given in full by the Historical Section of the Turkish General Staff as follows :—

	KILLED. Germans and Austrians.	KILLED. Turks	WOUNDED. Germans and Austrians.	WOUNDED. Turks	MISSING. Germans and Austrians.	MISSING. Turks	TOTAL.
Officers	2	10	2	12	4	26	56
Other Ranks..	5	284	7	1,064	37	994	2,391
					Grand Total		2,447

The commander of the Austro-Hungarian artillery detachment, Hauptmann Ritter von Truzschewski, was among the killed.

NOTE II.

TELEGRAMS BETWEEN SIR A. MURRAY AND THE C.I.G.S.

From—General Officer Commanding-in-Chief, Egypt,
To—Chief of the Imperial General Staff.
No. O.A. 377.   28th March 1917.

We have advanced our troops a distance of 15 miles from Rafah to Wadi Ghazze, to cover construction of railway. On the 26th and 27th we were heavily engaged east of the Ghazze with a force of about 20,000 of the enemy. We inflicted very heavy losses on him; I estimate his casualties at between 6,000 and 7,000 men, and we have in addition taken 900 prisoners including General Commanding and whole Divisional Staff of *53rd Turkish Division*. This figure includes 4 Austrian officers and 32 Austrian and 5 German other ranks. We captured two Austrian 4·2-inch howitzers. All troops behaved splendidly, especially the Welsh, Kent, Sussex, Hereford, Middlesex and Surrey Territorials, and the Anzac and Yeomanry mounted troops.

From—Chief of the Imperial General Staff,
To—General Officer Commanding-in-Chief, Egypt.
No. 31854, cipher.   30th March 1917.

Reference my letter O. 1/45/151 of 11th January. As a result of your recent success and our progress in Mesopotamia the situation has materially altered since the instructions quoted above were issued. The Turks, according to my information, have not now south of Jerusalem a force of more than 30,000 fighting troops, and their supply and transport situation makes it very doubtful if they can maintain more than 60,000 men south of that place. At present, indications point to fact that Turks are anxious about situation on Tigris and on Persian frontier and are diverting reinforcements to that theatre. In these circumstances, and as you are assured of reinforcements during the summer, your immediate objective should be the defeat of the Turkish forces south of Jerusalem and the occupation of that town. Your progress must, of course, depend upon the state of your communications, and until you are satisfied in that respect I do not wish to press you to advance, and I know you will continue to perfect your communications with the utmost energy. I am satisfied that your recent operations have assured the defence of Egypt, and that you need not now lock up troops for the protection of the Canal except

CORRESPONDENCE WITH C.I.G.S.

against such damage as very small parties of raiders or enemy agents can effect. I hope this will enable you to concentrate more troops for offensive purposes. Your subsequent operations after you reach Jerusalem must depend largely on what the Russian Caucasus Army is able to achieve. I am assured that about the end of April they mean to advance on Mosul in force and if they do this it should prevent any considerable diversion of Turkish force against you, and may enable you to advance beyond Jerusalem. I will keep you fully informed of Russian plans and movements and will issue further instructions as may be necessary in due course.

From—General Officer Commanding-in-Chief, Egypt,
To—War Office.
No. A.M. 1741.   30th March 1917.

In view of probability of my having early in April to attack a number of strongly fortified localities, which will necessitate extensive preparatory bombardments with heavy artillery, I should be very glad if I might, as early as possible, be supplied with more ammunition for my 6-inch and 8-inch howitzers, my stock of which is low, and should be increased, in order to meet probable requirements, by at least 2,000 rounds 6-inch and 1,500 rounds 8-inch. In view of the urgency of this demand I would suggest that these might perhaps be supplied from France, in order to facilitate shipping arrangements, and expedite arrival in this country. Further, with reference to your No. 30329, A. 2, 2nd March, in reply to my No. A.M. 1648, 1st March, as, in the course of these operations, use of gas shell will possibly be necessary, I trust that the supply of additional gas shells asked for in above-quoted telegram may now be arranged and their despatch treated as a matter of great urgency.

From—Chief of the Imperial General Staff,
To—General Officer Commanding-in-Chief, Egypt.
No. 31898, cipher.   31st March, 1917.

With regard to your fight on the 26th and 27th, War Cabinet wishes to have more details. State what force you employed and what enemy forces you have identified. As your operations affect other theatres, it is important we should always have this latter information as quickly as possible. It is always necessary also to send fuller particulars than you have yet furnished, though not necessarily for publication.

(Sir A. Murray's reply [numbered A.M.1749] to No. 31854 of the 30th March, sent on 31st, has been outlined in the text.)

From—General Officer Commanding-in-Chief, Egypt,
To—Chief of the Imperial General Staff.
No. A.M. 1751.   1st April 1917.

Your No. 31898, 31st March.
Intention—First, to seize the line of the Wadi Ghazze so as to protect the advance of railway from Rafah to Gaza. Secondly, to prevent at all costs the enemy from retiring without a fight, which we knew to be his plan as regards his troops in Gaza, Tell esh Sheria, and Beersheba, as soon as we approached a little nearer than Rafah. Thirdly, to capture Gaza by a *coup de main* if possible.

Command—General Dobell in command of whole force. General Chetwode in command of mounted troops and 53rd Division, acting as advanced troops to protect the march and to capture Gaza if possible. General Dobell had the 52nd and 54th Divisions as main body to secure Wadi and support Chetwode. Advanced General Headquarters at El Arish. All troops actively engaged for whom it was possible to provide water, munitions, and supplies.

Starting point—For the mounted troops, Rafah. Small oasis to the east for infantry wherever there was water. If the mounted troops had been placed closer to Gaza Turks would have evacuated without a fight, hence reason for keeping back, also easier to water and feed.

Weather—Morning of 26th, dense fog till 11 a.m. much delayed operations; 27th and 28th, hot winds, and temperature over 90 in the shade.

Water—No water between Deir el Balah and Gaza or to the north and east.

Operations on 26th—Gaza enveloped by dusk, and first-line trenches taken by 53rd Division; heaviest loss to enemy and 700 or 800 prisoners taken. Enemy blew up his wireless station and reported to von Kress that he must surrender. About 1 p.m. von Kress started his relief columns from Huj, Sheria and Beersheba, and also *53rd Division*, moved from Lydda, arrived El Majdal unexpectedly; our mounted troops assisted by armoured cars, all most brilliantly led, fought delaying action all day and, without much loss to themselves, inflicted very heavy losses on all these separate columns. Among other captures, they took the commander and staff of *53rd Turkish Division*, and I estimate the above enemy losses at over 5,000. Most probably Gaza would have fallen before dusk but for morning fog. Chetwode decided that he must not let his cavalry be enveloped by converging Turkish columns, so drew off towards main body and thus enabled Gaza to be reinforced during the night or early morning. Position of our 53rd Division at dusk on high ground, Ali Muntar, just south of Gaza, with some troops in the Turkish defences. 54th Division on prolonging ridge to Sheikh Abbas. Wadi Ghazze and right flank made secure by 52nd Division. Primary object attained.

Operations on 27th—Turks attacked 53rd and 54th Divisions and Camel Corps in entrenched positions. They were not in the least successful at any point, and again suffered the heaviest losses, e.g., Camel Corps nearly annihilated Turkish Cavalry Division. I estimate enemy losses at 3,000 on this day. Cavalry and camelry had to move back to El Balah to water, horses not having had any for 24 hours and camels for 4 days. The infantry managed on their water bottles.

It was obvious that if we could advance the 52nd, 53rd and 54th Divisions this evening, Gaza would have been taken, and the Turks must have retired, but want of water, fatigue of horses, and distance of railhead prevented this.

Operations on 28th—Enemy would not advance to attack again, and mostly occupied Gaza defences. Our cavalry remained in contact, and the infantry withdrew without a fight behind the 52nd Division's prepared position.

Troops of enemy engaged: The whole of *3rd Cavalry Division, 3rd and 16th Infantry Divisions*, and part of *27th* and *53rd Infantry Divisions*.

Our captures—Prisoners, 950; two 4·2-inch Austrian howitzers.

Our casualties—Killed, 47 officers, 351 other ranks. Wounded, about 2,900. Missing, probably prisoners, less than 200. Of the wounded, about 2,000 are slight cases, which I am informed will be able to rejoin shortly. The missing men probably fought their way after dark right into the streets of Gaza.

(The concluding paragraph of this message has been given in full in the text.)

From—Chief of the Imperial General Staff,
To—General Officer Commanding-in-Chief, Egypt.
No. 32017, cipher.   *2nd April* 1917.

War Cabinet have given careful consideration to your No. A.M. 1749, 31st March [the telegram of that date referred to above] and ask me to tell you that they think that, being at a distance, you may not fully realize the great importance of your operations. Everyone is now feeling the strain of the war, and this strain will certainly increase; therefore, the moral effect of success is of great importance, both in strengthening the hands of the Government and in making the public more ready to bear their burdens. For a variety of obvious reasons, success in Palestine will have a very inspiring effect in Christendom. War Cabinet are anxious therefore that your operations should be pushed with all energy. The general situation of the Turks must also be considered. There is much unrest in Constantinople, and undoubtedly the Turks are more exhausted by the war than any of our enemies, and success on your part, combined with recent events in Mesopotamia, must have great effect. I do not underrate in any way the fighting capacity of the enemy opposed to you, but after careful consideration of what the enemy can do, I see no reason why, with the reinforcements detailed for Egypt, you should not be completely successful if you can employ offensively all the troops at your disposal. Let me know at once if you are not satisfied as to this. Requisite drafts will receive every attention. I am asked by the War Cabinet to enquire further whether you are getting all that you require as regards guns, munitions, transport, and war material generally, and you may rest assured that we will do our utmost to meet your demands.

Am I to understand that you have definitely decided to lay your line along the coast to Jaffa, in preference to a linking up with the Beersheba railway? If so, report reasons for this, and also give statement of railway proposals in general. If you have decided to go to Jaffa, I am informed that you will have material to take you there.

NOTE III.

THE EVACUATION OF THE WOUNDED.

The evacuation of wounded in earlier operations had been a matter of difficulty in the desert, but the improved arrangements described in Chapter XVI made it possible to handle the heavy casualties of the First Battle of Gaza.

Prior to the battle El Arish became the chief centre for the reception and evacuation of wounded. No. 2 (Australian) Stationary Hospital moved there on the 10th March with an advanced medical stores depot, and a special hospital siding was constructed. There were two hospital trains on the line, one of which brought wounded to El Arish, while the other evacuated them to Qantara the following day. Nos. 53 and 54 Casualty Clearing Stations were established at Rafah, together with a hospital for prisoners of war. The Desert Column had a convoy of 21 Ford Ambulances, while light cars were obtained for the carriage of sitting cases. Ten of these cars crossed the Wadi Ghazze to evacuate wounded to the dressing stations. To aid the evacuation of wounded of the 53rd Division, a total of 25 sandcarts and 30 cacolet camels were sent from the 52nd and 54th Divisions. With this additional transport the field ambulances were practically clear by the evening, but it was found that the two hospital trains were inadequate for evacuation on the railway line.

In preparation, therefore, for the second attack on Gaza, a number of motor ambulance cars for the field ambulances of the three infantry and two mounted divisions were sent up by rail. Special arrangements were made for the operations of the mounted troops. Dressing stations were formed at Tell el Jemmi, and a convoy of 36 motor ambulance cars sent to Abasan el Kebir. In addition a camel convoy was formed to clear the dressing stations.

CHAPTER XVIII.

THE SECOND BATTLE OF GAZA.

(Maps 2, 13, 14. 15 ; Sketch 16.)

The Situation after the First Battle of Gaza.

Maps 2, 14. Sketch 16. The problem confronting the British Commander-in-Chief changed completely after the First Battle of Gaza. Gaza itself at the time of that battle was an outpost held by a strong detachment, on the flank of a line of communication passing far to the east. It now speedily became the strongest point in an entrenched position which ran through it from the sea and along the road to Beersheba as far as Abu Hureira, a distance of 12 miles. To prepare for a new attack time was necessary to the British, but the period of three weeks' quietude which intervened was, of course, invaluable to the enemy, and under German tutelage he took full advantage of it. In the early part of April British air reconnaissance reported almost daily the construction or extension of works in the sand-dunes, round the town, and along the Gaza–Beersheba road. No attempt was made to establish a continuous line of defence, but the position was well chosen, with a long field of fire, all approaches being within the beaten zone of one redoubt and generally of more than one. Large camps sprang up to show that the Turkish forces had closed in.[1]

The War Office was informed of these new conditions and of the estimate that the enemy's strength was 34 battalions and about 100 guns. The numbers were not greater than had been expected, and the information did not warrant any change in the instructions issued to Sir A. Murray. Beersheba was known to be lightly held, but an attempt to turn the Turkish left flank appeared out of the question owing to the impossibility of supplying water to any considerable force in that direction.

Both Sir A. Murray and Sir C. Dobell recognized that their next operation would be of a nature entirely different

---

[1] At Tell esh Sheria, for example, 236 tents increased to 500 within a week ; at Kh. Kufiye, 4 miles east of Gaza, there were 400, and at Kh. el Bir, 3 miles south-east of Gaza, 300.

Sketch 16

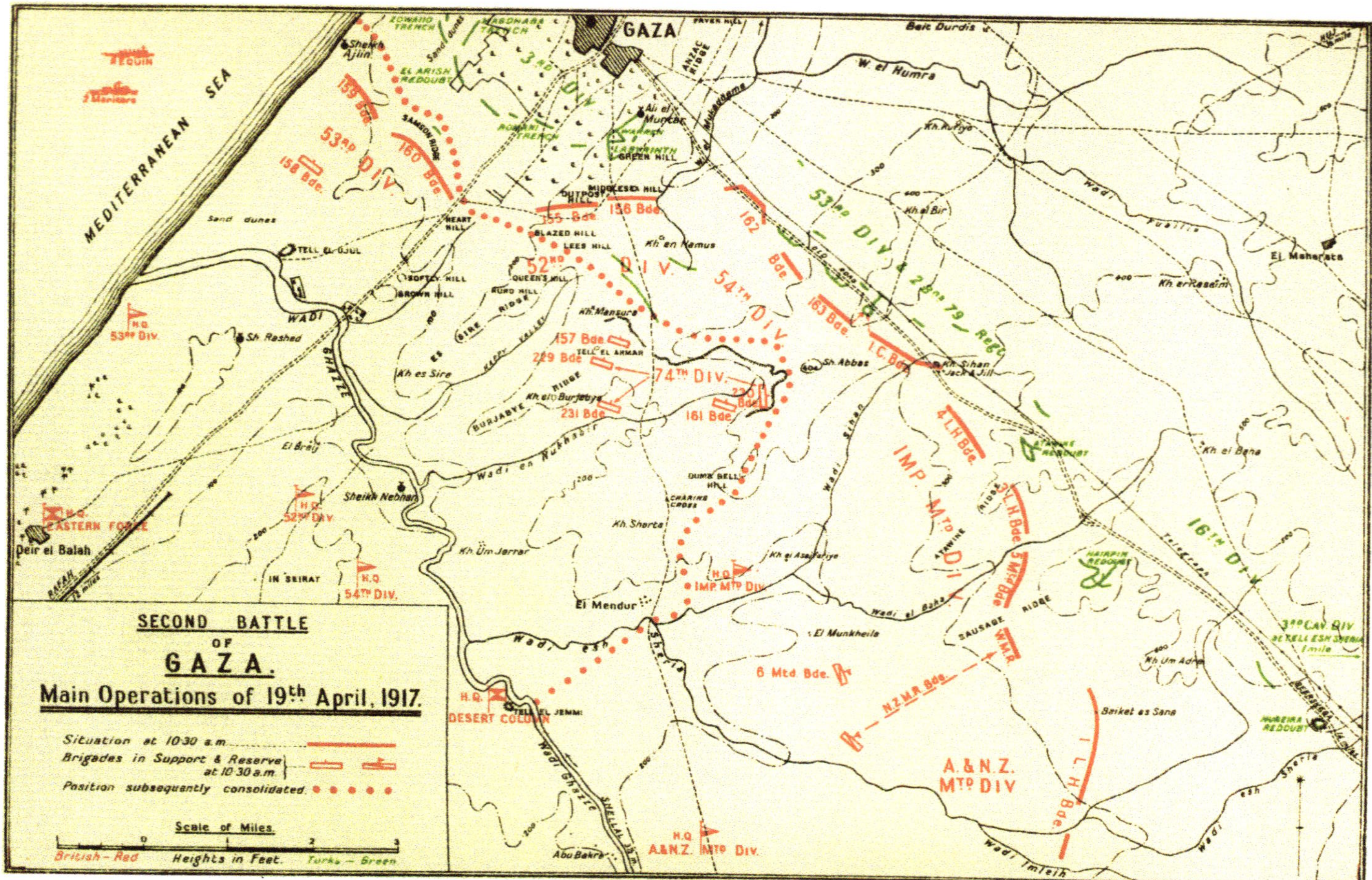

to the last. There was no question now of a *coup de main*; a deliberate attack upon a strongly defended position, an attack largely dependent upon the support it received from artillery, was in prospect.

1917.
April.

Thus three weeks passed in active preparation on both sides, the Turks evidently realizing that the British were little likely to rest content with their present situation. On the ground and in the air both sides carried out reconnaissances, but there was no aggression except by aerial bombing. On the 12th April hostile aircraft twice bombed Rafah, but caused little damage and only six casualties. The British machines bombed the Huj area and Kh. el Bir on the same date, dropping about a thousand pounds of bombs in each case. On the 1st April the British carried out an important ground reconnaissance of the country immediately east of the Wadi Ghazze between the Wadi esh Sheria and the sea, three battalions, one from each of the 52nd, 53rd, and 54th Divisions, being engaged. On the following day about a thousand Turkish infantry advanced to the right bank of the Wadi Ghazze, but quickly retired under the fire of the British artillery.

In order to permit the employment of all available troops the first step was to extend the railway. By the 5th April railhead had reached Deir el Balah, 5 miles from the Wadi Ghazze, where the headquarters of the Eastern Force was established. Reservoirs were constructed in the wadi to hold 67,000 gallons of water, which was borne to railhead in tank trucks and pumped a distance of 5 miles through a small pipe across the In Seirat Ridge. The wells at Deir el Balah also furnished a considerable supply. During this period of hard work the weather fortunately remained reasonably cool. The health of the troops was good and their spirits had recovered from the disappointment of the First Battle, in which victory had so narrowly eluded them.

To relieve Sir C. Dobell and his staff during the coming operations of responsibility for troops 150 miles away, the southern section of the Canal Defences was transferred on the 4th April to the direct command of G.H.Q.

The shortage of artillery could now be partially remedied owing to the approach of railhead to the scene of action. It will be remembered that only the right sections of the three heavy batteries had been employed in March, the transport of the left sections being required to carry ammunition. It was now possible to bring up the full complement of twelve 60-pdrs., but the only other additional heavy artillery available was the 201st Siege Battery, consisting of two 8-inch and two 6-inch howitzers. With regard to field artillery, the third brigades of the 53rd and 54th Divisions were brought up from the Canal Defences, but not the absent sections of the 18-pdr. batteries already at the front, which remained four-gun batteries during the battle.[1] The 74th Division (Major-General E. S. Girdwood), now complete except for artillery and one field company, R.E., was also brought up, and on the 7th April took over the outpost line along the Wadi Ghazze from the 54th Division. The 1st and 4th L.H. Brigades, absent at the First Battle of Gaza, had orders to rejoin the A. & N.Z. and Imperial Mounted Divisions on the eve of the new offensive. A detachment of the Tank Corps with eight tanks had also arrived.[2] The only other accession of strength was a supply of 4,000 rounds of 4·5-inch gas shell, not previously used in this theatre. The 52nd, 53rd, and 54th Divisions, almost up to establishment when the First Battle of Gaza was fought, were now on an average nearly 1,500 below it.

The R.F.C. had had a trying experience in March combating the superior aircraft possessed by the enemy. During the First Battle of Gaza only two German Halberstadt machines appeared, but these attacked British aeroplanes on every possible occasion with complete success, killing one observer and wounding two pilots, while six British machines were seriously damaged and two brought down. The total number of serviceable aeroplanes at the disposal of the 5th Wing[3] prior to the Second Battle of Gaza (exclusive of five in Arabia) was 25 : 17 B.E.2's and 8 Martinsydes. The

---

[1] See Note at end of Chapter XVI.

[2] The tanks were of early pattern and considerably worn, having been used for instructional purposes in England. It was found that they worked well enough in the sand, provided that the treads were kept dry instead of being greased as was customary. The sand then passed through them and fell away almost like liquid.

[3] At the opening of the Second Battle of Gaza the 5th Wing was distributed as follows :—

Wing Headquarters..	Rafah.
Advanced Headquarters	Deir el Balah.
No. 14 Squadron H.Q. and " A " Flight ...	Rafah.
" B " Flight ..	Deir el Balah.
No. 67 Squadron A.F.C.	Rafah.
" X " Aircraft Park	Abbassia.
Advanced Aircraft Park	Qantara.

latter were the best fighting aeroplanes available, but were 1917.
found to be liable to overheating in this climate. Br.- April.
General W. G. H. Salmond, commanding the Middle East
Brigade R.F.C., pointed out to the Director of Air Organization that the German policy was to apportion some of their
best types to each of their detachments and urged that
superior numbers in aircraft did not atone for mechanical
inferiority. The War Office promised to despatch some
Bristol monoplanes and Vickers Scouts of later pattern,
but none of these arrived until after the Second Battle of
Gaza.

Despite the superiority of the Turkish—or rather
German[1]—machines, the British did excellent work during
the period. In addition to the tactical reconnaissances
which discovered the new Turkish system of defences,
strategical reconnaissances were carried out, one of which
reported (on the 7th April) the beginning of a railway branch
from Et Tine[2] towards Gaza. A large number of photographs were taken, with the aid of which a new map, on the
scale of 1/40,000 and partially contoured, was printed in time Map 13.
for the Second Battle of Gaza.

The Plan of Attack.

General Dobell was directed by the Commander-in-Chief Map 14.
to frame a plan of attack upon the new Turkish position. Sketch 16.
They had discussed the problem generally and agreed that,
while an advance from the eastward offered better prospects
of success, the difficulties of water supply ruled this out of
account and limited them to a frontal attack on Gaza itself.
It will later be shown that Sir E. Allenby's capture of
Beersheba, which led to a great victory in the autumn of
1917, was preceded by extensive pipe-laying and development of wells to the east. Such operations appeared in
April to be beyond the resources of the force.

On the 3rd April General Dobell submitted his plan.
This included an infantry frontal attack, but by three
divisions instead of one, as in March. Two divisions were
to attack Ali Muntar from Mansura and Sheikh Abbas, while

---

[1] There were only six Turkish aeroplanes in the whole *Fourth Army*
at this date.

[2] Five miles south-west of Wadi Sarar Junction (Sketch 9). Et Tine
is shown on Map 2, 25 miles west of Jerusalem, but the old Turkish railway
is not marked on this map.

a third advanced through the sand-dunes on the seaward side of the town. The right of the attack was, as before, to wheel up to envelop the ridges covering the town from the east, and by this enveloping attack it was hoped to destroy the enemy's right. The Desert Column, consisting now entirely of mounted troops, that is, the A. & N.Z. and Imperial Mounted Divisions and the Camel Brigade, was to protect the right of the infantry from an advance by the enemy in and beyond the entrenchments at Atawine and Abu Hureira, on the Gaza–Beersheba road. This was to be effected by an advance of part of the mounted troops against those entrenchments, while a portion was held in reserve to take advantage of the hoped-for gap, either for pursuit or to surround Gaza from the north.[1] Finally, it was intended, when Gaza was captured, to hold a position north and east of the town with two divisions, while the third cleared up the town itself, the remaining troops returning to the Wadi Ghazze or Deir el Balah for water.

The operation was to be carried out in two stages. The first stage was to be a general advance, to which no strong opposition was anticipated, to a position between two and three miles beyond the Wadi Ghazze from which the actual attack could be launched. This line ran from Tell el Ujul near the shore, across the Es Sire Ridge and along the Mansura Ridge to Sheikh Abbas, and would, therefore, cover artillery positions east of the wadi. Two divisions, with a third (the 74th) in reserve, would advance east of the Es Sire Ridge, and one between the Rafah–Gaza road and the shore. When this line was reached it was to be entrenched and wired, and a strong point for a brigade constructed at Sheikh Abbas. The mounted troops meanwhile were to operate to the east and south-east to prevent interference by the enemy from the direction of Abu Hureira and Tell esh Sheria.

The second stage was to begin as soon as preparations were complete, at least one clear day between the two stages being necessary. It was to consist in the frontal attack by the three divisions already described and further covering

---

[1] Some of the subordinate commanders were of opinion that an attack in depth along the coast offered far more favourable opportunities to the infantry. This view was considered by General Dobell, but rejected, principally because it gave small scope for the co-operation of the large mounted force.

operations by the mounted troops. Between the two stages a heavy bombardment was to be carried out. Warships, which had not taken part in the First Battle of Gaza, because it had been feared that their fire would endanger the infantry, were to bombard Ali Muntar and take the Turkish defences in enfilade.

On the 10th April more definite information as to the enemy's dispostions inclined Sir C. Dobell to modify this plan. He telegraphed to G.H.Q. that the enemy appeared to have three regiments in Gaza, two regiments east of the town, two at Hureira, one at Tell esh Sheria and one in the neighbourhood of Huj. These detachments were well placed for mutual support, and would probably render impossible his original plan of wheeling in his right from Sheikh Abbas to envelop the Gaza position and destroy the enemy's right. He proposed to carry out the first stage as already arranged. This would have the effect of making the enemy disclose his intentions as to the use of the Atawine detachment and the force between it and Gaza. Sir C. Dobell might attack them directly by swinging his line slightly north-east, while containing Gaza with one division only. This appeared to be the only practicable method of creating a gap for the mounted troops, and, the gap once made, he considered that Gaza must fall and that there was a prospect of destroying its garrison. If the detachment at Hureira reinforced Atawine, he would still be strong enough to deal with the latter, while he would then expect the Desert Column to capture Hureira. If the Hureira detachment did not move, he would have all the more chance of creating a gap for the Desert Column. In certain circumstances also, he might decide to transfer his weight to the left and attack Gaza mainly on the coast side. To carry out either of these projects it might be necessary to make a longer pause than he had originally intended on the Sheikh Abbas–Mansura line, but neither would entail a radical alteration in the first stage of the operations. Sir A. Murray left him a free hand in the matter.

The final estimate of the enemy's rifle strength between Tell esh Sheria and Gaza was 21,000 ; including 8,500 at Gaza, 4,500 at Kh. el Bir and its neighbourhood, and 2,000 at Atawine.[1]

---

[1] This figure was not far out. There were 18,000 rifles on the front including the small Beersheba detachment. See Note at end of Chapter.

The First Phase of the Attack.

Map 14.
Sketch 16.

The first phase was fixed for the 17th April.[1] The preliminary movements began on the previous evening, the infantry divisions moving down to the crossings of the Wadi Ghazze at 5 p.m., to be across and ready to advance at 4.15 a.m. The Desert Column had also moved off early in the evening and was in its position of assembly by 2 a.m. on the 17th: the A. & N.Z. Mounted Division as far inland as Shellal, where the Rafah–Beersheba track crosses the Wadi Ghazze, 14 miles south of Gaza; the Imperial Mounted Division at Tell el Jemmi, near the junction of the Wadi esh Sheria with the Wadi Ghazze. For the first time since their formation they were at establishment as regards units, the 1st and 4th L.H. Brigades having joined them from Khan Yunis in the evening. The Imperial Camel Brigade was at Abasan el Kebir, $4\frac{1}{2}$ miles south-west of Khan Yunis.

The 52nd and 54th Divisions were grouped as the "Eastern Attack" under the orders of Major-General W. E. B. Smith, commanding the former division. General Smith's objective was a line from Sheikh Abbas through Mansura to Kurd Hill on the Es Sire Ridge, which line he was to seize as rapidly as possible and consolidate. The 54th Division was to attack on the right, the 52nd on the left. The 53rd Division (Br.-General S. F. Mott)[2] was to cross the wadi west of the Rafah–Gaza road. It was to secure the right bank and push forward an outpost line in the dunes to continue that of the 52nd Division.

During the first phase the Desert Column was to demonstrate against Abu Hureira, with the object of preventing the enemy from moving troops thence to Gaza, and also to protect the right of the 54th Division during the capture of Sheikh Abbas. The A. & N. Z. Mounted Division was to water three brigades at Shellal and then advance in the direction of Abu Hureira as soon after daylight as possible, but not to make a dismounted attack. The fourth brigade was to develop the supply of water at Shellal, whither it was anticipated the division would return at night, leaving an outpost line well forward. The Imperial

---

[1] The Eastern Force orders for this phase are given in Appendix 12.
[2] Major-General A. G. Dallas had resigned the command of the division after the First Battle of Gaza owing to a breakdown in health.

Mounted Division at Tell el Jemmi was to despatch one brigade across the Wadi Ghazze, to move up the Wadi esh Sheria and endeavour to surprise the Turkish outpost at Kh. Erk, 3 miles S.S.W. of Hureira, at dawn on the 17th.

1917.
17 April.

General Dobell's battle headquarters remained at Deir el Balah; that of General Chetwode moved to Tell el Jemmi. Sir A. Murray again brought up his railway train, this time to Khan Yunis, where he was in telephonic communication with the battle headquarters of the Eastern Force.

The Eastern Attack advanced without difficulty over ground thoroughly explored during the First Batle of Gaza. Its objective, held by Turkish outposts only, was captured at the slight cost of 300 casualties and one tank. The 54th Division had very few losses, but the leading tank accompanying the 163rd Brigade was thrice hit by shells and put out of action.[1] The allotted position was occupied by 7 a.m. The 52nd Division met with rather more opposition. On the 157th Brigade's front was a standing Turkish outpost at El Burjabye. This had been driven out night after night by strong patrols, so that a similar incident did not now cause the enemy to suspect a general advance. On occupying Mansura Ridge, however, the brigade came under considerable artillery fire from the neighbourhood of Ali Muntar. The enemy's guns were active at intervals throughout the day, but not sufficiently so to hinder the work of consolidating the new position. The withdrawal from that held on the 27th March, the maintenance of which would probably have involved losses higher than were now incurred, was therefore amply justified.

The Desert Column had no difficulty in carrying out its orders. The 5th Mounted Brigade of the Imperial Mounted Division crossed the Wadi Ghazze at 2.30 a.m. and occupied Kh. Erk with little opposition before dawn. A patrol of the Worcester Yeomanry, under 2nd-Lieutenant R. F. M. Harvey, succeeded in reaching the Gaza-Beersheba road north of Kh. Um Adra, between the Hairpin and Hureira Redoubts, and cut the telegraph line, dragging away over

---

[1] Only two tanks came into action on this date, both with the 163rd Brigade. They moved up from Dumb-bell Hill, starting at 4.30 a.m., and turned westward along the Sheikh Abbas Ridge. Two tanks allotted to the 52nd Division were prepared to assist the infantry if called upon, but were not required.

334 SECOND GAZA

a hundred yards of wire a distance of a mile and removing insulators. The A. & N.Z. Mounted Division, pushing out the N.Z.M.R. Brigade in the direction of Beersheba to protect its right flank, advanced towards Hureira, driving in enemy outposts. Only its advanced troops ever came into action, for the enemy showed no disposition to leave his entrenchments, though after the 22nd Mounted Brigade had remained some time in close observation of Hureira, troops were reported moving up the road from Beersheba. At dusk the two divisions were withdrawn across the Wadi Ghazze, an outpost line being left out from the right of the 54th Division to Bir Qamle on the wadi, $3\frac{1}{2}$ miles south of Hiseia.

1917.
18 April. The 18th April was spent by the British in bombardment of the Turkish positions from land and sea, and in preparations for the main attack, one of the most important of which was the transport of ammunition and water across the Wadi Ghazze. The mounted troops repeated the action of the previous day, but saved their horses as much as possible in view of the calls to be made upon them on the morrow. The enemy all along the front remained remarkably quiet.

The Plan of the Second Phase.

Map 15.
Sketch 16. The first phase having been successful, it was now for Sir C. Dobell to decide upon the exact method to be employed in the second. In any case surprise was out of the question. After the preliminary bound the enemy could be in no doubt that the main attack was yet to come, and was equally prepared to meet it at any point within the British infantry's range of action.

The passive attitude of the enemy in face of the demonstrations by the Desert Column on the 17th had made it probable that Sir C. Dobell need apprehend no flanking attack from Atawine or Abu Hureira, and that it would be within the capacity of his mounted troops at least to pin the enemy closely to his positions on the right. He therefore returned to his original scheme and decided to make his main attack from Mansura and Sheikh Abbas, rather than, as second thoughts had suggested, containing Gaza and wheeling north-east against the Turkish left. Once again the plan was to capture Ali Muntar and wheel left on

GAZA—BEERSHEBA ROAD
TANK REDOUBT
LOWER ROAD

Tank Redoubt from Sheikh Abbas.
(Area of advance of 54th Division & Imperial Camel Brigade in Second Battle of GAZA).

Gaza. But on this occasion the attack was to be made on a broader front, extending to cover the route taken by the A. & N.Z. Mounted Division in the First Battle of Gaza, penetrating the Turkish line between Kh. el Bir and Kh. Sihan, and here making a gap through which a portion of the Desert Column, held in reserve for the purpose, could pass. This was the role of the Eastern Attack, consisting of the 54th and 52nd Divisions. Meanwhile, the 53rd Division in the dunes was to capture the defences west of Gaza. The 74th Division was to be held in reserve. Of the seven tanks now available, five were to accompany the Eastern Attack and two the 53rd Division. The attack was to take place on the 19th April.[1]

The naval assistance was to be given by the French coastguard ship *Requin*,[2] which had, it will be remembered, played a prominent part over two years earlier in the defence of the Suez Canal, and by two monitors, *M.21* and *M.31*. The heavy artillery was directly under the orders of Eastern Force and to be employed chiefly for counter-battery or against strong points which held up the advance of the infantry. The divisional artilleries were in the hands of the divisional commanders, except for three 18-pdr. brigades of the 52nd, 53rd and 54th Divisions. Of these the 263rd Brigade (52nd Division) was attached to the 54th Division until 7.30 a.m. on the 19th, when it came under the orders of the 74th Division for the defence of Sheikh Abbas Ridge; the 267th Brigade (53rd Division) was attached to the 52nd Division until the same hour, when it returned to its own division; and the 272nd Brigade (54th Division) formed part of the Eastern Force artillery until 6.30 p.m. on the 18th, when it came under the orders of the 74th Division. During the first phase the heavy artillery had been employed in shelling Turkish heavy gun emplacements, while the *Requin* fired fifty rounds on Ali Muntar. The second phase was to be preceded by a two hours' bombardment of the Ali Muntar

---

[1] Eastern Force orders for the second phase are given in Appendices 13 and 14.
[2] The reason for the employment of a French ship was that operations had now passed out of the British naval zone, which ended at El Arish, into the French. The ships were protected by a screen of drifters and trawlers, *Requin* having a special escort of two French destroyers. They were needed, for in the course of the afternoon a submarine appeared and fired a torpedo at *Requin*, which just missed her. The submarine was driven off by the small craft before she could make another attempt.

position by the heavy artillery and the warships. During this preliminary bombardment the field howitzers were to fire gas shell for the first 40 minutes, employing high explosive for the remainder of the two hours. The gas shell was to be directed against enemy battery positions and the woodland area south-west of Ali Muntar. Ten minutes before the infantry attack the 18-pdrs. were to open.

The Eastern Attack, under the orders of Major-General Smith, was the main operation. The 54th Division, to which it was now decided to attach the Camel Brigade in order to broaden the frontage of attack, since it seemed improbable that the Imperial Mounted Division would be able to pierce the enemy's line, was to advance north from Sheikh Abbas against the Turkish position at Kh. Sihan and Kh. el Bir. On its left the 52nd Division was to attack the Ali Muntar position, including the Labyrinth and Green Hill. If all went well the 54th Division was eventually to wheel left and attack the ridge north-east of Gaza, leaving one brigade facing north-east to protect its right flank. The 53rd Division in the coast sector was to attack simultaneously, timing its advance by that of the Eastern Attack. Its first objective was a great dune known as "Samson Ridge," half-way between the Wadi Ghazze and the town, which would give an excellent view of the enemy's position. As the Eastern Attack progressed, it was then to capture the Turkish defences between Gaza and the sea.

The Desert Column was to operate on the right of the Eastern Force, the Imperial Mounted Division receiving orders to "act dismounted against Atawine with a view to "pinning the enemy to that place," while the A. & N.Z. Mounted Division covered its right flank against attack from the direction of Hureira. The secondary role of the latter division was to push through, mounted, should a gap occur in the enemy's line. The light armoured motor batteries and the 7th Light Car Patrol were attached to the A. & N.Z. Division : the 17th Motor Machine-Gun Battery to the Imperial Division.

By the morning of the 19th all was ready for the second phase. The cisterns in the Wadi Ghazze were full of water and 8,000 filled *fanatis* (about 100,000 gallons) had been dumped behind the line at Mansura. The weather had been fairly cool during the 17th and 18th, the temperature rising to about 90° after noon. The daily temperature depended

LAUNCH OF ATTACK

on the wind; fortunately there was no sign of a recurrence of the dreaded *Khamsin*, which had so sorely tried the troops on the 27th March.

**1917.
19 April.**

THE ATTACK OF THE EASTERN FORCE.

At 5.30 a.m. the bombardment began, the warships shelling the rear of the enemy defences and the heavy artillery concentrating on the most important points.[1] At 7.30 a.m. both switched their fire respectively to north and north-west of Gaza, north and north-east of Ali Muntar, to avoid endangering the infantry, which began its advance at this hour. At 7.20 the 18-pdr. batteries established a barrage on certain points to be attacked. There were not enough guns to cover the whole front, and even as it was the barrage was thin.

**Map 15.
Sketch 16.**

The advance of the 54th and 52nd Divisions began punctually at 7.30 a.m. The 163rd Brigade on the right of the 54th Division was directed north-east, its right on a Turkish redoubt one mile north-west of Kh. Sihan, its frontage 1,500 yards. On its left was the 162nd Brigade, with its left on the point where the Wadi Mukaddeme crossed the Gaza–Beersheba road. The 161st Brigade was in divisional reserve. The Camel Brigade moved simultaneously on the right of the 54th Division against Kh. Sihan. On the left the 52nd Division advanced, its leading brigade, the 155th, moving along the Es Sire Ridge, while the 156th followed, echeloned to the right rear and prepared to swing up to attack Green Hill and Ali Muntar. The 157th Brigade was in reserve to the Eastern Attack.

It was speedily evident that the fire of the warships, the heavy artillery, and the field howitzers firing gas—mainly directed during the preliminary bombardment, as it had been, against the trenches—had in no way silenced

---

[1] The *Requin* fired on Ali Muntar, one monitor on the Warren, on the western slope of the ridge, and one on the Labyrinth. The 15th Heavy Battery bombarded gun positions and trenches about Kh. el Bir; the 10th Heavy Battery the ridge east of Gaza up to Fryer Hill; the 91st Heavy Battery El Arish Redoubt, Magdhaba Trench and batteries west of Gaza; the 6-in. howitzers of the 201st Siege Battery Outpost Hill and Middlesex Hill on the Es Sire Ridge, and the 8-in. howitzers Green Hill, south of Gaza. There were available for all purposes, including reserve, 500 rounds per 60-pdr. and 6-in. howitzer and 400 rounds per 8-in. howitzer. The total supply for the field artillery of the infantry divisions was 600 rounds per 4·5-in. howitzer, and 600 rounds per 18-pdr.

the enemy's artillery. From Mansura and the Sheikh Abbas Ridge the ground to the north-east drops very slightly, then rises again equally slightly as the Gaza–Beersheba road is approached. In sharp contrast to the country between the Mansura bluff and the wadi, this is remarkably open and devoid of cover. As the brigades of the 54th Division advanced they came under well-directed artillery fire and, on approaching the Turkish trenches, under intense machine-gun fire also. The attack was carried out with admirable steadiness, the leading battalions moving straight on their objectives, despite heavy casualties.

On the right the 163rd Brigade (Br.-General T. Ward), led by a tank directed on the Turkish redoubt one mile north-west of Kh. Sihan, gained a ridge 500 yards from the enemy's trenches at 8.30 a.m. Half an hour later the tank, followed by part of the right battalion, the 5/Norfolk, entered the redoubt, killing or driving out the garrison and taking 20 prisoners. The Turks immediately concentrated the fire of several batteries on the redoubt, destroyed the tank, and caused casualties so heavy in the ranks of the 5/Norfolk that the party was unable to withstand the counter-attack which followed. The remnants fell back to the ridge from which they had advanced. The 4/Norfolk on the left fared no better, and was pinned to the ground also about 500 yards from its objective, after losing two-thirds of its numbers. The 8/Hampshire had been thrown in and had also suffered very heavy losses without being able to carry the assault forward. These three battalions had lost 1,500 men, including two commanding officers and all twelve company commanders.

On the left the 162nd Brigade (Br.-General A. Mudge) attacked with the 4/Northampton on the right, the 10/London on the left, and the 11/London in support behind the centre. Heavy casualties occurred from the first from artillery fire from behind Ali Muntar, from machine-gun fire, and also from that of mountain guns which must have been close up among the enemy's entrenchments. The 4/Northampton was held up 500 yards from the enemy's trenches. A handful of men, including Lewis gunners, worked their way forward almost to the Turkish parapet and shot down a number of the enemy at pointblank range, but this small party was eventually destroyed. The 10/London made the greatest advance of all that black day. The right half

54TH DIVN. HELD UP 339

battalion, endeavouring to keep touch with the 4/Northampton, became separated from the left and was held up in front of the Turkish works, but the left, faced by no connected line of trenches, fought its way across the Gaza–Beersheba road at 8.30 a.m. By rifle and Lewis-gun fire it drove out of action a Turkish infantry gun, which was hastily withdrawn to the ridge north of Ali Muntar. A deed of extraordinary gallantry was accomplished by Sapper Sore, of the brigade signal section, in cutting the telegraph line beside the road. He climbed a pole and cut one wire, but was then brought to the ground by fire from a range of under three hundred yards. Undaunted, he climbed the pole again, cut a second strand, and was in the act of cutting the third and last when he was blown to pieces by a shell fired from a mountain gun a few hundred yards away.

1917.
19 April.

The left of the 10/London was now completely isolated, there being a gap of 800 yards between it and the right half battalion, while it was far ahead of the 52nd Division on its left. Two machine-gun sections were pushed out to cover the left flank on the Wadi Mukaddeme, but the position remained hopelessly exposed. The situation was somewhat eased by the subsequent advance of the 52nd Division's right, but the party was eventually forced to fall back across the road. A counter-attack by two Turkish battalions compelled the whole battalion to fall back another 600 yards, but was then brought to a standstill, the machine-gun sections on the Wadi Mukaddeme swinging round to fire north-east and doing considerable execution.

At 1 p.m. General Hare ordered the 161st Brigade (Br.-General W. Marriott-Dodington) in reserve to reinforce the line held by the 163rd Brigade. The 5/Suffolk of the 163rd, supported by the 6/Essex of the 161st, was ordered to make a fresh attack on the redoubt from which the 5/Norfolk had been driven. At 2.20 p.m. these battalions began their advance, but had not become seriously engaged before General Hare ordered the whole line to stand fast.

On the right of the 54th Division the Camel Brigade, reinforced by one battalion of the 161st Brigade, was to attack from Kh. Sihan up to but exclusive of the redoubt a mile north-west of it. It had not been employed during the first phase and had come up the previous night to Dumb-bell Hill, due south of Sheikh Abbas. It advanced in conjunction with the original attack of the 54th Division, and men of the 1st Battalion on the left of the line entered the redoubt[1] at the same moment as the 5/Norfolk, the leading companies having lost half their effectives. Almost immediately the tank, repeatedly hit by shells, burst into flames. The enemy's artillery fire killed most of the men who had entered the redoubt; the few who remained alive were captured by the Turkish counter-attack already described. On the right the 3rd Battalion crossed the Gaza-Beersheba road and temporarily established itself on two hummocks known as "Jack and Jill," east of Kh. Sihan. When the 4th L.H. Brigade on its right was forced to give ground before a Turkish counter-attack, the men of the 3rd Battalion were likewise compelled to withdraw across the road, the battalion then slightly refusing its right.

At 3 p.m. General Hare, as already stated, ordered his division and the Camel Brigade to stand fast. He was concerned lest the strong counter-attacks in progress against the Imperial Mounted Division should uncover his right, in which case he considered it might be necessary to swing it back towards Sheikh Abbas. Moreover it was becoming apparent that, however gallantly the infantry might struggle, there was not a sufficient volume of artillery fire to carry the assault through positions strong in themselves and most stubbornly defended. Whenever a small breach was made the troops which had made it were so thinned by the enemy's fire as to be unable to resist the furious counter-attacks repeatedly launched by the Turks.

The 52rd Division began its advance at the same time as the 54th, but was less exposed to view as it moved up the Es Sire Ridge; nor, with its right brigade echeloned in rear of the left, did it present so broad a front. The 155th Brigade (Br.-General J. B. Pollok-M'Call) moved along the spine of the ridge to avoid the deep nullahs on either flank, 4/Scots Fusiliers on right, 5/K.O.S.B. on left, 4/K.O.S.B. in support. The 5/Scots Fusiliers acted as a left flank guard to protect the advance against counter-attacks from the woodland on the western slope of the ridge. No great difficulties were encountered till the leading troops and the tank which accompanied them reached the gullies

---

[1] This redoubt, subsequently known as "Tank Redoubt," was, as has been stated, outside its objective, but the 163rd Brigade appears to have swung slightly to its left, though, as we have seen, men of the 5/Norfolk also entered the redoubt.

Looking north from Lee's Hill over GAZA and Lambeth Wood.

MEDITERRANEAN SEA Sand dunes Sheikh Redwan GAZA

halfway between Queen's and Lee's Hills.¹ Into one of these the tank unfortunately dived nose first, and was lost for the day. The second tank took its place, and by 8.15 a.m. Lee's Hill was occupied. From this point the troops moving against Outpost Hill came under artillery fire and intense machine-gun fire both from their front and left flank. The 5/K.O.S.B., though wheeling slightly away to the left of its objective, succeeded in occupying the Turkish lunette on Outpost Hill at 10 a.m. after the tank had entered it. The right battalion, the 4/Scots Fusiliers, had no such good fortune against Middlesex Hill to the north-east, and finally was brought to a halt 300 yards from the hill, after suffering very heavy losses.

1917.
19 April.

By now the shortage of shell began to make itself felt. Middlesex Hill, Green Hill and Ali Muntar were within a comparatively small area; could they have been subjected to a really intense bombardment it is quite possible that they would have been captured by the 52nd Division, which would then, with its third brigade in hand, have been in a position dominating Gaza. As it was, such artillery fire as was directed on the Turkish batteries and machine guns was never sufficient to silence them. The woodland area west of the ridge was particularly troublesome. Though it had been bombarded with gas shell in the morning the enemy was either not driven out or reoccupied it later, and his fire continually galled the 155th Brigade.

An hour after the capture of the lunette on Outpost Hill the 5/K.O.S.B. was driven out. Fierce fighting followed, of which the details are not, nor can ever be, known, but it is believed that the redoubt changed hands several times, remaining in the possession of the Turks. At noon Br.-General Pollok-M'Call ordered the 4/K.O.S.B. to retake it, after half an hour's bombardment. Major W. T. Forrest advanced at the head of two companies, was joined at the foot of the slope by men of the 5th Battalion of the same regiment and of the 5/Scots Fusiliers, and led them forward in a desperate rush up the hill. The leader of the attack was mortally wounded on the parapet, but the lunette was captured after hand-to-hand fighting. There was no room

---

¹ In the descriptions of the battles of Gaza new names appear with each new attack. Very few were on the maps for the first battle, a number were added prior to the second, and still more before the third. In some cases names previously in use were dropped out.

in the work for all the attackers, and those left outside suffered heavily. Nevertheless, Outpost Hill was held all the afternoon, despite continual counter-attacks and the fact that there was no communication with it. At 6.20 p.m., when all the senior officers had become casualties, the 70 survivors were withdrawn, only a few minutes before the 7/H.L.I. of the 157th Brigade came up the ridge. So heavy was the Turkish fire, however, that it is doubtful whether this reinforcement could have held the hill.

The first check to the 155th Brigade had occurred at about 10 a.m. and had resulted in the 156th Brigade (Br.-General A. H. Leggett) on its right also being held up. When the right of the 155th advanced to the slope of Middlesex Hill, the 156th was again enabled to move forward. The left battalion, the 8/Scottish Rifles, was, however, speedily held up by fire from Middlesex and Outpost Hills and the whole brigade remained in the same position for five hours, the men lying in the open with little cover under considerable fire, chiefly from Green Hill. The left of the 54th Division was out of sight till the Turkish counter-attacks already described drove it back to a point east of Kh. en Namus. At about 3 p.m. a slight withdrawal was carried out, seeing which the Turks instantly launched a heavy counter-attack from Ali Muntar. The divisional artillery was swiftly concentrated on the advancing enemy, who broke and fell back in disorder to his trenches.

At 1.45 p.m. General Smith ordered the 157th Brigade (Br.-General C. D. Hamilton Moore), in reserve below the Mansura Ridge except for one battalion already sent to the support of the 155th Brigade, to move up to Lee's Hill and Blazed Hill. General Hamilton Moore joined General Pollok-M'Call on Kurd Hill, and, after consultation and reconnaissance, reported that his brigade was fresh and ready to advance, but that he could not launch an attack before 4 p.m. General Smith considered that to begin a fresh attack with the reserve brigade at that hour would be fruitless. His opinion was confirmed by orders received at 4.40 p.m. from Eastern Force to discontinue the advance and dig in from east of Heart Hill, in touch with the 53rd Division, through Outpost Hill to the right of the 54th Division near Kh. en Namus.[1] The 157th Brigade then relieved the 155th,

---

[1] There is no record of the exact terms of this order.

BUNKER HILL · MEDITERRANEAN SEA · EL ARISH REDOUBT · HOG'S BACK

Dunes south-west of GAZA from Samson Ridge.

which had had a thousand casualties out of a strength of 2,500 and had lost particularly heavily in officers. That Outpost Hill was evacuated before the garrison could be relieved has already been recorded. The 157th Brigade, therefore, took up a line just south of it.

The attack of the 53rd Division east of the Rafah–Gaza road began ten minutes before that of the other two divisions. On the right the 160th Brigade was to capture Samson Ridge, on the left the 159th Brigade to occupy a line from that height to Sheikh Ajlin on the shore, each brigade being assisted by one tank. The advance on the second objective, from Romani Trench to Zowaiid Trench, was to take place in conjunction with that of the 52nd Division on Ali Muntar.

The attack on Samson Ridge progressed very slowly, owing to machine-gun fire from the woodland area which had likewise delayed the progress of the 52nd Division. It was not till after 1 p.m. that the ridge was captured at the point of the bayonet, with 39 prisoners. The 159th Brigade on the left met with little opposition till within 800 yards of its objective, where it waited, in accordance with orders, for the capture of Samson Ridge. The enemy on its front then fell back, and Sheikh Ajlin was occupied without difficulty. A half-hearted counter-attack on Samson Ridge was beaten off. The division made no further advance, the reason given being that the 52nd Division was unable to take its objective and check the fire from the high ground to the east. But it appears that the men of the 53rd Division still felt the effects of their losses, disappointments and fatigue in the battle fought three weeks earlier, for their advance, even up to Samson Ridge, had been much slower than that of the other two divisions. They had, however, suffered upwards of six hundred casualties, chiefly in carrying Samson Ridge.

THE OPERATIONS OF THE DESERT COLUMN.

While the 54th Division was shattering itself against the Turkish defences, the mounted troops were fulfilling their rôle, which was to engage the Turkish defences along the Gaza–Beersheba road as far as Hureira and to cover the infantry's right flank.

The Imperial Mounted Division advanced at 6.30 a.m., or one hour before the commencement of the infantry attack, on a front extending from the right of the Camel Brigade to the Wadi el Baha, 7 miles south-east of Gaza. The 5th Mounted, 3rd and 4th L.H. Brigades, from right to left, were in front line, the 6th Mounted Brigade in divisional reserve. The A. & N.Z. Mounted Division had orders to place one brigade (the 22nd Mounted) about Tell el Fara, on the Wadi Ghazze, 4 miles south of Hiseia, in order to cover the right and protect the engineers at work on the wells at that point ; to despatch one brigade (the 1st L.H.) towards Abu Hureira ; holding two (the N.Z.M.R. and 2nd L.H.) in reserve, to be employed mounted. The brigades of the Imperial Mounted Division and the 1st L.H. Brigade were to attack dismounted.

The wording of General Chetwode's order to General Hodgson, "to act dismounted against Atawine, with a "view to pinning the enemy to that place," left to the latter's discretion how far the attack was to be pressed. The frontage of the division was 2 miles, which meant that the firing line would be weak, especially as at least one quarter of the division's strength had to remain with the horses. It was obvious that this weakness must have an important effect upon the tactics of the Imperial Mounted Division. Nevertheless General Hodgson knew that he was expected to carry out considerably more than a demonstration and that, if opportunity came to him of piercing the Turkish position, it was to be taken.

The three brigades made steady progress at the beginning, that on the left being naturally greatest owing to the advance of the 54th Division and the Camel Brigade. By 8.15 a.m. the 4th L.H. Brigade (Br.-General J. B. Meredith) had secured a position overlooking the Gaza-Beersheba road near Kh. Sihan, where its left was in touch with the Camel Brigade The 3rd L. H. Brigade (Br.-General J. R. Royston) had begun its advance before it had received orders to do so, had come under fire from the right, and then been instructed by General Hodgson to halt until the brigades on either flank advanced. By 9.15 it was close to the Atawine Redoubt and had captured 70 prisoners.

It was soon apparent that a long, narrow spur, parallel to and south-east of the Wadi el Baha, to which the name of "Sausage Ridge" had been given, was an obstacle to the advance, as the enemy on it was able to take in enfilade the attack on Atawine. The fire of the Ayr and Somerset

Kh. Sihan — FOOTHILLS OF SHEPHELAH — Wadi Sihan — ATAWINE RIDGE
GAZA–BEERSHEBA ROAD

Khirbet Sihan and Atawine, from south of Sheikh Abbas.
(Area of advance of 4th Light Horse Bde. in Second Battle of GAZA.)

Batteries and all available machine guns was concentrated upon it, but the result of the Turkish machine-gun fire was that the 5th Mounted Brigade (Br.-General P. D. Fitzgerald), and in lesser degree the 3rd L.H. Brigade on its left, swung back their rights to face the ridge, thus creating a gap between the 3rd and 4th Brigades. The 5th Mounted Brigade succeeded by its fire in driving a Turkish battalion off the lower slopes of Sausage Ridge, without, however, appreciably improving its own position.

At 9.30 a.m. the N.Z.M.R. Brigade (Br.-General E. W. C. Chaytor) despatched the Wellington Regiment to assist the 5th in the attack on Sausage Ridge. This regiment occupied the southern end of the ridge, but the "Hairpin Redoubt" at its northern end, near the Gaza–Beersheba road, prevented further progress. To the east the 1st L.H. Brigade (Br.-General C. F. Cox) of the A. & N.Z. Mounted Division, advancing on Hureira, was able to occupy Baiket es Sana without difficulty. At noon the remainder of the N.Z.M.R. Brigade was ordered forward, the Canterbury Regiment coming into line between the Wellington and the 5th Mounted Brigade.

The series of Turkish counter-attacks against the infantry, which have already been described, spread down the road, and at 2 p.m. the Turks, in considerable strength and well supported by artillery fire, swept forward on the whole front held by the Imperial Mounted Division. The 3rd and 4th L.H. Brigades suffered considerable casualties, the latter being forced back some distance. The situation was serious, and the 6th Mounted Brigade (Br.-General T. M. S. Pitt) was ordered up to reinforce. The brigade advanced at a gallop, arriving in the nick of time; two regiments supporting the 5th Mounted Brigade, while one filled the gap between the 3rd and 4th. This support, with that of the 263rd Brigade R.F.A., brought the Turkish attack to a halt, and no further retirement took place until after the fall of darkness.

While the main Turkish counter-attacks were in progress between Gaza and Atawine a subsidiary counter-attack was launched from Hureira against the 1st L.H. Brigade at Baiket es Sana. A regiment of Turkish cavalry[1]

---

[1] The *3rd Cavalry Division* had moved up to Tell esh Sheria at the beginning of the British attack.

346   SECOND GAZA

also advanced up the spit of land between the Wadis esh Sheria and Imleih. Against these attacks the 1st L.H. Brigade gave some ground, but eventually brought the Turks on both flanks to a standstill by the fire of their Hotchkiss and Vickers machine guns, aided by that of the Leicester Battery. A squadron from the Turkish force which had been advancing between the two wadis now swung southward and joined another cavalry regiment and a body of Bedouin in an advance against the 5th and 7th A.L.H., 2nd L.H. Brigade (Br.-General G. de L. Ryrie), south of the Wadi Imleih. The latter, being on a wide front, fell back, covered by its machine-gun detachments, finally bringing the Turks to a halt.[2] The 22nd Mounted Brigade (Br.-General F. A. B. Fryer) on the extreme right was also engaged by Turkish cavalry, and by infantry moving up from Beersheba, but the latter soon withdrew without pressing its attack.

The repulse of the counter-attacks against the A. & N.Z. Mounted Division terminated the offensive operations of the mounted troops. They had fulfilled their role of protecting the right of the 54th Division and preventing the enemy from reinforcing his front against it. The decision to dig in along the position gained by the infantry divisions was followed by an order to the mounted troops to withdraw to a line from Dumb-bell Hill, on the edge of the Sheikh Abbas Ridge, through Munkheile, south of the Wadi el Baha, to Hiseia.

THE SITUATION AT NIGHTFALL ON THE 19TH APRIL.

Map 15.
Sketch 16.

As the afternoon drew on it was apparent that there was no prospect of success on any portion of the front. The troops of the Eastern Attack had striven most gallantly to attain their objectives, the 54th Division in particular having expended itself without stint. At a few points the enemy's front-line trenches had been taken, only to be promptly recaptured by determined counter-attacks. There had been neither gun-power nor ammunition sufficient to carry the attack further. The 52nd and 54th Divisions had

---

[2] This movement was conducted by a staff officer of the *3rd Cavalry Division*, Nogales Bey, a Venezuelan volunteer with the Turks, whose reminiscences have been published under the title of " Four Years beneath the Crescent," (Scribner).

both lost heavily. One brigade only of the former was intact, while one brigade of the 54th had had comparatively light casualties, and the 74th Division had not been engaged. On the right the mounted troops could in no case have played more than a secondary role, unless either the infantry had broken the Turkish line or the enemy had withdrawn troops from his left flank to support his right. This, as we have seen, he had not been compelled to do.

Sir A. Murray at Khan Yunis had been anxiously following the progress of the battle. "Since it was evident," he writes in his Despatch, "that the action could not be "brought to a conclusion within the day, at 4 p.m. I issued "personally instructions to the General Officer Commanding "Eastern Force that all ground gained must, without fail, "be held during the night with a view to resuming the "attack on the Ali Muntar position, under cover of a con- "centrated artillery bombardment at dawn on the 20th."

Despite the injunction to abandon no ground, it was necessary to adjust the line of the 54th Division, since its leading troops, lying out in the open in face of the Turkish defences, were in an impossible position. Under cover of the Camel Brigade, which had its right close to Kh. Sihan, the right was withdrawn to the neighbourhood of Sheikh Abbas, where it was in touch with a brigade of the 74th Division. At 7.45 p.m. the Camel Brigade withdrew to Charing Cross, south-west of Sheikh Abbas. On the front of the 52nd Division the line passed close to the foot of Outpost Hill, but the construction of a new position through Heart and Blazed Hills was begun. The 53rd Division maintained its hold on Samson Ridge, which represented almost the only gain of the battle not already attained in the first phase of the 17th April.

General Dobell issued orders for the renewal of the attack next day. When, however, he had heard from his divisional commanders what was the state of their troops and the ammunition supply, had learned that the casualties were estimated to be 6,000, he decided that a fresh assault would only result in further heavy losses, without hope of success. He therefore postponed the attack for twenty-four hours and reported to Sir A. Murray that in his opinion no further advance was possible, adding that General Chetwode and the divisional commanders all held the same view. Sir A. Murray was reluctantly compelled to agree that the decision was just, and, though as late as the 22nd he informed the War Office that he still contemplated a renewed offensive, the reinforcement of the enemy's position finally obliged him to abandon the project.

1917. 20 April. The night passed comparatively quietly, with intermittent bursts of Turkish artillery fire. The British infantry, weary as it was, dug vigorously in anticipation of a counter-attack on the morrow. No general counter-attack came, however: the most serious of a local nature being an attempt by a body of the enemy to work down the Wadi Sihan, which was defeated by the artillery fire of the 54th Division.

The casualties from the 17th to the 20th April were 6,444,[1] of which the 54th Division suffered 2,870 (the 163rd Brigade alone 1,828), the 52nd Division 1,874, the 53rd Division 584, and the Imperial Mounted Division 547. The total of casualties to animals, including camels, was 2,129.[2] About two hundred prisoners were captured by the British.

* * * * *

Thus ended the second attempt to capture Gaza, and the most considerable battle yet fought in this theatre. It has none of the interest of the first attempt, which was practically an encounter battle, with constantly changing situation and ever-unfolding opportunities on both sides. This was a dogged advance against imperfectly located entrenchments and in face of fire from hidden artillery, without adequate support from that arm on the side of the attackers: an advance which finally lost impetus owing to the lack of the necessary mechanical support. It needs no comment, save that it illustrates once more the high quality of Turkish troops in prepared positions and emphasizes the advantages of defence by areas as opposed to linear defence, at least by day and in clear weather. There were wide gaps in the Turkish position, but the redoubts were well sited for

---

[1]
	KILLED.	WOUNDED.	MISSING.
Officers	43	257	42
Other ranks	466	4,102	1,534

Of the missing by far the greater number were killed and remained lying out in front of the line consolidated by the British. The Turks claim only 6 officers and 266 other ranks as prisoners, two-thirds of them wounded.

[2] " Veterinary History of the War," p.154.

mutual support and permitted the retention of reserves for counter-attack outside the danger zone. Since the Turkish infantry did not flinch from counter-attack, the result was never in doubt.

NOTE.

THE BATTLE, FROM GERMAN AND TURKISH SOURCES.

Between the First and Second Battles of Gaza the Turks were re- **Map 15.** inforced by the two regiments of the *53rd Division* which had not taken **Sketch 16.** part in the former, four batteries and some cavalry. The *3rd Division*, which had marched from Jemmame to the relief of Gaza, was moved into the town. The *16th Division*, less one regiment, returned to its old station at Tell esh Sheria, a proportion being held north of Hureira. The *53rd Division* with two battalions of the *79th Regiment* (*16th Division*) was stationed about Kh. Sihan (thus accounting for the new camps observed about Kh. el Bir). The coast flank was now very strong, the regiments of the *3rd Division* having four battalions each, while the division had two machine-gun companies in addition to machine guns with the regiments. The artillery defending Gaza itself consisted of four batteries of field artillery, the Austrian mountain howitzer batteries, and a 15 cm.-howitzer. battery. The *3rd Cavalry Division* was at Jemmame, but appears to have moved into Tell esh Sheria on the evening of the 17th, and certainly operated from that place on the 19th. Beersheba was very lightly held, by only two battalions of the *79th Regiment* and a single battery. The Historical Section of the Turkish General Staff states that an advance on the railway north of that town would have " provoked a crisis."[1] In the area between Jaffa and Ramle was one infantry regiment, and some miscellaneous battalions and artillery, detained for fear of a landing, which had been fostered by a wireless message despatched for the purpose by the British.

The ration strength of the force is given as 48,845 ; 18,185 rifles,[2] 86 machine guns, 101 guns ; but only 68 guns were in action at Second Battle of Gaza, and only twelve of these were above field-gun calibre.

Kress ("Sinai," pp. 29-30) states that the naval bombardment, though it had a certain moral effect, did little material damage ; while the Turkish General Staff claims that the British counter-battery fire was inaccurate owing to the Turkish aircraft having prevented the British machines from locating the artillery. [As a fact, haze and the dust caused by the bombardment were obstacles far more serious to the British observers than were enemy machines. During the three days of the battle the British artillery machines carried out 38 flights and engaged 63 targets, of which 27 were batteries. One hundred and twenty-eight direct hits were recorded and three guns reported to be destroyed.] It is stated, however, that the gas bombardment had some effect. After the attack

---

[1] Rafael de Nogales ("Four Years beneath the Crescent," p. 341) states that the line between Tell esh Sheria and Beersheba was guarded only by a handful of Arab gendarmes.

[2] It is not clear whether the 1,500 sabres of the *3rd Cavalry Division* (really no more than a strong brigade) are included in this figure ; probably not. The rifle strength is so small in comparison with the ration strength that the latter probably applies to all troops in Southern Syria.

was over Kress contemplated an attempt to throw the British back across the Wadi Ghazze, but found that the fatigue of his troops and still more the shortage of munitions rendered this impossible.

The Turkish losses from the 17th to the 20th April (the same period as that for which the British are given) were, according to the Turkish Historical Section, as follows :—

	Killed.	Wounded.	Missing.
Officers	9	34	5
Other Ranks	393	1,330	242

a total of 2,013.

CHAPTER XIX.

AFTER THE SECOND BATTLE OF GAZA.

(Maps 2, 8 ; Sketch B.)

THE CONSOLIDATION OF THE POSITION.

ON the 21st April, by order of Sir A. Murray, Lieut.- General Sir Philip Chetwode, Bt., assumed command of the Eastern Force, Lieut.-General Sir Charles Dobell returning to England. Major-General Sir H. G. Chauvel succeeded General Chetwode in command of the Desert Column, and Br.-General E. W. C. Chaytor replaced him in command of the Australian and New Zealand Mounted Division.

1917.
21 April.
Map 2.

General Chetwode, like his predecessor, was of opinion that, owing to the strength of the enemy's position, the renewal of a direct attack with the forces at the disposal of the Eastern Force was not justified. In this view his subordinate commanders concurred. Sir A. Murray decided, however, to maintain, subject to minor tactical readjustment, the position gained on the northern and eastern side of the Wadi Ghazze. The first problem was, then, to make this position secure ; the second to reorganize the force, and particularly the infantry divisions, after its severe trials and heavy losses.

The prospect ahead was not a pleasant one. The hot weather was at hand and another summer was to be endured, if not in the heart of the desert, on its verge, where desert heat and desert winds were prevalent ; while to the strain induced by these conditions that of trench warfare was to be added.

There was, however, to be one important difference between the deadlock which had resulted here and that on the Western Front. In Palestine, as in France, each adversary had one flank upon the sea, but in this case, unlike that of the main theatre, each had the other flank open. On the British right the power to manœuvre was limited only by the difficulties of water supply ; the Turks, with Beersheba in their possession, were even less constrained in this respect on their left. In front of Gaza the British line, as finally consolidated, ran from Sheikh Ajlin on the shore, across Samson Ridge, bent back slightly to the Rafah–Gaza road at Heart Hill, crossed Lee's Hill, followed the edge of the plateau through Mansura to Sheikh Abbas, and there turned south almost at a right angle. As far as Lee's Hill the troops holding it were in close touch with the enemy; thence to Sheikh Abbas was a wide No Man's Land, varying from 1,500 to 3,000 yards. But from Sheikh Abbas the British front ran south, while the Turkish ran south-east along the Gaza–Beersheba road, the distance between the two gradually increasing until in the neighbourhood of Qamle on the Wadi Ghazze the British right was 9 miles from the Turkish redoubt at Hureira. And between the Wadi Imleih and the Wadi Ghazze was a great open plain, slightly undulating and continuing practically unbroken to within a few miles of Beersheba.

The front from Sheikh Ajlin and for some distance beyond the southward bend at Sheikh Abbas was held by the infantry in a continuous trench line strongly wired throughout.[1] But south of El Mendur Sir P. Chetwode determined to keep an open gateway for the exit of his mounted troops to patrol the plain mentioned above. He forbade the construction of continuous defences here, and actually had wire torn up from a long weak line which had been prepared, replacing it by strong points. In the event of an attack by the enemy on this flank, the main line of defence ran through Weli Sheikh Nuran, 3½ miles west of the wadi at Shellal; but this was to be occupied only in the last resort. General Chauvel was instructed to defend the water and crossings at Shellal obstinately and make the enemy pay dearly for every yard of progress. The G.O.C. Eastern Force adopted this plan not merely because it appeared better from the point of view of defence than the holding of a long, entrenched line—for, however far he stretched that line, the enemy, if able to advance at all, could have turned it—but because he desired to keep his mounted troops constantly employed in the open. In this arm the British were overwhelmingly superior; when the

---

[1] Sir P. Chetwode considered the possibility of blunting the Sheikh Abbas salient by advancing the line through Munkheile to the Wadi esh Sheria, south of that point, but abandoned the project because it would have involved vast labour in the construction of communication trenches, the ground here being completely exposed to view.

TURKISH REINFORCEMENTS

1917.
April.

time came for a renewal of the offensive it would probably prove the decisive factor. It therefore behoved them to keep it bright and ready for action.

Both sides set to work vigorously upon their defences. Those of the British from Sheikh Ajlin to below Sheikh Abbas were made very strong, though the work in its early stages was hindered by a particularly severe *Khamsin* accompanied by high temperature, which silted up the trenches of the 53rd Division in the dunes as quickly as they were dug. On the right flank strong points were constructed, and at Weli Sheikh Nuran part of the old Turkish system which had covered Shellal from the south-west was utilized to form a second defensive position.

On the Turkish side the work, superintended by German engineers, was done with energy and technical skill. Reinforced within a few weeks of the Second Battle of Gaza by the *7th* and *54th Divisions*, Kress not only perfected his defences between Gaza and Hureira, but began to extend them along the Gaza–Beersheba road and thence due east across his railway. East and south of Beersheba the Turks also prepared a position which made of that town a strong though somewhat isolated fortress on their left flank: a vast labour, since the entrenchments here had to be blasted from the solid rock.

The lesser length of their front was a considerable advantage to the British, for as soon as the work on the defences was well in hand and the danger of an immediate counter-attack was over, it was possible to withdraw formations in turn from the line. The heat could not be escaped, but camps near the shore, with daily bathing in the Mediterranean, afforded some relaxation and were of value in restoring the health of the troops. To fight the minor illnesses, which would have withdrawn men to hospitals far in rear, and especially the sores prevalent in this dusty, fly-ridden country, an advanced hospital for light cases was established.[1] This matter was of particular importance

---

[1] " Many thanks for saying you will help us over the medical arrange-
" ments. What I am working at now is the ' stitch in time ' ; that
" is, to catch men in the early stages of sickness or septic sores, who
" would ordinarily speaking be given ' medicine and duty,' but whom we
" now hope to send for a few days to a convalescent station near Rafah,
" where they will be quickly available if required."
General Chetwode to General Lynden Bell [C.G.S. to Sir A. Murray],
30th April 1917.

owing to the weakness of certain of the formations, above all of the 54th Division. Other diseases, such as a mild form of diphtheria, sand-fly fever, scabies, became more prevalent in front of Gaza than they had been in Sinai. Of malaria there were remarkably few cases, owing to the unremitting attention paid to the breeding-places of anopheline mosquitoes, the oiling of pools, and, where water was running, the raking out of weed. This last method ensured the speedy destruction of the pupæ by the heat of the sun. On the whole the troops before Gaza were kept in good health, for which tribute is due not alone to the efficiency of the medical services under Surgeon-General J. Maher, but to the cleanly habits of the British soldier.

This was in sharp contrast to the state of affairs on the side of the enemy. There were capable men—chiefly Syrians and Armenians—among the Turkish medical officers, but the carelessness of troops and the ignorance of commanders made their efforts of little avail. We learn from Kress that during the heat of the summer ten thousand men, that is, one quarter of the force's strength, were in the hospitals at one time. The German commander states, however, that much of the sickness was due to insufficient nourishment, the single metre-gauge railway being quite inadequate to supply the front.

On the 2nd May the command known as the Northern Canal Section was broken up and its place taken by the Palestine L. of C. Defences, under Br.-General H. D. Watson. This command extended from the northern part of the Suez Canal to Khan Yunis, and was therefore responsible for the defence of almost the whole of the railway and pipe-line. The troops consisted of the Imperial Service Cavalry Brigade, the Bikanir Camel Corps, the French and Italian Contingents,[1] and small detachments of Imperial Camel Corps, Yeomanry, Indian infantry, British West Indies Regiment, and artillery.

British Policy After the Second Battle of Gaza.

On the 22nd April Sir A. Murray telegraphed to the War Office his appreciation of the situation. He did not expect with his present force to be able to achieve more

---

[1] See later in this Chapter.

than a local success. For continuous offensive operations
he required at least the five complete and fully trained
divisions which he had previously reported to be necessary.
At present he had three only. The 74th Division, though
its material was of the best, had had insufficient training
for employment as infantry in the field; the units of which
it was composed had not long been formed into battalions
and brigades, and it had still no artillery. He had recently
grouped into a brigade, which was to be the nucleus of the
75th Division, four battalions from East Africa, Aden and
India, but they were only then assembling for training and
equipment, while those from East Africa and Aden were
very far from fit. He therefore considered that for a large-
scale and continuous offensive he needed two more fully
trained and equipped divisions, additional field artillery to
complete all divisions (including the 74th and 75th) to a
standard of three brigades each of two 18-pdr. and one
4·5-inch howitzer batteries; three additional 60-pdr. batteries; and two additional siege howitzer batteries, exclusive
of one already on its way from Salonika.

Such were his requirements for the moment, but if the
Turks continued to reinforce their front he would need a
proportionate increase. He concluded by stating that his
estimate of his requirements had never varied, but that he
fully recognized the more urgent demands of the main
theatre of war. If what he asked for could not be sent, he
was prepared with what he had to keep the enemy fully
occupied.

Sir W. Robertson in reply informed him that, in view
of the failure of his recent attempts to capture Gaza, of his
appreciation recorded above, and of the fact that a Russian
offensive projected in the Caucasus had been postponed,
the War Cabinet had decided to modify its recent instructions
that his immediate object was the defeat of the Turkish
forces south of Jerusalem and the occupation of that town.
For the present his mission was to be " to take every favour-
" able opportunity of defeating the Turkish forces opposed
" to him, and to follow up any success gained with all the
" means at his disposal, with the object of driving the Turks
" from Palestine, as and when this became practicable."
In a subsequent telegram the C.I.G.S. stated that it was
not then possible to send the two divisions demanded, but

that Sir A. Murray's requirements in field artillery would be met and that his heavy artillery would be brought up to a strength of six 60-pdr. and four siege howitzer batteries.

On the 7th and 12th May the Commander-in-Chief dealt with the question at greater length in letters to the C.I.G.S. He pointed out that the effective strength of the enemy in Southern Palestine on the 17th March had been estimated to be 19,000 rifles, forty to fifty guns, and 1,500 sabres; composed of the *3rd* and *16th Divisions* and the *3rd Cavalry Division*, with unattached regiments of other divisions and some German and Austrian artillery units. Since then the front had been considerably reinforced both by drafts and new formations. The following divisions were now believed to be in line between Gaza and Beersheba : *3rd, 7th, 16th, 53rd, 54th, 3rd Cavalry*, and part of *27th*, with other troops in reserve. The enemy had also received reinforcements in artillery and machine-gun units. It was therefore probable that his strength in Southern Palestine was 33,000 rifles, 2,200 sabres, 130 machine guns, and 120 guns; and in all south of Damascus 45,000 rifles, 2,200 sabres, 133 machine guns and 132 guns.

After describing his own position and stating his intention of constructing a branch railway from Rafah to Shellal, to enable operations to be carried out on a broader front, Sir A. Murray pointed out that the scope of such operations must necessarily be limited by the fact that he had still only three fully equipped divisions and that they were all under strength. In the case of the 75th Division he considered it doubtful whether any of the units from India, Aden or East Africa, of which it was to be composed, would be available to take the field before the end of the summer.

He stated in conclusion that, without complaining of either the strength or composition of his troops, he desired that the situation should be fully understood and that there should be no misapprehension as to the causes of the cessation of his advance. He was definitely of opinion that his strength was insufficient to attempt further offensive operations for the time being.

It was now, therefore, clear that either the projected invasion of Palestine must be abandoned or reinforcements must be sent to the E.E.F. The Prime Minister and the War Cabinet were not prepared to consider the former alternative. To them it appeared that the Palestine theatre

REORGANIZATION OF MOUNTED TROOPS 357

offered great opportunities in return for a relatively small expenditure of means, and that a strong and prolonged offensive might result in eliminating Turkey from the war. The check represented by the First Battle of Gaza, the definite reverse in the Second Battle, were but spurs to new endeavour. For the moment the infantry divisions demanded by Sir A. Murray could not be sent, but he was considerably reinforced in other arms. The value of mounted troops on this front was recognized, and it was decided to return the 7th and 8th Mounted (Yeomanry) Brigades, which had been transferred to Macedonia. These brigades arrived in June and early July, bringing the total of mounted brigades to ten : five Yeomanry, four Australian, and one New Zealand. Sir A. Murray then decided to reorganize his mounted troops into three divisions, each of three brigades, retaining one brigade as army troops. The new division, to command which Major-General G. de S. Barrow was sent from France, was given the title of the " Yeomanry Mounted Division," and consisted entirely of Yeomanry brigades. The name of the Imperial Mounted Division was changed, on the removal of one Yeomanry brigade, to " Australian Mounted Division." The mounted troops of the Desert Column now consisted of the following :—

1917.
May-June.

A. & N.Z. Mounted Division (Major-General E. W. C. Chaytor)—
1st and 2nd L.H. Brigades, N.Z.M.R. Brigade ;
XVIII Brigade R.H.A. (18-pdrs.)

Australian Mounted Division (Major-General H. W. Hodgson)—
3rd and 4th L.H. Brigades, 5th Mounted Brigade ;
XIX Brigade R.H.A. (18-pdrs.)

Yeomanry Mounted Division (Major-General G. de S. Barrow)—
6th, 8th and 22nd Mounted Brigades ;
XX Brigade R.H.A. (13-pdrs.).

Army Troops—
7th Mounted Brigade (two regiments) ;[1]
Essex Battery R.H.A.

The batteries attached to the mounted troops were four-gun. The field artillery despatched by the War Office enabled the infantry divisions to be equipped with six-gun

---
[1] The Derbyshire Yeomanry was retained in Macedonia.

batteries—the 53rd and 74th with eight, the 52nd, 54th and 75th with seven. The last-named division (Major-General P. C. Palin) was constituted on the 21st June from units sent from abroad or hitherto in Egypt. Each brigade had for the time being three battalions only, two Territorial and one Indian, as follows :—

232nd Brigade—
1/5th Devon, 2/5th Hampshire, 2/3rd Gurkhas.
233rd Brigade—
1/5th Somerset L.I., 2/4th Hampshire, 3/3rd Gurkhas.
234th Brigade—
2/L. North Lancashire, 1/4th D.C.L.I., 123rd Outram's Rifles.

The 29th Indian Brigade was broken up to supply the new formation with troops, and its place in the Southern Section of the Canal Defences taken by the recently formed 49th Indian Brigade, hitherto "force troops" of the Eastern Force.

Both France and Italy desired to show their flags in this theatre and had obtained permission to despatch contingents to serve in the E.E.F. The French detachment, which was the more important, arrived on the 25th May and consisted of three battalions,[1] with cavalry, artillery, engineers and medical units. The small Italian contingent, some five hundred strong, was sent up from Port Said to Rafah on the 13th June.

Finally, the War Cabinet decided to reinforce the E.E.F. by a division from Salonika, and the War Office selected the 60th (London) Division, consisting of second-line Territorial battalions, which had seen some service on the Western Front before being sent to the Mediterranean. The arrival of this division began on the 14th June.

Communications and Water Supply.

May 8.
Sketch B.
It was clear as soon as the War Cabinet decided considerably to augment the E.E.F. that the single-line railway across Sinai was to be taxed to the uttermost. It appeared to Sir A. Murray that the railway advisers of the C.I.G.S., with the well-ballasted tracks of Europe in their minds, might expect his line to carry more traffic than was within

---

[1] 5/115th Territorial Regiment, 7/1st and 9/2nd Algerian Tirailleurs

CAPACITY OF SINAI RAILWAY

its capacity, and he was anxious that his situation in this respect should be thoroughly understood. On the 7th May he wrote at length on this matter to the C.I.G.S. He explained that railhead, at Deir el Balah, was 140 miles from the Suez Canal at Qantara. Thirteen trains a day could now be despatched from Qantara to Deir el Balah, but of these six were "obligatory trains," required for the normal services of railway construction and maintenance, and hospital trains; leaving seven trains a day for supplies, stores, and the movement of troops. This service would just suffice to maintain a fighting force of five infantry divisions, together with the mounted troops and those on the Lines of Communication. When, therefore, the 74th and 75th Divisions were fully organized the system would be strained to its full limit. The Commander-in-Chief had not yet heard of the intention to reinforce the E.E.F. by the 60th Division, so did not include that formation in his calculations. Sea transport also he left out, valuable as it had hitherto proved, because, owing to the nature of the coast and the activities of German submarines, it was unreliable, especially in autumn and winter, when likely to be most needed.

It was therefore necessary to forecast the extent of future demands on the line, since the transport of troops to Egypt could obviously be effected far more rapidly than the expansion of its capacity. It was unlikely that further offensive operations would be instituted before the end of the summer, but during the next three months all efforts should be concentrated upon the improvement of communications. The alternative methods of accomplishing this purpose were either to increase the capacity of the single line by making additional crossing-places, enlarging stations, and providing more engines and rolling stock; or to double the line.

It was estimated that the former measure would permit an increase of three trains a day, or sufficient to maintain at the front a total of six infantry divisions, three mounted divisions and auxiliary services. The larger project would involve the provision of railway material of every description from the United Kingdom or elsewhere, for the State Railways of Egypt had already given all they could afford. The doubling of the line from Qantara to Gaza would probably take eight months. Sir A. Murray proposed to proceed with the minor scheme at once, while awaiting instructions regarding the greater, which must depend on the decision of the War Cabinet upon future policy in the theatre of war. His advice was that the line should be doubled. He asked for an early decision, so that no time should be lost, especially in view of the projected visit to Egypt of the Director-General of Transportation, with whom he desired to discuss the question in the light of the War Cabinet's decision.

The C.I.G.S. replied that, though it was as yet impossible to predict exactly what reinforcements would be sent, Sir A. Murray should be prepared to maintain at and beyond railhead six divisions and three cavalry divisions by July. It was considered by the railway authorities in the United Kingdom that the single-line railway, if fully developed, would be capable of maintaining one infantry division in excess of the figures quoted. Finally, he asked whether Egypt was making the fullest possible contribution to the requirements of war. Sir A. Murray informed him that, so far as the railways were concerned, the civil authorities had done their utmost and Sir G. Macauley had met all his demands. The larger question of Egypt's effort we must leave for the moment, to be discussed when we turn to consider the general state of the country after over two-and-a-half years of war with Turkey.

During this period the Inland Water Transport service was expanded, and began to produce excellent results, though the conditions could never permit them to equal those in Mesopotamia. Its expansion made for efficiency as well as economy, for longshore and canal work can be done better and more quickly by those whose life's business it is than by deep-sea sailors. Small craft under this organization were now to a great extent employed along the coast. From January to April only 5,000 tons a week were carried by this service; between April and July the average had risen to 26,000 tons. It was estimated that thereby about a hundred trucks a day were saved on the railway. The Suez Canal Company had given its consent to the construction of ocean wharves at Qantara, so that large ships could be unloaded there rather than at Alexandria. This was an important convenience, particularly in the case of shipping from India.

The problem of water supply was at least as important as that of communications. With regard to the

PIPE-LINE AND LOCAL WELLS

1917.
May-June.

pipe-line the curious situation had now been reached that only a fraction of the vast quantity of water pumped from Qantara—one-sixteenth, in fact—was drunk by the troops in contact with the enemy. The 12-inch pipe still extended no further than El Arish, but 6-inch, 5-inch, and 4-inch piping had been picked up from lines in rear no longer required, and laid to Abu Bakra, on the Wadi Ghazze south of Tell el Jemmi.

Yet only 36,500 gallons of the 600,000 pumped daily from Qantara reached pipehead, the remainder being required for the needs of the railway and of troops and labourers between the two points,[1] while 100,000 gallons were carried from Rafah to Deir el Balah by rail. In supplying the War Office with these figures Sir A. Murray stated that the output of pumps and filters had been estimated below their maximum power, in order to allow in the calculations a margin of safety. The daily supply to pipehead might be increased temporarily to 65,000 gallons. Though all possible precautions were taken, a certain danger of breakdown in the system must exist, and this would completely disorganize railway traffic and the supply of water to the troops. In these circumstances Sir A. Murray suggested that the pipe-line should be doubled.

Large supplies of water were now found locally. Stone-lined wells at Khan Yunis produced over 100,000 gallons a day. Wells at Deir el Balah produced a considerable quantity, but of inferior quality, and this was used only for animals. At Shellal 200,000 gallons of good water was available, and it had been decided to install pumps and piping to drive it forward in the direction of Abu Hureira. Deep boring was being instituted at various points along the Wadi Ghazze, while near its mouth shallow wells had been sunk which supplied water for two divisions. Though the fact is not mentioned in the official reports, it is of interest to record that ancient cisterns at Um Jerrar, on the bank of the Ghazze between the Wadis Nukhabir and Sheria, were reopened. This place is generally identified with the Gerar of Genesis,[2] where the herdsmen of Abimelech strove with the herdsmen of Isaac for the right to dig for water.

---

[1] A table showing the employment of water from the pipe-line is given in Note at end of Chapter.
[2] Sir Flinders Petrie, however, identifies Tell el Jemmi with the ancient city of Gerar. "Antiquity," September 1927, pp. 348–51.

Yet, though these local supplies were considerable, it was impossible to foresee what would be the effect of the hot weather upon them; some diminution seemed almost inevitable. Moreover, though the Turks, at least at the two extremities of their line, were fairly well supplied with water, there was little between their line and the Wadi Ghazze. The success of any offensive movement therefore depended on the speedy capture of Gaza or Beersheba, with the wells intact.[1]

Minor Operations.

Map 2.
Sketch B.
Neither side was for the moment in a position to institute operations on a large scale, but each attempted to harass the other by means of aerial bombing and minor enterprises. On the 24th April a squadron of the 7th A.L.H. surrounded and captured a troop of Turkish cavalry in the noonday haze, 5 miles south-west of Shellal. The German aeroplanes showed considerable activity. On the 4th May five of them appeared over Deir el Balah and dropped bombs which caused 30 casualties. Six days later the British aeroplanes carried out in retaliation a bombing raid on Beersheba, with apparent success.

Between the 7th and 14th May a detachment of Imperial Camel Corps[2] from the L. of C. Defences was despatched to Kossaima and El Auja, on the section of the Turkish railway south of Beersheba, to destroy wells. A large number were blown up and the masonry of a bridge also damaged by

---

[1] The Turks in May had but 40,000 men and 10,000 beasts to provide for, as against 100,000 men (including Egyptians of Labour and Camel Transport Corps) and 70,000 horses, mules and camels, on the British side. For this force they were able to produce about 250,000 gallons a day, giving a man rather over 4½ gallons and an animal rather over 6¼ gallons— the former a fairly good measure, the latter a niggardly one according to British estimates, but the country ponies of Palestine require less water than European horses. Thanks to German assistance, they were well equipped with pumping machinery. There were in or just behind Gaza five wells with motor pumps and the same number at Beersheba, with a dozen on the rest of the front, but for the most part some distance behind it. Their one great difficulty, in fact, was to supply the front about Hureira. There were also, it need hardly be added, numerous wells with pumps worked by hand. Boring, in some cases to a depth of 250 feet, was carried out by a German detachment of one officer and 68 men (*Bohr-Sonderkommando I*), to which a Turkish labour company was attached. ("Sinai": Range, ii, pp. 93–105.)

[2] Nos. 2 and 16 Companies, a detachment of the engineer field troop, and two motor ambulances.

explosives. A train was fired on near El Auja, but escaped. Five railwaymen were captured, who supplied the important information that they had instructions to pick up rails south of El Auja, for use upon the new branch from Et Tine to supply the front at Gaza, of which mention has already been made. The line south of Beersheba, though largely abandoned by the enemy, was capable of serving him in two ways: the fifteen miles or so of rails south of El Auja would be of considerable value to him, while by using the line as far as that place for the transport and supply of troops he might be able to launch a raiding attack on the British communications.[1]

1917. May.

Sir P. Chetwode therefore determined to carry out the destruction of this section of the railway upon a large scale. The operation was not easy, owing to lack of water, and to the risk of an attack from Beersheba. It was decided to despatch two columns: one against Asluj, 12 miles south of Beersheba, the other against El Auja. The former column, which was to march from Shellal on the Wadi Ghazze, through Khelasa, was to consist of the 1st L.H. Brigade as escort to the engineer field squadrons of the A. & N.Z. and Imperial Mounted Divisions; the latter, starting from Rafah, of the Imperial Camel Brigade, including its engineer field troop. The engineers, to whom a number of picked men from the regiments were attached, were carefully trained for several days, and the whole work was mapped out and organized in advance as a drill. During the operation the Imperial Mounted Division was ordered to demonstrate south-west of Beersheba, while a wire-cutting bombardment was carried out against the Gaza defences.

The demolition parties accompanying the northern column reached Asluj at 7 a.m. on the 23rd May, and by 10 a.m. seven miles of railway had been made unserviceable, alternate rails on both sides being cut in half by the explosion of a small charge. The imposing 18-arch ashlar bridge at Asluj was destroyed, every second arch being blown clean out from the haunches. The Camel Brigade, which left Rafah early on the 22nd and followed the line of the Egyptian frontier to Auja, was delayed by the difficulties of the route and the fatigue of its camels, and did not reach the railway

23 May.

---

[1] The patrol found excellent masonry buildings, barracks, a hospital and large reservoir at this place.

until 11.45 a.m. on the 23rd. However, as the line was now interrupted further north, this detachment was able to work in security. In all 13 miles of rails were damaged, and seven bridges cut. The columns returned unmolested by the enemy.

This was the biggest operation carried out, but there were numerous raids on the pattern of those familiar on the Western Front. On the 18th May offensive patrolling began with the bombing of the Turkish trenches on " Umbrella Hill," an advanced Turkish position west of the Rafah-Gaza road, so called from a flat-topped tree on its crest, and destined to obtain notoriety in the Third Battle of Gaza. On the 5th June the enemy captured or killed the whole of a section of the 5/Scots Fusiliers, which occupied a post in advance of the main line near the same point.[1] On the evening of the 11th, the 5/K.O.S.B. avenged this loss by a brilliant raid on the most easterly Turkish post on the shore, 12 wounded prisoners being taken and all the remaining Turks in the post—at least fifty—being killed, while the raiding party had no casualties. Opposite Umbrella Hill a feint attack, with dummy figures, was staged to divert the enemy's fire. A long series of raids, particularly by the 52nd and 54th Divisions, followed: not all completely successful, but resulting in the establishment of a definite British superiority in No Man's Land.

By the month of June the troops, despite the heat, had thrown off the ill effects of their defeat in the Second Battle of Gaza, and, thanks to vigorous instruction, the Eastern Force was better trained than when it entered on that offensive. The weapon was being made sharp which was in the autumn to strike so heavy a blow.

Egypt and the War.

In answer to Sir W. Robertson's question whether Egypt was " pulling her weight " in the war, Sir A. Murray touched upon a very important political problem. So far Egypt had, without doubt, borne little of the strain of the war. But then her position was unique among the nations taking part in it, for she was a belligerent neither by virtue

---

[1] 2nd-Lieut. J. M. Craig, 5/Scots Fusiliers, who headed a rescue party, was awarded the Victoria Cross for gallantry in bringing in wounded men under intense fire.

of being an independent ally nor, strictly speaking, as a member of the British Empire. Sir A. Murray and the newly appointed High Commissioner, Sir R. Wingate, had given anxious consideration to this question and had decided that there were only two means by which the country could render greater assistance : personnel and further support from her railways.

With regard to the former Sir A. Murray called attention to Sir J. Maxwell's proclamation of the 6th November 1914, with its assurance that Great Britain took upon herself the sole burden of the war without calling on Egyptians for aid therein. Despite this there were serving under voluntary engagements 15,000 men of the Egyptian Army, mainly in the Sudan, where their excellent work has been recorded, but also three battalions with the E.E.F., and 98,000 labourers, of whom 23,000 were overseas. No great increase could be expected under voluntary enlistment, while, if it were obtained, it might result in a decreased production of cotton and food. Compulsory recruitment also might affect unfortunately the existing internal situation, which was still fairly satisfactory.

In the case of the railways it did not appear that more line could be picked up for use in Sinai without adversely affecting the conduct of the war in other respects; for, in a country where there were few wheeled vehicles and hardly any metalled roads outside the large towns, the railways were almost the sole means of transporting produce such as cotton, sugar, cereals, and forage to the centres of consumption and the ports. Sir G. Macauley was, however, prepared to pick up the line from Alexandria to Dabaa—the Khedivial Railway, mentioned in connection with the campaign against the Senussi—should there be urgent necessity.

The Egyptian people, generally speaking, had from the first disliked martial law, lightly as it was administered, and their dislike had grown no weaker as time passed. But it had been found to be absolutely necessary, in order to give the military authorities some measure of control over foreign European residents, to allow them to take precautions against enemy agents and to intern at least such enemy subjects as showed themselves dangerous. It also gave them a certain power—though less than they required—to control prostitution and the sale of liquor. Venereal disease can be as wasting to an army as the weapons of the enemy;

unlimited liquor, especially bad liquor, is a serious, if lesser, evil. Besides, drink leads men, their minds stupefied, to haunts that when sober they would avoid. Unfortunately the profitable trades of liquor-vending and prostitution were both largely in the hands of Europeans of a low type, who were partially protected, even against the working of martial law, by the Capitulations. The limitation of hours during which drink could be sold, the shutting of those drink-shops which broke the regulations, gradually produced an effect. Venereal disease remained a curse throughout the war, but its prevalence decreased to a great extent when the bulk of the force moved away from Egypt.

The Government of the Sultan of Egypt had, as has been stated in earlier chapters, from the first co-operated loyally with the military authorities, and continued to do so. But a change was appearing gradually in the temper of the country; the earlier good feeling was vanishing and that discontent was breeding which was to come to life in the revolt of two years later, when the war was over.

The causes of this unhappy change were numerous. One was that the campaign had been carried beyond the Sinai frontier. The Turks had been driven off Egyptian soil, and many Egyptians, hitherto ready enough to meet British demands for supplies and labour, felt that the war no longer concerned them. What was Palestine to Egypt? Then, again, the Egyptian Government, as the calls for labour increased with the expansion of the force, introduced, instead of conscription, what amounted to the old *Corvée*—forced labour—in new form, though differing very markedly from its predecessor, in that labour was now highly paid by the British. Each district was required to find a certain number of recruits, and the Government were not over particular as to the fashion in which local *mudirs* obtained them. The departure to rejoin their former regiments of many British officials with long service in Egypt and a thorough knowledge of its people also had unhappy effects.

These misfortunes of war may be conveniently mentioned here, though they did not reach serious proportions until the winter of 1917, a period which belongs to the second volume of this history. And, as we have anticipated in this respect, it may be added that the transfer of G.H.Q. from Cairo to the front rendered necessary by the autumn campaign in Palestine, which removed the Commander-in-Chief from close touch with the civil authorities, contributed in some degree to the difficulties of the situation. General Sir R. Wingate, actually the senior general officer, by "Army List" dates, in this theatre, suggested that, in view of the complications caused by the prolonged enforcement of martial law in a friendly country, he should be entrusted with its administration. It was, however, decided that this function must remain in the hands of the Commander-in-Chief. Yet another ill effect upon friendly relations was the death in October 1917 of Sultan Hussein of Egypt, a firm and loyal friend to Great Britain.

The growing unrest, part political, part religious, part economic, necessitated the retention of troops in Egypt, but had no great effect upon the course of the war, since garrison battalions sufficed for the maintenance of order and security. The brevity of this record must not obscure the fact that throughout the campaign the Egyptian Government followed what they conceived to be their duty, without deviation or compromise. Still less must be forgotten the invaluable service rendered in Sinai by the Egyptian Labour and Camel Transport Corps, or the even greater service they were to render and the hardships they were to undergo in Palestine.

NOTE.

TABLE SHOWING USE OF WATER FROM THE PIPE-LINE.

The plant at Qantara supplied to Romani daily	600,000 gallons.
Of this the railway and troops at Romani required 100,000 gallons.	
Of the 500,000 thus available the pumping plant at Romani could force to El Abd	480,000 ,,
Here railway and troops required	75,000 ,,
Leaving available to pump to Mazar	405,000 ,,
Here railway and troops required	75,000 ,,
Leaving available to pump to Arish	330,000 ,,
Here railway required	100,000 ,,
Leaving available for distribution east of Arish	230,000 ,,
Arish supplied to Deir el Balah by rail	100,000 ,,
Leaving available to pump to Rafah	130,000 ,,
Estimated railway requirements to railhead	93,500 ,,
Reached pipehead	36,500 ,,

CHAPTER XX.

Sir A. Murray's Recall.

**1917.
11 June.** The commander who had confronted the early difficulties with forces which he had judged and reported to be inadequate, who had made all the essential preparation for the invasion of Palestine, was not destined to reap the harvest of his labours. Like the commanders of many other British "advanced guards" sent to open a campaign with insufficient resources, he was superseded because he had failed to achieve the success expected. On the 11th June Sir A. Murray received a telegram from the Secretary of State informing him that, while fully appreciating the good work he had accomplished, the War Cabinet considered it desirable to make a change in command, and had decided to appoint General Sir E. Allenby to succeed him. He was to return to England after handing over command to General Allenby, who would sail for Egypt within a few days.

At the close of this definitely marked period of the operations it is fitting to reconsider shortly their inception and development.

For the first fifteen months of war with Turkey the defence of the Suez Canal was perforce conducted by Sir J. Maxwell upon its banks. There followed the phase of the first months of 1916, when an elaborate system of more distant defence was constructed. This was designed to prevent the enemy from bringing the Canal under gun fire, and in preparation for resistance to that large-scale Turkish offensive which was expected to follow the evacuation of Gallipoli. This period was also that in which the battle-worn and depleted units from the Dardanelles were landed in Egypt, to be restored and re-equipped, to take their places in the defences, and then, when they were again ready for active service, and when danger on the scale first contemplated had faded away, to be transported to France and elsewhere, leaving only four infantry divisions in the country.

Then came the third phase, which led so far, but began merely as a natural development of the second. The advance into Sinai was made with the sole object of occupying the Qatiya basin, in order to deny that area and its water to the enemy. There followed a check inflicted by the enemy at Qatiya in April and an attack by a Turkish expeditionary force at Romani in August. That apparently foolhardy venture, undertaken against heavy odds, was in fact a dangerous threat to the British, because in the climatic conditions the Turkish infantryman was a most formidable foe ; because the sun and the desert were his allies. Its complete defeat definitively robbed the enemy of the initiative. Then the British advance was continued towards El Arish, still with no intention of invading Palestine, but in accordance with the principle enunciated by the Commander-in-Chief, that " the true base of the defensive zone of Egypt against " invasion from the east was not the 80 or 90 miles of the " Canal Zone, but the 45 miles between El Arish and El " Kossaima."[1]

During the remainder of the summer heat, during the months of autumn and early winter, rail and pipe and wire road were driven forward across the desert, the desert itself being for the moment the most serious opponent to be met and conquered. The enterprise was in this phase an " engineer's war " and, it may fairly be said, typically British : resolute in the extreme, pursued with great material resources and without limit as to cost. No difficulties called a halt, scarce even a pause. The rails and piping were drawn from the four continents of Europe, Asia, Africa and America ; that is, from the home country, from India, from Egypt herself, and from the United States. The objective was attained by the year's end, and then, the enemy being again within striking reach, heavy blows were struck with the mobile forces at Magdhaba and Rafah.

Before these actions were fought or El Arish reached the Commander-in-Chief was asked to submit his proposals for action beyond that place and to state what additional troops he required for the purpose. He was at the same time instructed to make the maximum effort possible during the winter. He outlined his proposals. He stated that he needed two more infantry divisions, one to advance to the frontier at Rafah—though that much he was prepared to attempt with the four then at his disposal—and one more

---

[1] See p. 171.

for a subsequent advance into Palestine. He was next informed that the troops for which he had asked could not then be spared and that his primary mission was still the defence of Egypt; and a little later he was told that the inception of operations on a large scale in Palestine must be postponed until the autumn of 1917. In early March of that year one of his four divisions was withdrawn to France.

At almost the same moment the enemy, who had been holding a position at Shellal, suddenly evacuated it and withdrew to Gaza and Tell esh Sheria. To prevent the Turks again avoiding contact by a repetition of these tactics, which the Commander-in-Chief considered probable, and to bring them to action, he then ordered his lieutenant to carry out the *coup de main* against Gaza, that so narrowly failed to reproduce on a greater scale the successful cutting-out operations of Magdhaba and Rafah.

Again the War Cabinet changed its policy, influenced, it would seem—apart from the favourable aspect of affairs in Mesopotamia—less by the Commander-in-Chief's actual reports of the battle which he had just fought than by the tone of his telegrams and his estimate of the enemy's losses. He was now instructed to make his object the defeat of the Turks south of Jerusalem and the occupation of that city. His reply was cautious; he repeated his earlier statement of his requirements, with a word of warning that, should the enemy hold a series of strong positions, heavy fighting and serious losses must be expected. But the War Cabinet now believed that he was in a position to defeat the enemy, and was naturally eager for a success to give new heart to the people at home, strained and made uneasy by the cost and apparently meagre results of the offensive on the Western Front. He was urged to conduct offensive operations with the greatest possible vigour. In the interval of necessary preparation the Turks were reinforced, but not heavily, the complete change in the military situation being brought about rather by the fact that they were given time to prepare a strong defensive position. With any resolute opponent this would have been important; in the case of the Turk it was doubly so. He has often shown himself lacking in the qualities of good subordinate leadership, mental elasticity and vigour, so valuable in warfare of manœuvre, but his resolution in defending prepared positions and in local counteraction to retain them has always been unquestionable.

The sequel was the Second Battle of Gaza, with the immediate strategical result and the effect upon military policy which have been described.

There have been no major operations, by the standard which the war created in Europe, to describe in this narrative. There are three short battles only: Romani, First Gaza, Second Gaza. The attack on the Suez Canal, though potentially of more consequence than any of these, was practically unimportant because this almost hopeless Turkish enterprise did not develop into a considerable battle and because the reserves on neither side were committed. The other engagements, whether officially designated " affairs," as Wadi Majid, Wadi Senab, Halazin, Qatiya, Magdhaba, or " actions," as Agagiya and Rafah, were all on a small scale. None the less is the period notable in the annals of the Great War and British military annals generally.

The earliest conditions were those of improvisation, political as well as military. Hardly were they stabilized and the enemy's attempt upon the Empire's most vital communications repelled, when another campaign, that of Gallipoli, transformed Egypt into a great base and denuded her of fighting troops. Danger from the east was at the same time reduced, for Gallipoli also deprived the enemy in Palestine of offensive power; but the command in Egypt was left ill prepared to face the attempted invasion from the west by the Senussi. That involved a campaign in which, while numbers were not great, distances were vast and the issue of no small moment. Before it had been brought to a successful conjuncture by Sir J. Maxwell, to be completely liquidated by Sir A. Murray, the divisions from Gallipoli and additional troops from the United Kingdom had arrived. For a few weeks there was concentrated in Egypt the largest British army ever collected in the course of the war in any theatre but that of France.[1] The evacuation of Gallipoli had freed a large Turkish army; the project of a British landing in the Gulf of Iskanderun to cut Turkish

---

[1] The combined ration strength of the M.E.F. and Force in Egypt, exclusive of hospital patients, was approximately 275,000 on the 2nd March 1916. The ration strength of the E.E.F. on the 28th October 1917, the eve of the Third Battle of Gaza, was less by over 50,000. It is true that in the latter case there is not included a total of about 70,000 unattested Egyptians, but we are here referring to troops. During the Gallipoli campaign the high-water mark, including troops on the islands and in the Egyptian bases, was little above 200,000.

communication with the East had been vetoed; and it was anticipated that the enemy would repeat his attack on the Suez Canal upon a scale vastly greater than that of the previous year. An offensive was, in fact, contemplated by him, but, we now know, magnified unduly in the imagination of both Turks and Britons—by would-be attackers as well as defenders. Yet the moment was one of uncertainty, and it appeared advisable to retain a great reserve in Egypt until Turkey had disclosed her intentions. The army assembled on the Canal and in the Delta was the Empire's strategic reserve.

Meanwhile Egypt had become the principal base of a new campaign in Macedonia, had sent a force to the rescue of Aden, and the bulk of her original Indian garrison to Mesopotamia. All this time—and this was a permanent condition—the command was unavoidably drawn into the current of politics, occupied with the administration of martial law and with countering the devices of intrigue.

That phase passed; the concentration dispersed; the battle with the desert began. This, apart from its engineering achievements, is made chiefly notable by the work of the light horse and mounted rifles of Australia and New Zealand, these young nations laying the foundation of a record which will not be forgotten in the history of mounted warfare. In its midst broke out the revolt of the Arabs in the Hejaz, to be assisted by British counsel, British officers, British munitions of war, food and gold, to be thenceforth, up to the last day of fighting, a thorn in the enemy's side. The advance across Sinai and into Palestine was brought to a halt before Gaza, and this phase ended with a rebuff.

This was the past, and despite the last check, much had been accomplished to brighten the present and create hope for the future. Sinai had been cleared of the enemy, and all danger to the Suez Canal removed. The physical difficulties of the road to Palestine had been subjugated. No enemy was behind; Egypt herself, if there were sullenness among a section of her people, was quiet and prosperous. The Arab Revolt had been fostered and supported until it had become an important factor in the war. All was prepared for Britain, if she so desired, to put forth in this theatre efforts far greater than before and to concentrate against that Ally of the Central Powers, who here stood in arms against her, strength enough for decisive victory to be ensured.

APPENDICES.

APPENDIX 1.

TABULAR RECORD

EGYPT AND

From Outbreak of

Operations.	Battles.	Actions, etc.
		SUDAN.
Operations against the Sultan of Darfur (1st March–31st Dec. 1916).	.. ..	Affair of Beringia ..
		Affair of Giuba ..
		WESTERN
Operations against the Senussi (23rd Nov. 1915–8th Feb. 1917)	.. ..	Affair of the Wad Senab.
		Affair of the Wad Majid.
		Affair of Halazin ..
		Action of Agagiya..
		Affairs in the Dakhla Oasis.
		Affairs near the Siwa Oasis.

* The nomenclature and dates are those contained in the Official Report

OF OPERATIONS.

PALESTINE.

War to June 1917.*

Limits.		Forces engaged.	
Chronological.	Geographical.	British.	Enemy.
22nd May	Area covered by Lieut.-Col. Kelly's Force of the Egyptian Army.	8 guns, Egyptian Mtn. Arty; 14 Maxims; 8 Coys. Inf. (13th and 14th Sudanese and Arab Bn.).	The Sultan's Slave Army, 3,600 strong, with Auxiliaries.
6th Nov.	.. .. ..	1 Mtn. gun, 150 rifles, 13th Sudanese.	Remnants of Sultan's Army, a few hundreds strong.

FRONTIER.

11th–13th Dec. 1915.	Area covered by force under Lieut.-Col. J. L. R. Gordon.	Notts. Bty. R.H.A.; 2nd Comp. Yeo. Regt; 15th Sikhs (part of); 6th R. Scots (part of).	1,000–1,500 Senussist Regulars Auxiliaries 2 guns.
25th Dec. 1915	Area covered by the two columns under Major-General A. Wallace.	Notts. Bty. R.H.A.; Comp. Yeo. Bde.; 15th Sikhs; 1st N.Z. Rifle Bde.; 2/8th Middlesex.	3 Bns. (1,000 rifles) Senussist Regulars; Auxiliaries; 4 Mtn. guns.
23rd Jan. 1916		Notts. Bty. R.H.A.; "A" Bty. H.A.C.; Comp. Yeo. Bde.; 15th Sikhs; 2nd S. African Inf.; 1st N.Z. Rifle Bde.; 6th R. Scots; 2/8th Middlesex.	4 Bns. (1,200 rifles) Senussist Regulars; Auxiliaries; 4 Mtn. guns.
26th Feb. 1916	Area covered by the Force under Brig.-General H. T. Lukin.	Dorset Yeo.; Bucks Yeo. (1 Sqdn.); Notts. Bty., R.H.A.; ½ S.A. Inf. Bde. (1st and 3rd S.A. Inf.); 6th R. Scots; Sabres 400, rifles 2,000.	1,600 Senussist Regulars; Auxiliaries; 4 Mtn. guns.
17th–22nd Oct. 1916.	.. .. ..	Imperial Camel Corps; Light Armoured Cars; Light Car Patrols.	
3rd–5th Feb. 1917.	Siwa Oasis to Munassib.	Light Armoured Cars; Light Car Patrols.	1,200 Senussists; 2 Mtn. guns.

of the "Battles Nomenclature Committee." (H.M. Stationery Office, 1922.)

APPENDIX 1

EASTERN FRONTIER

I. THE DEFENCE

Operations.	Battles.	Actions, etc.
Defence of the Suez Canal (26th Jan. 1915–12th Aug. 1916).	.. .. ..	Actions on the Suez Canal.
		Affair of Qatiya ..
	Battle of Romani ..	.. .. ..
Operations in the Sinai Peninsula (15th Nov. 1916–9th Jan. 1917).	.. .. ..	Affair of Magdhaba
		Action of Rafah ..

* 4th–6th Aug. are the limits given in the Report. This excludes the

APPENDIX 1

AND PALESTINE.

OF EGYPT.

Limits.		Forces engaged.	
Chronological	Geographical.	British.	Enemy.
3rd–4th Feb. 1915.	East of the Suez–Qantara Railway.	R.F.C. (1 flight); 1 French Seaplane Flight; Imperial Ser. Cav. Bde.; Herts Yeo.; Westminster Yeo.; D.L.O. Yeo. (1 Sqdn.); Bikanir Camel Corps; 2 Btys., 42nd Divl. Arty.; 5th Bty., Egyptian Army; 10th Indian Div.; 11th Indian Div. (part of); N.Z. Inf. Bde. (part of).	Fourth Army. H.Q.; VIII Corps HQ.; Parts of 29th Cav. Regt. and of 10th, 23rd and 25th Divs. Two 6-in. hows.; 9 batteries Field Artillery; Irregulars. 25,000 men.
23rd April 1916	East of the Suez Canal and north of El Ferdan Station.	5th Mounted Bde.; Bikanir Camel Corps (part of); 4th and 5th R. Scots Fus. (part of). 2nd L.H. Bde.	32nd Regt. 6 Coys. Camelry 6 guns. 3,650 men.
4th–14th Aug. 1916.*	East of the Canal and north of Ismailia.	R.F.C.; A. and N.Z. Mtd. Div. 3rd L.H. Bde.; 5th Mtd. Bde.; 42nd Div.; 52nd Div.; 158th Bde. (53rd Div.); Casualties—1,130.	Expeditionary Force H.Q. 3rd Division; German "Pasha I" Formation; 1 Regt. Camel Corps. 16,000 ration strength; 12,000 fighting strength; 30 guns. Casualties—About 5,500 (including 4,000 prisoners).
23rd Dec. 1916	South and east of Bir Lahfan.	R.F.C.; A. and N.Z. Mtd. Div. (less 2nd L.H. Bde.); Imperial Camel Bde.; Inverness and Somerset Btys. R.H.A.; Hong Kong and Singapore Mtn. Bty.; Casualties—146.	2nd and 3rd Bns., 80th Regt. (27th Div.); 1 Mtn. Bty.; Casualties—Practically all captured (1,282 prisoners, 4 guns).
9th Jan. 1917..	North and east of Sheikh Zowaiid.	R.F.C.; A. and N.Z. Mtd. Div. (less 2nd L.H. Bde.). Artillery—Leicester, Inverness and Somerset Btys. R.H.A.; 5th Mtd. Bde.; Artillery—"B" Bty. H.A.C.; Imperial Camel Bde.; Artillery—Hong Kong and Singapore Bty.; No. 7 Light Car Patrol. Casualties—487.	31st Regt. (3rd Div. 1 Mtn. Bty.; Casualties—Practically all captured (1,635 prisoners, 4 guns).

pursuit, the fighting of Qatiya, and the hard fought action at Bir el Abd.

378 APPENDIX 1

II. THE INVASION

Operations.	Battles.	Actions, etc.
The First Offensive (24th March–19th April 1917).	First Battle of Gaza	.. ..
	Second Battle of Gaza	.. . .

[1] Australian and New Zealand troops are included under this heading, though they did not at this period carry swords.

APPENDIX 1

OF PALESTINE.

Limits.		Forces engaged.	
Chronological.	Geographical.	British.	Enemy.
26th–27th March	North of the line, Beersheba–Deir el Balah.	*Eastern Force* (Dobell): 5th Wing, R.F.C.; Desert Column (Chetwode)—A. and N.Z. Mtd. Div. (less 1st L.H. Bde.), Imperial Mtd. Div. (less 4th L.H. Bde.) Imperial Camel Bde., 53rd Div. and 161st Bde. (54th Div.), 7th Light Car Patrol, 11th and 12th L. Armoured Motor Btys.; 54th Div. (less 161st Bde.); 52nd Div. (not engaged but 2 brigades in area); Right Sections, 10th, 15th and 91st Heavy Btys. (60-pdrs.); Sabres—8,500;[1] Rifles—25,000 (19,000 without 52nd Div.); Guns—92. Casualties—3,967; Captures—837 prisoners, 2 guns.	*Expeditionary Force* (Kress von Kressenstein). Garrison of Gaza (Major Tiller)—125th, 79th, 2/81st Regts., German 10 cm.-Bty., 2 Austrian Heavy Mtn. How. Btys. (12), 2 Turkish Btys.; 3rd Cav., 3rd, 16th, 27th (part of), 53rd (part of) Divs. Sabres—1,500; Rifles—16,000; Guns—74. Casualties—2,447: Captures—246.
17th–19th April	North of the line, Beersheba–Deir el Balah.	*Eastern Force* (Dobell): 5th Wing, R.F.C.; Desert Column (Chetwode)—A. and N.Z. Mtd. Div., Imperial Mtd. Div. 52nd, 53rd, 54th Divs.; 74th Div. (without Arty. and not engaged); Imperial Camel Bde.; 10th, 15th, 91st Heavy Btys. (60-pdrs.); 201st S. Bty. (8-in. and 6-in. hows.); Palestine Det. Tank Corps; 7th Light Car Patrol; 11th and 12th L. Armoured Motor Btys.; 17th Motor Machine Gun Bty.; Sabres—11,000; Rifles—24,000; Guns—170. Casualties—6,444;[2] Captures—200.	*Expeditionary Force* (Kress von Kressenstein) 3rd Cav., 3rd, 16th, 27th (part of), 53rd Divs.; Sabres—1,500; Rifles—18,000; Guns—101. Casualties—2,013;[2] Captures—272.

[2] Casualties in each case are from 17th to 20th April.

APPENDIX 2.

ORDER OF BATTLE
OF THE
EGYPTIAN EXPEDITIONARY FORCE, APRIL 1916.

GENERAL HEADQUARTERS.

Commander-in-Chief	Lieut.-General (temp. General) Sir A. J. Murray, K.C.B., K.C.M.G., C.V.O., D.S.O.
Chief of the General Staff	Major-General A. L. Lynden-Bell, C.B., C.M.G.
Deputy Adjutant-General	Major-General J. Adye, C.B.
Deputy Quartermaster-General	Major-General W. Campbell, C.B., D.S.O.

Attached—

Major-General, Royal Artillery	Colonel (temp. Major-General) S. C. U. Smith.
Engineer-in-Chief	Colonel (temp. Brig.-General) H. B. H. Wright, C.M.G.

HEADQUARTERS OF ADMINISTRATIVE SERVICES AND DEPARTMENTS.

Director of Army Signals	Brevet Colonel (temp. Brig.-General) M. G. E. Bowman-Manifold, D.S.O.
Director of Works	Lieut.-Colonel (temp. Brig.-General) E. M. Paul.
Director of Supplies and Transport.	Lieut.-Colonel (temp. Colonel) G. F. Davies.
Director of Railways	Temp. Colonel Sir G. Macauley, K.C.M.G.
Director of Ordnance Services	Colonel P. A. Bainbridge.
Director of Remounts	Brig.-General C. L. Bates.
Director of Veterinary Services	Colonel (temp. Brig.-General) E. R. C. Butler, C.M.G.
Director of Medical Services	Colonel (temp. Surgeon-General) J. Maher, C.B.
Director of Army Postal Services	Major (temp. Lieut.-Colonel) P. Warren, C.M.G.
Command Paymaster	Colonel J. C. Armstrong.

INSPECTOR-GENERAL OF COMMUNICATIONS AND LEVANT BASE.

Commandant and Inspector-General of Communications	Major-General (temp. Lieut.-General) Sir E. A. Altham, K.C.B., C.M.G.

Australian and New Zealand Mounted Division.

G.O.C.	Colonel (temp. Major-General) H. G. Chauvel, C.B., C.M.G.
G.S.O.1	Major (temp. Lieut.-Colonel) J. G. Browne.

APPENDIX 2

1st Australian Light Horse Brigade (Western Force).

G.O.C. .. .. Lieut.-Colonel C. F. Cox (acting).
    1st Regiment Light Horse ;
    2nd Regiment Light Horse ;
    3rd Regiment Light Horse ;
    Attached—4th Regiment Light Horse.

2nd Australian Light Horse Brigade.

G.O.C. .. .. Colonel (temp. Brig.-General) G. de L. Ryrie, C.M.G.
    5th Regiment Light Horse ;
    6th Regiment Light Horse ;
    7th Regiment Light Horse ;
    Attached—12th Regiment Light Horse.

3rd Australian Light Horse Brigade.

G.O.C. .. .. Brevet Lieut.-Colonel (temp. Brig.-General) J. M. Antill, C.B.
    8th Regiment Light Horse ;
    9th Regiment Light Horse ;
    10th Regiment Light Horse ;
    Attached—11th Regiment Light Horse.

New Zealand Mounted Rifles Brigade.

G.O.C. .. .. Brig.-General E. W. C. Chaytor, C.B.
    Auckland Mounted Rifles Regiment ;
    Canterbury Mounted Rifles Regiment ;
    Wellington Mounted Rifles Regiment ;
    Attached—Otago Mounted Rifles Regiment (less 1 sqdn.).

Divisional Troops.

Artillery .. .. III (T.F.) Brigade, R.H.A.: Leicester and Somerset Batteries.
    IV (T.F.) Brigade, R.H.A.: Inverness and Ayr Batteries.
Engineers .. .. 1st Australian Field Squadron.
Signal Service .. .. .. 1st A. and N.Z. Signal Squadron.
A.S.C. .. .. H.Q., Light Horse Divisional A.S.C.
    Light Horse Supply Column (M.T.).
Medical Units .. .. .. 1st, 2nd and 3rd L.H. Field Ambulances, N.Z. Mounted Brigade Ambulance.

IX CORPS.

G.O.C. .. .. Major-General (temp. Lieut.-General) Sir F. J. Davies, K.C.B., K.C.M.G.
Brigadier-General, General Staff   Brevet Colonel (temp. Brig.-General) H. E. Street, C.M.G.
Brigadier-General, Royal Artillery   Lieut.-Colonel (temp. Brig.-General) C. H. de Rougemont, M.V.O., D.S.O.
Chief Engineer .. .. Colonel (temp. Brig.-General) E. H. Bland.

APPENDIX 2

Corps Troops.

Mounted Troops   *8th Mounted Brigade.*
G.O.C.   Colonel (temp. Brig.-General) A. H. M. Taylor, D.S.O.
1/1st City of London Yeomanry;
1/1st County of London Yeomanry;
1/3rd County of London Yeomanry;
1/1st London Signal Troop;
" B " Battery, H.A.C.;
No. 9 Field Troop;
1/1st London Mounted Brigade Field Ambulance.

Signal Service   " HH " and " KK " Cable Section.
London Pack Wireless Section.
Northern Wagon Wireless Section.

42nd (East Lancashire) Division.

G.O.C.   Major-General Sir W. Douglas, K.C.M.G., C.B.
G.S.O. 1   Major (temp. Lieut.-Colonel) A. Crookenden.
C.R.A.   Brig.-General A. D'A. King, D.S.O.
C.R.E.   Lieut.-Colonel S. L. Tennant.

125th Infantry Brigade.

G.O.C.   Colonel (temp. Brig.-General) H. C. Frith.
1/5th Lancashire Fusiliers;
1/6th Lancashire Fusiliers;
1/7th Lancashire Fusiliers;
1/8th Lancashire Fusiliers;
125th Brigade Machine-Gun Company.

126th Infantry Brigade.

G.O.C.   Major (temp. Brig.-General) A. W. Tufnell.
1/4th East Lancashire Regiment;
1/5th East Lancashire Regiment;
1/9th Manchester Regiment;
1/10th Manchester Regiment;
126th Brigade Machine-Gun Company.

127th Infantry Brigade.

G.O.C.   Lieut.-Colonel (temp. Brig.-General V. A. Ormsby, C.B.
1/5th Manchester Regiment;
1/6th Manchester Regiment;
1/7th Manchester Regiment;
1/8th Manchester Regiment;
127th Brigade Machine-Gun Company.

Divisional Troops.

Mounted Troops   1 Sqdn. Duke of Lancaster's Yeomanry.
13th Cyclist Company.
Artillery   1/1st E. Lancashire Brigade, R.F.A.
1/2nd E. Lancashire Brigade, R.F.A.
1/3rd E. Lancashire Brigade, R.F.A.
1/4th E. Lancashire (How.) Brigade, R.F.A.
42nd Divisional Ammunition Column.

APPENDIX 2

Engineers	.. .. ..	1/1st E. Lancashire Field Company, R.E.
		1/2nd E. Lancashire Field Company, R.E.
		1/2nd W. Lancashire Field Company, R.E.
Signal Service	.. .. ..	42nd Divisional Signal Company.
A.S.C.	.. ..	42nd Divisional Train.
Medical Units	.. .. ..	1/1st, 1/2nd and 1/3rd E. Lancashire Field Ambulances.
Attached	.. ..	*3rd Dismounted Brigade.*
G.O.C.	.. ..	Lieut.-Colonel Lord Kensington, D.S.O. (Acting).

1/1st E. Kent Yeomanry;
1/1st W. Kent Yeomanry;
1/1st Sussex Yeomanry;
1/1st Welsh Horse;
1/1st Norfolk Yeomanry;
1/1st Suffolk Yeomanry;
Machine-Gun Company;
3rd Dismounted Brigade Signal Troop;
1/1st Eastern and 1/1st S. Eastern Mounted Brigade Field Ambulances.

54th (East Anglian) Division.

G.O.C.	.. ..	Colonel (temp. Major-General) S. W. Hare, C.B.
G.S.O. 1	.. .. ..	Major (temp. Lieut.-Colonel) E. C. Da Costa.
C.R.A.	.. .. ..	Colonel (temp. Brig.-General) G. W. Biddulph.
C.R.E.	.. .. ..	Major D. Griffiths.

161st Infantry Brigade.

G.O.C.	.. ..	Colonel (temp. Brig.-General) F. F. W. Daniell.

1/4th Essex Regiment;
1/5th Essex Regiment;
1/6th Essex Regiment;
1/7th Essex Regiment;
161st Brigade Machine-Gun Company.

162nd Infantry Brigade.

G.O.C.	.. ..	Lieut.-Colonel (temp. Brig.-General) A. Mudge.

1/5th Bedford Regiment;
1/4th Northampton Regiment;
1/10th London Regiment;
1/11th London Regiment;
162nd Brigade Machine-Gun Company.

163rd Infantry Brigade.

G.O.C.	.. ..	Major (Hon. Colonel, temp. Brig.-General) T. Ward.

1/4th Norfolk Regiment;
1/5th Norfolk Regiment;
1/5th Suffolk Regiment;
1/8th Hampshire Regiment;
163rd Brigade Machine-Gun Company.

Divisional Troops.

Mounted Troops	1 Sqdn. 1/1st Hertfordshire Yeomanry (with H.Q. and Machine-Gun Section).
Artillery	1/1st E. Anglian Brigade, R.F.A. 1/2nd E. Anglian Brigade, R.F.A. 1/3rd E. Anglian Brigade, R.F.A. 1/4th E. Anglian Brigade, R.F.A. 54th Divisional Ammunition Column (1 officer and 35 other ranks).
Engineers	2/1st E. Anglian Field Company, R.E. 1/2nd E. Anglian Field Company, R.E. 1/1st Kent Field Company, R.E.
Signal Service	54th Divisional Signal Company.
A.S.C.	54th Divisional Train (Supply details only).
Medical Units	2/1st, 1/2nd and 1/3rd E. Anglian Field Ambulances.
Attached	*20th (Indian) Infantry Brigade.*
G.O.C.	Brig.-General H. D. Watson, C.M.G., C.I.E., M.V O.

2/3rd Gurkhas;
58th Rifles;
Alwar Infantry;
Gwalior Infantry.

29th Indian Infantry Brigade.

G.O.C.	Colonel (temp. Brig.General) P. C. Palin.

23rd Pioneers;
57th Rifles;
Patiala Infantry;
No. 10 Co. Q.O. Sappers and Miners;
110, 121 and 135 Indian Field Ambulances;
7th and 26th Mule Corps.

II AUSTRALIAN AND NEW ZEALAND ARMY CORPS.

G.O.C.	Major-General (temp. Lieut.-General) Sir A. J. Godley, K.C.M.G., C.B.
Brigadier-General, General Staff	Major (temp. Brig.-General) C. W. Gwynn, C.M.G., D.S.O.
Brigadier-General, Royal Artillery	Lieut.-Colonel (temp. Brig-General) W. D. Nichol.
Chief Engineer	Major (temp. Brig.-General) W. B. Lesslie.

Corps Troops.

Signal Service	No. 24 Airline Section. "FF" and "NN" Cable Sections. 1st Australian Ammunition Park. 1st Australian Supply Column. Royal Australian Reserve Naval Bridging Train. 14th Fortress Company, R.E.

APPENDIX 2

4th Australian Division.

G.O.C.	Major-General Sir H. V. Cox, K.C.M.G., C.B., C.I.E.
G.S.O. 1	Captain (temp. Lieut.-Colonel) D. J. C. K. Bernard.
C.R.A.	Lieut-Colonel (temp. Brig.-General) C. Rosenthal, C.B.
C.R.E.	Major (temp. Lieut.-Colonel) G. C. E. Elliott.

4th Australian Infantry Brigade.

G.O.C. .. Colonel (temp. Brig.-General) J. Monash, C.B.
    13th Battalion;
    14th Battalion;
    15th Battalion;
    16th Battalion;
    4th Machine-Gun Company.

12th Australian Infantry Brigade.

G.O.C. .. Major (temp. Lieut.-Colonel) D. J. Glasfurd.
    45th Battalion;
    46th Battalion;
    47th Battalion;
    48th Battalion;
    12th Machine-Gun Company.

13th Australian Infantry Brigade.

G.O.C. .. Lieut.-Colonel D. W. Glasgow, D.S.O.
    49th Battalion;
    50th Battalion;
    51st Battalion;
    52nd Battalion;
    13th Machine-Gun Company.

Divisional Troops.

Mounted Troops	"B" Sqdn., 13th Light Horse Regiment. 4th Divisional Cyclist Company.
Artillery	X Field Artillery Brigade. XI Field Artillery Brigade. XII Field Artillery Brigade. XXIV Howitzer Brigade. 4th Divisional Ammunition Column.
Engineers	4th Field Company. 12th Field Company. 13th Field Company.
Signal Service	4th Divisional Signal Company.
Pioneers	4th Pioneer Battalion.
A.S.C.	7th, 14th, 26th and 27th Coys., A.A.S.C.
Medical Units	4th, 12th and 13th Field Ambulances.

APPENDIX 2

5th Australian Division.

G.O.C.	Colonel (temp. Major-General) Hon. J. W. McCay, C.B.
G.S.O. 1	Major (temp. Lieut.-Colonel) C. M. Wagstaff, C.I.E., D.S.O.
C.R.A.	Lieut.-Colonel (temp. Brig.-General) S. E. Christian, C.M.G.
C.R.E.	Major (temp. Lieut.-Colonel) A. B. Carey, C.M.G.

8th Australian Infantry Brigade.

G.O.C. .. Colonel (temp. Brig.-General) E. Tivey, D.S.O.

29th Battalion ;
30th Battalion ;
31st Battalion ;
32nd Battalion ;
8th Machine-Gun Company.

14th Australian Infantry Brigade.

G.O.C. .. Colonel (temp. Brig.-General) G. G. H. Irving.

53rd Battalion ;
54th Battalion ;
55th Battalion ;
56th Battalion ;
14th Machine-Gun Company.

15th Australian Infantry Brigade.

G.O.C. .. Lieut.-Colonel (temp. Colonel) H. E. Elliott.

57th Battalion ;
58th Battalion ;
59th Battalion ;
60th Battalion ;
15th Machine-Gun Company.

Divisional Troops.

Mounted Troops	" C " Sqdn., 13th Light Horse Regiment. 5th Divisional Cyclist Company.
Artillery	XIII Field Artillery Brigade. XIV Field Artillery Brigade. XV Field Artillery Brigade. XXV Howitzer Brigade. 5th Divisional Ammunition Column.
Engineers	8th Field Company. 14th Field Company. 15th Field Company.
Signal Service	5th Divisional Signal Company.
Pioneers	5th Pioneer Battalion.
A.S.C.	10th, 18th, 28th and 29th Coys., A.A.S.C.
Medical Units	8th, 14th and 15th Field Ambulances.

APPENDIX 2

11th Division.

G.O.C.	Major-General E. A. Fanshawe, C.B.
G.S.O. 1	Captain (temp. Lieut.-Colonel) J. F. S. D. Coleridge.
C.R.A.	Colonel (temp. Brig.-General) G. S. Duffus.
C.R.E.	Major (temp. Lieut.-Colonel) F. A. K. White.

32nd Infantry Brigade.

G.O.C. .. Brevet Lieut.-Colonel (temp. Brig.-General) T. H. F. Price.

9th West Yorkshire Regiment;
6th Yorkshire Regiment;
8th West Riding Regiment;
6th York and Lancaster Regiment;
32nd Brigade Machine-Gun Company.

33rd Infantry Brigade.

G.O.C. .. Colonel (temp. Brig.-General) J. F. Erskine.

6th Lincolnshire Regiment;
6th Border Regiment;
7th South Staffordshire Regiment;
9th Notts and Derby Regiment;
33rd Brigade Machine-Gun Company.

34th Infantry Brigade.

G.O.C. .. Colonel (temp. Brig.-General) J. Hill, D.S.O.

8th Northumberland Fusiliers;
9th Lancashire Fusiliers;
5th Dorsetshire Regiment;
11th Manchester Regiment;
34th Brigade Machine-Gun Company.

Divisional Troops.

Mounted Troops	1 Sqdn. 1/1st Hertfordshire Yeomanry.
	11th Cyclist Company.
Artillery	LVIII Brigade, R.F.A.
	LIX Brigade, R.F.A.
	LX Brigade, R.F.A.
	CXXXIII Brigade, R.F.A.
Engineers	67th Field Company, R.E.
	68th Field Company, R.E.
	86th Field Company, R.E.
Signal Service	11th Divisional Signal Company.
Pioneers	6th East Yorkshire Regiment.
A.S.C.	11th Divisional Train (Supply details only).
Medical Units	33rd, 34th and 35th Field Ambulances

APPENDIX 2

No. 3 Section Canal Defences.

G.O.C., etc. .. .. Headquarters, 52nd Division.

Corps Troops.

Mounted Troops .. .. *5th Mounted Brigade.*
G.O.C. .. .. Colonel (temp. Brig.-General) E. A. Wiggin, D.S.O.
    1/1st Warwick Yeomanry ;
    1/1st Gloucester Yeomanry ;
    1/1st Worcester Yeomanry ;
    1/1st S. Midland Signal Troop ;
    " A " Battery, H.A.C. ;
    No. 7 Field Troop ;
    1/1st S. Midland Mounted Brigade Field Ambulance.
Engineers .. .. .. 220th Army Troops Company, R.E.
Signal Service .. .. .. No. 21 Airline Section.
                                                  " WW " Cable Section.

52nd (Lowland) Division.

G.O.C. .. .. Major-General Hon. H. A. Lawrence.
G.S.O. 1 .. .. .. Lieut.-Colonel F. W. J. Walshe.
C.R.A. .. .. Lieut.-Colonel (temp. Brig.-General) F. L. Parker, C.M.G.
C.R.E. .. .. Major (temp. Lieut.-Colonel) R. L. Waller.

155th Infantry Brigade.

G.O.C. .. .. Lieut.-Colonel (temp. Brig.-General) J. B. Pollok-M'Call.
    1/4th Royal Scots Fusiliers ;
    1/5th Royal Scots Fusiliers ;
    1/4th King's Own Scottish Borderers ;
    1/5th King's Own Scottish Borderers ;
    155th Brigade Machine-Gun Company.

156th Infantry Brigade.

G.O.C. .. .. Brevet Colonel (temp. Brig.-General) L. C. Koe.
    1/4th Royal Scots ;
    1/7th Royal Scots ;
    1/7th Scottish Rifles ;
    1/8th Scottish Rifles ;
    156th Brigade Machine-Gun Company.

157th Infantry Brigade.

G.O.C. .. .. Brevet Colonel (temp. Brig.-General) H. G. Casson, C.M.G.
    1/5th Highland Light Infantry ;
    1/6th Highland Light Infantry ;
    1/7th Highland Light Infantry ;
    1/5th Argyll and Sutherland Highlanders ;
    157th Brigade Machine-Gun Company.

APPENDIX 2

Divisional Troops.

Mounted Troops	H.Q. and " C " Squadron, Royal Glasgow Yeomanry.
	52nd Cyclist Company.
Artillery	1/2nd Lowland Brigade, R.F.A.
	1/3rd Lowland Brigade, R.F.A.
	1/4th Lowland Brigade, R.F.A.
	1/5th Lowland Brigade, R.F.A.
	52nd Divisional Ammunition Column (1 officer and 35 other ranks).
Engineers	2/1st Lowland Field Company, R.E.
	2/2nd Lowland Field Company, R.E.
	1/2nd Lowland Field Company, R.E.
Signal Service	52nd Divisional Signal Company.
A.S.C.	52nd Divisional Train.
Medical Units	1/1st, 1/2nd, 1/3rd Lowland Field Ambulances.
Attached	*1st Dismounted Brigade.*
G.O.C.	Temp. Brig.-General the Marquess of Tullibardine, M.V.O., D.S.O.

1/1st Scottish Horse;
1/2nd Scottish Horse;
1/3rd Scottish Horse;
1/1st Ayr Yeomanry;
1/1st Lanark Yeomanry;
Machine-Gun Company;
1st Dismounted Brigade Signal Troop;
1/1st Scottish Horse and 1/1st Lowland Field Ambulances.

WESTERN FRONTIER FORCE.

G.O.C.	Major-General W. E. Peyton, C.V.O., C.B., D.S.O.
G.S.O. 1	Major (temp. Lieut.-Colonel) R. E. M. Russell, D.S.O.
C.R.E.	Major (temp. Lieut.-Colonel) D. M. Griffith, D.S.O.

Force Troops.

Mounted Troops	*6th Mounted Brigade.*
G.O.C.	Lieut.-Colonel (temp. Brig.-General Viscount Hampden, C.M.G.

1/1st Buckinghamshire Yeomanry;
1/1st Berkshire Yeomanry;
1/1st Dorsetshire Yeomanry;
1/2nd S. Midland Field Troop Signal;
No. 6 Field Troop;
1/2nd S. Midland Mounted Brigade Field Ambulance.

Attached	1/2nd County of London Yeomanry.
Royal Flying Corps	No. 17 Squadron.
Artillery	1/1st Berkshire Battery, R.H.A.
	1/1st Nottinghamshire Battery, R.H.A.
Infantry	1st Bn. British West Indies Regiment.
	2nd Bn. British West Indies Regiment.
	3rd Bn. British West Indies Regiment.

APPENDIX 2

Signal Service	2nd Mounted Divisional Signal Squadron. No. 42 Airline Section. " UU " Cable Section. No. 6 Pack Wireless Section.

North-Western Section.

G.O.C., etc.	Headquarters, 53rd Division.

53rd (Welsh) Division.

G.O.C.	Colonel (temp. Major-General) A. E. Dallas, C.B.
G.S.O. 1	Lieut.-Colonel G. A. S. Cape.
C.R.A.	Colonel (temp. Brig.-General) A. H. Short, C.B.
C.R.E.	Major (temp. Lieut.-Colonel) R. P. T. K. Hawkesley.

158th Infantry Brigade.

G.O.C.	Major (temp. Brig.-General) S. F. Mott. 1/5th Royal Welch Fusiliers ; 1/6th Royal Welch Fusiliers ; 1/7th Royal Welch Fusiliers ; 1/1st Herefordshire Regiment ; 158th Brigade Machine-Gun Company.

159th Infantry Brigade.

G.O.C.	Colonel (temp. Brig.-General) J. H. du B. Travers, C.B. 1/4th Cheshire Regiment ; 1/7th Cheshire Regiment ; 1/4th Welch Regiment ; 1/5th Welch Regiment ; 159th Brigade Machine-Gun Company.

160th Infantry Brigade.

G.O.C.	Colonel (temp. Brig.-General) W. J. C. Butler. 1/4th Royal Sussex Regiment ; 2/4th Royal West Surrey Regiment ; 2/4th Royal West Kent Regiment ; 2/10th Middlesex Regiment ; 160th Brigade Machine-Gun Company.

Divisional Troops.

Mounted Troops	1 Sqdn., 1/1st Hertfordshire Yeomanry. 53rd Divisional Cyclist Company.
Artillery	1/1st Cheshire Brigade, R.F.A. 1/1st Welsh Brigade, R.F.A. 1/2nd Welsh Brigade, R.F.A. 1/4th Welsh Brigade, R.F.A. 53rd Divisional Ammunition Column (1 officer and 35 other ranks).
Engineers	1/1st Welsh Field Company, R.E. 2/1st Welsh Field Company, R.E. 2/1st Cheshire Field Company, R.E.
Signal Service	53rd Divisional Signal Company.
A.S.C.	53rd Divisional Train.

APPENDIX 2

Medical Units .. .. .. 1/1st, 1/2nd and 1/3rd Welsh Field Ambulances.
Attached .. .. *4th Dismounted Brigade.*
G.O.C. .. .. Colonel (temp. Brig.-General) E. A. Herbert, M.V.O.
 1/1st Shropshire Yeomanry ;
 1/1st Denbigh Yeomanry ;
 1/1st Cheshire Yeomanry ;
 1/1st Glamorgan Yeomanry ;
 1/1st Montgomery Yeomanry ;
 1/1st Pembroke Yeomanry ;
 Machine-Gun Company ;
 4th Dismounted Brigade Signal Troop ;
 1/1st Welsh Border and 1/1st S. Wales Mounted Brigade Field Ambulances.

22nd Mounted Brigade.

G.O.C. .. .. Lieut.-Colonel (temp. Brig.-General) W. Bromley-Davenport, D.S.O.
 1/1st Lincolnshire Yeomanry ;
 1/1st Staffordshire Yeomanry ;
 1/1st East Riding Yeomanry ;
 Signal Troop ;
 Mounted Brigade, A.S.C. ;
 Mounted Brigade Field Ambulance.

Provisional Infantry Brigade (less Headquarters).

 1/6th Royal Scots ;
 2/5th Devonshire Regiment ;
 2/7th Middlesex Regiment ;
 2/8th Middlesex Regiment ;
 2nd Garrison Battalion, Liverpool Regiment ;
 2 Naval 4-inch guns ;
 1/2nd Kent Field Company, R.E. ;
 17th Motor Machine-Gun Battery ;
 No. 1 Armoured Train.

South-Western Section.

G.O.C. .. .. Colonel (temp. Brig.-General) H. W. Hodgson, C.V.O.
Mounted Troops .. .. *1st Australian Light Horse Brigade* (see p. 381).
 1 Sqdn. Egyptian Army Cavalry.
Infantry .. .. 2nd Garrison Battalion, Cheshire Regiment.
 1 Company and Machine-Gun Section, Egyptian Army.
Signal Service .. .. .. Detachment, 2nd Mounted Divisional Signal Sqdn.
 Emergency Sqdn., Royal Naval Armoured Car Division.
 H.Q. and Nos. 1, 2 and 3 Light Armoured Motor Batteries.
 No. 2 Armoured Train.

GENERAL HEADQUARTERS TROOPS.

Mounted Troops .. .. Imperial Camel Corps.
 Bikanir Camel Corps.
Royal Flying Corps .. .. *5th Wing Royal Flying Corps.*

APPENDIX 2

Commander . . . . . . Lieutenant-Colonel W. G. H. Salmond.
    No. 14 Squadron ;
    No. 17 Squadron (with Western Force) ;
    2 Kite Balloon Sections (Naval).
Artillery . . . . Heavy Artillery.

XX Brigade, R.G.A.

10th, 15th and 91st Heavy Batteries, R.G.A.
1 Heavy Battery and 1 Section Heavy Battery, Royal Marine Artillery.

Stokes Gun, Batteries of—
125th, 126th, 161st and 162nd Brigade Batteries.

Anti-Aircraft Artillery—
Nos. 30 and 38 Anti-Aircraft Sections.

Mountain Artillery—
4th Highland Mountain Battery, R.G.A.

Armoured Cars—
Nos. 11 and 12 Armoured Motor Batteries.

Engineers . . . . . . 115th, 116th and 276th Railway Companies, R.E.

Signal Service . . . . . . G.H.Q. Signal Company.
Nos. 14 and 15 Airline Sections.
" NA," " NB," and " VV " Cable Sections.

Unallotted—
Southern Motor, W/T Station ;
No. 5 Pack Wireless Section.

A.S.C. . . . . 338th, 493rd and 619th Mechanical Transport Companies, A.S.C.

Transport . . . . . . Camel Transport Corps.
59th, 62nd, 70th and 191st Camel Corps.

LINES OF COMMUNICATION DEFENCE TROOPS.

Mounted Troops . . . . *Imperial Service Cavalry Brigade.*
G.O.C. . . . . Major (temp. Brig.-General) M. H. Henderson.
    Mysore Lancers ;
    1st Hyderabad Lancers ;
    Kathiawar Signal Troop ;
    124th Indian Cavalry Field Ambulance.

Infantry . . . . 1st Garrison Battalion, Essex Regiment.
2nd Garrison Battalion, Royal Welch Fusiliers.
1st Garrison Battalion, Devonshire Regiment.
1st Garrison Battalion, Royal Scots (less 2 companies).
1st Garrison Battalion, Liverpool Regiment.
1st Garrison Battalion, Royal Irish Regiment.
19th Garrison Battalion, Rifle Brigade.
20th Garrison Battalion, Rifle Brigade.
21st Garrison Battalion, Rifle Brigade.
22nd Garrison Battalion, Rifle Brigade.
1st Garrison Battalion, Royal Warwickshire Regiment (Khartoum).

APPENDIX 2

Alexandria District.

G.O.C.	Colonel (temp. Brig.-General) R. C. Boyle, C.B.
Coast Defence Artillery	84th Siege Battery, R.G.A. 92nd Company, R.G.A., Mex Battery. Ras el Tin Battery. Silsileh Battery. " Y " Battery Royal Malta Artillery.

Lines of Communication Units.

Headquarters, Inspector-General of Communications (see p. 380).

Infantry	1st Garrison Battalion, Notts and Derby Regiment. 1st Garrison Battalion, Northamptonshire Regiment. 2 Companies, 1st Garrison Battalion, Royal Scots (Cyprus).
Signal Service	Nos. 12 and 23 Airline Sections.
Engineers	13th Base Park Company, R.E. 46th Advanced Park Company, R.E. 3rd Lancashire Army Troops Company, R.E. 1/3rd Devon Army Troops Company, R.E. No. 5 Siege Company, Royal Anglesea R.E. Nos. 2, 3, 4, 5 and 6 Egyptian Works Companies.
A.S.C.	10th Australian Reserve Park. Indian Mule Cart Corps. Labour Companies—Nos. 24 and 27 Egyptian Labour Corps. Depot Units of Supply—Nos. 40, 41, 47, 48, 49, 50, 51, 52, 53, 54, 55, 56, 62, 63, 65, 66, 104, 105, 136, 137, 143, 144, 145, 146, 147, 175, 176, 177, 178, 180, 182, 190, 191, 193, 194, 195, 200, 201, 202, 217, 218, 219, 220, 228, 229, 230, 231, 258, 259, 260, 261, 262, 263, 265, 266, 268, 269, 270, 276, 360, 373, 374, 376, 377. Nos. 16, 17, 18, 19, 20, 21, 22, 23, 24, 25 Australian. Railway Supply Detachments—Nos. 17 and 56, 1st and 11th Australian. Field Bakeries—29th, 36th, 40th, 42nd, 50th, 51st, 55th, 71st, 4th and 5th Australian. Field Butcheries—10th, 11th, 29th, 32nd, 40th, 42nd, 51st, 52nd, 4th and 5th Australian. 345th and 347th Mechanical Transport Companies, A.S.C. Royal Naval S.A.A. Column (275th Company, A.S.C.). No. 6 (Auxiliary) Transport Company A.S.C. Base Horse Transport Depot (No. 137 Company, A.S.C.). Base Mechanical Transport Depot (No 500 Company, A.S.C.).

APPENDIX 2

Medical Units .. .. .. Nos. 18, 21, 22, 24, 29, 30, 31, 46, 52, 53, 54, 80, 89, 90, 91 and 93 Sanitary Sections.
Nos. 13, 24, 26, 53, 54, and 2nd Australian Casualty Clearing Stations.
Nos. 15, 17, 19, 21, 27, 31, 3 Australian, New Zealand General Hospitals.
Nos. 16, 17 and 18, 1st and 2nd Australian, 1, 2 and 3 Canadian, and Camel Transport Corps Depot Stationary Hospital.

Ordnance Units .. .. .. Nos. 11, 16, 26, 27, 31, 32, 38, 39, 47, 55 and 58 Companies, A.O.C.
No. 9 Company, A.O.C. (Egyptian Section).
3 Ordnance Travelling Workshops.

Veterinary Units .. .. Nos. 11, 17 and 18 Veterinary Sections.
Base Depot Veterinary Stores.
Advanced Base Depot Veterinary Stores.
Base Veterinary Hospital.
Nos. 16, 20, 21 and 22 Veterinary Hospitals.

Postal Units .. .. .. Advanced Base Post Office.
1 Base Postal Detachment and 11th Postal Detachment.

APPENDIX 2

GENERAL ORGANIZATION.
GENERAL HEADQUARTERS.

- General Headquarters Troops.
- No. 1 Section (IX Corps).
- No. 2 Section (II A.N.Z.A.C.).
  - A. and N.Z. Mounted Division.
  - Administered by—
    II A.N.Z.A.C.
    1st A.L.H. Bde. with S.W. Section.
    Divl. H.Q.
    2nd A.L.H. Bde. } Attached No. 3 Section.
    N.Z.M.R. Bde.
- No. 3 Section.
- Western Frontier Force.
  - North-Western Section.
  - South-Western Section.
- L. of C. Defence Troops.
- Inspector-General of Communications.
  - Alexandria District.
  - Cyprus Garrison.
  - Lines of Communication Units.

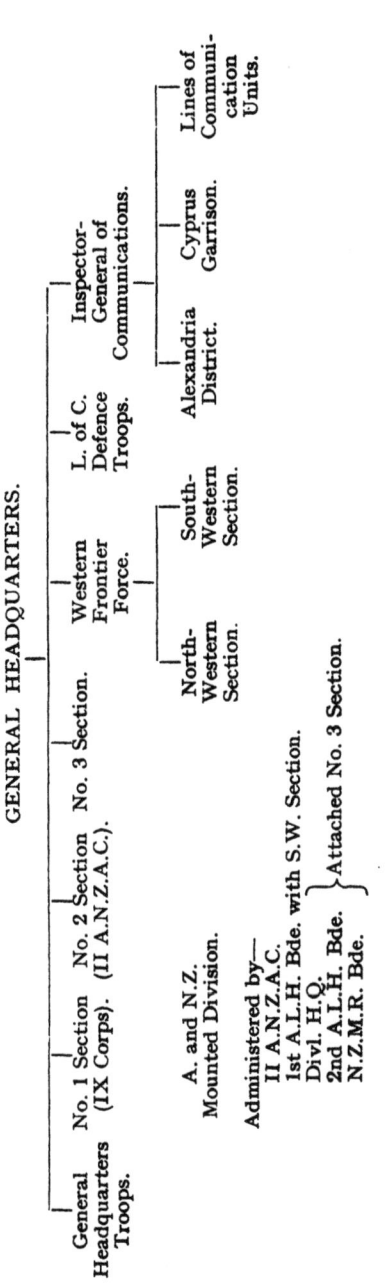

APPENDIX 3.

ORDER OF BATTLE

OF THE

EGYPTIAN EXPEDITIONARY FORCE, APRIL 1917.

GENERAL HEADQUARTERS.

Commander-in-Chief	Lieut.-General (temp. General) Sir A. J. Murray, K.C.B., G.C.M.G., C.V.O., D.S.O.
Chief of the General Staff	Major-General A. L. Lynden-Bell, C.B., C.M.G.
Deputy Adjutant-General	Major-General J. Adye, C.B.
Deputy Quartermaster-General	Major-General W. Campbell, C.B., D.S.O.

Attached—

Major-General, Royal Artillery	Colonel (temp. Major-General) S. C. U. Smith, C.B.
Engineer-in-Chief	Colonel (temp. Major-General) H. B. H. Wright, C.B., C.M.G.

HEADQUARTERS OF ADMINISTRATIVE SERVICES AND DEPARTMENTS.

Director of Army Signals	Brevet Colonel (temp. Brig.-General) M. G. E. Bowman-Manifold, D.S.O.
Director of Works	Colonel (temp. Brig.-General) E. M. Paul, C.B.
Director of Supplies and Transport	Lieut.-Colonel (temp. Brig.-General) G. F. Davies, C.M.G.
Director of Railways	Temp. Colonel Sir G. Macauley, K.C.M.G., C.B.
Director of Ordnance Services	Colonel (temp. Brig.-General) P. A. Bainbridge, C.M.G.
Director of Remounts	Brig.-General C. L. Bates, C.M.G., D.S.O.
Director of Veterinary Services	Colonel (temp. Brig.-General) E. R. C. Butler, C.M.G.
Director of Medical Services	Colonel (temp. Surgeon-General) J. Maher, C.B.
Director of Army Postal Services	Major (temp. Lieut.-Colonel) P. Warren, C.M.G.
Command Paymaster	Colonel F. W. Hill.

EASTERN FORCE.

G.O.C.	Major-General (temp. Lieut.-General) Sir C. M. Dobell, K.C.B., C.M.G., D.S.O.
Brig.-General, General Staff	Brevet Lieut.-Colonel (temp. Brig.-General) G. P. Dawnay, D.S.O., M.V.O.
Brig.-General, Royal Artillery	Colonel (temp. Brig.-General) A. H. Short, C.B.
Chief Engineer	Major (temp. Brig.-General) R. L. Waller.

APPENDIX 3

Force Troops.

Mounted Troops .. .. *Imperial Camel Brigade.*
G.O.C. .. .. Major (temp. Brig.-General) C. L. Smith, V.C., M.C.
    1st (A. and N.Z.) Battalion ;
    2nd (Imperial) Battalion ;
    3rd (A. and N. Z.) Battalion ;
    Hong Kong and Singapore Camel Battery ;
    Brigade Signal Section ;
    Brigade Field Troop ;
    Brigade Machine-Gun Company ;
    1/1st Scottish Horse Field Ambulance.

Imperial Service Cavalry Brigade.

G.O.C. .. .. Major (temp. Brig.-General) M. H. Henderson.
    Mysore Lancers ;
    1st Hyderabad Lancers ;
    Kathiawar Signal Troop ;
    124th Indian Cavalry Field Ambulance.

Artillery .. .. XCVI Heavy Artillery Group (four 4-gun 60-pdr., one siege battery).
    Nos. 30, 38, 55, 85, 96 Anti-Aircraft Sections.

Machine Gun Corps .. .. " E " Company, Heavy Section (Tanks).
    Nos. 11 and 12 Light Armoured Car Batteries.
    17th Motor Machine-Gun Battery.
    Nos. 1 and 3 Armoured Trains.

Engineers .. .. .. 220th and 555th Army Troops Companies.
    No. 10 Company (Queen's Own) Sappers and Miners.
    1/23rd and 2/23rd Sikh Pioneers.
    360th Company, R.E. (water unit).

Signal Service .. .. .. G.H.Q. Signal Company.
    Pigeon Section.
    N 14, N 15, N 23, N 24 and No. 61 Airline Sections.
    BR, NA, NB, NN Cable Sections.
    No. 9 Wagon and London Pack W/T Sections.

52nd (Lowland) Division.

G.O.C. .. .. Brevet Colonel (temp. Major-General) W. E. B. Smith, C.B., C.M.G.
G.S.O. 1 .. .. .. Major (temp. Lieut.-Colonel) G. W. V. Holdich, D.S.O.
C.R.A. .. .. .. Lieut.-Colonel (temp. Brig.-General) E. C. Massy, D.S.O.
C.R.E. .. .. .. Temp. Major (temp. Lieut.-Colonel) L. F. Wells.

155th Infantry Brigade.

G.O.C. .. .. Lieut.-Colonel (temp. Brig.-General) J. B. Pollok-M'Call, C.M.G.
    (For Troops, see Appendix 2.)

156th Infantry Brigade.

G.O.C. .. .. Temp. Lieut.-Colonel (temp. Brig.-General) A. H. Leggett, D.S.O.
(For Troops, see Appendix 2.)

157th Infantry Brigade.

G.O.C. .. .. Brevet Colonel (temp. Brig.-General) C. D. H. Moore, D.S.O.
(For Troops, see Appendix 2.)

Divisional Troops.

(As in Appendix 2, save that the Cyclist Company is omitted and the Artillery now consists of 261st, 262nd and 263rd Brigades, R.F.A.)

53rd (Welsh) Division.

G.O.C. .. .. Major-General A. G. Dallas, C.B., C.M.G.
G.S.O. 1 .. .. .. Major (temp. Lieut.-Colonel) A. E. M. Sinclair-Thomson, D.S.O.
C.R.A. .. .. .. Lieut.-Colonel (temp. Brig.-General) R. E. A. Le Mottée.

158th Infantry Brigade.

G.O.C. .. .. Major (temp. Brig.-General) S. F. Mott.
(For Troops, see Appendix 2.)

159th Infantry Brigade.

G.O.C. .. .. Colonel (temp. Brig.-General) J. H. du B. Travers, C.B.
(For Troops, see Appendix 2.)

160th Infantry Brigade.

G.O.C. .. .. Colonel (temp. Brig.-General) W. J. C. Butler.
(For Troops, see Appendix 2.)

Divisional Troops.

(As in Appendix 2, save that the Artillery now consists of 265th, 266th, and 267th Brigades, R.F.A.)

54th (East Anglian) Division.

G.O.C. .. .. Colonel (temp. Major-General) S. W. Hare, C.B.
G.S.O. 1 .. .. .. Major (temp. Lieut.-Colonel) A. H. C. Kearsey, D.S.O.
C.R.A. .. .. .. Colonel (temp. Brig.General) H. G. Sandilands, C.B.
C.R.E. .. .. .. Major (temp. Lieut.-Colonel) A. W. Stokes, M.C.

161st Infantry Brigade.

G.O.C. .. .. Lieut.-Colonel (temp. Brig.-General) W. Marriott-Dodington.
(For Troops, see Appendix 2.)

APPENDIX 3

162nd Infantry Brigade.

G.O.C. .. .. Brevet Lieut.-Colonel (temp. Brig.-General) A. Mudge.
(For Troops, see Appendix 2.)

163rd Infantry Brigade.

G.O.C. .. .. Major (Hon. Colonel, temp. Brig.-General) T. Ward.
(For Troops, see Appendix 2.)

Divisional Troops.

(As in Appendix 2, save that the Artillery now consists of 270th, 271st, and 272nd Brigades, R.F.A.)

74th (Yeomanry) Division.

G.O.C. .. .. Brevet Lieut.-Colonel (temp. Major-General) E. S. Girdwood.
G.S.O. 1 .. .. .. Major (temp. Lieut.-Colonel) P. S. Allan.
C.R.E. .. .. .. Major (temp. Lieut.-Colonel) R. P. T. Hawkesley.

229th Infantry Brigade.

G.O.C. .. .. Colonel (temp. Brig.-General) R. Hoare.
16th (R. 1st Devon and R. N. Devon Yeo. Bn.) Devonshire Regiment;
12th (W. Somerset Yeo. Bn.) Somerset Light Infantry;
14th (Fife and Forfar Yeo. Bn.) Royal Highlanders;
12th (Ayr and Lanark Yeo. Bn.) Royal Scots Fusiliers;
4th Machine-Gun Company.

230th Infantry Brigade.

G.O.C. .. .. Major (temp. Brig.-General) A. J. McNeill.
10th (R.E. Kent and W. Kent Yeo. Bn.) East Kent Regiment;
16th (Sussex Yeo. Bn.) Sussex Regiment;
15th (Suffolk Yeo. Bn.) Suffolk Regiment;
12th (Norfolk Yeo. Bn.) Norfolk Regiment;
209th Machine-Gun Company.

231st Infantry Brigade.

G.O.C. .. .. Major (temp. Lieut.-Colonel) W. J. Bowker, C.M.G., D.S.O.
10th (Shrop. and Chester Yeo. Bn.) Shropshire Light Infantry;
24th (Denbigh Yeo. Bn.) Royal Welch Fusiliers;
24th (Pemb. and Glam. Yeo. Bn.) Welch Regiment;
25th (Montgomery and Welsh Horse Yeo. Bn.) Royal Welch Fusiliers;
210th Machine-Gun Company.

APPENDIX 3

Divisional Troops.[1]

Mounted Troops	Sqdn., 1/2nd County of London Yeomanry.
Engineers	5th Royal Monmouth Field Company, R.E.
	5th Royal Anglesey Field Company, R.E.
Signal Service	74th Divisional Signal Company.
A.S.C.	74th Divisional Train.
Medical Units	229th, 230th and 231st Brigade, Field Ambulances.

DESERT COLUMN.

G.O.C.	Major-General (temp. Lieut.-General) Sir P. W. Chetwode, Bt., C.B., D.S.O.
G.S.O. 1	Major (temp. Lieut.-Colonel) V. M. Fergusson, D.S.O.
Brig.-General, Royal Artillery	Colonel (temp. Brig.-General) A. D'A. King, C.B., D.S.O.
Chief Engineer	Major (temp. Brig.-General) R. E. M. Russell.

Australian and New Zealand Mounted Division.

G.O.C.	Major-General Sir H. G. Chauvel, K.C.M.G., C.B.
G.S.O. 1	Major (temp. Lieut.-Colonel) J. G. Browne.
C.R.A.	Brevet Lieut.-Colonel (temp. Colonel) J. F. Laycock, D.S.O.

1st Australian Light Horse Brigade.

G.O.C.	Lieut.-Colonel (temp. Brig.-General) C. F. Cox, C.B.

1st Regiment Light Horse ;
2nd Regiment Light Horse ;
3rd Regiment Light Horse ;
1st Australian Light Horse Signal Troop ;
1st Australian Machine-Gun Squadron.

2nd Australian Light Horse Brigade.

G.O.C.	Colonel (temp. Brig.-General) G. de L. Ryrie, C.M.G.

5th Regiment Light Horse ;
6th Regiment Light Horse ;
7th Regiment Light Horse ;
2nd Australian Light Horse Signal Troop ;
2nd Australian Machine-Gun Squadron.

---

[1] The 74th Division had as yet no artillery.

APPENDIX 3

New Zealand Mounted Rifles Brigade.

G.O.C. .. .. Colonel (temp. Brig.-General) E. W. C. Chaytor, C.B.
Auckland Mounted Rifles;
Canterbury Mounted Rifles;
Wellington Mounted Rifles;
New Zealand Mounted Rifles Signal Troop;
New Zealand Machine-Gun Squadron.

22nd Mounted Brigade.

G.O.C. .. .. Colonel (temp. Brig.-General) F. A. B. Fryer.
1/1st Lincolnshire Yeomanry;
1/1st Staffordshire Yeomanry;
1/1st East Riding Yeomanry;
22nd Mounted Brigade Signal Troop;
18th Machine-Gun Squadron.

Divisional Troops.

(As in Appendix 2, save that batteries are not brigaded, Mounted Divisional Ammunition Column is added, Nos. 26 and 27 Australian Units of Supply are substituted for Light Horse Supply Column, and 1/1st North Midland Mounted Brigade Field Ambulance is substituted for 3rd Light Horse Field Ambulance.)

Imperial Mounted Division.

G.O.C. .. .. Colonel (temp. Major-General) H. W. Hodgson, C.V.O., C.B.
G.S.O. 1 .. .. .. Major (temp. Lieut.-Colonel) H. C. S. Ward.
C.R.A. .. .. .. Lieut.-Colonel the Marquess of Exeter.

3rd Australian Light Horse Brigade.

G.O.C. .. .. Colonel (temp. Brig.-General) J. R. Royston, C.M.G., D.S.O.
8th Regiment Light Horse;
9th Regiment Light Horse;
10th Regiment Light Horse;
3rd Australian Light Horse Signal Troop;
3rd Australian Machine-Gun Squadron.

4th Australian Light Horse Brigade.

G.O.C. .. .. Lieut.-Colonel (temp. Brig.-General) J. B. Meredith, D.S.O.
4th Regiment Light Horse;
11th Regiment Light Horse;
12th Regiment Light Horse;
4th Australian Light Horse Signal Troop;
4th Australian Machine-Gun Squadron.

APPENDIX 3

5th Mounted Brigade.

G.O.C. .. .. Colonel (temp. Brig.-General) E. A. Wiggin, D.S.O.
1/1st Warwick Yeomanry;
1/1st Gloucester Yeomanry;
1/1st Worcester Yeomanry;
5th Mounted Brigade Signal Troop;
16th Machine Gun Squadron.

6th Mounted Brigade.

G.O.C. .. .. Lieut.-Colonel (temp. Brig.-General) T. M. S. Pitt.
1/1st Bucks Yeomanry;
1/1st Berks Yeomanry;
1/1st Dorset Yeomanry;
6th Mounted Brigade Signal Troop;
17th Machine Gun Squadron.

Divisional Troops.

Artillery .. .. 1/1st Notts and 1/1st Berks Batteries, R.H.A.
"A" and "B" Batteries, H.A.C.
Mounted Divisional Ammunition Column.

Engineers .. .. .. Imperial Mounted Division Field Squadron.

Signal Service .. .. .. Imperial Mounted Division Signal Squadron.

A.S.C. .. ..

Medical Units .. .. .. 3rd Light Horse, 4th Light Horse, 1/1st S. Midland Mounted Brigade and 1/2nd S. Midland Mounted Brigade Field Ambulances.

NORTHERN CANAL SECTION.

G.O.C. .. .. Colonel (temp. Brig.-General) H. D. Watson, C.M.G., M.V.O. (in addition to his duties as G.O.C., 20th Indian Brigade).

Mounted Troops .. .. 1/2nd County of London Yeomanry (less 2 sqdns.).
16th Company Imperial Camel Corps (attached from 4th Battalion).

Infantry .. .. *20th Indian Infantry Brigade.*
Alwar Infantry.
Gwalior Infantry.
Patiala Infantry.
Signal Section (British).
121st (Indian) Field Ambulance.

1st Bn., British West Indies Regiment.
2nd Bn., British West Indies Regiment.
1st Garrison Bn., Notts and Derby Regiment (2 companies).
19th Garrison Bn., Rifle Brigade.

Medical Units .. .. .. 1/1st Lowland Mounted Brigade, Field Ambulance.

APPENDIX 3

Delta and Western Force.

G.O.C.	Brevet Colonel (temp. Brig.-General) H. G. Casson, C.M.G.
Mounted Troops	Bikanir Camel Corps.
	Nos. 8 and 10 Companies, Imperial Camel Corps.
	"B" Sqdn., 1/2nd County of London Yeomanry (attached Imperial School of Instruction, Zeitoun).
Infantry	2nd Garrison Battalion, Royal Welch Fusiliers.
	2/7th Battalion, Northumberland Fusiliers.
	6th Garrison Battalion, Royal Welch Fusiliers.
	20th Garrison Battalion, Rifle Brigade.
	21st Garrison Battalion, Rifle Brigade.
	1st Garrison Battalion, Royal Warwickshire Regiment.
	1st Garrison Battalion, Devonshire Regiment.
	1st Garrison Battalion, Royal Irish Regiment.
	1 Coy., 3rd Infantry Battalion, Egyptian Army.
Artillery	Detachment, Royal Marine Artillery (2 Naval 4-in. guns).
	No. 2 Armoured Train.
	Detachments, R.F.A., dismounted (three 15-pdr. Q.F., two 15-pdr. B.L.C., two 15-pdr. Ehrhardt and two 9-pdr. Krupp guns.)
	Nos. 1, 2 and 3 Light Armoured Motor Batteries.
	Six Light Car Patrols (Ford cars).
Signal Service	Western Force Signal Company.
	No. 42 Airline Section.
	"UU" Cable Section.
	Pigeon Section (detachment).
	No. 6 Wagon and No. 6 Pack W/T Sections.
A.S.C.—	
Mechanical Transport	5th, 6th and 29th Reserve Field Ambulance and Workshop Units.
	Western Force Mechanical Transport Supply Company.
	Advanced M.T. Supply Depot (Samalut).
	No. 303 (M.T.) Company, A.S.C.
Camel Transport	"H" and "O" Companies, Egyptian Camel Transport Corps.

Alexandria District.

G.O.C.	Colonel (temp. Brig.-General) R. C. Boyle, C.B.
Coast Defence	No. 103rd Local Company, R.G.A. Ras el Tin Fort.

APPENDIX 3

Artillery	Royal Malta Artillery (detachment). Quarantine and Chatby Batteries. Mex Fort.
Infantry	5th Battalion, British West Indies Regiment. 1st Garrison Battalion, Liverpool Regiment. 2nd Garrison Battalion, Cheshire Regiment.

GENERAL HEADQUARTERS TROOPS.

Royal Flying Corps ..	*Middle East Brigade, R.F.C.*
G.O.C.	Brevet Lieut.-Colonel (temp. Brig.-General) W. G. H. Salmond, D.S.O.
Staff Officer, 1st Grade	Major (temp. Lieut.-Colonel) P. R. C. Groves.
5th Wing	Nos. 14 and 67 (Australian) Squadrons.
20th Reserve Wing ..	Nos. 21, 22, 23, 57 and 58 Reserve Squadrons.
Engineers	Railway Operating Division. 115th and 116th Railway Companies, R.E. 2 Companies, Railway Bn. Sappers and Miners. Topographical Section, R.E.
Signal Service	" M " (L. of C.) Signal Company. Nos. 12 and 62 Airline Sections. " BQ " and " BS " Cable Sections. Northern Wagon, Southern Motor, and No. 12 Pack W/T Sections.
A.S.C.—	
Mechanical Transport	H.Q., A.S.C. Motor Boat Company. Two Advanced M.T. Sub-Depots (Ismailia and Qantara). 52nd, Highland Mounted Brigade, 6th Reserve and 29th Field Ambulance and Workshop Units.
Camel Transport ..	Nos. 1 and 2 Camel Transport Depots. " O " and " R " Companies, Egyptian Camel Transport Corps.

SOUTHERN CANAL SECTION.

G.O.C.	Brevet Colonel (temp. Brig.-General) P. C. Palin, C.B. (in addition to his duties as G.O.C., 29th Indian Brigade).
Mounted Troops ..	4th (A. and N.Z.) Battalion, Imperial Camel Corps (less 15th Coy., attached 3rd Bn. and 16th Coy., attached N. Canal Section, and with 13th Coy. from 3rd Bn. attached).
Engineers	14th Army Troops Company, R.E. 496th (Kent) Field Company (less detachment).

APPENDIX 3

Infantry .. .. *232nd Infantry Brigade.**
G.O.C. .. .. Major (temp. Brig.-General) H. J. Huddleston, D.S.O., M.C.
    2nd Loyal North Lancashire Regiment;
    1/4th Duke of Cornwall's Light Infantry;
    1/5th Devonshire Regiment;
    2/5th Hampshire Regiment.

29th Indian Infantry Brigade.
    2/3rd Gurkhas;
    3/3rd Gurkhas;
    123rd Rifles;
    Brigade Signal Section (British);
    123rd Indian Field Ambulance;
    Indian Brigade Supply Column;

49th Indian Infantry Brigade.
G.O.C. .. .. Lieut.-Colonel (temp. Brig-General) E. R. B. Murray.
    58th Rifles;
    1/101st Grenadiers;
    1/102nd Grenadiers;
    110th Indian Field Ambulance;

    1st Garrison Bn., Notts and Derby Regiment (less 2 companies);
    1st Garrison Bn., Northampton Regiment.
A.S.C. .. .. No. 900 Company, A.S.C. (Auxiliary Horse Transport Company, Ismailia).

Cyprus Detachment.
    1st Garrison Bn., Royal Scots.

LINES OF COMMUNICATION UNITS.
(Controlled by G.H.Q.)
Royal Flying Corps .. .. "X" Aircraft Park (5th Wing).
    "X" Aircraft Depot (Depot for al Middle East Units, R.F.C.).
Engineers .. .. .. 13th and 46th Base Park Companies, R.E.
    1/3rd Devon Army Troops Company, R.E.
Signal Service .. .. .. Base Signal Depot.
A.S.C. .. .. Field Bakeries—18th and 19th.
    Field Butcheries—17th.
    Supply Companies—Nos. 18, 19, 20, 21, 22, 23, 24 and 25.
    Horse Transport—137th, 671st and 313th Companies, A.S.C.
    Mechanical Transport—500th, 644th, 772nd, 894th, 895th, 904th, 905th, 906th, 907th Companies, A.S.C., Scottish Horse and 22nd Mounted Brigade Field Ambulance and Workshop Units.

---

* This was the only brigade yet formed of the 75th Division. The 2nd Loyal North Lancashire and 1/4th Duke of Cornwall's Light Infantry were temporarily attached to Eastern Force.

APPENDIX 3

Medical Units	Nos. 24, 29, 30, 80, 89 and 91 Sanitary Sections. No. 35 Motor Ambulance Convoy. Nos. 26, 53 and 54 Casualty Clearing Stations. Nos. 15, 17, 19, 21, 27, 31, 14 Australian and 5 Indian General Hospitals. Red Cross and Egyptian Government Auxiliary Hospitals. Nos. 24, 26, 36 and 2 Australian Stationary Hospitals. Miscellaneous Hospitals—Ras-el-Tin, Citadel, Infectious, Anglo-American, Nasrieh Schools, Red Cross, Turkish Prisoners', Egyptian Hospitals. Convalescent Homes and Depots—Mustapha, Montaza, Abbassia, Actea N.Z. Convalescent Home. Nos. 5, 6 and 7 Advanced Depots Medical Stores. R.A.M.C. Base Depot. Nos. 5 and 8, Abbassia and Levant Base Depots Medical Stores. Alexandria, Suez and Ismailia Military Bacteriological Laboratories. Hospital Barge, *Indiana*.
Remounts	Nos. 1, 2, 3, 48th Squadron, 4 Australian, Remount Depots, Nos. 1 and 2 Camel Remount Depots.
Veterinary	Nos. 16, 20, 21 and 26 Veterinary Hospitals. Convalescent Horse Depot. No. 3 Base Depot Veterinary Stores. Abbassia and Qantara Advanced Base Depots Veterinary Stores. No. 26 Veterinary Hospital (acts as Base Depot). Nos. 1, 2 and 3 Camel Hospitals. Nos. 54 and 55 Mobile Veterinary Sections.
Ordnance	Nos. 9, 11, 16, 26, 27, 31, 32, 38, 44 and 56 Companies, A.O.C. Nos. 37, 38 and 39 Ordnance Mobile Workshops. Nos. 4 and 5 Light Armoured Batteries Workshop.
Postal Units	Advanced Base Post Office. One Base Postal Detachment. 11th Postal Detachment.

APPENDIX 3

GENERAL ORGANIZATION.
GENERAL HEADQUARTERS.

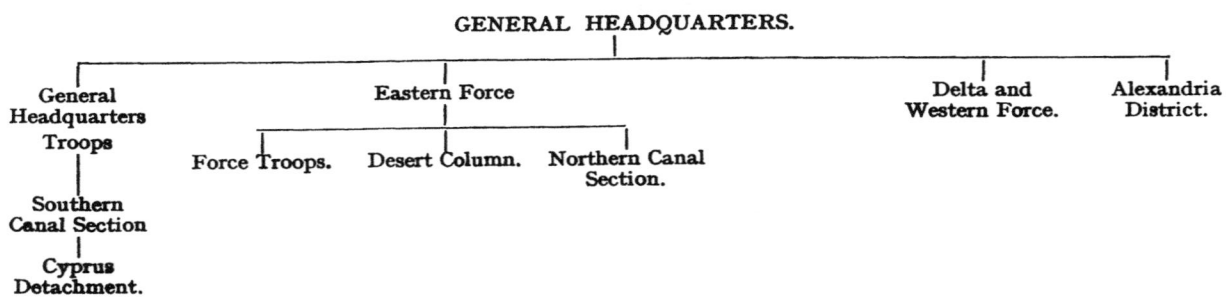

- General Headquarters Troops
- Southern Canal Section
- Cyprus Detachment
- Eastern Force
  - Force Troops
  - Desert Column
  - Northern Canal Section
- Delta and Western Force
- Alexandria District

1st Garrison Bn., Essex Regiment, at Khartoum.

APPENDIX 4.

THE STAFF AND ADMINISTRATIVE SERVICES IN EGYPT IN THE EARLY STAGES OF THE WAR, WITH A NOTE ON THE CAMEL TRANSPORT CORPS.

The large numbers of troops which arrived in Egypt during the first eighteen months of the war caused heavy strain upon the staff and administrative services, which remained for a considerable time without increase beyond the establishment required for the peace-time garrison, equivalent in strength to an infantry brigade and attached troops. The General Staff at the outbreak of war consisted of a single G.S.O. 2nd grade, and it was not till the question of the evacuation of Gallipoli arose that a full General Staff, on a war footing, with a brigadier-general (Br.-General N. Malcolm) at its head, was formed. On the administrative side the work was heavier, and a brigadier-general in charge of administration (Br.-General H. B. Stanton) was appointed in March 1915.

Embarkation duties were onerous from the first, and increased almost daily. Yet the total embarkation staff consisted of eight officers for the three ports of Alexandria, Port Said, and Suez. Military landing officers were detached from units in the command, until partially disabled officers became available for the service. Between August 1914 and the end of 1915, 28,099 officers, 787,193 other ranks, and 178,546 animals passed through the hands of the embarkation authorities.

The General Manager of the Egyptian State Railways was a retired officer of the Royal Engineers, Major Sir George Macauley. Both he and his senior assistants, Major R. B. D. Blakeney, Deputy General Manager, and Captain G. C. M. Hall, Traffic Manager, had experience of earlier operations in Egypt, which proved invaluable. It was owing to this experience and to the military training of these officials that the railway administration was able to adapt itself to military requirements without change of system, and that the entire service could be left in their hands. Sir G. Macauley was later responsible for the construction of the military railway across Sinai.

The work of the medical services has been mentioned in some detail in the text. The greatest difficulties which they had to face in the early days were due to the vast miscalculation of the casualties which the M.E.F. incurred in the landings at Gallipoli. It was calculated that these would be at the outside 10,000, to be divided between Egypt and Malta. In fact, in less than three weeks after the 28th April, the date of arrival of the first wounded from the Peninsula, over 15,000 casualties were landed in Egypt alone. By the end of July the total had reached 30,000. The Suvla Bay landing and the contemporary operations on the other fronts resulted in the arrival of 20,000 more, but by this time the resources of Egypt had been organized on a large scale, and ample assistance had arrived from the United Kingdom.

The work of the remount and veterinary services was made extremely difficult by the fact that the bulk of the horses belonging to the whole eleven infantry divisions eventually employed on Gallipoli, as well as those of the light horse and yeomanry which fought there dismounted, were left in Egypt.

Mention has been made from time to time in the text of the Camel Transport Corps, of which some further details may be of interest.[1] The

---

[1] The following details are taken chiefly from " A History of the Transport Services of the Egyptian Expeditionary Force," by Brevet Lieut.-Colonel G. E. Badcock, (Rees).

small organization formed by Sir J. Maxwell for use as second-line transport to the troops engaged in the defence of the Suez Canal was quite different from its successor, the regular Camel Transport Corps, since in the former case the camels and their drivers were hired through the Ministry of the Interior. In December 1915 orders were issued by the Force in Egypt for the formation of ten companies, each consisting of 2,020 camels. The personnel of each company consisted of ten British officers (including a medical and a veterinary officer), ten British N.C.O's., and 1,168 Egyptians. The corps was under the command of Colonel C. H. Whittingham, with the title of Inspector. By September 1916, when the advance into the desert after the Battle of Romani had begun, thirteen companies were on service. The Depot was established at Ein esh Shems, near Cairo, and early in 1917 transferred to Qantara, where it remained till the end of the war.

Officers were drawn from Government officials, British civilians, from the A.S.C., and, in greater numbers, promoted from the ranks chiefly of the Yeomanry and Australian troops, after attending a course in elementary Arabic.

The companies were employed either as first-line transport to a division or in special columns. The number of camels employed as first-line transport diminished after Sinai had been left behind and greater use could be made of wheeled transport, being about 4,000 to a division in the first half of 1916 and 2,000 in the summer of 1917. By the following year it had decreased to 1,200. The camels were of many types: Egyptian, Somali, Algerian, Syrian, Sudani, Indian, with various sub-divisions. Almost all had slightly different characteristics and required different treatment.

During the period covered by Volume I, the organization of the Camel Transport Corps worked well within its capacity, and it was not until after the Third Battle of Gaza that serious strain was put upon it. In scale, as in efficiency, it was not the least notable of the administrative achievements carried out by the E.E.F.

APPENDIX 5.

THE HISTORY OF SENUSSISM.

Early History.

Sidi Mohammed-ben-Ali-es Senussi (so called from the Senus Mountain in Algeria), the founder of the confraternity, was born in Algeria towards the end of the eighteenth century. He first practised as a lawyer, devoting much attention to religious questions. Obliged by the Turks to leave the country, he retired to Morocco. About 1822 he returned to Algeria, preaching a doctrine enjoining simplicity of life. From Algeria he journeyed to Egypt, where he had no great success. He next went to Mecca, but, after a long stay, had to leave owing to the revolutionary nature of his teaching in 1843. He had previously founded several hostels for use of the sect, termed *Zawiets*. In Mecca also he had met Sidi Ahmed Idris, the great-grandfather of the Idrissi (see Chapter XII), and from their friendship dated the close connexion between the two families.

After leaving Mecca, Sidi Mohammed returned to Egypt. In 1855 **Sketch A.** he established himself in the Oasis of Jaghbub or Jarabub, west of Siwa in the Libyan Desert, which became the headquarters of the confraternity. This was assigned to him as a residence by the firman of the Sultan. He developed the place agriculturally, built reservoirs, carried out irrigation. He died in 1859, and was buried with great pomp in a mausoleum in the mosque of Jaghbub. There have since been pilgrimages to his tomb, and Jaghbub has to a great extent superseded Mecca as a place of pilgrimage with the followers of Senussism.

The Senussists preach the return to the original teaching of the Prophet, freed from all heresies. They, like the Wahabis, form a Puritan party in Islam, and they are very strict in many matters concerning the discipline of life. Tobacco smoking, for example, is forbidden among them. From the point of view of doctrine, however, they are latitudinarian, and a man may be a Senussist without abandoning the Moslem order to which he belongs. Colonization and cultivation have been the methods adopted to spread their doctrines, though one of their most important principles has been the avoidance of civilized races. They have always taken part in slave-dealing.

Sidi Mohammed's Successor.

Mohammed-el-Mahdi was about fourteen years of age in 1859 when he succeeded his father, who bequeathed to him an immense ascendency in northern Africa, with *Zawiets* from Morocco to Arabia. He was, according to the authorities, an undoubted descendant of the Prophet, bearing between his shoulders the Naevus, said by Moslems to have marked Moses, Christ, and Mohammed.

At first he followed quietly the principles of his father, with little alteration. About 1870 there was a great spread southward of his influence, the Sultan of Wadai and many of his subjects accepting his teaching. He refused to have anything to do with the Mahdi in the Sudan, and warned his followers against the latter's doctrines. He had always been regarded with anxiety by the Porte. Receiving a hint that the Sultan wished to lay hands on him and force him to live in Constantinople, he moved from Jaghbub with his immediate followers to the even less accessible Oasis of Kufara in 1895. In 1898 or 1899 he moved from Kufara to the small Oasis of Guro, south-west of the Tibesti Mountains. There he came in contact with the French, who were approaching from the Congo. To his alarm, he was again in touch with a European power, and this time a Frankish one. The French arrival near Lake Chad disturbed him, and, as Wadai was cooling towards him, he tried to effect an alliance with Ali Dinar in Darfur. In this he had not much success, but he founded some *Zawiets*, and the Senussist influence was a factor in the revolt of Ali Dinar during the war. Having proclaimed a holy war against the French, he was utterly defeated, after several indecisive battles. He died at Guro in 1902.

Sketch A.

Despite his battles, he and his sect were till now certainly pacific in intention. He was bound to come into conflict with the French, because they were penetrating territory under his influence. The official French view of the sect was that it was often blamed unreasonably for acts of isolated fanatics. It had rendered great services to the natives of the wandering tribes between Tripoli and the Central Sudan by sinking wells, improving rest-houses, repopulating oases and securing trade-routes, as well as by giving an elementary education. Since the Senussists take Christians and even Jews into their rest-houses, they cannot be considered intolerant. Few cruelties are recorded against the second Grand Senussi, but he hated the Frank fanatically. His person was considered so sacred that he was usually veiled, and his intercourse with the world was conducted through a vizier.

The Third Senussi.

Mohammed-el-Mahdi left two young sons, the elder, Mohammed Idris, being fourteen years old at the time of his father's death. El-Mahdi had also a number of nephews, of whom the eldest, Ahmed-es-Sherif, was about thirty. The latter was elected by the brethren as his successor, owing to the youth of his sons.

The new Senussi returned to Kufara to avoid contact with the French. He continued to exercise the same influence as his predecessor over all Libya and the *Zawiets* outside it. He retained to a great extent his influence in Wadai, but made no striking progress with Ali Dinar in Darfur. He never established any hold upon the Hejaz, though he had some hundreds of adherents there. In Egypt proper there were only three *Zawiets*. Mohammed Idris had, at the outbreak of hostilities between his uncle and the British, reached man's age, and was moreover intelligent and moderate, so that the position of Sidi Ahmed was not without difficulties.

The Tripolitan War.

The Senussi took no prominent part in the Tripolitan War, as his friendship for the Turks was not warm. After it was over, however, he gave assistance to Aziz Bey el Masri, a Turkish officer who remained behind with a small party. There was some ground for the belief that in this he was egged on by the Khedive. On 14th January 1913 the Turkish governor and most of his troops left Tripoli, but the troubles of the Italians were by no means over.

In May 1913 the Italians, who had gained numerous small successes, were defeated by the Arabs and Turks near Derna (the Action of Etangi). In June Derna was reinforced, while on the other hand Aziz Bey left the Arab force with 600 regulars, apparently owing to quarrels with the Senussi. He eventually entered Egypt, where he was allowed to remain. The Italians then took the offensive and occupied Etangi.

In January 1914 the Senussi was in south-east Cyrenaica, and had suffered several reverses owing to the new energy which the arrival of General Ameglio had brought to the Italian troops. At this date it was believed the Arabs had the following troops :—

Derna district ..	3,000 regulars (paid by the Senussi) ;
	6,000 volunteers (self-supporting), commanded by the Senussi and a Turkish officer.
Benghazi district	3,000 regulars ;
	5,000 volunteers.
Tripoli district ..	600 negroes ;
	800 Zowai Arabs ;
	1,000 Tuaregs.

Later information suggests that these figures were exaggerated, and that the Senussi had not more than 10,000 men.

All these were armed with modern rifles and had a fair supply of ammunition. The Senussi had a cartridge factory which turned out 1,000 rounds a day.

Desultory operations between the Arabs and the Italians, the former hard to hit because of their mobility in the desert, the latter secure behind their fortifications, were in progress during the first half of the Great War.

APPENDIX 6.

TELEGRAPHIC ORDER BY HEADQUARTERS No. 3 SECTION.

G.S. 192.   4th August.

Anzac Mtd. Divn., 3rd A.L.H. Bde., 42nd Divn., No. 2 Section, 160th Bde., 126th Bde., Qantara Outposts.

Result of to-day's operations has placed us in a most favourable position. Enemy's attempt to outflank our position at Romani has been defeated. Several strong attacks have been beaten off. Our troops took

Map 10.
Sketch 10.

the offensive in evening and drove enemy off occupied positions, capturing 400 to 500 prisoners and one machine gun. Information points to enemy having recognized failure to penetrate our line and having drawn back to line of entrenched position running from Hod el Enna round Bir Qatiya to Abu Hamra with covering troops in front. Section Commander intends first of all to push the enemy southwards to the line Katib Gannit to Hod el Enna and secondly if opportunity offers to make a general advance on the northern flank with all available force in the direction of Abu Hamra and Er Rabah. At the same time a strong enveloping movement against the left flank of the enemy's position will be made from the direction of Dueidar. In accordance with this, all troops will move at 4 a.m. as follows.

Anzac Mounted Division will press forward all along the line with its right directed on Bir el Enna and its left in close touch with 52nd Division advancing on the line Katib Gannit to Mount Meredith. The 3rd A.L.H. Brigade will push out towards Bir en Nuss and attack Hod el Enna from the south, keeping in touch with Anzac Mounted Division or the 5th Mounted Brigade on its left flank. The 5th Mounted Brigade under the orders of G.O.C. 42nd Division, will assist in linking up the right of the Anzac Mounted Division and the 3rd A.L.H. Brigade. 42nd Division will move forward in full strength on the line Canterbury Hill to Mount Royston to Bir el Enna in close support of Anzac Mounted Division's right flank, and will drive back any opposition which delays the advance of the cavalry. 52nd Division will operate in a similar manner towards Mount Meredith. The G.O.C. 52nd Division will also organize his troops for a combined forward movement in the direction of Abu Hamra. This movement will only be undertaken if the situation is clear and under instructions from Section Headquarters, but all preparations for this must be complete. If an attack is made from the east and south, he will counter-attack with all available troops with the object of driving the enemy in a south-easterly direction towards Er Rabah and Umm Ugba. The above general instructions will be acted on with the utmost vigour and close touch will be maintained between all formations to facilitate necessary modifications should action of enemy demand. Reports of situation will be sent to Section H.Q. as soon as possible every clock hour.

(Copy not timed, apparently issued about 7 p.m.)

APPENDIX 7.

TELEGRAPHIC ORDER BY HEADQUARTERS No. 3 SECTION.

G.S. 216. 5th August (10.45 p.m.).

Anzac Mtd. Divn., Qantara Defences, No. 2 Section, D.D.M.S., R.F.C., Signals, Q., 42nd Divn., 52nd Divn., O/C Railways.

Map 10.
Sketch 10.
Information and air reconnaissance both confirm that enemy has retired leaving rear guard with artillery to hold position on line Er Rabah to Qatiya to Bir el Hamisah, strength probably one regiment. Our cavalry were unable to advance beyond Qatiya to-day. Captures to date are nearly 3,000 prisoners with four guns and some machine guns and 22 Germans. Pursuit will be continued to-morrow. Anzac Mounted Division less two brigades will move at daylight and press forward vigorously against retreating enemy. They will attack any bodies of enemy found and endeavour to cut off retreat of men and material. 42nd Division will advance at 4 a.m. and occupy line Bir el Mamluk to ruins of Qatiya inclusive as early as possible, supporting cavalry with full strength if required. 52nd Division, less one brigade, will advance from Abu Hamra at 4 a.m.

and occupy line Er Rabah to ruins of Qatiya not inclusive as early as possible, supporting cavalry with full strength if required. Both divisions will be responsible for protection of their own outer flanks. Railhead will be established as far forward as possible and supply will be from railway for all above troops. Section Headquarters will move to Romani at 12 noon, up to which hour reports will be sent to Qantara as usual.

Divisions will arrange for direct communication to the Section Report Centre at that place. The G.O.C. 52nd Division will nominate an officer to command the Romani-Mahamdiyah defences and notify his name to Section Headquarters. Acknowledge. Addressed 42nd, 52nd, Anzac Mtd. Divn., repeated R.F.C., D.D.M.S., No. 2 Section, Signals, Qantara Defences, Q.

APPENDIX 8.
Secret.

EASTERN FORCE ORDER No. 33.
BY
LIEUTENANT-GENERAL SIR CHARLES DOBELL, K.C.B., C.M.G., D.S.O., Commanding Eastern Force.

Headquarters Eastern Force.
24th March 1917.

1. The enemy's main body is in Tell en Nejile–Huj area, south of the **Map 12.** Wadi el Hesi, covered by detachments about Gaza, Tell esh Sheria, Abu **Sketch 14.** Hureira, and Beersheba. He appears to dispose of two weak divisions and fragments of two other divisions—the equivalent in all of between $2\frac{1}{2}$ and 3 divisions. One of these divisions appears not to number more than 6,000 rifles.

2. The General Officer Commanding intends to drive the enemy out of Gaza and hopes to destroy his advanced detachment at that place.

3. The Desert Column will move forward in the early hours of the morning of 26th March against the enemy at Gaza. The G.O.C. Desert Column will dispose his mounted troops so as to block the enemy's lines of retreat from Gaza, and to watch for any movement of his main body towards Gaza from the Tell en Nejile–Huj area, or of the Tell esh Sheria–Abu Hureira detachment along the main Gaza–Beersheba road or roads to the north of it.

He will then attack the enemy's force occupying Gaza.

4. (*a*) In order to pass the mounted troops round the enemy's position, it will be necessary for G.O.C. Desert Column to move them through the outpost position of the 54th Division soon after dawn on the 26th March.

The 54th Division will be ready to move at 5.30 a.m. on the 26th. As soon as the mounted troops of the Desert Column are clear and over the Wadi Ghazze, the division (less one infantry brigade, one field artillery brigade, and one field ambulance) will move from In Seirat to a position of readiness in the neighbourhood of Sheikh Abbas to be selected by the Divisional Commander. G.O.C. 54th Division will not disperse his troops at Sheikh Abbas more than is unavoidable, but will select a position suitable for defence against an attack from the east and south-east, and will make arrangements so as to enable it to be occupied and rapidly strengthened if necessary. He will also reconnoitre his lines of advance against a hostile force moving on Gaza from the Tell esh Sheria–Abu Hureira direction.

G.O.C. 54th Division will also make every effort to develop a supply fwater in the Wadi Ghazze, between Abu Im Teibig[1] and the bend in the Wadi east of El Breij, both inclusive.

(b) The Brigade Group, 54th Division, left at In Seirat, in accordance with the foregoing order, will for the time being be directly at the disposal of the General Officer Commanding Eastern Force.

5. The 52nd Division will await orders at Khan Yunis, for the protection of which place G.O.C. 52nd Division will be responsible. The division will be ready to move at the shortest notice, with two complete " mobile rations " on the man, and the Divisional Commander will make every endeavour to arrange that, by leaving behind non-essentials carried in his first-line transport, by loading additional forage on artillery vehicles etc., he may be able to carry one day's marching ration for animals in his first-line transport, in case it is necessary for him to move forward.

6. When the enemy's force at Gaza is disposed of, and if the G.O.C. Desert Column finds an opportunity for the use of his mounted troops in pursuit, the 1st Imperial Camel Brigade will revert to the direct command of the General Officer Commanding Eastern Force. G.O.C. Desert Column will report the exact position of this brigade as soon as possible after the dispositions of the mounted troops preliminary to the main attack on Gaza are completed.

7. The following is the disposition of the Royal Flying Corps.

A permanent contact patrol of one aeroplane will be maintained with the Desert Column, reporting direct to battle headquarters Desert Column. G.O.C. Desert Column will be responsible for transmitting information received from this contact patrol to Eastern Force headquarters, or battle headquarters, as the case may be. Five aeroplanes will be detailed for general reconnaissance, reporting to battle headquarters Eastern Force ; all information gained by these aeroplanes of movements of the enemy main body (at present in the Tell en Nejile–Huj area) or of his central detachment (at present in the Tell esh Sheria–Abu Hureira area), or of the approach of enemy troops from the Lydda–Ramle area, will be dropped at battle headquarters Desert Column, as well as at battle headquarters Eastern Force.

Six aeroplanes will be detailed for co-operation with the artillery. A wireless receiving station is allotted to the heavy artillery, three to each division, and two to each mounted division.

Six aeroplanes will be detailed for patrol duties.

8. *Special Communications.*—A Shore Signal Station, for intercommunication between the Navy and the Army will be established at 6 a.m. on March 26th at a point 200 yards north of the well at Sheikh Shabasi. This station will be connected by wire with battle headquarters Eastern Force.

Communication with the Navy can also be obtained by wireless from battle headquarters Eastern Force. As soon as Gaza is occupied, G.O.C. Desert Column will make arrangements for opening a Signal Station at some convenient place on the beach. The Sheikh Shabasi Signal Station will close down as soon as the new station is opened. In the event of battle headquarters Eastern Force moving before Gaza Shore Signal Station is opened, arrangements will be made for the Sheikh Shabasi station to be connected to the nearest signal office.

9. A note regarding the supply of ammunition is issued as an annexure to this order.

10. *Medical Arrangements.*—A Casualty Clearing Station will be established at Khan Yunis to which patients will be evacuated from the

---

[1] On the left bank of the Wadi, opposite Um Jerrar.

front. This Casualty Clearing Station will be laid out on the 25th ready to be set up, but no tents will be pitched on that day. G.O.C. 52nd Division will arrange to pitch the tents on the morning of the 26th.

The 54th Division will form a dressing station if required near In Seirat, on the Gaza–Rafah road as near as possible to Deir el Balah.

The 52nd Division will form a dressing station at Khan Yunis if required.

Evacuation will take place from the dressing stations to the Casualty Clearing Station at Khan Yunis by motor ambulance convoy.

D.D.M.S. Desert Column has at his disposal 21 Ford motor ambulances for use as an ambulance convoy. In the event of motor ambulances not being available for evacuation purposes, the A.D's.M.S. 54th and 52nd Divisions will use their own transport.

11. ─────────────────
To G.O.C. Desert Column;
G.O.C. 52nd Division;
G.O.C. 54th Division;
G.O.C. 74th Division;
Commandant, Khan Yunis;
only.

Special instructions are issued with this order regarding supply arrangements.

12. Battle headquarters Eastern Force will be established by 6 a.m. on the 26th March about Point 310 north-east of In Seirat.

The Officer in Charge of Signals Eastern Force will arrange to connect the battle headquarters of Eastern Force and Desert Column by wire as early as possible on the 26th.

G. P. DAWNAY,
Brigadier-General, General Staff, Eastern Force.

APPENDIX 9.

Secret.

DESERT COLUMN ORDER NO. 25.

BY

LIEUTENANT-GENERAL SIR P. W. CHETWODE, BT., C.B., D.S.O.

Commanding Desert Column.

March 25th 1917.

Reference Map : Sheet Rafah 1/125,000.

1. The enemy, whose estimated strength is about 2,000, is holding Gaza from a position about Ali Muntar, round to the olive groves to the south and south-west of the town.   **Map 12. Sketch 14.**

There are enemy forces at Hureira (10 miles S.E.), Tell esh Sheria (14 miles), Kh. el Akra, 2 miles N.E. of Huj (11 miles), and Tell en Nejile, on the railway 8 miles east of Huj (17 miles).

All the above distances from Gaza unless otherwise stated.

2. The Desert Column, closely supported by the 54th Division, will attack the enemy at Gaza to-morrow.

3. The enemy's position will be attacked by the 53rd Division, assisted, if necessary, by a proportion of cavalry.

4. The rôle of the I.C.C. and Cavalry is :—
   (a) To prevent the escape of the Gaza garrison by surrounding them ;
   (b) To observe the enemy known to be in the direction of Huj, Hureira, etc.
   (c) To attack these enemy detachments if they issue from their trenches and move to the relief of Gaza, and to co-operate with the 54th Division should the latter advance to attack them.
   (d) To assist in the reduction of the Gaza garrison if the 53rd Division find difficulty in doing so.
   (e) To pursue the enemy in the Huj or Hureira area if news be received that he is retiring either during, or after, the action at Gaza.

5. In order to carry out the above, the following moves will take place on the morning of the 26th March :—
   (a) *Mounted Troops.*—(i) The I.C.C. Brigade will move so as to be ready to cross the Wadi at Tell el Jemmi at 5 a.m. and take up a position of observation a short distance N.E. of El Mendur. Area of reconnoitring responsibility will be from the Wadi Ghazze (inclusive) to the Gaza–Saba main road (exclusive).
   (ii) The A. & N.Z. Mounted Division, closely followed by the Imperial Mounted Division, will move round the rear of the 54th Division, who are about In Seirat, and be ready to cross the Wadi by their previously reconnoitred routes at 5 a.m.
   (iii) The leading division will move rapidly to the neighbourhood of Beit Durdis, where it will take up a position of observation, detaching sufficient troops to surround Gaza completely from Beit Durdis, through Jebaliye, to the sea. Area of reconnoitring responsibility will be from Huj (inclusive) by Najd, to Deir Sneid (inclusive).
   (iv) The other mounted division (less detachment mentioned in para. 5(b) below) will move to the neighbourhood of Kh. er Reseim, 4 miles S.E. of Ali Muntar, and take up a position of observation.
   Area of reconnoitring responsibility will be Gaza–Saba main road (inclusive) to Huj (exclusive).
   (v) It is important for the cavalry to reach these positions as soon as possible, and if the ground is difficult their guns must follow as best they can and join them later.
   The mounted formations will remain as concentrated as possible and make only such detachments as are necessary for the above.
   (b) *53rd Division.*—The 53rd Division, with 1 regiment (less 1 squadron) Imperial Mounted Division, will be in a position to throw a strong bridgehead across the Wadi by 5 a.m. in the neighbourhood of El Breij and seize the high ground Mansura–Esh Sheluf, and will attack Ali Muntar as soon as the G.O.C. can complete his reconnaissances, registration, and other arrangements.
   (c) 54th Division have instructions to follow the cavalry across the Wadi and take up a position of readiness about Sheikh Abbas.
   (d) No. 11 Light Armoured Motor Battery and No. 7 Light Car Patrol will follow the I.C.C. and endeavour to reach the neighbourhood of Er Reseim, remaining on the Gaza–Saba main road.

6. *Ammunition.*—(a) Wheeled echelon of D.A.C. will accompany the guns.

(b) The Camel Echelons of the Mounted Divisional Ammunition Columns will follow the I.C. Brigade on the morning of the 26th *via* Tell el Jemmi and El Mendur, to rejoin their Division, guides being sent back to lead them up.

(c) On arrival at Sheikh Abbas the 54th Division will dump three-quarters of its ammunition, and the empty camels will proceed to the west bank of the Wadi Ghazze at Sheikh Nebhan to refill from a dump which will be formed there by 52nd Divisional Ammunition Column.

(d) The D.A.C. of 60-pdr. sections attached to 53rd Division will move in accordance with instructions given by G.O.C. 53rd Division.

(e) The D.A.C's of 53rd Division and I.C. Brigade will accompany their formations under divisional or brigade arrangements.

7. *Medical.*—The 53rd Division will form a dressing station at Deir el Balah immediately after the departure of the troops, and a collecting station at the Wadi crossing on the Rafah–Gaza road.

Dressing stations will be formed by Mounted Divisions and I.C. Brigade at the following places :—

(a) A. & N.Z. Mounted Division on Gaza–El Faluje road somewhere west of Beit Hanun.
(b) Imperial Mounted Division on main Gaza–Saba road west of Kh. er Reseim.
(c) I.C. Brigade about the same spot as Imperial Mounted Division.

A convoy of motor ambulances under the D.D.M.S. will work from the 53rd Division collecting station to the Deir el Balah and westwards from the commencement of the action.

When Gaza is in our possession, motor ambulances will then work through the town to the Dressing Stations of mounted troops and thence to an improvised Casualty Clearing Station which will be established in the town itself.

8. *Trains.*—B Wheeled Echelons of Divisions will remain at Deir el Balah on the departure of the troops and will be ordered up later, under divisional arrangements, as required.

9. *1st-Line Transport.*—Commanders will arrange that such portions of 1st-Line Transport as are not actually required for fighting purposes shall move in rear of the fighting troops of their own Divisions.

10. *Water Development.*—The 53rd and 54th Divisions will arrange to have water developed in the Wadi as soon as possible after the passage of the fighting troops; the 53rd Division north of El Breij; the 54th Division south of it.

11. Desert Column Headquarters will follow the second Mounted Division and will be established about Sheikh Abbas, Pt. 325.

12. *Communications.*—Column signals will keep touch with Divisions by cable as far as possible. Cable wagons will accompany each Division, laying lines from Deir el Balah. These will be diverted into battle headquarters when this moves to Sheikh Abbas.

By this means communication will be maintained between Divisions and Column Headquarters while on the move.

Divisions will establish visual communication with Sheikh Abbas as early as possible. Till then, in the event of failure of the cable, a visual station on Hill 310 will transmit messages from Divisions to Column Headquarters while on the march.

13. Acknowledge.

V. M. FERGUSSON,
Lieutenant-Colonel, General Staff, Desert Column.

APPENDIX 10.

Secret.

OPERATION ORDER. NO. 27.

BY

MAJOR.-GENERAL A. G. DALLAS, C.B., C.M.G.,
Commanding 53rd Division.

25th March 1917.

Reference Map : Rafah Sheet Scale 1/125,000.

Map 12.
Sketch 14.

1. In accordance with the general situation and intention of the General Officer Commanding given in the Memorandum issued herewith, the Division will attack and drive the enemy from the Gaza position to-morrow.

2. In accordance with detail given in para. 5, the 158th Infantry Brigade and attached troops will commence to cross the Wadi Ghazze at 3.45 a.m. by prepared crossings " A " and " B," under the orders of Br.-General S. F. Mott, in accordance with instructions already issued to him, in preparation for his advance on Mansura.

The 160th Brigade and attached troops will commence to cross the Wadi Ghazze at 3.30 a.m. by crossings " D " and " E " under the orders of Br.-General W. J. C. Butler, in accordance with instructions already issued to him, and make good the Es Sire ridge for a depth of about 2,000 yards.

As soon as both Brigades have established the necessary bridgeheads, they will pass across the troops of their respective columns and report to Divisional Headquarters as soon as their Brigades are ready for the advance on the line Mansura–Esh Sheluf.

The 159th Infantry Brigade and attached troops will follow the 158th Brigade, so as to assemble in a covered position in the Wadi Ghazze as soon as the 158th Infantry Brigade and the Artillery are clear. Should the 158th Brigade not have cleared the Wadi Ghazze before daylight, the G.O.C. 159th Brigade will move into a position under cover in the Wadi Ghazze.

The 2/4th Royal West Kent Regiment will cross the Wadi Ghazze at 3.45 a.m. and will make good the Clay Bluff and establish a bridgehead to cover the crossing of the Right Section, 15th Heavy Battery R.G.A. At daylight the Regiment, Imperial Mounted Division, will cross the Wadi Ghazze under cover of the 2/4th Royal West Kent Regiment and will move forward, covering its flanks as may be dictated by circumstances.

The role of this Column is to divert the enemy's attention to this flank and prevent him reinforcing the Ali Muntar position. The O.C. will therefore demonstrate against him, but will not allow himself to be involved in a close hostile attack from which he is unable to extricate himself. Should the enemy attack in strength, this Column will adopt rear-guard tactics and will delay the enemy's advance as much as possible, the Cavalry paying special attention to the seashore.

This Column is responsible for the safety of the Right Section, 15th Heavy Battery R.G.A., and it will be under the command of Lieut.-Colonel N. Money, D.S.O.

3. *Divisional Cavalry.*—The Divisional Squadron (less one troop escort for G.O.C. Division and one N.C.O. and four men each for G.O.C's. 158th and 159th Brigades) will assemble on the main Rafah–Gaza road about 1 mile S.W. of the Wadi Ghazze at 2.45 a.m. to-morrow and will cross the Wadi Ghazze at 3.30 a.m. and make good the Pink House and Gardens and the high ground immediately east of it.

4. *Artillery.*—(*a*) As soon as the 160th Infantry Brigade has secured the Es Sire position and the 158th Infantry Brigade has sufficiently

APPENDIX 10

advanced to ensure their safety, the 265th and 266th Brigades R.F.A. followed by the Section of the 10th Heavy Battery R.G.A., will move forward from the position of assembly and will cross the Wadi Ghazze; the 266th Brigade R.F.A. will follow the 158th Infantry Brigade; the 265th Brigade R.F.A. and the Section of No. 10 Heavy Battery R.G.A. will follow the 160th Infantry Brigade.

They will pass the Wadi Ghazze by the crossings prepared under the arrangements of the C.R.E.

(b) Under orders of the C.R.A. the 265th Brigade R.F.A. will then support the advance of the 160th Infantry Brigade, the 266th Brigade R.F.A. that of the 158th Infantry Brigade, until these Infantry Brigades have made good the line Mansura–Esh Sheluf.

(c) The Section, 91st Heavy Battery R.G.A., will occupy a position in observation by 4.30 a.m. in the Wadi Ghazze north of the telegraph line.

The Divisional Squadron, Duke of Lancaster's Own Yeomanry, under Captain Bates, will make good the Red House and Gardens at the Wadi Ghazze, where it is crossed by the Gaza–Rafah road and will provide for the protection of the Section, 91st Heavy Battery R.G.A. in action, which it will do under the orders of the C.R.A. It will march to its position direct from its bivouac and will not join the divisional position of assembly.

(d) The Section, 15th Heavy Battery R.G.A., marching by the northern track, will occupy a concealed position of readiness south of the Wadi Ghazze and will cross by a specially prepared passage as soon as the O.C. 2/4th Royal West Kent Regiment has secured the Clay Bluff near the caves, 1 mile from the mouth of the Wadi Ghazze. It will be ready to cross at 5 a.m.

(e) When the line Mansura–Esh Sheluf has been reached, the distribution and further action of the Artillery will be communicated as the situation may demand.

5. The Division (less D.A.C., Divisional Train, Field Ambulances and Mobile Veterinary Section) will be assembled at a point just north of the I in In Seirat (Square J.3) by 2.45 a.m. to-morrow morning in the following grouping :—

Group I.—158th Brigade, 1 Section Field Company R.E., to be detailed by C.R.E., and 1 Bearer Sub-Division Field Ambulance, to be detailed by A.D.M.S., will be on the south. The Right Section, 10th Heavy Battery R.G.A. will follow this group from this point of assembly.

Group II.—160th Brigade, 1 Section Field Company R.E., to be detailed by C.R.E., and 1 Bearer Sub-section Field Ambulance to be detailed by A.D.M.S., north of 158th Brigade.

Group III.—159th Brigade, 1 Section Field Company R.E., to be detailed by C.R.E., and 1 Bearer Sub-section Field Ambulance to be detailed by A.D.M.S., in rear of 158th Brigade.

The 265th Brigade R.F.A., and Right Section, 10th Heavy Battery, R.G.A., will form up with the 160th Brigade and the 266th Brigade R.F.A. with the 158th Infantry Brigade.

Group IV.—One Regiment, Imperial Mounted Division, the 2/4th Royal West Kent Regiment, and a portion of a Bearer Subsection will assemble just south-west of Sheikh Rashed (Square J.2) at 2.45 a.m.

Ammunition, tools, signalling equipment, and medical stores will accompany units on 1st-Line Transport Camels.

6. First-Line Transport Camels, other than those mentioned in last sentence of para. 5, will remain in their present bivouacs until 5 a.m. on the open ground 300 yards north of Point 130 (I.2),[1] clear of the bivouac

---

[1] Point 130 is north-east of Deir el Balah.

areas, under suitable escorts, which will be commanded by an officer in the case of larger units.

An officer of the Divisional Headquarters Staff will direct them to their forward position of assembly, 500 yards south of that mentioned in para. 5.

(*b*) At 5 a.m. the D.A.C. will move from its bivouac area to the point of assembly mentioned in paragraph 5.

(*c*) At 4.30 a.m. the Field Ambulances (less Bearer Sub-sections mentioned in para. 5) will move from their bivouac areas to a position south of the position of assembly mentioned in para. 5, selected by the A.D.M.S., who will also select suitable sites forward of this position for Dressing Stations.

7. *Prisoners.*—Prisoners will be marched under escort to Point 210 El Breij, where they will be handed over to the A.P.M.

8. *S.A.A.*—Two hundred rounds S.A.A. will be carried on the man and regimental reserve S.A.A. will be completed from the D.A.C. before marching off.

9. *Supplies.*—(*a*) One complete day's supplies on mobile scale will be carried in addition to the iron ration on the man.

(*b*) The 1st-Line Transport Camels, carrying three days' emergency rations, will remain in their bivouac areas at Deir el Balah under small guards.

10. The Divisional Train will remain parked in the bivouac area and await orders.

11. *Water.*—All water bottles and *fanatis* will be completely filled before leaving bivouac areas.

12. *Divisional Headquarters.*—53rd Division battle headquarters will be established at a point on the 200 contour just south of the El in the word El Breij, at 3.15 a.m.

13. Acknowledge.

A. SINCLAIR THOMSON,
Lieutenant Colonel, General Staff, 53rd (Welsh) Division.

Issued at 9.15 p.m.

APPENDIX 11.

Secret.

OPERATION ORDER NO. 28.

BY

MAJOR-GENERAL A. G. DALLAS, C.B., C.M.G.

G. 20. 26–3–17.

Map. 12.
Sketch 14.

The Division will attack the Ali Muntar position as follows:—

160th Brigade along the main ridge from the south-west on Ali Muntar ;

158th Brigade from the east also on Ali Muntar ;

159th Brigade, less one battalion, on the hill north-east of Ali Muntar, indicated to G.O.C. 159th Brigade, at the same time covering the right of the 158th Brigade.

The Artillery of the Division will support the attack under orders of the C.R.A.

The G.O.C. 159th Brigade will detail one battalion in Divisional Reserve at Mansura.

A. SINCLAIR THOMSON,
Lieut.-Colonel.

APPENDIX 12

Secret.

EASTERN FORCE ORDER No. 40.

BY

LIEUTENANT-GENERAL SIR CHARLES DOBELL, K.C.B.,
C.M.G., D.S.O., Commanding Eastern Force.

Headquarters,
Eastern Force,
12th April 1917.

Reference Maps: Syria 1/250,000 Jerusalem Sheet; Gaza 1/40,000.

1. The enemy, strength about 20,000 to 25,000 rifles in all, is disposed **Map 14.** in a chain of detachments along the 16 miles Sheria–Hureira–El Atawine– **Sketch 16.** Khirbet el Bir–Gaza, holding apparently a small reserve 12 miles north-east between Huj and Tell el Hesi.

Of the above numbers he appears to have about 8,500 at Gaza, 4,500 about Khirbet el Bir and Kufiye, 2,000 at El Atawine, and the *16th Turkish Division* (about 6,000 rifles) about Hureira–Sheria.

2. The G.O.C. intends to advance the right flank of the force so as to seize and occupy the Sheikh Abbas–Mansura ridge, preparatory to undertaking further operations.

3. (*a*) G.O.C. Desert Column will move one Mounted Division to Shellal during the night Zero/1st. The remainder of the Desert Column will move to Tell el Jemmi during the night Zero/1st. Neither move will begin before dusk on Zero day.

The mission assigned by G.O.C. Desert Column to his leading division will be to operate against Hureira in such a way as if possible to immobilize the enemy's force there; and, if the enemy should leave or sufficiently weaken Hureira, to seize any opportunity which may offer, whether for attacking his troops on the march or for dealing decisively with a weak detachment left at Hureira itself.

G.O.C. Desert Column will dispose the remainder of his command in such a manner as best to protect the right flank and right rear of the 54th Division. Patrols about the line of the Wadis Sheria and Sihan (Tell el Jemmi–El Mendur–Baiket Abu Mailik–El Aseiferiye) will be taken as a general indication; but G.O.C. Desert Column will report his exact dispositions as soon as they are made.

(*b*) The attack on the Sheikh Abbas–Mansura position will be carried out under the orders of G.O.C. 52nd Division by the 54th and 52nd Divisions.

The objective of this attack will be from El Meshrefe to the Es Sire ridge about Kurd Hill, *via* Sheikh Abbas, the Sheikh Abbas ridge and Mansura.

G.O.C. 52nd Division will allot their definite objectives to the 54th and 52nd Divisions.

During the night Zero/1st both divisions will cross the Wadi Ghazze, with covering forces thrown out to the line (approximate) Sharta–El Burjabye–Es Sire to protect their passage.

The 54th Division will be on the right, moving by crossings C.11 to C.16, both inclusive. The 52nd Division will be on the left, moving by crossings north of and including C.17.

G.O.C. 52nd Division will have both divisions so disposed as to be ready to attack by 4.15 a.m. on first day.

G.O.C. 52nd Division will make special arrangements, in allotting the task of the troops on the Es Sire ridge, to meet the contingency of an enemy movement against his left flank.

On gaining their objectives both divisions will immediately consolidate the position gained as completely and as rapidly as possible. Should the enemy's artillery fire render the consolidation of a strong position above the Mansura cliff especially difficult by day, the lip of the cliff must be held and a position beyond (north-east of) it dug and wired during the night 1st/2nd.

Every effort must be made to ensure that the position is made strong enough by dawn on second day—with especial reference to gaining for the occupying troops immunity from hostile shell fire, and with obstacles where necessary—to enable it to be held in case of need by one division alone, with a strong flank thrown back towards Sharta. The necessity for this, with a view to subsequent operations, must be strongly impressed upon all ranks.

Similarly every effort must be made rapidly to improve and clearly to mark communications between the position and the Wadi Ghazze; to establish the necessary forward dumps of ammunition, stores, and supplies; to search for sources of water supply and, if found, to mark them and carry out any necessary development.

(c) The 53rd Division will not advance on first day beyond the general line Red House–Tell el Ujul–Money Hill–the coast between Marine View and Cheshire Clump.

During the night Zero/1st, G.O.C. 53rd Division will, however, complete and occupy a strong point in the gap between his own right and the left of the 52nd Division, north-east of, and covering the crossings at, the Red House. This must be strongly entrenched, wired, and provided with necessary communication trenches. It will be selected and occupied with a view to assisting in the protection of the left flank of the 52nd Division on the Es Sire ridge.

On first day, G.O.C. 53rd Division will arrange to show special activity in reconnaissance towards Samson Ridge and Sheikh Ajlin.

One Infantry Brigade and one Field Ambulance, 53rd Division, will be retained near St. James' Park from dawn on first day, ready to be placed at the disposal of G.O.C. Eastern Force. This Brigade will not be moved without previous reference to Headquarters Eastern Force.

(d) The 74th Division will be in General Reserve, with one brigade in its present outpost positions, and the remaining brigades concentrated behind it—one east of In Seirat near the Um Jerrar road, and one near the road leading to crossing C.23.

In case of the enemy attempting any movement against the right of the 53rd or the left of the 52nd Division, G.O.C. 74th Division will be prepared to act rapidly if he should receive orders to counter-attack such a movement. Should the occasion arise, the 272nd Field Artillery Brigade will be allotted to G.O.C. 74th Division for support of a counter-attack in this area.

(e) The Eastern Force Artillery will be disposed as stated in " General Instructions—Artillery," O.Z. 4/4, of 9th April, for counter-battery work, for action against known enemy observation posts, for support of the nfantry at special points, or to oppose any counter-attack on the left of the 52nd or the right of the 53rd Division.

(f) The Naval force will work in two groups :—
    (i) Monitors.
    (ii) *Requin.*

The principal objectives of the naval guns will be enemy guns beyond the reach of the Heavy Artillery Group ; Ali Muntar and, if required, the Labyrinth and its neighbourhood.

APPENDIX 12

(g) O.C. "E" Company Heavy Section Machine-Gun Corps, with three sections (6 tanks) will come under the command of G.O.C. 52nd Division from 6 p.m. on Zero day.

One section (2 tanks) will come under the command of G.O.C. 53rd Division from the same hour and date.

4. The O.C. 5th Wing will provide contact patrol aeroplanes and will carry out continuous close tactical reconnaissance during the hours of daylight on first day, and subsequently as may be necessary. He will be prepared to carry out distant reconnaissance as required.

5. G.O's.C. formations will arrange between themselves for interchange of the necessary liaison officers.

6. Understudies for Staff Officers will be nominated, and the necessary notifications issued to all concerned, under arrangements to be made by G.O's.C. Desert Column and Divisions.

7. Infantry Battalions on going into action will leave behind the officers and other ranks detailed in circular memorandum O.Z. 1/5 of April 4th as amended by O.Z. 1/23 of April 10th. This personnel will remain at the divisional dumps referred to in para. 9 below. G.O's.C. will make their own arrangements for calling up any officers and other ranks required to replace casualties as may be necessary.

8. One hundred and seventy rounds S.A.A., one complete day's rations on the mobile scale, and one iron ration will be carried on the man.

Grenades will be carried under divisional arrangements. Arrangements will also be made divisionally to provide up to 50 per cent. of the infantry with tin squares or triangles to be worn on the back, in order to indicate the position of the infantry to our artillery and aircraft; these can be made from the tins of biscuit boxes.

9. Packs and surplus equipment, stores, etc., will be collected and stored during Zero day under arrangements for the formation of divisional dumps to be made by G.O's.C. Desert Column and Divisions.

10. No maps will be carried into action other than the following :—
Syria 1/250,000 (Jerusalem Sheet), Sinai Peninsula Map 1/125,000 (Squared Rafah Sheet), and the Gaza squared maps, 1/40,000 and 1/15,000.

11. The reallotment of water areas, referred to in circular memorandum O.Z. 2/21 of 10th April, will take effect from 6 p.m. on Zero day.

12. The Desert Column will arrange to draw supplies from the Desert Column Supply Dump at Khan Yunis, or in the case of necessity from the Supply Depot at Deir el Balah Station.

Divisions and Eastern Force Troops, all of which are provided with train transport, will draw their supplies from the Supply Depot at Deir el Balah Station. If the distance from this Supply Depot becomes too great for the train transport, assistance must be given by the 1st-Line Transport in possession of units.

13. (a) Twenty-one Ford Motor Ambulance Wagons have been placed at the disposal of the Desert Column for evacuating casualties to the Casualty Clearing Station at Deir el Balah Railway Station.

(b) G.O.C. Desert Column will make his own arrangements for the establishment of dressing stations. Except in the case of the Desert Column, divisional dressing stations will be on the Gaza–Rafah road about 800 yards north-east of Deir el Balah Railway Station. Advanced dressing stations will be formed in forward areas under divisional arrangements, and their situation will be notified to D.D.M.S. Eastern Force. Serious cases will be sent direct to the Casualty Clearing Stations (situated on the beach loop line to the west of the Deir el Balah Railway Station).

(c) It is expected that motor ambulance wagons, some of which are now available, will be able to run between the dressing and advanced dressing stations for purposes of evacuation. Application will be made to D.D.M.S. Eastern Force for any motor ambulances required for evacuation from the dressing or advanced dressing stations.

14. In addition to the existing arrangements for synchronization throughout the force by means of the Signal Service, the W/T station at Eastern Force Headquarters will send out to the monitors and the *Requin*, daily at 12.30 p.m., the official time for use during operations.

G.O.C. 52nd Division will make special arrangements with regard to the synchronization of watches in the 52nd and 54th Divisions.

15. Eastern Force Headquarters will remain in its present position when operations begin.

16. Acknowledge.

G. P. DAWNAY,
Brigadier-General, General Staff, Eastern Force.

Issued at 10 p.m.

APPENDIX 13.
Secret.

EASTERN FORCE ORDER NO. 41.

BY

LIEUTENANT-GENERAL SIR CHARLES DOBELL, K.C.B., C.M.G., D.S.O., Commanding Eastern Force.

Headquarters,
Eastern Force.
16th April 1917.

Reference Maps : Palestine, 1/63,360 ; Gaza (X)a, 1/40,000.

Map 15.
Sketch 16.

1. The latest information regarding the enemy will be notified separately before the second phase of the operations.

2. In accordance with Secret Instructions E.S. 163 of the 15th April, the G.O.C. intends to attack the enemy on . . . .

3. The attack will be preceded by a bombardment of the enemy's position which will begin at Zero hour and will be continued for two hours.

The Royal Navy and the Heavy Artillery will engage the following objectives :—

(a) *Requin* .. .. Ali Muntar Ridge.
One Monitor .. .. .. The Warren.
One Monitor .. .. .. The Labyrinth.

(b) *Heavy Artillery Group*—
15th Heavy Battery .. Guns and trenches W.10 and W.5.
10th Heavy Battery .. The Quarry and the Ridge up to Fryer Hill—guns and trenches.
91st Heavy Battery .. El Arish Redoubt and Magdhaba trench.
201st Siege Battery, 6-inch Howitzers. Outpost Hill and Middlesex Hill.
201st Siege Battery, 8-inch Howitzers. Labyrinth and Green Hill.

After Zero plus two hours the ships and heavy artillery will lift their fire on to targets in the area north and north-east of Ali el Muntar and north and north-west of Gaza.

Zero hour will be determined according to visibility, under arrangements made by B.G. R.A. Eastern Force, and will be notified to G.O.C. Desert Column and Divisional Commanders as soon as determined.

APPENDIX 13 425

4. The attack of the 52nd, 53rd, and 54th Divisions will be launched at Zero plus two hours.

5. The objective will be the enemy's positions between the Wadi running from Kh. Sihan to El Aseiferiye on the south-east, and the coast on the north-west.

The objective assigned to the 54th and 52nd Divisions, acting under the orders of G.O.C. 52nd Division, will be the enemy's positions between the Wadi above-mentioned (exclusive) and the Ali Muntar group of works (inclusive). G.O.C. 52nd Division will allot their definite objectives to the 52nd and 54th Divisions.

The objective allotted to the 53rd Division will be the enemy trenches in the sand dunes south-west and west of Gaza as far as the line of the Mazar–Magdhaba–Rafah trenches.

6. (a) The Desert Column, less the division operating against Hureira from Shellal, will push forward on the right of the 54th Division up the Atawine ridge, against the group of works which have been located there. G.O.C. Desert Column will make every effort to clear this ridge—if necessary leaving his horses and camels behind and operating dismounted. The remaining Mounted Division of the Desert Column will be brought from Shellal to the neighbourhood of El Mendur under instructions issued separately.

(b) The 54th and 52nd Divisions will advance to drive the enemy out of the Kh. el Bir series of works and trenches, and to clear the Es Sire–Ali Muntar ridge as far north as the line Kh. el Bir–Australia Hill.

(c) The 53rd Division will first attack and make good the line Samson Ridge–Sheikh Ajlin. Special arrangements for co-ordination of the attacks of the 52nd and 53rd Divisions have been made between General Officers Commanding concerned, so that the final stage of the attack of the 52nd Division on Middlesex Hill may be as nearly as possible simultaneous with the final stage of the 53rd Division's attack on Samson Ridge–Sheikh Ajlin. When these preliminary objectives have been gained, the 52nd Division will move forward to the attack of the Ali Muntar group of works simultaneously with the advance of the 53rd Division to the attack of the Mazar–Magdhaba–Rafah trenches and the enemy's works in front (west) of them.

Direct communication by wire and visual will be established between G.O's.C. 52nd and 53rd Divisions, in addition to their communication through Eastern Force Headquarters.

(d) The 74th Division will move across the Wadi Ghazze by crossings C.8 to C.13 and C.20, so as to be assembled between Sharta and the Wadi Nukhabir not later than 5 a.m.

The Division will move forward thence to the Sheikh Abbas ridge so as to take up a position of readiness behind it by Zero plus one hour, with outposts on the Sheikh Abbas ridge from Hill 300 (Y.1 and 2) to the Sheikh Abbas ridge at W.20.

The 263rd Field Artillery Brigade will be transferred from the 54th Division so as to come under the orders of G.O.C. 74th Division at Zero plus two hours on the . . .

G.O.C. 54th Division will inform G.O.C. 74th Division of the exact position of this brigade. The 272nd Field Artillery Brigade will come under the orders of the G.O.C. 74th Division from 6.30 on the previous evening, and will then cease to form part of the Eastern Force Artillery.

7. The attack will be pressed home in accordance with instructions already issued in Secret Memorandum E.S. 163 of the 15th April. When the right of the Eastern Attack has made good its objective, immediate steps will be taken to establish and consolidate a strong flank on a line running approximately north and south through Kh. el Bir.

As soon as it is clear that the Ali Muntar group of works has been taken, the 52nd and 54th Divisions, less such troops as are found to be required for the flank about Kh. el Bir, will go forward to clear the northern portion of the Ali Muntar ridge (Anzac Ridge).

Simultaneously with this movement the 53rd Division will push forward between Gaza and the sea from the Mazar–El Arish–Magdhaba–Zowaiid–Rafah line of trenches, to make good the area west of the town, but keeping clear of the town itself so far as possible.

G.O's.C. 52nd and 53rd Divisions will keep each other informed of their progress direct as well as through Eastern Force Headquarters, so that the commencement of their respective movements towards their final objectives may be synchronized.

8. G.O.C. 74th Division will establish communication by cable and visual with G.O.C. 52nd Division, as soon as the 74th Division reaches Sheikh Abbas. In the event of serious difficulty in communication between the 52nd Division and Eastern Force Headquarters, G.O.C. 52nd Division is empowered in emergency, or in case of immediate decision being required in order to exploit success, to call upon the 74th Division to act as he may consider necessary in either contingency. Unless, however, he is satisfied that the situation on the right flank has been cleared up, either by the complete success of the 54th Division or by the definite location of the Turkish *16th Division*, he will not move more than two infantry brigades and one field artillery brigade under this authority without first having received sanction from Eastern Force Headquarters.

In any case, should the occasion arise for the exercise of this authority, G.O.C. 52nd Division will be responsible for ensuring that a report notifying his action shall reach Eastern Force headquarters at the earliest possible moment.

9. G.O.C. Desert Column will, after the initial movements of the operation, act on the instructions already given in Secret Memorandum E.S.163 of the 15th April.

10. Special instructions regarding the Royal Flying Corps will be issued in due course, if the arrangements are varied from those made for the first phase of the operations.

11. If all the objectives are gained before nightfall, the 54th and 74th Divisions will take up defensive line facing approximately east, on the ridge running from the west of Kh. Kufiye, between Kh. el Bir and Kh. Sihan, to Sheikh Abbas. The 52nd Division will be disposed facing north-east and east with its left astride the northern portion of the Anzac Ridge. The 53rd Division will concentrate in the area Jebaliye–Sheikh Redwan–Meshahera.[1]

G.O.C. 53rd Division will detail the necessary troops to take charge of and control Gaza unless parties of the enemy are still holding out in the town at nightfall, in which case this work will be undertaken on the following morning.

In any case, all Commanders will take measures to keep their troops clear of the town until G.O.C. 53rd Division reports that the necessary measures for its control have been established.

12. In the event of the action not being brought to a conclusion within the day, the troops will hold the ground gained and will consolidate their positions during the night, preparatory to continuing the action on the following morning.

In this event, Divisions will be watered in accordance with the instructions contained in O.Z. 2/21 of the 10th April. The water dump (filled *fanatis*), established in the neighbourhood of Tell el Ahmar–Mansura

---

[1] The village of Jebaliye and the shrine of Sheikh Redwan are north of Gaza.

will, however, be available for troops of the 52nd and 54th Divisions if necessary; also for any troops of the 74th Division who may have been called on by the G.O.C. 52nd Division in accordance with the conditional authority given above in para. 8. The use of the water dump for this purpose will be at the discretion of G.O.C. 52nd Division. Every endeavour is, however, to be made to ensure that this water dump is not drawn upon unnecessarily and that in all cases in which it is possible animals are sent back to water at the divisional water areas referred to in the instruction above quoted, and that water is brought up from those areas for the troops.

13. Instructions are being issued separately with regard to supply arrangements after divisions reach positions referred to in para. 11 above.

14. The Casualty Clearing Stations will remain at Deir el Balah Station and the main dressing stations as stated in amendment to Eastern Force Order No. 40, dated April 15th 1917.

Any change in the above locations will be notified to all concerned. The positions of divisional advanced dressing stations, as altered from time to time in accordance with the requirements of the situation, will be notified to D.D.M.S. Eastern Force without delay.

15. The date left blank in the above orders will be notified in due course.

16. Eastern Force Headquarters will remain in its present position.

17. Acknowledge.

G. P. DAWNAY,
Brigadier-General, General Staff, Eastern Force.

Issued at 11.35 p.m.

APPENDIX 14.

Secret.

EASTERN FORCE ORDER NO. 43.

BY

LIEUTENANT-GENERAL SIR CHARLES DOBELL, K.C.B., C.M.G., D.S.O., Commanding Eastern Force.

Headquarters,
Eastern Force,
18th April 1917.

Reference Maps: Palestine 1/63,360; Gaza (X) 1/40,000; Gaza (Y) 1/15,000.

1. The latest information regarding the enemy will be issued to all concerned from time to time as it is received.

Map 15.
Sketch 16.

2. In accordance with Eastern Force Orders Nos. 41 and 42, the enemy will be attacked all along the line at Zero plus two hours on the 19th April, after a heavy bombardment beginning at Zero hour.

3. G.O.C. Desert Column will arrange to recall his Mounted Division which is operating from Shellal in time to have it under his hand and ready for action in the neighbourhood of Tell el Jemmi–El Mendur by Zero plus two hours on the morning of the 19th. One Mounted Division will advance at Zero plus two hours, conforming with the advance of the 54th Division, in order to make a strong demonstration against the enemy on the Atawine

ridge. Under cover of this demonstration, G.O.C. Desert Column will endeavour to push forward guns into positions from which they may assist the attack of the right of the 54th Division. The other Mounted Division of the Desert Column will operate on the outer flank. The method of its employment is left to G.O.C. Desert Column, who will, however, be guided in his action by the necessity, first, for having this division ready to push through any break in the enemy's line, in order to exploit a success or to take up pursuit; and secondly, for generally assisting in the protection of the right flank of the force.

4. The objective assigned to the 54th Division will be extended south-east to include the Kh. Sihan group of trenches. The north-west limit of the area of the operations of the Desert Column will be a straight line drawn between Baiket Abu Mailik and Kh. Sihan, excluding those places.

In accordance with Eastern Force Order No. 42, para. 3 (a), the Imperial Camel Brigade will be attached to the 54th Division to assist G.O.C. 54th Division in dealing with this additional objective.

5. The dividing line between the area of operations of the 52nd and 53rd Divisions will be the track running through the B of Blazed Hill and along the north-western edge of the Lambeth Wood (Gaza (Y) 1/15,000).

6. The 74th Division (less the infantry brigade and section of a field company already moved forward to a position between Sharta and the Wadi Nukhabir), will act as ordered in Eastern Force Order No. 41, para. 6 (d), except that the detachment already referred to, together with the 263rd Field Artillery Brigade, will take up a position of readiness on and behind the Sheikh Abbas ridge, while the remainder of the Division will take up a position of readiness further west behind the Mansura ridge, reporting its exact situation as soon as located.

7. The 263rd and 272nd Brigades R.F.A. of the 74th Division will be located, by direct arrangements between G.O's.C. concerned, so as to be available for use during the preliminary bombardment (and subsequently until required to operate with their own Division) as follows:—

    263rd Brigade R.F.A. to cover the area bombarded by the 54th Division.

    272nd Brigade R.F.A. to cover the area bombarded by the 52nd Division.

For this purpose the Brigades will temporarily come under the orders of the C.R.A's. 54th and 52nd Divisions, respectively. They will, however, keep in touch with G.O.C. 74th Division; they will not be moved forward and will be released as soon as they are required to support any operations undertaken by the 74th Division.

8. The bombardment will be carried out by the Eastern Force Artillery in accordance with a time table which will be issued separately.

From Zero plus two hours the front will be divided into three zones:—

    Right Zone .. .. Atawine to Wadi el Mukaddeme.
    Centre Zone .. .. Wadi el Mukaddeme to Rafah–Gaza road.
    Left Zone .. .. Rafah–Gaza road to the Coast (including targets for *Requin* north-east of Ali Muntar).

O.C. 5th Wing R.F.C. will arrange for one aeroplane to co-operate during the bombardment with each of the 10th, 15th, and 91st Heavy Batteries R.G.A., from Zero hour.

9. O.C. 5th Wing R.F.C. will provide for continuous close tactical reconnaissance during the day and for distant reconnaissance under instructions already given and as required.

10. Acknowledge.

                                  G. P. DAWNAY,
                      Brigadier-General, General Staff, Eastern Force.

Issued at 1 p.m.

APPENDIX 15.

1. THE MEANING OF SOME PLACE-NAMES IN THE THEATRE OF OPERATIONS.

Arish, Wadi el	River of Egypt.
Aqaba	Ascent, pass.
Bahret Lut	Lot's Sea (Dead Sea).
Beersheba	Bir es Sabe = 7 Wells or Well of the Oath.
Gaza	The Greek form of the Hebrew " Azzah " (fortress).
Jaffa	Beauty.
Jerusalem	Yĕrûshālēm (Heb.) = City of Peace, Place of Safety. El Quds (Ar.) = The Holy Place, The Sanctuary.
Khartoum	Spur of a hill, sandspit, " snout."
Muntar, El	The Watch Tower.
Palestine	Philistina.
Quds, El (Jerusalem)	The Holy Place.
Timsah (Lake)	Crocodile.

II. A GLOSSARY OF TERMS FOUND IN SOME COMPONENTS OF PLACE-NAMES (ARAB AND HEBREW) IN THE THEATRE OF OPERATIONS.

Abar (pl. of Bir) .. Wells.
Abd .. Slave, negro.
Abu .. Father (of); often—possessor (of).
Abyad (fem. Baida) .. White.
Ahmar (fem. Hamra) .. Red.
Ain (pl. Ayun) .. Spring.
Aqaba-t .. Ascent, pass.
Aulad (pl. of Walad) .. Children (of), tribe.

Bab (pl. Biban) .. Gateway, door, strait.
Bahari .. North.
Bahr .. Sea, or large river.
Beit, Beth (Heb.) .. House or tent, dwelling.
Beni, Bani .. Sons (of), tribe.
Bir (pl. Abar, Biyar) .. Well, tank, rock-cistern.
Birket, Birka-t .. Pool, lake, or pond.
Borg, Burj, Burg .. Tower, watch-tower.

Colours (Colour = Lon) :—
   White = Abyad (fem. Baida).
   Red = Ahmar (fem. Hamra).
   Green = Akhdar (fem. Khadra).
   Yellow = Asfar (fem. Safra).
   Blue = Azraq (fem. Zarqa).
   Black = Aswad (fem. Sôda).
   Purple = Argowani.

Compass, Points of :—
   North = Bahari, Shimal.
   South = Qibli, Ganub.
   East = Sharqi (fem. Sharqiya).
   West = Gharbi.

Darb .. Road or track.
Deir .. Monastery.
Ed, Edh, El, En, Er, Es, Esh, Et, Eth, Ez   The.

Gara .. Small hill, dark in colour.
Gebel (Egyptian maps) .. Mountain.
Ghadir .. Pool, pond, temporary water-pan.

Hamra (fem. of Ahmar) .. Red.
Hod .. Depression in sand full of palms, trough.

APPENDIX 15

Ibn (pl. Beni)	Son (of).
Jebel, Gebel	Mountain, hills, desert.
Kharm, Khareim	Artificial mound, vineyard.
K(Q)asr	Fort, large house, palace.
Kathib, (pl. Kathaiib, Kutban)	Moving sand-dune or sand-hill.
Kebir (fem. Kubra)	Great, large.
Khabra-t	Flooded area, hollow where rain-water collects.
Khan	Inn, caravanserai.
Khirbet (Kh.)	Ruins.
Khulil, El	The friend.
Khartum	Spur of a hill, sand-spit, lit. " snout."
Medina-t	Town.
Moiya-t	Water (a little), watering-place.
Maghara-t	Cave, cavern.
Mitla	Rising ground, ascent.
Nahr	River.
Nagb, Neqb, Naqb (dim. Engeib; pl. Nuqub)	Mountain pass, steep camel-track.
Natron Lakes	Soda lakes.
Qalat	Castle, citadel.
Qantara-t	Bridge.
Qarya-t (Ar.), Qiryath (Heb.) (dim. Qreiya-t)	Village (in Egypt), ruins.
Qasr, Qo(u)seir	Fort or palace, castle.
Rijm, Rujm	Stone heap, ruins.
Sabakha, Sabkhet	Salt lake, marsh, or bog.
Sawana-t	Gravel mound, flinty plain.
Shaluf (Shalufa-t)	Bluff.
Sharqi (fem. Sharqiya)	East.
Shatt	River, river bank, landing-place.
Sheikh (Sh.)	Chief, elder, saint.
Shellal	Cataract, waterfall.
Tell (Ar.) (pl. Tulul) (dim. Tuleil)	Mound (especially covering ruins).
Tel (Heb.)	Mound (especially covering ruins).
Um, Umm	Mother.
Umshash (pl. of Mashash)	Water holes.
Wadi	Watercourse (normally dry), valley.
Wely	A saint's tomb.
Zawiet Zawai(e)t Zawya(e)t Zowai(e)t	Monastery, priory, hamlet, Senussi religious centre and school.

GENERAL INDEX.[1]

Abbas (Egyptian Gunboat), 106
Abbas Hilmi, Khedive of Egypt, deposed, 17 ; 109
Abdul Hamid (former Sultan of Turkey), 86, 211
Abdulla, the Emir, 213, 221, 226, 228, 236
Abu el Lissal, the Affair of, 239
Aden, Turkish threat to, 67 ; Turkish attack on, 221
Adye, Maj.-Gen. J., 136, 137, 153
Aenne Rickmers (later *Anne*) (Seaplane Carrier), 28, 60, 160 (*f.n.*)
Agagiya, the Action of, 126, 371
Alexander the Great, 135, 281
Alexandretta, projected landing at. *See* Iskanderun
Alexandria District Command, 275
Ali, the Emir, 225, 228, 234, 236
Ali Dinar. *See* Darfur, Sultan of
Allenby, Gen. Sir E. H. H., 76, 86, 228 (*f.n.*), 329, 368
Altham, Lieut.-Gen. Sir E. A., 75, 97, 244
Aqaba, occupation of, 240
Arab Bureau, the, 216
Arab Revolt, outbreak of the, 225, 372
Arabi Pasha, revolt of, 9
Armenians, 21, 81, 86
Armoured Car Division, R.N., 110, 119, 121, 123
Armoured Cars, light, 138, 140, 142, 275
Artillery, at Romani, 180 ; at First Gaza, 285, 296, 304 ; at Second Gaza, 327, 335, 337, 341, 348
Arundell, Captain R. T., 42
Askold (Russian Light Cruiser), at Haifa, 22 ; 60
Asquith, Mr. H. H., 79, 81, 82, 234 (*f.n.*)
Auda Abu Tayi, 239, 240
Australia, contingent to be sent to Egypt, 19 ; contingent arrives, 20 ; contingent for Gallipoli, 55 ; light horse sent to Gallipoli as infantry, 58 ; shortage of rifles for contingents, 88 ; Composite Light Horse Regiment on Western Frontier, 107, 110, 112, 114, 119, 121 (*f.n.*)

Austrian Batteries, 202, 321
Aziz Bey el Masri, 235, 411

Babtie, Surgeon-Gen. W., 75
Bacchante (Cruiser), 61, 63, 64
Baghdad Railway, 20 ; gaps in, 21, 22, 26, 76
Bailloud, Gen., 71
Baker, Captain M. G. Lloyd, 163, 169
Balfour, Mr. A. J., 219
Balfour, Captain D., 147
Balfour Declaration, the, 219
Barlow, Major C. L., 264
Barrow, Maj.-Gen. G. de S., 357
Ben-my-Chree (Seaplane Carrier), 160 (*f.n.*), 226
Benn, Captain Wedgwood, 160 (*f.n.*)
Beringia, the Affair of, 150
Birdwood, Maj.-Gen. (later Lieut.-Gen.) W. R., 55, 56, 79, 94, 156
Blakeney, Major R. B. D., 408
Boisragon, Lieut.-Col. G. H., 62
Bouvet (French Battleship), 56, 61
Bremond, Col. E., 236
Britannia (Cunard Liner), 74 (*f.n.*)
Butler, Br.-Gen. W. J. C., 287, 293, 296
Byng, Maj.-Gen. (later Lieut.-Gen.) Hon. J. H. G., Commanding Force in Egypt, 11 ; 156

Camel Transport Corps, formation of, 23 ; 123, 280, 314, 367, 408
Carden, Vice-Admiral S. H., 55, 64
Carew, Mr. G., 50 (*f.n.*)
Casson, Br.-Gen. H. G., 153
Casualties—
British, in defence of Suez Canal, 50 (*f.n.*) ; on 29th April 1915, 64 ; at Wadi Senab, 110-3 ; at Wadi Majid, 117 ; at Halazin, 122 ; at Agagiya, 128 ; at Beringia, 151 ; at Qatiya, 168-9 ; at Romani, 198-9 ; at Sheikh Othman, 223 ; at Magdhaba, 257 ; at Rafah, 270 ; at First Gaza, 315 ; at Second Gaza, 348

---

[1] Names in orders of battle and orders, which appear in appendices, are not indexed.

433

434 GENERAL INDEX

Casualties (*continued*)—
  Turkish, in attack on Suez Canal, 50 (*f.n.*); on 29th April 1915, 64; on 23rd Nov. 1915, 72; at Wadi Senab, 113; at Wadi Majid, 117; at Halazin, 122; at Agagiya, 128; (Ali Dinar's) at Beringia, 151; at Qatiya, 168; at Romani, 199; at Mecca and Jidda, 226; at Taif, 227; at Wejh, 237; at Abu el Lissal, 240; at Magdhaba, 257; at Rafah, 270; at First Gaza, 315, 322; at Second Gaza, 350
Chauvel, Maj.-Gen. (later Lieut.-Gen.) Sir H. G., 169, 183, 188, 189, 191, 192, 193, 196, 197, 198, 201, 245, 253, 254, 255, 256, 257, 262, 264, 265, 267, 268, 274, 292, 297, 298, 299, 300, 305, 306, 307; assumes command of Desert Column, 351; 352
Chaytor, Br.-Gen. (later Maj.-Gen.) E. W. C., 179, 188, 189, 197, 200, 254, 255, 256, 264, 268 (*f.n.*), 276, 345
Cheetham, Sir Milne, 11, 17 (*f.n.*)
Chetwode, Lieut.-Gen. Sir P. W., Bt., 246, 252, 253, 256, 262, 263, 265, 268, 270, 283; his orders for First Gaza, 284; 285, 288, 289, 290, 294; orders Gen. Dallas to launch his attack, 296; 297; orders mounted troops to attack Gaza, 298; 303, 305; orders withdrawal of mounted troops, 307; 309, 310, 311, 316, 333; his orders for Second Gaza, 344; 347; assumes command of Eastern Frontier Force, 351; 352, 353 (*f.n.*); orders raid on Sinai railway, 363
Chope, Captain A. J. H., 20
Clayton, Lieut.-Col. (later Br.-Gen.) C. G., 216 (*f.n.*)
Clematis (Cruiser), 114, 115
Clio (Sloop), in defence of Suez Canal, 30, 37, 38, 45
Cochran, Captain L. F. A., 46, 47
Colston, Lieut.-Col. Hon. E. M., 155
Coventry, Lieut.-Col. Hon. C. J., 164, 166
Cowans, Gen. Sir J., 320
Cox, Br.-Gen. C. F., 255, 266, 345
Cox, Br.-Gen. (later Maj.-Gen.) H. V., 57, 91
Craig, 2/Lieut. J. M., 364 (*f.n.*)
Ctesiphon, Battle of, 85

Dallas, Maj.-Gen. A. G., 153, 246, 284; his orders for First Gaza, 285; 288 (*f.n.*), 289, 290, 293, 295, 296, 302, 303, 307; protests against abandoning position, 309; 310; orders withdrawal from Ali Muntar, 311; orders re-occupation of Ali Muntar, 312; 313, 314, 316, 317, 332 (*f.n.*)
D'Amade, Gen., 56
Darfur, Sultan of, 135, 147, 148, 151, 152
Darfur, unrest in, 67; 135; invasion of, 148; annexation of, 152
Davies, Lieut.-Gen. F. J., 156
Dawnay, Br.-Gen. G. P., 313
Delage, Lieut. de Vaisseau, 29 (*f.n.*), 49 (*f.n.*)
Delta District Command, 153, 275
Demir Hissar (Turkish T.B.), 61
D'Entrecasteaux (French Cruiser), in defence of Suez Canal, 30, 42, 44, 54 (*f.n.*); 64
Derby, the Earl of, 320
de Robeck, Rear-Admiral J. M., 64, 79
Desaix (French Cruiser), 54
Desert Column, formation of, 246; 256, 276, 283, 286, 290, 295, 296, 305, 307, 311, 330, 331; at Second Gaza, 332, 335, 336, 343; 351; reorganized, 357
D'Estrées (French Light Cruiser), 64
Destrem, Lieut. de Vaisseau, 29 (*f.n.*)
Dieckmann, Regierungsrat (German Official), 77 (*f.n.*), 85 (*f.n.*), 86 (*f.n.*)
Diel, Lieut. (German Officer), 229
Djemal Pasha, Ahmed, *Biyuk*, appointed Commander-in-Chief in Syria, 34; advances against Suez Canal, 35; his aims, 36; 51, 52, 85, 220, 235, 270 (*f.n.*)
Djemal *Kuchuk*, 34, 50, 237
Djemal, Mohammed (Djemal III), 237
Dobell, Maj.-Gen. (later Lieut.-Gen.) Sir C. M., 153, 244, 262, 270, 273, 281, 283; his orders for First Gaza, 284; 285, 288, 289, 295, 296, 298, 303, 305; orders 54th Div. to withdraw from Sheikh Abbas, 306; 309, 310, 311, 313; orders withdrawal across the Ghazze, 314; 316, 326, 327; his plan for second attack on Gaza, 329, 331, 334; 333; advises against new attack at Second Gaza, 347; relieved of command, 351

GENERAL INDEX 435

Dodington, Br.-Gen. W. Marriott-, 295, 312, 339
Doris (Light Cruiser), exploits on Syrian coast, 22, 29 (*f.n.*), 54
Douglas, Maj.-Gen. Sir W., 190
Dowson, Mr. E. M., 155
Dufferin (*R.I.M.S.*), 62, 66, 228

Eastern Frontier Force, formation of, 244 ; 274, 276, 280, 283, 286, 290, 295, 304, 313 ; at Second Gaza, 332, 336, 342 ; 351, 364
Egypt, British occupation of, 7, 9 ; proclamation of martial law in, 16 ; proclaimed a Protectorate, 17 ; Survey, Department of, 34 ; lack of war-time restrictions in, 72 ; position regarding war, 364 ; recruiting in, 365 ; discontent in, 366
Egypt, Sultan of. *See* Hussein Kamel Pasha
Egyptian Army, organization of, 2 ; pack-gun battery in Canal Defences, 23
Egyptian Expeditionary Force, formation of, March 1915, 97 ; 154 ; dispositions of, 27th July 1916, 203
Egyptian Labour Corps, 247, 367
Ellison, Maj.-Gen. G. F., 75
Empress (Seaplane Carrier), 160 (*f.n.*).
Engineers, work on Canal Defences, 33
Enver Pasha, 65, 78, 235, 278 (*f.n.*)
l'Escaille, Lieut. de Vaisseau de, 29
Euryalus (Cruiser), 60, 63, 64, 235
Eyres Monsell, Commander B. M., 130

Fantasse (Pl. *Fanatis*), 193
Feisal, the Emir, 220, 227, 228, 233, 236, 237
Fiki Ali (Sudanese Chief), 146, 147
Fischer, Major (German Officer), 35
Fitzgerald, Br.-Gen. P. D., 345
FitzGibbon, Lieut. R. A., 40
Flying Corps, Royal, detachment in Egypt in 1914, 28 ; 77, 108, 151, 155, 159, 166, 177, 179, 193 ; at Romani, 203 ; 234, 245, 252, 264, 276, 306, 327, 328, 362
Force in Egypt, the, 11 ; relief of pre-war garrison of, 14, 29 ; dispositions prior to Turkish attack on Canal, 31 ; casualties in defence of Suez Canal, 49, 50 (*f.n.*) ; services to M.E.F., 57 ;

Force in Egypt (*continued*)—
weakness of, 59 ; composition of 9th July 1915, 68 ; weakness of Dec. 1915, 85 ; despatches Indian troops to Basra, 87 ; reinforcements promised to, 88 ; ration strength of 7th Dec. 1915, 88 ; limitation of command of, 95 ; amalgamated with M.E.F., becoming E.E.F., 96 ; 154 ; administration of, 408
Forest, Major W. T., 341
Fournet, Admiral Dartige du, 54, 64, 86
Fox (Light Cruiser), 226
France, aspirations of in Syria, 218 ; intervention of in Hejaz, 236 ; sends contingent to Palestine, 358
Frankenburg und Proschlitz, Oberst von, 34, 51
French, Field-Marshal Sir J. D. P., 59
Fryer, Br.-Gen. F. A. B., 299, 346
Fulton, Lieut.-Col. H. T., 125

Gallipoli Campaign, the, opening of, 55 ; landing in Suvla Bay, 60 ; effects upon Egypt, 64 ; failure of Suvla Bay landing, 69 ; 73 ; evacuation of Anzac and Suvla decided on, 87 ; evacuation of Gallipoli, 88 ; 371
Garland, Major, H., 238
Garrison Battalions, 274
Gas Shell, 336, 337, 341, 349
Gaulois (French Battleship), 56
Gaza, First Battle of, 283, 370
Gaza, Second Battle of, 329, 371
Geoghegan, Br.-Gen. S., 41, 42, 46, 47
George V, H.M. King, 320
German Contingent. *See* Pasha I
German Military Mission to Turkey, 4, 26
Girdwood, Br.-Gen. (later Maj.-Gen.) E. S., 188, 190, 328
Giuba, the Affair of, 151
Godley, Lieut.-Gen. Sir A. J., 156
Goliath (Battleship), 63
Goltz, Field-Marshal von der, 4
Gordon, Lieut.-Col. J. L. R., 110, 111, 114, 115, 116, 117, 122
Grant, Col. P. G., 91
Grant-Dalton, Captain S., 177
Grobba, Lieut. F. (German Officer), 229 (*f.n.*).
Gumpenberg, Baron von, 66
Gwatkin-Williams, Captain R. S., 133

436　　　　GENERAL INDEX

Hagen, Hauptm. von dem, 47
Haig, Gen. Sir D., 94
Halazin, the Affair of, 121, 371
Haldane, Lieut.-Col. C. L., 53
Hall, Captain G. C. M., 408
Hamilton, Gen. Sir Ian, 55, 56, 57, 58, 59, 71, 76
Hampden, Br.-Gen. Viscount, 131
Hardinge (R.I.M.S.), in defence of Suez Canal, 30, 41, 43, 45, 50; at Jidda, 226
Hare, Maj.-Gen. S. W., 293, 339, 340
Harper, Captain R., 198
Harvey, 2/Lieut. R.F.M., 333
Henri IV (French Battleship), 54 (*f.n.*), 61
Hilal (brother of the Senussi), 109
Himalaya (Armed Merchant Cruiser) in defence of Suez Canal, 30
Hodgson, Br.-Gen. (later Maj.-Gen.) H. W., 142, 274, 297, 299, 300, 305, 306, 308, 344
Hogarth, Commander D. G., 216 (*f.n.*), 221
Holbrooke, Lieut. N., 104
Holy War. *See Jihad*
Horne, Maj.-Gen. (later Lieut.-Gen.) H. S., 85, 89, 90, 156, 161
Howard, Major T. N., 47
Huddleston, Captain (later Br.-Gen.) H. J., 146, 151, 152
Hussein Ibn Ali, Sherif of Mecca (later King of the Hejaz), 102, 209, 210, 212, 213, 214, 215, 216, 217, 219, 220, 221, 225, 232, 234, 240
Hussein Kamel Pasha, created Sultan of Egypt, 17; attempted assassination of, 63; 367

Idris, Mohammed, 103, 140; treaty with, 144; 410
Idrissi, the, 208, 209, 210, 230, 409
Imam of Sana'a, the, 209, 210, 230
Imperial Strategic Reserve, 97
Indian Army, organization of, 1
Indian Expeditionary Force " E," 2
Indian Imperial Service Troops, 2
Inflexible (Battle Cruiser), 56
Inland Water Transport, 360
Intelligence, British, 49, 81, 157, 216, 225, 248, 251, 273, 280, 310, 326, 331, 356
Irresistible (Battleship), 56
Iskanderun, Gulf of, projected landing in, 20, 77, 371
Ismailiyeh, 21
Italy, situation of in Cyrenaica, 65; sends contingent to Palestine, 358

Ja'far Pasha el Askeri, 104, 105 (*f.n.*), 106, 112, 113 (*f.n.*), 118, 119 (*f.n.*), 126, 127, 128, 235
Jauréguiberry (French Battleship), 54 (*f.n.*)
Jeanne d'Arc (French Cruiser), 64
Jihad (Holy War), 10, 18, 51, 66, 70 (*f.n.*), 101, 105, 148, 205, 212, 214

Kelly, Lieut.-Col. P. V., 148, 149, 150, 151, 152
Khadir Bey, 256
Khadri Bey, Major, 199 (*f.n.*)
Khairi Bey, 229, 230
Khalifate, the, 206
Kharga Detachment, 137 (*f.n.*)
Khedive. *See* Abbas Hilmi
Kitchener, Field-Marshal Earl, 1 Consul-General in Egypt, 10, 11; Secretary of State for War, 13; 14, 19, 20, 21; suggests landing at El Arish, 22; his instructions to Sir J. Maxwell, 49; his instructions to Maj.-Gen. Birdwood, 55; 56, 57, 58, 60, 65; sends reinforcements to Egypt, 69; 71, 76; comes out to the Ægean, 77; 78; his views on landing in Gulf of Iskanderun, 79; 80, 81, 82; his views on defence of Egypt, 83; sails from Mudros, 84; impressed by danger of Egypt, 88; 90; his instructions to Sir A. Murray, 95; 96, 98, 120, 148; his negotiations with Sherif Hussein, 213; 217
Klinghart (German Engineer), 21
Kress von Kressenstein, Oberst Freiherr, Chief of Staff to VIII Corps, 34, 50 (*f.n.*), 51, 52; 71 (*f.n.*), 85, 89, 157, 170, 181, 194, 199, 202 (*f.n.*), 252 (*f.n.*), 270 (*f.n.*), 276 (*f.n.*), 277, 278 (*f.n.*), 309, 310 (*f.n.*), 320, 354
Kut, 1915, Battle of, 78; siege of, 85

Lapeyrère, Admiral Boué de, 12
Lawrence, Maj.-Gen. Hon. H., 161, 169, 179, 182, 184 (*f.n.*); orders counter-attack at Romani, 187; orders general advance at Romani, 190; 191, 193, 194, 196, 198, 200
Lawrence, Captain (later Lieut.-Col.) T. E., 233 (*f.n.*), 235, 236, 239, 240
Lefroy, Major H. P. T., 310 (*f.n.*)
Leggett, Br.-Gen. A. H., 342
Le Mottée, Br.-Gen. R. E. A., 294 295

GENERAL INDEX

Levant Base, 73, 97, 99
Light Car Patrols, 138, 140, 142
Liman von Sanders, Gen., 4, 51, 157, 158, 199 (*f.n.*), 202, 220, 233 (*f.n.*), 321
Linberry, Commander T. J., 43
Lines of Communication Defences, Palestine, constituted, 354 ; 362
Lloyd George, Mr. D., 234 (*f.n.*), 250, 259, 260, 356
Lucan, Br.-Gen. the Earl of, 107, 118, 119, 125, 126, 127, 129, 130, 131
Lucas, Sir Charles, 224 (*f.n.*)
Lynden-Bell, Maj.-Gen. A. L., 353 (*f.n.*)

Macauley, Col. Sir G., 91, 360, 365, 408
McDiarmid, 2/Lieut. G., 167
MacDonald, Sir M., 91
M'Grigor, Br.-Gen. C. R., 56
McKenzie, Lieut. W. H. P., 308 (*f.n.*)
Maclachlan, Major T. R., 39, 47
M'Mahon, Sir H., appointed High Commissioner for Egypt, 17 (*f.n.*) ; 50, 72, 79, 83, 102, 214, 215, 217, 220, 232, 233
MacNamara, Major C. C., 146
McNeill, Lieut.-Col. (later Br.-Gen.) A. J., 137 (*f.n.*)
Macedonian Campaign, the, opening of, 70 ; 74, 98, 372
Magdhaba, the Affair of, 251, 369, 371
Maher, Surgeon-Gen., J., 354
Mahon, Lieut.-Gen. Sir B., 94, 153
Malcolm, Br.-Gen. N., 123, 408
Malone, Squadron Commander C. L'Estrange, 160 (*f.n.*)
Mangles, Captain C. G., 140
Mansoura (Armed Tug), in defence of Suez Canal, 43
Massy, Major S. D., 28
Mauretania (Cunard Liner), 74 (*f.n.*)
Maxwell, Lieut.-Gen. Sir J., Commanding Force in Egypt, 13 ; reports to Lord Kitchener, 15 (*f.n.*) ; 17, 19, 20, 22, 23, 27, 28 ; has information of German plot, 35 (*f.n.*) ; 48 ; unable to counter-attack Turks, 49 ; his difficulties lightened by Turkish repulse, 50 ; reports possibility of a second attack, 54 ; instructed to prepare force for Gallipoli, 55 ; 56, 57, 58, 59 ; anxieties of, 65 ; has evidence of Senussi's intrigues, 66 ; 67, 69 ;

Maxwell, Lieut.-Gen. Sir J. (*continued*)—
points out weakness of Egypt, 70 ; his policy in Egypt, 72 ; 74 ; purchases for Levant Base, 75 ; 76 ; his plans for meeting renewed Turkish offensive, 77 ; his views on evacuation of Gallipoli, 78 ; 79, 81, 83, 84, 85, 86, 87 ; promised reinforcements, 88, 90 ; reports on Canal Defences, 91 ; 93, 94 ; limitation of command of, 95 ; ordered to return to England, 96 ; 98, 99, 102, 105, 120, 121 (*f.n.*), 123, 124, 125, 129 (*f.n.*), 136, 137, 141, 154, 156, 213 ; urges co-operation with Arabs, 217 ; 222, 365, 368, 371, 409
Mecca, capture of, 225
Mediterranean Expeditionary Force, formation of, 55 ; base of established in Egypt, 56 ; has call on garrison of Egypt, 57 ; returns to Egypt, 88 ; becomes E.E.F., 97, 99 ; 154
Mehemet Ali, 11, 208
Meissner Pasha (German Engineer), 76, 85
Meldrum, Lieut.-Col. (later Br.-Gen.) W., 181
Meredith, Lieut.-Col. (later Br.-Gen.) J. B., 185, 186, 274 (*f.n.*), 344
Minerva (Light Cruiser), in defence of Suez Canal, 30 ; at Tor, 53 ; 60
Misurata (Italian Armed Yacht), 140
Mobile Column (at Romani), 181, 183, 184, 187, 190, 194, 196, 198, 201
Mohammed (the Prophet), 205
Mohammed Saleh, 142, 143, 144
Money, Lieut.-Col. N., 285 (*f.n.*)
Money's Detachment (at First Gaza), 285, 287, 296, 303, 312, 314
Monitors (*M*.21, *M*.31), 335, 337 (*f.n.*)
Monro, Lieut.-Gen. Sir C. C., 76, 77, 79, 81, 83, 94, 95
Montcalm (French Cruiser), 63, 64
Moore, Br.-Gen. C. D. Hamilton, 342
Moorina (Transport), 106, 118, 120 133
Morandière, Enseigne de Vaisseau Potier de la, 38 (*f.n.*)
Morgan, Captain M. H. L., 40
Morgani, Sayad Sir Ali, 214
Mott, Br.-Gen. (later Maj.-Gen.) S. F., 287, 288, 293, 332
Mudge, Br.-Gen. A., 338

GENERAL INDEX

Murray, Lieut.-Gen. (later Gen.) Sir A. J., C.I.G.S., 90; G.O.C., M.E.F., 95; his instructions from C.I.G.S., 97; 98, 99, 137, 139; orders raid on Siwa, 142; 149, 154; suggests advance to El Arish, 157; 159; appreciation by Feb. 1916, 170; 175, 178, 181, 182, 183, 199, 200, 201, 232, 233, 234; moves Headquarters to Cairo, 243; appreciation by Oct. 1916, 246; 250, 251; correspondence with C.I.G.S., 258; 262, 272; his estimate of troops required, 273, 318, 369; demands better aeroplanes, 276; 279, 280; orders attack on Gaza, 281; 289, 314; his reports after First Gaza, 317; his correspondence with War Office after First Gaza, 322; 326; orders renewed attack on Gaza, 329; 331, 333; orders ground gained at Second Gaza to be held, 347; 351; his views after Second Gaza, 354; reorganizes mounted troops, 357; discusses railway organization with C.I.G.S., 359; 361; his views on political affairs in Egypt, 364; recall of, 368

Napoleon I, 8, 89, 218, 281
Napoleon III, 218
Nasir, Sherif, 239, 240
Nasariyeh, 21
Neufeld, Karl, 228
Newcombe, Lieut.-Col. S. F., 235
New Zealand, contingent to be sent to Egypt, 19; contingent arrives, 20; Mounted Rifles sent to Gallipoli as infantry, 58
Nicholas, Grand Duke, 159
Nivelle, Gen. R., 320
Nogales, Rafael de, 346 (*f.n.*), 349 (*f.n.*)
Nuhr-el-Bahr (Egyptian Gunboat), 106
Nuri Bey, 65, 104, 109, 113 (*f.n.*), 126, 140
Nuri esh Shalaan, 209 (*f.n.*), 239

Ocean (Battleship), in defence of Suez Canal, 30, 45; 56, 60
Omdurman, Battle of, 9
Othman, Khalif, 206

Palin, Br.-Gen. (later Maj.-Gen.) P. C., 246, 358

Palmes, Lieut.-Commander G. B., 42
Panouse, Col. the Vicomte de la, 82
Pasha I (German formation), 202
Ped-rails, 180 (*f.n.*)
Peirse, Vice-Admiral R. H., 19; attacks Syrian ports, 22; 60, 107
Pennefather-Evans, Major G., 117 (*f.n.*)
Petrie, Sir Flinders, 361 (*f.n.*)
Peyton, Maj.-Gen. W. E., 57, 124, 125, 129, 130, 131, 134, 136, 140, 153
Philomel (Light Cruiser), 54, 61, 64
Picot, M. Georges, 218
Pipe-line in Sinai, 175, 242, 272, 276, 279, 360, 367
Pitt, Br.-Gen. T. M. S., 299, 345
Pollok-M'Call, Br.-Gen. J. B., 340
Proserpine (Light Cruiser), in defence of Suez Canal, 30; 64

Qatiya, the Affair of, 162, 369, 371

Rabenfels (later *Raven*) (Seaplane Carrier), 60, 160 (*f.n.*)
Rafah, the Action of, 262, 369, 371
Railways (British), 93, 137; in Sinai, 160, 170, 243, 259, 272, 276, 279; railhead reaches Deir el Balah, 327; 358, 365
Railways (Turkish), between Constantinople and Palestine, 26; 76, 85, 211, 212, 329; raid on, 23rd May 1917, 363
Range, Dr. Paul (German Official), 51, 362 (*f.n.*)
Rasheed (Egyptian Gunboat), 108
Rashid, Sa'ud Ibn Abd el Aziz Ibn, 209, 235
Requin (French Coastguard Ship), in defence of Suez Canal, 30, 41, 42, 43, 45; 61, 64; at Second Gaza, 335, 337 (*f.n.*)
Ridalla Selim Dadur (Bedouin Sheikh), 72
Rigg, Captain H. M., 41
Roberts, Captain F., 167
Robertson, Gen. Sir W. R., 95, 99, 120; agrees to occupation of Qatiya, 157; 178, 234, 250; orders postponement of invasion of Palestine, 272; orders invasion of Palestine, 318; correspondence with Sir A. Murray after First Gaza, 322; modifies Sir A. Murray's instructions, 355; 364
Romani, Battle of, 179, 369, 371
Romieu, Col., 86

GENERAL INDEX 439

Rothschild, Baron, 219
Royal Naval Air Service, 159
Royle, Captain L. V., 120, 133, 143
Royston, Col. (later Br.-Gen.) J. R., 186, 189, 196, 198, 254, 299, 300, 301, 308 (*f.n.*), 344
Rushdi Pasha, Prime Minister of Egypt, 17
Russell, Captain R. E. M., 33
Russian Revolution, the, 279 (*f.n.*)
Ryrie, Br.-Gen. G. de L., 291, 346

Saint-Louis (French Battleship), 54 (*f.n.*), 64
Salmond, Col. (later Br.-Gen.) W. G. H., 177, 329
Salonika Campaign, the. *See* Macedonian Campaign.
Sampson, Commander C. R., 160 (*f.n.*)
Sarrail, Gen., 95
Sa'ud, Abdul Aziz Ibn, 209
Sazieu, Lieut. de Vaisseau de, 49 (*f.n.*)
Scott, Lieut.-Col. W. H., 193
Seaplane Detachment, French, at Sir J. Maxwell's disposal, 28; breakdown of machines of, 49; 60
Senussi, the, 10, 65, 66, 83, 102, 103, 105, 108, 113, 120, 122, 125, 126, 133, 134, 135, 139, 140, 141, 142, 143, 144, 145, 148, 249; history of his Sect, 409
Shaw, Maj.-Gen. D. L. B., 222
Sinclair-MacLagan, Col. E. G., 55
Sinai Peninsula, the, evacuation of, 13; cleared of the enemy, 258; steps in reoccupation of, 271 (*f.n.*)
Siwa, the Raid on, 142
Skeen, Major, O. St. J., 40
Slessor, Lieut., J. C., 151
Smith, Lieut.-Col. (later Br.-Gen.) C. L., 181, 201, 254, 292
Smith, Maj.-Gen. W. E. B., 187, 188, 189, 193, 332, 336, 342
Snow, Lieut.-Col. C. L., 104, 105, 110
Sore, Sapper, 339
Souter, Lieut.-Col. H. M. W., 126, 127
Southern Force, the, 136, 153
Spear-point Pump, 176
Stanton, Br.-Gen. H. B., 408
Steuber, Obergeneralarzt, 202 (*f.n.*)
Stotzingen Mission, the, 228
Subar Singh, Havildar, 61
Sudan, British administration in the, 10; minor operations in the, 145

Suez Canal, the, 7; importance of, 8; freedom to navigation of, 11; measures for defence of, 23; cut to inundate Desert, 25; disposition of troops defending, 15th Jan. 1915, 31; Turkish demonstrations against, 61, 63; quietude of in summer of 1915, 71; requirements for defence of, 83; new method of defence of, Dec. 1915, 88; work on new defences of, 95; progress of defences of, 155; 368
Suez Canal, Actions on the, 37; failure of Turkish attack on, 47; 371
Suez Canal Company, 12; assistance of to Gen. Wilson, 25; 360
Suffren (French Battleship), 56
Sutton, Lieut.-Col. F. G. H., 42, 44
Swiftsure (Battleship), flagship at Suez, 19; in defence of Suez Canal, 30, 44, 45; 60
Sykes, Sir Mark, Bt., 218, 231
Sykes-Picot Agreement, the, 217

Taif, capture of, 226
Talbot, Col. Hon. M. G., 141, 144
Tanner, Lieut.-Col. W. E. C., 131
Tara (Armed Steamer), 106, 120; rescue of prisoners of, 133
T.B. 043, in defence of Suez Canal, 42, 43
Teiresias (Holt Liner), 64
Thompson, Major H., 167
Thomson-Glover, Lieut. J. W., 41
Tiller, Major (German Officer), 309, 310 (*f.n.*), 316
Tipton, Captain R. J., 177
Todd, Lieut.-Col. T. J., 178
Townshend, Maj.-Gen. C. V. F., 78, 85
Transport, reorganization of, 273
Travers, Br.-Gen. J. H. du B., 287, 294
Triumph (Battleship), 60
Turkey, outbreak of war with, 15
Turkey, Sultan of, position in Islam, 9, 16; proclaims Holy War on Allies, 18, 66; 205, 216
Turkish Army, reorganization of, 3; organization of in Syria, 26; advances against Egypt, Jan. 1915, 28; approaches Suez Canal, 30; attacks Suez Canal, 40; retreats from Suez Canal, 48; losses of in attack on Suez Canal, 50; troops of employed in attack on Suez Canal, 50; demonstration of against Suez Canal, 62; projected second invasion of

440 GENERAL INDEX

Turkish Army, reorganization of, (*continued*)—
Egypt by, 158; force of at Qatiya, 170; advances against Romani, 179; attacks at Romani, 185; retreats from Romani, 191; troops of at Romani, 202; troops of in Arabia, 212; attacks Aden, 221; in the Hejaz, 225, 232, 237; in Syria and Palestine, 248, 260; reinforced, 277; desertions from, 277; withdraws from Shellal, 278; dispositions of prior to First Gaza, 280; advances to relief of Gaza, 306; action of at First Gaza, 321; entrenches on Gaza–Beersheba road, 326; strength of prior to Second Gaza, 331; dispositions of at Second Gaza, 349; receives reinforcements, 353; water supply of, 362 (*f.n.*)

Turkish Army—
First Army, 158
Second Army, 158, 159
Fourth Army, 26, 34, 71 (*f.n.*)
Fifth Army, 158

Turner, Major C. E., 187
Tussum Post, Turkish attack on, 41, 51
Tyndale-Biscoe, Br.-Gen. J. D., 59, 107, 114, 119, 121 (*f.n.*)

Van Ryneveld, Captain H. A., 177
Venizelos, E., 71

Wadi Majid, the Affair of the, 114, 371
Wadi Senab, the Affair of the, 110, 371
Wallace, Maj.-Gen. A., 45, 107, 110, 111, 113, 115, 116, 118, 120, 121, 123, 124, 153
War Committee, 100
Ward, Captain E. S., 163
Ward, Br.-Gen. T., 338
Watson, Br.-Gen. H. D., 29, 354

Watson, Br.-Gen. (later Maj.-Gen.) W. A., 47, 63, 139, 153
Wejh, the capture of, 236
Wemyss, Rear-Admiral (later Vice-Admiral) Sir R. E., 55 (*f.n.*), 149, 182, 235, 263
Western Desert (of Egypt), unrest in, 65; pacification of coast area of, 134; invasion of oases by Senussi, 136; the motor car in, 138; the oases cleared, 139; 249
Western Frontier Campaign, the, outbreak of, 107, 371
Western Frontier Force, 107, 109, 113, 119, 120, 123, 124, 125, 134, 139, 153, 275
Westminster, Major the Duke of, 132, 133
Whittingham, Col. C. H., 409
Wigan, Major J. T., 110
Wiggin, Br.-Gen. E. A., 161, 162, 164, 168, 169, 189, 300
Wiggin, Captain W. H., 166
Wilkie, Major A. H., 271
Williams-Thomas, Major F. S., 163
Wilson, Maj.-Gen. A., G.O.C. Canal Defences, 19; not deceived by Turkish feints, 30, 31, 45; 48
Wilson, Lieut.-Col. E. C., 228, 234, 235, 236
Wingate, Gen. Sir R., Governor-General of the Sudan, 11, 58 (*f.n.*), 67, 145; orders invasion of Darfur, 148; 149, 214, 220, 221, 227, 232, 233, 365, 367
Wire road in Sinai, 243, 369
Wright, Col. H. B. H., 91
Wright, Major H. L., 296 (*f.n.*)
Yorke, Lieut.-Col. R. M., 165, 169 (*f.n.*), 189
Younghusband, Maj.-Gen. Sir G., 67, 223, 224

Zeid, the Emir, 221, 233 (*f.n.*), 236
Zekki Pasha, Br.-Gen., 34

INDEX TO ARMS, FORMATIONS, AND UNITS.[1]

Artillery—
  Batteries, Field—
    1/5th Lancashire—62; 19th Lancashire—39
  Batteries, Garrison (Heavy)—
    10th—286, 288, 296, 337 (f.n.); 15th—285 (f.n.), 286, 296, 337 (f.n.); 91st—286, 288, 296, 337 (f.n.); Royal Marine —108
  Batteries, Garrison (Siege)—
    201st—328, 337 (f.n.)
  Batteries, Horse—
    Ayrshire—180, 181, 186, 198, 344; Berkshire—67, 223, 300; H.A.C. "A"—108, 119, 121 (f.n.); H.A.C. "B"—67, 223, 265, 267; Invernessshire—193, 254, 258, 265; Leicestershire—180, 186, 265; Nottinghamshire—107 (f.n.), 110, 112, 114, 115, 120, 121, 125, 127, 300; Somersetshire —189, 197, 254, 265, 344
  Batteries, Mountain—
    5th Egyptian—39; Hong Kong and Singapore—130, 131, 134, 245, 252 (f.n.), 254, 267, 277
  Brigades (Field)—
    260th—180 (f.n.); 262nd—180 (f.n.); 263rd—180 (f.n.), 335, 345; 265th—288, 295, 296, 302 (f.n.); 266th—288, 295, 296; 267th—275, 335; 271st—293, 295, 302; 272nd—275, 335
  Brigades (Indian Mountain)—
    III—14

Camel Corps—133, 134, 137, 139, 146 (f.n.), 147, 150 (f.n.), 151, 245, 246, 275, 362

Camel Corps, Bikanir—13, 15, 20, 48, 62, 63, 72, 107, 160, 161, 195, 275, 354
——, Egyptian—13
Camel Brigade, Imperial—252, 253, 254, 255, 257, 263, 264, 265, 266, 269, 283, 286, 287, 292, 298, 300, 307, 309, 332, 336, 337, 339, 340, 347, 363
——, Regiments—
  1st Bn., 266, 267, 340
  2nd Bn., 266, 267, 277
  3rd Bn., 269, 340
Cavalry—
  Brigades (Australian)—
    1st Light Horse—180, 183, 184, 185, 186, 188, 190, 191, 192, 194, 196, 245 (f.n.), 247 (f.n.), 254, 255, 256, 262, 263, 264, 265, 266, 268, 274, 332, 344, 345, 346, 346
    2nd Light Horse—168, 180, 181, 183, 184, 185, 186, 188, 190, 191, 192, 194, 196, 197, 245, 247 (f.n.), 274, 276, 291, 298, 299, 344, 346
    3rd Light Horse—180, 183, 184, 187, 190, 192, 193, 195, 196, 197, 198, 201, 245, 247 (f.n.), 254, 255, 256, 264, 265, 266, 269, 274, 299, 300, 301, 308, 312, 344, 345
    4th Light Horse—69, 273, 274, 332, 340, 344, 345
  Brigades (British)—
    Yeomanry—
      1/1st North Midland Mounted (later 22nd Mtd. Bde.), 108, 136
      1/2nd South Midland Mounted (later 6th Mtd. Bde.), 120, 123, 130, 131

---

[1] Formations and units from orders of battle and orders, which appear in appendices, are not included in this index.
  As practically all Indian infantry regiments have been given new titles, it has been thought advisable to insert these in shortened form after the old, in square brackets. Otherwise it might not be easy some years hence to identify the regiments concerned. In many cases the old designations have been retained, e.g., 125th Napier's Rifles is now 5/6th Rajputana Rifles (Napier's), but these are unnecessary for the purpose of identification, and have been omitted to save space.

442   Index to Arms, Formations, and Units

Cavalry (*continued*)—
  Brigades (British) (*continued*)—
    Yeomanry (*continued*)—
      5th Mounted (formerly 1/1st South Midland Mtd. Bde.), 161, 180, 184, 187, 188, 189, 190, 192, 194, 195, 196, 198, 247 (*f.n.*), 263, 265, 266, 267, 274, 292, 300, 308, 333, 344, 345
      6th Mounted (formerly 1/2nd South Midland Mtd. Bde.), 134, 247 (*f.n.*), 274, 277, 299, 300, 308, 344, 345
      7th Mounted (formerly 1/1st Notts and Derby Mtd. Bde.), 357
      8th Mounted (formerly 1/1st London Mtd. Bde.), 357
      22nd Mounted (formerly 1/1st North Midland Mtd. Bde.), 134, 247 (*f.n.*), 274, 292, 298, 299, 301, 314, 334, 344, 346
  Brigade (New Zealand)—
    New Zealand Mounted Rifles, 178, 180, 184, 187, 188, 190, 191, 192, 195, 196, 197, 198, 247 (*f.n.*), 254, 255, 264, 265, 266, 267, 268, 270, 274, 276, 292, 298, 299, 334, 344, 345
  Brigades (Indian)—
    Imperial Service, 15, 22, 47, 48, 63, 247 (*f.n.*), 275, 354
  Divisions (Australian)—
    Australian and New Zealand Mounted, 156, 169, 180, 181, 187, 188, 190, 252, 253, 263, 274, 276, 283, 284, 287; at First Gaza, 290, 297, 298, 299, 300, 303, 308; 330; at Second Gaza, 332, 334, 336, 344, 346
    Imperial Mounted, 274, 283, 286, 287; at First Gaza, 292, 298, 299, 308, 309; 330; at Second Gaza, 332, 336, 340, 343, 344, 345; becomes Australian Mtd. Div., 357; 363
    Australian Mounted (formerly Imperial Mtd. Div.), 357
  Divisions (British)—
    Yeomanry—
      Yeomanry Mounted, 357
      2nd Mounted, 57, 58, 59, 67 (*f.n.*), 69, 87, 107 (*f.n.*)

Cavalry (*continued*)—
  Regiments (Australian)—
    1st Light Horse, 178, 185, 267
    2nd Light Horse, 185, 188, 194, 267
    3rd Light Horse, 188, 194, 256, 267
    4th Light Horse, 274 (*f.n.*)
    5th Light Horse, 161, 168, 180, 184, 188, 197, 299, 346
    6th Light Horse, 178, 186, 188, 291, 301
    7th Light Horse, 186, 188, 191, 291, 308, 346, 362
    8th Light Horse, 160, 255, 269
    9th Light Horse, 160, 178, 193, 255
    10th Light Horse, 178, 254, 255, 256, 267, 300
    11th Light Horse, 246, 274(*f.n.*), 277
    12th Light Horse, 246, 274 (*f.n.*)
  Regiments (British)—
    Yeomanry—
      Berks, 120, 300
      Buckinghamshire (Royal Bucks Hussars), 114, 115, 116, 120, 121 (*f.n.*), 125, 128
      Derbyshire, 114
      Dorset (Queen's Own), 120, 121 (*f.n.*), 125, 126, 128
      Duke of Lancaster's Own, 48 (*f.n.*), 114, 120, 121 (*f.n.*), 288
      Gloucestershire (Royal G. Hussars), 161, 163, 165, 187, 188, 189, 266, 267, 285 (*f.n.*)
      Herts, 48 (*f.n.*), 114, 120, 121 (*f.n.*)
      1st City of London (Rough Riders), 114, 246
      1st County of London (Middlesex, D. of Cambridge's Hussars), 178
      2nd County of London (Westminster Dragoons), 48 (*f.n.*) 120
      Scottish Horse, 69
      Surrey (Queen Mary's Regiment), 120, 121 (*f.n.*)
      Warwickshire, 161, 165, 197, 266, 267, 269
      Worcestershire (The Q.O.W. Hussars), 161, 163, 166, 189, 264, 266, 292, 333

INDEX TO ARMS, FORMATIONS, AND UNITS 443

Cavalry (*continued*)—
  Regiments (New Zealand)—
    Auckland Mounted Rifles, 184
      (*f.n.*), 187, 197, 255, 257,
      264, 266, 267, 299 (*f.n.*)
    Canterbury Mounted Rifles, 197,
      254, 255, 266, 267, 299, 345
    Wellington Mounted Rifles, 180
      (*f.n.*), 186, 188, 191, 254, 255,
      265, 266, 267, 269, 299, 345
  Regiments (Indian)—
    Aden Troop, 222, 223
    Hyderabad Lancers, 62
    Mysore Lancers, 72
Coastguard, Egyptian, 14, 20, 108, 118
Corps, British—
  VIII Corps—156
  IX Corps—156, 160
  XV Corps—156, 160, 161
  I Anzac Corps—56, 156
  II Anzac Corps—156
Cyclists, 52nd Divl., 187

Divisions (Australian)—
  1st—88, 98, 156
  2nd—69, 88, 98, 156
  3rd—156 (*f.n.*)
  4th—98
  5th—98
Divisions (British)—
  10th—60 (*f.n.*), 71
  11th—60 (*f.n.*), 98, 156
  13th—60 (*f.n.*), 98, 156
  14th—88
  22nd—79
  26th—79
  27th—79, 80
  28th—79, 80
  29th—55, 56, 98, 156
  31st—79 (*f.n.*), 88, 98, 156
  42nd (East Lancashire), arrival in Egypt of, 14 ; 15, 16 ; artillery in Canal Defences, 23 ; 57, 58, 98, 156 ; at Romani, 179, 181, 184, 189, 190, 191, 195, 201 ; 259, 272, 279
  46th—79 (*f.n.*), 88, 98, 156
  52nd (Lowland)—60 (*f.n.*), 98, 156, 162 ; at Romani, 175, 180, 190, 192, 195, 201 (*f.n.*) ; 252, 253, 259, 273, 279, 283, 286, 287, 310, 313, 317, 327, 328 ; at Second Gaza, 332, 333, 335, 336, 337, 339, 340, 341, 343, 346, 347 ; 358, 364
  53rd (Welsh)—60, 80, 88, 98, 156, 179, 272, 273, 279, 283, 284, 285, 286, 287, 288 ; at First Gaza,

Divisions (British) (*continued*)—
  53rd (Welsh) Division (*continued*)—
    293, 299, 301, 303, 305, 307, 309, 310, 312, 313, 314, 315, 316, 319, 327 ; 328 ; at Second Gaza, 332, 335, 336, 342, 343, 347 ; 353, 358
  54th (East Anglian)—60, 80, 88, 98, 156, 272, 273, 279, 283, 284, 285, 286, 287 ; at First Gaza, 293, 307, 309, 310, 311, 313, 314, 317, 327 ; 328 ; at Second Gaza, 332, 333, 335, 336, 337, 338, 339, 342, 346, 347 ; 354, 358, 364
  60th (London)—358, 359
  74th (Yeomanry)—273, 319 (*f.n.*), 328, 330, 335, 347, 355, 358, 359
  75th—319 (*f.n.*), 355, 358, 359
  Royal Naval—55, 56, 62, 80, 88
Divisions—
  New Zealand—98
  New Zealand and Australian—88, 98 (*f.n.*), 156
Divisions (Indian)—
  Lahore—14
  Meerut—14, 72 (*f.n.*)
  10th—2 ; formed in Egypt, 20, 22 ; 67, 156
  11th—2 ; formed in Egypt, 20, 22 ; 67

Engineers—
  Field Squadrons—
    1st Australian—253, 363
    Imperial Mounted Divl.—363
  Field Companies—
    1st East Lancashire—33, 39
    2nd East Lancashire—33
    Kent—130
    2/2nd Lowland—161
    3rd Australian—33
    10th Coy. Q.V.O. Sappers and Miners, 33
  Military Works Department, Egyptian Army, 33
Infantry—
  Brigades (Australian)—
    2nd—45
    3rd—55
    5th—70
    8th—88
  Brigades (British)—
    125th—184, 192, 194, 195
    126th—184, 191 (*f.n.*)
    127th—184, 189, 192, 194, 195
    155th—180, 193, 194, 195, 311, 337, 340, 341, 342

Infantry (*continued*)—
  Brigades (British) (*continued*)—
    156th—180, 188, 189, 190, 194, 337, 342
    157th—180, 193, 194, 195, 311, 333, 337, 342, 343
    158th—179, 180, 285, 287, 288, 293, 294, 296, 297, 301, 303, 311, 314
    159th—136, 285, 287, 294, 295, 296, 297, 301, 302, 303, 311, 316, 343
    160th—285, 286, 287, 293, 294, 296, 297, 301, 302, 303, 312, 343
    161st—108, 293, 295, 296, 302, 303, 312, 314, 317, 337, 339
    162nd—337, 338
    163rd—314, 333, 337, 338, 339
    229th—273, 275, 283
    230th—273, 275
    231st—273, 275
    232nd—358
    233rd—358
    234th—358
    1st Dismounted (Yeo.)—180
    2nd Dismounted (Yeo.)—134
    3rd Dismounted (Yeo.)—134
    4th Dismounted (Yeo.)—134
  Brigades—
    New Zealand—30
    South African—121 (*f.n.*), 124, 130, 134
  Brigades (Indian)—
    Garhwal—72 (*f.n.*); Sirhind—14, 15, 19; Lucknow—15; 20th—275; 22nd—39, 47; 28th—59, 61, 67, 70, 85, 87, 222, 223, 224; 29th—57, 58, 59, 88, 358; 30th—59, 61; 31st—45, 47 (*f.n.*); Imperial Service (32nd)—15, 29; 49th—358
  Regiments—
    Infantry of the Line and Territorial—
      Cameronians (Scottish Rifles) 7th Bn., 190, 191
      ——, 8th Bn., 190, 191, 342
      Cheshire, 4th Bn., 303
      ——, 7th Bn., 302
      Devonshire, 5th Bn., 358
      Duke of Cornwall's Light Infantry, 4th Bn., 275, 358
      Essex, 4th Bn., 303
      ——, 5th Bn., 303
      ——, 6th Bn., 303, 312, 313, 339
      ——, 7th Bn., 312, 313

Infantry (*continued*)—
  Regiments (*continued*)—
    Infantry of the Line and Territorial (*continued*)—
      Fusiliers—
        Scots, Royal, 4th Bn., 162, 167, 340, 341
        ——, 5th Bn., 161, 167, 340, 341, 364
        Welch, Royal, 5th Bn., 294, 301, 302
      Hampshire, 8th Bn., 338
      ——, 2/4th Bn., 358
      ——, 2/5th Bn., 358
      Herefordshire, 1st Bn., 301, 303, 312
      Highland Light Infantry, 7th Bn., 342
      Kent, West. *See* Queen's Own Royal West Kent.
      King's Own Scottish Borderers, 4th Bn., 340, 341
      ——, 5th Bn., 340, 341, 364
      London Regiment, 10th Bn., 338, 339
      ——, 11th Bn., 338
      ——, 2/3rd Bn., 58 (*f.n.*)
      Loyal Regiment (North Lancashire), 2nd Bn., 275, 358
      Middlesex (Duke of Cambridge's Own), 2/7th Bn. 107 (*f.n.*), 118 (*f.n.*), 119, (*f.n.*)
      ——, 2/8th Bn., 107 (*f.n.*), 114, 115, 116, 121 (*f.n.*)
      ——, 2/10th Bn., 302, 312
      Norfolk, 4th Bn., 338
      ——, 5th Bn., 338, 340
      Northamptonshire, 4th Bn., 338
      Queen's Own Royal West Kent, 2/4th Bn., 285 (*f.n*).
      Queen's Royal Regiment (West Surrey), 2/4th Bn., 312
      Scots, Royal (The Royal Regiment), 6th Bn., 107 (*f.n.*), 111, 121 (*f.n.*), 125
      Somerset Light Infantry (Prince Albert's), 5th Bn., 358
      Suffolk, 5th Bn., 339
      Surrey, West. *See* Queen's Royal Regiment
      Sussex, Royal, 4th Bn., 293, 302
      Wales, South, Borderers, Brecknockshire Bn., 222

Index to Arms, Formations, and Units

Infantry (*continued*)—
Regiments (*continued*)—
Infantry of the Line and Territorial (*continued*)—
Welch, 4th Bn., 303
———, 5th Bn., 302
Regiments (Overseas Dominions)—
Australian, 7th Bn., 45
———, 8th Bn., 45
British West Indies, 1st Bn., 275
———, 2nd Bn., 275
———, 5th Bn., 275
New Zealand, Auckland Bn., 30
———, Canterbury Bn., 30
———, Otago Bn., 30
———, Wellington Bn., 30
———, Maori Bn., 58 (*f.n.*)
———, N.Z.R.B., 1st Bn., 107 (*f.n.*), 113, 116, 117, 118 (*f.n.*), 121, 130
———, N.Z.R.B., 2nd Bn., 107
South African Infantry, 1st Bn., 124, 125, 127, 131
———, 2nd Bn., 121, 125, 131, 132
———, 3rd Bn., 124, 125, 127, 131, 132
———, 4th Bn., 130, 131
Regiments (Egyptian)—
2nd Bn., 53, 160
7th Bn., 146 (*f.n.*)
Regiments (Indian)—
2nd Q.V.O. Rajputs [1/7th Rajput], 30, 39, 41, 42, 87 (*f.n.*)
3rd Brahmans, 39, 87 (*f.n.*)
6th Jat [1/9th R. Jat], 87 (*f.n.*)
9th Bhopals [4/16th Punjab], 59, 87 (*f.n.*)
14th Sikhs [1/11th Sikh], 30
15th Sikhs [2/11th Sikh], 107, 108, 110, 111, 114, 115, 116, 117, 118 (*f.n.*), 119 (*f.n.*), 121, 123
27th Punjabis [3/15th Punjab], 47, 63
33rd Punjabis [3/16th Punjab], 15 (*f.n.*)
41st Dogras [3/17th Dogra], 87 (*f.n.*)
51st Sikhs [1/12th Frontier Force], 62, 70, 87 (*f.n.*)
53rd Sikhs [3/12th Frontier Force], 62, 70, 87 (*f.n.*)

Infantry (*continued*)—
Regiments (Indian) (*continued*)—
56th Rifles [2/13th Frontier Force Rif.], 61, 87 (*f.n.*)
58th Vaughan's Rifles [5/13th Frontier Force Rif.], 277
62nd Punjabis [1/1st Punjab], 39, 40, 47
69th Punjabis [2/2nd Punjab], 58
89th Punjabis [1/8th Punjab], 46, 58
92nd Punjabis [4/8th Punjab], 39, 42, 46, 87 (*f.n.*)
123rd Outram's Rifles [4/6th Rajputana Rif.], 358
125th Napier's Rifles [5/6th Rajputana Rif.], 59, 87 (*f.n.*)
128th Pioneers [3/2nd Bombay Pioneers], 33, 39, 40, 47, 87 (*f.n.*)
Alwar Infantry, 15 (*f.n.*)
Gwalior Infantry, 15 (*f.n.*)
Patiala Infantry, 15 (*f.n.*)
1/5th Gurkha Rifles, 38, 59, 62
1/6th Gurkha Rifles, 30
2/2nd Gurkha Rifles, 72
2/3rd Gurkha Rifles, 358
3/3rd Gurkha Rifles, 358
2/7th Gurkha Rifles, 48, 53
2/10th Gurkha Rifles, 39, 42, 59
Regiments (Sudanese)—
9th Bn., 146
11th Bn., 146 (*f.n.*)
13th Bn., 150 (*f.n.*), 151
14th Bn., 150 (*f.n.*)
Arab Bn., 150 (*f.n.*)
Equatorial Bn., 146

Machine Gun Squadrons—
3rd Australian L. H., 254
New Zealand, 198
Machine Gun Companies—
160th, 181
161st, 181
Motor Batteries and Patrols—
Cav. Corps Machine-Gun, 123, 132
7th Light Car Patrol, 263, 267, 269, 271 (*f.n.*), 301, 308, 336
11th Light Armoured M.B., 301
12th Light Armoured M.B., 301
17th Motor Machine-Gun, 336

Tank Corps (then known as Heavy Section, Machine-Gun Corps), 328, 333, 335, 338, 340, 341

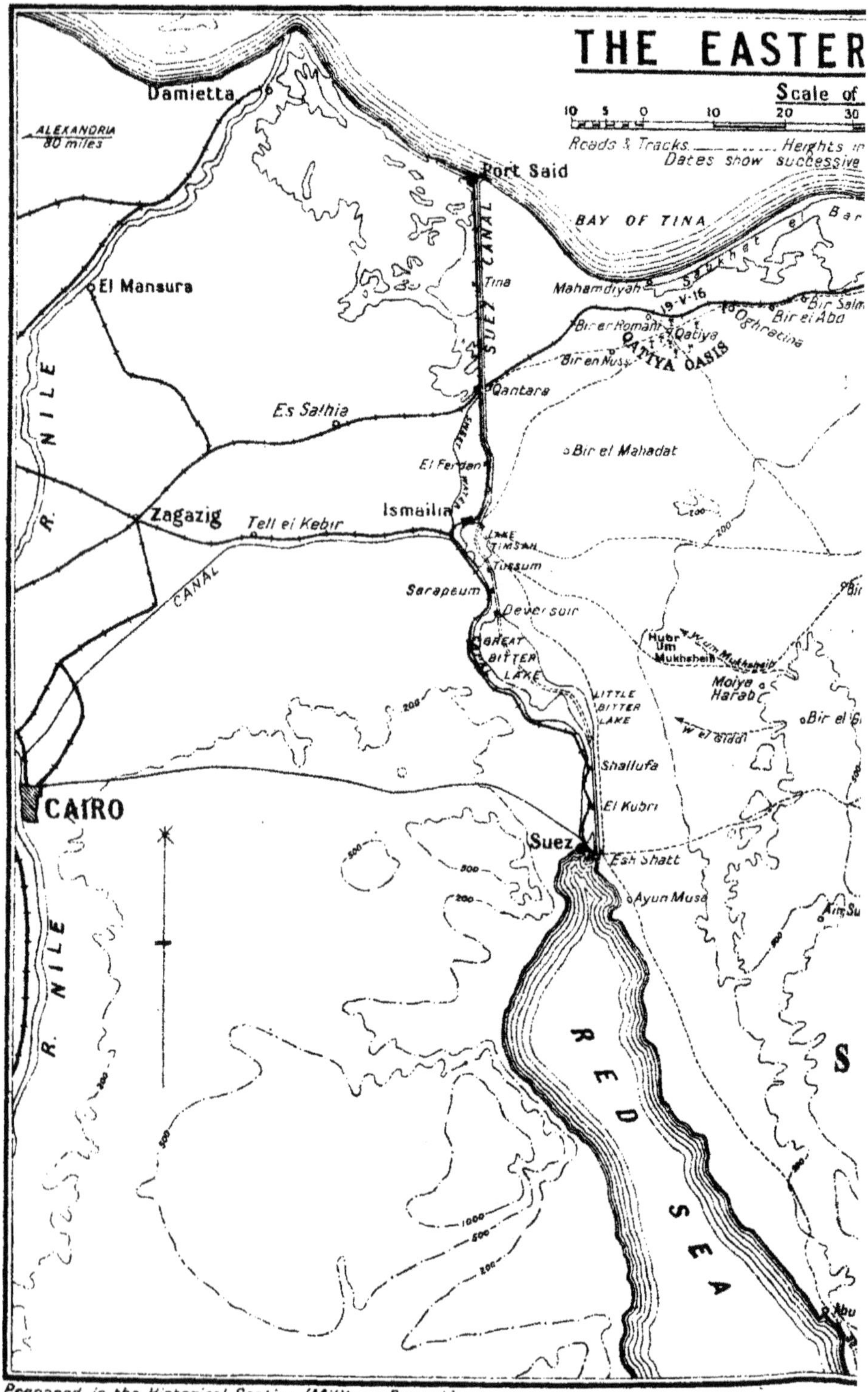

Prepared in the Historical Section (Military Branch).

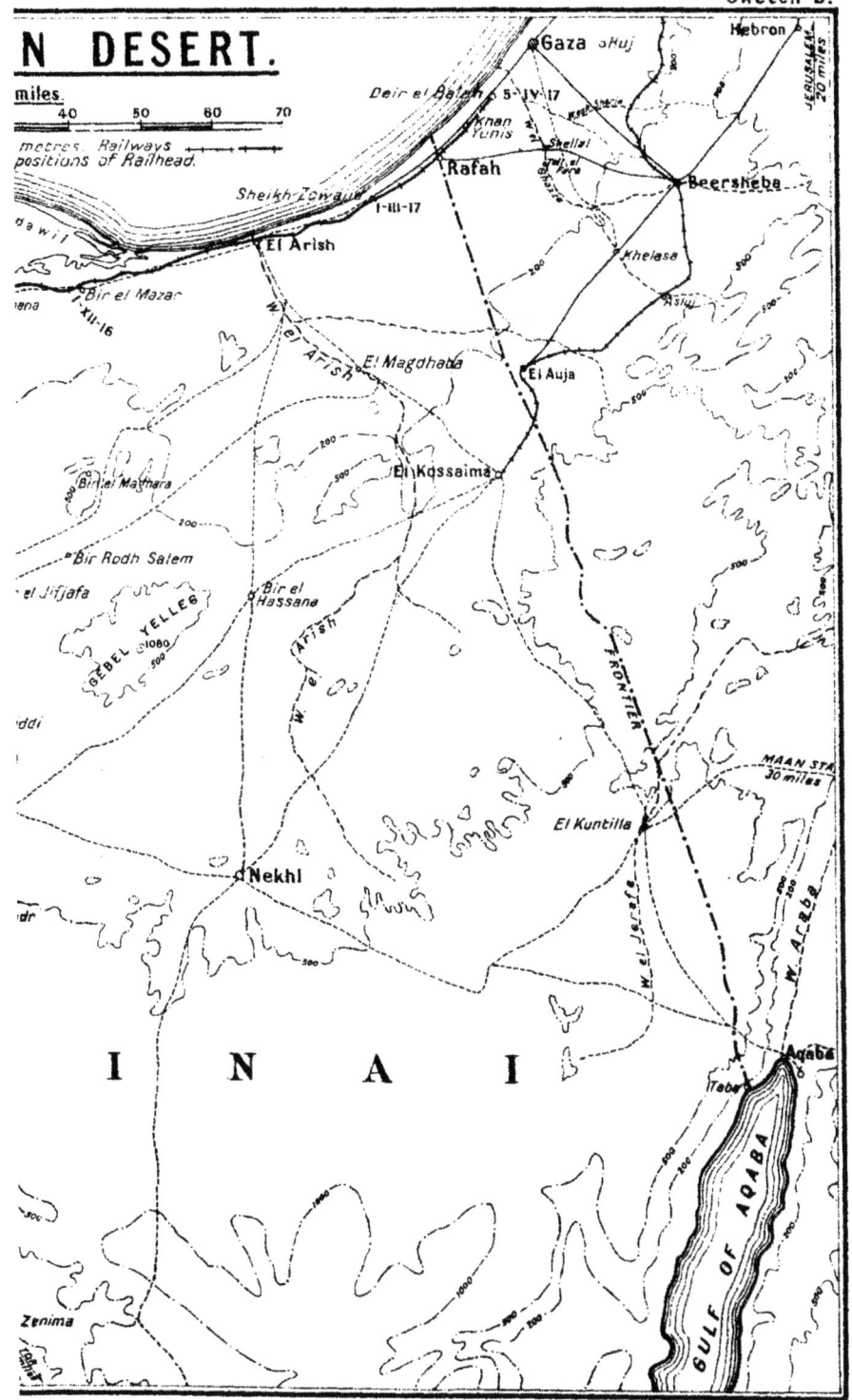

Sketch B.

Lightning Source UK Ltd.
Milton Keynes UK
UKHW020012131021
392107UK00007B/82